The Cult of Draupadī

Alf Hiltebeitel

The Cult of Draupadī

2

On Hindu Ritual and the Goddess

The University of Chicago Press
Chicago and London

40.00

Alf Hiltebeitel is professor of religion at George Washington University. He is the author of *The Cult of Draupadī*, volume 1, *Mythologies: From Gingee to Kurukṣetra*, published by this Press, and *The Ritual of Battle: Krishna in the Mahābhārata*. He has translated works by Mircea Eliade and Georges Dumézil.

Library of Congress Cataloging-in-Publication Data
(Revised for vol. 2)
Hiltebeitel, Alf.
The cult of Draupadī.
Includes bibliographical references and indexes.
Contents: v. 1. Mythologies : from Gingee to Kuruksetra—v. 2. On Hindu ritual and the goddess.
1. Draupadī (Hindu mythology) 2. Mahābhārata—Criticism, interpretation, etc. 3. Draupadī (Hindu mythology)—Cult. I. Title.
BL1138.4.D72H55 1988 294.5′2114 87-27036
ISBN 0-226-34045-7 (v. 1)
ISBN 0-226-34046-5 (v. 1 : pbk.)
ISBN 0-226-34047-3 (v. 2)
ISBN 0-226-34048-1 (v. 2 : pbk.)

∞ The paper used in this publication meets the minimum requirements of the American National Standard for Information Sciences—Permanence of Paper for Printed Library Materials, ANSI Z39.48-1984.

The University of Chicago Press, Chicago 60637
The University of Chicago Press, Ltd., London

Printed in the United States of America

00 99 98 97 96 95 94 93 92 91 5 4 3 2 1

To Caesar Titus Rajan
in memory of our friendship

Contents

Maps and Figures

Maps

Figures

Plates

Tables

Acknowledgments

A first draft of this second volume was written in 1982–84, in the same period as the first draft of volume 1. Proper acknowledgment requires that I rethank the institutions that made that writing, and the research behind it, possible: the American Institute of Indian Studies for a 1974–75 year's grant; the National Endowment for the Humanities for a 1977 summer stipend; the Joint Indo–U.S. Subcommission on Education and Culture for a year's grant in 1981–82; and the Guggenheim Foundation for support for writing in 1982–83.

Further research beyond what went into volume 1 was made possible during 1986 and 1987 summer trips to film and produce a video on Draupadī festivals (Hiltebeitel 1988b), and again during a January-to-June visit in 1990. The 1986 visit was largely funded by a Dilthey Faculty Fellowship from George Washington University and the University of Wisconsin Year in India Program. The 1987 and 1990 visits were sponsored by the American Institute of Indian Studies.

A thorough rewrite, and the addition of much new material, mainly bibliographical, was enhanced by a June-through-December 1989 fellowship from the Woodrow Wilson International Center for Scholars. A final, third draft, incorporating results from 1990 fieldwork, was then made possible by a July–August 1990 extension of the Wilson grant. Aid from the George Washington University Faculty Research Facilitating Fund has continued to support this project along the way.

I am deeply grateful to all these institutions for their support, but especially, as far as this volume goes, to the AIIS for keeping me in the field, and the Wilson Center for providing a castle tower and a stimulating intellectual atmosphere in which to find my words.

Eveline Masilamani-Meyer is due my foremost thanks for agreeing to be this work's first reader and critic (in its second draft), and for insisting that I learn more about the Draupadī cult around Thanjavur. To do that meant not only learning much from her, but benefiting from her knowledge of Draupadī temples in that area on several joint field trips. She is also to be thanked for her patience in translating some of the tapes that resulted from that fieldwork.

To Madeleine Biardeau, thanks continue to be due for the provocation of her now published work on the sacrificial post (1989a), for inviting our joint presentation of papers on Indian "gardens of Adonis" at the 1986 Centenary Celebration of the fifth Section, Religious Sciences, at the École Pratique des Hautes Études of the Sorbonne (Biardeau 1988, Hiltebeitel 1988c [revised as chapter 4 of this work]), and for repeated encouragement at points when it has counted most.

I also owe special thanks to Lee Weissman for sharing my last two months of fieldwork in 1990, enriching it through his insights, and helping me with both fieldwork and textual study in Tamil. To Abbie Ziffren I owe the same kind of thanks for aid and encouragement during work in Washington.

For both tangibles and intangibles that have affected this volume, I also thank the following friends and colleagues: David Shulman, Pon Kothandaraman, Wendy Doniger, David Knipe, Velcheru Narayana Rao, A. K. Ramanujan, Randy Kloetzli, Gananath Obeyesekere, Brenda E. F. Beck, E. Sundaramurthy, Fred Clothey, Guy Richard Welbon, Deborah Soifer, Doris Srinivasan, Frédérique Apffel Marglin, Paul Courtright, Ákos Östör, Indira Peterson, Krishnamurthy Hanur, John Samuel, N. Deivasundaram, P. Venugopala Rao, Harry E. Yeide, Jr., and Sarasvati Venugopal.

To my sister Jane Hiltebeitel Gould, immense thanks for her painstaking and affectionate work on the figures, and the same to my son Simon and to Brenda and Bob Mayes for their work on the maps. The photographs, unless otherwise noted, are my own. Thanks to David M. Brent for his editorial encouragement and perspicacity.

Fieldwork assistance in 1990 was provided by Satish Nath, R. S. Kumar, J. Rajasekaran, and, as mentioned above, by Eveline Masilamani-Meyer and Lee Weissman. Thanks to all, but special thanks here to Rajasekaran, not only for making fieldwork an enriched adventure, but for his work with me on the Draupadī festival video in both 1986 and 1987.

Fieldwork with C. T. Rajan continued from 1975 to 1987. He died in 1988 at the age of forty-eight. On my 1990 visits, I could have brought no sadder news to the friends we made in common at Tindivanam, Maṅkalam, Mēlaccēri, and Tailāpuram. This book is dedicated to his memory.

Conventions

With few exceptions, Tamil terms follow the transcriptions of the *Tamil Lexicon* and Sanskrit terms the transcriptions found in most Sanskrit dictionaries. Where terms from other Indian languages are cited, I generally follow the transcriptions of my sources, though often, perforce, selectively. Names of Tamil districts, Taluk towns, and informants are given without diacritics in the manner that one finds them most readily on maps, or in the way they are written using an English alphabet. I have kept to the District and Taluk names of the 1961 Census for the sake of consistency with volume 1, despite recent renamings. No names of villages or individuals have been disguised. Names and terms from the *Mahābhārata* and other Sanskrit texts are generally given in their more familiar Sanskrit forms, rather than in Tamil. But I make exceptions where it is a distinctly Tamil significance that is involved, as in the case of Vīrapattiraṉ. Both forms are generally cited, however, when a term first appears.

1 Introduction

This volume on Draupadī cult ritual follows a simple structure. It takes the order of a Draupadī festival from beginning to end. It thus mirrors the second part of volume 1 of this study, which does the same thing for Draupadī cult mythology. For those whose primary interest is in ritual, it can, of course, be read independently of the first volume, since where the myths are pertinent to understanding the rituals, I repeat them in outline.

While the structure itself is simple, however, Draupadī cult ritual has its own complexities that have required choices of focus and interpretative strategy. I began this research with the intention of studying one festival from beginning to end: first that of the Sowcarpet temple in Madras, where I did fieldwork in 1975, and then that of the Tindivanam temple, studied in 1975, 1977, and 1981–82. Already by 1977, however, it was apparent from these two festivals that Draupadī cult rituals can be very different. Having also attended some of the major ceremonies by that time at Pondicherry and Veḷḷimēṭupēṭṭai and mined the bibliographical sources then available on Draupadī festivals elsewhere, the project of investigating the principles of order behind this rampant diversity virtually imposed itself (cf. Hiltebeitel 1988a, xvii–xviii). Some of these principles are discussed elsewhere in this volume, and need only be mentioned here: a differentiation between festivals in cities, towns, and villages; the construct of a core area centered on the medieval royal Nāyakate of Gingee and its nearby Mēlaccēri temple, said to be Draupadī's "original shrine" (*āti pīṭam*); regional variation; diffusion; styles and types of ritual authority and expertise (local/itinerant, ancestral/text-based); variations linked with different festivals' main sponsoring castes; and historical change and the impact of modernity. These interpretative issues and principles arose largely out of coming to terms with the limits and possibilities of field study of the Draupadī cult itself.

Other principles, however, have emerged in writing this book. One set has been fashioned through trying to figure out how to proceed with an ordered discussion of Draupadī cult rituals themselves. While I have kept one festival—that of the Tindivanam temple—at the center of discussion throughout this book, I have had to reckon with the fact that no Draupadī festival could be profitably discussed in its absolute ritual entirety. There is first the minutiae of it all. Occasionally I must try to give the flavor of the minuscule ritual details, but by and large that is not my interest. More interesting on the level of the single festival is the process of replication within the ritual cycle. Rather than attempt to be exhaustive, however, I have chosen to emphasize the processual sweep of the festival. Circling in on Draupadī cult rituals, our perspective will be like that of Kṛṣṇa's mount, the celestial bird Garuḍa, who, as we shall see, shows an inclination to look in on ceremonies at two ritual sites: the *paṭukaḷam,* or ritual "battlefield," and the firepit (*tīkkuḻi*). Thus, of the mass of rituals that constitute a Draupadī festival, the ones that this book will focus on most sharply are those that occur in, or in connection with, these two ritual arenas. I will be briefer with rituals that occur elsewhere, most notably those whose primary focus is the third major ritual arena, the Draupadī temple, but also the drama-linked rituals that occur onstage and offstage in the *Terukkūttu,* or "street dramas." These choices are made easier by the fact that temple rituals have been a leading focus of two recent studies of single Draupadī festivals: one by Tanaka, going into rich detail and interpretative discussion about temple *pūjā*s and *apiṣēka*s (Sanskrit *abhiṣeka*), the unctions of the temple icons, at the 1982 festival in the town of Udappu in western Sri Lanka (1987, 172–259); the other by Shideler, giving further details on these matters as well as a singular emphasis on iconography, *alaṅkāra*s (decoration of the icons for processions from the temple), and processions themselves (1987, 105–27) at the 1986 festival in Pondicherry. Similarly, Frasca (1984, 1990) and I (1988a) have drawn out many of the ritual implications of the Terukkūttu. But my reasons for concentrating on the paṭukaḷam and the firepit are not that they are underrepresented in the literature. Rather, it is that these two arenas define what is most ritually distinctive about Draupadī festivals. Be it noted, however, that all four of these arenas are interconnected. They are joined above all by interlinking rituals, but also by overlapping symbolisms and interchangeable—that is, substitutional and compensatory—configurations. To the extent that I do focus on temple ritual in the first six chapters, it will thus be selectively. The purpose will be to introduce the paraphernalia of the Draupadī temple and its festival cycle as a whole, and to show how the opening temple rituals provide surprising and indispensable keys for further exploration of the interconnections between the temple cultus and the more climactic and "spectacular" rituals of these two other terrains.[1]

Because the battlefield and firepit rituals differ from one festival to another, however, discussion must also attend to the problems of regional variation, and of substitution and compensation. Within the core area, these processes can be studied under fairly close controls. But outside it, and in the cities, one encounters rituals that are not only substitutional or compensatory, but strikingly different. In some urban cases the differences seem to be best accounted for by "diaspora" surroundings, in which the cult's rituals lose some of their distinctiveness and take on colorings of the Brahmanical "great tradition." Regional variations, on the other hand, seem primarily to build from within by developing secondary Draupadī cult options into primary ones. I will argue that it is the latter process that characterizes the remarkable variations just south of the core area, in what may provisionally be called the Thanjavur region, where I have concentrated most of my additional Draupadī cult fieldwork since the writing of volume 1 (see map 1 and table 1).

All the while, there is also the *Mahābhārata* to draw from: to take its myth and reshape it to varying ritual needs. If there is one principle that has emerged here, it is that the most singular and durable features of Draupadī cult ritual are those that tie in not with the classical story as such, though it is hardly ignored in the ritual, but with figures and episodes from the Draupadī cult folk tradition.[2] This should hardly be surprising in itself. What should be surprising is that these singular and durable features of what is ostensibly the ritual of a "folk" or "popular" cult are precisely the ones that take us beyond folk traditions, as such, to the classical and even Vedic ritual systems of Hinduism.[3] Where Draupadī cult ritual in-

1. I use the term "spectacular" in the sense developed by Tarabout with reference to goddess festivals of southern Kerala. These bring about collective participation and involve the creation of elaborate ritual constructions and performances not only for "viewing" by the public at large, but also as offerings, "given to the viewing" of the goddess: offerings that in many cases recapitulate the symbolism of the "sacrifice of battle" (1986, especially 2–6, 461, 477–79, 610–11). See further chapter 7.

2. For a brief summary of the *Mahābhārata* and a genealogical table differentiating its classical and folk heroes as they bear upon the Draupadī cult, see Hiltebeitel 1988a, xxi and 449.

3. For a good discussion of current usages of the terms "folk" and "popular religion," see Bell 1989, especially 42–43, which outlines a recent "third stage" position that is closest to many of the intentions behind this study.

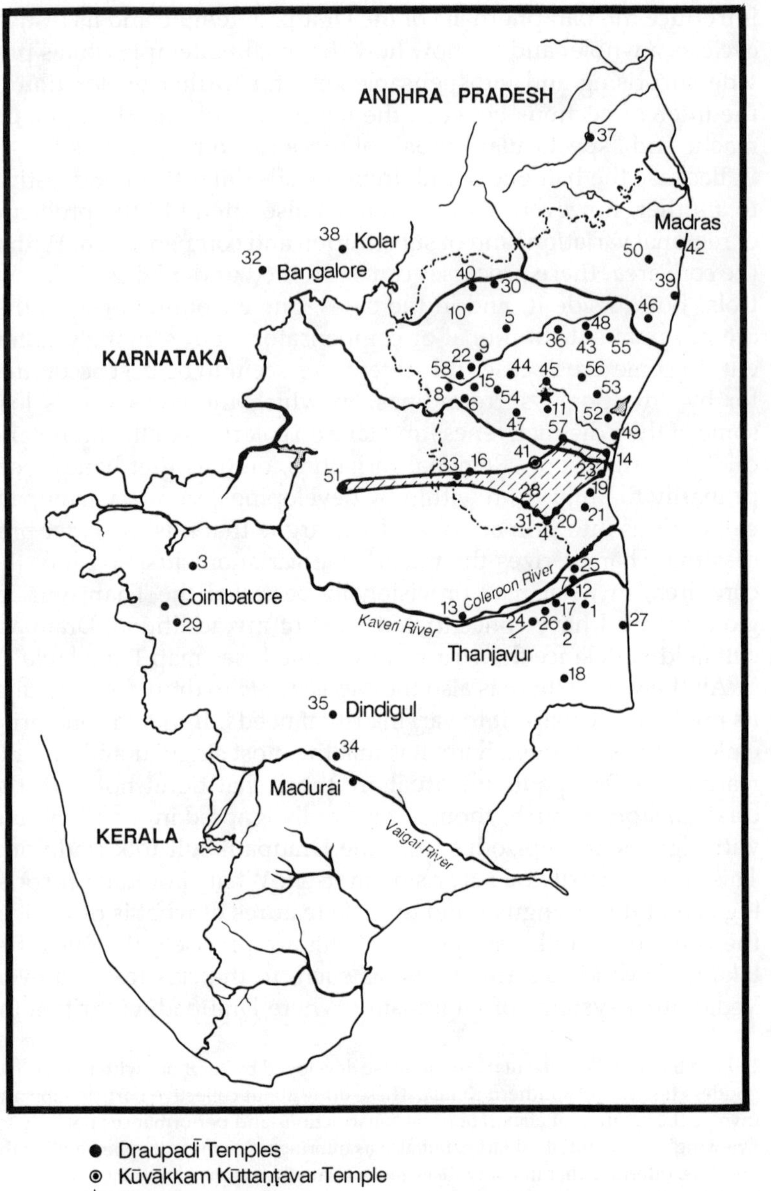

● Draupadī Temples
◉ Kūvākkam Kūttaṇṭavar Temple
★ Gingee
Shaded area indicating transitional zone between Gingee core area and Thanjavur area
1 For Numbered Sites, see Table 1.
-•- Boundaries of Chingleput, South Arcot, and North Arcot Districts

Map 1. New 1990 fieldwork sites and other major temples mentioned in the text.

Table 1. New 1990 Fieldwork Sites and Other Major Temples Mentioned in the Text

New Draupadī Cult Fieldwork Sites (1990)

1. A̱lakar Tirupputtūr, Kumbhakonam Taluk, Thanjavur District
2. Ammāpēṭṭai, Thanjavur Taluk, Thanjavur
3. A̱ṉṉūr, Avanashi Taluk, Coimbatore District
4. C. Kīraṉūr, Vriddhachalam Taluk, South Arcot District
5. Cantavācal, Polur Taluk, North Arcot District
6. Cāttaṉūr, Chengam Taluk, North Arcot District
7. Cattiram Karuppūr, Kumbhakonam Taluk, Thanjavur District
8. Chengam, Chengam Taluk, North Arcot District
9. Kāppalūr, Polur Taluk, North Arcot District
10. Karaṭikuṭi, Vellore Taluk, North Arcot District
11. Kōṉalūr, Gingee Taluk, South Arcot District
12. Kumbhakonam, Kumbhakonam Taluk, Thanjavur District (two temples)
13. Lalgudi, Lalgudi Taluk, Tiruchirappali District
14. Matukkarai, Pondicherry State
15. Mēlkarippūr, Chengam Taluk, North Arcot District
16. Muṭiyaṉūr, Kallakuruchi Taluk, South Arcot District
17. Muttāṉi, Papanasam Taluk, Thanjavur District
18. Pattukkottai, Pattukkottai Taluk, Thanjavur District
19. Perumattūr, Cuddalore Taluk, South Arcot
20. Poṉṉēri, Vriddhachalam Taluk, South Arcot District
21. Puvaṉakiri, Chidambaram Taluk, South Arcot District
22. Tenmakātēvamaṅkalam, Polur Taluk, North Arcot
23. Tēvaṉāmpaṭṭaṉam, Cuddalore Taluk, South Arcot
24. Thanjavur, Thanjavur Taluk, Thanjavur District (two temples)
25. Tirumaṅkalakkuṭi, Tiruvidaimarudur Taluk, Thanjavur District
26. Tiruppālatturai, Papanasam Taluk, Thanjavur District
27. Vaṭukku Poykaiyūr, Nagapattinam Taluk, Thanjavur District
28. Vayalūr, Vriddhachalam Taluk, South Arcot District
29. Veḷḷalūr, Coimbatore Taluk, Coimbatore District
30. Vellore, Vellore Taluk, North Arcot District
31. Vriddhachalam, Vriddhachalam Taluk, South Arcot District (three temples)

Other Major Temples Metioned

32. Bangalore City, Karnataka
33. Chinna Salem, Kallakuruchi Taluk, South Arcot District
34. Cōḻavantāṉ, Nilakkottai Taluk, Madurai District
35. Dindigul, Dindigul Taluk, Madurai District
36. Iruṅkal, Cheyyar Taluk, North Arcot District
37. Kalahasti, Kalahasti Taluk, Chittoor District, Andhra Pradesh
38. Kolar, Kolar Taluk, Kolar District, Karnataka
39. Kovelong, Chingleput Taluk, Chingleput District
40. Kūttampākkam, Vaniyampadi Taluk, North Arcot District
41. Kūvākkam (Kūttāṇṭavar Temple), Ulundurpet Taluk, South Arcot District
42. Madras City
43. Māṉāmpāṭi, Kanchipuram Taluk, Chingleput District
44. Maṅkalam, Tiruvannamalai Taluk, North Arcot District

Table 1 (*continued*)

45.	Mēlaccēri, Gingee Taluk, South Arcot District
46.	Mutikai Nallāṉkuppam, Chingleput Taluk, Chingleput District
47.	Nallāṉpiḷḷaipeṟṟāḷ, Gingee Taluk, South Arcot District
48.	Perunakar, Kanchipuram Taluk, Chingleput District
49.	Pondicherry, Pondicherry State
50.	Pūṉamalli, Sriperumbudur Taluk, Chingleput District
51.	Salem, Salem Taluk, Salem District
52.	Tailāpuram, Tindivanam Taluk, South Arcot
53.	Tindivanam, Tindivanam Taluk, South Arcot
54.	Tiruvannamalai, Tiruvannamalai Taluk, North Arcot
55.	Uttiramērūr, Kanchipuram Taluk, Chingleput District
56.	Veḷḷimēṭupēṭṭai, Tindivanam Taluk, South Arcot District
57.	Villupuram, Villupuram Taluk, South Arcot District
58.	Vīrāṇantal, Chengam Taluk, North Arcot District

troduces its greatest innovation into the *Mahābhārata* story—with reference to posts, weapons, fires, sacrificial victims, effigies, and forts—we find that the rituals draw their inspiration from the cult of the Hindu temple and the Vedic sacrifice.

These findings have of course required an argument, which has in turn woven itself into the design of the book. The argument is simply that Draupadī cult rituals cannot be interpreted on their own. They require considerable delving into other Hindu ritual traditions. In part this is because of the cult's links with the *Mahābhārata* itself, since the *Mahābhārata* sustains what can be called a thorough *bhakti,* or devotional, rereading of the forms, themes, and implications of Vedic ritual. In the hands of Draupadī cult ritualists, the epic continues to be a means of integrating not only "new" Vedic elements, but also features of other Indian ritual systems. The Draupadī cult may thus be regarded, perhaps to a singularly high degree but certainly not uniquely, as a palimpsest of Hindu ritual. To unlayer this material in an orderly way, the argument will thus proceed as follows.

After chapters 2 and 3 set the stage, sticking to the Draupadī cult alone through an overview of its temple ritual and festival cycle, chapters 4 to 6 will open the discussion of Vedic elements in Draupadī cult ritual: in particular, those that concern a rapport between sacrifice and battle. Chapter 7 will then move from Vedic rituals of battle to a discussion of battlefield rituals in popular Hinduism. Here I will attempt to situate Draupadī cult rituals in the context of their closest analogues, ones found not only in other Tamil cults, but also in what seems to be a ritual continuum from at least Kerala to Bengal.[4] By this time, chapter 6 will have also introduced the connections between the Draupadī cult's ritual battleground and the design of the Hindu temple, a topic that will grow in importance in chapters 8 through 13. With these connections come the systems of *āgamic* temple ritual, including temple architecture, of the different sectarian traditions. Chapters 4 through 7 will thus provide the building blocks that will allow us to return to a head-on discussion, integrated with these prior materials, of the Draupadī cult battlefield and firewalking rituals in the remainder of the book, chapters 8 through 15.

This is not to say that the Vedic sacrifice, the Hindu temple cult, and popular battlefield rites are the only paradigms that bear upon Draupadī cult ritual. I will also continue, as in volume 1, to stress the rapport between Draupadī cult rituals and the royal fall festival of Navarātri-Dasarā, with its continuities as well in village goddess festivals, particularly the village buffalo sacrifice (1988a, 44–48, 61–64, 144, 319–27, 434). The cults of other Tamil "village" and lineage goddesses will also continue to be pertinent. I should add that I am also well aware that Tantric and Śākta ritual systems have had their impact on Draupadī cult ritual. I have noted it where I have found the connections to be striking. Finally, I am further well aware that issues of Dravidian and tribal Hinduism bear upon any discussion of the Hindu goddess, and that certain scholars have taken them up with an eye to larger comparative issues connecting the Hindu goddess with the ancient goddess cults and mythologies of West Asia and the Mediterranean. Elsewhere, I have made my own attempts to contribute to these discussions, and I continue to do so in this volume, particularly in chapters 4 and 11 on the comparative question, and in chapters 4 to 6 on the tribal one. Suffice it to say at this point that my approach has become cautionary and at some points critical. I believe that what has been put together linking the Hindu goddess with tribals and the ancient world, including the Indus Valley culture, needs some deconstruction. I do not think the enterprise is futile, just that the gaps are too great to sustain many (though not all) of the claims that have so far been made. I am not in favor of an orthogenetic interpretation of Hindu ritual to the exclusion of such other influences, or for that matter of Indo-

4. Clearly one could also extend the discussion further into Karnataka; see chapter 8, section A, chapter 11, section D, and Prabhu 1977, 88, 99, 107. The lack of such rituals in connection with the *Ālhā* folk epic in the Hindi heartland of the North (Schomer 1989, 142) underlines a different ritual situation there that might bear further investigation.

European continuations. I do think, however, that it is the Vedic-Hindu continuum that has the most to tell us about Draupadī cult ritual. Where this work seeks to address a scholarly gap, it is in the comparative study of Hindu ritual traditions, across both time and space.

Finally, whereas in volume 1 I attempted to leave out all possible discussion of Draupadī cult ritual to reserve it for this volume, I cannot say that I have returned the favor by leaving out all possible discussion in this volume of Draupadī cult myth. While I am not unsympathetic to arguments for the integrity and autonomy of ritual, and while much that goes on in Draupadī cult ritual *can* and *will* be discussed without reference to myth, much else, and often what is most interesting, cannot be discussed without myth, and in particular, as I have already said, without reference to the Draupadī cult's folk *Mahābhārata*. If there are cases where myth is irrelevant to ritual, this is not one of them.

2 Draupadī Temples and Their Ritual Officiants

If the epic mythology of the Draupadī cult confronts us with an embarrassment of variations, its rituals only intensify the problem. At least for the Gingee core area, discussion of the myths could be correlated with the principle of "levels of performance" among informants: from the *pāratiyārs* (*Mahābhārata*-reciters) to the Terukkūttu dramatists and other itinerant cult specialists to the local temple personnel (Hiltebeitel 1988a, 135–46). Outside the core area, however, where the Terukkūttu troupes do not circulate, these levels are reduced to two: the pāratiyārs and the local people. So it is in the Thanjavur region, to the core area's immediate south. If the festivals there include a small selection of dramas, it is the villagers themselves who perform in them, usually in roles that are traditional to their families. Sometimes the pāratiyārs take leading parts, or even act as directors (see plate 1).[1]

When we turn to the ritual cycle, however, such levels are less revealing than they are for the myths. Indeed, ritual might be regarded as a leveler among such levels. One is just as likely to obtain important ritual exposition from informed local participants as from the itinerant specialists. Where they contradict each other, as they often do, they will still cooperate in the performance of a ritual even though they have different stories as to what it is about. Each festival is, above all, a local performance, and whereas different

1. The one example I observed, "Aravāṉ's Sacrifice" at Cattiram Karuppūr (May 24, 1990), drew a high-spirited village audience to something approximating a high-school play, directed by the pāratiyār S. Nagarajan, who played Draupadī. See Cēturāmaṉ 1986, 134; also reinforced in interviews with him and with R. Raju, National School of Drama, Delhi, in April 1990. Other dramas done with some frequency in this region are "Dice Match and Disrobing," "Arjuna's Tapas," "The Fight over the Cattle Raid," "Draupadī the Gypsy," and "Eighteenth-Day War." They are done not in a succession of nights, as in the core area, but at an appropriate point in the development of the Pāratam.

pāratiyārs and drama troupes will usually instruct and entertain the local audiences from one year's festival to the next, the local ritual cycle remains largely the same. In the ideal case, its paraphernalia and overall plan are kept from year to year, and its local participants continue to perform the same ritual roles that their forefathers did.

It is, in fact, tempting to say that the best ritual information comes from the local people. I will always be grateful to V. S. Purushottama Chettiyar, chief trustee of the Tindivanam Draupadī temple, for frequently dropping in unexpectedly on my evening interviews with the visiting pāratiyārs during the 1977 and 1981 Tindivanam festivals and puckishly interjecting information that would offhandedly contradict the visiting expert, or introduce seeming irrelevancies that were of interest to him but would take me some time to realize just how interesting they could be to me.[2]

But one must not overweigh the value of local informants. The pāratiyārs and dramatists are always part of the ritual cycle wherever they go. In some places they take on ritual roles that are elsewhere performed by local residents.[3] They know a great deal about ritual variations and are quite willing to discuss norms and departures from them. They sometimes claim to base their views on a *śāstra*, or manual, of which there are no doubt some in written form. But since no one could produce or tell me how to find one, the shastraic claims also seem to function as an oral tradition of their own (cf. Reports . . . 1854, 25, 31). On matters of norms, dramatists seem quite flexible, while certain pāratiyārs can be quite prickly. V. M. Brameesa Mudaliyar privately described some "omissions" in the 1981 rituals at Tindivanam as "violations" (*aṭappiṭi:* "violence," literally "holding to what is contemptible"). His is a clear instance where varied professional exposure, backed by long experience and training, supports informed synthesis and learned judgments (see also Hiltebeitel 1988a, 436). We shall return to him, and a tour I took with him, later in this chapter, and again in chapter 11. In contrast, when V. Govindaswami, the Tindivanam Draupadī temple priest or *pūcāri,* joined me on a tour of some other South Arcot Draupadī temples, he was surprised and not a little baffled by the considerable differences in temples and festivals only thirty miles from his own. Even supposing that there are au-

2. His most important cues will be cited in chapters 8 and 14.

3. See already Hiltebeitel 1988a, 43–51 and 168–82, on alternation between dramatists and local people in processional "street dramas."

thoritative shastraic traditions on Draupadī cult rituals, however, one problem is that the pāratiyārs and others who (orally) transmit them remain to some extent influenced in interpreting them by the forms the rituals have traditionally taken at the temples of their own native and surrounding villages.

We have, in any case, no assured access to any "classical" form of the Draupadī cult ritual cycle (see Appendix, nn. 24, 25). Every temple has fashioned its own festival from what seems to be an amazing array of basic options and innovative possibilities. It is a process that must have involved migrations and the establishment of new temples and ritual cycles based on old models but with new distinguishing features; accentuations and enlargements of specific rites out of local pride; the development of regional consistencies; selective borrowing, abandonment, and revival of specific rites; adoptions and adaptations of elements introduced by contact with the cults of other deities, especially other goddesses; flirtations with modernity; and so on.[4] In a sense, we are faced with distilling what is essential from so much variety when variety is its essence. But we cannot content ourselves with the extreme position that every local solution has equal significance. Our primary focus will be on the relative homogeneity, sustained amid remarkable diversity, of the Draupadī cult within its Gingee core area. We shall not, however, miss the opportunity to draw inferences from fieldwork, by myself and others, on Draupadī festivals outside this area—particularly in Thanjavur District to the south—to gauge such regional consistencies and variations. Moreover, the notion of a core area inevitably poses problems of diffusion (Hiltebeitel 1988a, 23–51).

In this regard, it will be worth restating the basic parameters of these problems, described in volume 1, and indicating a few modifications now required by the findings of more recent fieldwork. Volume 1 argued that the Draupadī cult consolidated between the late thirteenth century and the end of the fourteenth century (probably in the early fourteenth century) in the region of Gingee (South

4. The Tindivanam temple constructed a concrete effigy of Duryodhana in the 1960s, but it was destroyed in the early 1970s because, according to Purushottama Chettiyar, it attracted ghosts and troubled the public at night. South and west of the core area, one also finds permanent large prone effigies of Aravāṉ rather than Duryodhana: at Chinna Salem (see plate 13), Reṭṭipāḷaiyam near Thanjavur (Eveline Masilamani-Meyer's information), and Muṭiyaṉūr near Kallakuruchi (L. Sundar's information). Draupadī temples at Nallāṉpiḷḷaiperṟāḷ and Mutikai Nallāṉkuppam have been fitted with television sets in their outer walls.

Arcot District, Tamilnadu), that the Gingee region is thus the "core area" of the cult, and that the dispersal of the cult has gone through three main historical phases:

1. A diffusion throughout the Gingee core area itself, coincident with the emergence and self-definition of Gingee as a Hindu kingdom (or, more precisely, a Vijayanagar Nayakate), with a high concentration of this dispersal involving the carrying of the cult into rural villages and the founding therein of new temples. It is in this area that the cult has had its most intense regional diffusion: both "horizontally" across the terrain, and "vertically" through the caste system.[5]

2. The carrying of the cult beyond the core area. This no doubt had already begun during the period of Hindu rule in Gingee, but it intensified after that rule ended, in about 1648, with the takeover of Gingee by a succession of increasingly distant outside rulers: Bijapuri Muslim rule from 1648 to 1677, Maratha rule from 1677 to 1697, and Mughal rule, increasingly nominal, from 1697 to 1801. From 1718 on, the Gingee Fort was abandoned as a regional political center, with Mughal overlordship centered in nearby Arcot while the real centers of regional power continued to shift to French Pondicherry and British Madras. In these conditions, which were extremely harsh for the Gingee area and resulted in depopulation within it and migrations away from it, Draupadī cult diffusion was directed primarily to the larger towns and cities in surrounding kingdoms and districts within present-day Tamilnadu and neighboring states. In most of these areas the cult has had minimal rural village spread, as distinct from its diffusion through the core area. But the Thanjavur area must now be recognized as an important exception.

3. Under colonial conditions, the cult extended its diaspora to areas beyond South India, such as Fiji, Singapore, Malaysia, Réunion, Mauritius,[6] South Africa,[7] and Sri Lanka. With the likely exception of Sri Lanka,[8] none of these migrations seems to have occurred before the nineteenth century.

5. These terms are drawn from Srinivas 1965, 213–24 and passim, and Tanaka's discussion thereof (1987, 15–16).

6. Chellappan 1990, 1: Draupadī temples founded in 1859 and 1878.

7. Fisher 1974, 31, shows an Indian woman with "her cheeks and tongue pierced by fine gold needles . . . for an annual ceremony to the Hindu fire god, Dhrobathie." An *Observer* editor informed me that the photograph was shot in South Africa.

8. Hiltebeitel 1988a, 39–40; Tanaka 1987, 78, 331. Tanaka says the Draupadī temple at Udappu (Puttalam District, North Western Province, Sri Lanka) is traced by contemporary informants to seventeenth-century migrations from South India.

I will still hold to the hypothesis of diffusion from Gingee. But two new considerations are now in order. It has become apparent from my most recent fieldwork that in Thanjavur District (and extending into the eastern parts of Tiruchirappalli District), there are many more *village* Draupadī temples than I suspected. The generalizations about the limits of rural spread within the core area were made on the basis of information gathered from 1961 Census sources. Even from that information, however, I had already anticipated that the rural spread of Draupadī temples was continuous from the core area south into the Thanjavur Delta and was largely limited to these two contiguous regions (see Hiltebeitel 1988a, 24, map 1 and p. 40). It is all the more remarkable, then, that the cult is so different from the one area to the other. We have already noted the absence of itinerant Terukkūttu troupes in the Thanjavur region, and we shall observe further differences as they emerge in our discussion. The argument for diffusion from Gingee has thus become more complicated, and will be returned to in chapter 13, by which point all the major variations will have been covered.

Second, our assessment of the Muslim impact on the Draupadī cult through the presence in it of Draupadī's Muslim guardian and horseman, Muttāl Rāvuttaṉ (Hiltebeitel 1988a, 17, 21), has been made more complex by the recent findings of Susan Bayly (1989). Islam took root in the Tamil hinterland as early as the thirteenth to fourteenth century (ibid., 86), and by the fourteenth century Muslim traders supplied West Asian horses to the Pandyan rulers (ibid., 78). After the fall of Bijapur to the Mughals in the late seventeenth century, new Muslim warrior elites, speaking Dakhni, a southern variant of Urdu, moved south to settle in Tamil fortress towns like Gingee. There they were joined by Tamil-speaking Muslims claiming warrior status, who used the title Rowther or Rāvuttar/Rāvuttaṉ ("horseman"), as in Muttal Rāvuttaṉ. A parallel is found among eighteenth-century southern Tamil poligar chieftains, for whom having Muslim soldiers in their service was part of the process of domain building (ibid., 97–98). Rāvuttar shrines in these kingdoms came to provide "a focus for . . . clan-based martial populations" like the Maravars (ibid., 395). Similarly, Muttāl Rāvuttaṉ "shrines" became part of the "little kingdom" domain building reflected in Draupadī temples, where they were set within her "royal" temple compounds. As in the southern poligar domains, Draupadī's "Rowther" was worshipped by "martial" populations—especially Vaṉṉiyars—among her devotees. When this happened in the Draupadī cult's formation remains uncertain, but the fact that Draupadī's Muslim "horseman" serves her not only in the Gingee core area but, as we shall see, in the Thanjavur region still suggests that their connection goes back to the earliest phases of the cult's formation and diffusion and is older than the seventeenth- and eighteenth-century developments just mentioned.

With such considerations in mind, however, the three historical phases still allow us to identify certain effects of diffusion within, and "through," the cult. Though it is not possible to be sure what elements of the Draupadī cult go back to its constitutive period in the Gingee core area, certain elements today either are not found in the Draupadī cult beyond that region, or else are more highly concentrated, or have singular features, in the core area. Most of these core area elements, and especially the rituals among them, pose the possibility of discrete studies of diffusion that range beyond the Draupadī cult, since few are "unique" to it. One "unique" feature, however, a myth looked at in volume 1, is worth reexamining in this context as an exemplary case in point. Widely known through the core area but unknown beyond it, it describes how Draupadī was born a second time to come to the aid of an ancient king of Gingee to help him—aided by her guardian-to-be, Pōttu Rāja—to defeat the demon Acalammācuraṉ (or some such name). For current reference, I update the discussion by summarizing in this volume's Appendix the version of this myth found in a text called *Tiraupatātēvi Māṉmiyam*, "The Glorification of Draupadī Devī" (Ilaṭcumaṇappiḷḷai 1902). An important Draupadī cult document, this text provides the only known literary version of this story.

The myth identifies Draupadī's second advent with the stabilizing of the Gingee kingdom in a remote past, well before what can be identified as Gingee's actual history, and explains the founding of her "original temple" in Mēlaccēri village just outside the capital (Hiltebeitel 1988a, 29–30, 82, 88). I stressed the way this myth reflects a Hindu "little kingdom" ideal that finds similar, or at least comparable, expressions in the regional cults of other Indian "folk" deities of "royal" and "dominant caste" clans (that is, *kuladevatā*s, "clan deities"). In particular, there appeared to be the common denominator that cults of this type were consolidated in the process of early contacts with Islam (ibid., 21, 100–102). One might further see these developments as "locative" traditions in the sense proposed by Jonathan Z. Smith (1978, xiii), involving archaicization of "native" traditions, revival of myth, emphasis on the saving power of kingship over and against monstrous demons (a hundred- or thousand-headed one in the case of Draupadī's opponent), and moreover, within the core area, the ritual and mythic localization and poetic vernacularization (by Villiputtūr Āḻvār, ca. 1400) of the

Mahābhārata itself. It would be not only possible but fruitful to investigate these developments as part of a bhakti continuum, with such "locative" expressions in tension with more universal "utopian" sectarian and pilgrimage traditions, which become increasingly dissociated from royal values, concerns, and possibilities, and even from the aspiration to rule. Moreover, over time and space, it can be shown that the Draupadī cult loses this locative dimension. In the second phase of diffusion outside the core area, and particularly in the Thanjavur area, not only are the Gingee setting and mythology forgotten, but the myths and rituals are reshaped, often losing something of their royal, landed ideology, and sometimes conforming with more Brahmanical and pan-Hindu models. In the third phase of diffusion, outside India, one finds, at least in Fiji, the cult transformed into an expression of what could certainly be called a "utopian" vision of pan-Hindu unity.[9]

Beyond such variance over time and space, one other useful heuristic that I have found for clarifying broad differentiations between the festival cycles of Draupadī temples is the simple but usually quite revealing one, already mentioned in chapter 1, of classifying them according to whether the temples are in villages, large towns, or cities. Though I will discuss numerous temples and festivals of each type, I will for each variety take one as the temple and festival of reference. Mēlaccēri, or "Old Gingee," where Draupadī has her "original" temple, will for obvious reasons be our most remembered village, though for the Thanjavur area, we shall also familiarize ourself with the festival at Cattiram Karuppūr. Tindivanam will be our exemplary town. And Madras, the only major city within the core area and the site of at least ten Draupadī temples, will be represented primarily by the Sowcarpet temple near the center of the city, about a mile west of Georgetown and Parry's Corner. I attended much (but never all) of the course of these festivals: at Mēlaccēri in 1982 and 1986 (recorded on videotape; Hiltebeitel 1988b); at Cattiram Karuppūr in 1990; at Tindivanam in 1977 and 1981; and at Sowcarpet in 1975. Preliminary and follow-up fieldwork was done in all cases with my chief informants, at Mēlaccēri and Tindivanam as recently as 1990. I will move back and forth among these festivals, and among others from within the three basic types. This differential key will raise issues that overlap at points with those raised by the rapport between the core area and

9. See Brown 1984, 238–39, on pan-Indian involvement in this South Indian rite; similarly, Babb 1974; Tanaka 1987 (see n. 17 below). On uprooted "utopian" forms of bhakti under Muslim rule in the North, see Hein 1986.

the Draupadī cult diaspora, but by and large they will be different issues. Each will serve to highlight the consistent organizational principles and rituals that distinguish one Draupadī festival from another, and each will support the premise that, precisely where it differs, an "other" festival usually has structures and ceremonies that compensate for what it seems to be missing.

A. Festival Organization

Though the organization of a Draupadī festival is vital to its success in any circumstances, one has the impression that it is in the towns that organization poses the most crucial challenges. Village festivals, where successful, can rely upon traditional offices being passed on hereditarily (*paramparai*), often within a small set of participating castes. Such transmission becomes more problematic for town and urban Draupadī festivals. But whereas urban festivals succeed or fail by their ability to generate enthusiasm, as at Sowcarpet, within a particular residential quarter,[10] town festivals are most successful when they are able to negotiate a diversified sponsorship that takes in some "village"-wide representation of the town as a whole. This has been achieved at Tindivanam, Kalahasti, and Pondicherry, while at other comparable "headquarter" towns, Draupadī temples have fallen into total (Wandiwash) or relative (Tiruvannamalai Forest Draupadī Temple, Chidambaram, Vellore) disuse or have kept only small followings within the "hamlets" and castes that have traditionally supported the temples (Cuddalore, Villupuram, other temples at Tiruvannamalai).

In other words, while the villages surely retain what is most traditional within the cult, core area towns, where they have been successful, are interesting for the ways they magnify and extend the cult's structural and organizational principles. The Tindivanam festival is an especially rich example in this regard. As Brameesa Mudaliyar's remarks indicate, its ritual cycle is certainly not uniformly "classical." But it has other merits that make it ideal as a representative example. Tindivanam is centrally located within the Draupadī cult core area, only about twenty miles east of Gingee. Its festival is ambitiously organized, and would seem to have been conceived and developed, at least in its current form, with an eye to amplitude and completeness, as is evidenced by its sponsorship

10. Besides Sowcarpet, other Madras city Draupadī temples continue to hold festivals at Muthialpet, Teynampet, and Kilpauk, but the Mylapore temple has not held a festival for many years.

of a full eighteen nights (evoking the eighteen-day *Mahābhārata* war) of Terukkūttu dramas (Hiltebeitel 1988a, 144, 164–66). Moreover, the cult has prospered at Tindivanam in recent years. Brameesa Mudaliyar claimed that the crowds at the 1981 festival's culminating day ceremonies were the largest he had ever seen at the five hundred Draupadī festivals he had attended. The 1977 festival's crowds were no smaller: both, according to sober local estimates, were in the range of 10,000 to 15,000 people. But the number of firewalkers had grown from about 360 in 1977 to 800 in 1981 (the temple sells tickets to the firewalkers, so these figures are quite accurate). The latter figure is among the largest I have heard of and by far the largest I have witnessed, though it is again mainly in comparable Taluk towns that similar figures have been mentioned. My assistant C. T. Rajan learned from local informants at Kalahasti that there were about 1,000 firewalkers there in 1979, and in 1986 the Kalahasti temple pūcāri told me that 3,000 crossed the coals in the 1986 festival. The only mention of large numbers at a village Draupadī festival was at Vīrāṇantal, where, to the dismay of my informant, who would have preferred a calmer scene, there were said to have been 1,000 firewalkers in 1987 and other recent years. In 1990 the same informant said there had been no festival there since 1986 because the last one had been so hectic.

The organizational drive of the Tindivanam Draupadī temple is evident from the maximal thoroughness of its forty days of *Pāratam* (Sanskrit *Bhāratam*, that is, *Mahābhārata* recitation), eighteen nights of Terukkūttu, and well-structured rituals. It is also apparent from its success in enlisting support and involvement from different local communities: not only from a wide range of castes, but from various economically and ritually defined groups as well. This is borne out in the variety of groups and individuals who serve as sponsors (*upayatārs*) of the eighteen (or alternatively eighteen plus one) Terukkūttu dramas. As Tanaka has shown, upayatārs (or *upayakkāraṉs* in the form he cites from Sri Lanka) figure in the originally Vedic ritual function of *yajamāna* (Tamil *ecamāṉ*) as "sacrificer" and sponsor of rites.[11] Meanwhile, this essentially royal function is complemented at Tindivanam by the involvement of an

11. Tanaka 1987, 146–48 (observing that upayakkāraṉs are less active in the rituals than *bhaktas*); 178–79 (*upayam* as "gift" or "endowment"); 251, nn. 3, 4, and 6. Like the Vedic yajamāna, upayakkāraṉs in Udappu must be married, linking them, like the sacrificer, to householders' concerns with *kāma*, the ability to "control and enjoy female sexuality," and "desire" for the fruits of sacrifices (179, 251, n. 6, citing Malamoud in Biardeau and Malamoud 1976, 157). Cf. also Reiniche 1979, 87–88; Tarabout 1987, 602.

Aiyar Brahman, who daily decorates the chief processional images—usually Draupadī's and that of a companion figure prominent in the night's drama—that are taken by bullock cart on nightly tours through the streets of the town.[12] These processions of the deity through the town (*cāmi ūrvalam*) present Draupadī as a royal persona, sovereign during her festival over the town she traverses (Hiltebeitel 1988a, 3); they announce each night's play, bring the goddess before her worshipers' homes, and draw the town (or village) into the narrative progress of the Pāratam as both epic story and mode of worship distinctive to this epic goddess. At Tindivanam, the correlations between the patronage of the upayatārs, the nightly dramas, and the decoration of the icons reveal a number of creative solutions to the problems of retaining a basic festival structure while diversifying patronage in changing conditions. The list of dramas for 1981 (little changed from 1977, when the first play was omitted) is given in table 2.

The choice of icons has, of course, in each case some correlation with the night's drama, a point that ties the *alaṅkāra*s, or icon decorations, to the *Mahābhārata* in ways that clearly differentiate Draupadī festivals with Terukkūttu from festivals where such dramas are lacking. In festivals without dramas, the alaṅkāras take on an independent importance of their own, and show Draupadī and other epic figures in forms that identify them not so much with the epic as with the larger Hindu pantheon.[13] It should be noted that the Tindivanam list refers only to the primary icons that are decorated for the processions. Undecorated wooden icons of Pōttu Rāja, Kṛṣṇa, and the Pāṇḍavas are also sometimes taken out on an additional bullock cart that accompanies the main one. The choices of Draupadī's chief processional companion (or replacement, in the single case of Subhadrā, for the enactment of the latter's wedding) hold only a few instructive surprises: the frequency with which Arjuna appears before the war but not during it; Draupadī's appearance with Kālī for Aravāṉ's prewar sacrifice being her only procession with another female. What is significant for now is the design behind the sponsorship of the plays.

A comparison with the list of sponsors for the thirteen plays at Mēlaccēri village reveals two contrasts. First, at Mēlaccēri there is little, if any, evidence of an attempt to correlate identifying traits of

12. The Brahman's roles here are more extensive than at most village Draupadī temples. Brahman participation will be noted where it occurs and discussed especially in chapters 4 through 6; see also n. 19, below.

13. See Hiltebeitel 1988a, 48–49, on contemporary festivals at Dindigul; Shideler 1987, 111–22, on those at Pondicherry.

Table 2. The 1981 Tindivanam Festival: Dramas, Sponsors, and Icons

Day	Drama	Sponsor	Icons
1	Kaṇṇaṉ Jalakkirīṭai, "Kṛṣṇa's Water Sports"	Yātavas (= Yādavas, Kōṉārs), milkmen, cattle and buffalo herders	Draupadī and Kṛṣṇa
2	Arakkumāḷikai, "The Lacquer House"	Kottaṉārs, masons	Draupadī and Bhīma
3	Vilvaḷaippu, "Bending of the Bow"	Vaṉṉiyars	Draupadī and Arjuna
4	Turōpatai Mālaiyīṭu, "Draupadī's Marriage"	Vāṉiyar Ceṭṭiyārs, oil sellers	Draupadī and Arjuna
5	Cupattirai Mālaiyīṭu, "Subhadrā's Marriage"	Reṭṭiyars (Reḍḍis) from Jakkampēṭṭai Hamlet	Subhadrā and Arjuna
6	Irājacūya Yākam, "Rājasūya Sacrifice"	All castes of Tindivanam: donations collected through whole town, overseen by the temple trustees	Draupadī and Dharma
7	Cūtu Tukilurital, "Dice Match and Disrobing"	Vaṇṇāṉs (Dhobys), washermen	Draupadī and Kṛṣṇa
8	Arccuṉaṉ Tapacu, "Arjuna's Tapas"	Vāṉiyar Ceṭṭiyārs, oil sellers	Draupadī and Arjuna
9	Arccuṉaṉ Tēvappaṭṭam Peṟutal, "Arjuna Obtains a Divine Diadem"	Vaṇṇāṉs, washermen	Draupadī and Arjuna
10	Kīcaka Cammāram, "Slaughter of Kīcaka"	Vaṉṉiyars from Muruṅkappākkam Hamlet	Draupadī and Bhīma
11	Virāṭa Paruvam, "Book of Virāṭa" (= Māṭupiṭi Caṇṭai, "Fight over the Cattle Raid")	Erikoṭi Village residents (in 1981 only one: Devaraj Goundar, a Vaṉṉiyar)	Draupadī and Arjuna
12	Kiruṣṇaṉ Tūtu, "Kṛṣṇa the Messenger"	Double bullock cart drivers (iraṭṭaimāṭṭuvaṇṭikkārar)	Draupadī and Kṛṣṇa
13	Aravāṉ Kaṭapali, "Aravāṉ's Sacrifice"	Handcart pullers (kaivaṇṭikkārar)	Draupadī and Kālī
14	Pōrmaṉṉaṉ Caṇṭai, "Pōrmaṉṉaṉ's Fight"	Govinda Reddi, truck fleet owner	Draupadī and Pōttu Rāja-Pōrmaṉṉaṉ
15	Apimaṉṉaṉ Caṇṭai, "Abhimanyu's Fight"	Milk Society, cow and buffalo owners who pool money and resources in a cooperative	Draupadī and Abhimanyu

Table 2 *(continued)*

Day	Drama	Sponsor	Icons
16	Cayintavaṉ Caṇṭai, "Saindhava's [Jayadratha's] Fight"	Tea shop proprietors	Draupadī and Jayadratha
17	Tuṟcātaṉaṉ Caṇṭai, "Duḥśāsana's Fight"	Elumalai Brothers (Vaṉṉiyars)	Draupadī and Bhīma
18	Karṇamōṭca, "Karṇa's Salvation"	Paṇiceyvaṉs, funeral attendants, conch-blowers in funeral processions	Draupadī and Karṇa
19	Patiṉeṭṭām Pōr, "Eighteenth-Day War" (death of Duryodhana)	Shopworkers (of provision stores, "fancy stores," general merchants, etc.)	Draupadī and Bhīma

the upayatārs with the plays they sponsor. The only singular feature of the Mēlaccēri list is the sponsorship of "Eighteenth-Day War" by two groups of Harijans, which does not suggest any evident correlation, unless it be with the play's "handling" of numerous deaths, including Duryodhana's. At Tindivanam, on the contrary, certain correlations are unmistakable. It is obviously fitting that the Yādavas should sponsor the "Water Sports" of the Yādava hero Kṛṣṇa, that masons should contribute for "the Lacquer House," and that washermen should lend a hand for Draupadī's "Disrobing."[14] It is also significant that the Paṇiceyvaṉs, blowers of the conch (a symbol of Viṣṇu's) at funeral processions, should sponsor the play in which Karṇa dies attaining *mokṣa*, "salvation," through a vision of Kṛṣṇa atop Garuḍa (see Hiltebeitel 1988a, 410–13). Other possible correlations can also be entertained. For instance, sponsorship of *Pōrmaṉṉaṉ Caṇṭai* by a Reddy or Reṭṭi, a traditionally land-owning caste from Andhra Pradesh, suggests another signpost within the Draupadī cult of Pōttu Rāja's Telugu affinities and origins (cf. ibid., 83). But most interesting is the sponsorship of Yudhiṣṭhira's *rājasūya*, or royal consecration, sacrifice. Just as in the epic and the corresponding drama, all the kings of the earth must give their tribute to Yudhiṣṭhira for the performance of this sacrifice, so all the castes of Tindivanam make their donations to sponsor this performance. Like all the kings of the earth, "all the

14. At Mēlaccēri a group of Ceṭṭi families sponsored "Water Sports" and a group of Vaṉṉiyar families "Dice Match and Disrobing."

castes" are thus drawn into the drama cycle to contribute the "wealth" that not only supports the sacrifice that makes Dharma the sovereign king, but also excites the irreversible jealousy of Duryodhana. Moreover, it is the temple trustees who oversee this collection, and thus serve as the true upayatārs. This recalls Tanaka's findings that "when a particular rite in a festival is sponsored by the village as a whole," the temple administrative committee (*mutatis mutandis,* the trustees) "plays the role of sacrificer" (Tanaka 1987, 181; see above, n. 11).

Such correlations at Tindivanam are evidence of a deliberate adaptive design, one that has made the *Mahābhārata* "relevant" to changing social conditions and drawn creatively upon the town's character as a commercial center.[15] Indeed, not only do "all the castes" confer their symbolic wealth; the "Fights" of Abhimanyu and Jayadratha are sponsored by the Milk Society and the tea shop proprietors, and "Eighteenth-Day War" by a cross section of shop workers and general merchants. The contrast with typical village festivals is striking here. At Tindivanam, only three of the nineteen dramas were sponsored by Vaṉṉiyars, the Draupadī cult's staunchest patrons, particularly in South Arcot. At Mēlaccēri, the corresponding figure (for the 1981 festival) was seven out of thirteen (or nine out of thirteen, if one counts sponsorship of two plays by neighboring villages, where the support was no doubt mainly from Vaṉṉiyar families). Nor at Mēlaccēri or any other village was there any evidence of new commercial groups or unions sponsoring performances.[16] Thus, whereas in villages Draupadī is less a "village goddess" than a lineage goddess (*kuladevatā, kuladevī*), the Tindivanam temple has flourished, quite ironically, by making its festival approximate that of a "village goddess" on an updated, townwide scale.[17]

15. An opportunity was perhaps missed, however, by the double bullock cart drivers, who might have sponsored Arjuna's recovery of the cattle.

16. The other drama-sponsoring communities were Ceṭṭis, Vāṉiyar Ceṭṭis, Reṭṭis, Nāyuṭus, and Harijans. Similar data were gathered at Veḷḷimēṭupēṭṭai village (in 1977), where three of eight dramas were sponsored by Vaṉṉiyars, with the rest by Ceṭṭis, Vaṉiyar Ceṭṭis, Reṭṭis, and Nāyuṭus.

17. For comparable data involving sponsorship of the main rituals (though not dramas) at a town-scale Draupadī festival at Udappu, Sri Lanka, see Tanaka 1987, 178–79, 339–43, on major changes in the patronage system since 1950, from general patronage by the villagers, mostly "Sea Vēḷāḷar" (Katal Vēḷāḷar) fishermen, to control in recent years by the wealthier members of this community, and since 1979 by two Columbo merchants of Indian origin, not connected with either fishing or the village.

B. Draupadī Temples and Their Personnel

We have already observed some of the more important functions of Draupadī temple "trustees," the English term that is widely adopted into Tamil as an equivalent of *tarumakarttā*, "manager or trustee of a Hindu temple" (*Tamil Lexicon*). They are men of financial responsibility and high status among the local adherents to the cult, patrons of the temple and its festival, chief festival organizers, and embodiments of the function of yajamāna in both domestic and "royal" aspects, at Tindivanam notably as overseers of the patronage by "all the castes" of the performance of Yudhiṣṭhira's Rājasūya. As in related terms like *tarumakāriyam*, "act of charity" (ibid.), *taruma* (Sanskrit *dharma*) has here the connotation of "charity," just as upayatār connotes one who makes a gift or endowment (see n. 11).

Commonly a Draupadī temple will have five trustees, although this number may go up or down from year to year. It is also not unusual in villages for a temple to have one chief trustee, and for those with other titles to join him in overseeing the festival and temple administration. The Tindivanam temple had seven trustees in 1977 and five in 1981. Surprisingly, most of the trustees at Tindivanam were Kōmati Ceṭṭiyārs: four of seven, and then three of five (including the chief trustee, the aforementioned Purushottama Chettiyar) in those two years. Two others were Vaṉṉiyars and one, in 1977, a Reṭṭi. Most if not all of these trustees have shops (grain shops for the Ceṭṭiyārs) at a major crossroad near the temple. It may be noted that the Kōmati Ceṭṭis, like Reṭṭis, hail originally from Andhra and still speak Telugu in their homes. They also represent themselves as vegetarians and Vaiśyas, unlike the Reṭṭis and Vaṉṉiyars, who both eat nonvegetarian food and claim a Kṣatriya heritage. It would seem that the Tindivanam grouping reflects an alliance of the Tamil Vaṉṉiyars not only with originally Telugu-speaking communities, but with communities recognized for somewhat greater wealth and status. Factors such as these no doubt lie behind the organizational and economic successes of the Tindivanam temple, in particular, what might be called the partial commercialization of the upayatār function. Most other core area temples have rather different combinations of trustees. Of those on which I gathered information, ten were dominated by Vaṉṉiyars (evenly distributed between South Arcot, North Arcot, and Chingleput Districts), three by Kōṉārs or Yādavas (also equally distributed, Mēlaccēri being the most important example), and two by Mutaliyārs (both in North Arcot, where they outnumber the other two communities). The only other temple I have found to be controlled by Ceṭṭiyārs is that at Veḷḷimēṭupēṭṭai.[18]

There is, as might be expected, some correlation between the caste of the controlling trustees and that of the pūcāri, the temple priest. Thus at Mēlaccēri, the pūcāri is a Kōṉār; and at Māṉāmpāṭi, a Mutaliyār temple in Kanchipuram Taluk, Chingleput District (but at a crossover point near Cheyyar District, North Arcot), the pūcāri is a Mutaliyār. But it is at least as common for the pūcāri to be a Vaṉṉiyar while the majority of overseers of the temple are of a different community. So it is at Tindivanam, where the position has passed to V. Govindaswami from his father. It is, in effect, a pattern that was noted by T. A. Nayakar when he remarked that Vaṉṉiyars are usually given the role of carrying the "fire pot" on their heads "as a relic of [their] origin from fire" (1891, 42–43; cf. Hiltebeitel 1988a, 35–38). Though various pots or *karakam*s are carried at different times in a festival, his observation seems to refer to the pot that is carried over the firepit. This job is usually done by the temple pūcāri, as is the case at Tindivanam (see plate 35). I have noted only two cases where a Vaṉṉiyar-controlled temple has a non-Vaṉṉiyar pūcāri: at Cantirampāṭi (Wandiwash Taluk, North Arcot), where the pūcāri is a Kōṉār, and at Pūṉamalli (Sriperumbudur Taluk, Chingleput District), just outside Madras, where a Vaṉṉiyar has recently been replaced by a Paṇṭāram. Only in Madras city temples have I found such exceptional figures as the Liṅgāyat pūcāri at the Mylapore Dharmarāja Temple, the Aiyar Brahman Kurukkaḷ at the Dharmarāja-Vināyakar Temple in Muthialpet, and, according to the 1961 Census, a Brahman priest at the Elephant Gate temple, where no festival had been held for the previous thirty years (Nambiar 1965, 177). It may be noted that in all four of these latter cases from in or around Madras, the role of pūcāri has been assumed not by a member of a prominant "village" caste, but by individuals from groups defined by specifically religious functions.[19]

At the next level of involvement, that of aiding the pūcāri and performing hereditary roles at festivals, the preponderance of Vaṉṉiyars usually increases still further. Here Tindivanam is no

18. See also Moses 1961, 84: the Cuṇṇāmpukuḷam Draupadī temple (Ponneri Taluk, Chingleput District) "is the exclusive property of the Chettiars and Vanniars." See further Hiltebeitel 1988a, 32–39.

19. Paṇṭārams are traditionally those who arrange flowers and sell garlands for temple *pūjā*s (offerings); Liṅgāyats are a Śaivite sect, originally from Karnataka, who

exception, as all but one of the people who have such roles are Vaṉṉiyars, the other being a Kōṉār. Some of these roles involve titles, whose use seems to have considerable local variation, as well as what might be called popular applications. The variants, however, are of the greatest importance for understanding the rituals—especially those of the festival's culminatiing day—and must be looked at closely.

While I questioned countless informants about the nature of these offices, the pāratiyār Brameesa Mudaliyar, familiar with the practices at numerous temples and, as ever, a keen observer, was one of the few to offer any kind of synthetic overview. In fact, a tour he once took with me to five Draupadī temples just north and east of Kanchipuram was undertaken in part to test his theory: a test that met with as much variation (which he greeted with good-humored shrugs) as confirmation. In any case the norm, as he saw it, was that a temple should have four titled offices: *kaṇāccāri* (pronounced *gaṇāchāri*), *camayam*, *kuntam*, and *kumāravarkkam*.

In its literal meaning, a kaṇāccāri is a "teacher common to all, a teacher of the people" (Sanskrit *gaṇācārya*). It should be noted that this office is not unique to the Draupadī cult. Elliot mentions a *gaṇāchāri* who ties the *tāli*, or wedding necklace, around a village goddess in Karnataka (1860, 1:408; cf. Hiltebeitel 1985a, 174 and n. 11). "Ganachari" is an office of quite high rank in Liṅgāyat *panchāyat*s, or councils (Thurston and Rangachari [1904], 1965, 4:271). And in night processions for Vīrabhadra in the town of Rajahmundry in East Godavari District, Andhra, those who are possessed are called *gaṇācāri*s (Knipe 1989, 139), singling them out from the deity's general "host," or *gaṇa*. This set of functions—ceremonial prominence in the worship of village deities, supervision at marriages (whether divine or human), high rank in community councils, affinities with possession—may look to be a rather stray assortment, but as we shall see, they all have counterparts in the role of the kaṇāccāri at Draupadī festivals, at least in one place or another. *Camayam* (Sanskrit *samayam*) seems to be used in its sense of "arrangement" or "observance": perhaps the person in charge of

---

not infrequently take on priestly functions; Kurukkaḷ can be a term for Brahman priests at Śaiva and goddess temples and for "Śaiva Vēḷāḷa priests who minister to Non-Brahmans" (*Tamil Lexicon*). The Muthialpet temple Kurukkaḷ claims to be an Aiyar Brahman. Generally, Kurukkaḷs make this claim, while Aiyar Brahmans deny them that status. For our purposes, although Brahmans who participate in the Draupadī cult are probably in most if not all cases Kurukkaḷs, within the cult they are considered full Brahmans and will be so referred to here.

arrangements concerning observances.[20] *Kuntam* (or *kontam*) is the short form of *vīrakuntam*, the name for the odd-numbered, multi-tined lance that figures in the mythology of Pōttu Rāja–Pōrmaṉṉaṉ (see fig. 11; Hiltebeitel 1988a, 81, 85, 387, 391). One would thus expect that the person who bears this title should have some connection with this ritual implement. Finally, *kumāravarkkam* means literally "lineage" or "progeny" (*Tamil Lexicon*), or, if one breaks it down, the "class of youths" (Sanskrit *kumāravarga*). As a single title, it thus seems to refer to one who represents or supervises the continuity of the lineage. As an office, however, it has a history of being part of the "Poligar system" in Tamilnadu, an "essentially feudal and military" system in which the Poligar "was required to fulfil obligations to the imperial house like the payment of annual tribute, maintenance of a standing army and attendance at the Imperial Court on important and ceremonial occasions, in return for assignments of land to him, which he enjoyed" (Mahalingam 1972, xxxi–xxxii; cf. also 171 and idem [1940] 1975, 1:195–202). While imperial organization must have only rarely been as thorough as these words suggest, and especially rare with regard to the fractious Poligars,[21] the "institution of *Kumāravargam*" is not in question: "It would appear that the kings, chieftains, Poligars, and other rulers gave some of their leading ministers, officers, and others the status of the prince of the ruling house as a result of which they came to be called *Kumāravargam*" (Mahalingam 1972, xxxii) in the sense of "youths" or "sons" of the (royal) lineage, or "princes." Thus Dirks takes the term to mean "group of sons," implying a "highly privileged, perhaps connubial, circle of the king's sons," an "elite corps of the [Madurai] Nayaka's supporters" (1987, 101, 106, 111). Says Mahalingam: "This reminds one of the practice that obtained in earlier periods of South India under the rulers of the Cāḷukya, Hoysaḷa and Vijayanagar dynasties where prominent officers connected with the administration were treated as sons, *piḷḷais* or members of the royal family" (1972, xxxii). These remarks will help us to see how this title, relayed into the cult of a goddess

20. *Camayam* in Malayalam refers to the "decoration and dressing" of the king (the Raja of Cochin, the Zamorin of Calicut), as well as that of certain icons; see Tarabout 1986, 444 and n. 22.

21. Dirks 1982, 659, traces the rise of Poligars (Pāḷaiyakārs: those who "ruled over *pāḷaiyams* [literally, armed camps]" as "small kingdoms") of southern Tamilnadu to the period after "the collapse of the great Cōḻa empire in the thirteenth century," and their periodic flourishing after that to later eras (Vijayanagar, Nayak, late eighteenth century) of imperial decline.

of lineages with "royal" aspirations at the village level, could be taken in varying individual and group senses.

There are several problems, however, in working from these four names, not the least of which are that one of them, kuntam, is rarely found as a single ritual office, that kumāravarkkam has its single and plural variant meanings and extensions, and that the four are not always separated as a group from other Draupadī temple offices.[22] Moreover, they were found at only one temple—Uttiramērūr—in the combination, and with approximately the associations, that Brameesa Mudaliyar, with whom I visited this temple, had set forth as the norm. Since he had something to do with eliciting this information, it may have been teased a bit into its desired shape. In any case, whatever one finds "on the ground," this does not diminish the significance of authoritatively stated norms. I thus turn first to Brameesa Mudaliyar's account as an "ideal" case. It is also noteworthy that the most similar descriptions I obtained also came from other pāratiyārs.[23] I will then take up the actual situation at Tindivanam, which is more representative of the arrangements of most of the temples studied.

According to Brameesa Mudaliyar, the four titles identify their bearers with four different *Mahābhārata* figures and with four ceremonial implements. The kaṇāccāri impersonates a Rākṣasa (Arakkaṉ) in the *Mahābhārata* named Cañcakattakaṉ, and in the rituals he carries a pot (*cempu*) of water. The camayam represents the Brahman-warrior Kirupaṉ or Kirupāccāri (Sanskrit Kṛpa), maternal uncle of Aśvatthāman, and carries a vessel-like plate or offering tray (*tāmpūlat taṭṭu*) with turmeric powder on it. The kuntam office is connected with Aśvatthāman himself, and the person who fills it carries the weapon by the same name, that is, the kuntam or *cūlam* (Sanskrit *śūlam*), or "trident." And the kumāravarkkam is identified with the Yādava hero Kirutavarmaṉ or Kirutavaṉmaṉ (Sanskrit

22. The Tindivanam pūcāri mentioned a *nimantam*, which by itself means "service in a temple," as one of those who, along with the kaṇāccāri and camayam, takes responsibility for the icons. The five "highest positions of management" Frasca found at Iruṅkal were "the Tarumakarttā (care-taker), three Kumāravarkkam (important lineage heads), and one Kaṇṇācāri [sic] (temple leader)" (1984, 275).

23. V. Venugopala Aiyar and M. C. Venkatesha Bhagavatar linked some of these ritual offices with Kaurava survivors. On the other hand, N. M. Adikeshava Bharatiyar indicated an alternative set of correlations between ritual offices and implements: the camayam handling the alaku and kāppu wristlets (see chaps. 3–5), the kumāravarkkam handling firepit preparations; the kaṇāccāri as general supervisor overseeing what others leave out; and the tarumakarttā representing the temple in testing the heat of the firepit with the goddess's tummy sash, or *maṭi* (see chap. 14). On pāratiyārs interviewed in this study up to 1986, see Hiltebeitel 1988a, 78, n. 11.

Kṛtavarman), and carries a sword (*katti* or *alaku*). Brameesa Mudaliyar attributes important ritual roles to these four figures that go beyond the carrying of these implements and link up with a distinctive variant of Draupadī cult epic mythology in which the four heroes are the lone survivors of the Kaurava army who attend the dying Duryodhana as his "bodyguards" (*kāval*).

These learned correlations between officiants, ritual implements, and epic figures are unfamiliar to local temple personnel whom I have interviewed about these various titles. At Tindivanam, for instance, one finds not four titles but two: kaṇāccāri and camayam. These offices are not usually identified with specific figures in the *Mahābhārata*, but where they are, it can just as easily be with the Pāṇḍavas as the Kauravas. Thus at Marutāṭu (Wandiwash Taluk, North Arcot), the offices are said to derive from hereditary jobs in the Pāṇḍava kingdom. And at Kūttampākkam, Biardeau (1989b, 120) found that the original kaṇāccāri was said to have been the leader of the Pāṇḍava army. This "original marshal" is thus an alternate for Pōrmaṉṉaṉ–Pōttu Rāja, who figures most prominently, at least in core area Draupadī cult mythology, as the Pāṇḍavas' marshal (see Hiltebeitel 1988a, 110, 383–86, 392–93, 429), while the actual kaṇāccāri officiant can thus be regarded as one of Pōttu Rāja's ritual stand-ins or companions. In this light, it is further significant that the implements the kaṇāccāri and camayam carry are not the water pot and turmeric plate, as Brameesa Mudaliyar attested, but the two implements he attributed to the kuntam and kumāravarkkam: the kuntam (trident, etc.) and the katti (sword, perhaps fittingly, for a "prince"). At Tindivanam, the kaṇāccāri holds the kuntam; and until recently the katti was held by the camayam (the office has been discontinued). The kuntam, or more commonly vīrakuntam, is one of the most prominent of the ritual implements Pōrmaṉṉaṉ is said to have brought into the service of Draupadī, and while the sword is never mentioned among the weapons he delivers (Hiltebeitel 1988a, 386–89), this is no doubt because he never gives it up: that is, he always carries it in his hand. Moreover, both offices at Tindivanam have belonged consistently to Vaṉṉiyars, as they do at Mēlaccēri and at most other core area temples, including Uttiramērūr.

These facts describe a general pattern that applies, with the inevitable modifications, to numerous temples throughout the core area.[24] At Tailāpuram, for instance, the implements carried by the

24. At Cōḻavantāṉ, the kaṇāccāri and camayam are Nāyuṭus (on whom, in Madurai District, see Hiltebeitel 1988, 49 and n. 26). The kaṇāccāri at Cōḻavantāṉ acts the part of Bhīma at the festival; cf. ibid., 49–50.

two officiants are reversed. At Villupuram, the kaṇāccāri was said to carry both the kuntam and sword, plus the whip (*cāṭṭi* or *vīra-cāṭṭi*), statistically the most prominent of all the ritual weapons that come to Draupadī from Pōrmaṉṉaṉ (Hiltebeitel 1988a, 387), which the kaṇāccāri holds aloft in the kuntam's prongs. At Marutāṭu, the kaṇāccāri, an Ācāri, or artisan, carries the kuntam while the camayam, a Vaṉṉiyar, carries a bell. In addition to these roles, which are performed at processions and in major rituals, the kaṇāccāri and camayam will assist the pūcāri, see to the daily upkeep and requirements of the temple, bring flowers and carry water for various ceremonies, look after the temple's "public relations," and may even sponsor Terukkūttu dramas (as at Mēlaccēri) or serve as "philanthropists." The kaṇāccāri may also have ritual roles that are unique to him, as we shall see. These officiants may also play important roles in the ritual cycle that do not involve their bearing of weapons.

Most problematic, in any case, is the kumāravarkkam. Though such an individual office has been described at more than one temple, at many temples it is not the office of an individual but the designation of a group. At Pūṉamalli, an elderly Vaṉṉiyar informant, who had recently been deposed as his Draupadī temple's chief trustee, offered a correction of the usage. The term, he said, was not kumāravarkkam but *kumāramakkaḷ* or *kumāravarkaḷ*, "the youths," or, given the honorific, "the honorable youths." It referred, he said, to all the Vaṉṉiyars who do firewalking, including the carriers of the various ritual implements.[25] Another rather general definition was given by the Tindivanam pūcāri, who said the kumāravarkkam, or "class of youths," is "all the public who participate in the ceremonies." There are, however, more specific "classes of youths" in Draupadī cult ritual whose roles seem to reflect local and regional variation on what might be called an indispensable kumāra function. One is the group known in some places as *vīrakumāra*s, "heroic youths," who undergo sword-pressing and whipping ordeals. Another, the most arresting for our purposes, is the identification given by an elderly Vaṉṉiyar schoolteacher who serves as camayam at the Draupadī temple at Nallāṉpettāḷ (Chingleput Taluk, Chingleput District): the kumāravarkkam, he says, is the group of five that ritually enacts the war-ending ordeal of the five sons of Draupadī. As we have seen, *kumāravarkkam* also has the

25. A "Brahmin eye-witness" of a firewalk for "Thanthoni Amman, the tutelary deity of the village of Peralur," similarly refers to "the fire-walkers—otherwise known as *kumara makkal*" (Firewalking . . . 1900, 319).

connotation of a "group of sons." It should also be noted in this context that one of the Tamil meanings of *kumāra* is a boy of sixteen, an age that Draupadī cult informants attribute not only to the five Draupadeyas, or sons of Draupadī, but to the other Pāṇḍava sons who die in the war—Abhimanyu and Aravāṉ—as well.[26] For the moment, let us just observe that the ritual function of the kumāras is not so much that of bearing the weapons. With the exception of the sword pressers, who do both, the function of these last two "classes of youths" is to receive the weapons as victims. Since, as we shall see, kaṇāccāris, camayams, and other officiants, including trustees, can also be among the "youthful" sons of Draupadī, one can say that these offices span the continuum from sacrificer to victim.

In view of the function of whipping, however, one other role must be mentioned here: that of the bearer of the whip. As we have seen, during certain ceremonies a whip may be coiled through the prongs of the kuntam and be borne along with that implement by the kaṇāccāri. But on other occasions, a different individual wields the whip (sometimes a thicker and longer one, but of the same type), cracking it over the raised wrists of the devotees. Strength and impetuosity are among the evident qualities sought in such a person. The chief whip bearer at the Sowcarpet temple in Madras admitted that taking liquor had been part of his routine at festivals, though he had given it up after it resulted in an accident during the firewalk.[27] And it may well be that insofar as liquor is drunk before festival ordeals, the whip bearers are among the more likely to be involved. In any case, whatever the physical and convivial qualities of the whip bearers, this combination of traits is connected with a state of possession, which the whip bearers at some moments seem to simulate rather than enter, but which they control or regulate in others. The office is normally said to be hereditary, and is usually

26. See Hiltebeitel 1988a, 328: the "proper time" for marriage, as well as for death in battle. According to the Ñāṉavēl Terukkūttu Troupe of Tēvikāppuram (1988a, 337 n. 5; cf. 341), Caṅkuvati, the Pāṇḍavas' younger sister, is also supposed to be sixteen when she marries Pōrmaṉṉaṉ, but this is mysterious, since her mother Mādrī is supposed to have died as a suttee with Pāṇḍu before any of the Pāṇḍavas ever married and began to sire the children who are also said to have been sixteen at the same time as she was. According to the Tēṉmakātēvamaṅkalam temple pūcāri, Caṅkotari (a variant name: "Conch Belly") was born from the fateful last union of Pāṇḍu (cursed to die in coitus) and Mādrī. When Mādrī committed suttee on Pāṇḍu's pyre, Kṛṣṇa saved the fetus, put it in a conch shell, and asked Samudrarājaṉ, king of the ocean, to raise her until she was needed.

27. He was carrying two little girls on his shoulders; they were burned when he fell and had to be hospitalized but did recover.

held by Vaṉṉiyars. Moreover, just as there are sometimes several whips being used simultaneously, so there are often several who have the office of whip bearer. At Tindivanam, as at most other temples, there was no particular title that went with this office, though the two chief whip bearers at the firewalks I attended there—one a Vaṉṉiyar in 1977, the other a Mutaliyār in 1981—both claimed the office hereditarily.

At Mēlaccēri, however, whip bearing was a function of at least one of a group of five men with the title cimmācaṉapuli, "Tiger of the Lion Throne." The title does not, from what I can gather, refer explicitly to the whip bearers. Rather, the individuals who bear it participate in a variety of the ritual functions already covered. The combination of lion and tiger in the name, however, evokes possession-related traits of Draupadī's two guardians: the "tiger-faced" and lion-subduing Pōttu Rāja (Hiltebeitel 1988a, 79–80, 252, plate 19, 334–36, 365), and Muttāl Rāvuttaṉ with his alternating tiger and lion mounts (ibid., 121, 123–25, 244, plate 8). The cimmācaṉapulis do take part in rites that involve possession. Also, according to a Mēlaccēri cimmācaṉapuli named Muniswami Nayakar, the title was given to the ancestors of the current cadre in the days of the Gingee Nāyaks, when the present cimmācaṉapulis' forefathers were among those who led the Nayaks' armies in battle. Heading the army is a trait more specifically of Pōttu Rāja in his identity as Pōrmaṉṉaṉ, leader of the Pāṇḍava army (ibid., 383–93).[28]

C. Draupadī Temples in Karnataka: A Mirror Situation

To summarize this diffuse situation, and to hold up to it a possible adjustive lens, it is helpful to look at the way Vaṉṉiyars run their Draupadī festivals in neighboring Karnataka. Vaṉṉiyars are called Tigalas in Kannada, a name that Bangalore Draupadī cult informants told me they found disrespectful and thus rejected. But the caste is discussed under the entry "Tigala" in Nanjundayya and

28. Tanaka describes a similar office called cūrapuli, "fierce tiger" or "Hero-tiger," at the Kālī festival at Udappu, Sri Lanka, a village that also has its Draupadī festival. The two cūrapulis are ritual impersonators of, and are possessed by, Kālī's two guardians, Kātaṉ (Kāttavarāyaṉ?) and Vairavar (Bhairava), and carry the sword and trident, respectively (1987, 267, 276). They are also linked with Kālī's lion mount and, according to Tanaka, evoke the demon devotee (ibid., 273–74 and n. 16). Cf. Tarabout 1986, 511 and n. 12: a cortège of Untouchables who, drunk and disguised as tigers, perform a tumultuous "game of tigers" (*puli kaḷi*), sometimes joined by Muslims with whips, as part of the "battle formation" formed in certain goddess festivals in Kerala.

Iyer's *Mysore Tribes and Castes*. These authors tell us that "Tigala is the Kannada term for a Tamil-speaking man" (1931, 4:609; cf. Hasan 1970, 146–47), which suggests that Vaṉṉiyars probably find the term disrespectful because it typecasts them as outsiders and, even more unpalatably, as a group that stands out among other Tamil settlers for sticking to their former country's rural ways. Their "chief profession being vegetable and other petty gardening," including betel leaves, flowers, and fruits (ibid., 609, 610, 623), it is clear that they do not have the landed dominant caste status in Karnataka that they do in various parts of the Draupadī cult core area in Tamilnadu. For our purposes, what is arresting here is the possibility that in maintaining their caste and Draupadī cult traditions in such a climate, Kannada Vaṉṉiyars might have conserved elements that can be traced back to the core area, to a time (seventeenth to eighteenth century?) *before* their migration to Karnataka, and might have consolidated them into a durable structure, one which seems likely to have both archaic and adaptive aspects.[29]

Nanjundayya and Iyer's account gives the impression of summarizing matters for Vaṉṉiyars throughout Karnataka (or Mysore, as it was then called), and it seems that as far as the caste itself goes, we may take the description to be just such an attempted synthesis of information from a wide area of the state. It is thus the authors' evident intent to say that Vaṉṉiyars in general, including "the earliest immigrants among them," who speak Kannada and live in Tumkur District bordering Bangalore District on the northwest, worship "the eldest of the Pāṇḍava brothers," Dharmarāya (that is, Dharmarāja), "as their patron deity" (ibid., 609). If this is so, Tumkur Draupadī festivals would be an interesting subject for further research. But where Nanjundayya and Iyer turn to the Dharmarāja-Draupadī cult and its festivals, it is clear that their main information comes from a temple in a "city" (ibid., 621). Of the four Draupadī (or Dharmarāja) temples in Bangalore, this is most likely the Dharmarāya Temple at Hulsoor Gate.[30]

Karnataka Vaṉṉiyars have a tightly knit caste organization. The "caste headman" is called the *gauda*, a Kannada term used not only in "an honorific sense," but as the name of a cultivator and cattle-

29. On Bangalore temples in the context of Draupadī cult diffusion, see Hiltebeitel 1988a, 39–40.

30. I visited these four temples in 1975 with the guidance of Professor K. T. Pandurangi. The Hulsoor Gate temple, with its ambitious Karagam festival, is described in Hasan 1971, 148–50, and Munivenkatappa 1965; the Dharmarāya temple within the Ekambareśvara temple complex and the Kalassipalaiyam temple, each with firewalking ceremonies, are described in Richards 1910. The fourth, a Dharmarāya

breeding caste, the Gaudas, who use the term as well for their village and regional headmen (Thurston and Rangachari [1904] 1965, 2:269). They have no doubt adapted this gauda system to their own parallel usages. Not only does each local Vaṉṉiyar community have a gauda as the head of its caste council, but the Vaṉṉiyars also "have divided themselves into sections by the tracts of country inhabited by them, and each section, called a *kattemane,* is under the jurisdiction of a headman, or Gauda, with a council of elders" (Nanjundayya and Iyer 1931, 4:617). It is not indicated whether there are distinctive names for the offices that join the gauda at this regional level. But at the local level, the gauda's associates would seem to have come straight from the Draupadī cult of Tamilnadu:

> They have a Gauda at their head, and one learned in their caste and religious beliefs, styled *gaṇāchāri,* as next to him. The *pūjāri* of the temple of Dharmarāya is the latter's deputy, and they have a *yajman* besides. The Gauda, the elders of the caste, and the *yajman* form an ordinary [i.e., local] caste-council, while *gaṇāchāri* and the *pūjāri* form additional members. . . . [Decisions are] not final, as an appeal is open to the larger council at the headquarters of the *kattemane.* (ibid., 617)

Nanjundayya and Iyer mention virtually no functions of the gauda that are not done conjointly with the gaṇāchāri. Together, they see to it that the bride-price of one and a half rupees and other presents are brought by the groom's family to the bride's house (ibid., 612), arbitrate marriage disputes and divorces (ibid., 611, 615), and oversee funerals (ibid., 622). Moreover, "in the absence of the Gauda in Council, the *gaṇāchāri* is entitled to take his place, and to exercise his privilege of giving the casting vote" (ibid., 617). That local caste councils are comprised so largely of Dharmarāja temple officiants suggests the high degree to which the Draupadī cult has been linked with the perpetuation of the caste's identity in Kannada-speaking areas. As we turn to the cult itself of the Vaṉṉiyars' patron deity Dharmarāya, we meet with the participation not only of these familar offices, but also of others.

For the Draupadī-Dharmarāja festival described, the gaṇāchāri "is the grand master of ceremonies," observing strict rites of daily

temple at Kilari Road, is administered by Yādavas or Kōṉārs. Krishnamurthy Hanur has prepared a paper in Kannada titled "'Karaga' in the surroundings of Bangalore" (Draupadī festivals are known there as Karagam festivals), which he summarized for me at the Institute for Asian Studies, Tiruvanmiyur, Madras in January 1990. Some of his observations will be mentioned.

purification and pollution-avoidance. The pūjāri, likewise under similar restraints, conducts the worship under the gaṇāchāri's supervision (ibid., 618). Little is said of the *yajman,* but one may suppose that his role corresponds to the "sacrificer" function of the Tamil tarumakarttā, or chief temple trustee. Most revealing, however:

> There are others taking part in the celebrations, who are known as *Komaramakkalu,* i.e., young children, over a hundred in number. These have to bathe and observe fasts and be strict in the matter of meals. Their food is to be prepared by their wives only, who, before the commencement of the festival, subject themselves to a purificatory ceremony, by having their tongues touched with a burning turmeric root, and by drinking *tīrtha,* or holy water. All these men and women keep aloof from other persons during this period, so as to preserve their holy state. If any of the women has her monthly sickness in the interval, she remains outside for three days when she bathes, and meanwhile her husband has to cook his own food. (ibid., 619)

As at certain Tamil Draupadī temples, we have a plural form of kumāra (the Kannada singular is *komaramaga;* ibid.) that refers to a distinctive cadre of "youths" as performers of specific festival ordeals. And indeed, as we shall see in chapter 11, the sword feats of these Bangalore komāramakkalu (ibid., 619–20) are but a variant of one of the kumāra functions, already mentioned, that one finds in Tamilnadu. These "youths" seem invariably to be married, which suggests that the title is primarily a ritual one. As to the festival itself, let us just note at this point that most of our officiants come together regularly. "On each day of the festival, the *Gaṇāchāri,* the *Pūjāri* and *Komaramakkalu*" go from the temple to a well, where the "youths" receive the pūjāri's and gaṇāchāri's blessings, and then return to the temple carrying some rather familiar things in procession. They are listed as five, though with an "etc.": an umbrella, whip, bell, seal, and "*bhandarada pettige,* i.e., a casket containing turmeric powder" (ibid., 619). The latter is none other than the *paṇṭāra peṭṭi* or *pūcai peṭṭi,* the pūcāri's turmeric box that we have met in Tamil variants as one of the five ritual weapons carried with Draupadī, or brought to her by Pōttu Rāja–Pōrmaṉṉaṉ (Hiltebeitel 1988a, 338, 386–90). The processional carrying of these implements is clearly itself a *ritual* variant of their mythic comings and goings.[31]

31. As shown in Hiltebeitel 1988a, 386–88, these lists of five are elastic (the Bangalore Ekambareśvara temple provides the sole example of the bell in that discussion);

Meanwhile, on the night of the festival's "most important ceremony," the bringing of the karakam pot to the temple, the procession includes not only these officiants, but also the gauda and yajman (Nanjundayya and Iyer 1931, 4:620). It can hardly be coincidental that these two—the community's "political" and ritual headmen—should present themselves specifically as sponsors of this ceremony.

This sideline view from Karnataka of Draupadī cult offices is instructive at a number of points. Clearly the connection between ritual titles and processions of ritual weapons recalls similar correlations in Tamilnadu. It seems likely that Vaṉṉiyar traditions in Karnataka preserve in a time-tested, hardened form one of several types of Draupadī cult ritual organization that can be found in the core area. Yet in that more intensive region of the cult, where itinerant bardic and dramatist performers have circulated from temple to temple and festival to festival, types as such are rather fluid and difficult to disentangle from each other. It does, however, seem worth pursuing the possibility that if the Karnataka traditions preserve a ritual variant distinctive to Vaṉṉiyars, as they clearly do, then in the core area itself the variants that link the term *kumāra* with a title that refers to groups of youths might also be significantly associated with Vaṉṉiyars. That, in any case, is a hypothesis that fits such facts as I have found. Meanwhile, it raises the complementary hypothesis that the variants that link the term *kumāra* with the specific office of kumāravarkkam might be more distinctive of another important community in Draupadī cult circles, the Vēḷāḷar Mutaliyārs, like Brameesa Mudaliyar himself. We shall return to this problem in chapter 11.

---

see further below, chapter 6. The umbrella suggests royal pretensions. The seal is uncertain. Cf. the plaque carried by a washerman amid similar processional paraphernalia at the Singapore Draupadī festival (Babb 1974, 22). A picture, sent to me by Babb, shows a black "plaque" atop a pole, and wrapped around it, apparently, a tapered whip of the familiar type.

3 The Ritual Cycle and the Temple Icons

There is no way even to mention every ritual that occurs in a typical Draupadī festival, much less cover them all in my fieldwork. Many rites take place simultaneously. Much also occurs in, or at least in relation to, the home. When core area temples themselves announce their festivals on posters, they normally mention only flag hoisting, the sequence of dramas, and the spectacular rituals of the culminating day. But that is only a shorthand.

A. A Core Area Festival in Outline

At this point, an outline that shows where most core area rites fit into a total scheme will help to give some sense of what will be discussed and what will be left out. To that end, I have used the Tindivanam festival as an example, with dates from the 1981 program, to construct table 3. Unmarked entries indicate ceremonies performed at Tindivanam that I did not observe. Single asterisks (*) indicate ceremonies observed at Tindivanam, whole or in part, in either 1977 or 1981. If I observed ceremonies elsewhere, but not at Tindivanam, that is indicated by double asterisks (**), and the site is given in parentheses. Triple asterisks (***) indicate ceremonies observed both at Tindivanam and at other sites. A few ceremonies not performed at Tindivanam but done elsewhere will be indicated by parentheses. The table restricts itself to rites that are typical of the core area, for which I take the Tindivanam cycle as expansively representative. I will not include ceremonies found only outside the core area. Though important to my total discussion, they would only make the table unnecessarily confusing and must be treated in the proper context—that is, as alternatives to and variations on the core area rites.

As can be seen, such a festival cycle involves numerous movements back and forth between the temple and the other ritual

Table 3. The Tindivanam 1981 Festival in Outline

Preliminary (No set dates)	Contracts made with pāratiyār and leader of Terukkūttu troupe. After negotiations, the performers accept the offering of betel (*tāmpūlaṅ-koṭuttal*) and some advance money from a leading trustee. (**Mēlaccēri)
Ca. June 2	Flag hoisting (*koṭiyēṟṟam;* Sanskrit *dhvajārohaṇam*). (**Mēlaccēri)
	Sowing of nine grains (*navatāṉiyam;* Sanskrit *navadhānya*).
Ca. June 12	Arrival of pāratiyār; beginning of Pāratam narration (*Pāratak katai ārampam*) about 4:00 P.M., under temporary pantal in front of temple. (**Mēlaccēri)
Ca. June 15	Dispersal of navadhānyam seedlings in temple tank. (**Veḷḷimēṭupēṭṭai)
July 5	Sunday. Birth of Dharma (*Taruma piṟappu*). The pāratiyār has brought the epic story to this point; Dharma's icon is brought out under pantal for worship, and jaggery is distributed to the public.[1]
July 12	Sunday. *Birth of Draupadī (*Turōpatai piṟappu*). A square, three-tiered earthen fire altar (*ōmakuṇṭam;* Sanskrit *homakuṇḍa*), painted in blue wash with white markings, is built near the pāratiyār's dais, to its north. A Brahman officiates (recalling the two Brahmans hired by King Drupada, Draupadī's father). In front (east) of the altar, the Brahman prepares a copper pot with mango leaves around the rim and a coconut set in the top and places it between himself and the altar on a plantain leaf and three kilos of rice. Flowers removed from a garland are placed at the corners of the altar and its intermediate points. A *pampai* drum is beaten continuously. The pūcāri, dressed in a reddish-orange ankle-length *vēṣṭi,* sets straw in the altar and lights the fire, which the Brahman feeds with ghee and incense. The Brahman then invokes Draupadī with folded hands. Her wooden processional image, its hair in a bun (*koṇṭai, kūntal*) and decked in flowers, is brought out from the temple and rocked three times over the flames to signify her birth from the sacrificial fire. The pāratiyār recites his version of the story (see Hiltebeitel 1988a, 81–82, 386).[2] Once born like this, Draupadī is then set before the altar, facing east. After incense sticks are set in bananas before her, everyone shouts "Govinda!" The goddess is worshiped with coconut, flowers, and a garland and taken in procession, while sweets are distributed to children who remain behind.
Not done	(Local or "old style" "street drama" enactment of "Death of Baka," such as often introduces the drama cycle). (Hiltebeitel 1988a, 169–82)

1. Jaggery, or brown sugar, seems to be an offering particular to birth ceremonies; see Thurston and Rangachari [1904] 1965, 3:492 (among Koravas).
2. On Draupadī's birth from fire, see Hiltebeitel 1988a, plate 28 (a Bangalore fresco: her hair loose, emerging with weapons); cf. Shideler 1987, fig. 5 (a Pondicherry fresco: her hair up in a bun, born without weapons).

Table 3 *(continued)*

July 14	Tuesday. Arrival of Terukkūttu troupe. The pūcāri welcomes them with the waving of a camphor flame (*tīpārātaṉai;* Sanskrit *dīpārādhanā*). The cycle of eighteen nights of dramas begins next night.
July 17	Friday. Marriage of Draupadī (*Turōpatai tirumaṇam*).
	Tying of *kāppu* amulets on leading officiants (*kāppu kaṭṭutal*). (** Mēlaccēri)
	***Sowing of new navadhānya seedlings in small pots called *pālikai*.
	***Placement of a tall bamboo bow, variously called "Arjuna's bow tree" (*arccuṉaṉ vil maram*), "turmeric tree" (*mañcaḷmaram*), or "drama tree" (*kūttu maram*), on north side of drama stage. (Hiltebeitel 1988a, 196–97).
	At 7:00 P.M., icons of Draupadī and Arjuna Perumāḷ, as the printed announcement of the ceremony calls him, are decorated for their marriage beneath the pantal. These icons are not the wooden ones of these deities but their *pañcalōkam* ones: that is, icons made of five metals (gold, silver, copper, iron, and lead). Two brightly painted marriage pots are also prepared. The pāratiyār brings the narrative up to this point. One local group acts as the bride's party and another as the groom's party. Again the Brahman presides. He ties kāppu on the wrists of the pūcāri, kaṇāccāri, nimantam,[3] and the man who carries the sword in processions.[4] These ceremonies close by about 9:00 P.M., at which point the bamboo "drama tree" is set in a hole dug beside the stage and the play "Draupadī's Marriage" begins.
July 18	Saturday. Pāratam is moved from the Draupadī temple to a Rāma, Sītā, and Lakṣmaṇa temple, the Bhajana Kōvil, where communal singing is done, in a hamlet of Tindivanam called Jakkampēṭṭai. The Reṭṭis of this hamlet sponsor the drama "Subhadrā's Marriage" this same evening.[5]
July 20–21	Draupadī's wooden processional icon is dressed with its hair loose and without flowers.[6]
	***"Dice Match and Disrobing," the night's drama, can be the scene of intense audience possession rituals. (Hiltebeitel 1988a, 234–37, 263–81; 1988b)

3. See chapter 2, n. 22.
4. Recall from chapter 1 that this role used to fall to the camayam.
5. See chapter 2, section A.
6. At Mēlaccēri, with only pañcalōkam icons, a yellow screen is put up before Draupadī on her chariot so that she will not have to witness her own defilement (Hiltebeitel 1988b, part 1; 1989c). At Singapore, her saree is changed from yellow to red on this occasion (Babb 1974, 8).

Table 3 *(continued)*

	***Duḥśāsana actor does homage to Draupadī both on stage and in temple, begging forgiveness for dishonoring her.[7]
July 21–22	***Erection of Arjuna's *tapas,* or penance, pole and rituals within the drama "Arjuna's Tapas."
July 23–24	Kīcaka actor, in drama "Slaughter of Kīcaka," also does homage to Draupadī on stage and in temple, before dishonoring her. Further audience possessions may occur.
July 26–27	During performance of drama "Aravāṉ's Sacrifice," actor personifying Aravāṉ does homage to Draupadī in temple. Further audience possessions possible. Draupadī's wooden processional icon tours with one of Kālī.
July 27–28	During "Pōrmaṉṉaṉ's Fight," the temple's ritual implements, used in the drama, are identified with the weapons Pōrmaṉṉaṉ brings from his kingdom of Śivānandapuri and makes over to Draupadī via the disguised Arjuna and Kṛṣṇa. (Hiltebeitel 1988a, 342 and plate 23)
July 31	Friday. *On the afternoon before the drama "Karṇa's Salvation," Pāratam recitation is performed on that topic at a Tindivanam Māriyammaṉ temple. The pūcāri of this temple is a relative of the Draupadī temple pūcāri and cooperates in the performance of some of the subsequent rituals.[8]
August 2	Sunday. Paṭukaḷam-related ceremonies and firewalking: ***The driving out of the bulls (*māṭu miraṭṭal*) ***The opening of the eyes of Aravāṉ (*Aravāṉ kaṇtiṟappu*) and Aravāṉ's battlefield sacrifice (*Aravāṉ kaḷappali*) ***The death and rising of the "young Pañcapāṇḍavas," Draupadī's children ***The dying, or lying down, of Duryodhana (*Turiyōtaṉa paṭukaḷam*) ***The retying of Draupadī's hair (*kūntal muṭittal*) ***Firewalking (*tīmiti*), with numerous subrites Pālikai seedlings set on roof of Pōrmaṉṉaṉ *maṇḍapa* (enclosure for Pōrmaṉṉaṉ's stone icon) to desiccate Many private rituals, especially vows, are carried out concurrently with these ceremonies throughout this culminating day. One noteworthy detail from the 1981 Tindivanam festival is that this day fell on the eighteenth of the Tamil month of Āṭi, the day of *Āṭip-perukku,* a festival popular especially in the Kongu, Tiruchirappali, and Thanjavur regions of Tamilnadu for the "flooding"

7. At Mēlaccēri, where the temple is far from the stage, the actor does not visit it during the play.
8. The Draupadī and Māriyammaṉ temple pūcāris also cooperate at Mēlaccēri, but there they are of different castes and unrelated.

Table 3 *(continued)*

	(*perukku*) of the Kaveri River that comes after the onset of the southwest monsoon. Āṭip-perukku and festivals for Draupadī clearly share common themes.[9] But though the Tindivanam trustees were aware that they had chosen that festival's date for the culmination of their festival, they said they were not guided by the coincidence. They always select a Sunday for tīmiti, which eliminates the possibility that it could occur regularly on Āṭi eighteenth. Elsewhere, too, Sundays are common, but the usual choice of dates for Draupadī cult ceremonies ranges over several months, the peak months being Cittirai (April–May) and Vaikāci (May–June), followed by Āṭi (July–August).[10]
August 3	Monday. *Funeral rites (*karumāti*), including milk sprinkling (*pāl viṭutal, pāl teḷittal*), for the "corpses" on the paṭukaḷam.
August 6	Thursday. Coronation of Dharma (*Tarumar paṭṭāpiṣēkam*). (**Pondicherry)
Discontinued	(Leave-taking [*viṭaiyaṭṭi*] with festive throwing of turmeric water [*mañcaḷ nīr tiruviḷā*]. Sometimes done at Draupadī festivals [e.g., Sowcarpet], as at those for other goddesses, but discontinued at Tindivanam within recent memory because it got too rowdy [it was compared to Holi, which involves rambunctious throwing of reddened water and red powders]. Also not done at Mēlaccēri.)
Not done	(Offerings to guardian deities [*kāval pūjā*], not assigned a specific day at Tindivanam.)
August 18	Tuesday. Flag lowering (*tuja avarokāṇam;* Sanskrit *dhvaja avarohaṇam*) and removal of kāppu wristlets from main officiants.

arenas: the drama stage, paṭukaḷam, and firepit. In chapter 2 we accounted for the main persons involved in these movements. Let us now begin to look more closely at how such ritual movement also transpires through the temple icons.

B. A Temple and Its Icons

The plan of the Tindivanam Draupadī temple (map 2) provides a suitable point of reference and can be compared with the maps of

9. See discussion in chapter 12, section A.

10. The Census publications on the temples and festivals of Tamilnadu (Chokalingam 1973–74; Nambiar et al. 1965, 1966, 1968a, 1968b, 1968c, 1969; Nambiar, Karup, et al. 1968) yield the following figures on the monthly incidence of Draupadī festivals in the state: January or Tai 7; February or Māci 11; March or Paṅkuṉi 21; April or Cittirai 62; May or Vaikāci 46; June or Āṉi 28; July or Āṭi 33; August or Āvaṇi 10; September or Puraṭṭāci 3; October or Aippaci 2; other months 0. See Appendix: Draupadī stipulates the first of Cittirai for her firewalk.

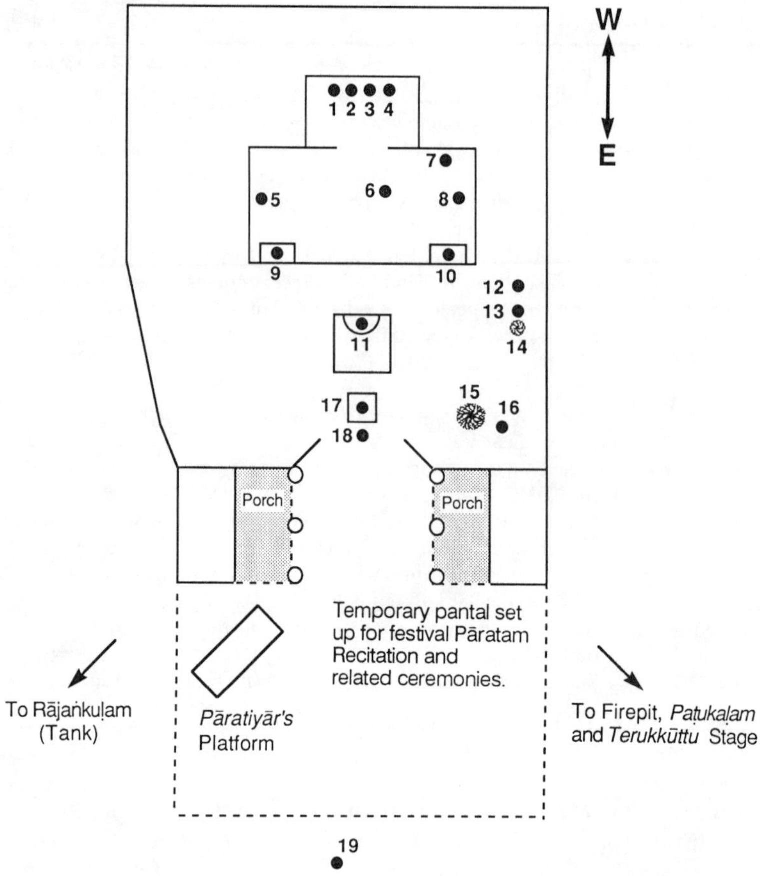

1. Vināyakar
2. Dharma
3. Draupadī
4. Kuntī
5. Wooden Processional Icons (5 Pāṇḍavas, Draupadī, Subhadrā, Kṛṣṇa on Garuḍa, Pōttu Rāja)
6. Fish carved on stone ceiling
7. Ritual Implements
8. *Pañcalōkam* Processional Icons (Dharma, Draupadī, Arjuna, Kṛṣṇa)
9. Vināyakar
10. Añjaṉeyar (Hanūman)
11. Pōrmaṉṉaṉ Maṇḍapa
12. Stone image of Murukaṉ with Vaḷḷi and Devayanī
13. Muttāl Rāvuttaṉ
14. Pavaḷamallipū Bush
15. Margosa Tree
16. Well
17. Flagstaff
18. Balipīṭha
19. Stone Posts (N. with Añjaṉeyar and Kāttavarāyaṉ; S. with unidentifiable figures)

Map 2. Tindivanam Draupadī temple.

the Mēlaccēri and Chinna Salem temples in volume 1.[11] The map shows the temple as it was from 1975 to 1984, since which some recent changes must be noted. From the outside, Draupadī temples often have little to distinguish them from other Hindu temples, although there are exceptions.[12] At Tindivanam, one should appreciate the *Mahābhārata* emphasis, defined as such by local informants, in the unusual placement of figures of Vināyakar, or Gaṇeśa (scribe of the *Mahābhārata*), and Añcaṉēyar, or Hanumān (who appears on Arjuna's chariot flag during the war), in niches on the front face. The fish embossed on the ceiling of the front hall, or *mukhamaṇḍapa*, is also said to represent Draupadī's connection with the fish that Arjuna must shoot to win her hand in marriage (Hiltebeitel 1988a, 200–211). Highly curious are two stone posts set at some distance in front of the temple, slightly off-line to the south from the east-west axis that extends out from the inner sanctum, and said to be boundary stones for the temple. Leaving their discussion for chapter 5, it is enough for the moment to say that my interest in these objects caused considerable amusement. I have found no other Draupadī temples with such "boundary stones," nor have I found any other with Muttāl Rāvuttaṉ's icon set beneath a *pavaḷamallipū* bush, said to have been planted because it produces flowers only after 7:00 P.M. and drops them on the deity before 5:00 A.M., a means of honoring this guardian god's nighttime vigilance in a spontaneous and natural fashion. But then what is so rewarding about visiting Draupadī temples is that one must expect such surprises, including seeing them removed. In 1990 the icons of Muttāl Rāvuttaṉ and Subrahmaṇya had been taken from their position northeast of the temple and set in new niches at the back, on the northwest and southwest, respectively. Meanwhile, Muttāl Rāvuttaṉ's place beneath the night-flowering bush was given to a small shrine for the Seven Virgins. The change was said to have been initiated by the official appointed by the state-run Hindu Religious and Charitable Endowments Board to administer the temple. His alleged purpose was to make it easier to circumambulate the

11. Hiltebeitel 1988a, 92, 111. For plans of other Draupadī temples, see Richards 1910, 33 (Bangalore, within the Ekambareśvara complex); Frasca 1984, 284 (Iruṅkal); Shideler 1987, 192 (Pondicherry); Tanaka 1987, 130 (Udappu); Babb 1974, map 2, opening pages (Singapore).

12. Some temples (e.g., Dindigul, Kaḷampūr [Polur Taluk, North Arcot]) have porches over their entrances showing distinctive painted sculptures of *Mahābhārata* characters. Others show a head of Aravāṉ somewhere on the roof or outer wall (Hiltebeitel 1988a, 249, plate 15; 328; also at Cantavācal, Tēṉmakātēvamaṅkalam), or, in Thanjavur District, large heads of Aravāṉ in separate maṇḍapas, or standing independently, to the temple's southeast, facing north.

temple, but he obviously had no idea that Muttāl Rāvuttaṉ belongs at the northeast—a point I shall return to in chapter 6.

Although every temple has, again, its special features, one finds icons of five main types: fixed stone icons (*mūlavar, mūlavikkirakam*) in the inner sanctum (*mūlastāṉam*), fixed stone icons at boundary points for guardian deities (*parivāra tēvatai,* kāval), processional icons (*uṟcavar, uṟcavavikkirakam, uṟcavamūrtti*) made of five metals (pañcalōkam), processional icons made of wood, and large wooden animal "mounts" or "vehicles" (*vākaṉam*) for procession of the deities. All of this is commonplace for Hindu temples and festivals, large and small and far and wide. But a few points of emphasis may be noted.

Most Draupadī temples, especially in villages, are too poor to afford pañcalōkam (pronounced, as in Sanskrit, *pañcaloha*) icons, and thus have only wooden ones. An important exception must be made here for Mēlaccēri, which is the only temple I have found that has just pañcalōkam processional icons (see plate 2). Since there is little to differentiate Mēlaccēri today from other villages economically, one may suspect that these icons go back to the Draupadī cult's more glorious past in this once royal village. Some Draupadī temples have both pañcalōkam and wooden processional icons and make distinctions as to their uses. I have already noted a few such differentiations at Tindivanam. Thus the more valued pañcalōkam icons may be taken out only at especially important ritual events or may even be set in front of the main stone icon in the inner sanctum and receive regular worship with it (as at Chinna Salem, Tēvaṉampaṭṭaṇam, and Cattiram Karuppūr).

Animal vākaṉams are uncommon in core area temples. As was seen in chapter 2, Draupadī, the Pāṇḍavas, and other deities are usually borne about not on animal mounts but on vehicles (bullock carts, palanquins) that represent a chariot (*tēr, ratha*), and in particular Draupadī's war chariot.[13] In this vein, one should appreciate that the ritual implements or "weapons" that were discussed in chapter 2 are actually a sixth type of icon. Indeed, let us keep in

13. In the core area, one seems to find animal vākaṉams (though never without some form of chariot as well) mainly at larger Draupadī temples, such as at Pondicherry (Shideler 1987, 86, 120) and in Madras (e.g., Ālantūr, Muthialpet). There seems to be a correlation between animal vākaṉams with temples that have processions, but no Terukkūttu; see Moses 1961, 84. At Siruvallikuppam (Villupuram Taluk, South Arcot), however, the reportedly five-hundred-year-old temple may have both dramas and vākaṉams; it is said to have an eighteen-day festival in Cittirai, a Vaṉṉiyar pūcāri, and horse and lion vākaṉams: Nambiar et al. 1966, 310. Outside the core area, as with the horse and lion vehicles at Cōḻavantāṉ, vākaṉams are probably more common.

mind that in the regional folk epic cult of the heroes of Palnāḍu, similar "reliquary weapons" are considered to be "deities" (*daivālu;* Roghair 1982, 27 and plate 1).

Reserving further discussion of stationary guardian deities and ritual weapons mainly for chapters 5 and 6, let us attend to the main stationary and portable icons.

Surprisingly, among the deities with fixed images in stone, there is much less consistency for those in the sanctum than for the guardian deities—usually Pōttu Rāja and Muttāl Rāvuttaṉ—who protect them at the temple boundaries. Thus at Tindivanam, each of the four in the mūlastāṉam—Vināyakar, Dharma, Draupadī, and Kuntī—can be found separately in the sanctums of other Draupadī temples. But I have seen only one other temple, at Vīrāṇantal, with exactly the same cluster. Moreover, even in such cases where the mūlastāṉam icons are identical, their configurations and settings may vary instructively (compare plates 3 and 4). Thus at Tindivanam, the left-to-right order is Vināyakar, Dharma, Draupadī, and Kuntī, while at Vīrāṇantal it is Draupadī, Kuntī, Dharma, and Vināyakar, with Draupadī set to the front, and specifically below the smaller Kuntī (both pairs of female figures have yellow-orange sarees). Moreover, both temples have in recent years constructed a much larger masonry image, in relief against the back wall, in an aureole with a leonine "face of glory" (*kīrtimukha*) at its top that emerges from the mouths of two aquatic creatures. At Tindivanam the figure is a standing Draupadī holding her parrot (Hiltebeitel 1988a, 263–64) on a closed lotus bud (ibid., 220) and attended by two serving maids who stand to the arch's side, while at Vīrāṇantal it is of Dharma seated in royal ease with three ritual implements known as "fire posts" (*akkiṉikampams*) outside the arch just to his right. Moreover, at Tindivanam the masonry Draupadī stands directly behind her central mūlavar (of her standing, with the same closed lotus and parrot), defining the shrine as a Draupadī temple, whereas at Vīrāṇantal the masonry Dharma sits directly behind his central icon (seated, with sword), identifying the shrine as a Dharmarāja Kōyil.

One can see that aside from the central icon, there does not seem to be much here to distinguish a Draupadī temple from a Dharmarāja temple. As we shall see in chapter 6, the differences that do occur seem to be centered on iconographic features of the temple, though there are hints that they may tie in with larger matters of ritual and myth. But for the most part, what goes on in the festival at large, and, in particular, outside the temple, is centered on Draupadī, with whom the Pāratam festival itself is usually identified (Hiltebeitel 1988a, 5; 1988e, 34). "Draupadī temple" is also the more inclusive term, and can be freely used for a Dharmarāja temple. Either one of them or the other has been found in the sanctum of every temple, and often they are both present. Of the sixty-two temples for which I have complete information on the mūlavikkirakams, sixty have Draupadī in the sanctum, while thirty have Dharma. The only two without Draupadī are at Tūci (Cheyyar Taluk, North Arcot) and Veḷḷalūr, where Dharma is alone in the sanctum. So usually Draupadī is there, with or without him. Meanwhile, of the remaining thirty, twenty-seven have Draupadī alone in the sanctum, three of these with double Draupadī images (Vīrapāṇṭi [Tirukoyilur Taluk, South Arcot], Aṉmarutai [Wandiwash Taluk, North Arcot], Thanjavur East Gate) and one with three (Nallāṉpettāḷ). In such cases only one is the main image, commonly distinguished by its height or, if it is in the core area, its origins from Gingee (Hiltebeitel 1988a, 66–67). Curiously, however, one of the temples with a single image of Draupadī alone in the sanctum is called a Dharmarāja temple (Cuddalore). Of this plurality of twenty-seven, eleven are in Thanjavur District, where having Draupadī alone in the sanctum is a norm that has so far found no exception.

After Draupadī and Dharma, there is a considerable drop-off in the number of times one finds other deities in the sanctum: Kṛṣṇa (counting one Mahāviṣṇu) and Sahadeva 9; Vināyakar 7; Arjuna, Bhīma, and Nakula 6; Kuntī 5; Subhadrā 3; Vyāsa 2; and one each for Pōttu Rāja (Māmaṇṭūr, Cheyyar Taluk, North Arcot), Viṣṇu-Durgā (Mēlaccēri), and Caṅkuvati (Tēṉmakātēvamaṅkalam). Here we need note only certain unusual configurations and patterns. As was mentioned in volume 1 (74), Mēlaccēri is unique in the way it accentuates Draupadī's virginal character, and also her affinities with Kṛṣṇa and his Kōṉār-Shepherd traits. It is also the sole temple that combines Draupadī with female deities only (again, all in yellow sarees). And they are females, moreover, of what might be called Kṛṣṇa's "family": Kuntī (his aunt), Subhadrā (his sister), and Viṣṇu-Durgā (that is, Durgā with the emblems, such as conch and *cakra,* or discus, of Kṛṣṇa/Viṣṇu).[14] With only female deities, Draupadī's *āti pīṭam* or "primal temple" (Hiltebeitel 1988a, 30) at Mēlaccēri has something of the flavor of a Śākta shrine (*pīṭam,* Sanskrit *pīṭha*), while Draupadī's positioning with Viṣṇu-Durgā reminds us not only that the conch and cakra work themselves into Draupadī

14. Cf. Hiltebeitel 1988a, 74, 91–92, for another explanation, drawn from a local Mēlaccēri informant.

cult folklore as parts of a kind of free-floating iconography that is only superficially "out of the goddess's hands,"[15] but also that Gingee has been called Draupadī's *avatāra* or "descent" (Hiltebeitel 1988a, 65). Subhadrā's appearances in the sanctum are never, in my sample, without Kuntī. Meanwhile, among male deities, the Pāṇḍavas appear five times as a group, most notably at Māṉāmpāṭi as five small rectangular slabs. But the only one aside from Dharma ever to appear separately is Sahadeva, presumably for his knowledge of astrology (ibid., 321). Finally, while Kṛṣṇa is found seven times in the inner sanctum, four of these instances are in Madras, and two others are in cities outside the core area (Bangalore and Salem).[16] One may suspect that this is further evidence for urban and extra-core area Brahmanization akin to that which Tanaka has documented at Udappu, Sri Lanka. There, Brahman priests came to serve at the Draupadī temple in the late nineteenth century (1987, 80–81). Then, in a major reform in 1950, when the temple was renamed after Pārthasārathi, or Kṛṣṇa as "Charioteer of Arjuna," Draupadī was replaced in the inner sanctum of what had been her own temple by Kṛṣṇa and his consorts Rukmiṇī and Satyabhāmā, and was moved into a narrow passage linking the sanctum with a prayer hall (ibid., 128–30, 334–43).

Passing over the stationary guardian deities for now, the usual set of pañcalōkam figures is Draupadī, Kṛṣṇa, and Arjuna, as at Chinna Salem (Hiltebeitel 1988a, map 5, p. 111). Draupadī regularly carries a parrot on a closed lotus bud, and Arjuna bears his bow Gāṇḍīva (looking much like Kōtaṇṭarāmaṉ, Rāma with the bow Kōdaṇḍa). According to the *Tiraupatātēvi Māṉmiyam,* each should have a triple-bend posture appropriate to their getting married (see Appendix, n. 14). Kṛṣṇa can be four armed with cakra and conch (Mylapore, Pondicherry), two armed with his flute (Māṉāmpāṭi), represented as Pārthasārathi (Kolar), or with his two consorts Ruk-

15. On the cakra, see Hiltebeitel 1988a, 226 (Draupadī stanches Kṛṣṇa's bleeding after he has cut his finger hurling the cakra to decapitate Śiśupāla). According to the pāratiyār S. Nagarajan, it was Aravāṉ's "wisdom" (*arivu,* providing one of the etymologies of his name), having watched the war for its eighteen days, to tell the Pāṇḍavas and Draupadī that it was not their prowess or vows that he saw in action at Kurukṣetra, but only the conch blowing, the cakra beheading, and the skull-bowl (*kapāla*) collecting the blood. Variants mention only the cakra and kapāla (cf. Hiltebeitel 1988a, 445; also the pāratiyār K. Muttuswami Pillai who performed at the 1990 Kūttāṇṭavar festival at Kūvākkam). Though Draupadī never holds these iconic emblems in her hands, she has them at her disposal (cf. 1988a, 377, 425). The conch (*śaṅkha,* Tamil *caṅku*) also surfaces in the name of Caṅkuvati, Pōrmaṉṉaṉ's wife, who serves Draupadī (344–49; above, chap. 2, n. 26).

16. The core area exception is at Cantirampāṭi, Wandiwash Taluk, North Arcot.

miṇī and Satyabhāmā (Mēlaccēri). Of my sample of ten temples with such five-metal figures, all of them have at least these three deities, to whom others may then be added: Dharma twice (at Tindivanam and Pondicherry), and others only once (Subhadrā and Pōttu Rāja at Mēlaccēri [see plate 2]; Bhīma, Nakula, and Sahadeva at Kalahasti; and a sixteen-armed Parāśakti at Pondicherry). It is striking that Arjuna should be so inconspicuous in the inner sanctum, where Dharma is prominent, and yet figure so centrally among the pañcalōkam icons. The inference is unavoidable that relative to Draupadī, Dharma and Arjuna represent alternative principles. Dharma is the stationary figure; the sanctum is either his throne room, from which he rules and wages war, or the place where he is reenthroned with Draupadī once she is vindicated and the war is over. But Arjuna carries out the missions in the world at large that make the establishment of *dharma* (and Dharma) and the vindication of the goddess possible.[17] Moreover, it is also no accident that the highly valued pañcalōkam icons consistently feature Arjuna, Draupadī, and Kṛṣṇa. Their movement outward from the temple into the world is analogous to the "descending" function of the avatāra. At the heart of the *Mahābhārata*, and in the Draupadī festivals that enact it, their actions in the world are conjoint (Hiltebeitel 1985c). As I have argued elsewhere, it is these three who figure as multiforms, if not outright avatars, of Śiva, the goddess, and Viṣṇu: the three gods of bhakti Hinduism.[18]

Most Draupadī temples, however, do not have five-metal icons and thus make do with wooden ones for all processional purposes, including rituals that are reserved for pañcalōkam icons elsewhere. The wooden icons are worth a full study in themselves for their variations in style and symbolism. There appears, for instance, to be a prevalence in South Arcot (especially in its northern and eastern districts) of bright colors (often intensified in recent years with the use of acrylic paints), dramatic poses, idealized rounded faces, and enlarged eyes that can be contrasted with a more static and grotesque cartoon-faced style in many North Arcot temples. Such differences are not only regional but micro-regional, yet one also has to reckon with the fact that a craftsman who both makes and repairs such icons, the sculptor N. Dandapani, does so for temples

17. Compare the discussion in chapter 2 of the touring of the icons introducing the dramas at Tindivanam.

18. Arjuna is the only one for whom this is not obvious; see Hiltebeitel 1980c, 151–68, especially 153; 1982b, 81–82; 1988a, 207–8, 223, 445 n. 11, 448 and Index, s.v. Arjuna and Śiva; 1984a, 1–6, 23–25. See also Appendix, n. 8.

of other folk deities beside Draupadī, especially Māriyammaṉ (Hiltebeitel 1988a, 104, 335–56, and passim), and nowadays can find work as far afield as Madras, a considerable stylistic distance from his home near Tailāpuram. In any case, I note here only some important patterns and details.

The full complement of wooden processional icons at Tindivanam can, as is so often the case for this temple, be taken as both typical and ample: Draupadī, Subhadrā, the five Pāṇḍavas, Kṛṣṇa, and Pōttu Rāja. Except for Subhadrā, whose icons are not uncommon, and with the proviso that Pōttu Rāja is often called Pōrmaṉṉaṉ, all the rest are found quite regularly, while beyond these ten figures, others are rare. Some temples keep a permanent wooden head of Aravāṉ, but the prevalent practice, within the core area, is to make a new clay head for each festival, and destroy it at the end. Some temples, however, keep their clay head, or collect several clay heads over the years, without destroying them. Otherwise, many of the additional epic figures I have found as wooden processional icons were at one temple, Chinna Salem, where the impressive array consisted of all the above except Dharma and Subhadrā, plus the following: Abhimanyu, Parikṣit (called Paracuttu Mahārājaṉ), and Janamejaya, who together represent the Pāṇḍavas' descent through three generations from Arjuna; Alli, one of Arjuna's additional wives; Kuntī; and Caṅkuvati, wife of Pōrmaṉṉaṉ. All of these Chinna Salem figures can be found in the Draupadī cult's lunar dynasty family tree (1988a, Appendix 1). There were also two unfamiliar goddesses among the Chinna Salem icons, Vālāmpāḷ and Muttu Kumāratti. We shall find a clue about Vālāmpāḷ, however, in chapter 13. Of these additional figures, only Abhimanyu (Kolar, Vīrāṇantal), Caṅkuvati (Kāppalūr, Cantavācal), and Janamejaya (Vīrāṇantal) have been found as icons elsewhere. The latter, seated in a howdah on an elephant, is brought out to listen to Pāratam recitation, just as the epic Janamejaya heard the epic's recitation during his interrupted snake sacrifice. Otherwise, the rare additional wooden figures that have been found include Vyāsa (Kāppalūr, Tiruvannamalai Tiruviḷaiyāṭal Street Temple); Allimuttu, the son of Pōrmaṉṉaṉ and Caṅkuvati (Salem); Mantatevī, said to be Kuntī's elder sister (Salem);[19] Droṇa (Kolar); a four-armed Vīrapattiraṉ or Vīrabhadra (Vaṭukku Poykaiyūr) who will be discussed in chapter 6; and Kōṭṭai Kāḷi, or Kālī of the Fort (Villupuram), who will be met again in chapter 13. Beyond this, other epic fig-

19. I could find out nothing about this otherwise unknown figure. Perhaps the name is a deformation of Mādrī, Kuntī's junior co-wife.

ures may be represented—as Jayadratha and Karṇa are at Tindivanam—by a temporary decoration of one of the Pāṇḍava icons.

Other than in the evident possibilities here for giving ritual embodiment to local folk epic variations, what is most striking are certain features of the main recurrent ensemble of the Pāṇḍavas, Kṛṣṇa, Pōttu Rāja, and Draupadī. All together, these features give the impression that the function of the wooden icons is to represent these deities as they extend the temple's activity, throughout the festival, into the village or town and the world at large. Moreover, in contrast to the pañcalōkam icons, which are rare in any case and used only selectively where icons of both types are found, one could say that the wooden icons are avataric not in the higher devotional, triadic sense mentioned above, but in a lower sense. That is, it is in these forms that the deities are represented as taking on their changing, even "living," epic destinies, and above all handling and confronting the sacrificial overtones of the *Mahābhārata* war. At this level one finds the closest parallel not in bhakti triads, but at Kārempūḍi (Guntur District, Andhra Pradesh), the ritual battlefield site at the center of the hero cult of the *Epic of Palnāḍu*. In each case one meets the same configuration: the goddess (Draupadī or Ankālamma), an incarnation of Viṣṇu (Kṛṣṇa or Brahma Nāyuḍu), Pōttu Rāja (Telugu Pōta Rāju), and "Heroes" (the Pāṇḍavas and company, and the Heroes of Palnāḍu, in each cult linked with Śiva).[20]

That this basic ensemble of wooden processional icons is oriented toward the war is, of course, guaranteed at Draupadī festivals, at least within the core area and to the north (Andhra) and west (Salem, Bangalore) of it, by the invariable inclusion of the red-faced Pōttu Rāja–Pōrmaṉṉaṉ among them. Since Draupadī and Kṛṣṇa are found regularly among both sets of portable icons, and since the Pāṇḍavas are represented by Arjuna among the pañcalōkam figures, Pōttu Rāja—the only one found only in wood (except at Mēlaccēri)—gives the wooden ensemble its special character. Indeed, it is his icon that leads the others in processions: knife or sword in his right hand and either severed head or subdued animal in his left, it is he who leads Draupadī and the Pāṇḍavas' army not only in myth (Hiltebeitel 1988a, plates 17 and 19 and 383–93),

20. See Roghair 1982, 91–92, on the significance and uniqueness of this configuration in the Palnad region, citing the verse: "Heroes are Śiva Lingas; Viṣṇu is Cennuḍu/Pōta Rāju is Bhairava; Ankama Śakti is Annapūrṇa." Cennuḍu is Cennakeśvara of Mācerla, the epic-linked regional form of Viṣṇu and patron deity of the people of Palnāḍu, of whom Brahma Nāyuḍu is the incarnation. On the heroes and Śivalingas, see 142–46.

but also in the cult's battlefield rituals. In fact, one sometimes finds that he is the only icon in wood, as at Kalahasti.[21]

Accentuations of character through skin color are one obvious way the wooden icons differ from the pañcalōkam ones, highlighting not only their lower material value, but also their expressiveness of emotional states, such as desire, heroism, and anger, and their symbolism of violence and impurity. Indeed, with facial colorings and exaggerated eyes, the wooden icons are more like the same epic figures as they are portrayed in the Terukkūttu. Moreover, in some cases there are important definitional differences between the pañcalōkam and wooden icons. At Tindivanam, Draupadī's wooden icon has hair, as in plate 7 and on the paperback cover of volume 1: hair to let loose for the play "Dice Match and Disrobing" and to put up on the paṭukaḷam. In contrast, the pañcalōkam icon is crowned, without hair, for the crossing of the firepit.[22] In her wooden icons, Draupadī is usually red faced, though her skin tone ranges from golden yellow to rose pink. She often wears a nose ring. More often than not she looks quite demure, but she can also glower or menace.

The wooden Pāṇḍava icons are usually a full group of five, rather than being represented primarily by Dharma, as in the sanctum, or by Arjuna, as among the pañcalōkam icons. If all but Dharma are included, as at Chinna Salem and Lalgudi, it only reinforces the symbolism that Dharma's true place is in the sanctum while the Pāṇḍavas as a whole range beyond it.[23] Each Pāṇḍava has his own range of facial and bodily skin colorings: Dharma is usually golden yellow, though sometimes flesh colored; Bhīma is usually red, though sometimes green or blue; Arjuna is usually green, though sometimes blue or a fleshy pink; Nakula and Sahadeva are usually fleshy pink, but occasionally red. Each also has his special iconographic emblems. Three of the Pāṇḍavas are defined by their weapons: Bhīma by his mace (he sometimes bears a knife as well); Arjuna by his bow and arrow (occasionally by a lance); and Nakula by a sword and shield (he sometimes also rides a horse). Sahadeva, however, carries an astrological manual in his left hand, and sometimes a parrot (here in the role of astrologer's companion) in his

21. At the Mylapore temple in Madras, his is the only wooden icon that has been kept in good condition. A weathered Draupadī and Arjuna have only continued to age through more than a decade and a half of my visits.

22. But at Mēlaccēri and Cattiram Karuppūr, where Draupadī has no wooden icon, her pañcalōkam icon is supplied with a wig for her paṭukaḷam rebraiding.

23. This pattern is repeated among the pañcalōkam icons at Kalahasti, which include all the Pāṇḍavas but Dharma.

right. And Dharma usually has a staff and book. Rarely, Arjuna has variant forms. Weaponless, he performs tapas (as at Tailāpuram, Villupuram, and Kiḷiyaṉūr) wearing a loincloth and a *rudrākṣa* necklace and has a Śaivite mark of three horizontal white lines on his forehead (otherwise all the wooden icons of the Pāṇḍavas have Vaiṣṇava *nāmams*, or sectarian marks, on their foreheads). He also has his hands joined over his head like the figure in the panel showing Arjuna's tapas at Mahabalipuram. At Tailāpuram, there is also an additional wooden icon of Arjuna in the otherwise unknown (for him) disguise of a snake charmer.

It is Dharma, however, who is the most interesting of the wooden Pāṇḍavas. In one case (Kilpauk) the icon shows him seated in the royal manner typical of his portrayal in the inner sanctum, much as his pañcalōkam icon sits at Pondicherry. The Kilpauk icon bears no staff, but at Pondicherry the staff is his *daṇḍa,* or rod of sovereignty and chastisement. More interesting, however, is a quite common representation of Dharma that to my knowledge is found only in wood. In this, he is golden skinned, in a vēṣṭi from the waist down to the ankles, and with his staff turned into a walking stick (see plate 5). This is said to be the form he takes during his year incognito, under the name Kaṅkupaṭṭar or Keṅkupaṭṭar, at the end of the Pāṇḍavas' thirteen years of exile.[24] The first part of the name derives from Kaṅka, the name that Yudhiṣṭhira actually assumes during his year in disguise in the Sanskrit epic and which means "heron." In Tamil, *kaṅku* means eagle or kite (*Tamil Lexicon*). The second part of the name, *paṭṭar,* equivalent to Sanskrit *bhaṭṭa,* means learned man, scholar, or Brahman (ibid.). Thus Dharma's wooden icon, in contrast to the ways his icons portray him elsewhere, depicts him as the "Kite-" or "Heron-Brahman," a learned Brahman in the form of a bird of prey. Here one must recall Biardeau's insight that Yudhiṣṭhira's name "Heron" carries connotations of impurity and death, associations with Yama, and foreshadowings of Dharma's destructive role at Kurukṣetra, for it is particularly in assuming this name during the year he must spend incognito in the kingdom of Matsya, "Fish," that he takes on the disguise of a bird that *eats* fish (Biardeau 1978, 92–99, 104).[25]

For Draupadī cult informants, Yudhiṣṭhira not only is named

24. The former is the spelling in Irākavamūrtti 1979, 24, the latter in *Kīcaka Cammāra Nāṭakam* 1962, 10. The usual pronunciation is Keṅkupaṭṭar.

25. All this ties in further with the god Dharma's connections with the crane, Baka, as indicated in Hiltebeitel 1988a, 202 (but I must correct my statement there that it is the name "Crane," i.e., Baka, that Yudhiṣṭhira adopts during the year incognito).

after his father, Dharma, but Dharma is unequivocally identified as Yama, who is also known as Dharmarāja, the god of death. In this vein, according to the chief trustee of the Vīrāṇantal temple, the reason there is no processional image of Dharma there (as also at Chinna Salem) is that if Dharma were ever taken out of the temple, he would destroy the world. Thus he is not even taken out during his coronation (*paṭṭāpiṣēkam*). What is most instructive and intriguing for us here is that when Dharma *is* taken out as Kaṅkupaṭṭar, he should "descend" from the temple into the world not as a warrior, or even as a regnant king, but in a disguise that refers to this hidden, chaotic nature of his rule. His kingdom is one in which the big fish eat the little fish, and where the big fish makes his only appearance as a devouring crypto-Brahman. Thus, as Dharma takes on this guise, the festival-performing village that his icon tours takes on something of the character of the kingdom of Matsya, which the war will devour. And the village also serves during the festival as a living "chaotic" metaphor for the connection between battle and the mixing of castes.[26] It is thus through this "low" form that Dharma reigns over the impurity and death that are both the causes and results of the battle of Kurukṣetra. Indeed, borrowing from the *Bhagavad Gītā,* one could say that his presence in this guise suggests an explanation of how Kurukṣetra can be a *dharmakṣetra,* a field of *dharma,* with the impurity of bloodshed and acts of *adharma,* including caste confusion, that occur there.

Finally, there is Kṛṣṇa. His color is usually blue, though not infrequently green.[27] Of the four aspects in which I have seen him as a pañcalōkam icon, only one recurs in wood, and that rarely. This is his flute-playing form (Veṇugopāla), which I have seen three times: at Kolar, Vaṭukku Poykaiyūr, and in a very striking and beautifully executed image at Vīrāṇantal, where he is four-armed,

26. On similar festivals in Kerala as scenes of asuric reign and chaotic mixture of castes, cf. Tarabout 1986, 82, 253–54, 479, 492, 497, 522. See also Hiltebeitel 1988a, 169–82.

27. In the *Tiraupatātēvi Māṉmiyam* (Ilaṭcumaṇappiḷḷai 1902, 39), Draupadī prescribes that Dharma should sit in the lotus position, left hand hanging at his knee, right hand holding a scepter (no color indicated); Bhīma, of the color of clouds, should have a knife or sword (katti) in his left hand, a mace in his right, and stand in an heroic posture; Arjuna, white in color (*veṇṇiṟam*), should bear the Gāṇḍīva bow, a half-moon arrow, and be crowned; Nakula, lotus-colored, should hold a lance (*īṭṭi*) and a riding crop and wear a red turban; Sahadeva (no color), should have a parrot in his left hand and in his right a book describing the story (*carittiram*) of Kṛṣṇa; Draupadī (no color) should have her left hand hanging, her right bearing a female parrot on a blue lotus; and Kṛṣṇa should be lying down on a lotus pedestal on his left side, with a pillow, holding a red lotus in his right hand.

playing the flute with his two right hands, the back one of which also holds the cakra, while he dances on the hood of the serpent Kaliya, holding the latter's tail in one left hand and the conch in the other. One normally associates Kṛṣṇa's flute-playing with his early *līlās*, or "sports," with the Gopīs, and not with the *Mahābhārata*, much less its war. But the Terukkūttu should caution us here, for as Kṛṣṇa guides the reins of Arjuna's war chariot in their fight with Karṇa, he has been seen to be playing the flute (Hiltebeitel 1988a, 411).

In any case, the usual form in which one finds Kṛṣṇa among the wooden processional icons is four armed, bearing cakra and conch with his back hands, showing the gesture of "fear not" (*abhaya*) with his right forehand, and riding his solar bird, Garuḍa (see plate 6). Garuḍa himself has a golden human face with a mustache, human lips (no beak; cf. Tarabout 285–87, fig. 38, pl. 17), a pair of wings, and also a pair of arms and hands that reach forward and upward so that their palms support (or come up just below) Kṛṣṇa's feet. A platform in back of this double image holds Kṛṣṇa in a position that gives the appearance that he is riding Garuḍa.[28] Now, as we saw in volume 1, Garuḍa makes some dramatic appearances in the Terukkūttu dramas that stage the Draupadī cult's *Mahābhārata:* first at the battlefield sacrifice of Aravāṉ (Hiltebeitel 1988a, 330–32) and then at the death of Karṇa (ibid., 412–13). In the latter instance, Karṇa achieves *mokṣa*, or salvation, because he has a dying vision not only of Garuḍa, but of Kṛṣṇa in the form of Mahāviṣṇu riding Garuḍa. But no matter how beatific, Garuḍa is also a bird of prey, generally identified in Tamilnadu as the Brahmany kite (ibid., 413). What is veiled in Yudhiṣṭhira in his disguise as Kaṅkupaṭṭar is thus open with Kṛṣṇa. As his wooden processional icon circles out from the temple to the ritual warsites of the paṭukaḷam, he rides, bestowing the ultimate blessings, upon his winged harbinger of death.

28. Sometimes the Garuḍa is a fully separate image, as at Ciṉṉapāpucamuttiram and Teynampet.

4 Offering Sprouts

Draupadī festivals begin rather unspectacularly, with ordinary temple rites that are performed at the beginnings of festivals for other deities as well. The dramas and spectacular rituals that quicken the tempo, unfold the festival's connections with the *Mahābhārata,* and build up to its climax all take place away from the temple, though, as we have seen, the temple interacts with them through, among other things, the duties of its officiants and the movements of its processional icons. But the temple's rapport with what goes on beyond it is not defined solely by its spatial extensions into the other arenas. The temple also provides the base line for the festival's temporal rhythms. As was shown in volume 1, the Terukkūttu is framed within the time allowed for Pārata Piracaṅkam, and Pārata Piracaṅkam is set within the temple rituals that precede and follow it. The model applies most readily to the core area, but even beyond it, where the dramas are performed by local people, the same schema still applies, though the dramas are not done on consecutive nights. Taken in series, then, this means that the temple controls both ends of a ritual thread that passes through five phases:

1. It is the site of opening ceremonies that are not intrinsic to the *Mahābhārata.*

2. It remains the main venue of the often long segment of Pārata Piracaṅkam that precedes the beginning of the dramas and that calls for no more than minimal ritual activity in the temple, and none outside it, unless at a temporary alternate site.

3. From the beginning of the dramas to their end, which leads directly into the climactic war-ending rites of the paṭukaḷam and firepit, ritual activity heightens as it extends outward from the temple.

4. The pāratiyār usually remains to close out the postwar seg-

ments of his Piracaṅkam, such as the coronation of Dharma; during this period ritual activity draws back into the temple.

5. Upon conclusion of Pāratam, when the pāratiyār has in ordinary cases left for home or his next job, most of the festival-closing rites center, as with the opening rites, in and around the temple alone (cf. Hiltebeitel 1988a, 139–40).

The chief opening and closing rites are, in fact, symmetrical: flag hoisting and flag lowering, donning and removing kāppu wristlets, and sowing and dispersing sprouts. Although susceptible to considerable variation, depending above all on a festival's length and complexity, they are nonetheless quite standard at Draupadī festivals. Generic to South Indian festivals for numerous deities, and traceable even as a complex to classical āgamic prototypes, these rites nonetheless take on their own Draupadī cult specifics and colorings.[1] Against this wider background, we will explore these rites in this and the next two chapters, not only looking at such colorings themselves, but also anticipating their shadings of the more dramatic rituals that they frame. Even though the flagstaff rites, linked most inseparably with the wristlet ceremonies, mark the true beginning and end of a festival, I will turn to the sprouting rites first because of their nuclear character, and because of the exemplary methodological issues that they raise for the study of Draupadī cult rituals as a whole.[2]

A. South Indian Gardens of Adonis Revisited

The little rite before us is known under many names, the most typical for Tamilnadu being *navadhānya* (Tamil *navatāṉiyam*), "nine grains"; *aṅkurārpaṇa*, "the casting or offering of sprouts" (Sanskrit); *mūlappari*, apparently referring to the tender seedlings; *pālikai*, the "little pots" in which the navadhānya is sown, a term that can also mean "young damsel" (*Tamil Lexicon*) and that, from a Sanskrit derivation, could mean "the Protectress" (Biardeau 1989b, 142 n. 28); and *pāli*, seemingly a shortened form of pālikai, found several times in my fieldwork, and once explained (by the pūcāri of the

1. On flag hoisting, the tying of a cord (*pratisarābandhana*) on the deity's wrist, and the offering of sprouts as a complex in Vaiṣṇava Vaikhānasa āgamas and related texts, see Gonda [1954] 1969, 244–62; cf. Janaki 1988, 132 n. 6: flag hoisting, sprout sowing, and drumming as interrelated initial functions in Śaiva āgamas.

2. The following is a reworking of Hiltebeitel 1988c, presented at the same panel as Biardeau 1988, which has inspired some of my revisions. An earlier presentation of this material was given at the 1979 meeting, on plants, of the Conference on Religion in South India, at Martha's Vineyard.

Mēlaccēri temple) as describing the *action* of placing the navadhānya on the ground (apparently from the Tamil verb *pāli,* "to give"). All these meanings will take on substance in our discussion. The rite's nuclear character is shown by the way it is always a small part of much larger ceremonies, so much so that one may easily overlook it or find it literally cropping up unexpectedly before one's eyes (as described in Zanen 1978, 1).

As several authors have observed, the premature sprouting and then discarding or abandoning of seedlings occurs in rituals in both the South Asian and ancient Mediterranean worlds. The seeming similarities between the rites have generated rather varied scholarly responses: from the comparativism of Sir James Frazer (1907, 182–216), who saw the rites as sympathetic magic—"charms to promote the growth and revival of vegetation" (ibid., 194)—and linked to the mythologies of "dying and rising gods" such as Adonis; to the diffusionism of Josef Haekel and his predecessors (see Haekel 1972), who propose missing links from tribal India and the Indus Valley civilization; to the structuralist anti-comparativism of Detienne (1972, 1977), who insists that the Greek data require their own interpretation. A brief article by M. Zanen (1978) attempts to reopen the comparative question from the vantage point of the great interpretative gains made by Detienne. But Zanen has ignored a considerable body of pertinent Indian material already in the literature,[3] and his own data are too sketchy to support his comparisons. Moreover, he is perhaps too cavalier in rejecting the possibility of diffusion by supposing there could be no meaningful contacts between two such "totally different culture areas" (1978, 1). One purpose of this chapter is thus to revisit the comparative question by pushing a bit further into the Indian data. My own fieldwork on

3. Such rites are also performed at temple founding and dedication ceremonies in South Indian Brahmanical temples (Rangachari 1930, 115–20; Diehl 1956, 96; Clothey 1983, 187); at marriage ceremonies among a full spectrum of castes from Brahmans to Untouchables (Srinivas 1942, 95–100, on Māḍiga Untouchables; Thurston and Rangachari [1904] 1965, 1:279–94, on Brahmans; Nanjundayya and Iyer 1928–35, 4:613–14, on Vaṉṉiyars); upon departing and returning from a journey (Gold 1987, 198–99, 230–31, 259–60); and widely during the nine days of spring and fall Navarātri ceremonies honoring the goddess (Babb 1975, 132–40; Frazer 1907, 201; Haekel 1972, 168; Biardeau 1984, 9; Crooke 1914, 6:457; 1915, 47; Kane [1930–62] 1975, 5:183; Flueckiger 1983, 31–32; cf. Thurston and Rangachari [1904] 1965, 4:388, involving worship of the Pāṇḍavas' mother Kuntī). For South India, see Oppert 1893, 478–80; Richards 1920, 118; Zanen 1978; Whitehead 1921, 64–65; Fuller 1980, 337; L. Dumont 1957, 386; Diehl 1956, 96–97, 176, 185, 262–64, 297; Tarabout 1986, 346; Thurston 1906, 2; Nishimura 1987, 11, 18, 71–72, 94. This list makes no claim to exhaustiveness.

the South Indian Draupadī and Kūttāṇṭavar cults will provide the main focus. I begin, however, not with any presumed Indian primordium such as the Indus Valley, tribals, or folk religion, or with the notion of autonomous "culture areas," but with the conceptual and practical worlds of Vedic ritual.

Śatapatha Brāhmaṇa 5.3.3.2–10, which describes the *devasū* offerings—a preliminary ceremony in the rites of consecration (*abhiṣecanīya, abhiṣeka*)—of a king within the Rājasūya sacrifice (see Heesterman 1957, 68–78; Gonda 1987, 211–14), provides a useful point of departure. To my knowledge, the ceremony has not been linked with later Indian "sprouting" rituals of the type we will be treating. The context of the devasū offerings is the royal yajamāna's *dīkṣā*, or "consecration," in preparation for which a victim is offered to Agni and Soma (5.3.3.1). Then the eight devasū are prepared, each one a "cake" (*puroḍāśa*) or "pap" (*caru*) made of different grains or seeds, and offered to different male deities who are invoked to "quicken" or "impel" the king's assorted powers. In addition, a ninth cake is prepared of an unnamed substance for Agni-Soma. A numerology of "nine grains" is thus detectable. Most intriguingly, however, the first two cakes are made from "fast-grown" (*plāśuka*) and "quick-grown" (*āśu*) rice, varieties that taxed the commentator Sāyaṇa, who described the first as "rice which has sprung up again and ripens very rapidly," and the second as "rice ripening in sixty days" (Eggeling 1966, 3:69, nn. 2 and 4). Let us note that this is a rite for a man about to become king: presumably a youth, or a man whose youthful powers are being "quickened" by these offerings (cf. Gonda 1987, 212–13). Moreover, these ceremonies form part of his dīkṣā, the rite that involves the construction of the womblike hut that is one Vedic prototype for the *garbhagṛha* ("womb-house") of the Hindu temple (in Tamil temples, the *mūlastāṉam*). There the yajamāna offers himself up to a death and new birth that finds something of a reversal in the plants of quickened growth, which provide the seeds for the "cakes" that are offered on his behalf. The Vedic rite thus has elements that almost certainly provide a basis for further elaboration of "sprouting" rites in connection with marriages, temples, and particularly temples of the goddess (see n. 3). In the latter, the nine grains often ripen in the garbhagṛha itself. And at goddess festivals they are offered—even if only implicitly—on behalf of a symbolically royal yajamāna, whether it be a king at Dasarā, a village headman, or the chief trustee(s) of a temple. Moreover, as is the case in navadhānya ceremonies performed in goddess temples, the grains offered must finally be understood as sacrificial victims.

So it is with the grains in another *Śatapatha Brāhmaṇa* passage (1.2.3.6–7), which describes how the "sacrificial essence" (*medhas*) passed from man (*puruṣa*), after he was offered up, to the horse, ox, sheep, and goat, and thence into the earth, from which it was dug in the form of rice and barley: "And as much efficacy as all those sacrificial animals would have for him, so much efficacy has this oblation (of rice & c.) for him who knows this" (Eggeling [1882] 1966, 1:50–51; cf. Gonda 1987, 22–23). The offering of grains thus has the same essence and just as much efficacy as the offering of the gamut of victims from goats to man (puruṣa). Furthermore, rice in South India and *javārā* (variously identified as wheat, millet, or barley) in Central and Western India[4] are the grains in navadhānya-type ceremonies, each also figuring among the devasū offerings, with barley (*yava:* apparently the etymon of *javārā*) offered to Varuṇa (*Śatapatha Brāhmaṇa* 5.3.3.9).

Let us admit that we do not know what precise connection this Vedic rite might have to later navadhānya rituals, and that on the basis of current information any attempt to reconstruct a historical connection would be all too tentative.[5] But I would posit that it is the prominence of navadhānya-type rituals in the Navarātri, the implicitly if not explicitly royal festival to the goddess Durgā (see n. 3), that provides our likeliest link between the Rājasūya and the widely documented occurrence of navadhānya rituals in the cults of village, caste, and lineage goddesses, Draupadī included. Yet I would not argue that all the elements of the latter ceremonies can be traced through these links back to Vedic models. The transformation of Vedic rituals into āgamic paradigms for the royal, and then village, cult of the goddess will not account for everything. If, as I hope to show, there is purpose in pursuing the question of structural affinities between Indian and Greek sprouting rites, we must not rush to find quick solutions to the questions of historical and cultural connections (Mediterranean/Indian, Aryan/Dravidian). Let us regard the Vedic rite as one among the many transformations such rites have taken, rather than simply as a privileged Indian prototype. With this in mind, we can refresh our memories of the Greek Gardens of Adonis.

First the myth. As I will argue for the Indian materials, even

4. See Haekel 1972, 168 (Gerste, barley); Babb 1975, 134 (wheat); Gold 1987, 198 (*juvārā:* "usually of millet"); Flueckiger 1983, 28 and n. 3 (*javārā,* wheat, to which barley, rice, and pulses may be added).

5. A Dharmaśāstra rite has a rather intermediary look: dedicated to Viṣṇu, it invokes the goddesses Earth, Rāka, and Sinīvalī in connection with the planting pots, as well as Soma, king of plants (Gonda [1954] 1969, 259).

though the rites occur in festivals with many different myths and are rarely mythologized themselves (that is, directly tied in with the primary cult myths), the sprouting rites are still symbolically expressive of the different cults' underlying mythic themes.

Adonis was born of an incestuous seduction by Myrrha of her father Thias, a king of Assyria. Fleeing her father's wrath once he found out that he had lain with her, Myrrha, with the aid of the gods, was turned into a myrrh tree, from which ten months later Adonis was born. Immediately after birth, while still an infant, Adonis aroused sexual desire in Aphrodite and Persephone, and Zeus was led to decree that the two rival mistresses must share Adonis, each for one half of the year, Aphrodite in this world, Persephone in the underworld. But at adolescence, nearing full maturity, Adonis was gored to death by a wild boar after having been hidden by Aphrodite among lettuces.

Detienne argues that the Frazerian interpretation of Adonis as a dying-rising "fertility god," and of his "gardens" as intended to magically further the cycle of the agricultural season, are inadequate to account for the myth and the rite. The "gardens of Adonis" were sown during the "dog days" of summer, the canicular period of the heliacal rising of the constellation Sirius, the "dog star," variously dated from July 20–27 (Detienne 1977, 100). According to the Greeks, this is a period when plants are burned and die, when fields are sterile, a time for drought, thirst, and fevers. This time, when the sun is "closest to the earth" and threatening it with desiccation (ibid., 9, 106), coincides with the only time for the harvesting of frankincense and myrrh, spices the Greeks mythologized as being attainable only during the hottest season, and from Arabia. Adonis, born from Myrrh (Myrrha), is like the plants in his gardens: not a figure of mature fertility but one of sexual precocity and sterility. In one instance cited, he is "compared to a young man whose premature death is reminiscent of those plants 'which grow rapidly in a pot of earth, a basket or some kind of wicker receptacle, and are then cast into the sea where they soon disappear'" (ibid., 101, n. 21). Similarly, Plato asks in the *Phaedrus,* "And now, tell me this: if a sensible farmer had some seeds to look after and wanted them to bear fruit, would he with serious intent plant them during the summer in a garden of Adonis and enjoy watching them grow up into fine plants within eight days?" (ibid., 103). Let us now review some of our Indian data with the implications of such a question in mind.

In the Draupadī cult, one common pattern—found primarily at shorter festivals of ten days or less—is for the navadhānya to be linked with the opening ceremonies so that the period of the plants' sprouting covers the span of the main festival activities. Such a case occurs at the Muthialpet Dharmarāja-Vināyakar temple, a Draupadī temple in Madras City. On flag hoisting day, sand is taken from the base of the temple's *vaṉṉi* or *śamī* tree at the northwest corner of the temple compound and set in nine dishlike pots with tapered bases (pālikai). These are arranged on a high platform within the temple's "sacrificial hall," or *yākacālai*, a small masonry structure with open latticework around the upper walls except for the western wall, which has the door that opens toward the east-facing temple. The nine grains are sown in the pots on the platform.[6] Following Biardeau, one may appreciate that the term *yākacālai* (Sanskrit *yāgaśāla*) retains the usage of āgamic ritual, in which *yāga* replaces the Vedic term *yajña*. In this perspective, the high altar within the "sacrificial hall" (a recurrent feature at both Brahmanical and popular temples) can be regarded as a transformation of the *uttaravedi*, the "superior" or "higher" altar of the Vedic sacrifice (Biardeau 1988, 94).

The Muthialpet temple pūcāri, a Kurukkaḷ, then ties threads (said to be the deities' veins) around an additional nine pots (Sanskrit *navakalaśa*), pours rice, water, and milk in them, and invokes the "nine rivers"—that is, all the rivers—into them with mantras. Three of these pots are said to belong to Dharma, Draupadī, and Kṛṣṇa, but the nine together also represent the "nine planets," or better, the nine planetary deities, who govern astrological destinies. On each day of the ten-day festival, the main deity dressed for procession is brought twice before the growing navadhānya, and each day firewood (peepul, vaṉṉi, banyan, and *erukku*, a milky shrub) is brought and a sacrificial fire made in the *akkiṉikuṇṭam* (firepit),

6. Lists of nine grains show quite some variation. From itemizations gathered at Tindivanam, Mēlaccēri, Tailāpuram, and Kūvākkam, and compared with those in Thurston and Rangachari [1904] 1965, 1:281; Oppert 1893, 478; Eichinger Ferro-Luzzi 1977, 551; and the *Tamil Lexicon* (s.v. *navatāṉiyam*), the following are mentioned in relative order of frequency: *kaṭalai* (chick-pea or Bengal gram) is mentioned in all lists; *nel* (rice, paddy), *uḷuntu* (black gram), and *tuvarai* (pigeon pea or "red gram") in all lists but one each; *avarai* (field bean) in all but two lists; *payaṟu* (green gram), *moccai* (hyacinth bean, climber), and *kārāmaṇi* (cowpea or chowlee bean) occur in over half the lists; *paṭṭāṇi* (garden pea, gray or field pea), *irāki* (or *rāki*, a grain or cereal), sesame, and *kampu* (red millet) are mentioned at least twice; *eḷḷu* (gingelly), *nilakkaṭalai* (peanut), *perum payaṟu* (chowlee bean), and *cōḷam* ("great millet") are mentioned once. The chapbook drama *Turōpatai Kuṟavañci* also mentions cōḷam and various other millets of different colors. In all, at least sixteen distinct plants are named. A list from Sri Lanka has six of the above plus *kaṭuku* (mustard), *koḷḷu* (horse gram), and *kaupi* (unidentified) (Tanaka 1987, 250 n. 32). The variants no doubt reflect local crop selections.

more revealingly called also the *yōṉikuṇṭam* ("womb [-shaped] pit"), within the yākacālai in back (to the east) of the navadhānya "altar." The *yoni-*, or really vulva-shaped, firepit (it has a channel to the north like a yoni pedestal for a liṅgam), seems especially pertinent in a goddess temple, particularly through the links with firewalking that will be noted shortly.[7] But it is also one of several ways of representing the firepit within a yākacālai, another being to have three pits, recalling the three Vedic sacrificial fires (Biardeau 1988, 94).

Finally, on the culminating tenth day at Muthialpet, the water stored in the *kalaśam* pots beside the navadhanya dishes is brought from the yākacālai to the temple and used for an *apiṣēkam* ("consecration") of the three main processional deities: Draupadī, Arjuna, and Kṛṣṇa. Wood and water used for the lighting and spreading out of the coals of the firewalking pit are also taken from the yākacālai. And the nine dishes of navadhānya are taken on a morning procession, and then in the afternoon placed around the borders of the firepit—two at the entrance and exit sides (east and west), and two on the northern border and three on the southern. These represent the security offered by the nine planets to those who cross over the coals. It would seem that the seedlings are thus in effect offered up at the firepit, to be singed and desiccated by the heat of the coals. After this the pots are returned to the yākacālai, marking the conclusion of their use in the festival.

At Muthialpet, as at many other shorter festivals, the navadhañnya rites thus coincide with the other festival-framing rites of flag hoisting and wristlet (kāppu) tying. As we shall see in chapters 5 and 6, these rites often require the temporary services of Brahmans. The Muthialpet Kurukkaḷ's Brahman status may help explain the prominence of the navadhānya ceremonies at this Madras temple, and may also explain their unusually extensive integration with wider features and aspects of the temple (sand from the vaṉṉi tree) and the festival (presentation of the processional icons, offering of seedlings at the firewalking pit). At the Kalahasti Draupadī temple, the navadhānya ceremonies in the yāgaśāla are done not by an *arcaka* or pūjāri from the temple's main community, the Vanne Reddis, but by a Brahman. In this regard, Biardeau indicates that in the normal situation, only a Brahman would enter a yāgaśāla, not to mention officiate within it (1988, 94). At Draupadī temples with non-Brahman pūcāris, yākacālais are accordingly less common,

7. Cf. Tanaka 1987, 210: the altar as both vagina and mouth of Agni, recipient of oblations.

and the navadhānya ceremonies themselves are often performed by these non-Brahman priests, and not in a yākacālai but in the sanctum. For now, let me only remark that where such rites coincide with flag hoisting and wristlet tying, they mark a link between the navadhānya and Pōttu Rāja, Draupadī's primary iconic guardian, who figures prominently in connection with the flagstaff.

It is more common, however, especially at longer festivals, for the navadhānya to be sown not at flag hoisting, but at the ritual and dramatic enactments of Draupadī's wedding. Where this is the case, there is still a link with the tying of kāppu, for whereas the chief temple officiants would have donned them at flag hoisting, at enactments of Draupadī's marriage it is common for the additional cadre of those who vow to undertake the rite of firewalking to put them on as well. In such circumstances, there is usually (Tindivanam providing something of an exception; see below) no apparent link between the navadhānya and Pōttu Rāja, for whom I have found no accentuated place at Draupadī's wedding. But a link between the navadhānya and Pōttu Rāja often does resurface at the closing navadhānya ceremonies of the festival, as at Veḷḷimēṭupēṭṭai village.

A brief description of the Veḷḷimēṭupēṭṭai ceremony will allow us to underscore some of the consistencies and variations in the performance of navadhānya rites in Draupadī festival settings. Here flag hoisting precedes the main ten-day segment of heightened festival activity by several weeks. But the ten-day segment itself begins with narrative, ritual, and dramatic enactment of the epic scene of Draupadī's wedding. Firewalkers put on kāppu wristlets like the main officiants before them, and the sowing of the nine grains coincides with Draupadī's wedding. Like most Draupadī temples, the Veḷḷimēṭupēṭṭai temple has no separate yākacālai, so instead the grains are planted in the northwest corner of the temple's inner sanctum, called the *navatāṉiya mūlai,* or "navadhānya corner." Furthermore, they are sown not in separate pots, but in a pile of moistened soil or sand (see Hiltebeitel 1988d, plate 1, p. 89). And instead of nine kalaśam pots being interspersed with them, a single large clay pot is set in the center of the mound of navadhānya. The latter, however, called the *apiṣēka śakti karakam* (the pot for the goddess's consecration), replicates the nine kalaśam pots' function of providing water for abhiṣekas. Every evening (or morning) it is taken to a nearby tank, filled with fresh water, and redecorated with new flowers and mango leaves before it is returned to the cella for the next day's pūjās. The notion of the inner sanctum itself as a garbhagṛha, or "womb-house," would seem to replicate the proximity of the nine grains to the yōṉikuṇṭam, the womb-shaped firepit in the Muthialpet yākacālai. Or better, as part of the yākacālai, the yōṉikuṇṭam replicates the garbhagṛha.

The closing ceremonies at Veḷḷimēṭupēṭṭai, however, once again relate the nine grains to Pōttu Rāja and the lowering of the flag. These rites occur on the day following the firewalk. But meanwhile, during the evening of the firewalk, the nine grains, having sprouted to a height of about four inches in their corner of the garbhagṛha, remain in place while the inner sanctum itself becomes the scene of extremely *heated* activities, some having erotic associations, which will be discussed in chapter 14. In effect, the firewalk marks the ritual end of the nine grains' sprouting within the temple, for in the next day's ritual sequence, the nine grains—here represented by only one grain, nel or paddy—are placed on a large tray and carried in procession, by a woman, to the temple reservoir or tank (see Hiltebeitel 1988d, plate 2, p. 90). The navadhānya tray is not alone in this procession, however, as other women also carry baskets containing their preparations for cooking *poṅkal* (rice cooked in milk in a mud pot until it boils over, symbolizing abundance). And all are led by the processional icons. Pōttu Rāja is carried first, but facing backward toward the images of Draupadī and Arjuna, the navadhānya, etc. Other temple officiants hold aloft certain processional paraphernalia: one, the multi-tined lance called vīrakuntam with a lemon impaled on its central prong, and two others a pair of temple flags. Mythically, these "weapons" belong to Pōttu Rāja.[8] When the procession reaches the edge of the tank, the three icons are placed to watch the following ceremony. Standing with his feet in the water, a man scrapes two miniature enclosures for growing paddy (*taṇṇir pāttis*) into the mud of the bank.[9] He and various women then assist in setting the "nine grains" (actually rice plants) into the mud, and a pūjā is performed. A betel leaf, several coins, and a rupee note are placed beside a little tower of mud with turmeric powder mixed into it, and then *neem* (margosa) leaves are placed around the tower. After a short prayer, all shout "Govinda" and return to the temple with the poṅkal preparations for the concluding rites. This little ceremony, carried out against a background of elevated weapons, pennants, and icons backed by tall borassus palms against a blue sky, has a serenity and coolness that contrasts with the hot ceremonies of the previous

8. See Hiltebeitel 1988a, 392–93, and below, chapter 6.

9. This form of the rite was also described in 1986 as the one familiar from previous Mēlaccēri festivals but went unperformed there in 1982 and 1986.

night. But one realizes that the sprouts of navadhānya, having survived the "hothouse" atmosphere of the garbhagṛha, are now being consigned to their death at the water's edge. Moreover, the inevitable *premature death* of these beautiful sprouts is coincident with the women's preparation of poṅkal from *matured* rice. It is thus most intriguing that I was told that if the paddy grew, it would be a sign of good augur, but if it died something bad would happen. Clearly it could not really grow.[10] But it was not a question of good or bad augur for the village, but of good or bad augur for the just (dharmic) rule of the five Pāṇḍavas, Draupadī's husbands. The cry "Govinda" implies here that the growth will be a miracle overseen by the god Kṛṣṇa, the Pāṇḍavas' ally. And "in reality," the sprouts need remain green only until the coronation of Dharma (Yudhiṣṭhira, the eldest Pāṇḍava), which at Veḷḷimēṭupēṭṭai takes place *ritually* later that same evening.

A third and final example of Draupadī cult navadhānya rites needs to be considered for only a few more particulars. At Tindivanam, the Draupadī festival is of grand proportions. As many as forty days may come between flag hoisting and the beginning of epic dramas and related rituals. Once the latter do begin, the enactments of Draupadī's marriage do not occur until the third of the eighteen nights of drama, sixteen days before the firewalk, which occurs on the day the eighteen nights of drama are over. There are thus about fifty-eight days between flag hoisting and firewalking day, and the festival continues for six more days of wind-up ceremonies after that. Here the navadhānya ceremonies are in effect doubled, and at the points we would now expect. The navadhānya ceremony *proper* begins with flag hoisting. Then the beginning of a similar rite is set to coincide with Draupadī's wedding. That a larger festival should double these rites in a way that reinforces their two primary ritual settings of flag hoisting and marriage certainly confirms that these two contexts are of great significance.

At flag hoisting, the sowing of navadhānya again follows variants of the rites of the flagstaff and the tying of the protective amulet or kāppu. Sand and soil for the nine grains are placed in the inner sanctum of the temple, though not in the northwest corner but the northeast, the "the corner of Caṉi," or Saturn (*caṉi-mūlai*), the most baleful of all the "nine planets," whose astrological influence these rites propitiate. The affinity between the nine planets and nine grains, which we have seen before at Muthialpet and

10. Zanen 1978, 3, remarks that "the seedlings did not drown in the river, they even sprouted during the following days." This must have been a short respite.

shall remark on again, is widely attested in the Draupadī cult and elsewhere (cf. Diehl, 1956, 297; Eichinger Ferro-Luzzi 1977, 551). According to the Tindivanam temple pūcāri, a purification ceremony (*puṇṇiyāvatāṉam*) that forms part of the prior flag hoisting makes the nine planets auspicious for the navadhānya ceremony. The latter now continues with the sowing of a little paddy into the soil, and then the nine grains. The pūcāri, V. Govindaswamy, an exuberant and emphatic man, claims that the grains sprout within three days and within seven to ten days are a foot tall! If the grains sprout in a good manner, then it is understood that everyone will live well; if each and every grain is favored it means a good life for all that year. After ten to fifteen days, with the sprouts still thriving, the pūcāri and his entourage take them down to the "Gaṅgā" (actually, the Rājaṅkuḷam tank near the temple) and consign them to the water. There are no miniature paddy fields made for them, and in fact, according to the pūcāri, "no ceremony": when the sprouts die, they are just thrown away. Indeed, there is no significance to their dying. In fact, he says, they reach the full growth that one hopes for from them, and that is that.

The second ceremony on the day of Draupadī's marriage obviously replicates features of the first. Two large and highly decorated clay pots called *cāl karakam* are set down so that they flank a group of pālikai, the small tapered navadhānya pots already noted. Cāl, from the verb *cāl, cālu,* "to be abundant, full, extensive," means a "large water pot," but also "fullness, abundance," "furrow in ploughing," and the "track of a sower in passing and repassing while sowing grain" (*Tamil Lexicon*). The pālikai are seeded with navadhānya, the nine grains being no different, the pūcāri insisted, from those sown earlier in the inner sanctum. Here again we see the little pots for the nine grains placed beside one or more bigger pots, but this time there is a clear resonance of an opposition that may be implied in our other examples as well. Whereas the big pots represent fullness of growth, and at least in this case full-scale agriculture, the seedlings remain symbols of rapid but aborted growth. As observed at Tindivanam in 1981, there were six pālikai between the two cāl karakams (see Hiltebeitel 1988d, plate 3, p. 91), but the number is not fixed. There may be five, six, or seven, the number five—mentioned at Mēlaccēri—reminding us that Draupadī has five children. As part of the same ceremony, a few people—all important temple officiants: the pūcāri, kaṇāccāri, and nimantam (who has responsibility during the festival for the temple icons)—don the kāppu wristlet. (At Tindivanam, firewalkers—numbering in the high hundreds—do not put on kāppu until firewalking day itself.) After the pālikai are seeded, the sprouts grow at Tindivanam for the sixteen days between Draupadī's marriage and the firewalk, surviving well, and rising—according to the same pūcāri—in a good year to the height of the pots (again, about a foot). Here the navadhānya *are* linked with Pōttu Rāja at Draupadī's marriage, for they are stationed directly in front of the Pōrmaṉṉaṉ maṇḍapa, Pōrmaṉṉaṉ being, of course, a variant name for Pōttu Rāja. Indeed, as the pūcāri himself further insisted, they are set at the "center" of the line of sight between Pōrmaṉṉaṉ, from his maṇḍapa, and Draupadī, from within her inner sanctum. Thus both watch over their growth: Draupadī, it seems, taking a maternal interest, as they are seeded at the time of her marriage, and Pōttu Rāja overseeing their inevitable sacrifice, in which he himself is in this case clearly implicated. For after the firewalk, the pālikai are placed *on top of* the Pōrmaṉṉaṉ maṇḍapa, where they are left to die. Later, at no specific date, they are taken down without fanfare. One cannot miss here the alternate outcomes of the two similar rites within this one festival: in one case the sprouts are consigned to the water, in the other left on a rooftop to desiccate in the sun.

Finally, for the last example from my own fieldwork, I turn to the navadhānya rites as they are included within festivals of the god Kūttāṇṭavar. His cult is closely related to Draupadī's, since both are rooted in the same general areas, in some cases they engage the same specialist performers (pāratiyārs and Terukkūttu dramatists), and they even, in certain cases (as at Tailāpuram), hold joint festivals. Moreover, Kūttāṇṭavar is identified as Aravāṉ: the son of Arjuna and the serpent (*nāga*) princess Ulūpī, and a figure whose important place in Draupadī cult ritual will be the subject of chapter 9. Most pertinently, for the moment, it is the sixteen-year-old Aravāṉ-Kūttāṇṭavar who offers the battlefield self-sacrifice (*kaḷappali*) to Kālī that assures the Pāṇḍavas' victory at Kurukṣetra, but not before Kṛṣṇa has disguised himself as Mohinī, the Enchantress, and quickly married Kūttāṇṭavar on the battlefield to secure him the proper funeral and afterlife that he would be denied as an unmarried child.[11] Like the ideal Draupadī festival, Kūttāṇṭavar's major festivals at Kūvākkam and Kottaṭṭai (Chidambaram Taluk, South Arcot) last eighteen days. The ritual enactments of the marriage and battlefield sacrifice, with its scenes of mutilation, dying, and rebirth, occur on the sixteenth day at Kūvākkam and on the eighteenth at Kottaṭṭai. These are also the days when thousands of

11. See Hiltebeitel 1988a, 317–32 and below, chapter 9. Opinions vary as to whether the marriage is consummated.

men take the vow to impersonate Kṛṣṇa-Mohinī in his/her marriage to Kūttāṇṭavar. Most of them are local farmers who fulfill their vow by wearing a saree for the day and putting on bangles and a tāli (wedding necklace); but many of them are eunuchs (*ali*s) who come from far and wide to dress first as the brides and then as the widows of this self-mutilating god. It is also on this day that the navadhānya enters into play.

While Kūttāṇṭavar's sacrifice and death in battle are ritually represented, the eunuchs who have "married" him carry on lamentations for the doomed god, their husband, leading his chariot to a grove of trees called the *a̱lukaḷam*, or "weeping ground." At Kūvākkam, it is there, after a final crescendo, that their dirges cease. The eunuchs then leave the a̱lukaḷam to don the white sarees of the widow. The a̱lukaḷam has been the site of a small open-air "temple" (*kōyil*) on which a little mound of pāli, or naradhānya, has been growing since it was sown on the festival's second day. The sowing of the nine grains coincides with the ritual marriage of two Harijans, one of whom impersonates Mohinī and the other Kūttāṇṭavar, and from the second day on, it is the Harijan bride who guards the growing sprouts from browsing goats and other intruders. During the evening of the fifteenth day and through the sixteenth day, before the chariot reaches the weeping ground, farmers come to take clumps of the sprouts to mix with their seeds to bring about good crops. By the time the chariot arrives there, marking Kūttāṇṭavar's death, the sprouts are all gone. Meanwhile, at Kottaṭṭai, the navadhānya (again called pāli) has other instructive variations. On the first day, the nine grains are sown on a five-by-five-foot plot of ground on the a̱lukaḷam, and fenced off to prevent intrusion by animals. By the eighteenth day, the sprouts have grown to about a foot. There on the a̱lukaḷam, as part of the scene of lamentation over the slain god, when Kūttāṇṭavar's chariot (tēr) is pulled over the navadhānya, the eunuchs begin their most intense weeping. Then, both they and the transvestite farmers cut their tālis and break their bangles (symbols of their widowhood upon the god's death) and throw them onto the navadhānya crop.[12] After this, the sprouts are left to dry out and die naturally. Thus at Kūvākkam they are uprooted, but to benefit the crops, while at Kottaṭṭai they are left green, but only to desiccate amid the cut and broken symbols of death and widowhood. The paradoxical complements of ag-

12. At Kūvākkam, the thousands of cut tāli strings are strung over a special post (the *veḷḷikkāl*, or "silver post") implanted at the eastern boundary of the outdoor a̱lukaḷam "temple." The bangles are smashed at the base of this post.

ricultural life and sacrificial death are obvious in each case. We need pursue the Kūttāṇṭavar ceremonies no further than to note that at each festival, the day on which the sprouting rites conclude coincides not only with the god's death, but also with his revival at a nearby Kālī temple.

One may suspect a correlation between the premature death of these seedlings and the premature death of Kūttāṇṭavar, both on the same "weeping ground." In the Draupadī cult there are also affinities between the seedlings and Draupadī's children, whom her cult calls the "young Pañcapāṇḍavas" (*iḷam pañcapaṇṭavarkaḷ*). For one thing, a connection of this type is intensified where the sowing of the grains coincides with the celebration of Draupadī's marriage: the growth of the sprouts in the yākacālai, or "womb-house," of her temple parallels the conception (rather mysterious in her cult, since she is a virgin) and growth of her children. Furthermore, the navadhānya and the "Young Pañcapāṇḍavas" have parallel destinies. Like Aravāṉ-Kūttāṇṭavar, they too are "sprouts," destined to die young and unmarried, victims of cruel sacrificial deaths on the battlefield. Moreover, the death-revival parallelism between the sprouts and Kūttāṇṭavar has its counterpart in the Draupadī cult, which has rituals that imply the revival of the "Young Pañcapāṇḍavas."[13] One should also appreciate that in each of these cults, the complex of myth and ritual connected with their sprouting rites emphasizes varying forms of collaboration and complementariness between Viṣṇu (Kṛṣṇa, Mohinī, the cry "Govinda") and the goddess (Draupadī, Kālī).

B. Comparisons

At this point, then, we have unfolded some of the underlying structural continuities, and certain distinctive theological and mythological themes and ritual practices, that are connected with the

13. See below, chapter 11. See also the connections between sprouts and youths in the Ind-Pithoro ceremony (a navadhānya variant that forms part of a tribal transformation of Navarātri-Dasarā) performed by the Rathwa of Gujarat: baskets (called *jawara*, "barley") of nine grains are represented by nine youths, who must fast during the nine-day period, then handle the baskets on the culminating day in a ceremony followed by the violent possession of a *barwo* (shaman-priest), who swings a sword around the nine baskets, thrusts it into the earth between them, then sacrifices goats and cocks, and finally disperses the grains in a nearby body of water (Haekel 1972, 167–70). Cf. Hiltebeitel 1988a, 193–94: Droṇa trains the Kaurava and Pāṇḍava youths in a yākacālai, again suggesting an affinity between youths (as battle offerings) and sprouts.

navadhānya rites of the two cults studied most closely in my fieldwork. Now, with regard to our wider "comparative" issue, certain things should be striking. According at least to Zanen, "In the ritual of Adonis, the prematurely withering plants can only evoke the young god" (1978, 5). In the absence of an Indian Adonis, however, Zanen thought the Indian rites lacked the meanings of "death" and "transitoriness" and sought out other meanings instead—most notably "cooling"—for the submersion and dispersal of the sprouts (ibid., 4–5). Yet we have seen two cases where the Indian rites are linked with rather striking mythic counterparts to Adonis: figures who not only are sexually immature or precocious, but have little or no sexual experience (see n. 11). Similarly, even though the navadhānya rites may be connected with the agricultural cycle—as with the paddy field divisions at Veḷḷimēṭupēṭṭai or the mixing of Kūttāṇṭavar's pāli with the farmers' seeds at Kūvākkam—it is still only *by contrast* with the fruits of "real" agriculture: the coinciding poṅkal at Veḷḷimēṭupēṭṭai, the anticipated good crops at Kūvākkam. This is just as it is in Greece. Says Detienne, "the gardening of Adonis stood for a negation of true cultivation of plants and was an inverted form of the growing of cereals as represented, in a religious context, by the principal power responsible for cultivated plants, namely Demeter" (1977, 103). This "negation" is at the core of a series of oppositions that emerge clearly in the structure of the Greek rites, and find remarkable analogues in India. Let us attempt to refine Zanen's structural comparison, modifying only slightly his "code" headings but altering rather extensively what comes under his South India column, in the light of what we have found not only in our own field data, but also in the wider data in the available literature.

Greece	*South India*
I. *Cosmological Code*	
Dog days. Hottest period, earth closest to sun (ca. July 20–27). Normal agriculture suspended.	Usually in hot season (April to August), corresponding to spring Navarātri ceremonies and the predominance of goddess festivals in the hot season.[14]

Let us note that this period can be described in terms similar to those Detienne applies to the Dog Days of Greece: a time of seared

14. This, of course, excepts the cases where the sprouting is connected with the fall Navarātri; see n. 3. Zanen's example from Madurai occurs around the new moon day of Tai (December-January), and is unusual.

plants, sterile fields, fevers, drought, and also—in tune with Indian conventions about springtime (*vasanta*)—a time of "erotic madness" (Detienne 1977, 9, 122). One name for a Draupadī festival is Akkiṉi Vacanta Viḻā, a Spring Fire Festival.

II. *Agricultural Code,* 1

A. "Gardens" cultivated in pots during eight days.	"Gardens" cultivated in (or around) pots, usually for seven to ten days, and often specifically for eight or nine, though outdoor plots may grow for as long as eighteen days.
B. On the roofs of houses, closest to the sun.	In the inner sanctum of a temple, in a yākacālai, or within houses.
C. In plain sunlight; little water.	Little or no sunlight; water.
D. Before they can take root they dry up.	Plants are unable to develop. When dispersed, they may be "yellow-white" (Zanen 1978, 2, 3), brownish (Oppert 1893, 478), or still partially green.

Here Zanen remarks on the contrasts in the second and third items: "In the Mediterranean ritual the plants are exposed to the too excessive heat of the sun in that time of year. In Madurai, on the other hand, the plants are being deprived of sunlight" (Zanen 1978, 3). He thus notes that in each case one element necessary for the proper cultivation of crops is lacking: in Greece, water; in India, sun. We should note, however, that the rite at Tindivanam in effect doubles the navadhānya, placing the plants *between* enclosures, and ultimately setting them on top of the Pōttu Rāja–Pōrmaṉṉaṉ maṇḍapa, much like the rooftop desiccations in Greece. There is, however, a common element that cuts across the usual modes of destruction and corresponds to our modification of Zanen's "cosmological" contrast. In both cases—in accordance with the height of the hot season—the grains are submitted to the rigors of excessive heat. In Greece, they are placed "too near" the sun. In South India, they are either sown outdoors at the height of the hot season (for Kūttāṇṭavar) or are placed too near the overheated goddess, in her "womb-house" or in a yākacālai where, as at Muthialpet, they may grow beside a vulva-shaped yōṉikuṇṭam ("womb-firepit"). In either of these latter cases, one has a "hothouse" womb setting.

III. *Social Code*

A. "Gardens" cultivated by married women (here we must add that they were especially cultivated by lovers, concubines, and courtesans).	"Gardens" cultivated by temple personnel (Draupadī cult); by married women in their homes (Zanen 1978); by virgins (Fuller 1980, 337); by postmenopausal women (Nishimura 1987, 72); by a Harijan (Kūvākkam).
B. Ecstatic expressions of grief; illegitimate (excessive) sexual relations.	Abstinence from sex, special care for purity; ascetic vows and routines.

Here Zanen's Indian information comes from a temple cult of the goddess Cellattammaṉ, where the grains are tended by married women. But we see already that the situation is more varied. Perhaps, however, we should also detect a feminine part in our Draupadī cult examples, since the pūcāri and other temple personnel represent the goddess, and it is she who "really" tends the grains in her temple, in its yākacālai, or in front of it but within her line of vision. Similarly, the Harijan at the Kūvākkam Kūttāṇṭavar festival impersonates Kṛṣṇa-Mohinī as Kūttāṇṭavar's bride. In any case, the license/abstinence opposition, which at first looks so straightforward, is actually filled with complexities on both sides. In Greece, as Detienne makes clear, the Adonia must be viewed in relation to its antithesis, the Thesmaphoria. The Adonia rites were organized as a private cult in which women—supposedly sexually aroused during the hot season while men are dried up—act as courtesans and entertain their lovers. Their tending of miniature "gardens" of barley, wheat, fennel, and lettuce (the last symbolizing the precocious coolness and wetness of Adonis) has its structural antithesis in the Thesmaphoria rites, sacred to Demeter, the goddess of true cereal agriculture. In the latter, the women act like solemn matrons and abstain from sexual relations (Detienne 1977, 75–83, 99–110), like Zanen's South Indian counterparts.

It is thus not so much a case of Mediterranean–South Indian oppositions, but of two complementary Greek rites and two complementary faces of the multidimensional Indian rites. In India, the Adonia-type rites can be interior to the rites of marriage, and also to festivals that culminate in high-pitch events that evoke connections between sacrifice and sexuality. At goddess festivals, for which Draupadī's is here no exception, the purity and abstinence of those who perform these rites in the image of the goddess's own chastity may have, within the festival itself, counterimages of the *same* goddess that present her as licentious, a whore, sexually available to lovers outside marriage, erotically aroused and arousing (Hiltebeitel 1988a, 3–12, 220–33, 267–68). At Kūttāṇṭavar festivals, such oppositions become explicit. While ordinary farmers impersonate Kṛṣṇa as Mohinī and take on vows of chastity to marry Kūttāṇṭavar, the eunuchs impersonate the same god-turned-goddess—or as some of the eunuchs see it, god-turned-eunuch (some alis, or eunuchs, refer to Mohinī as Kṛṣṇa's "Ali avatāra")—and engage in nightlong revelries that are reputed to include sexual license, homosexuality (a potential Zanen [1978, 4] sees in the Adonia), and prostitution (which occurred in the Adonia at Byblos; ibid.). Indeed, they both "marry" a god no less doomed than Adonis, and the eunuchs lament him on the "weeping ground" in "ecstatic expressions of grief," something that Zanen thought the Adonia alone provided, without Indian parallels. The eunuchs are said to release a "flood of tears."

IV. *Agricultural Code,* 2

Withered, dried-up plants thrown into sea or springs. Quick dispersion during daytime.

Seedlings carefully placed into shallow water (tank or stream; the Gaṅgā); dispersed as *prasādam* ("grace" of the deity); tossed off without fanfare from Pōrmaṉṉaṉ's rooftop; sown with seeds by farmers; left to desiccate in place; usually by day, or at night (Zanen's example).

I have followed Zanen's argument that the dispersal of the plants in Greece (as also at Byblos and Alexandria) "can only signify the death of the god." And I have held that such a connection also applies to Kūttāṇṭavar and has pertinence in the Draupadī cult to the "Young Pañcapāṇḍavas." In the Indian cases, however, there is also a suggestion that the plants' manner of dispersal can be linked to the *revivals* of these youthful gods and heroes. Some have noted the tenderness with which the sprouts are placed in the water (Zanen 1978, 4; Oppert 1893, 477–80). At Veḷḷimēṭupēṭṭai, they are even called on to miraculously thrive. Or better still, at Tindivanam they are placed into the Gaṅgā: a symbol of a destiny beyond even rebirth in the attainment of mokṣa.

With these remarks, I conclude the attempt to follow Zanen's encodement to a more informed "structuralist comparativitism." I have, of course, tried to bring the Greek and Indian materials closer together than he did and have even found Indian themes connected with the navadhānya that have virtually forced a reconsideration, if not a revival, of some of the unfashionable ideas of Frazer. Indeed, we must face the fact that informants often link the ceremonies "sympathetically" with marital and agricultural fertility. Flueckiger calls instructive attention to two different interpretations of the rite—in each case called *bhojalī*—in adjacent areas of central India. In the Raipur area, where the sprouting rite is linked with Navarātri and tended mainly by married women, it is perceived as a ceremony through which the goddess grants fertility "both to the land (in the form of abundant crops) and to the participating women" (1983, 33). But in neighboring Chhatisgarh, where only unmarried girls carry the sprouts, reference to fertility is inappropriate. Though the girls' songs anticipate marriage, there is "a noticeable lack of direct reference to the fertility of either the land or the participants" (ibid., 35). The growth of the seedlings is associated instead with the vitality of the friendships that the girls formalize through the ritual. It is thus not so much a matter of *magically* stimulating the growth of plants as of having different ways of stepping into a rhythm: of songs "evoking in lilting poetic imagery [the sprouts'] over-drooping greenness" (Gold 1987, 199), or, with the nine planets, of getting a sense of good or bad augur. I would thus agree here with Detienne's critique of Frazer's interpretation of the Greek material, that the Indian rites cannot be taken—as many (Frazer, Gonda, Srinivas, Haekel) have done—as rites of sympathetic magic. The primary symbolism rather involves clearing away the ephemeral, precocious, and even abortive crop so that true agricultural or mature human fertility can proceed. But we should perhaps not be so quick, at least for India, to discredit the notion of a link between sprouting rites and "dying and rising gods." For the moment, it is enough to reopen the problem, since I will return to it in chapter 11.

We should also not leave the impression that the Greek and Indian rites are as close as all that. For one thing, unlike the Greek "Gardens of Adonis" and their mythology, the Indian materials betray no evident analogues with the Greek concern for spices and aromatics, or with a cool, moist plant like lettuce. Certain "cool" plants may figure in navadhānya-type rites, such as neem leaves and lemons. The cooling neem leaves may be present when the sprouts are laid to rest, as it were, in the water (as at Veḷḷimēṭupēṭṭai; cf. Babb 1975, 139). But lemons and neem have too many other resonances to be paralleled with lettuce. Oppert mentions that frankincense and myrrh are offered to the navadhānya pots (pālikai). But this seems nothing more than part of a conventional pūjā. India has no need for the spices of Arabia, and no reason to mythologize them, or spices in general, in relation to the nine grains. None of our heroes dies in a lettuce patch, or is the son of the myrrh tree, or anything similar. The plants in question are mostly grains (including rice), beans, and lentils: plants which as early as the Upaniṣads are already linked with concepts of reincarnation and—in shorter terms—regeneration and rebirth.[15]

Second, on the Indian side, the comparison with the Greek materials has to a certain extent misled us into a one-sided identification of the sprouts with Adonis-like male heroes. Such an identification, however, is only one *potential* mythologization of the Indian sprouting rites. The tender sprouts are also said to reflect in various ways upon the goddess. There are instances where they clearly represent her (Babb 1975, 134; Oppert 1893, 478). In Chhatisgarh, while the seedlings grow in a dark place for nine days (a variant of Navarātri, even though occurring at a different time), "they are worshipped by the women as a manifest form of the goddess *bhojalī dāī* (bhojalī mother)." On the final day, the unmarried girls carry the seedlings to the village pond, where they are immersed and "distributed as *prasād* (sanctified offerings distributed to worshipers)," or in some cases exchanged by the girls to formalize their ritual friendships (Flueckiger 1983, 28). The songs speak of the goddess as Pīlī Bāī, the "Yellow Woman": a reference "to the *bhojalī* seedlings, which are a yellow-green color from having been sprouted in a dark place," and probably also, according to Flueckiger, an allusion "to a bride, who has been bathed in turmeric and oil prior to her wedding day, leaving a golden hue on her skin" (ibid., 30, 40 n. 7). Similarly, the pūcāri at the Mēlaccēri Draupadī temple linked the sprouts with both the girl who marries and the children she will beget. If the sprouts grow well, she will beget children without any problems, and they will grow without handicap and acquire a good family life. But if the sprouts grow

15. On rice in ancestral rites, see chapter 9, section A; sesame seeds are the metaphor for reincarnation in the curious argument between Mahāvīra and Mikkhali Gosāla, founder of the Ājīvakas (Basham [1951] 1981, 45–48). Cf. *Chāndogya Upaniṣad* 5:10.3–4: those who embark upon the way of the Fathers are reborn on earth "as rice, barley, herbs, trees, sesame plants and beans." Pulses may also be included among the "many seeded" plants not to be eaten by Jains (Williams 1963, 110–11). Compare the Pythagorean notion, without connection to the Adonia, that connects beans with metempsychosis because they "serve as support and ladder for the souls (of men) when, full of vigor, they return to the light of day from the dwellings of Hades" (Detienne 1977, 50).

poorly, she will have difficulties bearing children and her family will be without peace and unity.

When one transposes this onto Draupadī, it suggests a double reference: on the one hand, to her mythological epic family, and on the other, to her "children" devotees. Yet Draupadī is not only the mother. She is also the virgin, the bride to be, and so on. All the more pertinent, then, are rites like those in Draupadī temples where the seedlings are sown in receptacles called pālikai, the "young maiden" or "protectress." I would suspect that the goddess's affinity with the sprouts is not only as a symbol of energy (*śakti*), fertility, and growth, such as Babb was told of, but also as a symbol of the violent offering of the goddess herself, the abused and suffering goddess (Satī, Reṇukā, Draupadī, etc.), in sacrifice. As Biardeau has argued, it looks as if the tapered form of the pālikai is ultimately one of a number of transformations of the Vedic altar—the *vedi*, proverbially shaped like a woman's waist—into a vertical, three-dimensional form: one that still serves as an altar for the offering of the sprouts themselves (1988, 114). For the moment, however, whether it be in the form of slender-waisted pots, as is widespread in the south; in a mound of dirt in a corner of the temple; in outdoor mounds or plots; or in the form of rounded pots, which seem prevalent in the north, the sprouts' receptacle is not only an altar, but a symbol for the earth: that is, the goddess Earth, whose sufferings in Indian mythology are legion, whose cycle of transformations from virginity to fruitfulness to barrenness and desiccation are evoked in other goddess's myths as well, and who must see all that sprouts forth from her come eventually to die. Moreover, not only do the receptacles have such variant shadings. So do the seedlings.[16] In cults and festivals (like Dasarā) that link sprouting rites with possession, and with real or symbolic animal sacrifice, the goddess who is tenderly placed in the water in the form of sprouts seems to be the *virgin* goddess who has withstood the heated dangers of demonic forces, and who must now yield to her *married* form as sovereign of true and fertile agriculture. And in marriage itself, the discarded sprouts seem to symbolize the abandonment of the chastity (and precocity?) of youth for either or both partners as they assume the full sexual potential and responsibility of marriage. Furthermore, these resonances seem to

16. Cf. Biardeau 1988, 115: the most visible victims are the sprouts, condemned not to see the light of day and to be uprooted and dispersed. But they are complementary to the pot-altars that represent the fecund goddess who must see her progeny destroyed. Each festival also miniaturizes the cycles of world destruction and renewal (paraphrased).

find their counterparts in the "quickening" of the king, the earth's husband, in connection with navadhānya-type rites that form part of his "rebirth" in the Rājasūya dīkṣā.

Last, although Greek "Gardens of Adonis" are connected with sacrificial practices and sacrifice-related themes,[17] it would probably be fruitless to seek out correspondences with the Indian "gardens" in this domain. The Greek and Indian sacrificial "codes" are rather different. Indian sprouting rites are persistently connected with rites of possession,[18] symbolic as well as real sacrificial killings, symbols of impalement (lemons on tridents, as at Veḷḷimēṭupēṭṭai; cf. Babb 1975, p. 136), and varieties of self-torture: flagellation, dancing with "a chain of festooned barbs," perforation of the body with needles or metal rods, hook-swinging, swinging on a seat of nails, and firewalking.[19] In the Kūttāṇṭavar cult, such themes center on the fact that the nine grains are brought to, or are grown at, the site where the hero dies after his "battlefield sacrifice" of cutting his body in thirty-two places and is lamented by his tāli-cutting and bangle-breaking "widows."

In the Draupadī cult, however, the links between the navadhānya and the cult's rites of sacrificial violence are more muted. The rite of dispersing the sprouts may have instead, as it does at Veḷḷimēṭupēṭṭai, an air of serene and peaceful beauty. But we should not be misled. We have found repeatedly that the nine grains are linked with the cult's primary symbols of sacrifice. At Muthialpet, they are made into towers that surround the firepit. More commonly still, they are linked—in diffuse but persistent ways—with Pōttu Rāja: sown after the raising of the flagstaff; set before his stationary image in his maṇḍapa; dispersed after they wither and die on his maṇḍapa's roof; and led by his portable processional image to their dispersal at the water's edge. Pōttu Rāja oversees and provides all the sacrificial weapons for the symbolic killings that are enacted within the Draupadī festival. The fact that he leads the navadhānya procession at Veḷḷimēṭupēṭṭai by facing backward toward the plants is highly suggestive that he is overseeing their

17. Frankincense and myrrh—brought down the ladders in the Adonia—are the same spices used in sacrifices to the gods. The Adonia may anticipate rites of sacrifice that are linked with true agriculture, among which would be the offering of pigs to Demeter (with the counternote that Adonis is gored to death by the tusk of a boar). On commonalities between the use of spices in sacrifice and marriage, see J.-P. Vernant in Detienne 1977, xx.

18. See Flueckiger 1983, 32, 40 n. 9; Gold 1987, 259–60, linking the goddess with Bhairuji-Bhairava; and Babb 1975, 136–39.

19. See Babb 1975, 136–40, including the chain; Francis 1907, 235, including the nail-seat swing; and Oppert 1893, 478–80.

sacrificial death as well. Normally he leads processions facing forward, as if leading an army toward the sites where the symbolic acts of sacrifice will occur.

We need not, however, draw our interpretation entirely from the imputed contextual connections that the navadhānya may have with other rituals, and with the underlying myths of various festivals. The Draupadī cult, perhaps uniquely, has its own folk epic myth of the nine grains. The episode is known in both ballad (Pukaḻēṇṭippulavar 1909) and dramatic (Taṇikācala Mutaliyār 1979) chapbook form. Let us recall the story from volume 1.

While in their period of concealment, the Pāṇḍavas and Draupadī live in a forest where there is nothing for them to eat. The forest setting for this "origin" of the navadhānya is intriguing: as Tanaka shows, there are reasons to suspect that the yākacālai, the ideal Brahmanical setting for sprouting rites, is identified with the forest or wilderness, and thus with hermitage life, asceticism, and "forest dwellers," or *vānaprasthas*,[20] all of which are part of the Pāṇḍavas' and Draupadī's forest experience. Meanwhile, in the Kaurava court, Bhīṣma tells Duryodhana that the Pāṇḍavas will seek some way to get fresh grains to sow in this forest for their food. Duryodhana orders that anyone who comes begging for fresh grains should be given only roasted ones. And he prepares to search out the Pāṇḍavas and catch them before they complete their one year of living incognito. Meanwhile, Kṛṣṇa visits the Pāṇḍavas, tells them of Duryodhana's plan, and urges that Draupadī disguise herself as a gypsy fortune-teller (*kuṟavañci, kuṟatti*), go to the Kaurava capital, predict the Kauravas' grim futures to their wives, and demand fresh seeds as payment. Draupadī does her part successfully, but when she and Arjuna return with the grains, Kṛṣṇa tells them they are roasted, not fresh. Nonetheless, he sows them anyway. Arjuna has no doubt that Kṛṣṇa can make them grow, but he asks him how he will do it. Kṛṣṇa replies that according to their various degrees of blackening and discoloration, each will become a different one of the nine grains. The roasted grains miraculously grow, to the eventual amazement of Duryodhana. The Pāṇḍavas and Draupadī are thus able to leave the forest, the metaphoric "yākacālai" where their nine grains have miraculously revived, and settle themselves into the kingdom of Matsya: literally the "Fish," and symbolically—according to the classical epic itself—

20. At the Kālī and Draupadī festivals at Udappu, Sri Lanka, the yākacālai, decorated with leaves from numerous trees, "looks as if [it] . . . is located in a forest (*kāṭu*)" (1987, 188; cf. 191, 217, 235, 251–52 n. 9). At Kūvākkam, the aḻukaḷam "temple" is in a grove (*tōppu*), directly beneath a large peepul tree.

the "womb" in which they successfully complete their dīkṣā-like period of concealment.[21]

This myth helps us, of course, to understand why people shout "Govinda" at Veḷḷimēṭupēṭṭai in expectation that the sprouts left on the bank of the tank will grow as a good augur for the Pāṇḍavas. The goddess Draupadī goes to obtain the seeds, but it is Kṛṣṇa who achieves the miracle of regeneration, an oft-repeated pattern of collaboration. But what is perhaps more striking is that the myth evokes so many themes of the classical Brahmanical sacrifice. As just noted, in linking the origin, sowing, and sprouting of the nine grains with the Pāṇḍavas' dīkṣā-like period of concealment, the myth provides a parallel to the connection between the dīkṣā and the "quickening" devasū offerings in the Rājasūya. The Pāṇḍavas too are kings who must be "quickened" and reborn through this period of concealment in the Matsya womb. Also, it is Kṛṣṇa who determines the outcome of this rivalry, not only through his miraculous seeding, but also through tricks and deceptions, just as he does elsewhere in the *Mahābhārata,* and as Viṣṇu (whom Kṛṣṇa incarnates) does in the classical and Brāhmaṇa mythology. More than this, the folk epic myth treats the nine grains as one of those sacrificial substances that become a stake in the endless rivalry between the gods and the demons, or their protégés the Pāṇḍavas and the Kauravas, in their efforts to obtain the "essence" of the sacrifice. We have seen that this essence is transmitted in Vedic ritual from animals to plants. More than this, the sacrificial essence that the Devas and Asuras strive over is the sap-full union of plants and water. When all the plants leave the gods for the demons, only the barley (*yava*) remains. But because the gods "put into the barley whatever sap there is in all plants," making barley thrive when all other plants wither, "they attracted to themselves all the plants of their enemies." One thus sprinkles water mixed with barleycorns to "keep from us the haters, keep from us the enemies" (*ŚB* 3.6.1.7–11; Eggeling [1882] 1966, 2:142–43). Here one has not only a prototype for the Pāṇḍavas' and Kauravas' rivalry over the navadhānya, but for the use of javārā, etymologically connected with *yava,* as the main plant in North Indian sprouting ceremonies.

I propose that in bringing us to see the navadhānya as another expression of the "essence" of the sacrifice, the folk epic myth,

21. See Hiltebeitel 1988a, 301–9. The forest setting of this agricultural wonder reminds one of the winter and desert settings of the "grain miracles" of Christian women saints and the Virgin Mary, always fleeing threatening males who seek to capture them (Berger 1985, 53–56, 89–91). I do not know, however, whether these legends are linked with medieval European variants of Gardens of Adonis.

with such Vedic prototypes, helps us to appreciate the "nuclear" significance of our sprouting rites in so many different ritual contexts and brings us as close as we may get to a general understanding of their distinctiveness as Indian variants of the Gardens of Adonis. The sprouting rite is always a prism of the larger ritual contexts that color it. But it is also one cogent element within a sacrificial complex that persists, as we shall now see by way of further examples, through countless modifications from Vedic to popular Hinduism.

5 Flag Hoisting and Tying of Kāppu

The true temporal brackets for Draupadī festivals are the ceremonies of flag hoisting and flag lowering. As in festivals for numerous other Tamil goddesses, flag hoisting, as we have seen, is sometimes linked with sprouting rites and, even more regularly, with wristlet tying.[1] My information on opening rites at Tindivanam is based on the description of the Draupadī temple's pūcāri and is thus less complete than what I can draw on from observation of the corresponding ceremonies at Mēlaccēri.[2] In outline, however, the two temples conduct matters in much the same way, and in a manner not only familiar from other Draupadī festivals, but also paralleled at festivals for other deities. I will describe the ceremony mainly as it occurs at Mēlaccēri, with details from Tindivanam in counterpoint.

A. Two Flag-Hoisting Ceremonies

Before the main ritual actors arrive at about 10:30 A.M., the Mēlaccēri temple grounds are already busy with preparations. The outer courtyard is cleaned, weeds are cut back, ropes are braided from hand-twisted strands of dried paddy stalks held taut between the ropemakers' two largest toes. Fresh bunches of mango leaves are brought to hang from the rope festoons (*tōraṇams*), soon draped from the upper corners of the temple facade, and to decorate the flagstaff. Coconuts are husked for offerings. Natural materials and traditional ways are stressed. Then various officiants arrive. At Mēlaccēri, a local Brahman with a Śrīvaiṣṇava *nāmam* comes first, ac-

1. Cf. Meyer 1986, 107–9, 234–35, on flagstaff and kāppu rituals at Aṅkāḷammaṉ festivals as frames for "core rituals"; cf. Reiniche 1979, 85, 93–97, 161, 206–7; Hiltebeitel 1985a, 183; Beck 1981a, 88, 110–11; and Nishimura 1987, 73–80.
2. See Hiltebeitel 1988b, part 1.

companied by a single assistant. Then comes a procession of about thirty people, featuring the pāratiyār, several trustees (others arrive separately), and the kaṇāccāri and camayam, each weaponless. A group of Untouchable drummers, playing the tambourine-shaped *paṟai* drum that is their trademark in this traditional procession-leading role, head the group up to the temple's outer gateway and then stand aside while all the others enter. The pāratiyār, carrying a copy of Villiputtūr Āḻvār's *Makāpāratam,* has come with his assistant because he will launch his recitation of the *Mahābhārata* immediately after flag hoisting, joining the two ceremonies as part of one ritual sequence. This conjunction, typical of shorter festivals, is of course different from what one finds at Tindivanam, where Pāratam begins about ten days after flag hoisting.[3]

Be it noted that at Mēlaccēri, the pūcāri, whose home is some distance away in neighboring Tindivanam district, did not arrive for flag hoisting. In contrast, at Tindivanam, where my information comes from the pūcāri himself, it is he who is the self-described central figure in the procession, led by a *mēḷam* (musical band) of drums and other instruments (though with no Untouchables), that comes (also without the pāratiyār) from a nearby Śiva temple. The pūcāri's charge in this procession is to carry a set of articles, known as the *varicai,* on a brass plate (*tāmpāḷam*) held on his head. The varicai consists of a five-meter length of cloth, two bunches of bananas, a hundred grams of turmeric powder, a big bundle of white fiber twine, provisions for a hundred leaves of betel nut, 1.25 kilograms of raw rice, camphor, sandal sticks, four small mud pots (one larger than the others, for apiṣēka of the icons and flagstaff), some darbha grass, ghee, and fire-lighting sticks of pipal, banyan, mango, erukku, and *nāyuruvi* woods.[4] As we shall see, all these items find either exact or close counterparts at Mēlaccēri, but there such items were not conspicuous in the procession or identified by one name.

One meaning of *varicai* is fixed rent, calculated on the ascertained average yield of cultivated land (*Tamil Lexicon*). According to the Tindivanam pūcāri, for whom this meaning was evidently primary, some years back certain philanthropists gave land to the Draupadī temple, and the varicai is paid for out of the income from those properties. But another meaning, with the basic sense of

3. See chapter 3, section A. Compare Babb 1974, 5–7.

4. As noted in chapter 4, erukku is used at the Muthialpet firepit. Nāyuruvi (*Achyranthes aspera*), a thicket and hedge plant (*Tamil Lexicon*), is also one of the nine types of sacrificial fuels (Winslow [1862] 1979).

"row," "order," or "regularity," has such additional senses as "distinctive mark of honour or privilege granted by a royal or other authority," and "present, especially to a daughter on marriage" (ibid.). The endowment of this rite by former benefactors of the temple is clearly in a tradition of royal temple patronage, and the festival is one in which Draupadī is ritually represented as a daughter (indeed, a princess) offered in marriage.[5] The varicai is thus both a present to her and a set of insignia that, like the flag-hoisting ceremony more generally, mark her sovereignty over the festival, and over the town in which it is performed.

Once the main officiants arrive, the temple sanctum is purified.[6] Unction or apiṣēka is performed over the icons,[7] and they are then freshly dressed, the female ones (four at Mēlaccēri, two at Tindivanam) given new yellow sarees. Water remaining in the large clay pot used for bathing the icons is then brought out to wash the flagstaff, which at Mēlaccēri is at this point set lengthwise on the ground. Surprisingly, there are many different types of flagpoles. Reflecting the relative wealth of the Tindivanam temple, the one there is covered in bronze (*veṅkalam*), round, and set erect permanently in a masonry platform that rises seven tiers to meet its base. Not all Draupadī temples have flagstaffs, but most do, in the form of semipermanent wooden poles, uncovered and thus open to the elements, similarly round but rather narrow, and also set standing in masonry bases (e.g., Tailāpuram, Maṅkalam). But at Mēlaccēri, a new one is cut and chiseled for each festival by a group of four carpenters, who must begin by selecting a suitable tree from the forest. The one made for the 1986 festival was from a *bilva* tree, and provided a pole that was markedly curved toward the top (there are in fact āgamic and purāṇic prescriptions that the tree chosen for a flagstaff should *not* be crooked [Gonda 1969, 246]). Other trees men-

5. Cf. Frasca 1984, 290; Moffatt 1979, 281; Reiniche 1979, 52; see also Appendix, nn. 5 and 24.

6. At Tindivanam, the pūcāri performs a purificatory ceremony (puṇṇiyāvataṉam [cf. chap. 4, sec. A], a corruption *puṇṇiyākavācanam;* cf. Tanaka 1987, 349; Beck 1981a, 88, 104) to ward off the year's evils since the last festival: he says it is the same ceremony that is performed to purify a home when a death has occurred in a family.

7. This apiṣēka differs from the elaborate ones done daily for Draupadī and the other three mūlavar icons at Tindivanam, which consist of nine apiṣēkas in sequence, the last of *corṇam,* or "gold," achieved by mixing turmeric, kuṅkum, and ash (*vibhūti*) in a vessel of water with flowers on top, placing a gold article from a devotee in the vessel, waving the floating flame before the goddess, removing the gold article and returning it to its owner, and dousing Draupadī and the other icons with the fluids. Most Draupadī temples cannot afford such elaborate pūjās, or even daily pūjās at all.

tioned as suitable were the *pū aracu* (the portia or tulip tree) and the vaṉṉi, the latter—rare, but important for further discussion—only "if available." The Mēlaccēri post was roughly hewn to show eight sides. Otherwise, it was fitted with the typical cross-plank frame, with three horizontal planks (*skandha*s or *yaṣṭi-phalaka*s) extending out from the pole and two vertical rods (*upadaṇḍa*s) connecting them (see fig. 1). A *tuvaca-t-tampam,* literally "flagpole," actually consists of both the pole and the cross-plank frame (see Janaki 1988, 133 and figs. 1–2). Once the Mēlaccēri post is lowered at the end of the festival, it is kept in the temple for some time (the 1986 one was still there in January 1990). But a new one will be made for the next festival, and a fresh hole will be dug for it, always in the same spot directly in front of the temple on its west-east axis.

While the Mēlaccēri temple's flagstaff is still glistening from its washing, several hands, both of men and women, come forth to put dots of red kuṅkum powder on its sides (mainly those that will face the four directions) and the joints in the upper cross-hatching. Mango leaves are fitted into the crossbar joints and tied in a circle around the main shaft at two points: about half a meter below the lowest of the horizontal bars at the top, and a foot above the ground-level point near the bottom. Meanwhile, the Brahman, seated within the temple's front-facing, twenty-four-pillared maṇḍapa, prepares a packet of kāppu wristlets. He ties a piece of turmeric root into each string, passes the string through a tray of turmeric powder, and sets it next to a mound of raw paddy on a banana leaf. The wristlets can be called "turmeric wristlets" (*mañcaḷ kāppu;* Frasca 1984, 274; Tanaka 1987, 199). At this time, all the stone-imaged "deities" under the twenty-four-pillared maṇḍapa—Pōttu Rāja and Muttāl Rāvuttaṉ in front and Vināyakar, the craftsman who built the temple, a caduceus serpent, and a many-hooded Ādiśeṣa in back, near the sanctum—are honored. Strings of jasmine, made into clumps, are placed atop each figure, and each is given a red forehead dot (*poṭṭu*). Then they are fed, each with a banana, a small cake, a serving of rice, and a flour lamp (*māviḷakku:* a ball of moistened flour indented so that it can hold oil and a wick). In core area Draupadī cult mythology, the rice and flour lamp are particularly associated with Pōttu Rāja–Pōrmaṉṉaṉ, for along with a goat, they are the things he requires, each in an exaggeratedly huge portion, before he will serve Draupadī as her chief guardian and army leader (Hiltebeitel 1988a, 345, 359, 370; 1988b). Here he is the first to receive these offerings, minus, of course, the goat. Then, after the food is removed, a camphor flame is set before each figure, and they are offered dīpārādhanā.

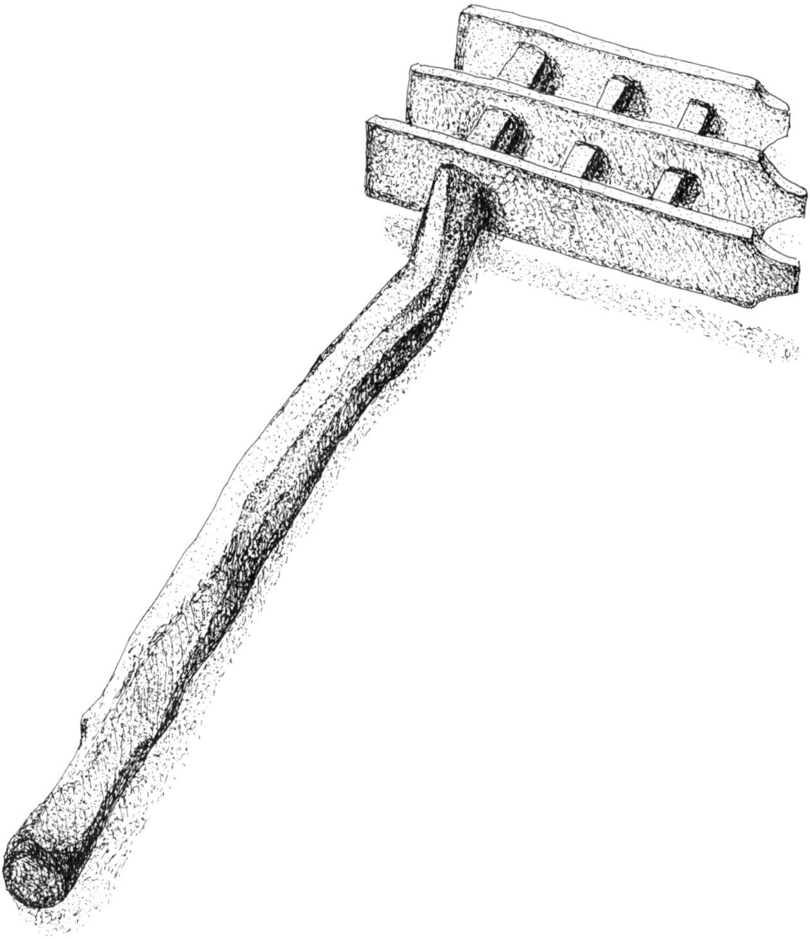

Figure 1. Mēlaccēri flagstaff, 1986 Draupadī festival.

Just outside the temple, front-center, two workers, one using a crowbar and the other his hands, now begin digging the hole for the flagstaff. Numerous large rocks have to be removed. A freshly cut and trimmed bamboo pole, about twenty-five feet high, is brought to the same spot. A yellow banner shaped like an elongated W (that is, with two pennant points and an indentation between them) is fixed to the top of this pole, and it is set down beside the flagstaff. Meanwhile, inside the temple, several bricks are taken up from the floor of the twenty-four-pillared maṇḍapa on the axial line that connects Draupadī in the sanctum, the images of Pōttu Rāja and Muttāl Rāvuttan̲, and the spot for the flagstaff. The dug-out area from which the bricks were removed is curbed with the detached bricks just above the floor level. The upraised bricks are then coated with mud to form the walls of a square offering pit, or ōmakuṇṭam. The Brahman now sits before this firepit altar, facing south, reciting in Sanskrit over the strings of kāppu.[8] A camphor flame is set on a leaf in the ōmakuṇṭam, and the Brahman then feeds the flame with firesticks, again reciting in Sanskrit, surrounded by a circle of seven of the temple's elders, including Gopāla Goundar, the chief trustee, and several other trustees, the kaṇāccāri, and the camayam. He then goes into the sanctum and returns with a stainless steel pot of *tīrttam* water (Sanskrit *tīrtha*), gathered from washing the icons, and some mango leaves. As a young man plays the pampai drum, the Brahman, again seated, goes around the circle of elders giving each a small amount of the tīrttam to swallow. Then he makes the same round twice again, first placing a poṭṭu of red kuṅkum powder on each one's forehead, and then a yellowish tan dot of turmeric powder (*vīrakantakam*) mixed with powdered raw rice atop each red dot. Each time he follows the same order of seniority, Gopāla Goundar coming second after a more elderly Kōṉār trustee.

The receiving of tīrttam and poṭṭu are conventional acts of temple worship, here preliminary to the actual tying of kāppu (*kāppuk kaṭṭutal*), which now begins. As the drumming continues, the Brahman puts the kāppu strings on a plate and carries them into the sanctum. There, as a bell is rung, he ties one around the right wrist of each of the four Mēlaccēri temple Ammaṉs, or goddesses. He then returns to the twenty-four-pillared maṇḍapa and presents kāppu to each of the deities within: Pōttu Rāja first, then Muttāl Rāvuttaṉ, Vināyakar, etc. Since most of these figures are without extending arms (the first two are in bas relief, two others are snakes), he lays these kāppu over the clumps of jasmine atop each image. Then he returns to the circle of elders beside the ōmakuṇṭam and sits down. To each one in turn, he offers the same coconut (a conventional symbol of the head), with a clump of jasmine on its top.[9] Each temple officiant, seated cross-legged, holds the coconut and bows his head toward it while the Brahman ties the kāppu around his right wrist. Then the officiant returns the

8. Cf. Tanaka 1987, 198, 242: the power of the kāppu derives from *mantras* chanted by priests or exorcists. Reiniche 1979, 161 further emphasizes that one meaning of *kāppu* is "invocation."

9. On the coconut as a symbol of the head, see Janaki 1988, 155; Bolle 1983, 38–39 (though with the errant claim that Draupadī "definitely is not associated with violence" [39]).

coconut to a tray of turmeric powder held in the Brahman's left hand, whence the Brahman passes it to another of the seven. During these ceremonies, the Brahman wears a darbha-grass ring, tied so that its two ends point upward from the back of the fourth finger of his right hand. Last in this series, the Brahman ties kāppu around one of the binding cords of the pampai drum. Longer kāppu strings are then tied around the full girth of the outer stone icons (Pōttu Rāja first, etc.) and the drums as well.

Finally, the Brahman comes outside for the flag hoisting, carrying a coconut and a sheaf of handwritten pages. A heavy cotton cloth, dyed yellow with turmeric, five meters high and two feet wide, is twisted and tied into a loop at one end. A long piece of twine is cut to hoist this flag from the looped end up to a ring set underneath, and at the outward end, of the bottom cross-plank of the frame-"flag" atop the still unraised flagpole. Before this is done, however, someone with a good memory recalls that the bamboo pennant should be raised first. It is tied to one of the outer pillars of the maṇḍapa, one of the two nearest the hole that is prepared for the flagstaff, just to its right (and north) as one faces the temple. Then several hands join in to set the base of the flagstaff in its hole and raise it carefully into position so that the upper cross-planks face inward toward the temple, in fact, over its roofs.[10] The long cloth flag is raised up to the ring at the bottom of the lowest crossbar of the frame-flag so that it hangs down freely, almost to the ground. This, literally, is the "flag hoisting" per se, but one should appreciate the replication, for so far there are three flags—the frame-flag, the cloth flag, and the pennant—to which we will soon add a fourth.

Now lofted, the cotton flag is loosely twisted into a long roll and held. While the hole is being filled in, the Brahman reads from his prepared text a long prayer in Sanskrit, calling first on Govinda, then various goddesses including Draupadī, the Pāṇḍavas, all of Viṣṇu's avatāras, and finally Draupadī and the Pāṇḍavas once again, and asking blessings on the temple and all its features.[11] Then the rolled-up flag is pulled taut from its ring at the outer end of the frame-flag, wound three times around the pole, and fixed in that position by several rounds of twine (see Janaki 1988, fig. 3).

10. For corresponding āgamic prescriptions on these matters, see Gonda [1954] 1969, 246, 248; Janaki 1988, 152.

11. He mentions a number of features the Mēlaccēri temple does not have: *dvārapālakas*, *vimānapālakas* (gate guardians and guardians of the tower over the inner sanctum; the temple does not even have a *vimāna*, much less guardians of it), *gopuram*, or gateway tower, and so on.

Mango leaves are set into the coils of flag and twine. Flag hoisting is over, and everyone goes back into the twenty-four-pillared maṇḍapa to listen to the beginning of Pāratam.

A few notes must suffice for Tindivanam. According to the pūcāri, the two main events are reversed: flag hoisting comes before the tying of kāppu. All five of the temple's trustees are present, but the chief trustee, Purushottama Chettiyar, technically regarded as *the* tarumakarttā, takes on the leading roles. He is asked to sit before the flagstaff—to show him respect, according to the pūcāri, but also to indicate his role as chief patron of the rite. A Brahman, called upon specially for these activities, places a darbha-grass ring on one of the tarumakarttā's fingers to indicate that he accepts responsibility for the ceremonies. Then he does the same for the other trustees, in order of their ages. Before the five-meter-long flag is wound around the flagpole "like a snake," the flagpole itself has lengths of darbha grass tied to the portions that the flag will touch.[12] No separate bamboo pennant was mentioned. Then comes kāppu tying, in the following order: the stone image of Pōttu Rāja in his "Pōrmaṉṉaṉ maṇḍapa"; the vīrakuntam, or "heroic lance"; the *koṭicīlai,* or portable pennant; Ampāḷ (the goddess: that is, Draupadī's mūlavar), Vināyakar, Añcaṉēyar, Murukaṉ, Muttāl Rāvuttaṉ, the *balipīṭha* (offering stone), and all the portable wooden icons. The koṭicīlai is of course our fourth type of flag, or flagpole: the one that will be carried aloft at rituals away from the temple. Let us also note that this list includes no human beings. As we have seen, the leading officiants at Tindivanam do not put on kāppu until the ritual celebration of Draupadī's marriage.[13]

The case of Tindivanam, however, only reinforces the fundamental connection between flag hoisting and kāppu tying. Although the leading officiants are not given kāppu at this point, the icons are, and they are certainly no less important. Moreover, the tying of darbha-grass rings on the fingers of the trustees appears to be a selective, elevated (at Mēlaccēri only the Brahman has such a ring), and preliminary substitute for the real kāppu kaṭṭutal of the main temple officiants that will occur at Draupadī's wedding.[14] At

12. A five-meter flag is also mentioned at Pondicherry (Shideler 1987, 131). But a twenty-meter flag at Chinna Salem suggests that there is the usual room for variation. Darbha grass can be considered as the hair of the flagstaff, conceived as a one-footed person (Janaki 1988, 161). Cf. also Reiniche 1979, 93.

13. See chapter 3, section A; chapter 4, section A.

14. Cf. Tanaka 1987, 199: the kāppu "has more or less the same effect as the *darbha* grass ring, but is more popular and stronger than it: while the *darbha* grass ring is rarely used by specialists other than Brahman priests, the *kāppu* appears in various

both Tindivanam and Mēlaccēri, the winding and binding of the flag around the flagpole replicates the tying of kāppu on the icons and leading participants. Indeed, at Tindivanam, the covering of the pole with darbha grass before the flag is wound around it is reminiscent of the darbha-grass finger ring. The binding of the flag seems to be the most conspicuous symbol of what all these tyings represent: in simplest terms, the commitment of the temple, the deities, and the leading officiants, in whatever order, to carrying out the festival. But there is also an evocation of the Vedic principle that what is offered is what is bound and tied.[15]

B. Other Temples, Other Goddesses

Beyond this, some useful things can be learned from what others have written about these rites. Keeping the discussion momentarily limited to Draupadī festivals, Shideler was apparently told at Pondicherry that the flagstaff represents "an absolutely fixed point, a center, to which the gods are bound in space as well as time. The mind travels up the flagpole west" across the horizontal planks of the frame-flag toward the *kumbha* finial that rises above Draupadī's mūlavar in the sanctum, and then back out across the main axis of the shrine to the complex in which the flagpole is placed between the stone image of Pōttu Rāja and the balipīṭha (1987, 97). This description helps clarify the rapport between the flagstaff complex, which I will return to shortly, and the spatial design of the temple as a whole.

Frasca has also brought to light valuable information about the practice of raising two flags. First, after the trustees and upayatārs have met and agreed to hold a Draupadī festival, that same night one of the participants in the meeting, unseen by anyone in the village, hoists a turmeric-colored flag "on a pole in the vicinity of the Tiraupatiyammaṉ temple. This is called the Tiruṭṭu-koṭi (flag raised undetected) that symbolizes that a festival will be conducted." Several days later, "another turmeric-colored flag will be raised on the flagpole. This flag, called the Mey-koṭi or 'true-flag,' signifies the true beginning of the festival" (1984, 277). The "undetected" flag's "secret" and perhaps "false" character (as opposed

ritual contexts such as village festivals and healing rituals." Similarly Diehl 1956, 88: they are "comparable" and "similar" amulets of protection while undertaking an observance.

15. See Tarabout 1986, 538–52, on the rapport between posts of varying kinds and symbols of tying.

to the "true" flag) suggests its smallness,[16] and indeed in the one case—at Maṅkalam—where I have found a similar practice (though without learning the terms Frasca mentions), the first flag was a yellow pennant on a pole that had been placed way up near the top of a huge pipal tree that rises about thirty yards from the entrance to the temple. I suspect that the reminder at Mēlaccēri that the pennant should be raised before the true flagstaff is a faint reminiscence of this sequence, though with nothing left of its concealment. I suggest that the nighttime placement of the "undetected" flag has the flavor of a symbolic military operation. For the festival of the heroes of Palnāḍu, two banners are hung in trees before the Temple of the Heroes: one for each of the factions whose rivalry the festival will reenact (Roghair 1982, 26). Along such lines, perhaps the "undetected" flag is a secret signal to those who will join Draupadī in performing the festival (ultimately the Pāṇḍavas), or even a decoy to mislead her opponents (ultimately the Kauravas).[17] What is important here is its rapport with the true flagstaff, which, as we shall see, also has martial implications. A rapport of this type between pennant and flagstaff is replicated in the fixed flagstaff's connections with the portable koṭicīlai pennants that will be carried during "battlefield" rituals. Indeed, as we have just seen, the koṭicīlai is one of the "icons" supplied with a kāppu during the flag hoisting at Tindivanam.

As to the kāppu, Frasca, distilling information from several core area informants, found three meanings to kāppu tying: it "initiates all of the men involved into a position of very intimate contact with the deity"; it commits those involved to a state of sexual purity and avoidance of "other types of ritual pollution (*tīṭṭu* in Tamil) such as meat eating"; and, as the term itself (from the root *kā*, "to protect")

16. The term *tiruṭṭu* also means secret, stolen, fraudulent.

17. Though I did not find parallels for them at Tamil Draupadī temples, I have in mind here Tanaka's findings (1987, 354; cf. Raghavan 1961, 75–77) at Udappu, Sri Lanka, where the Draupadī festival makes use of five "flags": one for the Kauravas (the main temple flag, called *uṭkoṭi*, or "inside flag," bearing the image of a cobra and eight auspicious objects); one for the Pāṇḍavas (*kontaṉ koṭi*), said to mean "cross-cousin flag" but more likely named after the vīrakuntam (sometimes written *vīrakontam*) or "heroic lance" (it is "7 ft long, and is like a fork with five prongs" on and through which are fixed five limes and a coiled whip, and to which is tied a red cloth, apparently giving it the status of a "flag"); a "sun flag" (*cūriyaṉ koṭi*) and "moon flag" (*cantiraṉ koṭi*) that accompany the Pāṇḍavas' "flag," suggesting a representation of the solar and lunar dynasties; and an "outside flag" (*veḷikkoṭi*) bearing an image of Hanumān, said to be Bhīma's flag. Hanumān should normally be on Arjuna's flag, but a ritualist impersonating Arjuna bears the Pāṇḍavas' kontaṉ koṭi, suggesting it may have an affinity (like the vīrakuntam) with Arjuna's (and Śiva's) pāśupata weapon.

suggests, it places the *kāppukkāraṉs* or kāppu-wearers under the deity's "protection" (1984, 274). It may even protect the wearer from death pollution within the family (Tanaka 1987, 242). One can also follow Tanaka here, who argues that the renunciatory values undertaken by the kāppukkāraṉs are those of persons temporarily transformed into the status of a *dīkṣitas*, those consecrated to undertake a sacrifice (1987, 202). In this vein, it is instructive that in Śaivite āgamas, a festival "is considered as the Dīkṣā that Lord Śiva Himself condescends to undergo in order to elevate the mental and spiritual levels of human beings at large" (Janaki 1988, 139–40). As regards the Draupadī festival deities, Shideler adds that the tying of kāppu on them is believed to bind them to the festival "until the flag is taken down" (1987, 132). Gods and humans, joint sacrificers, mingle as joint dīkṣitas. These meanings may all be brought together, and reinforced, at festivals where the kāppukkāraṉs undertake a set of personal restrictions, such as wearing a *mañcaḷ vēṣṭi* (turmeric-dyed dhoti), sleeping in seclusion from their homes (which have sexually polluting mattresses) in the precincts of the temple for the duration of the festival (Frasca, 274), eating vegetarian food, and so on. But though these additional practices are indeed common, one must not generalize, for there is much variation here, and sleeping in the temple, in particular, is not done at all Draupadī festivals. For instance, it is not done at Mēlaccēri.

Looking beyond Draupadī festivals, one can catch more of the meanings and practices associated with these rites, though far more in the case of flag hoisting than of kāppu tying. When done for other deities, the latter practice presents mostly just more of the same.[18] The main exception arises from contexts in which it is specifically associated with marriage, such as we have found at Tindivanam, where the chief ritual officiants don kāppu at the celebration of Draupadī's wedding. There is often an additional tying of kāppu for the mass of firewalkers on firewalking day, thus yielding three standard occasions for kāppu tying, all three of which may be differentiated in a long festival. Thus at Tindivanam, the first kāppu tying, at flag hoisting, is of the icons and implements (with a complementary rite for the trustees); the second, at Draupadī's wedding, is for the kāppukkāraṉs; and the third, on tīmiti day, is for the firewalkers. Alternatively, at shorter festivals, these moments may be variously combined.[19] But it seems that flag hoist-

18. See nn. 1, 8, and 14 above. On ascetic restraints and sleeping in the temple, see Beck 1981a, 87, 110–11 n. 29; Reiniche 1979, 85.

19. At shorter festivals, the firewalkers may join the other kāppukkāraṉs in donning kāppu from flag-hoisting day onward.

ing and the goddess's marriage are the two alternative occasions for the kāppu kaṭṭutal of the main officiants. This is the same pair of options we have found for the performance of sprouting rites, each case presenting its possibilities for doubling and symbolic overlap.

Where the setting for kāppu tying is the goddess's marriage, the sexual resonances of the rite are deepened. Marriages are themselves occasions for the wearing of kāppu (or *kaṅkaṇam* in Sanskrit) by the bride and groom. Like Frasca, Beck emphasizes the kāppukkāraṉs' "intimate contact" (1981a, 110) with a female deity, and underscores as well the dangers that this takes on in a marriage context. The festival for Māriyammaṉ at Kaṉṉapuram (Coimbatore District) celebrates a period during which the goddess's interactions with a demon are represented by signs of their marriage, including the opening-day tying of kāppu on their primary symbols: a pot for the goddess and a triple-pronged post (on which more, shortly) for the demon. On the same day, kāppu are tied on three male officiants. Beck brings out several latent metaphors in this ritual coincidence. "One interpretation, then, is that these men are like chaste, almost unwitting bridegrooms for the eight days of the festival" (1981a, 111). Indeed, couples wear the wristlets for the four days during which they are to keep apart, that is, remain sexually chaste, in the course of their wedding (Diehl 1956, 252, following Winslow [1862] 1979, s.v. *kā, kāppu*). At the Māriyammaṉ festival, the kāppu on the pot and the post may in fact symbolize that the "marrying" pot goddess and post demon actually remain chaste, or, more to the point, that the goddess remains chaste, despite their heated and dangerous interaction, and that the demon is an unwitting bridegroom no less than the kāppukkāraṉs.[20] Other ritual metaphors then arise from the dangers inherent in the forms this intimate contact may take. In contrast to the demon, the kāppukkāraṉs' ritual precautions, which at Kaṉṉapuram include the shaving of their pubic hair, would "seem to focus precisely on protecting the main participants from becoming attracted" to the goddess (Beck 1981a, 111 n. 29).[21] In this vein, other kinship metaphors

20. I suggest this on the basis of Biardeau's interpretation of festivals of this type (1989b, 166–202), which differs from Beck's on the status of the demon, the nature of the goddess's marriage, and the identity of her husband. Note that in the main Kaṉṉapuram Māriyammaṉ myth, the demon lusts for the goddess, but she does not marry him. She has also before this defeated a Mahiṣāsura multiform (Yama's vehicle, by that name; Beck 1981a, 94). The "unwitting bridegroom" theme finds its telling Draupadī cult analogue in Arjuna-Vijayāmpāḷ's "seduction" of Pōrmaṉṉaṉ–Pōttu Rāja, alias Mahiṣāsura (Hiltebeitel 1988a, 340–45, 358–82). Compare also Beck 1982, 54.

21. The kāppukkāraṉs should be married so as "to reduce sexual desire" (Beck

beside marriage may also be operative, above all the "desexualized" one of sonship, by which Draupadī cult kāppukkāraṉs sometimes take on the ritual identity of Draupadī's sons.

For flag hoisting and what I have called the flagstaff complex, however, the widening of our horizons beyond the Draupadī cult allows us to deepen our discussion considerably. Upon entering a Tamil temple, the usual (though by no means uniform) arrangement is that as one approaches on the axis leading into the sanctum, one will encounter three objects placed close together. First, one comes to the balipīṭha, or altar of sacrificial offerings; then the *koṭimaram* (literally, "flag-tree"), *koṭi-k-kampam* ("flag-post"), or tuvaca-t-tampam (Sanskrit dhvajastambha, "flagstaff"); and third, the deity's vehicle: the bull Nandi for Śiva, Garuḍa for Viṣṇu, the lion for the goddess, the peacock for Murukaṉ, the rat for Gaṇeśa.[22] Flagstaffs are common at the entrances to South Indian Hindu temples. The type we have discussed so far, with the inward-facing frame at the top, is found at Brahmanical temples for all major deities. Earlier pillars topped with animal enblems, also called *dhvajastambha* but without such frames, have an all-India antiquity traceable to the second century B.C.E., and a South Indian history going back at least to Brahmanical temples at Nagarjunakonda of the third century C.E. (H. Sarkar 1978, 230).[23] As far as I can tell, however, the inward-facing "flag tree" is South Indian. More demonstrably South Indian is the balipīṭha, found in Tamil and Kerala temples from the earliest periods, "sporadically in Andhra," and "in all probability . . . not associated with any architectural tradition of the north" (ibid., 93).

Metaphorically, this usual sequence can suggest for us, at least provisionally, that having first offered oneself at the balipīṭha, one can rally to the deity's banner and then ride the appropriate vehicle into the divine presence. If the order of the first two is reversed (see n. 22), it is just as sensible to think that one rallies to the banner before offering oneself. In whatever combination, the three ob-

1981a, 111); or, in certain rarer contexts, they may be chosen from among "sexually pure" unmarried youths, "for the self-control of married men before the festival cannot be relied upon" (Moffatt 1979, 255). See chapter 2, n. 11 on the function of kāma among upayatārs.

22. The most common variant is to encounter the flagstaff before the balipīṭha. The positions of the flagstaff and vehicle may also be reversed (Curtis 1973, 32).

23. The *dhvajastambha* with animal emblems or vāhanas on top can also be found at Brahmanical temples (for instance the Garuḍa-stambha at the Bhūvarāha Perumāḷ temple at Sri Mushnam, Cuddalore Taluk, South Arcot [Nambiar et al. 1966, temple plan and plate following p. 442]).

jects also constitute obstacles that guard the sanctum against the impure and undevoted. In terms of Śaiva Siddhānta theology, at the balipīṭha one sacrifices one's *āṇava malam,* the "taint of arrogance"; the flagstaff represents the causal (*kāraṇa*) aspect of Śiva as distinct from his subtle (*sūkṣma*) aspect in the sanctum (that is, the liṅgam); and Nandi (the animal vehicle for Śiva) "symbolizes the purified devotee" who has "surrendered all sense of ego" (Vanmikanathan 1971, 118; Curtis 1973, 34; Janaki 1988, 129).

At most core area Draupadī temples, these general schemes require only one modification, but a major one. In place of the bird or animal vehicle is a stone slab with a bas-relief of Pōttu Rāja. Having offered oneself and rallied to the banner, one enters the ranks of the army of devotees that Pōttu Rāja leads on behalf of, and ultimately into the presence of, the goddess Draupadī. We will observe other cases at non-Brahmanical goddess temples where a guardian replaces the vāhana in such ensembles. In the case of Pōttu Rāja, his icons sometimes show him subduing a lion, perhaps the very lion vāhana that would otherwise face the goddess from "his" position (see Hiltebeitel 1988a, 335).

C. The Most Beautiful Tree in the Forest

At Draupadī temples, however, the variations are no less revealing than the general pattern. And one of the most interesting of these is found at Mēlaccēri, where a new flagstaff is raised for each festival.

Ramachandra Rao sees the inspiration for the temple flagstaff in its representation of the deity as a conquering king: "A tall flagpost, richly decorated and elaborately installed, would mean a rich and prosperous temple commanding royal patronage. . . . God is the greatest of kings and the temple is His palace" (1979, 107); "Hoisting the flag suggests setting out to conquer" (ibid., 109). At the Brahmanical spring (*cittirai paurṇami*) festival for Śiva at Mel Ceval (Tirunelveli District), flag hoisting must be completed before the divinities (Śiva and the goddess) can go out from the temple in processions: that is, in their warrior and royal aspects, on a large chariot (Reiniche 1979, 95). Such a rule would also hold, at least implicitly, for Draupadī festivals, at which the only procession before flag hoisting is one *to* the temple, without the deities, and thus also without their "chariots." At Mel Ceval, flag hoisting is thus a necessary "rite of passage," a precondition for the deities' movement out from the sanctum to respond to personal, societal, and village concerns. It also announces the deities' dharmic and prosperous rule, and, according to the temple's Brahman pūcāri, paves the way for the festival to run its course without accidents by propitiating dangerous spirits who lurk around the flagstaff and balipīṭha (Reiniche 1979, 94–95). According to another officiating Brahman pūcāri from outside the village, the flagstaff comes to be the bearer of such harmful forces (*pēy* and *tēvatai,* demons and inferior divinities) because when the artisans went into the mountains to cut down the tree to make it, they brought back the demon who dwelt in it (ibid., 95, n. 18).

Reiniche surmises that her informant drew this theme from legends of popular divinities, and she provides a telling example about a familiar figure. After Cuṭalai Māṭaṉ committed the many violent and odious acts—including his demand for offerings of pregnant females: not only animals but also a girl he had raped—that led us to compare him to Muttāl Rāvuttaṉ (Hiltebeitel 1988a, 105–10), he took up residence in "the most beautiful tree in the forest," a *vaṉṉi-maram* or *śamī* tree (Reiniche 1979, 206). Here this Māṭaṉ ("Bull-Man") of the Burning Ground (*cuṭalai*), who is represented in Tirunelveli District by a pyramidal or conical pillar (Ramanayya [1930] 1983, 72–73 and fig. 16), joins company with the dangerous goddess Brahmaśakti, who resides in the tree's summit, and various other demons who surround it. As Reiniche notes, the story evokes the *Mahābhārata.* The Pāṇḍavas hide their fiery weapons in a śamī tree, whose wood serves to light the Vedic sacrificial fire, after worshiping the destructive goddess Durgā to begin their period of concealment in preparation for the sacrifice of battle (Reiniche 1979, n. 24, citing Biardeau CR 82:93–94; cf. Hiltebeitel 1988a, 296). Moreover, the "big śamī" in the epic is "close to the cremation ground" (*Mbh.* 4.5.12). This arouses the suspicion that Cuṭalai Māṭaṉ's pillars are themselves multiforms of the śamī-vaṉṉi tree as bearers of fire. *Vaṉṉi* means "fire" in Tamil, and the *vaṉṉimaram,* "fire-tree," has many resonances, including ritual use at marriages (Hiltebeitel 1988a, 35–37). In connection with Cuṭalai Māṭaṉ, it evokes one of fire's (Agni's) most destructive yet indispensable aspects as the devourer of corpses (*kravyāda;* see Malamoud 1989, 58–60), and implies an affinity between the crematorium and the battlefield.

Once Cuṭalai Māṭaṉ has taken up residence in this tree, Murukaṉ-Subrahmaṇya, who has just killed a demon at Tiruchendur, demands a flagpole (koṭimaram) before he will go on procession through the town. A team of carpenters, disregarding bad omens because of their faith in Subrahmaṇya's protection, head with ox carts into the forest to find the most beautiful tree, and come at last upon the "immense" vaṉṉi. Upon striking the trunk with the ax, they cut each others' legs, and Māṭaṉ joins in the hacking to produce a river of blood. The survivors then learn from a regionally prominent form of Aiyaṉār, who has dominance over such demons, that they must first make an offering to Cuṭalai Māṭaṉ. This done, they fell the tree. Māṭaṉ himself joins the procession back to Tiruchendur, helps to erect the pole, and obtains from Subrahmaṇya the right to receive offerings because he subdues the wicked (Reiniche 1979, 206–7). I assume that he remains identified with the flagstaff he helps to erect.[24]

This is a myth of the cutting of the flagstaff and its first and permanent erection. It is not an account of a recurrent flagstaff-implanting ritual, such as one finds at Mēlaccēri. Reiniche indicates that she does not know whether the śamī is habitually the tree chosen for temple flagstaffs (1979, 206, n. 25). We have seen that it is considered a rare option at Mēlaccēri. Indeed, the śamī is too rare to be a candidate for regular use in flagstaffs, making its mention in a myth all the more intriguing. But as we shall see, the vaṉṉi tree will provide an important link between the flagstaff and Draupadī's guardian Pōttu Rāja.[25]

In approaching this topic, one must take notice of the Tamil transformations of the rite of worshiping the śamī tree (*śamīpūjā*), which normally forms part of the royal ceremony of Dasarā or Vijayādaśamī. In North India, the śamī is worshiped at Dasarā, in connection with royal boundary rituals and the honoring of weapons, as an embodiment of the goddess of victory, ultimately Durgā, fresh from the celebration of her triumph over Mahiṣāsura in the preceding "Nine Nights" ceremony of Navarātri. In what may be a carryover from the Vedic Rājasūya, in which one subrite calls for the king to mount a chariot and shoot an arrow in the direction of a Kṣatriya "relative" in the symbolic role of a rival or enemy (Heester-

24. A similar story is told in Kanyakumari District about Veḷḷaikkāracāmi, the "White Man God": an Englishman who required a huge tree for the mast (called a koṭimaram, "flagstaff"; Perumal 1983, 38 ff.) of his merchant ship: "The woodcutters had of the opinion that, that tree was the spiritual abode of the demonish god Chenkitaaikkaran. When they fell the tree, they witnessed a kind of reddish liquid flowing out of the cuts [sic]" (ibid., 88). The god Ceṅkiṭāykkāraṉ eventually takes revenge against Veḷḷaikkāracāmi by having the mast fall on him in a storm, after which the two are worshiped jointly, with Veḷḷaikkāraṉ as the attendant. Thanks to Lee Weissman for alerting me to this text and story.

25. See Hiltebeitel 1988a, 133, 333, 389, and below, with bibliography. Cf. Beck 1981a, 121–22: in a Sri Lankan Tamil myth, when Durgā fought Mahiṣāsura, "he tried to escape by taking the form of a (*vaṉṉi*) tree," but "the goddess discovered the ruse and cut the tree down"—though with no suggestion that it became a flagstaff.

man 1957, 129–32, 138–39; 1985, 119), the king at Vijayādaśamī may either make an effigy of his enemy or bring him before his mind (Kane 1930–62, 5, 1:191). In Tamilnadu, where Vijayādaśamī is usually detached from any prior Navarātri that would explicitly link it with the *Devī Māhātmyam*, and thus the mythical and ritual killing of a buffalo, the śamī (or vaṉṉi) tree, still often associated with boundaries, has come to represent the "king's" adversary himself, or even a demon. In former times, actual Tamil kings may well have performed the rite much as in the North.[26] But in currently found rituals, the "kings" are usually deities, whether male or female, who represent the royal function. The god or goddess often rides a horse vāhana to a boundary location where his or her pūcāri, impersonating the deity, shoots arrows in various directions before aiming a sole arrow at a śamī tree, a banana or plantain tree, or some combination of śamī and banana (the banana tree alone apparently substitutes for the śamī). Instead of a śamīpūjā, the śamī and/or banana has thus come to represent the enemy himself, and the enemy, further demonized but still in tree form, is sometimes identified as Mahiṣāsura (Masilamani-Meyer in press-a, 14), or a demon named Vaṉṉiyāsuraṉ (Biardeau 1984, 12; 1989b, 281–86), whose name derives from the śamī-vaṉṉi.[27]

At some Draupadī temples, particularly ones having vaṉṉi trees in their compounds (Muthialpet, Kaḷampūr), such a ceremony is performed, separate from the temple's festival cycle, at the fall ceremony of Vijayādaśamī itself. In the one I observed at Muthialpet, Draupadī's portable icon is lavishly dressed, with her hair in a richly flowered bun, and taken with Arjuna's icon to the vaṉṉi, the temple's sacred tree (*sthalavṛkṣa*). There the pūcāri, an Aiyar Brahman Kurukkaḷ, first places a bow and three arrows in the hands of Arjuna's icon. Then, representing Arjuna, he shoots three arrows into the śamī. Finally he places the bow and arrow below the tree. The pūcāri explained that the shooting of the arrows was done so that Arjuna could prove his strength to Draupadī before marrying her, while the placement of the bow below the tree repre-

26. In 1892 the king of Ramnad went to a plain, and after circumambulating "the gods and goddess a number of times" (there is no mention of a śamī either as tree or goddess, and it may have been absent), "darted consecrated arrows in different directions amidst the loud applause of the vast crowd of spectators" (Breckenridge 1977, 88; Masilamani-Meyer in press-a; 15).
27. This summary relies mainly on works just cited by Biardeau and Masilamani-Meyer. See also Fuller and Logan 1985, 101–2; Tarabout 1986, 105–6 (involving a royal hunt in Kerala, likewise performed for various deities—Śiva, Skanda, Viṣṇu—and sometimes at Vijayādaśamī).

sented the Pāṇḍavas' concealment of their weapons in the śamī before they undertook their year of hiding. As we shall see, at certain Draupadī festivals this ritual also has variations within the festivals themselves.

Here, of course, the śamī is a sthalavṛkṣa within the temple and need not be cut to make a flagstaff. Its demonic status is barely hinted at by the fact that Arjuna shoots it to impress Draupadī. In any case, the erection for each festival of a new flagstaff, or the reestablishment of an old one, is probably not so rare, at least for non-Brahmanical village deities. Masilamani-Meyer, for instance, has found that at Aṅkāḷammaṉ temples permanent flagpoles are rare, and suggests that "they were not intended as permanent structures" (Meyer 1986, 235 n. 1, citing Ramachandra Rao 1979, 104, 106). Similarly, there are other Draupadī temples beside Mēlaccēri's to have flagpoles that are raised temporarily for each festival (e.g., Māṉāmpāṭi). There are, in fact, reasons to suspect that flag hoisting is originally more specific to festivals than it is to temples per se (H. Sarkar 1978, 230; Gonda [1954] 1969, 245–48, 255–59; Janaki 1988, 128, 153). The most revealing festival parallels, in any case, are to be found at certain Māriyammaṉ temples in Kongunad, where it is a question not precisely of a flagstaff, but of another kind of post—the three-pronged post mentioned earlier—that literally stands in its place.

For these festivals, a trunk or branch that forks off in three limbs must be found from a tree with milky sap (a *pālamaram* or *paccamaram*). It is cut to make a *kampam* ("post") of the required shape.[28] Brought back to the temple, which has no flagpole, it is erected in a freshly dug hole at the spot where a flagpole (koṭi-k-kampam) would be (Beck 1981a, 120): beside a permanent stone post called Kampattu Kaṟuppaṉ, "Kaṟuppu of the kampam-post," or in an apparent variant at one temple, Tūṇaicāmi (Sanskrit Sthūṇasvāmin), "the Post god." The axis that carries one into the sanctum then leads from the kampam and Kaṟuppu (or Tūṇaicāmi) past the balipīṭha and Māriyammaṉ's lion. The erection of the post is preceded by the tying of kāppu on leading officiants, on the post, and on a pot that represents the goddess in the two instances where it is clear that she and the post marry (Kaṉṉapuram, Ceṉṉimalai), and on every object but the post (the goddess, balipīṭha, Tūṇaicāmi) in the case were their marriage seems doubtful (Civaṉmalai). Before

28. This discussion draws from descriptions of three such festivals: at Kaṉṉapuram (Beck 1981a), Civaṉmalai (Biardeau 1989a, 23–31 and 1989b, 181–202) and Ceṉṉimalai (idem 1989b, 175–81). See n. 20.

the kampam is planted, a goat is beheaded. According to one of Biardeau's informants at Civaṉmalai, where the head is placed at the bottom of the hole before the post is erected on top of it, the goat is offered to the post (1989b, 190). At Ceṉṉimalai it is offered to Kaṟuppu (ibid., 177). Possessions and oracles follow. The post itself is a demon, with Untouchable affinities. The placements of an earthen pot in the kampam's forked crotch represents the goddess's interactions with the demon. The rituals portray either their marriage (though, as I indicated earlier, it is probably unconsummated) or the demon's holding the goddess captive. At Kaṉṉapuram and Civaṉmalai the kampam-Kaṟuppu-balipīṭha ensemble also marks the site for two later goat or ram sacrifices. The second one, the festival's main animal sacrifice, is supplied by a chief local landowner, and is apparently offered to the goddess, along with māviḷakku and poṅkal. And the final one is offered at the time of the uprooting of the kampam, at which time the head of the goat is placed in the bottom of the hole to be crushed with the post before the hole is filled in. Again, possessions follow as the post is taken away and submerged in a well or tank.

Thus the post not only may retain something of the demon in the tree from which it is cut, it may be a demon. And the demon's "conversion" to the service of the deity not only may occur in a founding myth, but also may be reenacted in the rituals that in some manner reflect the impropriety of his relations with the goddess, and the sacrifice—for the uprooting of the pole is the demon's death—that results from those improprieties. Indeed, the post not only is the demon, it is the sacrificial victim. In this regard, it is more than suggestive that in the same Kongu region, around Coimbatore, festivals for Arjuna's son Aravāṉ-Kūttāṇṭavar represent this "demon"-deity (Hiltebeitel 1988a, 410) by a kampam of the same three-pronged type, made of wood from the country fig tree (*ātti maram; Ficus glomerata*). The ritual enactment of his sacrificial death includes cutting up this post.[29]

One could surely draw more examples into this flagstaff-tree-demon-post continuum.[30] In a brief glance beyond Tamilnadu we are inevitably drawn to the Navakalevara ("New Body") festival, performed once every twelve or seventeen years, with its *vanayāga*, or "forest sacrifice," of four margosa trees to supply the wood for

29. See further chapter 9, and chapter 4, n. 12 for a variant use of a post in connection with Kūttāṇṭavar-Aravāṉ's sacrifice.

30. In the background, one must recall the festivals for Indra's banner (*indradhvaja*) referred to in the *Atharva Veda* and early classical (including epic) texts; see Hopkins

making the "new bodies" of the deities of the great Jagannātha temple at Puri, Orissa. None of the four icons made from the tree trunks—Jagannātha-Kṛṣṇa, Subhadrā, Balabhadra-Balarāma, or a post called Sudarśana (normally the name for Kṛṣṇa's discus)—is ever set in a flagstaff position outside the Jagannātha temple. But the actual vanayāga, or cutting of the trees, replicates such a configuration in the forest. For each cutting, the old "retiring" Sudarśana post is brought on a pole by a special low-caste officiant (of reputed tribal origins) and mythologically identified as Daita, or "demon") and set in the roots of the chosen tree, as if marking it for sacrifice. The first of the four trees to be cut is the one for the next Sudarśana post. A temporary *yajñaśāla,* or sacrificial pavillion with a thatched roof, is erected so that the tree stands to its east, just as a flagstaff would stand outside a temple. Here a temple is, as it were, brought to the forest; or a portion of the forest is made into a temple. Conversely, Reiniche observes that the bringing of a tree for the flagstaff makes for the presence of exterior forces from the forest in the sacred interior of the temple (1979, 95 n. 18).

Inside the yajñaśāla (or yāgaśāla), a square fire altar (vedi) is built, apparently in the center. One will recall the fire altar in the outer twenty-four pillared maṇḍapa at the flag-hoisting ceremonies of the Mēlaccēri Draupadī temple. In each case, such rites require Brahmans; those at Puri collaborate with a cadre of so-called Daitas and are linked closely with the king. In this "forest sacrifice," seeds are then sown in a rectangular bed to the north of the vedi. This is a variation on the sprouting rites that were discussed in chapter 4. Both rites thus feature Brahmans as prominent ritualists and evoke connections between the temple and the forest.[31] A pot represents Durgā at the western end of the forest yajñaśāla, opposite the tree: in the position, that is, of the garbhagṛha of what now amounts to a "forest temple" for Vanadurgā, "Durgā of the Forests."[32] At

[1915] 1969, 125–26; J. J. Meyer 1937, 3:93–134; Gonda 1967, 413–29; idem [1954] 1969, 255–59; and Dumézil 1973, 61–65. Its being "like the sacrificial post (*yūpa*)" (Gonda 1967, 417), its original mythic use on Indra's chariot to conquer the demons, its ostensibly royal character, and the occasion of the festival at the end of the rains as prelude to the season for wars (like Dasarā) are all instructive in the present context.

31. See chapter 4, section B, and nn. 20–21.

32. The forest is near a temple of the goddess Maṅgalā, at which the tree-searching group until recently made its headquarters. The chief officiants still sleep there and learn from the goddess in which direction to seek the trees for cutting. There is no need to look for an "aboriginal deity" behind Maṅgalā (Eschmann 1978c, 280), or an original rite without her (Tripathi 1978, 242). When the party arrives at Maṅgalā's temple, its accompanying pandits and Ācārya (the chief Brahman priest of the king) recite the *Durgāsaptaśatī* (that is, the *Devī Māhātmyam*) (ibid., 234–35).

the northeast corner of this pavilion, Narasiṃha, Viṣṇu's violent "Man-Lion" form, the presiding deity of the whole forest sacrifice, is invoked into a pitcher on a special maṇḍala. Throughout Orissa, Narasiṃha has a long history of being represented by (and on) sacrificial posts. Here he has no post, but he is identified with the Sudarśana post at the base of the tree by a mantra that is itself connected with pacification (*śānta*). The northeast, which seems here to be Narasiṃha's direction, is very important in these rites. Among other things, the forest where the margosa trees must be sought is to the northeast of Puri. All this is reminiscent of what might be called the "functions of the northeast" that involve pacifying the sacrifice. In the Draupadī cult these functions fall primarily to Pōttu Rāja's Muslim colleague Muttāl Rāvuttaṉ (Hiltebeitel 1988a, 126–27). Before the tree is cut, *bhūtas* (demons) who reside in or near the tree are offered lumps whose principal ingredient is a cut-up gourd, the standard substitute for an animal sacrifice. A Brahman of supposedly mixed-caste ancestry (from a Brahman male and a tribal chief's daughter), who earlier wears the garland from the Sudarśana post, then makes the first symbolic cut with a golden ax and goes into possession. After this the tree is cut down by carpenters and should fall in a northeast direction.[33] I will say more about the icons themselves in chapter 6, and in particular about Orissan posts. We will also return in later chapters to the theme of transposable temples. But for the moment it is enough to say that the wonderful documentation on these matters gathered by the Orissa Research Project needs to be reexamined in its entirety from a detribalized perspective. The operating assumption of that collaborative effort turns on the notion of the "Hinduization" of originally tribal rituals and ritual paraphernalia.[34] But the result is really an unsuccessful scholarly tribalization of Hinduism (cf. Biardeau 1989b, 66 and n. 6).

Turning back to Tamilnadu, only one more related instance need be mentioned, with a special point in mind. This is the case of Kāttavarāyaṉ, who best introduces us to the subject of impalement. It is his impalement stake, or *kaḻumaram,* rather than the three-pronged kampam, that one finds in the "post position" outside

33. From Tripathi 1978, especially 232, 234, 239–50, and 255 n. (on the Narasiṃha mantra's connections with śānta), plus Marglin 1985, 250 on the Brahman identity of the officiant who makes the first cut in the tree.

34. For the main essays that bear on these issues, see Tripathi 1978, 254; Eschmann 1978a, 85–90, 1978b, 101–4, 110–13, and especially 1978c; Eschmann, Kulke, and Tripathi 1978b, 170–71, 177–87, 191–93; and Kulke 1978, 130. See also n. 32 above as one of many points to be made in this connection.

Māriyammaṉ temples in Thanjavur District (Biardeau 1989a, 20–22; 1989b 132–60 and plates 52, 53, 55, 56, 59 and 60), while at certain Kāmākṣī temples in Tiruchirappalli District the kaḻumaram is a well preserved wooden post erected anew for each festival. Masilamani-Meyer describes the actual pole raised for festivals at Pāccūr, the village where Kāttavarāyaṉ's impalement is said to have occurred: "a sixty foot long square pole of hard wood (ebony or teak)" that was "not used for impaling people—which would in any case seem impossible at such height." Rather, "the person who was to die was placed on a small platform close to the top of the pole and there tied and fastened with hooks. He was then left to die without food and water" (1989a, 87–88). Elsewhere, Kāttavarāyaṉ's stake is often a post holding an apparatus for hook swinging (*ceṭil*), a rite that may itself be attenuated by suspending Kāttavarāyaṉ's ritual impersonator in a square frame (ibid.). Kāttavarāyaṉ's festivals in Tiruchirappalli District are called *kaḻuvēṟṟal,* which refers to the "mounting of the stake" by a man impersonating Kāttavarāyaṉ (ibid.).

For our purposes, the important matter is the persistence through all these variations of the *symbolism* of impalement, which comes out vividly in the myth.[35] The stake-tree, a *veṅkai,* or kino, tree (*Pterocarpus marsupium*), is born at the same time as the Brahman girl whom this Untouchable god-man of all castes covets, knowing as he does so that the stake will be his fate. Kālī oversees its growth, "raising it like a goldsmith's needle," its "inside diamond hard as ebony." It grows naturally to a height of sixty feet into a sculpted shape, "like a statue," without chisel or adze. Kāttavarāyaṉ, following Kālī's instructions, cuts down the tree himself with the help of a thousand demons. When he cuts it, streams of blood flow. He then places ashes on it, puts it in a cart, and brings it to Pāccūr. In the cutting and carrying, the story is highly reminiscent of the myth of Cuṭalai Māṭaṉ's flagstaff (see also n. 24), though also of the goat sacrifices at the raising of the three-pronged kampams in Kongunad and the role of Daita "demons" in the gourd- and tree-cutting rituals in the forests northeast of Puri. Kāttavarāyaṉ then invites carpenters (Ācāris) to "ornament" the stake according to his directions: with sharp nails and thorns, a huge hook as big as a thigh, and big baskets for his women. Disguising himself as Kaṅkāḷaruttiraṉ, a form of Rudra-Śiva (or

35. The following details are all from Eveline Masilamani-Meyer's translation of the *Kāttavarāyaṉ Katai,* which she is preparing for publication (in press-b). I thank her for her generous permission to cite this fascinating work. For summaries, see Masilamani-Meyer 1989a and Shulman 1989.

Bhairava) as a skeleton, he also places eighteen markings on it. It is then erected on a strong earthen platform. Before his impalement, the stake receives a pūjā—one pot of poṅkal per household and offerings of goats, chicken, pigs, opium, marijuana, intoxicating sweets, arrack, coconuts, millet, etc. The story also connects him with Kaṟuppu, the same "dark demon" whose stone stands permanently at the spot reserved for the mounting of the three-pronged kampams of Kongunad, and who figures as a guardian or parivāra deity at the Thanjavur and Tiruchirappalli temples where Māriyammaṉ and Kāmākṣī are linked with Kāttavarāyaṉ (Biardeau 1989a, 20–23; Masilamani-Meyer 1989a, 80, 95).

It may seem that with triple-forked trees, forest sacrifices, and impalement posts we are in danger of losing sight of the ordinary temple flagstaff. This is not the case, as a return to the Draupadī cult will show. We must, however, look further not only at the flagstaff but, once again, at the total configuration of which it is a part.

D. Draupadī Cult Posts for Pōttu Rāja and Vīrapattiraṉ

The ordinary Draupadī temple combination of balipīṭha, flagstaff, and Pōttu Rāja slab is susceptible to other variations besides those at Mēlaccēri. It is common to find Pōttu Rāja represented not only on the slab that shows him facing into the sanctum, but also on the squared base of the flagstaff's support column. Most interesting is the flagstaff at Uttiramērūr, which has Pōttu Rāja facing west (again, into the sanctum), Kṛṣṇa facing north, Draupadī east (as she does from inside the sanctum), and a seven-tined vīrakuntam facing south. At Tindivanam, the base of the flagstaff has a metal plaque of Pōrmaṉṉaṉ (i.e., Pōttu Rāja) facing west and one of Hanumān facing east, recalling the latter's association with Arjuna's flagstaff. At Pondicherry and Kīḻkoṭuṅkālūr, Pōttu Rāja faces both west and east.

If Pōttu Rāja is not the demon of the flagpole, he is at least its guardian, as can be seen by an instructive set of substitutions at Cōḻavantāṉ. The Draupadī temple there has no Pōttu Rāja in any form. It is beyond the core area, in Madurai District to the south. It has, however, a flagstaff and a Muttāl Rāvuttaṉ stone and tomb in the customary positions: on the central axis and to the northeast, respectively. The flagpole is set in an eight-sided concrete platform, and adjacent to the angle facing into the temple is a stone object on ground level, intermediary, in effect, with the base of the flagstaff and the position where Pōttu Rāja would ordinarily have

Figure 2. Kaṟuppu at the base of the flagstaff-post [kampam], Cōḻavantāṉ Draupadī temple.

his stone slab. The stone looks, however, distinctly like a much smoothed-out version of a balipīṭha, with a low, eight-sided base rising to a squat, conical, flat top for offerings of flowers. Its name is Kampat-t-aṭi Kaṟuppu, "Kaṟuppu at the Base of the Kampam," and the temple's chief trustee says that it protects the flag (see fig. 2).

Curiously, this Kaṟuppu is also more of a balipīṭha than a stone post, the form in which Kaṟuppu appears in Kongunad. But he is still the same "Kaṟuppu of the kampam" who marks the site of the three-pronged posts for Māriyammaṉ. As we have seen, either Kaṟuppu or the kampam may be offered the goat that is sacrificed when the three-pronged post is raised. In the Draupadī cult, there are no goat sacrifices to Pōttu Rāja (or Kaṟuppu at the base of the Kampam) at flag hoisting. But if flag hoisting has the connotations of a call to arms, a rousing of the army—which, as will become increasingly clear, it surely does—then one may recall that when Pōrmaṉṉaṉ agrees to become the leader of the Pāṇḍavas' and Draupadī's army, he requires a huge goat, flour lamp, and mound of poṅkal. Indeed, as we have seen, he is the first among those who receive a flour lamp and poṅkal, though not a goat, at the Mēlaccēri flag hoisting. The goat and its substitutes—in one case a rooster—are usually reserved for myth and drama.[36] However, one does find at temples west (Bangalore, Kolar) and southwest

36. Cf. Hiltebeitel 1988a, 346–47, and 1988b, part 1: Pōrmaṉṉaṉ's biting off the head of a rooster and drinking its blood are paralleled in the possession that comes between the first goat sacrifice and flag hoisting at Kaṉṉapuram: the priest who carries the kampam bites off the necks of small chicks and drinks their blood (Beck 1981a,

(Lalgudi) of the core area that the sacrifice of a goat by biting its jugular vein is done at some Draupadī festivals as one of the closing kāval pūjā offerings to guardian deities—either Pōttu Rāja or his alternate Vīrapattiraṉ (Vīrabhadra).[37] The closing kāval pūjā normally precedes the *lowering* of the flag rather than its raising.

Cōḻavantāṉ thus provides us with a case where our usual Draupadī temple ensemble is reduced to the flagstaff alone, with no recognized balipīṭha or Pōttu Rāja, yet with a Kaṟuppu who seems to substitute for both of them. Conversely, one also finds Draupadī temples where Pōttu Rāja is alone, as if standing for all three, or with just one of the other two. The three objects thus not only have an evident rapport, but a certain interchangeability.[38] These are subjects upon which we can shed no further light without examining a few rare but telling instances where Draupadī's Pōttu Rāja is not a figure sculpted on a slab, but a post.

Pōttu Rāja as a post is found most often in Andhra Pradesh, where the post itself is simply called Pōta Rāju, the Telugu spelling. Andhra Pōta Rājus are normally of śamī wood (Telugu *jammi;* Tamil vaṉṉi), though one also finds them in stone (Roghair 1982, plate 8; cf. Biardeau 1984, 14–16; 1989b, 9–11). Whatever the medium, such posts certainly have cutting, carving, installation, and renewal rites behind them, though for the present one can only imagine them, as none have been documented.[39] In Andhra villages, śamī-wood Pōta Rājus are found in two places, their functions linked through

88). Beck says he is possessed by the goddess and gives oracles for her. Most intriguingly, in touring the temple his possessions do not cease until he sees "the face of Pōttu Rāja" (ibid., 89), whose position to the northwest is to this north-facing temple as a northeast position would be to an east-facing temple.

37. Bangalore information from Krishnamurthy Hanur (see chap. 2, n. 30): the man impersonating Pōttu Rāja is a Tigala or Vaṉṉiyar, covered with ashes, turmeric on forehead, holding a sword in his right hand, with bells on his ankles for dancing around the temple. After he bites the goat, while still possessed, devotees touch rice balls to the blood on his mouth and take them home as prasādam. Cf. Hiltebeitel 1988a, 365 (Kolar). At Lalgudi (Lalgudi Taluk, Tiruchirappalli District), the biting is done by a Vēḷāḷar Piḷḷai possessed by Vīrapattiraṉ, who replaces Pōttu Rāja in this region. Though no story was known at Lalgudi in connection with this practice (it may be in the *Mahābhārata,* I was told), the man who bites the goat's neck and drinks its blood is then offered rice poṅkal, tender coconut water, and lemons. Recall that Pōrmaṉṉaṉ demands a goat as tall as a palm tree, poṅkal like a mountain, and a flour lamp like a hillock (Hiltebeitel 1988a, 345–79).

38. At Maṅkalam, for instance, one finds only a Pōttu Rāja slab and flagstaff, but no balipīṭha. The Duḥśālā-Kālī shrine within the Chinna Salem Draupadī temple has only a balipīṭha; cf. Reiniche 1979, 95 n. 18.

39. For parallel rites of installation and renewal elsewhere, see Biardeau 1989b, 83–92; Eschmann 1978c, 266 n. 2, 276–78. Probably the rituals for obtaining and

the village buffalo sacrifice. One is outside the goddess temple that marks the village boundary. The goddess in such cases will typically be one of the Seven Sisters who have Pōta Rāju as their younger brother. The other is in the center of the village, not connected with a goddess but set on a platform under a pair of trees that have been married to each other—usually a pipal as the male and a margosa as the female—and planted so that they will intertwine (Biardeau 1989b, 7–34).

Biardeau presents a number of arguments for interpreting the margosa and śamī as having a special affinity, with the margosa often serving as the śamī's substitute. We shall have occasion to recall this pattern. In connection with marriage trees, however, one sometimes finds the pipal and śamī post alone, suggesting that the post—despite its male identity in Andhra as Pōta Rāju—can also replace the margosa, in this case as the "wife." As we shall see, there is no contradiction in having female posts of this type, and the śamī, in its Sanskrit name, is "originally" feminine. But in most circumstances it will be the margosa that substitutes for the śamī, since the latter is both the rarer and documentably older (in ritual usages) of the two. In fact, even in the case of marriage trees, the śamī-pipal pairing may be the prototype.[40] As we have seen, the śamī has mythological associations with fire in the *Mahābhārata* episode where the Pāṇḍavas conceal their weapons. As Biardeau has shown, these associations are rooted in Vedic ritual, where the śamī and pipal (Sanskrit *aśvattha*) are related to each other through their joint production of the Vedic sacrificial fire. According to different Vedic—and eventually popular—sources and varying interpretations, either the Vedic firesticks are both made of pipal wood that is said to be *śamīgarbhāt,* "from the womb of the śamī," or else the vertical male stick is pipal and the horizontal female one śamī. Biardeau sees the marriage-tree combination of margosa (or śamī) and pipal, together in the center of Andhra villages, as a popular transformation of this Vedic symbolism, retaining the rapport between the two trees as a source of prosperity (*śrī*) through the sacrificial fire, but substituting them for an actual sac-

---

sculpting a stone post differ little from those for a wooden post. According to the Pāñcarātra āgamas, for instance, when one chooses a stone for an icon, one must disperse the hovering Bhūtas and propitiate the divinity (*devatā*) in the rock before the stone can be brought to the place where the sculpting will begin (H. D. Smith 1969, 26, 41–44). Conversely, the post-tree may grow in rock-hard wood "like a sculpture," untouched by chisel or adze, as in the Kāttavarāyaṉ myth.

40. This priority holds at least to the degree that the pairing is originally Vedic. On the pipal and margosa in Indus Valley seals, see Hiltebeitel and Hopkins 1987, 221.

rificial fire produced by firesticks. As a feature of village ritual, the latter would require Brahmans, who in Andhra do not participate in such village rites. The double appearance of the śamī post in Andhra villages is thus instructive. Outside the goddess temple on the margins of the village, the post, masculine, recalls the Vedic *yūpa*, or sacrificial post. And in the village center, masculine but still serviceable in a feminine function, it is part of an ensemble that evokes the sacrificial fire.[41]

Posts of the first type are also found outside Draupadī temples. It is very rare, however, to find them in the position of Andhra Pōta Rājus, directly before the sanctum, and a bit more common to find rough approximations of them in the northeast position associated with Muttāl Rāvuttaṉ. I will return to the relation between these two guardians and their posts in chapter 6. But for the present, I will discuss only posts in the "Pōttu Rāja position," as they are invariably the more finely sculpted. I will discuss the eight instances shown in figures 3 and 4, noting variations on these as they have been discovered in fieldwork. It is curious that in most of these cases the presence of such posts seems to involve dislocations or displacements of the normal alignment of the three objects—balipīṭha, flagstaff, Pōttu Rāja slab—contiguously in a row. It is also curious that the incidence of such posts often coincides with unusual variants of Pōttu Rāja's ritual and mythology. The posts in question are all in stone, though one is accompanied by another post in wood. I will proceed geographically from north to south: from the Andhra fringes of the northern parts of the core area, through its Tamil center, to the Thanjavur–northeastern Tiruchirappalli area to the south.

Transitionally significant is a pointed conical stake for Pōta Rāju at the Kalahasti Draupadī temple (where Telugu is the language spoken) in the Chittoor District of southern Andhra (fig. 3A). Heavily coated with turmeric and daubed with dots of kuṅkum, it is set in a concrete platform toward the front of the temple's outer maṇḍapa directly before the main icon of Dharmarāja in the sanctum, who is flanked by smaller figures of Draupadī and Arjuna. There is no flagstaff or balipīṭha, as if the post Pōta Rāju sufficed for all three. The pūcāri gives Pōta Rāju a typical Andhra pedigree as the younger brother of the "Seven Śaktis" (equivalent to the aforementioned Seven Sisters), but he also tells a highly modified yet

41. For Biardeau's treatment of the above, see 1989b, 9, 14, and 1984, 13–14, 17, on the two locations of the Pōta Rāju; 1989b, 81, 94–95, and 1984, 13 n. 4, on the complementary trees; 1989b, 50–62, and 1984, 4, on the Vedic firesticks; and 1989b, 63, 82, on the general absence of fire in the Andhra rituals.

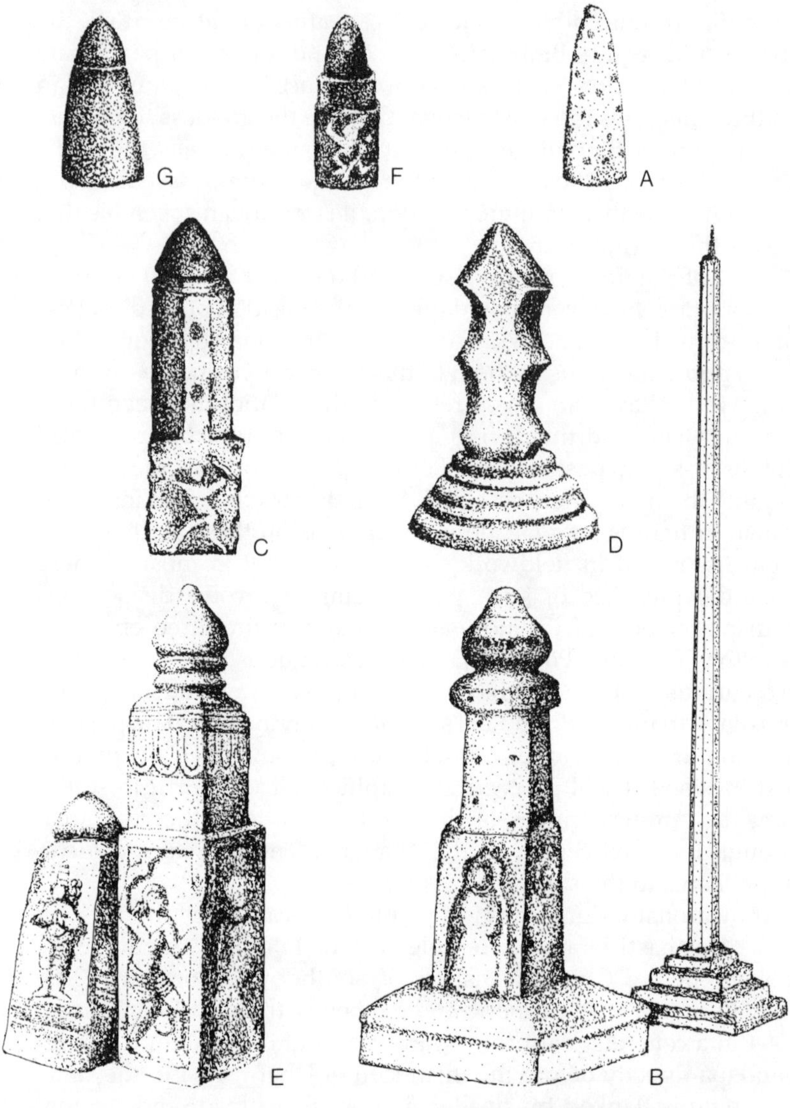

Figure 3. Draupadī cult posts: (A) Kalahasti; (B) Kūttampākkam (from Biardeau 1989b, photo 41); (C) Vīrāṇantal; (D) Tiruvannamalai; (E) Tindivanam (cf. Biardeau 1989b, photo 42); (F) Tailāpuram; (G) Kumbhakonam Hājiyār Street Draupadī temple.

easily recognized variant of the Pōttu Rāja–Pōrmaṉṉaṉ myth familiar at Draupadī temples in Tamilnadu. Pōta Rāju's father, named Maharṣi, was the guru of the Kauravas, and had astrological manuals that would help them win the *Mahābhārata* war. Kṛṣṇa and Sahadeva prevailed upon Pōta Rāju to try to obtain these for the Paṇḍavas. When the old sage refused them, Pōta Rāju cut off his father's head. He then brought the head, along with the manuals, to serve the Pāṇḍavas, and he became a "disciple" (*śiṣya*) of Dharma, as did "Muhammad Khan" (alias Muttāl Rāvuttaṉ), whose tomb is in the typical companion position to the northeast. The temple also has a wooden processional icon of Pōta Rāju showing him holding his father's head.[42]

At Tamil Draupadī (or, to begin to be more precise now, Draupadī and Dharmarāja) temples, the stone-post Pōttu Rāja of reference must be the one discovered by Biardeau at Kūttampākkam, Vaniyampadi District, North Arcot (fig. 3B), close enough to the Andhra border for her to have suspected a direct Andhra influence (1989b, 111, 117–18). As is often the case in North Arcot, the temple, to Dharmarāja, is in the hands of Vēḷāḷar Mutaliyārs rather than Vaṉṉiyars. It is this temple that has not only a stone post but also a wooden one, both on the same axis from the sanctum, with the stone one to the outside. Biardeau's Mutaliyār informant identified the stone post as Pōttu Rāja and the wooden one, thinner and much taller, as Akkiṉikampam (Sanskrit Agniskambha) or "Fire-post," an implement that he said was born with Draupadī, who held it in her hand when she emerged from the sacrificial fire of her birth. As Biardeau indicates, this akkiṉikampam thus has something of the status of Draupadī's brother, and doubles for her "true" epic brother Dhṛṣṭadyumna. Meanwhile, Pōttu Rāja in stone retains his identity as the Pāṇḍavas' brother-in-law through his marriage to their sister Caṅkuvati. But instead of a figure of Pōttu Rāja on the base of the post that faces into the temple, such as one might expect in an analogy with the bas-reliefs of Pōttu Rāja on slabs in the corresponding position, the four faces show what Biardeau takes to be various "heroes" (*vīraṉs*) of a type often shown at the base of posts for other Tamil goddesses (1989b, 123, 131–32).

At the beginning of the Kūttampākkam festival, a flagstaff (dhvajastambha) is erected outside the Pōttu Rāja maṇḍapa, farther out

42. See further Hiltebeitel 1989a, 344–48 and plate 39, and 1988a, 339, 343–44, 380–81, 446. At Cantavācal Pōrmaṉṉaṉ is called Śivānantapurirājaṉ. On other Muslim names for Muttāl Rāvuttaṉ, see ibid., 103–4, to which can be added Bhai (Hindi "Brother") at Poṉṉeri, and Muttāl Irāvaṇan (= Rāvaṇa!), a Muslim, at Cantavācal.

along the same axis. Apparently it is a temporary flagstaff, as at Mēlaccēri. Biardeau makes no mention of a balipīṭha. As part of the flag-hoisting ceremony, darbha grass is wound around the akkiṉikampam from top to bottom. Then it receives kaṅkaṇam (i.e., kāppu), as do the main officiants. One should note an incongruity here, and recall at this point that the spiral of darbha grass is usually placed around the flagstaff itself. As if to confirm this, a Brahman arrived at the Kūttampākkam temple to inform Biardeau that the true flagstaff is the akkiṉikampam/agniskambha itself, which should have been placed outside the stone post rather than inside it! The temple also has a wooden processional icon of Pōttu Rāju, of which one detail is mentioned: it is not brought into the maṇḍapa until *Mahābhārata* recitation reaches the beginning of the war, the theater appropriate to Pōttu Rāja as the Pāṇḍavas' marshal (Biardeau 1989b, 119–22). We must return to these matters, the Brahman informant included, but for the moment it is enough to note that this is the only Draupadī temple found so far where a wooden post is fixed in the same alignment as a stone one, and to appreciate that the interchangeability of post and flagstaff (even such an unusual flagstaff) has such authoritative local support.

Moving farther south into North Arcot, I have found three similar Draupadī cult stone posts: at Kāppalūr (Polur Taluk), Vīrāṇantal (Chengam Taluk), and Chengam itself. Let us consider the Vīrāṇantal one as our main example (fig. 3C). Andhra connections might be suspected here too, since the temple is primarily in the hands of Nāyuṭus, an originally Telugu-speaking community, with Vaṉṉiyars and Ceṭṭiyars in secondary roles. The post is in a beautiful east-west, see-through maṇḍapa just inside the temple's main eastern entrance, while a tall, red-painted wooden lamppost (*viḷakku tūṇ:* not a flagstaff, since it has no frame at the top) is at some distance outside the entrance, with Hanumān on the westward, inward-facing, base angle rather than Pōttu Rāja. There is no balipīṭha. Lined up between the post and the sanctum is a stone rat, the vehicle of Vināyakar, who is one of the deities in the sanctum (see plate 4). As at Kūttampākkam, the post shows a vīraṉ on the square base, though only on the angle facing the sanctum. Here, however, the vīraṉ, like the post itself, was identified with no hesitancy as Pōttu Rāja. Why does Pōttu Rāja have this shape? It is "custom" (*aitikam*), I was told. At the beginning of the festival, the first pūjā goes to Vēṭiyappaṉ, a regional, ancient guardian deity in the Tiruvannamalai area, who has a hero stone just inside the outer temple compound wall, just south of the entrance. The second pūjā then goes to the post Pōttu Rāja. According to my chief trustee informant, K. Venkatesan, "Without Pōttu Rāja there is no festival" (*Pōttu Rāja illāmal viḻā illai*). This is a sentiment I heard once before from the pāratiyār Brameesa Mudaliyar, at the conclusion of his account of Draupadī's second advent to Gingee (Hiltebeitel 1988a, 82).

The Vīrāṇantal temple has a rather large assemblage of wooden processional icons, some of which I remarked on in chapter 3. It is curious, however, that it has none for Pōttu Rāja. One surprise in Vīrāṇantal, however, is that a wooden processional icon of Pōttu Rāja is kept elsewhere, in a Kūttāṇṭavar temple (for Arjuna's son Aravāṉ-Kūttāṇṭavar). This temple is run entirely by Vaṉṉiyars. It has no Pōttu Rāja of any kind in front of it, though it does have a ruggedly hewn stone post to the northeast called Canyāci Īcuvaraṉ; diseased animals are brought to this post-deity so that he can cure them after he is offered an abhiṣeka. Pōttu Rāja's processional icon does, however, lead Kūttāṇṭavar's chariot in his processions, just as it leads the icons of Draupadī and the Pāṇḍavas at Draupadī festivals. Something of Pōttu Rāja's resultant split duty can be gathered from the Kūttāṇṭavar temple pūcāri's account of the Pāṇḍavas' alliance with Pōttu Rāja:

> Pōttu Rāja was promised that he could marry Dharma's sister Caṅkuvati, but Kṛṣṇa said he must kill his father first. Pōttu Rāja's father Alampācuraṉ [also called Cilampacuraṉ, "Anklet Demon," here] lived in Devaloka [the heaven of the gods], where he was doing penance. The instruments needed to kill him were with Tēventiraṉ [Indra] in Devaloka. Even Kṛṣṇa couldn't get them himself. If Pōttu Rāja could get them, use them to kill his father, and bring them back, he could marry Caṅkuvati and use the implements as the marshal (*cenāpati*) of the Pāṇḍavas' army. Pōttu Rāja did all this. His icon shows him holding the head of his father Alampācuraṉ. The implements—kuntam [trident], *koṭi* [flag], *maṇi* [bell], cāṭṭi [whip]—are now kept in the Draupadī [i.e., Dharmarāja] temple.

That the weapons are with Indra is intriguing, since usually they come from Pōttu Rāju's ancestral kingdom in Śivānandapuri, the City of the Bliss of Śiva. Other variations aside, this is the only instance I have met of a complete coalescence of the Cunītaṉ cycle, in which Pōttu Rāja helps Draupadī kill the Gingee Forest demon Acilōmaṉ/Acalammaṉ (see Appendix: Alampācuraṉ is clearly one of many variants on this name), and the Pōrmaṉṉaṉ cycle in which he kills his father in Śivānandapuri. Here it is the second cycle that provides the main narrative while the first supplies the names. The demon of the Cunītaṉ cycle has become the beheaded father of the

Pōrmannaṉ cycle: one more, no doubt inevitable, explanation for the head in the hand. Nowhere else has the father's name been a variant of Acalammaṉ, or his residence been in Devaloka.[43]

One striking feature common to all five of the temples mentioned so far—those at Kāppalūr and Chengam included—is that they are Dharmarāja temples. Draupadī joins Dharma in the sanctum, but he is the main deity, especially in his seated form against the rear wall. Only at Vīrāṇantal is there a rat vehicle, since the other temples do not have Vināyakar in the sanctum. At Chengam, Dharma shares the sanctum with Draupadī, and at Kāppalūr with Draupadī and Kuntī. At Chengam there is a balipīṭha but no flagstaff; at Kāppalūr the reverse. At each place, the stone post is identified as Pōttu Rāja, and has its own maṇḍapa covering it. At Chengam, it is noteworthy that between the Pōttu Rāja maṇḍapa and the sanctum, there are anthropomorphic images of Vīrapattiraṉ (Vīrabhadra) and a head of Karumāriyammaṉ to the south, and of Bhairava, a nāga, and an unidentified female to the north. One wonders whether Vīrapattiraṉ and Bhairava are there to compensate for the missing anthropomorphic representation of Pōttu Rāja on a stone slab. But the temple does have a wooden processional Pōttu Rāja, his body covered with gold leaf! Meanwhile, at Kāppalūr, the post Pōttu Rāja has five small stone cones set beside it. They look like little liṅgams, maybe representing the Pāṇḍavas, but the Kōṉār pūcāri said they were *cummā*, "nothing special." In this village, the portable wooden Pōttu Rāja is kept in a Kāḷiyammaṉ temple, where he is supposed to be Kālī's guardian as well as Draupadī's, making himself present at both festivals.

In this area, however, one cannot discuss posts of this type as if they were for Dharmarāja and Pōttu Rāja alone. At Vīraṇam village (Chengam Taluk), there is a similar post called Taṇṭamāri (Māriyammaṉ in the form of a staff, or *daṇḍa*) outside a Māriyammaṉ temple. At Kīḻiravantavāṭi village (Chengam Taluk), the post outside a Māriyammaṉ temple is simply called Ammaṉ, "Mother." A little farther southeast at Kārai village in Gingee Taluk (South Arcot), the post outside another Māriyammaṉ temple is called Nilaiyammaṉ, "Lady of the Door Frame." And in Tiruvannamalai itself, there is a temple for Ammaccārammaṉ (seated against the rear wall) and Reṇukā (her head only, set above ground before her) which has a

43. One is reminded of the Tindivanam pūcāri's version in which Pōrmaṉṉaṉ's father is the *demon* Pōttu Rāja (Hiltebeitel 1988a, 344). On the two-cycle problem see ibid., 76–88, 333–47, 377 (in relation to the heads); on Śivānandapuri, ibid., 338–44, 358–61, 390.

large figure of Pōttu Rāja in a shed to its southeast.[44] Just in front of the temple for the two goddesses is a post of the same type, which informants were unable to name. What is striking in at least three out of four of these cases is that the posts are identified as female. The Pōttu Rāja posts before Dharmarāja temples thus seem to be variants of a regionally popular gender-free form.

Continuing to move southward and eastward, deeper into Tamilnadu, our examples cease to be from Dharmarāja temples and are henceforth from Draupadī temples. First, still within the area just mentioned, at Tiruvannamalai, near the South Arcot border, is the intriguing Forest Draupadī Ammaṉ temple just south of the Ramana Maharshi Ashram. The temple, which must once have been one of the Draupadī cult's most splendid, is neglected and rapidly deteriorating. The large, old, unpainted wooden processional icons inside it—of Draupadī, the five Pāṇḍavas, and Mahāviṣṇu—are testimony to what must once have been grand festivals that have not occurred in many decades. On the east-west axis heading into it is a balipīṭha followed by a stone post—in the Pōttu Rāja position—shaped much like a spear point (see fig. 3D). The temple's evening pūjās are offered alternately by four members of one family of pūcāris, who also serve at other goddess temples in the town, including its other two Draupadī temples. According to one of these pūcāris, the post is called Stūpi, while another named it Cūlam. *Stūpi* (variant *tūpi*) means a "pinnacle, as of a tower, temple, palace, etc.; finial" (*Tamil Lexicon*), and also recalls the Buddhist usage *stūpa* or *tope* for a memorial or reliquary mound. *Cūlam*, Sanskrit *śūla*, means "spear." This post is not identified as Pōttu Rāja, who has his own separate maṇḍapa, one in which he is represented anthropomorphically on both sides of a slab. Here, rather than on the temple's east-west axis, he guards its southern entrance. But as we shall see, a pointed Pōta Rāju is an idea waiting to be realized.

At Tindivanam, now well into South Arcot, the Draupadī temple has a normal balipīṭha–flagstaff–Pōttu Rāja slab ensemble within the compound wall, while its two posts are outside and slightly south of the main axis (see map 2, fig. 3E). It is unlikely that either post ever had anything to do with Pōttu Rāja, though it is possible that the large one might at some point have been replaced by the current ensemble in front of the sanctum. As we saw in chapter 2,

44. This large processional Pōttu Rāja on a chariot, kept in a shed, is similar to the one at Maṅkalam (see Hiltebeitel 1988a, 366–67). The Tiruvannamalai one, however, is suffering from termite damage.

Telugu-speaking communities are among those that play prominent roles in the festival, but Vaṉṉiyars provide the temple's largest population. It would at this point be sheer guesswork to link any community with one temple feature, such as these posts. On the larger post, to the north (or right, facing the temple), the figures on the four-sided base were said by the pūcāri to be of Hanumān (east and south faces) and Kāttavarāyaṉ (north face). Biardeau (to whom I sent pictures of these posts) thinks that with the exception of the south-facing Hanumān, these identifications are unlikely and that the figures are again probably vīraṉs, or "heroes." She also identifies the figures on the base of the smaller post as vīraṉs, with the exception of the one facing eastward, whom she takes as a bhakta, possibly the donor of this smaller, perhaps votive post (1989b, 121–22 n. 5). According to the pūcāri, the posts are only boundary stones (*ellaikkal*) for the temple, and largely irrelevant to the festival, during which they receive no regular pūjās. Only on firewalking day do the figures on them receive a red forehead mark, or poṭṭu. If they are indeed vīraṉs, however, their recognition at this time only is interesting, since it implies a correlation between firewalkers and battle "heroes."

It is, in fact, only at the Tailāpuram Draupadī temple that one finds a combination of the post with a normal ensemble, moving inward, of balipīṭha, flagstaff, Pōttu Rāja slab (weathered beyond recognition), and post, nearest the sanctum, as a fourth (fig. 3F). The temple is in the hands of Vaṉṉiyars. Again, a single figure on the sanctum-facing base of the post is a running battle hero (vīraṉ), as at Vīrāṇantal. Here, however, the post is quite small and is without certain of the features that make the other posts more interesting.

Moving deeper into South Arcot, one begins to find a fluid situation marking a transitional zone between the Gingee core area and the Thanjavur area beyond it. Among the elements that differentiate these regional complexes, the pertinent one for the moment is the substitution of Vīrapattiraṉ for Pōttu Rāja, which one begins to find at Draupadī temples around Vriddhachalam: for example, at two of the three temples in Vriddhachalam town, and at C. Kīranūr nearby. At the Junction Road temple in Vriddhachalam, Vīrapattiraṉ is shown in bas relief on a slab, facing the sanctum, looking much like Pōttu Rāja. He appears to be strangling a goat or lion, but according to the pūcāri he is holding the head of Kuṇṭotaraṉ, one of Śiva's potbellied "host" who had disturbed Śiva's garden, thus provoking Śiva to create Vīrapattiraṉ from his wrath to behead him. At another Draupadī temple just west of Vriddhachalam at

Poṉṉēri, one does find a roughly hewn post, square at the base and then tapered toward the top, in the Pōttu Rāja–Vīrapattiraṉ position. It is identified with neither, however, but is called kampam, "post," and was said, without any clear explanation, to be used for the flagstaff (*koṭimaram*).

Finally, once one passes into Thanjavur and northeastern Tiruchirappalli Districts, Vīrapattiraṉ is the usual figure facing the sanctum, and Pōttu Rāja is unknown. Often he is called Akōra ("Fierce") Vīrapattiraṉ. Sometimes he is shown anthropomorphically, on a sanctum-facing slab, holding a goat-headed Dakṣa (Thanjavur East Gate Temple) or an unidentified goatlike animal (Pattukkottai). This befits Vīrabhadra's classical mythology as Śiva's agent of revenge against Dakṣa, who had ostracized Śiva—his son-in-law, the husband of his daughter Satī—from his great sacrifice (see Hiltebeitel 1988a, 373). At Pattukkottai, the weapon in Vīrapattiraṉ's right hand was called *cukkumākatai,* which seems to combine the *cukkumāttāṭi* ("the club or weapon of some inferior deities" [Winslow (1862) 1979, s.v.]) with the *katai,* or "mace" (Sanskrit *gadā*), the weapon of Bhīma. Held upright, it has two rings just below the top. The name agrees with what one finds on the only wooden processional icon of Vīrapattiraṉ I have located in the region. At Vaṭukku Poykaiyūr, his utsavamūrti is red-faced, kneeling, fanged, and four-armed (a feature not replicated on the stone slabs, or anywhere for Pōttu Rāja). His upper right hand bears a knife, his lower right hand a cukkumāttāṭi; a second cukkumāttāṭi leans against his chest; his upper left hand is empty; and his lowered left hand bears the human head of Dakṣa (see plate 7).

Like Pōttu Rāja, however, one also finds Akōra Vīrapattiraṉ in post-forms and multiforms. Some temples have conical stones in this position that are simply called *liṅgam*s (Ammāpēṭṭai, Cattiram Karuppūr). But at Vaṭukku Poykaiyūr, such a liṅgam, with a double indentation forming a ring below the curved top, was called Vīrapattiraṉ, Vīraṉ, and Draupadī's Muṉṉoṭiyaṉ ("Forerunner") by different informants. The conical post shown in figure 3, from the Hājiyār Street Draupadī temple in Kumbhakonam, Thanjavur District, is actually not identified as Vīrapattiraṉ (fig. 3G). But it is the third in a set of five figures that extend outward on the eastern axis from the sanctum. First, all three together on one platform, are a bhakta (waist up, hands folded); a shielded and sword-bearing warrior said to be the *kulateyvam,* or family deity, of the people who do ironing; and the post itself, said by the pūcāri to be related to offering sacrifice, but with no name that he could recall. Fourth stands an Añcaṉēyar pillar. And finally, in an arched niche set within the temple's eastern wall, is a fanged, flame-crested, human-sized, eight-armed Vīrapattiraṉ, a weapon in each hand, treading on a blue demon whose head is still intact. Probably, considering Vīrapattiraṉ's other post-multiforms in the region, this one "related to sacrifice" was originally connected with him.

Most fascinating and instructive, however, is the Akōra Vīrapattiraṉ of Lalgudi (see fig. 4). The side facing into the sanctum shows Vīrapattiraṉ standing on a lion, his right hand holding a raised (unidentified) weapon, and his left hand clutching the back of an elephant that he is in a position to strike. It appears to be a typical figure on a slab but for one thing. The top narrows to a ring that is surmounted by gumdrop-shaped extension that is said to be "like a crown" (*kirīṭam*). It is only when one looks at the outward-facing side of the same icon that one realizes this button is the top of a post, set in relief against the slab's flat back, that is much like the posts found farther north for Pōttu Rāja. Furthermore, incised into the post itself are two interesting details. First, just below the top are the sun and the moon. These are said to be symbols of Śiva, who created Akōra Vīrapattiraṉ from his sweat to kill Dakṣa, and also symbols of Akōra Vīrapattiraṉ's own vow to the sun and the moon that he would protect Draupadī, as Śiva ordered him to do.[45] Second, below the sun and the moon, set into a pedestal base, is what might be called a five-branched trident. The top and cross-pieces extend into actual tridents, while the two lower protrusions have a bladelike curve. This was said to be "like Akōra Vīrapattiraṉ's weapon," known here as a *vīrakumpam*, "heroic pot," but actually a multi-tined trident that is held aloft before Draupadī on her processions and otherwise kept in the southwest corner of the temple's mukhamaṇḍapam with another ritual implement, the whip. Clearly vīrakumpam is a variant name for vīrakuntam, elsewhere the "heroic lance" of Draupadī and Pōttu Rāja.[46] Before the Vēḷāḷar Piḷḷai bites the neck and drinks the blood of the goat during the kāval pūjā that closes the festival, he holds the vīrakumpam and gets possessed by Akōra Vīrapattiraṉ while hearing songs to Draupadī sung over this icon. Once possessed, he tours the town and the exterior of the temple before taking up the goat at the

45. There seems to be a necessary sequence between Vīrapattiraṉ's part in the Dakṣa myth and Śiva's command that he serve Draupadī, but informants at the temple were not sure and said they are just separate stories.

46. Another interesting variation on this name is Kuntammatēvi (Poomal Ravuttar Koyil Street temple, Thanjavur; Veḷḷalūr), identifying the vīrakuntam with Kuntī, who is considered to have her śakti in it. Like the posts and, as we shall see, the akkiṉikkampams, the implements can be female as well as male.

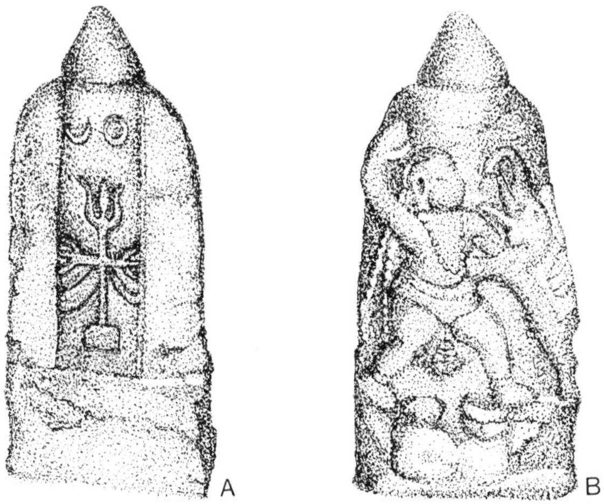

Figure 4. Post and anthropomorphic forms of Vīrapattiraṉ on back and front of one slab, Lalgudi: (A) post with trident, sun and moon, facing east and out from temple; (B) Vīrapattiraṉ standing on lion, holding and attacking elephant, facing sanctum.

temple entrance. Akōra Vīrapattiraṉ is said to receive the goat in this fashion at the end of the war (rather than at its beginning, as in the case of Pōrmaṉṉaṉ) for having served as Draupadī's guardian (kāval) while the war went on (see n. 37).

What is extraordinary about this Lalgudi Vīrapattiraṉ is that it unifies his post and anthropomorphic forms into one icon. Indeed, it further combines them with his chief weapon. It is also the clearest articulation of a post-shape, as distinct from a liṅgam-shape, that I have found for Vīrapattiraṉ. It may thus be significant that it is on the western side of the Thanjavur-Trichy region, since that could place it in a continuum with the Pōttu Rāja posts that extend down the western side of the core area through North Arcot.

Pōttu Rāja and Vīrapattiraṉ posts are no doubt to be found at other Draupadī cult temples. But certain patterns are unmistakable from this sample. The core area temples where the stone post displaces the usual slab-balipīṭha-flagstaff ensemble are Dharmarāja temples that are either in southern Andhra, or extend from that region into North Arcot, and are in the hands of either Vēḷāḷars or other groups besides Vaṉṉiyars, who predominate in South Arcot Draupadī temples. The Lalgudi temple—not a Dharmarāja temple but a Draupadī temple—is also run mainly by Vēḷāḷar Piḷḷais, while many of the Draupadī temples farther east in Thanjavur District are primarily in the hands of Vaṉṉiyars, as they are to the immediate north in South Arcot. Without further examples and more information, it would be premature to speculate on either the geographical or communal implications of these distributions. But the present alignments are suggestive.

More provocative is the post's one-to-one link with Dharmarāja over parts of Southern Andhra and North Arcot. I suspect an explanation is to be sought in the identification of the post with the sacrificer. In Dharmarāja temples, Dharma is the yajamāna, overseeing the sacrifice of battle from within the sanctum, which he must not leave (according to our Vīrāṇantal informant) lest he destroy the world. As we saw in chapter 2, in the Draupadī cult Dharmarāja is the incarnation of Yama, the god of death. As we learned at Kalahasti, the post Pōta Rāju is Dharma's "disciple." In principle, as we shall see, the post represents the sacrificer. At Draupadī temples, the yajamāna role is more diffused, and might be said really to belong to Draupadī. But Pōttu Rāja intercedes on her behalf, with myths to explain how he comes holding a head and bringing various weapons. It is thus quite logical that he would appear not as a post but as an armed hero in bas-relief. Moreover, insofar as the Draupadī cult posts are male, it is less logical that they should represent the sacrificer-goddess.

As to Vīrapattiraṉ, we must defer further discussion of his icons and the reasons for seeing him as a "substitute" for Pōttu Rāja to chapter 13, where we can familiarize ourselves more fully with his southern Draupadī cult mythology. Beyond such matters, however, Draupadī cult posts of all these types are best treated in relation to Biardeau's argument about the Vedic yūpa, parts of which I must now attempt to recapitulate.

6 Posts, Altars, and Demon Devotees

Outside core area Draupaḍī temples, on the margin between the temple and (if the temple has outer walls) its courtyard, whose eastern gate opens to the world, there is, then, normally an ensemble that is composed of three items that direct one, as one approaches the temple, westward, into the sanctum: the balipīṭha, the flagstaff, and Pōttu Rāja on a stone slab. In this chapter, I will argue that the rapport between these items requires the rare *post* Pōttu Rāja, rather than the more common *slab* Pōttu Rāja, to explain it. The same argument will also hold in principle for Draupadī cult Vīrapattiraṉs. In effect, it is the symbolism of the post that is "parceled out" (Lévi-Strauss 1971, 672) and magnified into these three aspects. This interpretation, in turn, will require a review of the scholarship that lies behind it: Madeleine Biardeau's trailblazing thesis that the Pōttu Rāja post is itself a replica of the Vedic sacrificial stake, or yūpa.[1]

A. The Yūpa: Some Further Chips

Let us organize our discussion around a series of points concerning the yūpa and its symbolism.[2]

1. *Position.* The yūpa is placed on the eastern margin of the *mahāvedi,* the trapezoidal "great altar" required for the exemplary Vedic animal sacrifice (*paśubandha*). The mahāvedi must itself extend eastward beyond the ordinary hour glass-shaped *vedi* "altar" and the three fires around it that are required for regular "solemn" (*śrauta*) sacrifices: that is, offerings of substances (grains, cakes,

1. This discussion draws primarily from Biardeau 1981c, 1984, 1988, and especially 1989b. I translate throughout.
2. Biardeau has offered a summary of her own in 1989b, 81–83.

ghee, etc.) other than animals (and, it should be added, *soma*—the divine plant pounded to make the drink of immortality—which also requires a mahāvedi, and which can be combined with animal sacrifices of increasing complexity). The yūpa is the outermost object on the direct axis that extends toward its easternmost position, from the domestic fire (*gārhapatya*) to the west, through the vedi and the offering fire (*āhavanīya*), and then, on the mahāvedi, through the "higher" or "further altar" (uttaravedi), which has centered upon it a square hole called the *uttaranābhi,* the uttaravedi's "navel." Fire transferred from the āhavanīya and placed on this high altar's "navel" becomes the new āhavanīya (offering fire) for the mahāvedi, and thus for the animal sacrifice, while for this same complex, the original āhavanīya now comes to serve as the gārhapatya fire (P.-E. Dumont 1962, 247).[3] Of all these constructions, the uttaravedi and new offering fire are nearest to the yūpa, and are prepared specifically for offerings that derive from the sacrificial animal (see map 3).

Biardeau comments that if, as the texts say, everything within the altar corresponds to the gods (*devayajanam*), the post, half in and half out, is only half divinized. In particular, its divinized side is the one that faces into the altar, or more particularly, faces the āhavanīya fire on the uttaravedi within it (1989b, 50). It thus mediates between the animal (which remains undivinized and tied on the outer side of the post), the gods (to whom the animal's omentum will be offered in the āhavanīya), and men, who move back and forth ritually, and of course spiritually, between both worlds. Malamoud also shows that the yūpa's position represents a boundary between the village and the forest (1989, 101). "By its rapport with all that is situated on the vedi, [the post,] if one may say so, has an inferior status" (Biardeau 1989b, 50). Mutatis mutandis, Pōta Rāju/Pōttu Rāja is an inferior deity represented by a post outside the entrance, on the eastern boundary, of goddess (or sometimes Dharmarāja) temples. Alternatively, and more commonly in the Draupadī cult, we find him in the same position, but figured on a slab, in various combinations with the flagstaff and balipīṭha. Vīrapattiraṉ at Lalgudi is in fact a deity facing in and a post facing out.

2. *The post as victim.* The yūpa, or more exactly the tree from which it is cut, is the first victim, consecrated to Viṣṇu, in the entire

3. For details such as these, and on the Vedic animal sacrifice in general, consult also Schwab 1886, which Biardeau draws on (1989b, 36–50); Kane [1930–62] 1975, 2, 2:1109–32; and Thite 1975, 132–51.

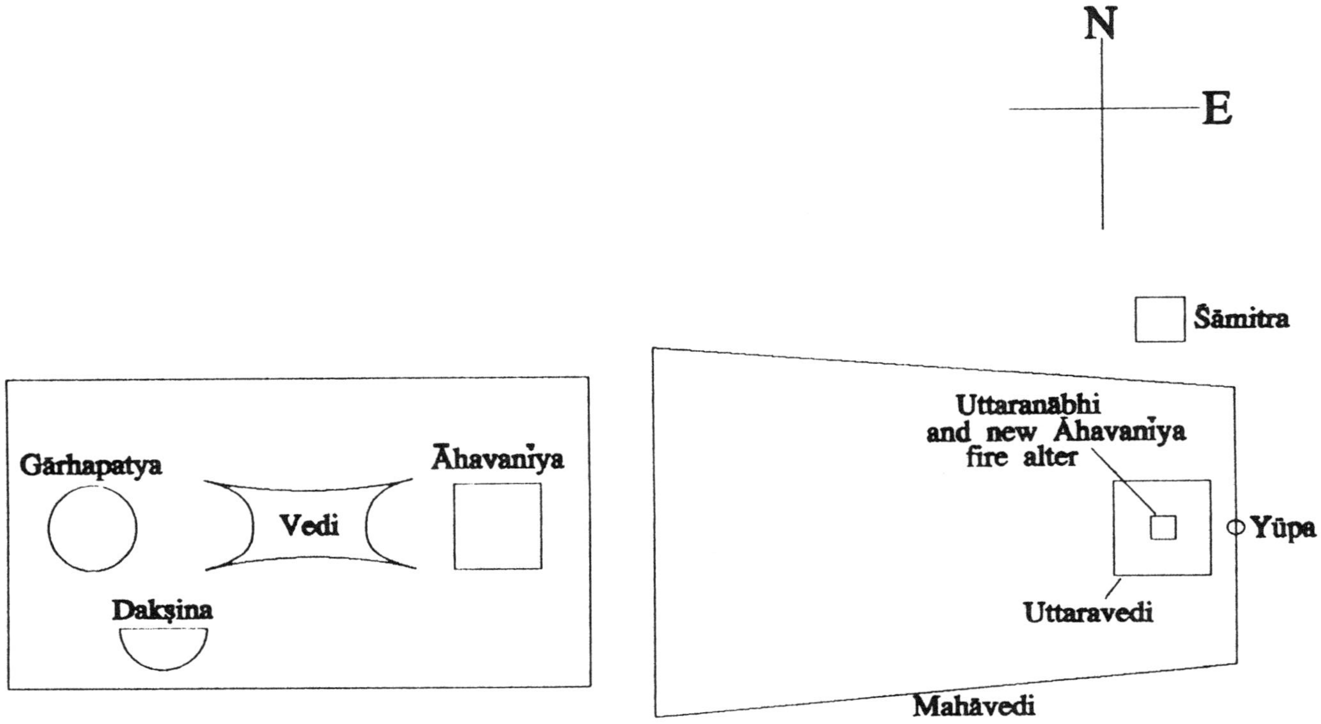

Map 3. Vedic altars.

ritual sequence of the Vedic animal sacrifice (Biardeau 1988, 111; cf. 1989b, 48–49). Among the precautions that assimilate its cutting to a sacrifice, the tree is anointed with ghee, its cutting point is marked by a blade of darbha grass, and when the tree is first cut or wounded, the first chip that falls—the *svaru,* of which more shortly—is reserved for further uses (1989b, 38). If one cannot quite say via the texts that the animal victim is identified with the post, one can at least say that the post is the means through which the animal submits to becoming a victim like the post itself. At Andhra temples to village goddesses, the post plays such a mediating role in the buffalo sacrifice. After the buffalo is taken around the temple and post, it is sacrificed elsewhere.[4] At Draupadī and Dharmarāja temples, the post shows Pōttu Rāja or other "heroes" at its base who are akin to those who participate, again elsewhere, in the rituals that reenact the *Mahābhārata*'s sacrifice of battle. Alternatively, it is complemented or "replaced" by the balipīṭha–flagstaff–bas-relief combination that likewise marks a boundary between the temple and the battlefield rituals outside it.

For the deeper connections here, however, one must turn to myth. The Pōta Rāju post outside goddess temples is none other than a materialization of an implicit formulation. It incarnates the victim—mythically the Buffalo Demon, ritually the sacrificial buffalo—who has submitted to a sacrificial death like the post itself and who, now represented in the form of a post, marks and mediates the Buffalo Demon's transfiguration into the semidivine form of an inferior divinity, the "Buffalo King." This is another way of getting to the same seminal point that Biardeau makes in her 1981 article: "In the end it seems indubitable, because perfectly logical, that Pōtu Rāju is identical with Mahiṣāsura, but a converted Mahiṣāsura" (1984, 19; cf. 1981, 238)—converted, through his death, from the goddess's demon foe to her semidivine guardian and demon devotee.[5] We have also seen that the post-as-victim rapport recurs in myths of flagstaff cutting. Or alternately, the post or flag-

4. At one Andhra village, after it has been led around the boundary goddess temple with its Pōta Rāju post, the buffalo is sacrificed near the second Pōta Rāju stake below the pipal-margosa marriage trees in the village center, before the boundary goddesses' portable icons (Biardeau 1989b, 14; 1984, 17–18).

5. Cited in Hiltebeitel 1988a, 77, as a key to Draupadī cult mythology. It is no less so to its ritual. Biardeau adds: "It is probable that the constitution of Pōta Rāju into the goddess's little brother has had as its condition the forgetting of his asuric identity" (1989b, 82). While forgotten, in the Draupadī cult it also remains residual in Pōttu Rāju's iconography (Hiltebeitel 1988a, 382 and n. 12, plate 26) and Pōrmaṉṉaṉ's myths and dramas (ibid., 363–72, 379–82, 390–93).

staff, once established outside a temple, has a guardian demon at its base in a position to protect it from recutting or to mark the spot of its yearly uprooting.

3. *The yūpa's form.* From what one can reconstruct of the shape of the Vedic yūpa, the Pōta Rāju post looks to be a stylization of it (Biardeau 1989b, 88–82). Wooden yūpas from the Vedic period, of course, have not survived. The oldest surviving yūpas are in stone, the earliest being a pair from the Kuṣāna period (one with an inscription probably from the first century C.E.) that were retrieved from the banks of the Yamuna River in 1910 at a village called Īsāpur, a suburb of Mathurā (Vogel 1910–11; Caland 1924; Chhabra 1947). These give us a good idea of certain main features, and for the most part conform to descriptions in the Vedic texts, which stipulate that the post have a rough, unhewn base, be eight-sided in the middle, and have a ring over a rounded projection from the top. The Īsāpur posts, like most of the other commemorative yūpas in stone, differ in being squared at the base, which suggests an important convention, even if it does not seem to be based on the earlier texts.[6] They are also girdled toward the middle by a rope that is tied at one end to form a noose. A second rope hung over the top probably represents one that had been used the previous day for goat sacrifices, which should be removed upward and replaced by a fresh one for the soma pressing (Caland 1924). Otherwise the only serious incongruities with textual prescriptions concern the top rings (*caṣālas*) and the exaggerated "tenon" portions that extend up through them. One top ring is square, the other eight-sided, as is the norm. But neither has the mortarlike (or female waist-like) inward curvature toward the middle that characterizes the caṣāla in the ritual texts. The streamlined stone caṣālas are set at an angle that would allow them, at least in the imagination, to fit over the apparently exaggerated curve and width of the tenons, which are likewise stylized in ways that do not conform to Vedic prototypes: rather than being rounded, they continue the octagonal shape of the shaft, and the cut-off top faces away horizontally rather than upward. A glance at Biardeau's composite drawing of a yūpa from the texts (1989b, 42) shows these contrasts, while the miniature Vedic yūpa preserved at the Vaidika Saṃśodhana Maṇḍala

6. Chhabra 1947, 81. It is not clear on what basis Biardeau speaks of a "roughly squared" ("mal équarrie") base (1988, 106), as shown in her drawing (1988, 108; 1989b, 42) reproduced in figure 4. Cf. Schwab 1886, 8: the bottom part (*uparam*) "remains unworked" ("bleibt unbearbeitet").

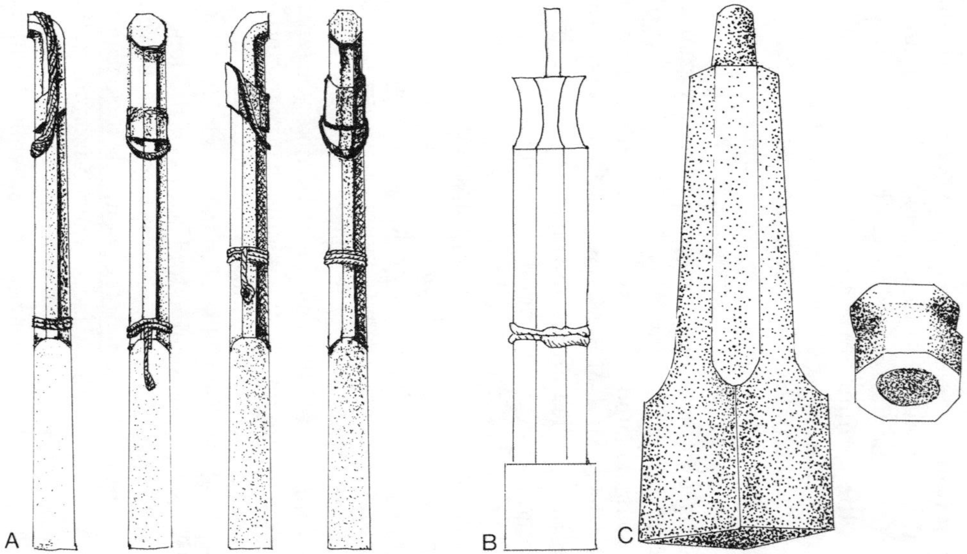

Figure 5. Vedic yūpas: (A) commemorative stone yūpas, Īsāpur (from Vogel 1910–11, plate 23); (B) according to specifications of Vedic texts (from Biardeau 1988, 108, fig. 1; cf. 1989b, fig. 2); (C) miniature wooden yūpa and caṣāla from Vaidika Saṃśodhana Maṇḍala Museum of Vedic sacrificial utensils, Pune (from Dharmadhikari 1989, 70).

museum of Vedic sacrificial utensils in Pune (Dharmadhikari 1989, 70–71) shows how close the current form is to a typical Pōttu Rāja (see fig. 5). According to T. N. Dharmadhikari, most of the Vedic implements at the museum were collected in Andhra Pradesh (personal communication, March 1990).

Pōta Rājus for Andhra village goddesses have what Biardeau takes to be variations on this shape. She considers the ring between the shaft and the top of the Pōta Rāju to be a stylized replica of the inwardly curved caṣāla. And she regards the Pōta Rāju's terminal knob to be an enlargement of the tenon on the end of the yūpa once the caṣāla has been fitted over the tenon's lower portions, so that the knob itself would probably reflect an interpretation of the post as a living being, with the shaft as body, ring as collar, and knob itself as head (1989b, 81–82; 1984a, 15). To this I would add that where the knobs are pointed (they often rise to modulated and even quite elongated points), further possibilities arise. One of these is impalement. The other, most readily suggested when the button rises to a point through an inward drop-like curvature of its own, is the image of a flame, such as one often sees rising from sacrificial altars and from the fronts of demons' diadems, including those of both Pōttu Rāja and Muttāl Rāvuttaṉ (Hiltebeitel 1988a, 120 on the latter). The flame-diadem could figure as a substitute for the head, as well as play on further resonances between the post and fire.

Several of the Draupadī cult posts are interesting from this perspective. The Kalahasti and Tiruvannamalai posts are most suggestive of impalement. The larger Tindivanam post has a nicely indented curvature for its "caṣāla" collar, as Biardeau has noticed (1989b, 121 n. 5), and its upper knob has the flame-drop shape. The Kūttampākkam and Vīrāṇantal posts also have nice rings, though less clearly set off from the other elements above or below them, and in addition they show the three-part segmentation authorized by the Vedic yūpa: square base (at least for the commemorative stone yūpas), octagonal main shaft, and rounded top (as do those at Chengam and Kāppalūr). Moreover, at Kūttampākkam it is not only the stone Pōttu Rāja that is of interest, but also the taller wooden post beside it, called Akkiṉikampam, or "Fire-post." It too is octagonal. Recalling that it was identified as this temple's "true flagstaff," it cannot be insignificant that flagstaffs may also fit these prescriptions. At Karaṭikuṭi (Vellore Taluk, North Arcot), one has the usual configuration of Pōttu Rāja on a slab, balipīṭha, and flagstaff, all set in one base, with the flagstaff on the outside (as the

Brahman said it should be at Kūttampākkam). This is not, however, an ordinary flagstaff, since it has no inward-facing frame. Rather, it is a tall post that is squared at the base, octagonal through the mid-portion, and topped by a ring and a flame-drop knob: in effect, an elongated Pōttu Rāja post. The more ordinary flagstaff at the Cuddalore (Tirupatiripuliyūr) Draupadī temple has a square base and an octagonal shaft. The Mēlaccēri flagstaff is octagonal from top to bottom.

4. *The yūpa, the patron of the sacrifice, or yajamāna, and the Brahmans.* Vedic texts speak of a rapport (especially in terms of height), and posit an identity, between the yūpa and the yajamāna (Biardeau 1989b, 37–38). At Draupadī temples, the fact that the tarumakarttā and chief temple office holders receive kāppu (or an equivalent) at the same time as Pōttu Rāja (whether or not he is honored along with a post or flagstaff ensemble) reflects a similar identification, one that we will have occasion to notice in concrete ritual terms. The Vedic yajamāna is also variously identified with the victim, who substitutes, or serves as a "ransom," for the sacrificer in the other world. The forest-village boundary position of the yūpa also evokes the rapport between the sacrificer and the victim, and the characterization of *human* victims as wild (like the yūpa tree) rather than domesticated animals (Malamoud 1989, 105–6). In the case of Pōttu Rāja, the identification is with a "former victim" and wild animal (the Buffalo Demon) turned devotee (the Buffalo King).

As a "king," Pōttu Rāja retains a royal dimension that is also open to the Vedic sacrificer. Yet the Vedic sacrificer, no matter what his *varṇa*, or caste, may also be a quasi-Brahman. "Not only the king but also the commoner is proclaimed a *brāhmaṇa,* a representative of the *brahmán,* at his consecration for the Soma sacrifice (*dīkṣā*)" (Heesterman 1985, 154). Indeed, as the *Śatapatha Brāhmaṇa* affirms for the Aśvamedha sacrificer, who must necessarily be a Kṣatriya king, "truly whoever sacrifices, sacrifices after becoming, as it were, a Brâhmaṇa" (13.4.1.3 [Eggeling translation (1882) 1966, 5:348]; Malamoud 1989, 40). Similarly, the king is addressed as *brahmán* in the Rājasūya sacrifice (Heesterman 1985, 151–52).

Pōttu Rāja is also a quasi-Brahman no less than a quasi-king. Indeed, he is often explicitly identified as a Brahman, in both the Draupadī cult (see Appendix, n. 17) and the Telugu *Epic of Palnāḍu* (Hiltebeitel 1988a, 79, 83, 347–48, 353–54, 377, 391). For present purposes, this Brahman status signifies that even if Brahmans do not participate in the rites, specifically those that concern posts and fires (which, as we have seen, may also invite distinctions in the ways that Draupadī temples perform their "nine grains" sprouting rites), Pōttu Rāju can substitute for the Brahmans as a "Brahman-king," or even as a Brahman-Untouchable. As we have seen, Brahmans are normally absent from village buffalo sacrifices in Andhra and are irregular at Draupadī cult flag-hoisting (and sprouting) rites, so this service is not insignificant. Incongruous as it may seem, Pōttu Rāja in effect makes—or better, keeps—the rites "Brahmanic." In fact, Pōttu Rāja's proverbially vast appetite, and the feeding of either his icons (as at Draupadī temples) or his ritual impersonators (as, for instance, at the festival of the heroes of Palnāḍu, in Andhra[7]), seems to be nothing but an ironic—indeed possibly self-consciously ironic—solution to the injunction that falls upon royal patrons of great festivals like Dasarā (which I regard as the Brahmanical counterpart to these hero cult festivals) to provide vast quantities of food to vast numbers of Brahmans.[8] Whatever limited functions they may perform at village and regional festivals, real Brahmans will not accept food from such festivals' Śūdra patrons. So Pōttu Rāja, in his various guises, stands in the Brahmans' stead and registers the ambiguity of his status in the food that he accepts: a menu that runs the gamut from the vegetarian fare offered to his icons facing into Draupadī's temples to the decisively nonvegetarian predilection for goat (or rooster) that he displays in some Draupadī cult dramas and extra-core area festivals.[9]

It may be added that it is precisely in such areas as these that the Orissa Research Project has turned its evidence inside out. That Brahmans are brought in to perform a fire sacrifice as part of the consecration of newly installed posts for the goddess is not—even in Khond (tribal) villages—"a first decisive step of Hinduization" of originally tribal posts (Eschmann 1978c, 270), but an indication that the post-fire combination would not be there at all were it not for the Vedic-Brahmanical-Hindu heritage. The nerve center for the carryover of such post traditions in Orissa is again the Brahmanical

7. Velcheru Narayana Rao indicates that it is a routinized function of the impersonators of Pōta Rāju at the Palnad Heroes' Festival to receive repeated food offerings (personal communication, November 1987). On Pōta Rāju's hunger in various myths and cults, see also Hiltebeitel 1988a, 344–66 and plate 25.

8. See Waghorne 1989, 411, and Radhakrishna Aiyar 1917, 178, on the daily feeding during Dasarā at Pudukkottai of "a large number of Brahmans."

9. See chapter 5, section D, nn. 36, 37. At Maṅkalam, where Pōtta Rāja is a vegetarian at two Draupadī temples, he receives meat curries and goat sacrifices as guardian of three village goddesses (Hiltebeitel 1988a, 366).

fall festival of Dasarā (Vijayādaśamī) or Durgāpūjā, at which the posts are used in connection with goat and sometimes buffalo sacrifices.[10]

At this point, in fact, the Orissa materials point us toward the solution of a problem raised at the end of the previous chapter about the relative prominence of posts in Dharmarāja and Draupadī temples and the status of the "divine" yajamāna of the sanctum. Outside goddess temples in Orissa, one finds posts of the same shape as in Andhra and among Draupadī cult Pōta Rājus. But a common type of Orissan post represents the goddess herself. Similarly, in Tamilnadu we have found such female posts outside Māriyammaṉ temples, and in the same North Arcot area of concentration as the Pōttu Rāja posts outside Dharmarāja temples. The Orissan posts are called Stambheśvarī (Sanskrit) or Khambheśvarī (Oriya), "Lady" or "Goddess of the Post." This goddess, and presumably her form as a post, begins her career as the tutelary divinity of two successive dynasties: the Śūlkīs in the sixth century, and the Bhañjas in the ninth. Like royal and dominant landed caste kuladevīs elsewhere, she is clearly a form of Durgā, and not an "autochthonous" (Kulke 1978, 130), "totemic" (Nandi 1973, 121–22), or "tribal" goddess (Eschmann 1978c, 267; Majumdar 1911, 446).[11] In current worship, the post goddess in front of the temple is sometimes regarded as the nonvegetarian sister of the goddess inside the sanctum, who is often identified as Durgā herself. She thus receives animal sacrifices, while the purer sister remains behind the sanctum's closed doors (Eschmann 1978a, 89; 1978c, 278).

10. I rely on Eschmann 1978a, 85, 93, 96; 1978c, 270–73, 276–78, 281–82; cf. Kulke 1978, 130–31; Majumdar 1911, 445, for information on Dasarā, but disagree with their conclusions. See specially Eschmann 1978c: it is "impossible" to assume penetration "from above" (266); similarly, Dumāls must be of tribal origin "because they worship posts as the Khonds do" (ibid., 271). Archer's study of the post-deity Bir Kuar also deserves examination from this angle: his wooden posts are made by carpenters of mixed Ahir (herder)-Brahman descent (1947, 82–85). Unlike landed dominant castes, whose post-deities face into goddess temples, the unlanded Ahir set them in open fields, to fertilize she-buffaloes (ibid., 25, 37). Bir Kuar's myth involves oppositions between the tiger and buffalo, and themes of impalement (ibid., 49–81); he has a Muslim attendant and dog (ibid., 35); and he receives goat sacrifices and votive clay horses (ibid., 36–45). His caṣāla-type collars are striking in plates 37 and 40; cf. Shah's (1985) treatment of Rathwa "tribal" memorial posts, and Haekel's presentation of the Rathwa sprouting rites—similarly part of a clear Dasarā complex; see chapter 4, n. 13.

11. Cf. Eschmann 1978a, 86 (one can hardly agree that her name "expresses the difficulty of Hindu mythology in naming her"), 94; Eschmann, Kulke, and Tripathi 1978b, 176. Eschmann 1978c, 266 admits that her argument is weak for the Saoras and must turn to the problematic Khonds.

Or one red wood (*rohiṇī*) post, worshiped by Brahmans, may represent Parameśvarī, the Supreme Goddess, while Khambheśvarī is worshiped as a black post by low-status Dumāls (Majumdar 1911, 445–46; cf. n. 9).

What has not been emphasized in connection with Khambheśvarī, however, is that as a post-female she is in some cases immediately complemented by post-males. According to Kulke, all the kings of the Śūlkī dynasty "combined their names with that of their tutelary deity," resulting in names like Raṇastambha ("Battle-Post") and Kulastambha ("Lineage-Post") (1978, 130; cf. Majumdar 1911, 443–44). The king identifies with the "Lady of the post" as her male counterpart; each is a multiform of the yūpa, her sphere being the buffalo sacrifice, his the sacrifice of battle. Equally interesting is the local legend of the Khambheśvarī temple at Aska (Ganjam District, near the Andhra border):

> In the forest there lived a *ṛṣi* or sage named Khambhamuni [the "Post-Sage"]. "Khambheśvarī appeared to him in a dream and expressed the desire to be worshiped by him. He agreed on the condition that she should live as a daughter in his house, which she did." But people soon had "suspicions about an old man living with a beautiful girl." At first he "refused to put things right," but finally disclosed her true divine nature, which she confirmed by miraculously escaping the people. Thereafter, however, "she played mischief" on Khambhamuni, testing and frightening him until he slapped her face in annoyance. She then announced that her "childhood play" was over, "that the old man would die, and that she would be worshiped on the spot by one of his sons," whose descendants "are not Brahmans" but "call themselves *śūdra munis*." (Eschmann 1978a, 93; summarized except where quoted)

The photograph showing a stone Khambheśvarī post outside this Aska temple also shows a wooden post "presiding over the sacrificial pit" (ibid., 94 and plate 63). Is this another Khambheśvarī, or is it Khambhamuni? The hint of an improper relation between the virgin goddess and this post-muni ancestor of "Śūdra muni" priests is, in any case, a variation on several themes that surface equally in the Telugu and Tamil mythologies of Pōta Rāju. One is the suggestion of an improper sexual relation, akin to the goddess's rapport with the buffalo and variously worked out in mythologies of combat, seduction, marriage, and caste and kinship strategies that rule out marriage (here the false father-daughter one) between the goddess and her male counterparts. Another is the mixed caste, and essentially "false Brahman," status of Khambhamuni and his descendants, for *muni* does indeed imply a Brahman, as when it is used for Pōttu Rāja (Hiltebeitel 1988a, 79), and especially, at least in Tamilnadu, when it refers to the type of powerful forest-based Brahman "sages" who often act as Brahmarākṣasas.[12] Like Pōttu Rāja with Draupadī, Khambhamuni is thus a quasi-Brahman who is instrumental in establishing the local worship of a royal lineage goddess. But what is most significant for now is that Khambheśvarī's role as sacrificer is mitigated through this post-muni's descendants, her priests, just as the earlier Stambheśvarī's sacrificial functions were mediated in battle by the king.

These Orissan strains allow us to get a better sense of the variations we have noted in the relative prominence of posts for Pōttu Rāja in Dharmarāja and Draupadī temples. If the ultimate sacrificer in the sanctum is Dharmarāja, what has been said so far makes perfect sense. Dharma is himself a king with a famous "Brahman complex" whose wooden processional icon—if he has one—tours Tamil villages at Draupadī festival time in his Brahman disguise (see chap. 3). Indeed, his disguise as the "Heron-Brahman," the eater of flesh, has behind it the mythology of the Brahmarākṣasa.[13]

Where Draupadī is the mūlavar in the sanctum, however, the post seems less common and, even where one finds it, less conspicuous. Pōttu Rāja, usually represented in bas-relief, has more the status of Draupadī's stand-in or substitute in handling the violent dimensions of the sacrifice. Still, Draupadī is the sacrificer. The eighteen-day war, and the Pāratam festival that enacts its sacrifice of battle, is by and for her (Hiltebeitel 1988a, 5 and n. 2). Similarly, in Durgā's combat with the Buffalo Demon, the goddess is the real royal patron of her own "sacrifice of battle," or better, "great fes-

12. On these complex figures, see Hiltebeitel 1988a, 178–79, 377–79; on the range of mythic options for relating the goddess and buffalo, see ibid., 266–77, 348–49 and n. 17: especially the "outraged Brāhmaṇī" myth that tells how in their former lives the goddess had been a Brahman woman and the buffalo an Untouchable who deceived her into marrying him—the only case in which they have sexual relations, but still deflected, to a former life. Cf. chapter 5, section C on the marriage between the three-pronged post and pot in Kongunad Māriyammaṉ festivals. On muṉi-Brahmarākṣasas, see Hiltebeitel 1988a, 179–80, on Baka as the Muṉi from Maṅkalam. See also Shulman 1980b; Biardeau 1967–68.

13. Baka, the typical Brahmarākṣasa, is the "Crane"; see chapter 3, n. 25. Note also that both Dharma and Pōttu Rāja have affinities with Yama, the former being his son (see chap. 3), the latter through common associations with death and through their different connections with the buffalo. Pulavar Keeran, who lectures on the purāṇas and *Mahābhārata* to urban Tamil audiences, simply identified Pōtta Rāja as Yama (personal interview, June 1975).

tival of battle" (*yuddhamahotsava; DM* 2.55).[14] The sacrifice of battle requires two yajamānas, each sharing with his or her opponent the possibility of becoming a victim (Biardeau and Péterfalvi 1986, 66; Hiltebeitel 1988a, 395–96, with further citations). Indeed, it is Durgā who must be the royal sacrificer because the gods have defaulted from this status, leaving Mahiṣāsura alone to rule the triple world and have jurisdiction (*adhikārān; DM* 2.6) over the sacrifice and its shares.[15] From the angle of Draupadī, which is the most pervasive angle in the Draupadī cult, the situation is very similar. And let us note that the pervasiveness of her angle will become clearest when we move to the rituals beyond the temple, where Pōttu Rāja's primary rapport is unmistakably with her. The myths are also told from this angle, and help to define it through their two cycles. In the Pōrmaṉṉaṉ cycle, the Pāṇḍavas have defaulted. The Kauravas, Draupadī's enemies, are in charge. The sacrifice of battle is up to her, and she must have her own special guardian, Pōrmaṉṉaṉ the "Battle King" (compare Raṇastambha, the "Battle-Post"), a multiform of the yūpa, as her marshal. Or in the cycle of the Pāṇḍavas' heir Cunītaṉ, the dispossessed king of Gingee, Draupadī stands in for this defaulted king herself, making her sacrificer function literal by serving as executioner of the hundred-headed Acalammācuraṉ. But she still requires the services of Pōttu Rāja, who must hold the last of the hundred heads lest it fall to the ground.[16]

This last account introduces a theme that can round out the present discussion. Should Pōttu Rāja drop the head, Draupadī would become not the victor in her sacrifice of battle but its victim. Whether it is Vedic ceremonial or the ritual of battle, the sacrifice requires an identity between the yajamāna and the victim, and the post is the point of mediation between the two. But the notion of the goddess as victim is only a latent possibility in the iconographies and mythologies cited so far. It has, however, one rich and striking development in the iconography of *satī* stones, the cenotaphs that commemorate suttees, or women who immolate themselves on their husband's cremation pyre. These sometimes show the suttee in relief in the form of a yūpa-type post, with only one human feature. Her right arm, with bangles, comes out horizon-

14. Both terms are used in this text. The gods use the term "great festival of battle" in lauding the goddess for her defeat of Mahiṣa. "Sacrifice of battle" (*yuddhayajña*) is used to describe the goddess's fight with Caṇḍa and Munda (7.24). The festival (*utsava*) is explicitly the nine-night fall festival that has become Navarātri (12.10–13).

15. The Śumbha-Niśumbha sequel in the *Devī Māhātmyam* makes this equally clear (5.1–5).

16. On the two cycles, see chapter 5, n. 43, and below, Appendix.

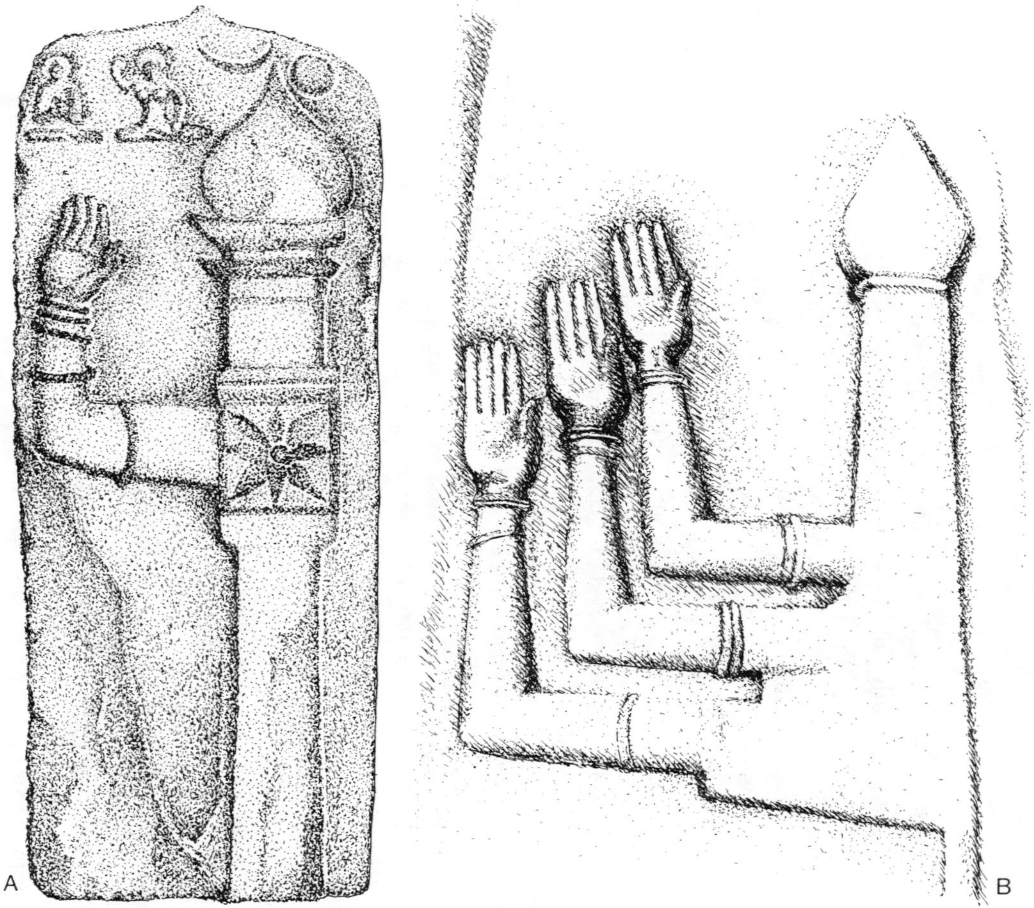

Figure 6. Bangle-armed posts on Satī stones: (A) Madras Government Museum; (B) Kandār, Maharashtra (from Settar and Sontheimer 1982, fig. 36).

tally from the right side of the post and is bent at the elbow so that, as her forearm rises vertically, she raises her right hand in a sign of fearlessness or benediction.[17] Above the post, the husband and wife may be shown reunited in heaven (see fig. 6). Satī is preeminently the goddess as victim, and suttees share her suffering. But why are suttees represented by a multiform of the yūpa? Let us recall that Satī, their prototype, enters her father Dakṣa's sacrificial fire because he does not recognize her husband, Śiva. Indeed, like Mahiṣāsura with Indra, Dakṣa rules Śiva out of a share in the sacrifice. Like the virgin and unmarried Durgā, then, Satī must be her own sacrificer. But unlike Durgā, Satī is the sacrificer as victim. She is without a male (king or husband) to sacrifice with and for her. In her wake, suttees, likewise without living husbands (often warriors who have ideally died in battle), are also their own sacrificers. Or, more precisely, the satī, as the sole survivor of the marital couple, enters the fire as joint sacrificer and joins the body of her husband in death as the cremation fire transforms each of them into an oblation (cf. Malamoud 1989, 60). Fittingly, the post thus represents her as sacrificer-victim; it is her bangled arm that rises from it, a symbol of marriage uninterrupted by death. Indeed, she becomes the post that implicitly faces the cremation fire, the fire of her own suttee, or self-offering. Insofar as the post mediates between her status as sacrificer and victim, and perhaps also because the post comes—as we shall see—to be associated with the containment or prevention of pain, particularly fiery pain, it attenuates her suffering and transforms it, and her, into an image of triumph and heavenly reunion with her husband. Not surprisingly, the knob on top often has the flame-drop shape, rising, as does the suttee, like a flame from an altar: a proposition that requires that the post, altar, and flame can be joined, ascendingly, in one body.[18]

17. On the raised hand, I follow Chidanandamurti 1982, 129, and Sontheimer 1982, 277–81, who agree, however, that the pillar's symbolism is yet to be explained. The bangles imply that she is still married and not a widow (cf. chap. 4, sec. A). Cf. Chidanandamurti 117–18: a Kannada satī story like Khambhamuni's and others involving improper sexual relations and personified posts and stones.

18. The flame-drop is most pronounced in the Madras Museum suttee stone, shown in figure 6. Many show no post, only the bent arm with raised hand; others show the hand on a vertical post. See the plates in Settar and Sontheimer 1982. The Lalgudi Vīrapattiraṉ post also shows the sun and moon, which may retain some trace of a connection between Vīrapattiraṉ and the post in the suttee of Satī. Recall also the connections between Cuṭalai Māṭaṉ, fire, and the post at cremation grounds (chap. 5, sec. C).

5. *Male-female symbolism.* A post that can be male or female must have a certain bisexuality. The relation between the caṣāla and the tenon-peg that passes through it at the top of the yūpa has, among other things, a sexual aspect. The caṣāla, which must come from the portion of the tree immediately above the top of the part that forms the yūpa, is repeatedly "imagined like a tree carrying fruits" which are to yield benefit in the form of the fruits of the sacrifice (Biardeau 1989b, 43–44; 1988, 108). An image of fecundity, it is thus also compared to the earth, and, with its inward curve, it has the now-familiar female waist–like shape of the vedi. Biardeau suggests that in relation to the yūpa and the tenon that extends through it, the caṣāla seems to be a figure of the female sexual organ, and thus of the wife of the sacrificer in conjunction with him, the latter as represented by the yūpa shaft and tenon (1988, 106–10; 1989b, 44). The yūpa and caṣāla together thus stand for the sacrificer and his wife: the "pair of lords" (*dampati*) that is indispensable for sacrifice, which is, as we have seen, oriented toward obtaining the fruits of desire. And insofar as the caṣāla and tenon have also been taken to evoke the mortar and pestle, Biardeau remarks that this fecundity is one that is brought about through sacrificial death and destruction (1988, 105, 108).

It has sometimes been proposed that the yūpa is thus phallic (Thite 1975, 137; J. J. Meyer 1937, 3 : 193–94). In the same vein, Bruce Tapper says that Pōta Rāju posts are "clearly phallic" and adds: "The overt use of a phallic form to represent the male figure suggests that the diamond-shape of a corresponding female figure is similarly an allusion to the female genitals" (1987, 175). What might strike us equally now is that the shape of the female figure in question looks to be an elongated replica of the ring (which Biardeau takes to be the stylization of the caṣāla) below the top of the corresponding Pōta Rāju (see fig. 7). In any case, it is true no less for Pōta Rāju than for the Vedic yūpa that it is an interpretative mistake to put the penis before the post, or sexuality before sacrifice. As Biardeau has further observed, there are reasons to think, at least as soon as we get to classical representations of the liṅgam and the yoni, that the liṅgam has been modeled on the yūpa. Especially in the case of votive liṅgams outside the garbhagṛha, the yoni pedestal has the same inward curvature as the tapered caṣāla. And the liṅgam has the same tripartite structure as the yūpa: four-sided at the base (identified with Brahmā), eight-sided in the midportion (identified with Viṣṇu), over which the yoni fits, and rounded at the top (identified with Śiva) (Biardeau 1981c, 111; 1988,

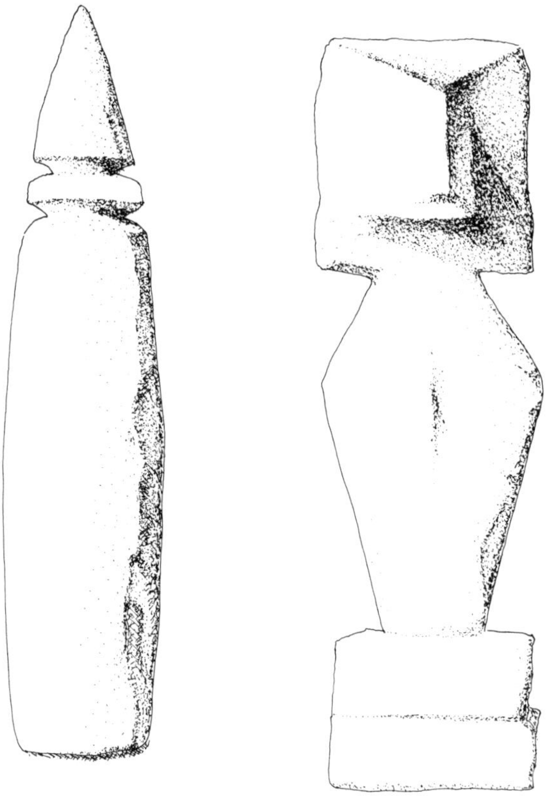

Figure 7. Portable icons of Pōta Rāju and local goddess Bandamma, Andhra Pradesh (detail from Tapper 1987, plate 8).

100–104, 109).[19] The visible rounded portion of the liṅgam thus has an affinity with the portion of the tenon-peg that extends beyond the caṣāla, which the Vedic texts identify with the highest heavenly realm.

In this light, how predictable it is that we should frequently find Draupadī cult images and myths portraying Pōttu Rāja, the erstwhile stake, carrying the liṅgam, or the liṅgam and yoni, on

19. Cf. discussion and illustrations in Snodgrass 1985, 322; Janaki 1988, fig. 10. Mitterwallner 1984, 21–22, 25–26 dates the fully developed tripartite liṅgas from the fifth century A.D. and *liṅgapīṭhas* (yonis) with recessed middle layers from the fourth to the sixth century. The principles behind these forms, however, produced related variations before this. The back-to-back articles of Mitterwallner and D. M. Srinivasan (1984) on early (including pre-Kuṣāna) liṅgams and the development of liṅ-

his head (see plate 8).[20] Indeed, Pōttu Rāja may be represented by liṅgam-like cones, as at Aṉṉūr. Nor is it surprising that, insofar as Vīrapattiraṉ is a substitute for Pōttu Rāja and a manifestation of Śiva himself, he should often be reduced to the shape of a liṅgam. Indeed, the liṅgam on Pōttu Rāja's head has its formal equivalent in the crownlike knob on the anthropomorphic face of the Lalgudi post-Vīrapattiraṉ (see fig. 4). In Pōttu Rāja's case, by analogy, it seems that the base of the post becomes, or corresponds to, the human form of Pōttu Rāja, while the ring and knob, alias the caṣāla and tenon, extend beyond this body-base and are transformed into the yoni and liṅgam. Furthermore, if the yoni corresponds to the caṣāla as altar (a connection that will follow shortly), the liṅgam corresponds to the flame that rises from it. One thus has another evocation of the combination of post and fire.

It should also not be surprising that the Tamil Śaiva Siddhānta tradition supplies a schema for the layout of a temple in which "the god's innermost sanctum corresponds to a human head, while the flagpole and *palipītam* [balipīṭha] are likened to the body's genital area" (Beck 1981a, 120).[21] Even more explicitly, the flagstaff and balipīṭha are liṅgams, two of five liṅgams—the *dhvaja liṅga,* or "flag liṅgam," and *bhadra liṅga,* or "prosperous liṅgam," respectively—that are found in every Tamil Śaivite temple, the other liṅgams being the one in the sanctum (which delegates its power to the rest), the *vimāna* tower (*stūpa liṅga*) that rises over the sanctum (recall the post called Stūpi at the Forest Draupadī temple in Tiruvannamalai), and the sacrificer or officiating priest.[22] Moreover, the flagstaff can have the same three-part division as the principal liṅgam: either all above ground, as at Karaṭikuṭi, or with the top representing Rudra, the middle Viṣṇu, and the interred base Brahmā (Reiniche 1979, 94). This "native" connection between the liṅgam

---

gam iconography could be reexamined from this perspective. Rings around the glans penis of early liṅgams receive little comment; see especially the eight-sided ring in plate 19 and the indentedness of the wreathlike ring in plate 2. The caṣāla could help to explain both, as well as the phenomenon of the rings more generally. See also the early liṅgam-altar (vedi) combinations in plates 4, 20, and 26.

20. See also Hiltebeitel 1988a, 82–83, 344, 380–82, 390 and plates 19 (the liṅgam and yoni are there in black, but very small), 26, and 27. Alternatively, the slab Pōttu Rāja at Villupuram is set in a yoni-shaped drainage stone (with the channel to the north as it should be), as if the anthropomorphic Pōttu Rāja were a liṅgam himself.

21. Cf. Beck 1976, 239–40, Vanmikanathan 1971, 117–21, and Curtis 1973, 32–34. Beck shows Bhairava in the northeast position of Śiva's left hand, which Śiva-Bhairava uses to hold the head of Brahmā.

22. Cf. Janaki 1988, 127–29: mūlavar as *sūkṣma liṅgam; vimāna* as *sthūla liṅgam;* balipīṭha as bhadra liṅgam; flagstaff as kāraṇa liṅgam.

and the flagstaff thus has behind it, whether consciously or not, the symbolism of the yūpa. And though this Śaivite tradition identifies both the flagstaff and balipīṭha as liṅgams, the former, if one may say so, is more of a liṅgam, and likewise more yūpa-like, then the latter. This brings us back to the flagstaff ensemble.

6. *Altars.* What is a balipīṭha? Everyone is in agreement that it is an "altar of offering." In vegetarian temples it will receive only flowers or sometimes cooked rice. But at temples that hold festivals with animal sacrifices, the balipīṭha, if there is one, may receive, for instance, the head of a goat (Brenda Beck, personal communication, 1989). Indeed, in an eleventh- or twelfth-century Tamil war poem, it receives the offering of a human head to Kālī (Nagaswamy 1982, 26). Balipīṭhas are found at temples for all bhakti deities. Most small temples have only one, but in temples that have more than one, the principal one (or ones) will be outside the entrance. At Avalūrpēṭṭai (Tiruvannamalai Taluk, North Arcot), Draupadī's temple has one at each corner, and each receives a pumpkin offering at the festival. Some larger Brahmanical temples will have them in the eight directions, "where attack by evil spirits and other malevolent agencies is thought to pose a serious threat" (Fuller 1987, 29, 30–31; cf. Ramachandra Rao 1979, 99).

No one, however, seems to have offered much on the balipīṭha's shape. Let us, at least initially, leave variations aside. The usual balipīṭha has first a stone or masonry platform topped by a lotiform altar, technically the *padmapīṭha,* or "lotus altar." The latter, the most distinctive feature, is normally of stone and has three components: a square base, a section like an upside-down cup with lotiform markings that widen downward toward the base and then curl outward and upward from the base in the form of eight petals, and a round and flattened stumplike top (see fig. 8). With its square base, eight-sided middle, and rounded top, it is easy to see how it can be identified as a liṅgam. But it is of course too squat and wide-bottomed to be a very convincing liṅgam.

That the balipīṭha can be called a bhadra liṅga, or "prosperous liṅgam," supplies a helpful consideration. The lotiform shape is the symbol of prosperity. The balipīṭha looks like a lotus with a severed stem placed upside down on a square base. But it still complements the three-part structure of the liṅgam-flagstaff. The connection between the square base and Brahmā evokes Brahmā's creative birth from the lotus. The flattened round top is a reduction of the top of the liṅgam, connected with Śiva, to a surface required for an "altar." And the midsection is still oriented to the eight

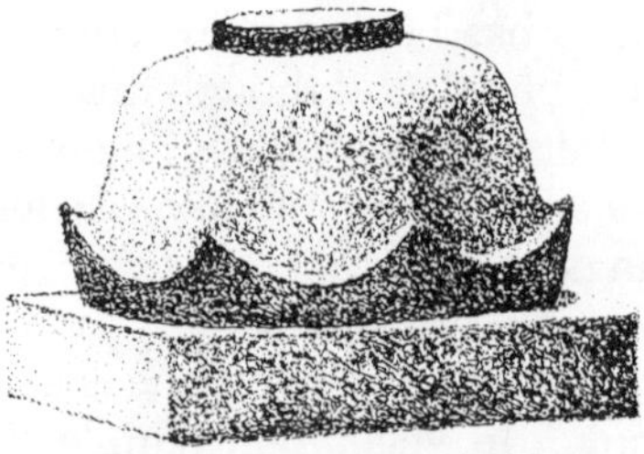

Figure 8. Typical balipīṭha, Tailāpuram Draupadī temple.

directions. But here is where the major difference lies. Instead of this eight-sided section, identified with Viṣṇu, being a symbol of Viṣṇu's royal sovereignty over space, it is more readily identified, through the lotus, with his feminine complement, Śrī-Lakṣmī, goddess of good fortune and prosperity. Whether separate or united, the two imply each other: the domain of sacrifice is the domain of royally ordered prosperity. The distinguishing characteristic of the balipīṭha is its evocation of the feminine.

As with the liṅgam itself, however, it is possible to look beyond such essentially āgamic and purāṇic symbolism, which can only help account for the form as it has become standardized, to Vedic forms involving the yūpa and their popular transformations. Indeed, noting that the balipīṭha marks the outer limit of a temple and that "flesh mixed with turmeric powder" is among the offerings it receives in "some canonical texts," S. K. Ramachandra Rao remarks: "Perhaps, it is a remnant of the Vedic *yupa,* and in many temples we do find *bali-pithas* which are merely crude stone blocks or wooden posts" (1979, 100). The Bow Song tradition of Tirunelveli District provides a fascinating case in point, except that the posts in question are of clay or brick. The so-called *pītam*s (pīṭhas) that serve as the main icons in open-air "temples" for the quasi-demonic "cut-up" deities of this tradition are like the obelisk-shaped posts for Cuṭalai Māṭaṉ, from the same district. But the Bow Song deities' posts are obelisks that rise to a squared-off platform that is then topped by a gently pointed "head" or "flame-drop" button (Blackburn 1988, plates 2 and 3, 37–38). Here the [bali-]pīṭha and the popular yūpa forms are fused. Though the icon has the profile of a post, it is probably called a pītam because it is the form through which the deity receives offerings. Instead of being outside the shrine as a guardian deity, it is the shrine.

The balipīṭha's affinities with the yūpa are, however, usually more positional and functional than formal. Fuller indicates that the balipīṭha is "situated at the boundary" between two "zones":

one inside the temple, characterized by purity and bhakti, and one outside, characterized by sacrificial activity (1987, 30). This could also apply—minus bhakti—to the yūpa's boundary position in separating animal sacrifice from the purer activities within the mahāvedi. In terms of form, however, one may gain some insight by turning to the rapport between the yūpa and the Vedic sacrificial altars.

As we have seen, the yūpa is aligned with three altars: the hourglass-shaped vedi, the trapezoidal mahāvedi (tapered toward the yūpa), and, closest to the yūpa, the square uttaravedi. It seems that the classical form of the balipīṭha results from trying out and combining all three shapes. Instead of being laid out horizontally on the ground like the vedi and mahāvedi, however, the balipīṭha incorporates these shapes into a vertical form. As with the pālikai pots, discussed in chapter 4, which transform the hourglass shape of the vedi into a vertical three-dimensional form to serve as the altars for seedlings, the balipīṭha seems to be another vertical transposition of the forms of Vedic altars. In this case, however, it combines all three altars. The verticality is already present in the uttaravedi, whose square form is further built into the balipīṭha's platform and base. The whole profile, often with ascending, narrowing gradations built into the platform up to the still narrower base, and rising via the upside-down lotus to the flat-topped stump, can approximate a flat-topped pyramid: that is, it can be trapezoidal in outline, like the mahāvedi. Or alternatively, though the term is used rather freely to describe platforms with recessed middles or "necks" (*kaṇṭhas*) between extended moldings, the platform may have an "hourglass" shape (H. Sarkar 1978, 93–96, 174; Harle 1986, 347), as in monumental raised balipīṭhas in Kerala that have their prototypes in early Pallava ones of Tamilnadu (H. Sarkar 1978, figs. 16, 17, 35).

Here we must recognize that the considerations that led to the design of the balipīṭha are also related to those that led to the hourglass shape of the yoni pedastal, which was itself called both a vedi and a pīṭha in early descriptions (Mitterwallner 1984, n. 81).[23] As with the pālikai seedling pots, the yoni pedestal and the balipīṭha seem to present us with another set of complementary moves, each involving additional modifications of the already upright form of the caṣāla, itself a formal complement of the vedi, into practical modifications for temple use of the Vedic altars. The liṅgam and

23. Cf. Biardeau 1988, 101–2 and photo 5.

yoni would thus represent these elements in union, and the flagstaff and balipīṭha would represent them separated, parceled out, with the balipīṭha in particular halved and truncated.

7. *Pointed yūpas.* As a symbol of death and killing, the yūpa is identified with the *vajra,* the ultimate weapon of the Vedic texts. "The sacrificial post is shaped like a wooden sword; the wooden sword is a thunderbolt" (*TS* 2.1.5.7ff.; Keith 1914, 1:139ff.). The post is also one of the vajra's multiforms. When Indra smote Vṛtra, the vajra became fourfold: the wooden sword (*sphya*) used to mark off the sacrificial terrain, the yūpa, the chariot, and the arrow. The passage, moreover, is interesting for the parallelism it draws between sacrifice and battle: "In consequence of this, the priests make use of two (of these pieces) at the sacrifice, and men of the military caste (*rājanyabandhu*) also make use of two of them in battle: viz. the priests make use of the sacrificial post and the wooden sword, and the men of the military caste [make use of] the chariot and the arrow (*śara*)" (*SB* 1.2.4.1–2; Eggeling [1882] 1966, 1:52; cf. Thite 1975, 133). Among these implements, at least two, the arrow and the wooden sword, are pointed and will be mentioned again. Indeed, we shall see that chariots can also be pointed. The yūpa's identification with the vajra is itself an evocation of impalement, in the general sense of piercing, which, I will argue, is sometimes to be distinguished from the function of cutting, with its sacrificial overtones of dismemberment. The vajra evidently has both resonances, being "thousand-spiked" and "hundred-edged" (*ŚB* 1.2.4.6).

Now ordinarily, a Vedic yūpa should be level at the top of its tenon. According to *Ṣaḍviṃśa Brāhmaṇa* 4.4.7, it should not be pointed (*śūla;* Thite 1975, 135; Bollée 1956, 98). But what is the use of having such injunctions if there are not to be exceptions? According to the same Brāhmaṇa, there is a sacrifice called Śyena, or Falcon, in which the yūpa should either be without a caṣāla or have a point like a sword (*sphya,* as above; *ṢaḍB* 3.8.16; Thite 1975, 134; Bollée 1956, 81). It is of a general type that can be called *abhicāra,* referring to what some have termed magic rather than religion, but that has agonistic elements that others have regarded as an archaic feature of Vedic religion. Such rites, which may be parts or modifications of larger well-known ceremonies or consist of contests between rival priests or yajamānas, involve sacrificing for the sake of defeating, and ultimately killing, a rival or an enemy (Thite 1975, 175–79). Of a number of these described in the *Ṣaḍviṃśa Brāhmaṇa,* Śyena, named after the swift falcon that catches its prey, is the most prominent. Apparently evoking the Agnicayana, in which the mahāvedi is shaped as a śyena bird that takes the sacrificer to heaven, numerous details of the Śyena represent symbolic means to attain victory over an enemy on earth.[24] The *havirdhāna* carts, on which the soma is placed the day before its pressing, become two-wheeled chariots hurled like a thunderbolt (which, as we have seen, is already pointed) against the rival (Thite 1975, 177).[25] The sacrificial grass should consist of reeds (*śara,* which also means arrow, as above) for hurting (*śīrtyai*) the rival. The animals dedicated to Agni Rudravat should be red. The priests should wear red clothes and red turbans, and their sacrificial threads should be around their necks rather than over their shoulders (*ṢaḍB* 3.8.18, 20, 22; Bollée 1956, 82–83; Thite 1975, 177–78). Furthermore, if the Agnicayana's *śyenaciti* (the falcon-shaped altar of bricks) provides the model (see n. 24), the pointed (*śūla*) yūpa would presumably be at the falcon's beak: the farthest eastward boundary point on the altar and (since the talons are not represented) the foremost point of attack.

The *Ṣaḍviṃśa* is no doubt late among Brāhmaṇas, but it is still a facet of the Vedic revelation. To put matters simply, the unusual pointed yūpa is really part of a cogent opposition within the Vedic sacrifice.[26] The regular unpointed yūpa is suitable for ordinary sacrifices, in which violence, particularly cutting and impalement, is carried out and represented away from the yūpa, and only in muted and sacrificially self-contained forms. But pointed, the yūpa becomes a symbol (though still not a means) of impalement. It is designed for representations of a sacrifice directed against a rival who may also have such means at his disposal—a rival, moreover, whom one may meet not in one's own self-contained sacrificial ter-

24. See Parpola 1983, 47–48; 1988, 252. The Śyena sacrifice seems to evoke the Agnicayana's śyena-shaped brick fire altar (*śyenaciti*) without actually involving the construction of such an altar.
25. This detail, cited by Thite, is not mentioned in Bollée's translation of the *Ṣaḍviṃśa*.
26. Note also that the yūpa "pointed downward" is a ritual means by which the gods seek to keep humans from attaining heaven (*AB* 2.1; Lévi 1966, 85; Malamoud 1989, 248): another "agonistic" myth with magical overtones. I do not follow Heesterman's notion that agonistic elements of the Vedic sacrifice are perforce "preclassical." This is a selective backward projection of agonistic elements that form *part* of the "classical" Brahmanic sacrifice. See Trautmann's excellent review (1988, 682–83) of Heesterman 1985, observing: "The pre-classical sacrifice is not directly known; it must be inferred"; note also the criticism of Heesterman's lack of interest in Indo-European continuities and his loyalty to Held 1935, which may affect his views of the *Mahābhārata* and agonistic themes.

rain, where violence can be muted, but on a mutual site of contention—a battlefield, magical or otherwise—where violence and bloodshed are not only inevitable but desired. In other words, the pointed yūpa directs one toward a type of sacrifice that goes on beyond the regular sacrificial altars. The *Ṣaḍviṃśa Brāhmaṇa* goes on to name a variety of sacrifices similar to the Śyena: the Arrow (*Iṣu*), Tongs (*Saṃdaṃśa*), and Thunderbolt (*Vajra*), each with its special mode of attack (3.9.7–3.11.8; Bollée 1956, 85–89; Thite 1975, 178–79). Needless to say, we have a model here for the sacrifice of battle. Indeed, Rāvaṇa's son Indrajit provides a vivid epic example of the use of such abhicāra rites in preparation for battle in the *Rāmāyaṇa*.[27] As for the *Mahābhārata*, it is no accident that one of the decisive functions of the marshals (*senāpati*s) in the war is to make daily determinations as to what battle array will best counter the formation of the enemy (Singh 1965, 147–48). Among these, the Śyena array is chosen by the Pāṇḍavas, with Bhīma in the beak, to overcome the *makara* (sea monster, crocodile) formation chosen by Kauravas on the fifth day of the war (*Mbh.* 6.65.4–8).

Now Kurukṣetra, the *Mahābhārata*'s battlefield, is called the vedi, or even the uttaravedi—the altar, or high altar, of the gods (e.g. *Mbh.* 3.81.177–78; 129.22). The *Mahābhārata* war is itself conceived of as a "sacrifice of battle" or "sacrifice of weapons" that is performed upon this altar, with the two sides rivaling each other as sacrificers, each desiring the opponent as sacrificial victim. In the Draupadī cult (at least in the core area), it is, of course, Pōttu Rāja–Pōrmaṉṉaṉ who becomes the Pāṇḍavas' marshal, which explains why his iconic form leads the processions of Draupadī's and the Pāṇḍavas' icons, and sometimes icons of their Kaurava opponents (see chap. 2), outside of the temple to the various ritual terrains that represent aspects of Kurukṣetra.

But Pōttu Rāja can also be a pointed stake. Indeed, this is the case not only for Draupadī's Pōttu Rāja, but for Pōta Rājus in Andhra. As I noted earlier, the latter's upper knob is often elongated to a point, as are some of the female posts before Māriyammaṉ temples: most specifically the one called Ammaṉ at Kīḻiravantavāṭi. Indeed, Whitehead even supplies a picture of a pointed Pōta Rāju (see fig.

27. Indrajit goes twice to the Nikumbhilā grove, which is "crowded with hundreds of yūpas" (*Rām.* 7.25.3), to make himself invisible in battle by offering a soma and fire sacrifice, along with a black goat seized by the neck, using a black iron ladle and weapons for ritual implements, and with his priests wearing red robes and red turbans (6.60.22–23; 67.5–7). As Vibhīṣaṇa tells Lakṣmaṇa, only by interrupting Indrajit's third attempt can he be defeated (71.13–22). Cf. Chhabra 1947, 80 n. 5.

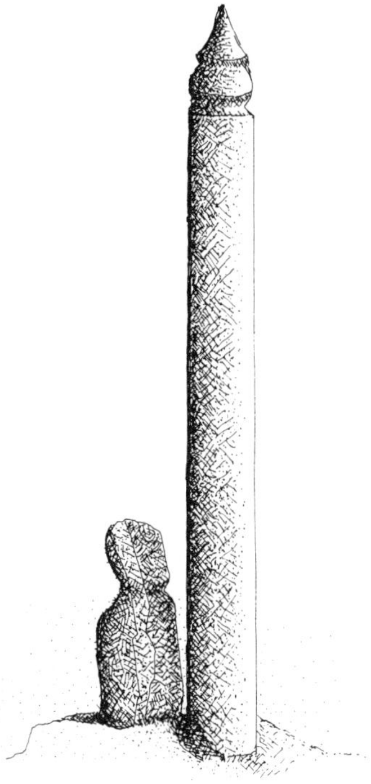

Figure 9. Whitehead's "stone symbol of Potu-rāzu with stake for impaling animals" (from Whitehead 1921, plate 4).

9) that he captions as a "stake for impaling animals" (1921, plate 4). It is possible that he only imagined this function on analogy with other impalement practices he describes elsewhere, since neither he nor anyone else has ever recorded the actual use of a Pōta Rāju post for impalement. But a connection between a post that symbolizes impalement and real impalement practices that do occur elsewhere is still to be suspected. Whitehead's apparent justification for the caption lies in his observation that the Pōta Rāju post "faintly resembles a spear," that the spear is a "common symbol of the village deities," and, most interestingly, that "it is called *sulam,* which in Telugu means spear" (ibid., 40). As we have seen, Cūlam (= *śūlam*) and Stūpi are alternate names for a spearlike post that stands in Pōttu Rāja's customary position at the Forest Draupadī temple in Tiruvannamalai. In this aspect the Telugu and Tamil Pōta Rāju posts would seem to have inherited the Vedic function of defining a type of battle-sacrifice that takes place away from the regular sacrificial terrain, a terrain that has been replaced, in these popular transformations, by the grounds and permanent features of the temple that the godling guards. Unless the goddess con-

quers her foe within her temple (a possibility, but one I leave for later discussion), she must in some fashion go out from her temple to encounter him. In Andhra, the ritual that represents this is the buffalo sacrifice, itself a reenactment of the goddess's combat with the Buffalo Demon.[28] In the Draupadī cult, the rituals are reenactments of the battle of Kurukṣetra. The functions of Pōttu Rāja's permanently placed icons and his processional anthropomorphic icons are thus clearly complementary. The first (whether the god is a post or bas-relief on slab plus flagstaff and balipīṭha) defines the limits of the goddess temple as a regular sacrificial ground, akin to the terrain of a regular Vedic sacrifice. The second leads beyond those limits to the grounds that represent the battlefield. Here we are of course talking about the relations between the fixed and the mobile, the permanent and the temporary, the ritually pure and the less pure, all of which are commonplace in Hindu festival ritual. But it is more complicated than this. It is also a question of Pōttu Rāja's weapons and Draupadī's processional chariot.

8. *Sacrificial weapons.* As we have seen, the ordinary Vedic yūpa is not pointed, which absolves it of any direct association with cutting or impalement. Without either being the instrument of killing or marking the actual place of killing, however, it is nonetheless an instrument of attenuated torture because of the animal's painful bondage to it. The victim is tied to the yūpa by its left leg, neck, and right horn (the goat is the prototype for the animal sacrifice, or paśubandha), thus imposing upon it what must have been an awkward and uncomfortable attitude of submission (Biardeau 1989b, 44–45, 47 n. 2, 50).[29] Then it is removed to the *śāmitra* fire, situated northeast of the mahāvedi, to be slaughtered (by suffocation or strangulation) and then butchered.

Within the ritual, the yūpa also has numerous sharp-pointed multiforms or extensions. First is the svaru, the chip kept from the

28. The pattern is clearer in some descriptions than others, and clearest in the one referred to in n. 4. In an analogous pattern, but in Tamilnadu, the two buffalo sacrifices at the Gingee Fort occur not outside the temples of any of the three goddesses involved, but at the fort boundary and the grazing ground at the old town center (Hiltebeitel 1985b, 184–86).

29. Biardeau suggests that the mainly South Indian practice of placing the right foreleg of the sacrificial buffalo or goat in the mouth of its severed head transforms these Vedic practices (1989b, 47 n. 18). But one may question the argument's shift from the left foreleg to the right, the latter being significant in some mythic explanations of the popular practice (see Hiltebeitel 1988a, 305 and n. 31 with bibliography; also Whitehead 1921, 51 n. 1 and 85).

first cut of the yūpa-tree (Schwab 1886, 11). Biardeau observes that in *Ṛg Veda* 3.8, a hymn to the sacrificial post, the term *svaru* "designates the post itself. In the ritual it seems to be no more than a reduction of the post, destined to replace it in certain manipulations that demand its mobility," a sort of "miniature mobile yūpa" (Biardeau 1989b, 38, 50). When the post is cinctured with a triple rope of *kuśa* grass around its middle, or at the level of the sacrificer's navel (the prototype of darbha grass around the flagpole), the svaru is fixed under this "girdle," in vertical parallel with the angle of the yūpa that faces the fire. Upon completion of the libations into the (new) āhavanīya, the *adhvaryu*, or Yajur Veda priest, takes the svaru from the girdle on the post, handles it together with a double-edged knife, steeps the svaru in the ghee left from the last libation, and passes one of the blades of the knife across the spout of the *juhū* ladle. The combining of the svaru with the knife clearly implies a function of piercing and cutting as extending from the yūpa (Biardeau 1989b, 45–46 n. 14). Let us also note that the svaru is given a fanciful etymology of "very sore" (*su-aru; ŚB* 3.7.1.24; Vogel 1910–11, 45), perhaps recalling the yūpa's association with the victim. As the animal stands bound to the yūpa, facing west (that is, situated outside the mahāvedi but facing it: a prefiguration of the demon devotee facing the sanctum), the adhvaryu then anoints it between the horns with the svaru and knife and hands the knife to the slaughterer (*śamitar*). He tells the śamitar to use the unanointed edge of the knife to carve the animal after it has been slain, while reserving the anointed edge for carving the meat when it is cooked. The adhvaryu then returns the svaru to the girdle on the yūpa (Biardeau 1989b, 44–48; cf. Kane [1930–62] 1975, 2, 2:1117–19). As Biardeau explains, the adhvaryu's touching of the animal with the svaru and knife "is the real putting-to-death, the one that counts" (1989b, 45, n. 14), the one that takes place while the animal is bound to the yūpa.

With the return of the svaru to the yūpa, other pointed implements now continue to extend the same symbolism. When the animal is untied from the yūpa, the adhvaryu touches it with the *vapāśrapaṇī*, the spits or skewers that he and the sacrificer will use to carry the omentum, once it is extracted from the butchered animal, from the śāmitra fire, outside the mahāvedi to the northeast, to the āhavanīya on the uttaravedi. There the adhvaryu will pass these skewers to another officiant who will use them to roast the omentum before offering it to Indra and Agni (Biardeau 1989b, 48). According to *Āpastamba Śrauta Sūtra* 7.19.1, the two vapāśrapaṇī spits are distinguished as follows: one is a two-pronged spit (*dviśūla*) on which the omentum is placed, and the other is a one-pronged spit (*ekaśūla*) on which it is pierced (C. Sen 1978, 112; Renou 1954, 133). As we have seen, the term *śūla* is used for the yūpa in sacrifices where the latter is pointed. Similarly, a sharp-pointed wooden spit used for roasting the heart or kidneys of an animal victim is called the *hṛdayaśūla,* the "heart śūla" (C. Sen 1978, 112; cf. 160; Kane 1975, 2, 2:1128). Most suggestive, however, is the use of the term in connection with the *Śūlagava* sacrifice, a Vedic domestic (*gṛhya*) rite performed yearly (in spring or autumn) on the paradigm of the animal sacrifice, in which a "spit ox" (*śūla-gava*) is taken to the northeast of the village—the śāmitra position—and offered to Rudra. A special "unplaned" or "unchiseled" (*ataṣṭa*) yūpa is prepared, apparently evoking Rudra's wildness (recall the unchiseled stake for Kāttavarāyaṉ), while the name of the animal probably refers to Rudra, the recipient, as *śūlin,* the deity "possessing the 'spit.'"[30] According to Macdonell and Keith ([1912] 1967, 2:393), the first mention of the śūla in its familiar role as the weapon of Rudra is *Ṣaḍviṃśa Brāhmaṇa* 5.11.3, the same text that delineates the magical use of pointed (*śūla*) yūpas: "'To Rudra hail', 'Hail to the Lord of Animals', 'Hail to him whose hand is with the trident'" (Bollée 1956, 112). The yūpa is thus not only a multiform of Indra's vajra but a prototype—when pointed—of Śiva's trident. As we have seen, it is also linked mythically with the arrow and wooden sword, bound up literally, in the ritual, with the svaru (that is, girdled to it), and metonymically with these and also with the two-edged sacrificial carving knife and the various spits, including the suggestive three-pronged combination of the dviśūla and ekaśūla. Given the propensity of the Vedic sacrifice to remove bloodshed, cutting, and impalement from the animal sacrifice, it looks as if such activities are retained, sub rosa, only in muted symbolisms extending from the ordinary yūpa. In this light, it is intriguing that the Brāhmaṇas derive the word yūpa from the root *yup,* meaning "to efface, to scatter, debar, conceal" (Thite 1975, 133, with numerous citations; cf. Malamoud 1989, 248).

Like the Vedic yūpa, Pōta Rāju is bundled up metonymically with mobile ritual implements, many of them pointed. In Andhra, he is commonly represented by a portable replica of his stationary post. It is carried in rituals, sometimes on a pole wrapped in mar-

30. See Gonda 1980, 435–37, especially n. 64; Kane [1930–62] 1975, 2, 2:831–32; C. Sen 1978, 160. The apotropaic functions of this rite, which seems to have drawn increasing Brahmanical disfavor, deserve study as a prototype for apotropaic functions of the buffalo sacrifice (on which see Hiltebeitel 1980a, 192–200).

gosa leaves.[31] In the *Epic of Palnāḍu,* he supplies the goddess Ankālamma and her heroes with a number of ritual instruments that include a pillar and dagger (Roghair 1982, 213–14). It is much the same, but more so, in the case of Draupadī's Pōttu Rāja. Whether he is represented by a post or as part of a flagstaff ensemble, Draupadī requires Pōttu Rāja's services not only so he can marshal her army, but also because he will bring with him the ritual weapons of her cult.

On the level of myth, these weapons have various sources. Pōttu Rāja normally brings the implements from the City of the Bliss of Śiva. But we have noted a variant in which they must be obtained from Indra. They are multiforms of the weapons that the gods give to Durgā to defeat the Buffalo King's former self, the Buffalo Demon. Or they are born with Draupadī from the rather abhicāra-like sacrifice of one of her fiery births: presumably her second birth, when she is born to kill the demon Acalammācuraṉ.[32] In this vein, let us hold up the mirror of one further, and unmistakable, parallel: in this case a myth from a village in Chingleput District (within the Draupadī cult core area) concerning the goddess Celliyammaṉ:[33]

> A demon (unnamed) performed a thousand sacrifices to Celliyammaṉ, and then demanded various boons, plus her four ritual weapons: the whip, pampai drum, flag, and trident. The goddess agreed only on condition that he sacrifice to her "a woman pregnant with her first child," thinking no woman would agree. But the demon convinced his own first-time-pregnant wife to be the offering. Celliyammaṉ then had to give him the boons and weapons, thus losing her *śakti,* or "power," and her kingdom and becoming his slave. Finally Viṣṇu took the form of Lakṣmī to seduce the demon, trick the weapons from him, and kill him. (Summarizing Moffatt 1979, 273)

This Celliyammaṉ myth allows us to attend to two matters: first the long-deferred rapport between Pōttu Rāja and Muttāl Rāvuttaṉ, and then the nature of the weapons themselves. At least as far back as this Celliyammaṉ myth takes us, the ritual weapons belong originally to her, the goddess. In offering her a woman pregnant

31. See Tapper 1987, 175 and plates 8 and 12 (see also fig. 7 above); Biardeau 1984, 14; 1989b, 10–13.
32. See Appendix, n. 12; chapter 3, n. 2; cf. Hiltebeitel 1988a, 386–93.
33. This myth should be compared with others discussed in Hiltebeitel 1988a, chapter 16, for which I should have remembered it, having earlier cited it in another connection (1980c, 169).

for the first time, however, the demon is more like Muttāl Rāvuttaṉ than Pōttu Rāja, although Muttāl Rāvuttaṉ only prepares such an offering (to Draupadī) and does not actually carry it out (when Draupadī changes her demand after feeling a sympathetic identification as a female with the would-be victim).[34] Unlike Pōttu Rāja, the demon also first obtains the weapons from the goddess, enslaves her, and as a result must be killed. He does not, apparently, become her guardian or demon devotee. What is interesting in our present context is that the weapons actually fall into the hands of the goddess's enemy, who can use them against her: a theme that is only latent in the Draupadī cult, in the notion, found in some variants, that Pōrmaṉṉaṉ's father (who, like Celliyammaṉ's demon, *is* killed), is a partisan of the Kauravas who must be prevented from aligning his son with the Kauravas as well. Finally, it is again Viṣṇu in female guise who tricks the demon and restores the weapons to the goddess, just as it is Kṛṣṇa and Arjuna, or sometimes just Kṛṣṇa alone, whose women's disguises trick Pōrmaṉṉaṉ so that the ritual weapons can be obtained for Draupadī (Hiltebeitel 1988a, 105–10, 340–42).

If Draupadī requires no *real* animal sacrifices *within* the time and space of her festival, she *allows* them—and, according to the myth of Muttāl Rāvuttaṉ and his pregnant sister, actually arranges for them—on its temporal-spatial periphery, the place where Muttāl Rāvuttaṉ is stationed at the northeast of her sanctum.[35] Now, among the Draupadī cult's representatives of inferior bhakti, Muttāl Rāvuttaṉ ranges toward the bottom. But inferior bhakti still has two potentials: it can be elevated, or it can be debased to include the crudest parodies of sacrifice such as the willingness to offer up pregnant women. Celliyammaṉ's demon foe represents this extreme in its execution. But Muttāl Rāvuttaṉ, magician and Muslim, represents it in its conversion and subordination to this higher bhakti ideal. It is thus his function to stand at the boundary between these possibilities. He partakes of his impure and illicit offerings, but he neutralizes their dangerous effects so that when they are returned to the offerers as prasādam, they are detoxified (Hiltebeitel 1988a, 126). Here one occasionally finds him represented anthropomorphically, but most often by little offering stones. I have found no Muttāl Rāvuttaṉs that are as clear in their replication of yūpa features as are the rare post–Pōttu Rājas, discussed in chap-

34. On this episode, see Hiltebeitel 1988a, 105–10; 1989a, 356–58, 367–68.

35. Some of this material relating Muttāl Rāvuttaṉ to Pōttu Rāja is dealt with at greater length in Hiltebeitel 1989a. Cf. also 1988a, 116–27.

ter 5. They do, however, clearly include simplified multiforms of the yūpa, as well as both rough and polished variations on the impalement stake (see fig. 10).

Meanwhile, as we have seen, the stationary icon of Pōttu Rāja that receives vegetarian offerings *usually* represents him in human form, and only rarely as the "yūpa" that so widely identifies him in Andhra. Thus in large part Pōttu Rāja relinquishes the sacrificial stake's explicit representation, however crudely, to Muttāl Rāvuttan̲, marking its movement from the center of a village goddess–type cult (such as one finds in Andhra) to its periphery in the cult of Draupadī. Nonvegetarian offerings are made to Muttāl Rāvuttan̲'s little stones outside the goddess's line of sight. Yet if the offerings to Muttāl Rāvuttan̲ are set off and apart at Draupadī festivals—above all, offerings of liquor and goats, but also cocks, hens, meat curries, spicy Bengal gram, marijuana, opium, chapattis, cigars, cheroots, cigarettes, and horse gram for his horse—they are still part of her cult.

Now, as I argued in volume 1, this periphery to which Muttāl Rāvuttan̲ is consigned is not without its precise ritual definitions, for the northeast is the position of such impurity-handling agents as the *kṣetrapāla* ("field-protector," e.g., Bhairava as temple guardian), the *nirmālyadevatā* (the deity, often a lower form of the temple's main deity, who receives the "residue of offerings," or *nirmālya*, of the main deity, guards it from violation, and handles its impurity), and ultimately, as is crucial here, the śamitar (1988a, 126–27). From what one can learn of the ritual operations at the Vedic śāmitra, it is there, to the northeast of the mahāvedi, that the śamitar cooks or roasts the limbs and other portions of the victim after cutting them: a process that must have included some handling of the victim's severed head, even if the texts are quiet on this point.[36] What is significant here is the rapport between the śamitar's fire and the yūpa, which is set at the eastern end of the mahāvedi. The yūpa corresponds to the typical position occupied by the temple flagstaff, which, as noted earlier, is connected with Pōttu Rāja, not Muttāl Rāvuttan̲. Let us repeat in this connection that the pan-Indian prototype of the head-holding kṣetrapāla is Bhairava, who holds the head of Brahmā and is commonly stationed at the northeast. Clearly, Pōttu Rāja's icons derive the head in hand, at least in part, from Bhairava's iconography. Yet at this point, if one recalls the Vedic model that keeps Draupadī's two guardians in their intimate

36. See C. Sen 1978, 110–11 and plans 3 and 5; Malamoud 1989, 212–16.

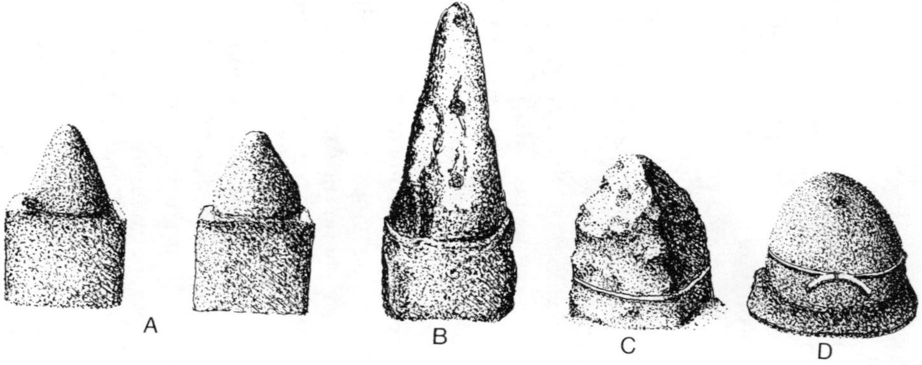

Figure 10. Stone images of Muttāl Rāvuttaṉ: (A) pair from Kovelong; (B) Villupuram; (C) Nallāṉpiḷḷaiperṟāḷ (with kāppu string); (D) Mutikai Nallāṉkuppam (with kāppu string and piece of turmeric root).

rapport, one sees the very opposite of the situation one might expect. In effect, Muttāl Rāvuttaṉ and Pōttu Rāja have made a trade. Out at the northeast periphery where the kṣetrapāla Bhairava would normally hold the head of Brahmā, and where the śamitar would dismember the sacrificial animal and thus have to handle the "head of the sacrifice,"[37] one finds Muttāl Rāvuttaṉ represented by crude multiforms of the sacrificial stake or stone that one might normally expect to find at the end of the central eastern axis of a village goddess temple, as in Andhra, or mutatis mutandis, of the mahāvedi. He also holds no head. And at the eastern end of this central axis, where one might expect to find the stake itself, one finds Pōttu Rāja, the erstwhile stake of Andhra, (usually) holding the sacrificial head instead. The post and the "head of the sacrifice" have thus, in the usual Draupadī temple configuration, reversed their positions. This reversal accords with the Draupadī cult's sacrificial logic, which imputes actual sacrifice to the cult's periphery, where it can be overseen by Muttāl Rāvuttaṉ, yet retains the symbolism of sacrifice at its center, where it is represented by the head in Pōttu Rāja's hand.

This trade, or reversal, brings us back to the weapons, for the head that Pōttu Rāja holds is also a weapon: in a sense, the ultimate weapon, since it recalls the head of Brahmā that Bhairava holds, which is itself a multiform of the *brahmaśiras* (head of Brahmā), the doomsday weapon of the *pralaya* (the "dissolution" of the universe). Should Pōttu Rāja release it, a great catastrophe would occur.[38] This head befalls him as a result of one or another of his mythic services to Draupadī and is not borne by any human officiants in a ritual context. In contrast, the rest of Pōttu Rāja's weapons are intimately linked with his incarnation of sacrificial activity and with the ritual dispersal of that activity to the officiants of the Draupadī cult. A number of ritual implements may be included in the list, which typically totals five. Four of the most common—whip, pampai drum, flag, and trident—were just noticed among the trove sought by Celliyammaṉ's demon. In the Draupadī cult, no matter which implements are included, six are mentioned with the highest regularity: vīracāṭṭi, or heroic whip; vīrapampai, or heroic pampai drum; vīrakantakam, or heroic turmeric powder; vīrakuntam, or heroic lance, also known as cūlam, trident; pūcai peṭṭi or paṇṭāra peṭṭi, the priest's container for turmeric; and koṭicīlai, pennant or portable flagstaff (Hiltebeitel 1988a, 387). Leaving aside

37. See especially Heesterman 1985, 45–58; Hiltebeitel 1988a, 328, 372.
38. See Appendix and Hiltebeitel 1988a, 373–78, 434, 448; 1989a, 366.

the pampai drum and the pūcai or paṇṭāra peṭṭi, the rest seem to be popularized multiforms of elements of Vedic sacrificial ritual.[39]

The vīrakuntam, or multi-tined "trident," is the preeminent mobile implement of impalement, with its apparent pointed (śūlam) precursors in the Vedic spits, skewers, and pointed posts, and its mediation through Durgā, who obtains it from Śiva in the *Devī Māhātmyam* and uses it there—and in most iconographic representations—to impale the Buffalo Demon while at the same time using the sword to behead him (*DM* 2.20; 3.39–42). Indeed, the double symbolism is revealing. At least in the hands of the goddess, the śūlam, like the yūpa, is not the actual instrument of killing but a means of bringing the victim to a fixed standstill. Thus even when it is carried, lemons are *fixed* on it (see fig. 11, plate 21). In this regard, it complements the long, tapered, turmeric-dyed coconut-fiber whips (cāṭṭi, vīracāṭṭi)—associated with Pōta Rāju both in Andhra and at Tamil Draupadī temples—that are often coiled in its prongs. As Biardeau has argued, the whip has its prototype in the rope that is used to tie the victim to the sacrificial stake. Besides their placement in the prongs of the vīrakuntams, the whips, among other things, are placed around Pōttu Rāja's icons (see plate 24) and used by his ritual impersonators, and they have a variant in the similarly shaped cotton wicks (*pot*) dipped in oil that the Potrājs in Maharashtra slowly burn while they disperse ash near a śamī tree as a token of the goddess's blessing at Dasarā (Biardeau 1984, 20–22). Meanwhile, the portable flag or pennant (koṭicīlai) is not just an extension of the permanent flagstaff, itself a multiform of the yūpa; in *Ṛg Veda* 3.8.8, the yūpa is already called the "flag" or "banner" (*ketu*) of the sacrifice (Gonda [1954] 1969, 81). Among the verses by which one invokes the yūpa for the animal sacrifice, it is said: "Erect, do thou protect us from distress with thy banner" (*ketunā; TB* 3.6.1; P.-E. Dumont 1962, 249). Finally, vīrakantakam as turmeric powder has many resonances that are best discussed later. For the present, it is enough to say that it has an anointing function in both buffalo sacrifices and Draupadī cult ceremonial that I take to be a reinterpretation of the use of clarified butter (*ghṛta, ghī*) for anointing the ritual implements (including the yūpa, at both its cutting and erection) and the victim in the Vedic animal sacrifice.

Let us note also that in the Thanjavur area, one finds similar lists of five weapons. For example, at Cattiram Karuppūr, the kuntam

39. According to the *Tamil Lexicon*, s.v., *pūcai-p-peṭṭi* also refers to a "case for the *liṅkam* [liṅgam] used in private worship."

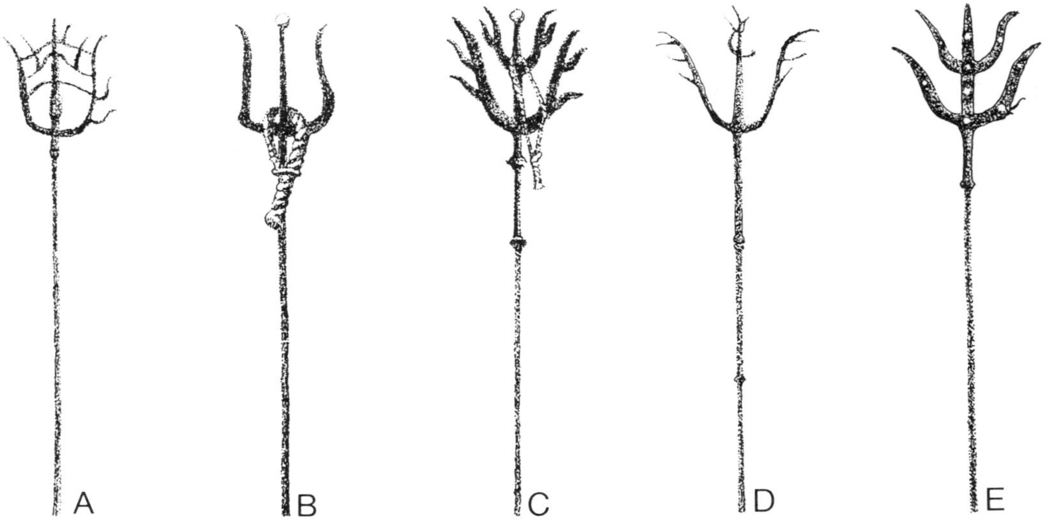

Figure 11. Multi-tined vīrakuntams or cūlams: (A) Mēlaccēri; (B) Tindivanam (with lemon on central prong and coiled vīracāṭṭi whip); (C) Veḷḷimēṭupēṭṭai (with lemon and whip); (D) Maṅkalam; (E) Perunakar.

(combining elements of the trident and cakra; see plate 21), cāṭṭai whip, pampai drum, *perampu* (a staff), and *karakam* (a pot), are mentioned together, and are all said to be Draupadī's. But we should recall that at Lalgudi, the vīrakumpam, equivalent to the (vīra-) kuntam, is also linked with Vīrapattiraṉ. Moreover, Vīrapattiraṉ is found at Pattukkottai and Vaṭukku Poykaiyūr with the cukkumāttāṭi. This clublike implement is linked with other guardian deities, and it evokes a pounding function that joins together with piercing (impalement) and cutting (dismemberment) as one of the three most prominent sacrificial idioms of Vedic ritual.[40]

B. The Yūpa, the Chariot, and the Ceremonies of the Flagstaff

To draw our material together, and to get from the temple to the paṭukaḷam, or ritual battlefield, we must now go back to "the most beautiful tree in the forest" (chap. 5, sec. C). To put matters simply, a śamī is chosen for the flagstaff at Tiruchendur because the Murukaṉ–Cuṭalai Māṭaṉ story retains an impulse from the royal folklore of the goddess's fall festival of Dasarā, the ceremony that marks the end of the rainy season and the opening of military campaigns. The provision of a śamī flagstaff outside the temple to enable the deity to go out on chariot processions can be drawn only from the *śamīpūjā,* or "worship of the śamī," that is one of Dasarā's central rites. As can be gleaned from ritual manuals like the *Nirṇayasindhu* (early seventeenth century) and the *Dharmasindhu* (ca. 1790), and from eyewitness accounts that also go back to the early seventeenth century, royal celebrations of Dasarā or Vijayādaśamī involve three basic rites: śamīpūjā, "worshiping the śamī"; *sīmollaṅghana,* "crossing the boundary" of the capital; and Aparājitāpūjā, worshiping the goddess under the name Aparājitā, the "Invincible." These three rites form part of one procession to the śamī tree. Feminine grammatically, as well as in its Vedic symbolism, the śamī is itself invoked as Aparājitā. And the "crossing of the boundary" occurs either before or after the śamīpūjā, depending on whether the śamī

40. In the Soma sacrifice, but also in the pounding of grains (sometimes linked with Pōttu Rāja; Hiltebeitel 1988a, 404). On the cukkumāttāṭi, cf. Hiltebeitel 1985b, 185–86 and 198 n. 54 (borne at the Gingee buffalo sacrifice with a cūlam, karakam, firebrand, and perampu stick); Biardeau 1989b, 144–46, 155 (connected with Kāttavarāyaṉ, and suggesting "a close symbolic unity between the impalement stake, the śūla, the cekkumāndaḍi, the banana stalk [called Agniskambha], and the person who gets possessed" [155]). Biardeau's spelling *cekku-* (the noun means oil press) might recall other acts of pounding grains.

is inside or outside the capital limit. In other words, the tree *is* the "unvanquished" goddess who is worshiped in conjunction with the crossing of the capital boundary.[41] Just as the erection of Cuṭalai Māṭaṉ's vaṉṉi flagstaff is necessary to mark a boundary of the temple before Murukaṉ can go outside it on royal chariot processions, so the śamīpūjā marks the crossing of the capital boundary as a rite that opens the season of battles for kings.

The link here with the *Mahābhārata* is thus not so much with the Pāṇḍavas' hiding their weapons in the śamī as with their retrieving the weapons from it to begin the battle of Kurukṣetra with the Kauravas. The story of the Pāṇḍavas' retrieval of their weapons from the śamī, however, is specifically a piece of Dasarā folklore, sometimes told to explain the origin of the ceremony. Classical versions of the *Mahābhārata* have no such episode. There one hears only of how the Pāṇḍavas hide their weapons in the śamī *before* entering the kingdom of Virāṭa; never of the weapons' retrieval upon *leaving* Virāṭadeśa, though this must have occurred for them to have launched the war.[42] We shall meet further Draupadī cult variations on this missing epic theme in chapters 8, 9, and 13. In any case, the śamī outside the city of King Virāṭa is somewhere near the capital boundary that the Pāṇḍavas must cross before leaving the city.

A summary of the śamīpūjā rites at Dasarā cannot, however, be complete without mentioning that they may combine with, or carry to conclusion, another ceremony: the *āyudhapūjā*, or "worship of the royal weapons." Normally this would occur on the ninth day of Navarātri, the "nine nights" festival sequence that ordinarily includes a buffalo sacrifice on the eighth or ninth night, and precedes Dasarā (which means the "tenth day") with daily recitation of the

41. This summary relies mainly on Biardeau 1984, 8–10; 1989b, 301–2, and Kane [1930–62] 1975, 5, 1:177–95. See also Kinsley 1986, 106–11.

42. For discussion, see Biardeau 1984, 7. See also Hiltebeitel 1988a, 296–301; Villiputtūr and Draupadī festival dramas follow the classical epic story. For an example of the Dasarā folklore, see Underhill 1921, 56. In classical epic accounts, the śamī is revisited only when Arjuna, disguised as a eunuch at the end of his year incognito, retrieves his bow, quivers, and arrows to turn back the Kaurava cattle raid. There is nothing about him returning these weapons to the tree so that they would be there for all the Pāṇḍavas to collect the weapons together, something the Dasarā folklore seems to require. Rao 1936b, 53, 55–56 n. 1, mentions another folk alternative that innovates in the placement of the weapons rather than the occasion of their retrieval: it is only a matter of Arjuna retrieving his weapons, which with the rest were "buried under" the śamī, "on the tenth day (*daśamī*) of Aśvin . . . , which, later, witnessed the battle of Kurukṣetra," and is celebrated as the victorious tenth "because it is the day of Vijaya, i.e., Arjuna, the Victorious." See also Sarojini Devi 1990, 275.

Devī Māhātmyam.[43] The weapons may, however, also be taken to the śamī, worshiped *with* it, and then carried back from the śamī to the palace.[44] This bundling of the śamī with the weapons in a pan-Indian royal ritual is unmistakably a missing link—a logical if not necessarily historical intermediary—between the two other orders of bundling that have concerned us. One cannot really get from the Vedic bundling of the yūpa with pointed sacrificial implements to the various bundles of weapons associated with Pōta Rāju–Pōttu Rāja–Pōrmaṉṉaṉ without considering the śamīpūjā.

Let us begin by noting that we are talking about potentially martial boundary rites in all cases. The various Vedic śūlas, and other piercing and cutting implements, extend the violent functions of the animal sacrifice beyond the yūpa, which stands on the boundary of the mahāvedi; and if the yūpa is itself pointed, the implements, including the chariot, can become "magical" weapons of warfare against a rival who is, by definition, beyond these boundaries (or, to mention another possibility that will concern us later, who must be kept from invading them). The goddess temples that have wooden Pōta Rāju posts outside them in Andhra are village boundary temples, a characterization that seems to hold for many Tamil Draupadī temples, especially the Vīrāṇantal temple, where Draupadī should not hear the household sounds of mortar and pestle, and the Mēlaccēri temple to the north of Gingee (Hiltebeitel 1988a, 72 and n. 5). In these cases, however, the boundary function is doubled, for Telugu and Tamil Pōta Rājus also mark the boundary of the temple itself. At Andhra limit temples, the buffalo sacrifice takes place beyond this boundary: sometimes just outside the temple, in sight of the goddess; sometimes at the second Pōta Rāju post beneath the "married" pipal and margosa trees in the village center (see n. 4). Two complementary practices bring out the latent martial character of these village rites: on the one hand, the remains of the sacrifice (especially the blood) must be closely guarded lest neighboring villagers steal its benefits (Whitehead 1921, 50–51, 69); on the other hand, the remains (principally blood-soaked rice, and sometimes the head) may be thrown over the boundary into the next village to turn the goddess's wrath toward the neighbors (ibid., 54, 67; cf. 39). Such contentious implications become explicit in the Draupadī cult, where the main ceremonies away from the

43. See Ramakrishna Rao 1921, 308; Masilamani-Meyer in press-a, 1; Fuller and Logan 1985, 85, 99.

44. The details on the āyudhapūjā forming continuity with the śamī pūjā are clearest in Ramakrishna Rao 1921, 305, describing Dasarā at Mysore; cf. also Rao 1936b, 145. See also Biardeau 1984, 9; Kane [1930–62], 1975, 5, 1:193.

temple reenact aspects of the *Mahābhārata*'s sacrifice of battle: the war overseen by Draupadī-Yākacēṉi, "She whose army is the sacrifice" (Hiltebeitel 1988a, 194, 338, 392).

The link, however, is not one just of a position, but of a specific tree: the śamī. The śamīpūjā of Dasarā provides a connection between the Vedic ritual, where the śamī is not one of the trees listed as suitable for making a yūpa, to the Pōta Rājus of Andhra, which *are* made of śamī. Here we must follow Biardeau's tentative route back through Orissa. There, as we have seen, one finds stone posts outside the temples of various royal lineages, and now "village goddesses" (*grāmadevatī*), including Khambheśvarī, the Lady of the Post. These are actively used in connection with goat and buffalo sacrifices at Dasarā or its variant Durgāpūjā. According to Biardeau, the śamī is now extremely rare in Orissa, but it is the tree of choice for making the yūpa (the Vedic term is used) for buffalo sacrifices at Durgāpūjā in an Orissan Sanskrit ritual manual. Such wooden posts, however, were to be set up only for the ceremony and were taken up and removed once it was over (Biardeau 1984, 14–15; 1989b, 67–79). In Orissa, the post's use at village and even "tribal" forms of Durgāpūjā, and its identification with the goddess Khambheśvarī, also suggests that it is a village-scale substitute for—or equivalent of—the śamī tree worshiped at Dasarā outside royal capitals (Biardeau 1989b, 66–67). In any case, in Andhra, as we have seen, the śamī post, as Buffalo King, is identified not with the victorious goddess but with the male buffalo victim: an alternative association that, it must be repeated, is not necessarily a derivative one, since the name of Pōttu Rāja, if not these ritual resonances, can be traced back to the Pallava period.[45] In both the Andhra and Tamil cases, the festival is no longer Dasarā or Durgāpūjā, but a spring festival, often bearing the earmarks (at least in the Draupadī cult) of a modification of a spring Navarātri plus Dasarā (Hiltebeitel 1988a, 44–45, 144). And the goddess is not Durgā but one (or some combination) of Pōta Rāju's seven sisters, the Andhra village goddesses, or, in our Tamil setting, Draupadī. In Tamil Draupadī and Dharmarāja temples, the śamī post once again becomes stone and is more often than not "replaced" by a flagstaff ensemble.

From Reiniche, however, we have learned what it means for a śamī to provide the tree for a flagstaff. And we have also seen that the Pāṇḍavas' retrieval of their weapons from the śamī tree is a widely diffused fragment of Dasarā folklore about the ceremony of

45. Hiltebeitel 1988a, 15–16 and n. 7. Michael Rabe (personal communication, 1989) indicates that Pōttu Rāja is a more common Pallava title than I suspected.

śamīpūjā. It is thus appropriate to ask whether Draupadī cult ritualists have done the same thing that their Tirunelveli counterparts appear to have done: that is, link this *Mahābhārata* mytheme with the ceremonies of the flagstaff. And indeed, it seems they have done so, only far more thoroughly. I restrict myself here as much as possible to ritual details, since I will take up Pōttu Rāja's mythological connection with the śamī again in volume 3.

Let us recall that flag hoisting coincides with honoring Pōttu Rāja in many forms: the slab showing his bas-relief receives offerings; he is often additionally represented on the base of the flagstaff, on the angle facing into the temple; and at Kūttampākkam in particular, his stone post is doubled by a wooden "fire post" (*akkiṉikampam*) that is treated as if it were the "true" flagpole. As we shall see, a "fire-post" is clearly a multiform of the "fire-containing" śamī. Moreover, the honoring of Pōtta Rāja at flag hoisting further coincides with the first honoring and use, for the festival, of the Draupadī cult's ritual weapons: the weapons that Pōttu Rāja, alias the śamī, has indeed brought mythically into the cult. Turmeric is used, among other things, to color the kāppu wristlets. A whip may be coiled in the tines of the vīrakuntam. The multi-tined vīrakuntam or cūlam, the portable flagstaff, or koṭicīlai, and the vīrapampai drum receive kāppu along with the stationary and portable icons of Pōttu Rāja, the other icons, and the main officiants who will carry (or play) these ritual weapons, away from the temple, during the festival. Insofar as flag hoisting marks the beginning of the Pāratam festival, it also represents the beginning of a reenactment of the *Mahābhārata* war. But this symbolism may be further doubled and intensified, as at Kūttampākkam, where Pōttu Rāja's portable icon is brought before the akkiṉikampam-"flagstaff" on the day that begins the actual recitation of the war. Finally, movement out from the temple with the ritual weapons will often be accompanied, again only after flag hoisting, by "chariots" for the deities, including one for Draupadī, as they open their equivalent of the military campaigns that follow upon the completion of the śamīpūjā of Dasarā. In short, Draupadī cult flag-hoisting ceremonies appear to involve elaborations of forgotten links between Pōttu Rāja and the śamīpūjā and, even more deeply and pervasively, of both of these with the Vedic yūpa and its pointed surrogates.

At this point, before we trace the movement from the temple to the paṭukaḷam any further, it is worth attempting a recapitulation of the rapport between the Vedic sacrificial terrain and the Draupadī temple. Henceforth I will attempt to build upon the following working premise: the goddess temple is an intermediary form between two sacrificial open-air terrains. On the one hand, it is a transposition of the mahāvedi, the terrain of the Vedic animal sacrifice. On the other hand, it is itself the model that is transposed onto the paṭukaḷam and other ritual battlefields like it. Note that the rapport being stressed is one with goddess temples, and that I shift from the specifics of the Draupadī temple to the generality of the goddess temple in making this proposition.

To buoy the first part of the argument, one would have to go further into the problematic area of continuities between the Vedic animal sacrifice, in which goddesses have a low profile, and the post-Vedic animal sacrifice *to* the goddess. Suffice it to say for now that our discussion of yūpas and related matters has brought out a number of such continuities, with the intention of showing that it is primarily in the cult of the goddess that the structures of the Vedic animal (and human) sacrifice have been reworked into popular (including Brahmanical) devotional Hinduism. One more piece to this puzzle may be cited here. As Jamison has shown, in Vedic literature, the uttaravedi is often addressed with a mantra that identifies "her" as "lioness" (*siṃhi(r) asi;* e.g., *VS* 5.12; *MS* 3.8.5), making "reference to a tale in which the Uttaravedi is transformed into a lioness and stands between the gods and Asuras" before siding with the gods and bringing them prosperity (*TS* 6.2.7.1 and variants). Jamison shows that the uttaravedi becomes fierce and devouring—a lioness—because she is made from the mahāvedi by the violent cutting of the earth (in press, chap. 3, sec. 2). Both the imagery and the myth supply prefigurations of Durgā, with her lion, supporting the gods against the demons.

As to the second part of the argument, I will continue to try to lend it precision. The reference to goddess temples in general, however, is called for because the layout of battlefield terrains—and such analogues as "forest sacrifices" and crematorium rituals—often ties in with goddesses other than Draupadī. At this juncture, however, a composite map will suffice to point out the correlations we have observed so far between the mahāvedi, the Draupadī temple, and—for one extended example that is due a few more words even now—the "forest sacrifice" to Durgā that supplies the icons of Puri (see map 4). The schema is meant to be no more than skeletal: a taxonomy of inter-linked species, and a model to be fleshed out and turned about in our discussion of the paṭukaḷam. Just one point for now: in moving from the (new) gārhapatya, the extended domestic fire of the Vedic householder-sacrificer, to the pot and the "womb-house" (garbhagṛha) of the

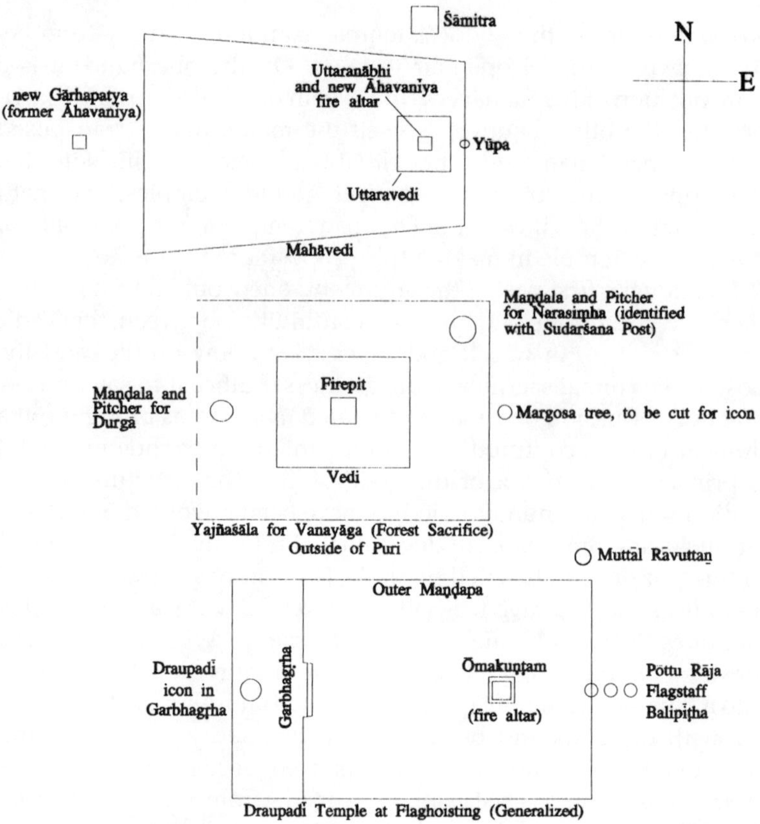

Map 4. Congruent plans: the Vedic great altar for animal sacrifice, the forest sacrifice for the Jagannātha icons, and a generalized Draupadī temple. The forest sacrifice is reconstructed from Tripathi (1978, 239–50). An alternative rectangular shape is also mentioned—thus the broken line. Exact positions of the vedi and pitchers are uncertain.

goddess-as-sacrificer, one retains a basic "domestic" symbolism at the source of each plan. Each is a house from which the sacrificer—whether male or female or sacrificial couple, and whether human or divine—triumphs over forces beyond. Let us also note that the śamī tree at Dasarā, in so many ways akin to Pōttu Rāja and the yūpa, is generally to the north, or northeast, of the capital, the royal home or palace: a sign that this ground plan must survive some turns in different directions.

This recapitulation is not complete, however, without attending to the relation between two more items, the chariots and the portable akkiṉikampams. Let us formulate the problem, once again, by going back to Orissa. There one finds portable wooden multiforms of the yūpa-like post that are described as *calantī pratimās*, literally "movable images." Representing one or another goddess, they may be dressed in a saree and go visiting other deities at Dasarā (Eschmann 1978a, 90 and plate 68). Most instructive, however, is the use of movable images at the great Jagannātha festivals of Puri, where the four icons are made from margosa trees cut in the "forest sacrifice" so that Jagannātha can go out of his temple on chariot processions as "Lord of the Universe." All four of these icons are actually calantī pratimās, since they go out on their huge chariots together. But one of them in particular, the Sudarśana, has been compared to other mobile posts, since that is unmistakably what it is. It has many revealing aspects and functions. As we have seen, it represents Viṣṇu as Narasiṃha, the Man-Lion, and is invoked by a Narasiṃha mantra. The old "retiring" Sudarśana is brought on a pole by a low-caste officiant to mark the site for the "forest sacrifice" of each of the four chosen trees. The tree for the next Sudarśana is the first one cut, and the ritual is the prototype for the felling of the others. The "mixed caste" (Brahman-"Demon") priest who wears the Sudarśana's garland strikes the first ax blow and goes immediately into possession. On some occasions, apparently including the "forest sacrifice" of the four margosa trees, it is the only one of the four images carried out of the temple.[46] Sudarśana, however, does not have its own chariot. At the Jagannātha festival, it is placed to the front left of the chariot of Subhadrā, the goddess. This is also the position in which one finds Pōttu Rāja in front of Draupadī's processional chariots at Mēlaccēri, and the (vīra-) kuntam in front of her chariot at Cattiram Karuppūr. For one thing, to be on the deity's left hand is to handle her or his impurities. Also, the left side corresponds to the northeast in a temple, assuming that the deity's ideal position is to face eastward (or to lie face up, head to the west, representing the sanctum, in a

46. See Eschmann, Kulke, and Tripathi 1978a, plate 21. Cf. Biardeau 1989b, 64–65: even more like Andhra Pōta Rājus than this portable Sudarśana (very much lengthened, and thinned in diameter from bottom to top) is a bas-relief of the Sudarśana post on the eastern Gopuram of the Liṅgarāja Temple at Bhubaneshwar (Eschmann, Kulke, and Tripathi 1978a, plate 46). The perspective of Eschmann (1978a, 89–90) and Eschmann, Kulke, and Tripathi (1978b, 185–87) that the Sudarśana was "originally" the portable image of an apparently once nonprocessional Jagannātha must be questioned. Rather, Sudarśana's character as portable post is the prototype for the other three deities. On saree wrappings for Khambheśvarī and Subhadrā, see Eschmann 1978a, 89; 1978b, 101–3; 1978c, 282; Tripathi 1978, 262–63.

conventional temple ground plan; see n. 21). Thus at Vīrāṇantal, Dharma accepts the service of Muttāl Rāvuttaṉ (locally called Āl Rājaṉ) by telling him that he may always remain at his left side. We will return to the chariot-temple homology in a moment.

It should be observed that whereas portable posts in Andhra may be identified as Pōta Rāju (Tapper 1987, 175), who is, after all, a post there in his permanent forms, portable posts in the Draupadī cult are not named after Pōttu Rāja. Since most Draupadī temples represent him anthropomorphically, such an identification would be unexpected. Thus a new name—akkiṉikampam—for the portable post. We have met this term before in the tall akkiṉikampam at Kūttampākkam, which is the only Draupadī cult akkiṉikampam I know of that is stationary.[47] Others are portable, with uses that will be discussed in chapter 14. One finds at certain temples that the term akkiṉikampam has been forgotten and replaced by *kuṭṭi-p-piḷḷaiyār,* "Little" or "Dwarf Gaṇeśa" (Tindivanam, Maṅkalam), *kalacam,* "pot" or "cupola" (Nallāṉpiḷḷaipeṟṟāl), or *śaktikumpam,* "śakti-pot" (Vaṭukku Poykaiyūr). A reason for these alternatives is that some of these posts look as if they have rounded "bellies," though in fact the post in such cases would appear to have been reduced to the flame-like drop, seen elsewhere on the top of the post-shaft and collar, now on a small base (see fig. 12). Moreover, some temples have no akkiṉikampam at all. The pāratiyār Brameesa Mudaliyar insists, however, that *akkiṉikampam* (or, as he put it, *akkiṉi stampam*) is the correct term, that such variants are popular misunderstandings, and that the festival uses of the akkiṉikampam are de rigueur: one "cheats" the Ammaṉ, he said, if it is omitted. It may be noted that the akkiṉikampams are especially large in the same area of North Arcot that one finds stone posts for Pōttu Rāja. Portable akkiṉikampams about three feet long are kept at Kāppalūr (where there is a stone Pōttu Rāja post), Karaṭikuṭi (where the flagstaff has the triple-sectioned shape of such a post), and Cantavācal. Whatever the setting, however, the name akkiṉikampam, "fire-post," recalls the śamī Pōta Rāju posts of Andhra, and the śamī's connections with fire, and may accentuate the flamelike drop shape. Brameesa Mudaliyar even compared the akkiṉikampam to

47. Eveline Masilamani-Meyer informs me (personal communication, 1990) that in Kongunad, the term akkiṉikampam is used alternatively with *viḷakku tūṇ* ("lamp post") for a post about six to eight meters high, set in a platform and rising to a flame-drop-shaped metal "cage" in which an earthen vessel is placed. A fire is lit in this pot at festivals. These "fire" or "lamp posts" are sometimes placed in the line of sight of a temple's main deity, beyond a Nandi and a balipīṭha.

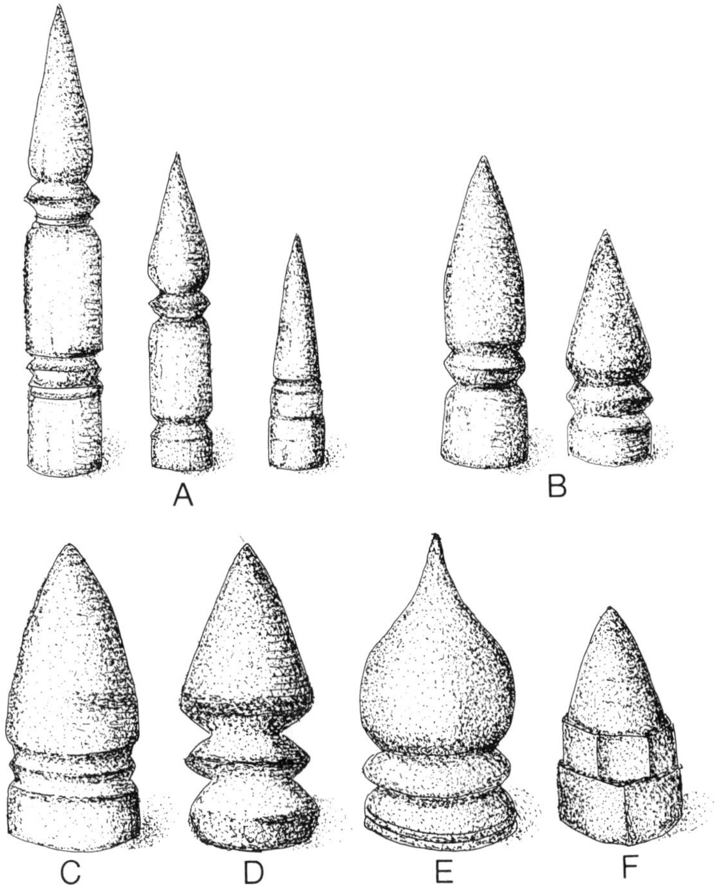

Figure 12. Akkiṉikampams (also called kalacam, kuṭṭi piḷḷaiyar, and śaktikumpam): (A) three from Vīrāṇantal; (B) pair from Mēlaccēri (1982, 1986); (C) Veḷḷimēṭupēṭṭai; (D) Mutikai Nallāṉkuppam; (E) Tindivanam; (F) Maṅkalam (one of four, 1982, all of same type that is unique in showing yūpa-like square base, octagonal midsection, and rounded top).

the Vedic firesticks.[48] Both he and my trustee informant at Vīrāṇantal also said that the akkiṉikampam is to be made from the wood of the *ātti,* or country fig tree. At Vīrāṇantal, the reason given for this was that the ātti has milky sap and a quick growth. As Biardeau has indicated, although the śamī is not a tree with milky sap, such

48. The precise nature of this analogy is uncertain. See chapter 14 for the akkiṉikampam's use at the firewalk.

trees are often chosen as substitutes for it in the making of varied posts (1989b, 90–91, 175).[49] The milky sap seems to impart a feminine dimension to the post's appeasing or cooling function.

Finally, as to the chariots (tēr, ratha) of Draupadī and the Pāṇḍavas, they may in rare instances, as at Pondicherry, be fairly elaborate, along the lines of the great chariots one sees at large Brahmanical temples. Nor should it be overlooked that when the temple's flagstaff frame is covered at flag hoisting with a cloth picture of Hanumān, as at Cattiram Karuppūr, it transforms the Draupadī temple itself into an image of a chariot, since in the *Mahābhārata* Hanumān positions himself on the flagstaff (*dhvaja*) of Arjuna's chariot. But the usual icon-bearing bullock cart is still a tēr, as is a palanquin for rituals that require a portable chariot (cf. Kalidos 1989, 20). Pōttu Rāja will normally lead these chariots in the form of his anthropomorphic wooden (or, as at Mēlaccēri, pañcalōkam) processional icon. Or, more commonly, at certain processions his ritual weapons and the akkiṉikampam may be held aloft near him, in the lead. Here we have the setting into motion of the processes of bundling and parceling out that begins at flag hoisting.

The rich symbolism of the chariot has mythical, ritual, philosophical, and even political depths that deserve further study as background to the use of chariots at festivals.[50] Like the balipīṭha and the flagstaff with the inward-facing frame, there is reason to suspect that the "car festival" (the usual term for the use of chariots in festivals) originates in the South.[51] As a quick glance at some well-reported Brahmanical temples shows, the tour of the chariot has different mythological referents. For Śiva at Mel Ceval, it recalls the god's destruction of Tripura, the Triple City of the demons, and evokes the pralaya, the dissolution of the universe (Reiniche 1979, 83–111; cf. Kalidos 1989, 28 n. 74). For Jagannātha of Puri, it signifies the god's sovereignty—along with Balabhadra, Subhadrā, and Sudarśana—over the universe, *jagat,* all that "moves." For the goddess Mīnākṣī at Madurai, it reenacts her conquest of the

49. Recall the forked posts in Kongunad, chapter 5, section C. Alternatively, at Kāppalūr and Karaṭikuṭi, the akkiṉikampam is made from *āla maram,* banyan.

50. See Hiltebeitel 1982c; 1984a, 12–17; Gonda [1966] 1969, 123–28; Singh 1965, 23–71; Miller 1974, 52–59; Parpola 1988, 199, 205–6.

51. D. C. Sircar, "probably a Dravidian religious institution," especially popular in the South and probably brought to the Puri Jagannātha festival "by the Gangas who had come to Orissa from the South" (1971, 59 n. 2). Cf. Kalidos 1989, 5–12: the temple car reached its "acme under Vijayanagar around the 15th century A.D." (5), with Chola and probably Pallava predecessors.

gods of the eight directions and her culminating combat with Śiva, which she must lose, along with her third breast, before she can marry him.[52]

On the humbler scale of village goddesses, the Andhra buffalo sacrifice may be followed by the goddess's ride to the village boundary. Impersonated by both a clay icon and a hereditary Untouchable Māla priest dressed in a saree, her chariot is equipped with posts on its corners and in its middle (totaling five or nine such posts) for the impalement (or alternatively, binding) of pigs, lambs, and fowl (Whitehead 1921, 58, 67, 69). The chariot (in one case made of margosa wood; ibid., 67) becomes both an altar and the means for impaling the victims.[53] One such chariot (called *korata*) is discussed and photographed by Herrenschmidt. Eggs or pigs are impaled on the stakes, the pig through its stomach and back. After it is buried for eight days, its blood is mixed with nine grains (1989, 94–95 and plates 3b and 4a). Let us also recall that in one Telugu myth, Pōta Rāju (alias the stake) even drives the goddess Reṇukā's chariot into battle (Hiltebeitel 1988a, 352, 359), thus importing the symbolism of this post-chariot rapport further into a battlefield context.[54]

Herrenschmidt's pig aside, one wonders whether some of these real chariot impalements are anal. I cite the sequence of the morning sacrifices at the culminating tenth day of the Kālī festival at Udappu, Sri Lanka, as the best documented case of this practice (Tanaka 1987, 289–97), and also as a parallel to much that preoccupies us elsewhere in this volume in milder forms. First, four roosters are beheaded at the village's cardinal points. Upon each beheading, one of the goddess's Cūrapulis, or "Heroic Tigers" (see chap. 2, n. 28)—possessed by Kātan (Kāttavarāyaṉ?) and Bhairava, and bearers of Kālī's weapons—"grabs the decapitated bird and sucks the blood from its neck" (ibid., 290). Then "a large black vil-

52. See Hudson 1971, 199; revised 1982, 115; and, especially on film, Hudson, Binford, and Camerini 1976. See also Harman 1989, 75: Mīnākṣī on her chariot turns south for her battles, and then northeast when she is finally disarmed of her bow after confronting an image of herself with Śiva as a married pair.

53. The combination of chariots with impalement also occurs widely with the attachment of a hook-swinging apparatus to chariots; see Powell 1914, 155, 157, 167–68, and below, chapter 7, section A.

54. The persistent chariot leading and charioteering by Pōta Rāju in both Andhra and Tamil contexts recalls the charioteer role of the Vedic purohita (literally, "the one placed before") and Brahman "chaplain" to kings (Heesterman 1985, 151). Pōttu Rāja is likewise a Brahman "minister" (usually *mantrin*) and "forerunner" (*munnoṭum piḷḷai;* Hiltebeitel 1988a, 79, 347). See Appendix.

lage goat (*ūr āṭu*)," which may represent the goddess's husband (ibid., 295), must shake after water is poured over it by the president of the temple committee in the role of sacrificer (ibid., 294) before it is decapitated in front of the temple. Again, one of the Cūrapulis "sucks the blood pouring from its neck," after which its head is set to face into the temple. Then, a five-foot stick (*kālmaram*) is set up at the balipīṭha outside the temple; a rooster is brought and doused with water, and when it shakes, "the priest gradually pierces it from its anus through to its mouth with the stick. It is then worshiped, covered with margosa leaves, and left at the *palipīṭham* for four hours," after which it was said "to revive, as if nothing happened to it"—a "miracle" effected by Kālī that Tanaka admits, rather noncommittally, he did not actually see (ibid., 296–97). I can only imagine this as ritual fiction and a rather grotesque comedy of innocence. In any case, the elements here are all familiar. The kālmaram, literally "leg-tree" (*kāl* also means pole or staff), that is used for the actual impalement is apparently homophonic with Kāttavarāyaṉ's "impalement stake," the kaḻumaram. It is set up beside the balipīṭha and near the severed head of the "black village goat" as the latter faces into the temple: an ensemble, that is, of post, balipīṭha, and goat's head in what Tanaka himself refers to as the position of the "demon devotee" (ibid., 295). And while Kālī "revives" the impaled rooster, it has been offered to the even more "demonic" and impure Pecci. It is worth noting in these cases that the black village goat, like the Andhra buffalo, is not impaled; only the smaller and apparently subordinate animals are, like the goats slain near the posts in so many other contexts, including buffalo sacrifices. It seems that real impalement and its pain are displaced from the real rival (the goddess's black goat/buffalo/"husband"/opponent) onto these smaller surrogates. But as with the Śyena sacrifice, with its pointed yūpa and its havirdhāna carts transformed into chariots hurled like thunderbolts against the rival, it is hard not to suspect that, where the impalement is that of a rival, there has been all along a symbolic undercurrent of this dire form of subjugation through sexual humiliation.[55]

55. The most prominent South Indian expression of this theme seems to be the Śaivite myth of the impalement of the eight thousand Jains who rival the saint Campantar for the patronage of the king of Madurai and suffer this punishment (in Cēkkiḻār's *Periya Purāṇa* version) for having attempted to burn the saint alive (Vanmikanathan and Mahalingam 1985, 239–62). The illustration in the Irattiṉa Nāyakar chapbook version of the *Periya Purāṇam* in prose (reproduced in Hudson 1989, 392) shows this to be an anal impalement, as does a fresco on the inner side of the northern outer wall of the Thanjavur Bṛhadīśvara temple. Other details and variants of

In any case, the chariot may also be an altar for the goddess's own suffering, and even impalement of a less drastic sort, as in an image shown by Whitehead, without explanation, of a goddess on a chariot with nails driven into her body (Whitehead 1921, plate 18, facing p. 89). As usual, the image one has of Draupadī must fall between these Brahmanical and "village" poles. On her chariot she will suffer, as when her portable icon (at Mēlaccēri) is screened from seeing her own disrobing on the Terukkūttu stage (Hiltebeitel 1988b, part 1; 1989c). But she will also be victorious. In all these cases, however, the chariot enables the deity's (or deities') movement from the purity of the sanctum into the conflicts of the world. In the Draupadī festival, a theme that is probably latent in many other instances thus becomes explicit, through the connection with the *Mahābhārata.* As Draupadī, and her cult's other deities, move on their chariots back and forth from the temple to the drama stage, paṭukaḷam, and firepit, they orchestrate the major movements of a sacrifice of battle.

---

this story brought out in Peterson 1989, including the claim that the Jains impaled themselves voluntarily after losing their debate (all sacrificial victims are alleged volunteers) and Padmanabh Jaini's response, in discussion, that Jains have no recollections of these events, could be further studied from this mythic angle: impalement appears to be a literalized symbol of anal fixation projected upon an enemy. A Western literary parallel can be found in Andric [1945] 1977, 41–58, and there are historical and folkloric parallels in the figure of Vlad the Impaler, or Dracula (Florescu and McNally 1973, 59–60, 68, 101, 113, 117, 123, and especially 76–80, 143, and 179 (a Zulu parallel).

7 Rituals of Battle

In the last three chapters I have argued that by looking at ordinary rituals that take place within and at the boundaries of the Draupadī temple, one can work back from them to Vedic sacrificial structures that carry the implications of a ritual of battle. Or in reverse, I have attempted to present examples of how Vedic ritual forms persist through classical and royal transformations into the ritual idioms of "folk" or "popular" Hinduism. So far, the Draupadī cult has been linked with the "popular" end of this continuum through comparisons with village goddess cults: particularly those involving buffalo sacrifices, and secondarily with other cults involving (more) explicit themes of impalement. One can, however, define the place of Draupadī cult rituals within this spectrum more precisely. Before we look at Draupadī cult paṭukaḷam and firewalking rituals directly, we should identify their place amid a class of popular Hindu festivals that include similar battlefield rituals, or rituals of battle.

To achieve this, and to allow for further comparisons on specific points, let us recall our Garuḍa for one last long-range view. We will first look briefly at other Tamil and Andhra rituals with similar profiles and terminology. These include cults familiar from earlier discussion, and important for all three volumes of this work: above all, the hero cults of the *Palnad* and *Elder Brothers* folk epics. Then we will examine two flanking traditions: one from Kerala, the other from West Bengal. With our discussion of materials from Orissa in chapter 6, we will have traced an arc from Bengal to Kerala. The Draupadī cult rituals that will be described in the following chapters will thus be placed in the most appropriate cultural and scholarly contexts. As always, the purpose will also be to show how, within these expanded horizons, these ritual traditions shed light upon each other.

A. *Kaḷam* Rituals

In volume 1, discussion of the Draupadī cult's vision of the *Mahābhārata* war as narration and drama led to mention of a number of the basic elements and connotations of the paṭukaḷam, the terrain on which this same epic vision is given expression in ritual. The term itself contains the word *kaḷam,* which has in both wider Dravidian and ancient Tamil usages the double connotation of "battlefield" and "threshing floor," as well as such further meanings as "open space" and "hall of sacrifice."[1] As denoting a sacrificial site, the same word recurs in the term *kaḷappali* (*kaḷam* + *pali,* "sacrifice, sacrificial oblation"). This term serves in the title of the episode "Aravāṉ's Battlefield Sacrifice" in Tamil versions of the *Mahābhārata,* a Terukkūttu drama, and, as we shall see, the ritual that opens the Draupadī cult paṭukaḷam ceremonies. When the dramas refer to the battlefield of Kurukṣetra, they can refer to it as the paṭukaḷam and sing of it as attracting our friend Garuḍa to both Aravāṉ's sacrifice and the death of Karṇa (Hiltebeitel 1988a, 331–32, 412).

If I dwelt at some length on the Tamil *Elder Brothers Story* and the Telugu *Epic of Palnāḍu* in volume 1, it was not only because of their affinities with the Draupadī cult *Mahābhārata,* but also in preparation for further discussion in volumes 2 and 3: in this volume, because each also has what may be called paṭukaḷam-type rituals, and in volume 3 because there is more to say about them in connection with the *Mahābhārata* and regional folk epics. In the cult of the heroes of the *Elder Brothers Story,* paṭukaḷam is the very term for the site of the shrines that mark the place of the heroes' deaths and the rituals that reenact them in the Viramalai Hills of Tiruchirappali District (Beck 1982, 47, 51–52). Meanwhile, in festivals within the Elder Brothers' cult that are celebrated at places beyond the Viramalai in Kongunad, where the folk epic is most popular, "paṭukaḷam ritual behaviour" is transposed to an "open space on which the possession and funeral rites occur [that] is metaphorically considered a paṭukaḷam" (Beck 1981b).

In the cult of the heroes of Palnāḍu, the term *kalli pāḍu,* according to Roghair, means "the horror and the desolation" and commemorates "the desolation that followed the horror of the final

1. See Choondal 1978, 8, 16 nn. 1 and 2, on wider Dravidian and other (including Bengali and Hindi) uses; Kailasapathy 1968, 241; Hart 1975, 34–35; and Parpola in press, sec. 3.2.3 on early Tamil usages in this double sense; cf. Hiltebeitel 1988a, 320–21, 402–4 and n. 13.

battle of the epic" on the field of Kārempūḍi (1982, 29). But Velcheru Narayana Rao, whose work on this cult and its folk epic is still continuing, informs me that while the meaning of *kalli* is uncertain, the second term is probably not *pāḍu*, or "desolation," but *paḍu*, or "falling," as when the weapons that represent the heroes are touched to the ground, ritually signifying their deaths (personal communication, November 1987). Tamil *paṭu*, "to lie down, die," and Telugu *paḍu*, "to fall, die," seem to be related, and though I have no hesitation in insisting that the rituals of this Palnad hero cult are of a "paṭukaḷam type," I suggest that it is likely that this defining term has at least a partially common etymology with the Tamil paṭukaḷam. Let us note, however, that while both of these cults have paṭukaḷam rites, neither has firewalking. Ritually, the paṭukaḷam is thus the point at which these two cults and the Draupadī cult have the most in common.

The term paṭukaḷam is also used for "lying down-battlefield-dying" rituals in the festivals of other Tamil goddesses. Reiniche describes two instances in a cult of Kāḷiyammaṉ, or Kālī, found mainly among weavers in Tiruchirappalli District (1987, 90, 93–94). In the same district, the term is also used for death and revival rites at Māriyammaṉ temples in Kaḷḷai and Nallūr villages (Kulittalai Taluk). There the paṭukaḷam rites for four Paṟaiyars follow directly upon the symbolic impalement of a fifth, whose wife stays in a basket below his impalement stake (*kaḻukumaram* or *kaḻumaram*) until a goat is sacrificed. After this the chief Paṟaiyar descends from the stake and revives the others. Then he tends to the goat's head, if it falls, during a competition (from which the Paṟaiyars are otherwise excluded) called *tarakkōl*, in which long poles or lances (*īṭṭi*) are used to carry and toss the goat's head from pole to pole around the temple and the village, the victor being the one who makes it back to the temple with the head on his pole.[2] The term may also be used for the cremation-ground rituals in the cult of Aṅkāḷammaṉ.[3]

2. Brief and misleading reference is made to the Kaḷḷai festival in Nishimura 1987, 6 n. 15, 67–68 (photos), 93, without mentioning the paṭukaḷam rites that are part of it (which some informants connected with the *Elder Brothers Story*, others with *Kāttavarāyaṉ*). Fieldwork was carried out with Lee Weissman (May, June 1990). Madeleine Biardeau informs me of a similar festival for Cellāṇṭiyammaṉ near the Samayapuram Māriyammaṉ temple (Lalgudi Taluk, Tiruchirappalli District; personal communication, June 1982), while Eveline Masilamani-Meyer found another for the goddess Muttalammaṉ with a different story near Natham village (Melur Taluk, Madurai District; personal communication, June 1990). In a long song to her, Māriyammaṉ is called "Princess of the battlefield" (Loud n.d., 48).

3. According to the chief trustee of the Aṅkāḷaparamēcuvari Kōvil, Mundakkanniyamman Koyil Street, Mylapore, Madras, questioned in February 1982. Meyer

Also closely related are the aḻukaḷam, or "weeping-ground," rituals of the Kūttāṇṭavar cult (see chaps. 4 and 9), which commemorate the lamentations over Aravāṉ-Kūttāṇṭavar's battlefield sacrifice to Kālī.

The analogies with Draupadī cult rituals are telling in these cults, and will be noted further. But they are not as extensive as those that link the Draupadī cult with the Elder Brothers and Palnad hero cults. These three main "paṭukaḷam" traditions share a suggestive configuration of elements: the centrality of the goddess, dominant caste patronage, regional folk epic development, and links with the *Mahābhārata*. While some of the other deities with paṭukaḷam-type cults have similar rituals, the only real common ground among the elements just mentioned seems to be the centrality of the goddess.[4]

For the moment, in fact, we might propose that where the similarities with the Draupadī cult are fullest, we are dealing with a five-element complex: (1) kaḷam rites, (2) the goddess, (3) dominant-caste patronage, (4) regional folk epic development, and (5) links with the *Mahābhārata*. We can thus "control our experiment" by looking not only at ritual traditions that share all these elements with the Draupadī cult, but at cults that share significant portions of that configuration. The richest comparative material outside the Palnad and Elder Brothers cults comes not from the Tamil paṭukaḷam-goddess traditions just mentioned, but from southern Kerala and West Bengal. These traditions have all of these elements in varying degrees but lack the integration of the whole through a regional folk epic that ties in closely with the *Mahābhārata*.[5] Their interest for this volume is thus in their richness of ritual.

1986, however, never mentions use of the term paṭukaḷam in her extensive treatment of Aṅkāḷammaṉ cult rituals. Correspondences between Aṅkāḷammaṉ and Draupadī cult mythologies are discussed in volume 1.

4. Kāḷiyammaṉ and Aṅkāḷammaṉ both have myths that confront the goddess and her "heroes" with opposing tyrannical kings, but these are not regional folk epics of the *Palnāḍu* or *Elder Brothers* type. Other than Māriyammaṉ's *Mahābhārata* and purāṇic identity of Reṇukā, she and Aṅkāḷammaṉ have only tangential epic connections: e.g., songs claiming that Aṅkāḷammaṉ was Draupadī in the previous Dvāpara yuga (Meyer 1986, 267, 273); or that Draupadī and the Pāṇḍavas sit royally in Māriyammaṉ's heavenly court (Loud n.d., 62). The Kūttāṇṭavar cult does have all four of these elements.

5. This statement is only provisional, for lack of detailed information. The southern Kerala tradition does in fact have a regional folk epic development, its "Northern Ballads," that is closely related to our complex, especially connecting the heroes to the goddess and the *kaḷari* or gymnasia (see below, and Tarabout 1986, 415–16, 418, 425; Zarrilli 1984, 15, 18–21). But to judge from available summaries and translations

B. The Original Battle Formation

The southern Kerala situation is fascinatingly diffuse. I can mention only those broad features that justify referring to it as a parallel. First are the uses of the term kaḷam. It is, of course, the same term in Malayalam as in Tamil, and has much the same range: threshing ground, battlefield, plus a distinctive altar for animal sacrifices with sixteen quadrilateral squares (Tarabout 1986, 146 and n. 37, 565). It is also used for images of the goddess drawn on the ground with powders of five colors (black, white, red, yellow, green) that represent her body as composed of substitutional "food" offerings (ibid., 251) and also an altar that, once it is destroyed by being swept up, can be given out as prasādam (ibid., 301–2; cf. Jones 1982, 271–77 and nn. 8 and 12). Moreover, kaḷam shares an overlapping semantic range, and a common etymology, with *kaḷari* (Burrow and Emeneau 1961, 98, #1160),[6] the term that in Kerala refers to the important institution, found mainly among the dominant-caste Nāyars, of the "gymnasium" or "training place" for the martial art of *kaḷari-payaṟṟu*.[7] The kaḷari "serves the function of both training center and temple" (Zarrilli 1979, 116). Training formerly occurred under a master of arms over twelve years, during the monsoon, after which one would be given a sword and standing in the local militia (Tarabout 1986, 416). One senses here a parallel to the movement from goddess temple to battlefield that is ritually orchestrated at the end of the monsoon through the rites of Dasarā.[8] As

(especially Mathew 1979, 83–104; Logan 1906, 98–102), the stories have only minimal reference to the *Mahābhārata* (in the only instance found, the hero Otēnan goes to his fatal duel wearing "A bracelet worked in with scenes / from Rāmāyanam and Bhāratam / High up on his right arm" [Logan 1906, 101]).

6. Eveline Masilamani-Meyer informs me that *kaḷari* is the term used for a long pillar in Madurai District. Barney Bate indicates that in the same district it can be a term for a village festival (personal communications, 1990).

7. Raghavan 1947, 44, however, says that *kaḷari* "has been derived" from Sanskrit *khalūrikā*, "a parade, place for military exercise," a derivation that Devi 1976, 414, accepts, citing Raghavan's study. After the Nāyars, kaḷaripayaṟṟu is next most prominent among Ilavas or toddy tappers; cf. the martial traditions among Bants and Biḷḷavas in Tulunad.

8. Most interesting in this regard is Tarabout's discussion of parallels between the three royal state festivals, all postmonsoon (though not all after the same monsoon), that reconfirm the king's sovereignty through forms of ritual combat: Onam (with a cult rendered by certain castes to their tools; 1986, 82) in central Kerala; Māmaṅkam in the north; and Navarātri as the apparent "equivalent" in the south (1986, 427–47, esp. 447). Cf. ibid., 42–47, 83, on dispersal of Dasarā elements and lack of "spectacle" comparable to other Kerala festivals; 121–22, 165–66 on uses of the *Devī Māhātmyam*.

buildings, the kaḷaris defined a prescribed ritual space, "all twice as long as they were wide," dug "1 kol (2½ feet) into the ground," walled by earthworks dug up from the pit, with places for weapons and deities, most notably a "virgin's corner" in the southwest for Bhagavati as the goddess of war (Zarrilli 1979, 116; Thurston and Rangachari [1904] 1965, 2:397; Raghavan 1947, 43). Most interesting, "In the past there were two types of kalaris, the payatt kalari, for practice and training, and the ankam kalari (somewhat larger), for mock fights or duels" (Zarrilli 1979, 116). This latter kaḷari is surely none other than a variant of the kaḷam as ritual battlefield, but with the emphasis on single combat (*aṅkam*).

The terms kaḷam/kaḷari set us on a chartable semantic course, and underscore a rapport not only among different Kerala rituals but also between those rituals and similar ones in Tamilnadu and beyond. But there is another Malayalam term that brings these same Kerala rituals together with still others under the heading of one "native concept." This is the notion of the "original *paṭayaṇi*." Paṭayaṇi itself means "army battalion, battle formation" and is used with reference to a specific style of festival found in central Travancore that includes nocturnal processions with torchlight dances and, at least traditionally, mock fights (Tarabout 1986, 211–12).[9] The term combines directly with kaḷam, in the form *paṭayaṇi kaḷam*, to refer to a hardened ground where such martial rituals are carried out, directly in front of the goddess's temple (ibid., 216–17).[10] The "original paṭayaṇi," however, is a maximal, and no doubt mythical, concept. "The prevalent conception is that in former times there existed an original and complete paṭayaṇi that would have included sixty-four different sequences: what one sees now are the scattered vestiges of this bygone paṭayaṇi; certain sequences have been 'preserved' only in a single locality, thus accounting for the diversity of styles" (ibid., 259; my translation). According to Tarabout, "This logic is extended to the ensemble of

9. From *paṭa*, "army, battle" and *aṇi*, "array, formation" (Tarabout 1986, 211). Cf. Tamil *paṭai*, "army," as in such relevant compounds as *paṭaittalaivaṉ*, "marshal" (see Hiltebeitel 1988a, 345, 426); *paṭaiyāṭci*, "army leader," "soldier" and name for Vaṉṉiyars (ibid., 38); and even *paṭaiyaṇi*, "a kind of dance with torch-light in hand" (*Tamil Lexicon*, s.v.).

10. One also finds in Kerala instances where *paṭa* serves as the base term for another functional equivalent to paṭukaḷam: *paṭanilam*, "battlefield," a depressed ritual ground for mock combats, in one case commemorating a supposed historical battle (Tarabout 1986, 440–42), in another, with an additional "pool of blood" nearby, possibly evoking the all-Kerala hero Paraśurāma's conquest of the Kṣatriyas at Kurukṣetra that resulted in his filling twenty-one lakes of blood (Tarabout 1986, 441; Thurston and Rangachari [1904] 1965, 2:59–60).

festivals of central Travancore," so that the term paṭayaṇi covers a whole range of rituals, some the specialties of different festivals, all susceptible to unceasing recombination according to different local formulations, that are understood as having originally been components of a single and comprehensive "primordial totality."

This concept is of double interest. The image of a fractured cult serves, as Tarabout says, to pay homage to the grandeur of the ancestors, to account for current forms as the result of decadence, and yet at the same time to authorize and even lend pride to variations that differentiate one local festival from another (ibid., 59–60). Although I have encountered no notion of an "original paṭukaḷam" (or paṭukaḷam plus firewalk) in Draupadī cult rituals, there is similar ritual fragmentation, and as we have seen, one often hears it accounted for by both local pride and the claims of visiting pāratiyārs and dramatists that local variations are departures from traditional norms. More important, though, the elements of this "original paṭayaṇi," taken as an ensemble, bear an affinity to the totality of rituals that one finds at Draupadī festivals. Not only does the "original paṭayaṇi" include paṭayaṇi and kaḷam rituals proper, but it also contains hook-swinging rites (*tūkkam*), which large images of Garuḍa are brought to watch and in which the last devotees to suspend themselves from the hooks (the goddess's teeth) impersonate Garuḍa himself; martial dances; the display of huge portable effigies of chariots, horses, elephants, and bulls that represent armies or kingdoms offering themselves and each other to the goddess; cock sacrifices (ibid., 259 and passim); mock battles; and revilement of the goddess (ibid., 405).[11] Moreover, further recombinant, at least at southern Travancore festivals (ibid., 263) and apparently at some central Travancore festivals as well (ibid., 240–41, 509), are rituals featured in southern Travancore that center on constructions representing the goddess by her hair (*muṭi*).

This last point is intriguing, especially in view of the rituals of Draupadī's hair (Tamil *muṭi, kūntal,* etc.) that take place on the Draupadī cult paṭukaḷam. In the southern Travancore festival that Tarabout treats most fully, the muṭi represents the goddess Bhadrakālī. It is a circular, open-pleated fan of fabric that surrounds a metallic mirror with an engraved image of the goddess in its center and stands on a table pīṭha, or altar. Through most of the festival it resides in a specially built "shelter of the muṭi." There it is joined for some time by the portable image of the goddess Bhagavati of

11. On the tūkkams and "parades of edifices," see Tarabout 1986, 263–321 and 461–522, respectively, and further discussion below.

the local Nāyar kaḷari, who is the same goddess, but in a more benign aspect.[12] On the culminating seventh day, after this portable image has been returned, the festival's closing ceremony calls for a Brahman officiant to detach the protective ring, called kāppu, that has tied the muṭi since the beginning of the festival. This Kerala usage might recall the "protective" significance of Draupadī's hair tying, though the term kāppu is not used in that context.

The untying of Bhadrakālī's muṭi marks the goddess's departure. Then, after other closing rites, it is taken out of the shelter and set facing south before a sixteen-square quadrilateral sacrificial kaḷam altar, into which is offered a combination of reddened water (lime mixed with kuṅkum) and two cut-up gourds, thus "inundating the ground with 'blood.'" Once this is done, the muṭi is lifted and demonstrated, after which the site remains dangerous and off-limits for a week. The sacrifice is supposed to appease the Bhūtas (demons) who form the goddess's entourage, but as Tarabout indicates, despite her stated departure, it must also satisfy the goddess, or at least the aspect of her that is betokened by her loosened hair, facing the inauspicious south. For the Brahman priest, the muṭi is deactivated with the untying of the kāppu, and the goddess leaves for her main temple at Kodungallur. But for the Nāyars as "sacrificers," the muṭi still represents a fraction of her active, dangerous power, and one, moreover, that in this "loosened" aspect presides over a sort of appended kaḷam "blood" sacrifice destined—at least openly—not for her, but for her Bhūtas (ibid., 145–49). One is struck by the way these ritual acts in Kerala are almost entirely mute when it comes to myth.[13] Clearly they have no narrative connection with Draupadī's *kūntal muṭittal* (chignon tying), and they seem even to invert its implications. Instead of marking the end of the kaḷam rites with a hair tying that returns the goddess, as in Draupadī's case, to a benign form, the tied muṭi shows the goddess in a relatively benign form until the end of the festival, when the ritual untying unveils her dangerous side, the aspect that calls for a final kaḷam offering. But as we shall see, in each case, it is in her

12. Using the term *iḷaṅkam*, equivalent to kaḷari, as the apparently preferred term in southern Kerala (Tarabout 1986, 137 and n. 30).

13. At least at this point, though the muṭi is not mythically mute through the entire festival: earlier, the muṭi's shelter is closed at the death of Pālakan (Kōvalaṉ of the *Cilappatikkāram*), then reopened after his resurrection (Tarabout 1986, 135). In a different Southern Kerala usage of the goddess's "muṭi," her dancer wears "a towering head gear over 20 ft. high" in procession to the temple, where it is "carefully removed and disposed of," upon which the goddess pronounces oracles, and benedictions (Raghavan 1947, 28).

"disheveled" form, facing south, that she presides over the symbolic blood sacrifice.

Tarabout's study must be savored to appreciate his finesse in combing out the knots that connect these "spectacular" festivals, and his insight in developing a comprehensive interpretation of their ensemble under the repeated refrain of the "sacrifice of battle."[14] I used this term somewhat metaphorically in volume 1, keeping discussion of ritual there to a minimum, to refer to features of Draupadī cult mythology. This volume has begun to give it some ritual specificity.

In this regard, Tarabout's treatment remains pertinent on some additional points. In terms of our five-element complex, we have seen how Kerala festivals of great variety form a unity as paṭukaḷam-like battlefield cults through the overlapping ritual and mythical idioms of the kaḷam and the paṭayaṇi. The same rituals are further unified through their dominant-caste patronage by the Nāyars,[15] and through their ritual and mythic dedication, in one form or another, to the goddess.[16] Here, however, important differences emerge from what one finds in the core area of the Draupadī cult and in the Elder Brothers and Palnad hero cults. The participation of the Nāyars in overlapping "martial" cults might, for instance, be compared with that of the Vaṉṉiyars of northern Tamilnadu in the cults of Draupadī, Kūttāṇṭavar (who is linked with a number of goddesses), and Paccaivāḻiyammaṉ (Hiltebeitel 1988a, 37 n. 8), not to mention their prominent involvement in the ten-day buffalo sacrifice to Ceñciyammaṉ, Māriyammaṉ, and Kāḷiyammaṉ at the Gingee Fort (Hiltebeitel 1985b), or the worship of Kāḷiyammaṉ, Māriyammaṉ and Nelliyammaṉ at the Maṅkalam Pōttu Rāja festival (Hiltebeitel 1988a, 366). The Tamil examples, however, concern cults of different goddesses, whereas the Kerala cults center on one goddess whose two aspects (benign and terrible) are reflected in her double name of Bhagavati/Bhadrakālī (Tarabout 1986, 109–10,

14. On the sacrifice of battle theme, see chapter 6, section A, 4; Biardeau in Biardeau and Malamoud 1976, 131–53; Tarabout 1986, 6, 170–74, 412, 427–36, 438–44, 458–61, 490–97, 521–22, 529, 560, 594. See also Reiniche 1987, 98–99.

15. Tarabout 1986, 149 (muṭi and kaḷam), 177 (festival of the "army leader" Tampuran as Nāyar "house" deity, akin to a kuladevatā), 215 and 243, 281 (paṭayaṇi), 262 (tūkkam), 439–42 (mock combats), 492, 504, 527–29 (parades of edifices), etc. Cf. also the role of the Nāyars in a Palghat area firewalking cult (336).

16. An interesting variation is Bhagavati's victory over Kongan, supposed king of the people of Kongunad in Tamilnadu, who rode a great buffalo into battle. The goddess emerged from her temple icon to kill them both. The battle is reenacted at night, with sham fighting, in connection with the Kongapada festival at Chittur (Ananthakrishna Iyer 1909–12, 2:71–75; Choondal 1978, 62–64).

134, 149, 172, 574–80). Moreover, Bhagavati/Bhadrakālī's chief demon-conquering myth, the one that finds distinctive retellings and additional episodes that tie in with her different types of festivals, is one that confronts her not with the Buffalo Demon Mahiṣāsura, but with her special Kerala antagonist, the demon Dārikan. The mythology of Mahiṣa and the ritual of buffalo sacrifice are relatively inconspicuous in Kerala, as I will mention again in connection with Dasarā rites there.[17]

No matter what demon the goddess fights, however, she has her army, and in one form after another, the participants define themselves as soldiers. In all cases, if it is not precisely a question of the goddess's army, it is probably always, in some sense, an army that offers itself, or dedicates its services, to her. Thus in the mock combats and parades of edifices, the festival armies of rival "kings" present and symbolically offer themselves, their opponents, their kingdoms, and the earth to the goddess, in the latter case holding up huge effigies of chariots, horses, elephants, and bulls on a sort of war-stage before her temple.[18] Taking Tarabout's interpretation a step further, I suggest that behind the "parades of edifices," with combinations of chariots, elephants, horses, and bulls, plus those on foot who form the paṭayaṇi, there is the specific image of the offering of the typical epic army with its four components of chariot riders, elephant riders, cavalry, and foot soldiers (with bulls, as Tarabout says, representing additionally the total populace of all classes). The unexplained single chariot at one festival, with two armies represented by all the other components (ibid., 519), also suggests a distant (perhaps forgotten) evocation of the single chariot of the *Bhagavad Gītā*.

More straightforwardly, the hook-swinging *tūkkakkārans* dress as if for combat as the goddess's soldiers (ibid., 264, 268, 290). Indeed, Tarabout's plate 15 (facing 269) shows them four abreast, hanging two each from the long poles that project forward and upward from the scaffold-base of a sort of chariot. Moving their legs as if running, four of them together convey the impression of horses pulling a stylized Vedic or epic war chariot, or a solar chariot (cf. ibid., 489; also Powell 1914, 159, 168–69). They thus seem to

17. On adaptations of the Dārikan myth to varied "spectacles," see Tarabout 1986, 131–32, 150–53 (muṭi), 192–93 (Tampuran), 214 (paṭayaṇi), 264, 294 (tūkkams), 347, 351 (firewalk), 373 (ritual obscenities), 526 (parade of edifices, variant). Raghavan 1947, 24–25 says the slaying of Dārikan "underlies the cult of the goddess."

18. See especially Tarabout 1986, 500, fig. 59, and 311 ("sacrifice of a multitude"), 412, 491–92, 521–22, convincingly stressing Vedic elements transfigured through bhakti with the theme of pralayic cosmic crisis.

combine the horse and chariot as offerings to the goddess, again reminding us, this time through a ritual of self-offering, of the combination of the chariot and impalement. They also identify, according to one myth, with the demon Dārikan: the hooks as the goddess's "teeth" recall that when Bhadrakālī defeated Dārikan, she bit him in the back to drink his blood (Powell 1914, 168).

Most interesting, though, are the paṭayaṇis, which, as we have seen, implicitly (or "originally") embrace all these other spectacles. Tarabout says they "always make reference to the army of the goddess, composed of Bhūtas" (1986, 211; see also 281, 290). But one finds modifications, such as festivals in which the paṭayaṇi represents Śiva's Bhūtas, dancing to appease the goddess after her killing of Dārikan (ibid., 214). There is no need here to account for the many variations on the theme of who it is that forms the goddess's army. We shall find similar variations in the festivals of West Bengal. As to who leads or marshals it, suffice it to say that there are as many candidates in Central Kerala as there are in the Draupadī cult *Mahābhārata,*[19] but that the figure who should be studied most closely in relation to Pōttu Rāja–Pōrmaṉṉaṉ and Vīrapattiraṉ is Ghaṇṭākarṇṇan, "Bell-Ear," whom Tarabout shows to be another "transfigured demon" and multiform of Vīrabhadra himself.[20] What is most important for us in the Kerala festivals is that the goddess's Bhūta army may also be composed of, or include within its ranks, the Kauravas.

Central Travancore is an area where temples and festivals of many types "are characterized by repeated references" to the *Mahābhārata* (Tarabout 1986, 224). In paṭayaṇi-type festivals in that region, the Kauravas are known as "Mountain Gods" (*maladēvan-*

19. On the successive and to some degree interchangeable series of the goddess's guardians—Ghaṇṭākarṇṇan, Vīrabhadra, Bhairava, Māṭan, Vetalan, Tampurān, etc.—see Tarabout 1986, 126, 163, 167–68, 175, 209, 309; also 505 on Bhūtan and Taṟa.

20. His name, "bell" plus "ear," has several connotations, including "bell-shaped ears" (cf. Kumbhakarṇa, "Pot Ears," brother of Rāvaṇa), "having bells in the ears," or, a "bell with a tongue," as in myths where he is created from Śiva's ear to lick smallpox sores off Śiva's or the goddess's body (Tarabout 1986, 151 and n. 4). Cf. Pōta Rāju–Pōrmaṉṉaṉ's tongue (Hiltebeitel 1988a, 339, 351, 363). Tarabout suggests he is a "personalized" (add "demonized") "form of the goddess's bell, considered as a weapon (and the 'large tongue' as nothing more than its clapper)" (1986, 154 n. 46). The bell is one of the ritual weapons linking Draupadī with Pōrmaṉṉaṉ (Hiltebeitel 1988a, 387). Ghaṇṭākarṇṇan is linked with Vīrabhadra as residing in the *dhanumaram,* or "bow tree" (ibid., 126, 163, 168), another demonized ritual "weapon" (ibid., 169); cf. Arjuna's "bow tree"; chapter 8; and identified with Yama's buffalo (ibid., 151 n. 2, 166). Ghaṇṭākarṇṇan's altar receives the blood of tūkkakkāran-warriors (ibid., 291, 293–98, 310–13).

mār). Imagined as cruel giants and "children of the dust" or "workers of the earth," their cult is maintained not by the Nāyars but by lower castes and is linked with sorcery and exorcisms. At the festival Tarabout documents, they are represented by Untouchable Kuṟavans, whose name is locally identified with the Kauravas and whom the Nāyars view as representing an image of diminution, incompleteness, and disorder.[21]

While a paṭayaṇi-kaḷam ground lies to the east of the goddess's temple, the Kaurava–Mountain Gods have a curious shrine to the temple's southwest: a masonry platform surmounted by a miniature, whitened cement, cottagelike "niche" that has little iron arrows (some bent) placed around it while other such arrows project helter-skelter from its roof, points outward. It appears either that the bases of the arrows have simply been set in the cement so that the emergent shafts and arrowheads can suggest a bristly image of impalement, or that the roof is represented as having been pierced from inside the building as if it were a fort that had been attacked from within. In any case, these Kauravas are the goddess's guardians: as Tarabout says, "a new example of 'guardian-demons.'" Four of them protect the cardinal directions, and one is identified as the goddess's servant and "young female buffalo" (Tarabout 1986, 216, 222–23, 256). Draupadī cult parallels are inviting: Could this be the Kauravas' sister Duḥśālā, who has her shrine to the south of Draupadī's temple at Chinna Salem (Hiltebeitel 1988a, 113, 118 and n. 24)? Or could it be Duryodhana's wife, the foremost among the hundred Kaurava wives whom Gāndhārī, the Kauravas' mother, refers to collectively as a "herd of buffaloes" (ibid., 232)?

During the ten-day paṭayaṇi, the Kaurava–Mountain Gods are featured at key points. On "the most important" eighth night, which features a "quasi-totality" of all the paṭayaṇi sequences (Tarabout 1986, 226, 246), the Kuṟavan in charge of the Mountain Gods becomes possessed by them in the night procession around the temple (ibid., 229). And on the last day, as closure to a series of elaborate offerings to the temple's subordinate deities, the Mountain Gods are honored by a rite called *ūrāḷi paṭayaṇi* (*ūrāḷi* is an

21. Tarabout 1986, 223 recounts a regional Kuṟavan-*Mahābhārata* story that looks like a distant variant-inversion of "Draupadī the Gypsy (*kuravañci*)": A Kuṟavan in Duryodhana's service goes to bewitch the Pāṇḍavas but is secretly devoted to them. He "pierces the brothers' shadow," but only partially, and thus puts them to sleep. His wife sees them inert, becomes furious, takes her own son, quarters him, and then goes to Kṛṣṇa, who brings them all back to life. For further details, see Raghavan 1947, 21; Varadarajan Pillai 1977, 63–64; Logan 1906, 78. Cf. Hiltebeitel 1988a, 301–9 and above, chapter 4.

honorific title for Kuṟavan leaders; ibid., 223). After the Kuṟavan officiant in charge invokes the Mountain Gods with offerings (including tobacco, "appreciated by inferior divinities in general"), he takes up an iron bow (with jingling bronze rings) and an iron arrow (like the arrows at the Mountain Gods' altar). When the Mountain Gods possess him, he plants the bow in the ground, brandishes the arrow, and announces that an error was committed earlier in the festival. These words are addressed to a member of the family (apparently Nāyar; ibid., 217) from whose house—one of those that owns traditional rights to the products of the land—the goddess comes (248–49). The Kuṟavan, possessed by the Kaurava-Mountain Gods, thus speaks for the goddess, whom the Mountain Gods guard, implying that the fault should be corrected in the future.

The Kauravas are thus part of the Bhūta army that guards the goddess. Indeed, in the same region there is a temple of Duryodhana as her army's chief: elaborate "parades of edifices" are danced before it, most notably with "horses" that are geometric, as elsewhere, but with the added feature of figurative horse heads, sculpted in wood (ibid., 483). At another temple, in Quilon, the priest, possessed by Duryodhana, dances on one leg for hours at the time of the annual festival, recalling, according to Tarabout, the fracturing of Duryodhana's leg by Bhīma (ibid., 223). This one-legged Duryodhana suggests either a prolongation of his death agony as a dance of self-offering to the goddess or his death and transfiguration (reborn?) into her disabled demon devotee.[22]

But where are the Pāṇḍavas? Tarabout did not do fieldwork on these two festivals accentuating Duryodhana, so his descriptions are brief, but it is striking that nothing is said about them other than the implications of *past* action by Bhīma. The Pāṇḍavas, however, are not forgotten. One option, not well developed, is to symbolize the Kaurava-Pāṇḍava opposition through two groups. The one case mentioned occurs among Untouchable Pulayans of central Travancore, who divide themselves into a "western" group descended from the Pāṇḍavas' slaves, and an "eastern" one from slaves of the Kauravas (Tarabout 1986, 224, 491; Thurston and Rangachari [1904] 1965, 7:20). There is, however, no indication of mock

22. It is not indicated whether this Duryodhana, like the Kuṟavan-Kaurava leader, gives oracles; cf. chapter 12, section B. In the Dharma *gājan*s of West Bengal (see sec. C below), some possessed Untouchable dancers hop on one leg while shouting a word that means "depraved," "debauched," "wicked," "disastrous" (Robinson 1980, 388–89; cf. 219, 267, 361).

combats between them, as there is in so many other Kerala contexts. Moreover, the opposition is not between the Kauravas and Pāṇḍavas themselves, or between their reincarnations (such as can be found elsewhere in regional folk epics), but between the Untouchable descendants of their "slaves." I suggest that this humble account of ancestral division among the Pulayans registers the fact that any ritual transposition of the direct opposition between the Kauravas and the Pāṇḍavas would have to involve the Nāyars.

In fact, this is what one finds, though for the clearest example we must once again move, as with the festivals accentuating the goddess's muṭi, from central to southern Travancore. For the Paṅkuni Utsavam festival at the great Padmanabhaswami (Viṣṇu-Nārāyaṇa) temple in Trivandrum, one of the large Nāyar houses is responsible for "recruiting" those who will perform a type of "danced combat" called *vēlakaḷi* (ibid., 448). The house is that of a former master of arms and marshal of the Rāja of Chempakasseri in central Travancore (Tarabout 1986, 50, 449), and the vēlakaḷi style is actually most prominent in central Travancore, where it is connected with reenactments of reputedly historical battles rather than with the *Mahābhārata* and is intertwined with rituals of the paṭayaṇi cluster. At Trivandrum, however, "the dancers are the Kauravas," while the Pāṇḍavas are represented by huge painted wooden effigies, all carrying maces. The two largest, six to eight meters high, are of a seated Yudhiṣṭhira-"Dharmaputra" and a standing Bhīma, while those of Arjuna and the twins are of decreasing sizes. Dharmaputra's position, with the left foot planted and the right ankle at a "royally easeful" rest over the left knee, is identical with that found in many images of Dharmarāja in the sanctums of Draupadī-Dharmarāja temples (see plate 4; Tarabout 1986, plate 25a).

During the Trivandrum festival, the Kaurava dancers gather twice a day to "execute their movements" before the immobile effigies, or more precisely between the effigies and the temple, for the effigies are set facing west into the temple. "Silently they stand . . . while the simulated conflict surges about them, advances, recedes, advances again, and finally fades away" (Cousins 1970, 200). The Pāṇḍavas' temple-facing position is normally one of temple guardians, and it may be suggested that the two types of festivals are complementary: whereas the Pāṇḍavas guard this Viṣṇu temple, the Kauravas guard temples of the goddess. Moreover, the Trivandrum temple is dedicated to Viṣṇu-Nārāyaṇa: the supreme, reclining form of Viṣṇu that seems to complement the goddess by overseeing the liberating, salvific dimensions of the sacrifice of battle, in which they collaborate together.[23] There is no mention of Bhadrakālī (or of images of Draupadī) at vēlakaḷis before Viṣṇu (cf. Raghavan 1947, 46–47), but one may suspect that these "Kauravas" are still a somewhat "Vaiṣṇavized" variant of the goddess's Bhūta army. Here again the ritual suggests ambiguity. On the one hand, the severe, mace-holding images of the Pāṇḍavas—particularly the Yama-like Yudhiṣṭhira, seated on his throne—suggest the Kaurava army's submission, defeat, and self-offering, not only to the Pāṇḍavas but also to Nārāyaṇa. In this vein, a large image of Garuḍa faces south over the same dancing ground (Tarabout 1986, 456). On the other hand, the ritual suggests the revival of the Kaurava army, born ever anew to challenge the Pāṇḍavas—a theme that is hinted at in Draupadī cult dramas when Duryodhana tries to revive his army at the end of the war (Hiltebeitel 1988a, 415). It is intriguing that the Pāṇḍavas, especially Bhīma but also Draupadī, are sometimes represented by effigies that are carried along with those of chariots, horses, elephants, bulls, and birds in the "parades of edifices" of central Travancore (Tarabout 1986, 485, 487, 491; Raghavan 1947, 46–47). Is one to interpret these effigies—as Tarabout does with the others—as sacrificial offerings? Or do they appear to mark the festival "army" as that of the ever-loyal Kaurava opposition, as in the vēlakaḷis?

As regards the apparent absence of regional folk epic development linked with the *Mahābhārata,* I offer two observations. First, the Northern Ballads themselves, drawing inspiration from the ideals of the kaḷari, place such a high premium on the single combat duel (*aṅkam*) between champions that they render the activities of armies inconsequential.[24] As folk epic, they thus present an unsuitable vehicle for *Mahābhārata* themes, leaving such possibilities almost entirely to the realm of ritual.

Second, whatever the ambiguities that attend the occasional presence of Draupadī and the Pāṇḍavas among the parades of edifices, the Kaurava-Pāṇḍava opposition seems to find no direct representation, whether in those rituals or in mock fights, of the two sides on a par. Where the Kauravas are the cruel Mountain Gods impersonated by Untouchable Kuṟavans, they are ritually opposed

23. I make this point only tentatively (cf. Hiltebeitel 1984b, 172; 1988a, 55 and n. 6, 346; 1988b, part 1), reserving further discussion for volume 3.

24. Devi 1976, 414, 416, 419, notes the "conspicuous absence of pitched battles" and of chariots in this literature and remarks that such a system, while it emphasized bravery, showed an "absence of efficient military organization" when faced with colonial forces.

to the Nāyars, but only in the context of criticizing their supervision of the festival. The Nāyars are not figured as the Pāṇḍavas. And where the Nāyars "recruit" the Kaurava army, the Pāṇḍavas are represented by immobile effigies. Epic figures—Droṇa, Arjuna, and Bhīma—serve as models for Nāyars (and others) training in kaḷari-payaṟṟu (Zarrilli 1984, 24; 1979, 116), but again without implying any ritualized opposition. This situation seems to mirror, and might also help to account for, the apparent lack of a regional folk epic transposition of such an opposition. According to Tarabout, the combination of Vedic elements reinterpreted through purāṇic and epic "prisms" in the relatively "Brahmanized" popular festivals of Kerala results from the Nāyars' relatively extensive interaction with the Namputiri Brahmans, and thus enhances the "(external) warrior aspect of the rites that connects them with the epics (and most often . . . with the *Mahābhārata*)" (1986, 554–55). For what it is worth, I suggest that the rich elaboration of a folk *Mahābhārata* at the level of ritual in Kerala, without regional folk epic development to close the circle, derives from this same collaboration between the Nāyars and the Namputiris. The rituals themselves involve regular collaboration with the Brahmans and are not only "spectacular" but highly public. They do not have the low visibility, back-country quality of Draupadī festivals or of the other kaḷam cults discussed above. Moreover, the Nāyars are, relatively speaking, unrivaled in their position of landed dominance in Kerala.

Finally, the paṭayaṇi cycle brings us back to the subject of impalement. After the Kaurava–Mountain Gods possess the Kaurava-Kuṟavan during the sequence of processions on the eighth night of Tarabout's exemplary paṭayaṇi, there follows a rite of "glorification" called *kāppoli*. Participants come before the goddess to the sound of drums and percussion instruments, shouting cries of acclamation and agitating various objects before her: these days fantastic masks and headdresses (*kōlam*) that represent different Bhūtas; formerly horses and bulls such as one finds elsewhere in the parades of edifices. This agitation of objects before the goddess has a revealing background in a "legendary anecdote" about the "original paṭayaṇi":

> In one village, presented as the place of "origin" of the paṭayaṇi, the festival opposed in open competition two groups of *kara*s [Nāyar residence groups]. One year, one of these groups sought to surpass the other by exhibiting and agitating a human corpse. The other group did not consider itself defeated, and did not

> hesitate to impale a living man on a stake for shelling coconuts. Since then that village no longer organizes a paṭayaṇi. (1986, 229)

As Tarabout observes, "If the human sacrifice by impalement is presented as an excess that places it beyond the limits of the kāppoli, it is nonetheless conceived of as the ultimate outcome of the logic of this glorification" (1986, 229–30). Amid all the spectacles in the paṭayaṇi cluster, the only one with a clear impalement symbolism is the tūkkam, with its "hook swingers" swaying from the goddess's "teeth." But now we see that the "original paṭayaṇi" is pervaded by this symbolism, coming to an end in its "original" village, to be fragmented into its many subrites once the logic of impalement took on its mythic reality.

As we saw in chapter 6, this mode of killing is evoked in connection with the myth of the goddess's impalement of the Buffalo Demon. One thinks especially of the Orissan accounts in which Durgā must straddle two hills to impale Mahiṣa, below her, with her trident: either because he has been cursed to die seeing (see 1988a, 369, n. 1), or blessed to attain liberation through kissing (Parpola in press, section 3.2.1), her vagina. This is not, however, to say that this complex is sufficient to account for impalement symbolism in general. In Kerala, as noted (see n. 8), there is a dispersal of Navarātri-Dasarā elements, and the mythology of Mahiṣāsuramardinī, though known, is largely in the background. The "original paṭayaṇi" involves not Durgā but Bhagavati-Bhadrakālī. In any case, the goddess is not the only deity to impale demon foes and have it reflected in festival ritual. Once again, we are led back to Śiva, whose affinities with impalement have Vedic precedents, and who gives the goddess her trident in the first place in the *Devī Māhātmyam* (2.20).[25] Before turning back to the goddess, we must thus look at one more type of festival that will recall our discussion of the connections between the yūpa, the liṅgam, and the symbolism of impalement.

C. The Demon and Lord of Arrows

The type of festival in question, found with regional variation throughout West Bengal, is known as *gājan,* which is said to mean "roaring."[26] There are actually two gājan traditions, one for Śiva and the other for a deity called Dharma, Dharmarāja, or Dharma

25. See chapter 6, section A, 8.

26. Robinson 1980, 29, 103, 252. Cf. B. K. Sarkar [1917] 1972, 73: "from the Sanskrit word 'Garjana,' meaning loud clamour"; N. N. Bhattacharyya 1975, 148. R. C. Sen

Ṭhākur: an intriguing name, to be sure, since, as we have seen, another Dharma-Dharmarāja lends his name to, and presides over, many "Draupadī temples." It would be worth exploring whether the connections between these and other Dharmarājas go beyond the resonances of the name.[27] In the light of scholarly controversies over the origins and nature of Dharma Ṭhākur, I do not, of course, mean to suggest that the Dharma gājan is simply a reflex of the Śiva gājan.[28] I would like to think, however, that this discussion will contribute to understanding their rapport.

The two cults overlap regionally, share common subrites, a common overall festival structure,[29] and, as we shall see, interlinked ritual and mythical terminologies. There is also the sense that the multiple subrites and variations from temple to temple, cult to cult, and region to region hark back to an original unity akin to the "original paṭayaṇi" of Kerala.[30] Most important for our purposes,

---

1833, 609, proposes the etymology "*Gā* or *Grāma; jana,* people," implying a village festival.

27. For a precursor on likely connections, see Chattopadhyay 1942, 129–30. In the Dharma cult, Yudhiṣṭhira is cited as Dharma's greatest worshiper in the Dvāpara yuga (each yuga has such a figure; ibid., 126). We have also just met Dharmaputra in Kerala. These Dharma cults, and also one in Rajasthan (Lindsey Harlan, personal communication, 1989), seem to connect Dharma with heroic death (for Draupadī's Dharmarāja, see chap. 5, sec. D). B. K. Sarkar [1917] 1972, 108 writes of Dharma gājan flesh piercing as a "semi-military feat" performed by "a class of men" who "furnished the Hindu Zamindars (landlords) of yore with their infantry." In the related regional folk epic, when the hero Lausen performs his battlefield sacrifice, "Death reigned everywhere." All others die with him, except a dog that "refused to die, reasoning that Dharma was apt to come" (Robinson 1980, 28): surely evoking Yudhiṣṭhira's refusal to abandon the dog that turns out to be Dharma when all others have died at the end of the *Mahābhārata.*

28. See Östör 1980, 221 n. 20, on supposed Buddhist or "tribal" backgrounds; R. M. Sarkar 1986, 51–55, 68–74, on affinities with various Vedic gods, Dharma's tortoise and solar and Ḍom Untouchable connections—plus the author's opinion that Dharma worship arose from pre-Aryan primitive fertility cult magic (70–71). Cf. Chattopadhyay 1942, 131–35: an original primitive human sacrifice; N. N. Bhattacharyya 1975, 141–64: "proletarian" and "primitive"; Robinson 1980, 6–7, critical of most such theories, but still looking for "tribal" origins (despite a cautionary note from Ralph Nicholas; 228–29), a Dharma gājan before syncretism with the Śiva gājan (ibid., 243), and "brahmanic interpolations" (ibid., 307; cf. 269, 285). Vedic counterparts to the goat sacrifice and drinking of a ritual intoxicant are cited (ibid., 230, 335), but "original non-Aryan" (ibid., 339) explanations are favored. It is intriguing, given the possible Soma analogy, that the procession of the sacred beverage may be the scene of "mock or actual fights" (N. N. Bhattacharyya 1975, 153).

29. R. C. Sen 1833, 609; Chattopadhyay 1942, 105–7, 127–28; Östör 1980, 142, 145, 199–200; R. M. Sarkar 1986, 123.

30. "More than one hundred rites comprise the Dharmapūjā as it is performed in different villages collectively. In no single village setting will each of these rites be

however, is that in terms of ritual, Dharma Ṭhākur himself would seem to be associated with Śiva precisely where it comes to matters of impalement. Following Östör (1980), I will center discussion on the cluster of rites at the gājan for Śiva-Ṣāṛesvar at Vishnupur in Bankura District, West Bengal. References to Dharma gājans will be based on more varied sources, with most of the festivals discussed being from Birbhum District, of the same state.[31] The Vishnupur Śiva gājan has the advantage of being connected with the royal traditions of that city, and is of regional centrality, while Dharma gājans are village festivals. Other Śiva gājans, however, are without royal patronage. In any case, one would need more information about the socioreligious background and interrelationships of the two cults before generalizing about such matters. I would suggest that if we are to find the right *preliminary* word to characterize the difference between them, it would be that the Śiva gājan is more "purāṇicized": not "Hinduized" or "Brahmanized."[32] Although only the Dharma cult has Untouchable Ḍom priests, who actually trace their ascent to the marriage of the son of the cult's Brahman founder and a Ḍom woman,[33] we shall observe that Brah-

---

found, since many are, practically speaking, functionally equivalent to certain other rites" (Robinson 1980, 176; cf. B. K. Sarkar [1917] 1972, 61–62, 80). Along with features discussed below, one finds at least two varieties of crematorium dance: *mashâna nâcha* ("crematorium dance"), in which bhaktas enact the goddess's crematorium dance with disheveled hair (B. K. Sarkar [1917] 1972, 55–56); and *mashâna-kridâ,* "crematorium play" in which they take up "dead bodies and severed heads, [and] dance a wild dance, known as Tândava" (ibid., 81; cf. 90, 188 and Robinson 1980, 257–61). These scenes evoke the pralaya (cf. n. 18 above), not "a sublimated expression of human sacrifice in head-hunting" (Robinson 1980, 258). Cf. the "pillaging of the crematorium" at Aṅkāḷammaṉ festivals (Meyer 1986, passim; Biardeau 1989b, 296–99; below, chap. 13, sec. C), also one of many rites within a total cult complex.

31. Robinson's emphasis on a "composite Dharmapūjā" and on a "cumulative conception" arising from four functional groups of rites (1980, 176–79) obscures the significance of sequences, but her work on Baruipur (linked with the Lausen folk epic as the site of the hero's battlefield sacrifice) is still the fullest ethnography (other than in Bengali) on one village Dharma gājan. See also Chattopadhyay (1942, 108–27; two festivals); R. M. Sarkar (1986, 147–76; five).

32. Cf. Bhattacharya 1971, 240. The notions of Sanskritization, Brahmanization, and Hinduization are all prominent in R. M. Sarkar 1986: e.g., 7, 23 n. 5, 49, 73; cf. Robinson 1980, 201, 244–45, 259). Whatever "primitive" or tribal (or Buddhist) elements his cult may include, however, Dharma's gājan (like Śiva's) is best interpreted as an ensemble with a Hindu structure for which a pre-Hinduized or pre-Brahmanized "primitive" precursor is figmental. Without purāṇic sources, the Dharma cult created a purāṇa of its own, the *Śūnya Purāṇa* (probably thirteenth century; Chattopadhyay 1942, 100).

33. Chattopadhyay 1942, 104–6, 111, 115, 125, 128; R. M. Sarkar 1986, 68, 72. On the

mans play similar pivotal roles—linked, as we would now expect, to threads, fires, "posts" (or their equivalents), and related sacrificial acts—in both cults.[34] Moreover, it would appear that in both cults they are called Gājane Brahmans for officiating in the gājan festivities and are of low status among other Brahmans because of their service to lower castes (B. K. Sarkar [1917] 1972, 76 and n. 1).

The Ṣāṛesvar temple once belonged to the Vishnupur kings, and as we shall see, the rāja was still honored in the festival at the time of Östör's fieldwork in 1969–70. The gājan of this temple is thus unique in being both a royal festival and a "community worship" for the entire town. It is the largest Śiva gājan regionally, with lesser ones held by other Śiva temples both within Vishnupur and in area villages (Östör 1980, 98–99). The main festival takes place over sixteen days in April–May, the month of Caitra at the end of the Bengali year, but the chief rituals occur only from the twelfth day on (ibid., 28). Dharma gājans usually culminate, after anywhere from eight days to a month, on the full-moon day of the month of Vaiśākha (May–June).

For our purposes, with little shading, one can characterize these festivals as combinations of temple-based rituals, "kaḷam" or battlefield rituals, and firewalking (or equivalents), much like what one finds at Draupadī festivals. As to my use of the term kaḷam here, for now let us note the following. The main rituals that will concern us at Vishnupur occur in and around a fallow rice paddy field and involve use of a winnow, a link that we have already met between "rituals of battle" and the threshing of grain (ibid., 127–31). A winnow is also an element in a special altar to Dharma (Robinson 1980, 324). Further, the Dharma gājan includes variations on "mock combat" (ibid., 259; cf. 268, 342; N. N. Bhattacharyya 1975, 153). One village has two wards, each with its own Dharma temple, that "stand against each other ceremonially" and engage in "keen competition" in different stages of the festival. Among the competitions is the staging of "grotesque" dramas performed by "comedian troupes" on decorated bullock carts, which members of the sponsoring faction pull into the other ward for the actual performance.

mixed ancestry of this priesthood, cf. the Orissan counterparts mentioned in chapter 5, sec. C, and chapter 6, section A, 1.

34. For the Dharma cult, see Robinson 1980, 189–96, 202, 305; R. M. Sarkar 1986, 154, 162, 167 (wristlet tying and equivalent scarves or threads around necks); Robinson 1980, 245–46, 265; R. M. Sarkar 1986, 149–51 (fire homa); Robinson 1980, 232; R. M. Sarkar 1986, 149–51 (goat and ram sacrifices); Robinson 1980, 83, 306–9, 316; R. M. Sarkar 1986, 153, 157, 162 (overseeing worship of impalement plank-"post," discussed below).

The cult shows little in the way of direct ritual or folk epic allusion to the *Mahābhārata,* but "sometimes special and attractive scenes from the Ramayana and Mahabharata are selected and the concerned parties dress accordingly" (R. M. Sarkar 1986, 147, 279–80). At another village, during one set of offerings, "a party of mummers came dressed up as Muhammadans, with beard and *loongi* . . . carrying an imitation *tajia* and shouting 'Hassen Hossain'," to which is added "a spirited display of sword and stick play" (Chattopadhyay 1942, 116). Thus Muslim Muharram themes are incorporated into the gājan. Dharma gājan rituals are also tied in, though sometimes rather loosely, with the martial folk epic about the hero Lausen, recounted in regionally variant texts called *Dharmamangals*.[35]

Ritual allusions to mythic and epic themes appear to be fragmentary in both gājans. But this does not diminish the significance of myths in the two cults. In accounts gathered by Östör, the Śiva gājan's rituals are considered to have been formerly "performed by the deities themselves," though in a revealingly fluid mythic continuum. One myth is that "a particular," but unfortunately unnamed, Asura did tapas until Śiva gave him the rule of heavens and earth. To break Śiva's meditation and end their distress, the gods "performed pūjās, lay on the ground and rolled around Śiva himself, lay on thorny bushes, pierced their tongues, and walked on fire." When Śiva rose from meditation, "all the wounds the gods had afflicted upon themselves appeared on his own body." Taking on the deities' sufferings, he then defeated the demon.

Alternatively, the first gājan "was performed by Śiva's companions—ghosts, *bhūtas*, *rākṣasas*, *piśācas*, and Bhairabas, the riders of the night—the creatures that populate the burning grounds and other inauspicious places." Śiva then joined the gājan and all the deities joined in to participate in his violent *tamasik* powers, and to secure this power for divine ends lest it fall to the demons. In both cases, whether their model is the gods alone or the gods and "companions" (Śiva's *gaṇa*), the gājan's performers take on the character of Śiva's "army." While the myths do not involve this "army" in actual combat with the demons, which in the first myth is left to Śiva and in the second is deferred to an indefinite future, the "pointed" sufferings of the gods are shared not only with Śiva but presumably with the defeated demon himself.

35. See n. 24; Robinson 1980, iii, 22–48 and passim; R. M. Sarkar 1986, 74–79; Chattopadhyay 1942, 103, 117, 121–22, 126.

Moreover, at least one secondary gājan draws its inspiration from another myth: after the gājan, Śiva returned to the goddess "intoxicated by the devotion of the gods and his companions," but with his body "marked in a frightful way." Seeing the goddess "moody and jealous" that he had experienced all this without her, Śiva cried out, "I will do gājan again." Thus an image of Durgā is carried in this gājan's processions (Östör 1980, 29–30). Presumably she takes on the sufferings too. Actually, as we shall see, the goddess's participation is subordinate but still vital to the Vishnupur gājan as well. The goddess's place in the gājan is complex, but it seems that the bhaktas, or devotees, can be the goddess's army no less than the army of Śiva (cf. R. C. Sen 1833, 611). Dharma also has a complex interplay with the goddess, with varying emphases on his androgyny (Robinson 1980, 237–38, 321–22), his ritual marriage to Muktā or Mukti (ibid., 324–33), his Pōta Rāju-like status as a brother to such village goddesses as Sitalā and Manasā (ibid., 320–21), his opposition to Durgā as protector of Lausen (R. M. Sarkar 1986, 76–78), and more besides (Chattopadhyay 1942, 111–20, 128; B. K. Sarkar [1917] 1972, 63, 68–69, 95–96, 185, 197–201).

Although the Śiva gājan myths highlight the gods, the goddess, and the companions as the models for gājan, and de-emphasize the demon, and the Lausen epic does nothing for demons either, there is an important myth that compensates in the other direction. Östör mentions it as forming part of the "exegesis given by bhaktas" of the Śiva gājan's dances and processions (1980, 31), but unlike the myths just cited, he does not work it into his interpretation. B. K. Sarkar, however, treats it as the main myth behind the Śiva gājan's flesh-piercing rites and processional dances. And R. C. Sen, in one of the earliest attempts to give a scholarly account of both gājans (though he describes mainly Śiva's), says some participants consider the festival "an act of piety and religion, in commemoration of the austerities performed by Vana Raja, a king and Daitya, who by acts of self-torture and denial obtained the special favour of Mahadeva, and who first introduced the festival" (1833, 610).

The demon in question, then, is the Asura Bāṇa (however spelled), or Bāṇāsura, the last in the famous Daitya line of "distinguished fiends" (Hopkins [1915] 1969, 51) that descends from Hiraṇyakaśipu, Prahlāda, Virocana, and his great father Bali, "the Sacrifice," the "good demon" devotee of Viṣṇu. His name means "the arrow." His myth is first fully told in the *Harivaṃśa* and retold more briefly in various purāṇas, one of which, the *Rudrasaṃhitā* of the *Śiva Purāṇa,* is interesting for its Śaivite retouches.[36] B. K. Sarkar suggests that the latter text stands closer to the gājan rituals ([1917] 1972, 107, 245), and he may be right, at least chronologically. But since the earlier *Harivaṃśa* account is far richer in features that correspond to the cult, it serves best for a summary of the myth:[37]

> One time, seeing Śiva's son Kumāra (Skanda-Kārttikeya) sporting in play, Bāṇa, son of the great Asura Bali, determined to undertake tapas to become a son of Śiva (*devadevasya putratvam; rudrasyāradhanārthāya; HV* 2.116.10–13). Śiva rewarded Bāṇa's tapas by making him a son of his and the goddess's, gave him a city called Śoṇitapura, "City of Blood," and promised his protection. Having soon defeated the gods with his thousand arms and found his strength now useless, Bāṇa grew arrogant and asked Śiva for more opponents. Śiva told how this would come about, and at the promise of battle Bāṇa was filled with joy, prostrated himself on the ground, and worshiped Śiva with his five hundred pairs of folded hands (*pañcāñjaliśatair;* 2.116.33).
>
> The battle eventually came about, following further inducements by the goddess that affected Bāṇa's daughter Uṣā. She and Kṛṣṇa's grandson Aniruddha fell in love through a shared dream that, nonetheless, left Uṣā "bathed in blood" (*śoṇitāktā;* 2.118.3), having lost her maidenhood.[38] Aniruddha was then spirited to her quarters for a "real" tryst. Bāṇa found out, however, and fought a preliminary battle with Aniruddha, ultimately using his illusory powers (*māyā*) to bind him with snake arrows, but refraining from killing him. Then Kṛṣṇa came to the rescue. There were additional combatants: Kṛṣṇa, Balarāma, and Pradyumna (Aniruddha's father and Kṛṣṇa's son) attacked riding on Garuḍa; Bāṇa, Jvara (the Fever demon), Śiva, Skanda, and Śiva's Pramathas or Gaṇas guarded the city.

36. B. K. Sarkar somewhat confusingly summarizes both accounts, not always making it clear what comes from which text, and identifying the *Śiva Purāṇa* portion as the *Dharma Saṃhitā* ([1917] 1972, 106–7, 245–47). Allusions to Bāṇa's Daitya genealogy (1.59.20) and his thousand arms and protection by Śiva (12.326.86–87) are found in the *Mahābhārata.*

37. This serves well to remind us that the nonsectarian outlook of the epics and *Harivaṃśa* is, in spirit, closer than the "sectarian" revisions of the purāṇas to the popular Hinduism of the cults: in this case, even with a Śaivite purāṇa and a Śaivite cult. See Biardeau 1976, 112–13, viewing the incident in this passage where Kṛṣṇa-Viṣṇu and Śiva become one as evidence of a presectarian Smārta universe structured around Viṣṇu.

38. See O'Flaherty 1984, 65–71, on this theme in the Bāṇa myth.

> Noteworthy is the point where Śiva withdrew and embraced Kṛṣṇa, revealing, as they became invisible, that in their yoga, Śiva and Kṛṣṇa are truly one (2.125.22–23; cf. n. 37).
>
> Bāṇa then challenged Kṛṣṇa directly, repeatedly "roaring" (*garjatas*, etc.; 2.126.45–49, etc.). Eventually, Kṛṣṇa set about to lop off Bāṇa's thousand arms with his discus. Śiva and the goddess interceded, however, asking Kṛṣṇa to let their son live, so Kṛṣṇa agreed to leave Bāṇa two arms and his life (126.117–20). Reduced to two arms, maddened with the blood that streamed from his body (126.132–33), Bāṇa continued to challenge Kṛṣṇa until Śiva convinced Kṛṣṇa to withdraw, which he did, at last going to free Aniruddha and arrange his nuptials with Uṣā. Meanwhile, Nandi, Śiva's bull, told Bāṇa to appear with his wounds before Śiva and dance, so as to bring about his well-being (*śreyas*). Bāṇa then danced, bathed in blood, and Śiva was pleased to grant him a series of boons: (1) that he be unaging and undying; (2) "that when [your] devotees dance [before you] as I [Bāṇa] have, anointed with blood, extremely afflicted, pained with wounds, it will result in birth as [your] son [or the birth of a son]";[39] (3) that he have relief for his afflicted body; (4) that he be first among the hosts of Pramathas and receive the name Mahākāla;[40] (5) that he be renowned for his strength and manliness; and (6) that he suffer no disfigurement of limbs after being reduced to two arms. Having granted all this, Śiva disappeared. (126.142–64)

This account provides numerous points of contact with the Śiva gājan that are absent from the *Śiva Purāṇa* version. The emphasis on Bāṇa's attaining sonship of Śiva (rather than just chieftainship of Śiva's Gaṇas[41]) points toward the gājan tradition that the bhaktas are "sons of Śiva."[42] Bāṇa's incessant "roaring" reminds one of the etymology of the name *gājan* (see n. 26). And his six boons, especially the second, provide explicit prototypes for the varieties of processional dancing with wounds that are so prominent in gājan

39. *Yathā 'haṃ śoṇitairdigdho bhṛśārto vraṇapīḍitaḥ / bhaktānām nṛtyatāṃ deva putrajanma bhavedbhava;* 2.126.152 (= Critical Edition 112.120 with minor changes). For *putrajanma bhaved* I follow B. K. Sarkar [1917] 1972, 246, since it makes more sense within the story and as prototype for the gājan. But "may [the devotees] have sons" (Dutt 1897, 803) is also possible.

40. Bāṇa's title of Mahākāla and status as Rudra's follower are known in *Mahābhārata* 1.536*, an apparent Northern Recension addition to *Mahābhārata* 1.59.20.

41. As in *Śiva Purāṇa, Rudrasaṃhitā* 51.1–2 (Shastri 1970, 2:1026).

42. "Sons of Śiva" is the title of Östör's film on the gājan; cf. Östör 1980, 129.

rituals.[43] The greater development of the part of Jvara, Fever, in the *Harivaṃśa* might also provide background for the equally prominent West Bengal cult of Jvarāsura, the Fever Demon.[44] In short, it looks as if the *Harivaṃśa* might also provide a classical sounding board for popular developments (including ritual exegesis of the gājan) of Bāṇa's story. But a few features of the *Śiva Purāṇa* account suggest further development of the story as the background of a cult. After Nandi encourages Bāṇa to dance wounded before Śiva, Bāṇa goes to Śiva's *temple*. There, "divested of his haughtiness [and] overwhelmed with love and devotion, . . . he performed the Tāṇḍava dance assuming various poses and postures" (*Rudrasaṃhitā* 56.7–10; Shastri 1970, 2:1051). B. K. Sarkar takes this account of Bāṇa's dance as a prototype for masked dances in the gājan ([1917] 1972, 245). In any case, Bāṇa now becomes Śiva's perfect demon devotee, and his battle, wounds, and dance supply an alternate myth in which those who identify with him as sons of Śiva can form not only an army of Śiva and the goddess, but an army of the demons in a "City of Blood."[45] We must keep Bāṇāsura in mind.

Turning now to gājan rituals, what is central for our purposes at Śiva's main gājan at Vishnupur transpires from the thirteenth through the fifteenth day. Earlier, the *pāṭbhakta*, or chief devotee, whose actions we must follow, has set and kept things in motion by distributing sacred threads to other devotees on the first day (Östör 1980, 106), worshiping the sun daily (ibid., 107), guiding the bhaktas with stories about Śiva and past gājans (ibid., 103), and, deep in the twelfth night, "dangerously" submerging himself in water with a pot on his head to bring it up full for installation in one of the subordinate Śiva temples to signify the goddess's joining the gājan (ibid., 115–21). On the sixteenth day he will then be responsible for the corresponding festival-closing rites involving the dispersal of the threads and the pot (ibid., 135).

On the thirteenth day, the pāṭbhakta, carrying a trident decorated with garlands and lotuses, joins a procession to a certain *gāmār* tree that "stands at the edge of a rice field two miles out of

43. Bāṇa's boons are treated passingly in the form of a short wish list, eight in all being mentioned, only one of which—"healing of wounds"—could refer to gājan practices (*Rudrasaṃhitā* 56.16–20; Shastri 1970, 2:1052).

44. In the *Śiva Purāṇa* account, it is reduced to five verses (*Rudrasaṃhitā* 54.28–32; Shastri 1970, 2:1043). On Jvarāsura in West Bengal, see Bang 1973; Dimock 1982; Nicholas 1978.

45. As with Pōttu Rāja's "City of the Bliss of Śiva" (see Hiltebeitel 1988a, 360), one does best to resist historical-geographical identifications of Bāṇa's mythical kingdom such as those mentioned without conviction in Shastri 1970, 2:1027 n. 318.

town" (ibid., 121–22). The gāmār is a "rare" and "thorny" tree ("the decorative tree *Gmelina arborea*": ibid., 222 n. 10; also known as "coomb teak": Robinson 1980, 264) with a white trunk resembling the ash-smeared body of Śiva (Östör 1980, 124, 145). When the procession reaches the tree, a pūjā is performed. First, "the pāṭbhakta touches a bundle of yellow threads to the sacrificial knife," then gives the bundle of threads, along with *bel* (wood apple) leaves (sacred to Śiva) and darbha grass, to other bhaktas who tie the leaves to the tree "at about waist height." Then at a spot just below the leaves, where a mixture of turmeric and mustard oil has been placed, a Brahman "paints a trident-like sign . . . with vermilion and oil" (ibid., 122). The Brahman then uses the sacrificial knife—shaped like the implement used for sheep and buffalo sacrifices (ibid., 225)—to cut three tubers in half, each with one blow. Then the pāṭbhakta uses the knife to cut off a small branch of the tree, and a large branch is removed by another bhakta. Back in the town, a pūjā to the (larger?) branch is performed at one of the related Śiva temples, and the wooden part of it is taken to a blacksmith. Before the following morning the blacksmith "will set three iron nails or spikes in the wood, placing the small pāṭā inside the larger pāṭā (board of nails)" (ibid., 123). The "small pāṭā" here is the branch of the gāmār, its thorns supplemented and incremented by the three nails. The larger pāṭā can be made of bel, *sāla* ("the forest tree," *Shorea robusta*), or *nīm* (margosa) wood and has "the length and width of an adult man" (ibid., 125; cf. 130). It too has nails thickly studding its middle portion, plus an iron neck-rest near the top, iron hoops for the ankles at the bottom, and two poles tied to it lengthwise so that it can be carried (ibid., 125).[46]

The ritual sequence on the fourteenth day, which culminates in the "highest moment" of the festival, the *Rātgājan*, or "gājan of the night," begins with evening worship of the sun. Just before sunset, the pāṭā with the gāmār branch and nails and several other smaller pāṭās are carried in procession to the fallow paddy field. There they are placed in the center of the field for a rite called *Sūryapūjā*, "honoring the Sun." "The trident is planted at the head of the middle pāṭā. Then the pāṭbhakta marks the trident and the pāṭā with vermilion and covers the head of the pāṭā with a mixture of vermilion, turmeric, and mustard oil. The rest of the bhaktas follow suit." After the pāṭbhakta and priest make various offerings to the pāṭā,

46. Curiously, *pāṭā* (written *pata*) is apparently the term used for hook-swinging rites, performed by devotees of Śiva, among Santal tribals in the Santal Parganas of Bihar (Archer 1974, 133–35 and plate 19). Cf. *alaku* as sword and needle (below, chap. 14).

accompanied by recitations, the bhaktas approach to offer fruits: "A small mountain of mangoes, bel fruit, and jackfruit quickly accumulates on top of the pāṭā. At the end of the Sūryapūjā the Brāhmaṇ takes most of these as his share of the prasad, but those pieces that are firmly spiked must stay there, as they are essential to the rituals later on" (ibid., 128). During the night the intensity of the festival mounts to its highest pitch, with people undertaking various vows. At one point a special group of devotees arrives called *bānnphurabhaktas*, "devotees with pierced tongues," who are "usually from the lowest castes" (ibid., 129).[47] Though not given the insignia of regular bhaktas, they dance with their tongues perforated by long iron rods (ibid., 129). Finally, a procession is formed with these bānnphurabhaktas in the lead, and the pāṭbhakta among those at the rear. Toward the middle are the *śālbhaktas*, who dance carrying the pāṭā on their heads, entering into trance with "wild and spasmodic" movements while they take up the pāṭā in turns. "Bhaktas explain that in the trance the pāṭā is Bhairab" (Bhairava), who "descends" on the bhaktas through the pāṭā and enters them through the head, inducing possession (ibid., 130). The fruits left on the nails of the pāṭā "go through the procession and are regarded as potent: barren women eat them later in the belief that this will bring about conception. When a fruit falls during the dance of the bhaktas women beseech the dancers to give it to them." It is also during this procession that the winnow (*cāluni*) is brought into play. Filled with fruits like the pāṭā, it too brings on trance. At the main gājan it is carried by younger bhaktas, and at one of the secondary gājans, by three women (ibid., 131). The procession ends only at sunrise at a Śiva temple, where the bānnphurabhaktas have the rods removed from their tongues and the pāṭbhakta performs a Śivapūjā.

The fifteenth day's "gājan of the day" (*dīngājan*) is hardly less intense, as the "night gājan" is preparation for a firewalk.[48] The pāṭbhakta leads the firewalkers into the firepit, and when they fall into trance, other bhaktas lead them into the Śiva temple to cool them with water kept for sprinkling the deity. At midday, the bhaktas then carry the pāṭās to a pond near the temple. In shallow water, after an offering to the sun-god Sūrya, "they hold the pāṭbhakta and gently lower him on the biggest pāṭā. Calling Śiva, the bhaktas lift the pāṭā high, and the pāṭbhakta rests with his back on the

47. Cf. Roghair 1982, 28–29: at the Palnad heroes festival, *katti sēva*, pressing a sword against the chest, is performed mostly by Untouchable Mālas.

48. Östör records no specific firewalking myth, other than that it was one of the things the gods did to arouse Śiva from his meditation (1980, 30).

bed of nails." Once at the temple the board of nails *and thorns* is lowered and the pāṭbhakta lifted from it: by Śiva's mercy, unharmed (ibid., 133).

This final ordeal by the pāṭbhakta brings to an end the series of rites that concerns us. But within this three-day sequence, there is also a rite called *jhāpbhānga,* "thorn breaking," that brings together even more of our elements. Östör discusses it in connection with the visit to the gāmār tree, which is presumably when it occurs:

> In this rite the spikes of the gāmār tree are set within a small piece of gāmār wood. The bhaktas build a linga of sand under the *asatva* tree (the sacred pipal). . . . The *sannyāsī-bhakta* [a colleague of the pāṭbhakta] then places three thorns from the tree on top of the linga and does pūjā. . . . Offerings of flowers and water are made, and the pāṭbhakta falls chest down on the spikes, invoking Śiva. It is through Śiva's or Bhairab's mahātmā ["power of divinity": glossary] that the thorns do not pierce his stomach. The spikes are set vertically, and the force of the fall is supposed to break the thorns; but without the pūjā and the influence of Śiva, the spikes would impale the pāṭbhakta. (Ibid., 124)

Here the liṅgam, a sand liṅgam with thorns, unmistakably joins its stake and trident multiforms among the implements of impalement.

I have chosen to keep commentary so far to an absolute minimum, as these rituals have what is by now a number of familiar features. Their further interpretation, however, requires that we fill out the picture with the corresponding features of the Dharma gājans. There are some rites for Dharma that do not appear to be performed for Śiva, most notably a goat sacrifice that reflects his character as a village deity;[49] further votive animal sacrifices that include not only goats but also ducks, fowl, and pigs (Robinson 1980, 228–30; R. M. Sarkar 1986, 70–71); and rites involving the fermentation of country rice liquor that, when carried in pots, brings on possession.[50] At least in the Vishnupur Śiva gājan, there is neither liquor nor animal sacrifice of any kind. But the first point to insist upon is that the Dharma gājan is similar to the Śiva gājan in elements, sequence, and structure.

49. On the goat sacrifice, see Chattopadhyay 1942, 109–10, 117–19, 124–27; Robinson 1980, 170–72, 230–31, 241–43; R. M. Sarkar 1986, 70–71, 157, 163–64, 169, 173–74; cf. also tables 7.2 and 7.6 and 319, indicating the prominence of the "dominant cultivating caste" Sagdops in sponsoring and overseeing the festivals. Robinson 1980, 228, says that Dharma gājans may also include buffalo sacrifices.
50. Robinson 1980, 94–96, 121–22, 335–46; R. M. Sarkar 1986, 152, 158, 170, 174.

Amid its many variations, toward its beginning, the Dharma gājan can include a trip to a gāmār tree for a cutting that will be taken to the blacksmith to be studded with nails. "In the old days," a thick branch would be cut into short lengths, fitted with nails, and "pressed against the chest by the devotees" (Chattopadhyay 1942, 102–3, 120). The worship of the gāmār in the Dharma gājan can further be connected with the honoring of weapons, in particular the trident (in the northeast) and arrows.[51] Moreover, if the gāmār and its rites seem to be sometimes omitted or "abbreviated" (Robinson 1980, 264) in the Dharma gājan, they appear to have a predictable substitute in a nīm or margosa tree: as ready a variant for the gāmār as for the śamī. At Baruipur, where such a nīm stands outside the Dharma temple, it is called Bāṇ Gosäin, "the spirit attendant of Dharmarāj who is believed to dwell in the nīm," to function "as the deity's familiar," and to stand "in for Dharma on certain ritual occasions" (ibid., 101). Moreover, if the personalized short lengths of gāmār are equivalent to the small pāṭās of the Śiva gājan, there is also a counterpart to the large pāṭā, called *Bāṇeśvar*, which is itself regarded as a multiform of Bāṇ Gosäin, the nīm. As Robinson puts it, the Bāṇeśvar, which I will return to shortly, is, "among other things, an outward and visible manifestation of the elusive spirit soul of the Bāṇ Gosäin; whereas the former is the Lord of Arrows, the latter is the Spirit of Arrows and, as such, the receiver of austerities offered to Dharma. Ritual austerities are dedicated to both Bāṇeswar and the Bāṇ Gosäin without distinction, as if the two are one" (ibid., 101–2). The Bāṇ Gosäin is the main example for Robinson of the interdependent relationship of the cult symbols, in that many of them, including the Bāṇeśvar, are carried before this tree (ibid., 102).[52] It also has a functional equivalence with Bhairab (Bhairava), in that some of the same rituals can be performed before either deity (ibid., 319).

Just as the pāṭā has an alternative name in the Dharma gājan, so the pāṭbhakta is usually called the *mūlbhaktya* (R. M. Sarkar 1986, 158) or *mūlasannyāsī* (B. K. Sarkar [1917] 1972, 74); but the term pāṭ-

51. A variant name for the gāmār, Gāmbhira, is also apparently an older or alternative name (in North Bengal) for the gājan cult. "In the course of this [Gāmbhira] worship, the glorious trident has to be worshiped in the north-east," along with other weapons, one each for the eight directions. Further, "in the Gambhîrâ the trident and the arrow are found to receive worship" (B. K. Sen [1917] 1972, 241). See further Östör 1980, 145.

52. Cf. R. M. Sarkar 1986, 149: the Bāṇeśvar "is also known as Bangosain and Baneswari," the latter a female identity not unlike the Orissan Khambheśvarī. Cf. N. N. Bhattacharyya 1975, 151 n. 1, 156.

bhakta is also used (Chattopadhyay 1942, 102, 108, 110, 120). As with the "night gājan" (and the eighth night of the paṭayaṇi sequences of Kerala), the point of highest intensity of the Dharma gājan occurs on one night (Robinson 1980, 410; R. M. Sarkar 1986, 152–53, 158–60), normally the full-moon night of the month of Vaiśākha. This is the night for acts of flesh piercing, above all involving metal rods (sometimes also knives) and thorns of "deadly" or "prickly nightshade."[53] These rites are combined with, and then more explicitly followed by, rites of fire. Thus, whereas in the Śiva gājan the firewalk follows the night of impalements, in the Dharma gājans such rites of flesh piercing are followed—though usually at the end of the same night rather than on the next day—by one or a combination of at least three different fire rites, the main ones being firewalking, "flower play" (*phul-khelā,* involving tossing about and playing catch with coals [= "flowers"]),[54] and "swing service" (generally called *dolan sevā,* being hung upside down from a crossbeam over a fire and offering flowers into the fire while swaying).[55] The structure is most evident when these variations are reduced to essentials, as at villages where "breaking thorns" (*jhāp bhānga*) remains the only flesh-piercing rite, followed by firewalking, the latter either alone (R. M. Sarkar 1986, 165–66), or in combination with dolan sevā (ibid., 170–71; cf. Chattopadhyay 1942, 120).

Finally, where a major rite is reserved for the next day, it is the *caṛak,* or hook swinging.[56] According to B. K. Sarkar, who wrote in

53. On the "awakening" of these thorns, see R. M. Sarkar 1986, 152, 165, 168. Alternatively, while certain rites with thorns may take place on this night, others may be performed on the day before or after it (Robinson 1980, 185, 277–78, 284–85). "Thorn games" are avoided by Brahmans (ibid., 278), but that does not make them "indigenous, non-brahmanic" (ibid., 285). Through the gāmār tree and the pāṭā or Bāṇeśvar, thorns are clearly part of the "Brahmanic" ensemble.
54. See R. M. Sarkar 1986, 153: the coals thrown back and forth "give the very appearance of numerous flowers cutting through the darkness" (1986, 153; cf. 175). Robinson 1980, 185, 265–68, however, indicates that the rite can occur on the morning after the full moon, and may also include walking on the coals, rubbing them on the body, and performing the rite before the Bāṇ Gosāin nīm tree. R. C. Sen 1833, 611, seeming to describe a Śiva gājan, deplores the procurement of fuel "by plundering gardens, and carrying off railings, loose doors, window frames, &c."
55. The rite has many variations with different names; see Chattopadhyay 1942, 109, 116 (with drawing); R. M. Sarkar 1986, 165–66, 170–71; B. K. Sarkar [1917] 1972, 81; Robinson 1980, 295–99 (including one on a "cart"). With the firepit coals probably also comparable (as elsewhere) to flowers, all three of these fire rites seem to involve an interplay between coals and flowers. For additional fire rites involving coals on the head, see Robinson 1980, 270–74.
56. Caṛak can be an independent gājan-like festival (Robinson 1980, 99–101, 363). At Dharma gājans, it can be "used as the focal point of the final celebration of the festival" (ibid., 364), as substantiated in R. M. Sarkar 1986, 160.

1917 about caṛak ceremonies in Śiva gājans, the practice had "of late been prohibited by law" ([1917] 1972, 87). R. M. Sarkar indicates that its discontinuation is still recalled at certain Dharma gājans (1986, 152, 165; cf. Robinson 1980, 100, 249). In any case, the fire rites may thus be bracketed by flesh-piercing rites, as at Vishnupur. Moreover, in the one village, where a continuing caṛak practice has been recently documented, while the hook swingers carry out their vow, "a few *Bhaktyas* are engaged in fanning the *Dharmaraj* in the temple to cool him down." It is said that during the "excessive painstaking feat" of hook swinging, Dharma "regularly perspires as sweat drops are often visible on the surface" of his "black slab" (R. M. Sarkar 1986, 279).[57] Whether it be Śiva or Dharma, firewalking or hook swinging, at both gājans these closing rituals emphasize that at the end, the deity absorbs his bhaktas' sufferings.

It is evident in both cults that the "bundled" metonymic connections between the various implements of impalement are akin to those that relate Pōta Rāju, the śamī, and the sacrificial stake. At Vishnupur, one has the tree, branch, trident, and sacrificial knife, plus the liṅgam with three thorns and pāṭā with three nails, both obvious equivalents of the trident (one portable, the other evoking the permanent and immobile icon in the temple). As Östör indicates, the "bundled" weapons are also interchangeable with objects carried by the bhaktas—canes and saplings of gāmār, bel, or margosa, with the canes, at least, being in turn "like the weapons of the deities" and "like the trident of Śiva" (ibid., 138). The pāṭā is also a form taken by Bhairava. The blacksmith's role in fashioning the iron nails and making the pāṭā may also remind us that in the Pāṇḍav Līlās of Garhwal, it is the ironsmith deity Kaliya Lohār, possibly another multiform of the śamī, who makes and maintains the Pāṇḍavas' weapons (Hiltebeitel 1988a, 133). Östör indicates that the blacksmith performs animal sacrifices in other pūjās, forges the sacrificial knives used later in the gājan, and figures in mythologies of impalement (1980, 145–46).

In the Dharma gājans, there is a similar interchangeability, noticed already in terms of substitutional patterns, between "thorn breaking" and flesh piercing with objects of iron made by the blacksmith (including the personalized gāmār staves with nails and the Bāṇeśvar, equivalent to the pāṭā), and between the Bāṇeśvar and the Bāṇ Gosāin nīm tree (which has nails set in it; Robin-

57. Dharma, theologically "formless" (Robinson 1980, 53–72, 96–97, 110), is represented in his temples not by an icon but by a "round, oblong, conical or even irregular" "piece of stone" (R. M. Sarkar 1986, 68), or like a tortoise (Chattopadhyay 1942, 105; N. N. Bhattacharyya 1975, 141).

son 1980, 202). Canes are also used in Dharma gājan processions. Rather than being the weapons of the deities, they are regarded as the weapons of the Untouchable bhakta soldiers in Lausen's army (Robinson 1980, 361; cf. Chattopadhyay 1942, 107). Both gājans may involve rites of falling on a row of knives (*bati*, Chattopadhyay 1942, 107; R. C. Sen 1833, 610–11). Moreover, the same term, *bāṇ* or *bāṇa*, "arrow," is used in both cults for a whole range of iron flesh-piercing implements, from those used to pierce the tongue (recall the bānnphurabhaktas), forehead, and sides (called, among other things, *triśūla bāṇa*s, or "trident arrows") to the "two iron Vāṇas [i.e., bāṇas] shaped like fishing-hooks" that are used to pierce the back for the caṛak or hook swinging.[58] Let us recall that Kāttavarāyaṉ's impalement stake, likewise homologized with the hook-swinging frame (ceṭil), is equipped with fishhooks as big as a thigh. The billhook, used by Lausen for his battlefield self-sacrifice, can also be called a bāṇ (Robinson 1980, 28, 301). Finally, where the Dharma gājan puts a cart into service as the altar-chariot for upside-down swinging over a fire, it too is an arrow: the *gāṛi bāṇ*, the "cart" or "chariot arrow."[59]

It would not be difficult to show that both gājans supply still further links to these metonymic chains. Our purpose, however, is to bring this discussion back to the affinities between these rites and the Draupadī cult rites and implements that come bundled with Pōttu Rāja and Vīrapattiraṉ (recall the multiple trident on his post at Lalgudi). With these irrepressible figures in mind, let us now look one last time at the gāmār tree and the pāṭā or Bāṇeśvar, the two ritual artifacts of the Śiva and Dharma gājans that most decisively orient and unify their highly proliferated symbolisms of impalement.

First, the gāmār functions like the śamī, even to the point of being a rare, "thorny" boundary tree. Its whitish trunk is compared to Śiva's ashes, another sublimation of fire. Similarly, the nīm, in its substitutional form as Bāṇ Gosāin, is proverbally a tree associated with cooling. As to the sand liṅgam with the three thorns of the gāmār, it is striking that it is placed beneath a pipal tree. In addition to the thorns' association with the liṅgam and the apparent "male" character of the tree (ibid., 156), the combination

58. B. K. Sarkar [1917] 1972, 103, 106. There are too many alternative names and groupings of the bāṇas to recount; cf. ibid., 97, 103–8; Chattopadhyay 1942, 107, 120–23; R. M. Sarkar 1986, 70–71, 73 (the claim that worship with "bodily tortures" is "pre-Aryan" is purely hypothetical), 143 n. 7, 153, 158, 208 n. 7; Robinson 1980, 286–90.

59. Robinson 1980, 295–97; see n. 55 and chapter 6, section B above.

recalls the marriages of the śamī and the pipal, or alternatively the margosa and the pipal, which Biardeau has traced through Orissa, Andhra (where such marriage trees mark the point where Pōta Rāju has his post in the centers of villages), and points farther south. Indeed, this would not be the only place where an impalement had the connotations of a marriage.[60]

As to the pāṭā, let us note first that in the Śiva gājan at Vishnupur, there seems to be a link between the pāṭā and the Rāja, since the visit to the king is intermediary to the pāṭā's preparation and its "sacrificial" uses. Whereas the Rāja (and now the community) would have the function of yajamāna (see Östör 1980, 146, 151), the pāṭbhakta, as preeminent "victim," appears to be his (or the community's) substitute in offering himself on the pāṭā. Moreover, when the bhaktas come to pay homage to the king, they show themselves to have one of the functions of his army: "They come to defend the king; they are like a bodyguard" (ibid., 125). The bhaktas thus form not only the army of Śiva, the goddess, and the demon, but also that of the king.

All this is highly instructive, because the pāṭā has the shape of a yūpa. Or more exactly, it has the shape of a Pōta Rāju, but a flat, horizontal Pōta Rāju, with its vertical element being the protruding thorns and nails rather than the top of the post. It is, at last and in brief, the *literal* transformation of the Vedic yūpa into an impalement post, and a portable impalement post to boot. This identification was initially made not so much on the basis of Östör's book as based on his film on the gājan (see n. 42), where the pāṭā is shown not only to have the length and width of a man (like the Vedic stipulation that the yūpa have the height of the sacrificer), but to have the form of a stylized, yūpa-shaped board with indentations at either side, toward the front end, marking off a "collar" and a pointed button-"head" (see fig. 13).

More than this, its equivalent in the Dharma gājan, the Bāṇeśvar, appears to have two main variations, each with its corresponding lessons. One, shown and described by Chattopadhyay, is "made of wood and shaped . . . like a post with a conical head, resembling a bulbous spear-head" and "studded with a number of nails generally." The Bāṇeśvar that Chattopadhyay illustrates—from Labhpur village, Birbhum District (1942, 108; see fig. 13)—seems to be conical, bulbous, and spearlike, but of a type that is without the "generally" found nails. It is in connection with this first type, however,

60. See Visuvalingam 1989, 438–45, discussing the story of Kāttavarāyaṉ; see above, chapter 4, section C; cf. B. K. Sarkar [1917] 1972, 87.

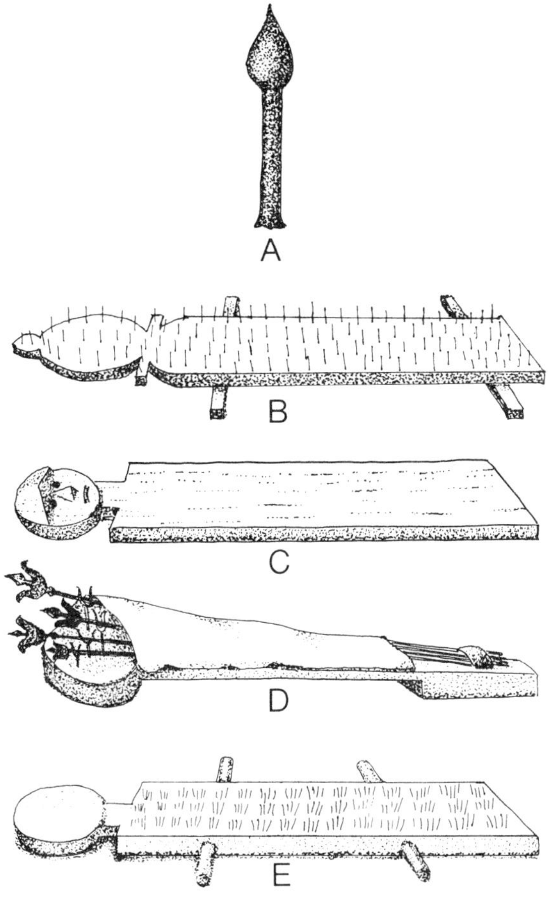

Figure 13. Pāṭās and Bāṇeśvars: (A) "spearlike" Bāṇeśvar, Birbhum, West Bengal (from Chattopadhyay 1942, fig. 1, p. 108); (B) Pāṭā, Vishnupur Śiva gājan (from photograph supplied by Ákos Östör); (C) "the Pāṭ also known as Bāṇeswar or Bāṇ Gosāiñ," Kandi, Murshidabad, Central Bengal (from A. Bhattacharyya 1952, fig. 2, p. 122, quoting caption); (D) "the Pāṭ of Ishurdi in Pabna, East Bengal," with "Śaiva influence evident in the tridents" (ibid., fig. 3, p. 126); (E) Pāṭ or Bāṇeśvar from Dāmrā, Burdwan District, West Bengal (ibid., fig. 1, p. 120). Drawings A and C–E from Dharma cult.

that Chattopadhyay took the first step in making the connection for us almost fifty years ago. Recalling Whitehead's description and picture (see above, chap. 6, fig. 9) of a Pōta Rāju post that "faintly resembles a spear and is called Sulam," Chattopadhyay says: "The photo published by him shows the spear to resemble closely the spearlike image of Baneswar" (ibid., 130).

The second, and more common, type of Bāṇeśvar is virtually interchangeable with the pāṭā. A. Bhattacharyya shows illustrations of four Dharma gājan Bāṇeśvars from different districts (1952, 120, 122, 126, 127; figs. 1–4), noting that the Bāṇeśvar may also be known as *pāṭ* (= pāṭā) or Bāṇ Gosāin (1952, 122). All have the rectangular body length, neck, and a rounded head, with a face on the head in one case, nails on the body in two, and tridents instead of nails on the fourth (fig. 13). R. M. Sarkar also describes one (in Birbhum District) as "a flattened wooden slab at one end of which there are a number of pointed iron sticks attached to it vertically," and "generally 4 to 5 feet in length" (1986, 149, 207 n. 4). Similarly, Robinson describes the typical Bāṇeśvar as "a yard-long plank of wood fashioned in the shape of an arrow" on four short legs that occasionally drop off, "made from *bel* wood which has thorny branches," and supplied with "nails sticking out from the tops and sides of its body" (1980, 80). Her photographs and descriptions show a "neck" and "head" at one end,[61] and the rituals suggest correlations with the neck of the chief bhakta during his investiture with a scarf or cloth necklace (ibid., 83) and the offered head of Lausen (ibid., 123–24). But most precious is Robinson's mention of "a cakra (wheel) design" that is "rather finely rendered" at a spot "near the top of the lower half" of the Bāṇeśvar's body, beside which are placed the Bāṇeśvar's longest spikes or nails. "This cakra is the 'energy' seat of the Bāṇeśwar; mangoes and cucumbers are fixed onto the cakra spikes" (ibid., 81).[62] I will return to this combination of a cakra with impalement spikes shortly.

The rituals involving the Bāṇeśvar in the Dharma gājan are clearly akin to those involving the pāṭā in the Śiva gājan.[63] Robinson writes repeatedly of the bhaktas' identification with it (1980, 83, 191, 202, 283). It is considered to be "the replica of Dharmarāj" (R. M. Sarkar 1986, 207 n. 4). Clearly his *portable* replica, it seems to precede or represent an invisible Dharma in processions and can also apparently have a trident as its substitute (Chattopadhyay 1942, 110, 112). "During the whole ceremony of Dharma worship

61. Robinson 1980, 83, 123–24, 168–69, figs. 38 (357) and 39 (358).

62. Robinson continues this sentence: "as if to depict the male sexual organs." This is intriguing, considering, among other things, affinities between the yūpa and the liṅgam.

63. I refer here only to the wooden Bāṇeśvar, which according to Robinson may be called Choṭa ("Small") Bāṇeśvar as distinct from a long rectangular stone called Baṛa Bāneśvar. The latter is taken out from the temple only once and is more instrumental in inducing possession (1980, 86, 139, 159–60, 211–12). But the wooden one is also linked with possession in various rites (ibid., 220, 301).

Baneswar becomes the constant companion of the *Bhaktyas* and every step of the festival is observed in front of it" (R. M. Sarkar 1986, 207 n. 4). As in the core area worship of Draupadī, "Without Pōttu Rāja there is no festival." Just as Pōttu Rāja is offered kāppu before Draupadī's worshipers, so it is "the custom for the *Bhaktyas* to offer sacred thread to the iron nails of Banesvar before taking the same for themselves."[64] When it is brought out of the temple a few days before the main night (either an old one is repaired or a new one is freshly fashioned), it is taken (often by the chief bhakta) to a tank and bathed. The chief bhakta may hold it above his head and dip under the water (ibid., 156). Childless women seek drops of water from this special bath, as the Bāṇeśvar is considered highly fertile, not only for humans but also for plants and animals.[65] It will be recalled that women desire the fruits on the pāṭā for the same reason. With the Bāṇeśvar, too, "Sometimes a number of fruits like mango, pineapple, guava, etc., are pierced on the nails" (ibid.). The hero of the cult's folk epic, Lausen, is conceived when his mother Rañjāvatī falls on such an object (a "spear studded plank"), or some equivalent ("on *kāṭāri* [curved knives] fixed on plantain stems") (Chattopadhyay 1942, 126, 103; cf. Robinson 1980, 26–28, 275, 285–86, 367). Linked not only with fertility but with "asceticism" (R. M. Sarkar 1986, 172), the Bāṇeśvar may be brought back to be placed beside Dharma within the temple (ibid., 168), or outside the temple beside an altar to Bhairava, with whom it thus seems to have an affinity, like the pāṭā (ibid., 156–57). At some gājans, a bhakta sits on a raft, goes into possession, and lies on four swords, after which the Bāṇeśvar is placed spikes-down on top of him, with a cloth over it. Other bhaktas then carry the raft in procession before setting it afloat with the sandwiched bhakta on it (Robinson 1980, 301–3).[66] At another gājan, on the culminating night, amid all the acts of flesh piercing, the Bāṇeśvar is taken on the shoulders of various devotees on a four- or five-hour round "through the village paths," while one of the bhaktas lies on top of it (R. M. Sarkar 1986, 152), like the pāṭbhakta in the Śiva gājan. Finally, on the closing day, it is once again taken to the tank and bathed, after which the bhaktas place their sacred threads on its

64. R. M. Sarkar 1986, 207 n. 4; cf. Robinson 1980, 83: the Brahman priest ties a scarf or cloth necklace around the neck of the Bāṇeśvar, then gives one to the chief bhakta, who puts it around his neck and extends it to the Bāṇeśvar's cakra. Cf. Robinson 1980, 306.
65. See R. M. Sarkar 1986, 162, 168, 173, 207 n. 3, 266–68, 298 n. 8; it is especially fertile when placed in conjunction with the (feminine) basil or tulasi plant (163).
66. The place in the festival sequence is not indicated.

nails (ibid., 153, 160, 166, 171, 175). Or alternatively, they may place them on the nails of Bāṇ Gošain's nīm tree (Robinson 1980, 202).

But why, after all, do we have a pāṭā in the Śiva gājan and a Bāṇeśvar in the Dharma gājan?[67] Here the information from these two overlapping traditions supplies the closest analogue yet found—and, let me insist, a confirmatory and in some measure explanatory analogue—to the transformation Biardeau posits to account for the unconscious rapport between Mahiṣāsura, the Buffalo Demon, and Pōta Rāju, the Buffalo King. Just as Durgā defeats Mahiṣāsura, so Śiva defeats the Asura Bāṇa. In both cases, these are purāṇic myths that pit the deities who oversee the cosmic order (Durgā, Śiva) against "world class" demons. Insofar as maintaining the cosmic order on earth is the prerogative of the king, these myths are further susceptible to royally sponsored rituals like Dasarā and the Śiva gājan at Vishnupur.

The story of Bāṇāsura, the "Arrow Demon," is not, however, part of the mythic exegesis of the Dharma gājan, but only, apparently, of the Śiva gājan.[68] There he is the prototypical demon-devotee of Śiva and the goddess. But, as if by compensation, Bāṇāsura has reemerged in the Dharma gājan, by another name and with no recognition of a connection between the two identities, as the "deity" Bāṇeśvar, the "Lord of Arrows."[69] Indeed, he has emerged doubly, for he has the additional form of Bāṇ Gosāin, the "Spirit of Arrows." As the transposition of a purāṇic demon into a folk cult, Bāṇeśvar is thus akin to Pōta Rāju. But unlike Pōta Rāju, the Bāṇeśvar in the Dharma cult is not a "demon" devotee and seems to have only minimal, if any, "guardian" functions. It would, in fact, be problematic for him to "become" Dharma's demon devotee, since he is already Śiva's. Indeed, the transformation is made more problematic mythically by the fact that Bāṇāsura, unlike Mahiṣāsura, never dies! Nothing of his demon alter ego remains except the fact that now, as Lord of Arrows, he is present for all the Dharma gājan ordeals that, in the Śiva gājan, he was the first to undergo as the Arrow Demon in the role of Śiva's exemplary

67. Crossovers in terminology would, however, be expected. Sarkar and Ghose 1972, 104 mention a Śiva gājan "Baneswar." *Pāṭ bhāṅgā* in Dharma gājans means falling on a bed of thorns (Robinson 1980, 284–85). Cf. above, n. 46.

68. Beyond what can be deduced from available sources, the nonreference to the Bāṇa story as background to the Dharma gājan was confirmed by Sandra Robinson (personal communication, June 1989).

69. On Bāṇeśvar as a "deity," see Chattopadhyay 1942, 108; R. M. Sarkar 1986, 150. N. N. Bhattacharyya's notion that he was originally "probably a primitive agricultural deity" connected with hoe cultivation is fanciful (1975, 156).

bhakta. Rather, like Dharma, for whom he is a "replica," Bāṇeśvar has no anthropomorphic form. His name, with the ending *īśvar,* seems to link him (like Bhairava) with Śiva (cf. Robinson 1980, 220).

It would thus be better to call Bāṇeśvar a "demon" god than a "demon" devotee, with the quotation marks in each case signifying that the prior demon identity is forgotten, or perhaps better displaced, since it cannot be assumed for either Bāṇeśvar or Pōta Rāju that the corresponding purāṇic myth is unknown. What is striking, however, is that in both cases it is on the village or folk level that the demon "survives," in each case as a multiform of the sacrificial stake, and as the central ritual artifact in a metonymic chain that connects a fire-sublimating tree (or even two such trees) with symbolic weapons of impalement.

As we have seen, in both gājans the iron implements of impalement are known as bāṇas, "arrows." It seems that the Dharma cult's Bāṇeśvar is from this angle nothing but the deification of the pāṭā (in the Śiva gājan alternately identified with Bhairava) as the Lord of all such ritual weapons. In fact, in terms of the complex under discussion, the practice of *bāṇ phoṛa* or *bāṇafodā,* literally "piercing with arrows," is the link between these cults.[70] As B. K. Sarkar puts it for the Śiva gājan, "the name of Vâṇafodâ was given to the practice after King Vâṇa [Bāṇa], who was its originator" ([1917] 1972, 107). And as R. M. Sarkar puts it, with what can only be unnecessary caution, for the Dharma gājan, bāṇafodā practices "may have some relationship" with the Bāṇeśvar (1986, 207 n. 4; cf. R. C. Sen 1833, 611). According to Robinson, bāṇ phoṛa is the "generic designation" for all the piercing rites, and "cult practitioners explicitly dedicate these observances to the Bāṇeśvar" (1980, 277).

The bāṇas have many remarkable uses, of which I note only the following, beyond what is mentioned above (see n. 58). Excepting the billhook, the fishhook-shaped bāṇas for hook swinging, and (in most cases) the rod that goes through the tongue, the other iron "arrows" are, in one way or another, weapons of fire (cf. Robinson 1980, 286). The "chariot arrow" has an altar of fire on it. The *kapāla bāṇa,* or "forehead arrow," is a short iron needle to which a small lamp is attached once it is set between the eyebrows (B. K. Sarkar [1917] 1972, 103). The bāṇas that are placed in the sides or the abdomen are joined together at their linked ends by a pipe, to which

70. Robinson gives two spellings, *bāṇ phōṭa* and *bāṇ phoṛa* (1980, 192, 288). Östör (1980, 129) takes the term *bānnphura* to mean "piercing the tongue," but I have found no other reference to tongue piercing having this name. It seems that the usage he cites is a modification—perhaps a reduction in meaning—of bāṇ phoṛa.

a trident may be attached, and the ends are then wrapped in cloth soaked in ghee or kerosene. As the bhakta dances in the night, resin or incense is thrown to heighten the flame.[71] Indeed, there is also a "trident with lamps for passing through the tongue" (Chattopadhyay 1942, 122; cf. Robinson 1980, 289). All this must make for brilliant spectacle when danced, in procession with the pāṭā or the Lord of Arrows, at night. Indeed, in one Dharma gājan the chief bhakta himself lies "pierced with flaming arrows" on the Bāṇeśvar, which is carried by other bhaktas who keep the flames ablaze, and surrounded by still others who dance with the flaming arrows in their sides (Robinson 1980, 286). Drawing upon another sacrificial idiom, ghee, like turmeric elsewhere, is used to prepare the flesh for piercing, as well as the rod itself, and is then rubbed over the hole to stop the bleeding when the bāṇa is removed.[72]

Here we must remember that the Pāṇḍavas' weapons and the ritual weapons of Draupadī's Pōttu Rāja are also fiery weapons, each having its source, via different myths, in the śamī or vaṉṉi ("fire") tree. Indeed, throughout the *Mahābhārata* war, one hears repeatedly that many of the arrows of Kurukṣetra are fiery and made of iron. To dance with such bāṇas is thus in more ways than one an enactment of a sacrifice of battle. Let us remember too that the Kauravas are demons represented in central Travancore by a houselike shrine pierced by iron arrows. The combustibility of arrows is further in evidence in the death of Bhīṣma, which B. K. Sarkar likens to bāṇ phoṛa rites and mentions as a possible classical analogue to them, along with the story of Bāṇa ([1917] 1972, 106). As Bhīṣma lies on his heroic bed of arrows that penetrate every inch of his body, he announces that the arrows will eventually serve to incinerate him as his funeral pyre (Biardeau and Péterfalvi 1986, 61, 66). The flaming bhakta on the Bāṇeśvar also seems to evoke such associations.

It is, however, still the myth of Bāṇāsura that will reward one more look, this time in connection with the Draupadī cult mythology of Pōttu Rāja–Pōrmaṉṉaṉ. Östör accentuates one "basic principle" in the Śiva gājan, that of *milan śakti*, "the power of union": "All action of the gājan is made possible by the union (*milan*) of Śiva and Durgā. The bhaktas are the means by which these two deities are brought together" (1980, 178–79). At one level, this oc-

71. B. K. Sarkar (1917) 1972, 104; Robinson 1980, 286–87, 289; R. M. Sarkar 1986, 153, 159, 208 n. 8.

72. See B. K. Sarkar [1917] 1972, 105; Chattopadhyay 1942, 122; R. M. Sarkar 1986, 143 n. 7, 208 n. 7. However, cf. Östör 1980, 130.

curs when the goddess is brought up from the water in the form of a pot atop the pāṭbhakta's head. On another, it is also brought about by Bhairava (ibid., 120, 178). During the dance with the pāṭā, not only does possession come from Bhairava through the spiked board, but the bhaktas help bring on the dancer's trance by hitting their canes together above it. This is called *ananda korā,* "making joy," for joy is "the basis of devotion to and possession by Bhairab, Śiva's 'deputy' in the gājan" (ibid., 138).

Reports on the Dharma gājan do not mention the term milan śakti, but it is clear at least in Robinson's account that something very similar takes place, although with a differently accented theology. On the eve of the main night gājan, there is a double representation of Dharma's marriage. A "full pot," the *pūr kalasī,* representing both Dharma and the goddess, and a heavy rectangular stone called the "Big Bāṇeśvar" are brought up out of the water from their bath, and taken in the lead of an ecstatic procession that Robinson calls a "psychodrama of sexual union" and a "dance of coition" (1980, 92, 318, 329). This heavy stone Bāṇeśvar has the most to do with the accompanying possession, but the wooden Bāṇeśvar is also present for possessions in other contexts, and the two are ultimately regarded as one (see n. 63). The woman who dances with the pot on her hip while the chief bhakta carries the heavy stone on his head is the leader of a group of women bhaktas called the *mahāmile*s, the "great mixing" or "great coming together" (ibid., 307). from the same root as *milan*. Meanwhile, a preparatory temple ceremony that is often omitted, but is described in the Dharma cult's ritual texts, celebrates a more abstract union of Dharma with his wife Muktā or Mukti (ibid., 324–34). I take this as an evocation of the fulfillment of the four goals of human life through the union of Dharma and the suitably "formless" Mokṣa, Liberation: a union further resolved in Dharma's androgyny that is also evoked in the ecstatic dance, where both the pot and the stone Bāṇeśvar are forms of Dharma through which he ultimately marries himself.[73] Popular Hinduism once again concerns itself with mokṣa, not only with the things of this world.

In the Śiva gājan, however, there is a third model, one that Östör does not explore, for the bhaktas' ecstatic dances of joy. This

73. On the pūr kalasī as Dharma and not a goddess, see Robinson 1980, 89–91; on Dharmas of two villages marrying each other, ibid., 322. Actually, Muktā also has a nonformless aspect: in her marriage song turmeric anoints her limbs, "flowers are curled in her hair knot, oleanders adorn her braid" (ibid., 326). Compare Draupadī's hair and the muṭi in Kerala.

is the dance of Bāṇāsura in his City of Blood. In the Dharma gājan, Bāṇa has the further transfiguration into Bāṇeśvar the Lord of Arrows: like Pōta Rāju, another multiform of Bhairava, and of the sacrificial stake. As we have seen, Bāṇeśvar is not only a horizontal stake with vertical implements of impalement. It has upon it a cakra: its energy center to be sure, but also the weapon of Kṛṣṇa. Within the Dharma gājan, this cakra on the Bāṇeśvar is surely another ritual trace of the myth of Bāṇa, whose "disarmament" results entirely from Kṛṣṇa's discus. Moreover, in the cakra's conjunction with spikes, the implements of impalement that resonate with Śiva and his trident, one is reminded of the *Harivaṃśa*'s evocation of the unity of Kṛṣṇa and Śiva as prelude to Bāṇa's defeat. While the bhaktas of both Śiva's and Dharma's gājans undergo flesh-piercing impalements from thorns and bāṇas that are multiforms of Śiva's trident, they are supplied in both cults with mythic models who undergo the more extreme "sacrifice" of dismemberment. For not only does Bāṇa lose his many arms; Lausen, using a billhook, cuts off his flesh in nine places, the last, at his neck, being his head (Robinson 1980, 28). There will be more to say about the relation between dismemberment and impalement, the discus and the trident, and their respective resonances with Kṛṣṇa and Śiva. Let us just note for now that both weapons are represented on this multiform of the sacrificial stake and recall that they may be similarly combined—especially in the Thanjavur area—on Draupadī cult vīrakuntams (see plate 21). Moreover, in Orissa, the Sudarśana post is named after the cakra and is cut from a tree that should have a "sign of the Cakra"—lines like spokes, with a small depression in the middle—upon it (Tripathi 1978, 237).

It may thus be that Śiva's connection with impalement, and with rituals that relate sacrifice and battle, both antedate and encompass the goddess's connections with such rites. But goddess festivals retain their centrality. Just as the *Mahābhārata* transforms the Vedic sacrifice into the "sacrifice of battle," goddess festivals, particularly Navarātri and Dasarā, are probably most pivotal in transforming the Vedic ritual into the "festival of battle." They are generally more explicit in their battle symbolism than the gājan, though the gājan is no less preservative of Vedic elements, most notably the stake. But of course gājan, as has been stressed repeatedly, is also a festival to the goddess. And most festivals of the goddess are also festivals to Śiva. Nor, as we have just seen, can one forget Viṣṇu and his avatāras. Though I know of no instances where Viṣṇu has his own kaḷam-type festivals (unless one thinks of Onam in Kerala, but that is the festival of his "good demon" opponent, Bali, "the Sacrifice," father of Bāṇa, "the Arrow"), he and his avatars can be as omnipresent on the ritual battlefield as he is in the Vedic sacrifice and the *Mahābhārata* war. These are all points that will have a bearing on our understanding of Draupadī cult paṭukaḷam and firewalking rituals.

8 Paṭukaḷam Configurations: Arjuna's Artifacts

Draupadī cult battlefield rituals have affinities with similar rituals in other cults, above all those of the Palnad and Elder Brothers hero cults, with which there are strong possibilities of cross-pollination, not only in myths but also in rituals.[1] On the one hand, I will argue that though there is considerable similarity and even a strong likelihood of cross-fertilization between the three traditions, one can identify unique Draupadī cult paṭukaḷam traditions, in particular, one distinctive to the Gingee core area. This Gingee tradition can be distinguished geographically, and also through the *overt* reference that its rituals make to the *Mahābhārata*. In contrast, the similar rituals in the other two cults are linked with the *Mahābhārata* only through the filter of their regional folk epics, a subject I reserve for volume 3.

Core area Draupadī cult traditions thus refer to a quite discrete set of *Mahābhārata*-inspired ceremonies when using the term *paṭukaḷam*. In the strict sense, festival posters and flyers use it to refer to those rites that take place, on the festival's culminating morning, around the effigy of Duryodhana. In some cases the announcements refer to this sequence as Turiyōtaṉa paṭukaḷam, "Duryodhana's lying down, or dying, on the battlefield." So there are good reasons to accentuate a Draupadī cult paṭukaḷam tradition in the singular.

On the other hand, such a usage obscures much of what is most characteristic of Draupadī cult paṭukaḷam rites. I use the plural here advisedly, because if one can speak of the Draupadī cult paṭukaḷam as a unity at all, one must decide between two options. One may take the term in the strictest sense, just mentioned, confine its usage to a hypothetical, ideal form of limited geographical distribution, and describe a number of *related* Draupadī cult rituals sepa-

1. On the myths, see Hiltebeitel 1988a, 342 n. 13, 348, 353–60, 377–78, 445; 1984b.

rately, as if they were each discrete units. Or one may take it in an encompassing sense in order to understand the nature of those *relations*. I have chosen the latter option because it opens the widest windows on ritual (and of course on these rituals in particular), and on the dynamics of the cult. This does not mean that I will neglect the distinctive paṭukaḷam rituals of the Gingee core area. But it does mean that I will launch this topic by exercising a broad-view option: and this in two ways.

First, within the Draupadī cult as a whole, there are a number of rites that may figure in place of paṭukaḷam rites in a strict sense. One may call these patterns substitutionary or compensatory. Beyond the core area, alternative rites proliferate. And within the core area, the cult has undergone transformations in large town and urban environments. We will see that in certain cases, it is the alternative rites that reflect the above-mentioned process of cross-pollination between the Draupadī cult and other hero cults. At some festivals certain of these rites may be covered through an extended use of the term *paṭukaḷam,* while at others, the alternative rites will occur without any use of the term, as if it had been eclipsed or had never existed. In view of these factors, I will use *paṭukaḷam* to stand both for itself and for its variations, whether they are components or equivalents.

Second, and in principle quite distinctly, there are reasons to think that even when *paṭukaḷam* is used in its strict sense as referring to the rituals around Duryodhana's effigy, the paṭukaḷam takes in more, ritually, than just those rites. We have already seen that *paṭukaḷam* has both a semantic and a ritual overlap with Aravāṉ kaḷappali, Aravāṉ's battlefield sacrifice, the topic of the next chapter. Not only are they both kaḷam rituals on one contiguous terrain but, as we shall see, they also mark the beginning and end of the battle of Kurukṣetra on that terrain. I will argue that this principle of overlap applies, at least ritually if not semantically, to three other rituals as well: Arjuna's drawing of the bow, his tapas, and his retrieval of the cattle from the Kaurava cattle raid: the subjects of this chapter. These are all episodes familiar from the dramas, but so too are Aravāṉ's sacrifice and the death of Duryodhana.[2] What the five have in common is that they all extend the drama out from the Terukkūttu stage onto the ritual terrain that includes the paṭukaḷam: either through the construction of large ritual artifacts that remain

2. For the dramas portraying these episodes, see Hiltebeitel 1988a, 195–201 (bow-bending), 282–86 (Arjuna's tapas), 299–300 (cattle raid), 320–29 (Aravāṉ's sacrifice), and 413–33 (death of Duryodhana).

in place through the festival (Arjuna's "bow tree" and "tapas tree"), or through separate rituals that in effect double the events staged in the drama by reenacting them on that separate ritual ground. Thus, though it may seem incongruous to treat the ritual components or equivalents of prewar episodes as part of a discussion of the Draupadī cult's battlefield rituals, the reason for doing so is that in each case the spectacular elements of these rituals form part of the ritual space of which the paṭukaḷam eventually becomes the center and raison d'être. At various festivals, it may be said that they encroach upon the paṭukaḷam terrain. In fact, with the proviso that its centrality is equal to, or perhaps interchangeable with, that of the paṭukaḷam, the same principle applies to the firewalking area. As we shall see, each of these components forms part of one continuous ritual space in the concluding karumāti rituals: the set of rites that will confirm this second sense in which the paṭukaḷam is best understood as the center of an inclusive ritual unity.

It must be acknowledged, however, that these remarks are in part tailored to allow the ceremonies at Tindivanam to serve as our main point of departure. At other Draupadī festivals, different sequencing of this span of paṭukaḷam-defined rites and different configurations of the paṭukaḷam space in relation to the other ritual terrains (temple, drama stage, firepit) are to be found at every turn. Such variations will be noted—I hope sufficiently. What makes the Tindivanam solutions so instructive is that the temporal and spatial condensations of the rituals there allow one to grasp the structural principles behind these connections. At other Draupadī festivals, the connections and even the rituals themselves will often be handled differently while the principles remain basically the same. With this in mind, we will first observe the outlines of the intersecting ritual locations at both Tindivanam and Mēlaccēri.[3] We will then turn to the three drama-related prewar rituals—involving the bow tree, tapas tree, and retrieval of the cattle—that, in effect, prefigure the paṭukaḷam as a battlefield terrain (see maps 5 and 6).

For the moment, one need only note that the Tindivanam temple is on the top of a ridge that rises between the large Rājaṅkuḷam reservoir (or tank) to the south and the paṭukaḷam area to the north. Dwellings line the base of this ridge along the south side of the paṭukaḷam, while commercial shops facing the east-west Gingee

3. Compare Frasca 1984, 329, figure 34, on the spatial arrangements of the festival at Iruṅkal. His map must be corrected to read "South" instead of "North." Otherwise the temple would face west, which it does not do according to his temple diagram on p. 284. Once this adjustment is made, Iruṅkal is conventional. A correction is made in Frasca 1990, figure 43, by repositioning the term "north."

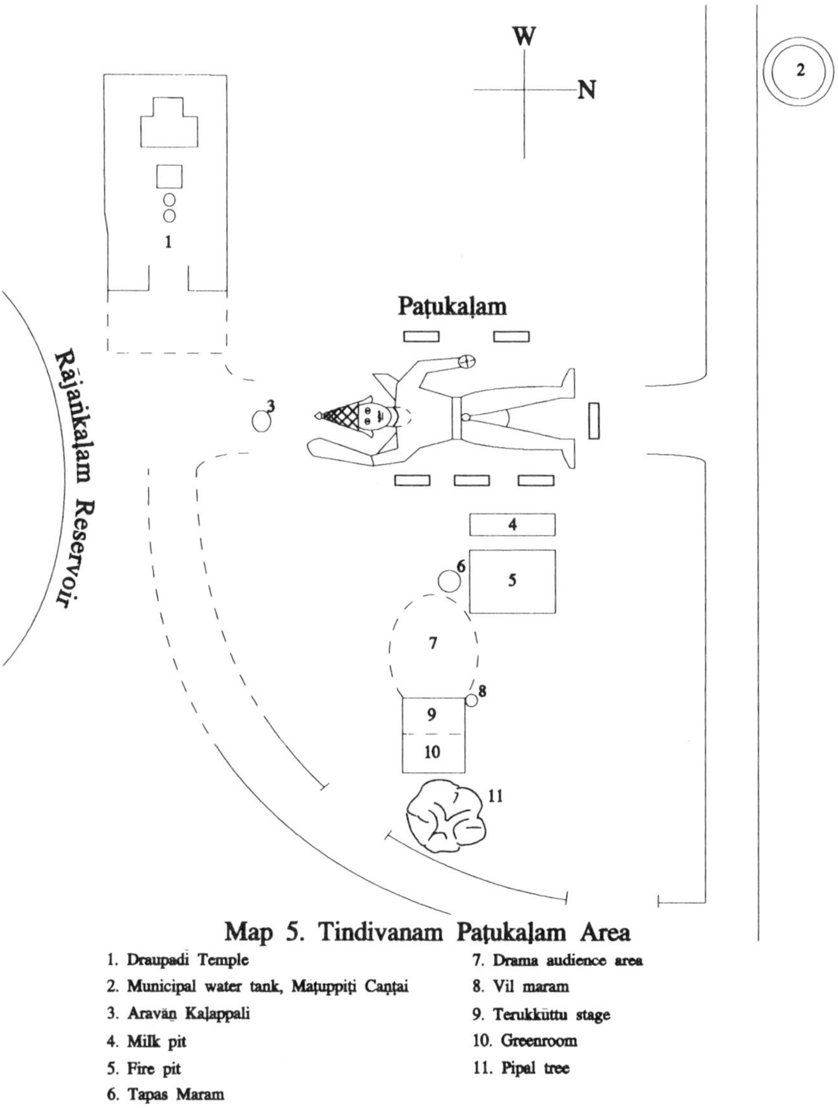

Map 5. Tindivanam paṭukaḷam area.

Road back onto it from the north. The paṭukaḷam itself is thus a plot of low-lying fallow ground that at other times of the year becomes a rainsoak, a web of crossing paths, a children's play area, and a dusty urinal. Having been a site for the epic's funerary rituals, it is inauspicious, though no longer haunted since the removal of a "permanent" concrete effigy of Duryodhana. Duryodhana's re-

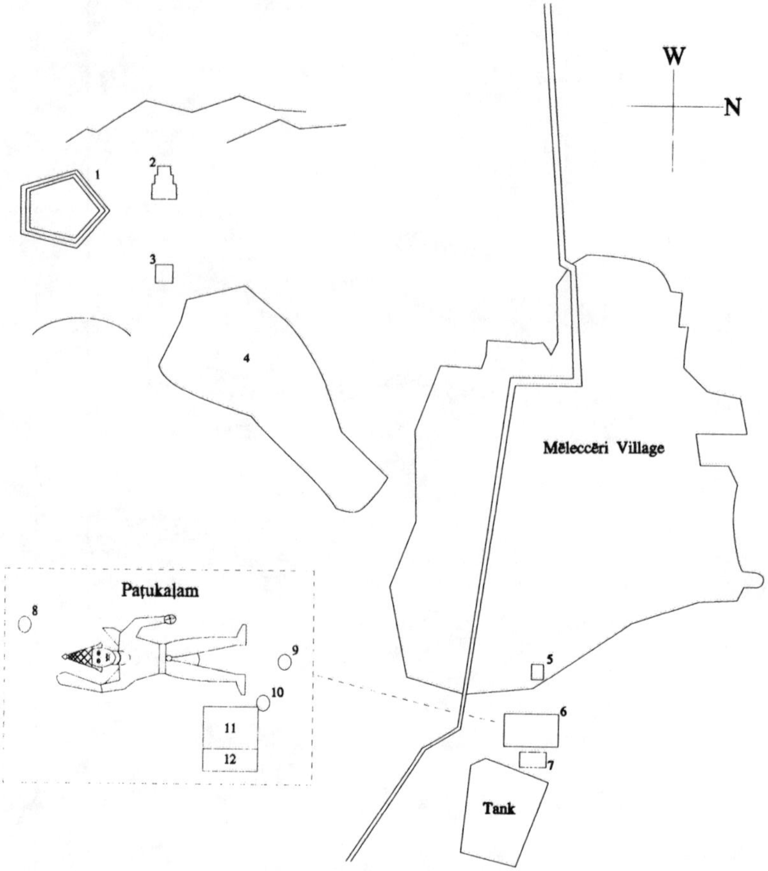

Map 6. Mēlaccēri village and ritual arenas.

mains are still present throughout the year, but only in the form of a long earthern mound, its features lost to trampling and erosion, such as one finds after most core area Draupadī festivals are completed. Around this dirt pile, however, there are still the six concrete platforms that serve in rites of dying and revival for the Young Pañcapāṇḍavas.[4]

4. Description as of 1982. By 1990 the western end of the area was used for lumber storage, and the concrete blocks had been removed. Cf. chapter 2 n. 4. The paṭukaḷam area is always an open space, often one marked by inauspicious associations. At Pondicherry, a clocktower site is used because "it was an empty lot at the end of town (when these festivals began)," and "the edge of town is the place to deal with demons and dangerous forces which are not desired within the town" (Shideler 1987, 156). A clocktower provides an intriguing backdrop for Kurukṣetra.

Meanwhile, at Mēlaccēri, it is enough to note that instead of one terrain for the four main intersecting arenas, there are two. The paṭukaḷam is adjacent to the drama stage in an open area at the eastern end of the village, while the firepit faces the temple about a mile to the southwest of the village amid the boulders and mountainous outcroppings that lead into the Mēlaccēri Forest (*kāṭu*).

A. Arjuna's Bow Tree and Tapas Tree

As indicated on maps 5 and 6, there are two "trees," both linked with Arjuna, that are set up in connection with the drama cycle but that remain in place through the ritual cycle: the bow tree (*vil maram*) and the tapas tree (*tapacu maram, tapas maram*). They are the only Terukkūttu props to take on such durative significance.[5] The bow tree is usually a tall bamboo, as high as forty feet (Frasca 1984, 288; Hiltebeitel 1988a, 197).[6] It is sent for by Draupadī's father, king Drupada, at about 1:00 A.M., during the drama enacting the *svayaṃvara*, or "self-choice," contest for Draupadī's hand in marriage. Drupada, who wants Arjuna to marry Draupadī but needs to spring him from a disguise so that he can do so, has heard that only a Pāṇḍava can bend this awesome bow. When the party arrives with the bamboo about an hour later, its trunk is set in a hole at the side of the stage, and it is erected with a long rope dangling from the top that will serve as the bowstring that the various contestants will try to pull taut and tie to the base: an easy task humorously made to look difficult, except that when Arjuna finally succeeds, he must do the tying behind his back. As the ritual extends little beyond the stage, I discussed most of my findings on it in volume 1 (196–97, 199–201). In contrast, Arjuna's tapas tree, which is set up for the play that portrays his asceticism to win weapons from Śiva, extends the drama beyond the stage and engages much greater local ritual involvement. I have thus reserved discussion of the tapas tree rituals for this chapter.

Let us begin by looking at what the two trees have in common. At Tindivanam, their placement suggests that their primary ritual

5. The only comparable prop I have observed is in the play "Kṛṣṇa's Water Sports": a small leafy tree cut to serve as the *piṉṉai* tree that Kṛṣṇa hides in with the Gopīs' sarees. At Mēlaccēri in 1986, it was removed after the play and the bow tree was set at the same spot the next night.

6. At Pondicherry, cf. Shideler 1987, 141, 148–49: without dramas, a carriage bears a five-meter mast, to which is fixed an eighty-centimeter fish at the top and a "yellow bow about three meters long." Arjuna's wooden icon holds a chain from the top of the bow to effect his archery feat with the fish target.

affinities are not with the paṭukaḷam proper, but with the two other arenas beside it: the bow tree with the drama stage, the tapas tree with the firepit. These primary associations appear to be conventional. The bow tree is alternatively known as the "drama tree" (*kūttu maram*) and is almost always placed toward the front left (from the audience's angle) of the stage (Hiltebeitel 1988a, 196–97). This would normally be the stage's northwest, since the stage conventionally faces west, as if toward the goddess as she looks out from her temple. It is, however, the vantage point of the goddess that counts. The temple itself will usually not be aligned directly with the dramas, so the goddess's temple icon would "see" the dramas only obliquely.[7] Or, more exactly, she will see them through her portable icon on her "chariot" that arrives to watch the plays, following the processional lead of Pōttu Rāja. Now, from the position of her chariot, which is itself her portable temple, as Draupadī watches the plays with Pōttu Rāja before her, also facing forward (as distinct from in the temple, where he faces Draupadī), the bow is to *her* northeast. This arrangement does not seem fortuitous. At Aṉmarutai, the prop for Draupadī's marriage is not a stage-side bow tree but a special wooden flagstaff set within the temple compound, just to the northeast of the Draupadī temple itself. For the play, an orange wooden fish is suspended from a ring under the bottom crossbeam of the flagstaff as Arjuna's target. Within the temple, this flagstaff is of course in the quadrant of Muttāl Rāvuttaṉ, who is represented at Aṉmarutai as a small square stone.

The tapacu maram, on the other hand, often marks the future site of the firepit. As is shown on map 5, at Tindivanam it will eventually rise from the middle of the firepit's south side. But at Veḷḷimēṭupēṭṭai, Maṅkalam, and Iruṅkal—in what seems to be the most recurrent arrangement—the tapas tree will stand to the firepit's northeast.[8] Mēlaccēri seems to require an instructive exception. The firepit and temple there are far removed from the stage and paṭukaḷam. Presumably the tapas pole, whose primary use is in the drama, could not be placed near the eventual site of this distant firepit, since one could not shift environments during the drama and move the play and the audience from one end of the village far past the other to the edge of the forest in the middle of the night. As if by compensation, the tapas tree at Mēlaccēri is

7. At Cattiram Karuppūr, however, the main entrance hall of the temple is used as the stage, with arrangements for hanging scenery and curtains. The sanctum faces east, the entrance north.

8. On Iruṅkal, see Frasca 1984, 329, fig. 34, and n. 3 above; on Maṅkalam, see plate 33.

placed very near the bow tree, about fifteen feet from it, offstage to the northwest. As Arjuna climbs the tapas pole, the bow tree sways right beside it. This of course reinforces the evident affinity between the two trees. More than this, being now in conjunction with the bow tree, the tapas tree is also to the northeast of the goddess on her chariot, just as in more ordinary circumstances it is to the northeast of the firepit. Finally, the tapas pole at Mēlaccēri is also aligned with the paṭukaḷam itself, providing its northern orientation in line with Duryodhana's feet. This is altogether suitable, since it represents Mount Kailāsa, in the "northern" Himalayas.

Beyond their respective primary affinities with the drama stage and firepit, then, the bow tree and tapas tree (or their substitutes) may also be "transplanted" to the temple and the paṭukaḷam. At different festivals, they are movable markers of the ways these ritual arenas intersect. Our problem for the moment, however, is to understand their relation to each other. They are obviously both Arjuna's. Beyond that, if we begin with the hints at associations of both "trees" with the northeast, a solution arises. The northeast is the direction of Śiva in his form as Īśāna. And as I argued in volume 1, Śiva is "the most prominant linking figure" between all the operatives of the northeast: the Vedic śamitar; the kṣetrapāla, and Bhairava (the exemplary kṣetrapāla) in particular, who is ultimately a form of Śiva's wrath; the nirmālyadevatā; and of course Muttāl Rāvuttaṉ, the ardent Śivabhakta with the Śaivite nāmam, who in one account even receives his boon of invulnerability (not unlike Arjuna) by performing tapas to Śiva (1988a, 115, 122, 127).

To this list, Draupadī cult ritual (though not myth) allows us to add the figure of Arjuna. This is not to say that Arjuna has no mythical links with Śiva. He does, and they are deep: both in the classical epic and in Draupadī cult enrichments.[9] It is just that Arjuna has no mythical associations, at least none that I know of, with Śiva-Īśāna's direction of the northeast. Draupadī cult ceremonialists have simply used conventional ritual idioms to set the rapport between Arjuna and Śiva in an appropriate ritual location. But in this frame, their rapport takes on new dimensions. The bow tree and the tapas tree are both artifacts that enable Arjuna, in the dramas, to pass difficult tests that set him on a par with Śiva. The bow tree, which he must string at Draupadī's svayaṃvara, comes from the Himalayas, and in varying accounts is brought by a great Śivabhakta or even belonged to Śiva himself (Hiltebeitel 1988a, 196

9. See Hiltebeitel 1980c, 151–58; 1984a, 24–26; 1988a, 82, 193, 207–9, 223, 283–86, 296, 298, 445 n. 11, 448. I will return to this matter in volume 3.

and n. 20). And the tapas tree, representing Mount Kailāsa, which is of course *in* the Himalayas, is the site of Arjuna's archery and wrestling contests with Śiva (disguised as a hunter), in which the outcomes are in both cases more or less even.[10] Moreover, if the bow tree shows Arjuna uniquely capable of stringing Śiva's (or his great devotee's) bow,[11] the tapas tree provides him with Śiva's ultimate missile, the *pāśupata,* which, as the play "Arjuna's Tapas" makes clear, is itself an arrow that fits Arjuna's bow.[12]

Erected to represent events before the war, the bow tree and the tapas tree thus stand as spectacular reminders of Arjuna's superhuman mastery of the supreme destructive power of Śiva. Their rapport with the paṭukaḷam, or ritual battlefield, even on its temporospatial periphery, is thus evident, for Arjuna is the supreme warrior-yogin at Kurukṣetra. What is striking, however, is that the weapons they represent are ones that Arjuna does *not* use at Kurukṣetra. He uses his own bow, Gāṇḍīva, leaving the bow tree, as it were, behind. And once he has obtained the pāśupata from Śiva, he holds it in reserve, never using it in the war itself, but only in its aftermath.

This is clarified in two variants of end-of-the-war scenes gathered since the writing of volume 1. In a performed (Pakkiripāḷaiyam troupe) version of "Eighteenth-Day War," before Draupadī ties up her hair, she sees Duryodhana dead with his fist closed, like a baby just born, and asks Kṛṣṇa how this can be: Is he still alive? Kṛṣṇa reassures her he is dead, telling her he died counting five undone things that he thought would have won the war. Among them, he could have taken earlier advantage of Aśvatthāman, who, as Śiva's chief protégé on the Kaurava side, could have released the pāśupata. Kṛṣṇa comments that each of the five things could have been countered by a weapon held in reserve by one of the Pāṇḍavas: in Arjuna's case, the pāśupata.[13] Then, according to the icon sculptor N. Dandapani, when Arjuna has to neutralize Aśvatthāman's pāśupata in the war's aftermath, he completely forgets he had won the pāśupata from Śiva and panics until Kṛṣṇa reminds him and tells him where and how it was concealed. Kṛṣṇa had cut open (*aṟuttu*) Arjuna's right thigh and put the weapon there. Arjuna then draws it out, neutralizes Aśvatthāman's missile, saves the

10. The wrestling match has many variants; see Hiltebeitel 1988a, 285–86.

11. Or any one of the Pāṇḍavas, as in the chapbook version of the play; see Hiltebeitel 1988a, 196.

12. See Hiltebeitel 1988a, 286, and, on film, 1988b, part 1. On the pāśupata, 1988a, 355–56, 372–79, 424–35, 444–48.

13. Hiltebeitel 1988b, part 2; 1989d; for other variants, see 1988a, 419–35.

world, and brings back Aśvatthāman's crown to satisfy Draupadī's demand for his head (cf. Hiltebeitel 1988a, 424–26).

Thus in relation to the paṭukaḷam, where Arjuna's part at Kurukṣetra gets little or no explicit ritual recognition, the two trees are usually the sole *ritual* reminders of his role there during the eighteen-day war. True, they are northeast only of Draupadī's chariot or the firepit, not of the paṭukaḷam itself. Erected before the paṭukaḷam is laid out, the trees usually define Arjuna's battlefield prowess rather than the paṭukaḷam space itself. They seem however, to share with other artifacts and persona of the northeast a symbolism that is as pertinent to the paṭukaḷam as to the firepit, which also can represent the battlefield: a destructive power that is not only peripheral and linked with Śiva, but muted, held in reserve, pacified, and contained—and associated with the containment of the further violence that could be unleashed by the *Mahābhārata*'s sacrifice of battle *were these artifacts not there.*

Against this background, we may now look more closely at the rituals of the tapacu maram: in particular, those at Tindivanam and Mēlaccēri and, thanks to Frasca, at Iruṅkal. As is common throughout the core area, the tree in question is a palmyra (*paṉai maram*). After a suitably tall and strong one is selected, a pūjā is done to it, it is cut and then prepared by a village carpenter (Ācāri) with a plank for a platform that is held in place by a thick metal rod (*kaṭapaṟai* according to Frasca) implanted in the top.[14] Sizes vary from about twenty to a hundred feet (the latter traditional at Māṉāmpāṭi), with those at Tindivanam and Mēlaccēri being about fifty feet high after the removal of the treetop, and including the four- or five-foot base that will be implanted in the ground. At Tindivanam in 1981, the bark was left on and the trunk was unpainted. In 1977, however, the bark was stripped and the trunk was prepared in the same fashion as the ones at Mēlaccēri in 1982 and 1986 (and at most other sites): painted with alternating red and white stripes from top to bottom. Log sections of casuarina wood, each about two feet long and an inch and a half in diameter, are set in holes to serve as steps. These are placed in two ascending rows, each successive step alternating from one row to the other, and about two and a half to three feet apart, so that when the pole is erected the two

14. I follow Frasca here. In his sketch of a tapas maram (1984, 299), the platform is larger and more elaborate than ones I have seen, with a turmeric-dyed dhoti extended to form an arched cover and banana tree cuttings at the side. At Mēlaccēri in 1986, the actors rejected as too dangerous three planks attached upward from the platform to form a rectangular frame. For *katapparai* (*sic*), Winslow [1862] 1979, 219 gives "crowbar."

rows project perpendicularly from it. At Tindivanam the two rows are at right angles (zigzag) to each other so that when the pole is raised, they extend north and west, with mango leaves tied to the tips of the steps. At Mēlaccēri, they extend from opposite sides of the tree, to the east and west, and mango leaves are tied to the trunk.

The number of steps varies. At Tindivanam, there were fourteen in 1977 and eighteen in 1981. Frasca shows sixteen in a drawing of the post at Iruṅkal (1984, p. 299). The hundred-foot-high post at Māṉāmpāṭi is approached by a rope ladder ("like a suspension bridge," according to informants), so there the number of steps would be over a hundred. The Mēlaccēri tapas maram of 1982 had fourteen steps, and the one there in 1986 had seventeen steps, the top being the eighteenth, each one set at a juncture between one of the eighteen sections of red and white on the pole. Though the number eighteen seems to have no especially high incidence of occurrence, we may refer to the 1986 Mēlaccēri pole as a useful example (see fig. 14).

The bottom section is red and becomes largely covered by the mound of earth that is built up from ground level once the pole is implanted.[15] At the top of the pole, the platform on which Arjuna will complete his penance is thus set above the final section of white. One need only recall Beck's classic article (1969) on the correlation between color and temperature in South Indian ritual to appreciate this design. Red commonly denotes heat, fire, life, blood, and fertility, but it is dangerous alone and is thus encompassed, surrounded, or set against a background of white, symbolizing coolness. Change or transformation is represented by the alternation of these colors and is always desired over stasis. Thus the alternation on this tapas pole begins with red at the bottom—which can be linked to the earth or to the eventual firepit at the base of the pole—and ends with white at the top, white being "auspicious where stability, well-being, and the absence of evil are primary concerns" (Beck 1969, 556). Alternatively, where the top segment is red, as at Mēlaccēri in 1982, it is still surmounted by the platform. In any case, tapas is a heat "built up as a result of sexual abstinence" and "diverted inward, focused, and finally directed at will by the practice of special yogic exercises" (ibid., 560).[16] These

15. The mound is no doubt an image of a yoni base, but there is no ritual suggestion of copulation between the post and the mound as at the Bisket Jātrā festival in Bhaktapur, Nepal; see Chalier-Visuvalingam 1989, 184.

16. Cf. Beck 1981a, 122–23, n. 68: the triple-forked kampam with the alternating hot (with fire) and cool (with water) pots, discussed in chapter 4, section C, "can be

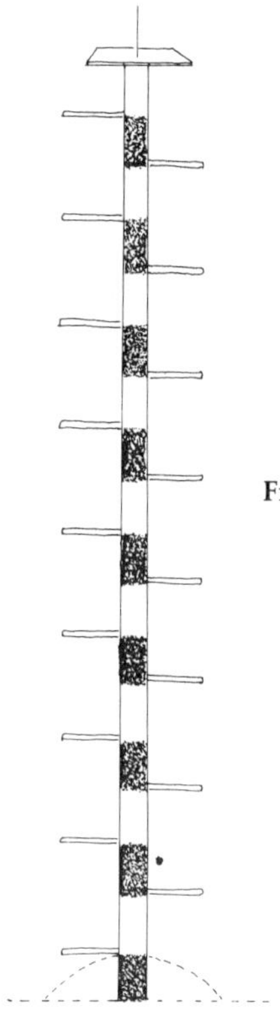

Figure 14. Tapas maram, Mēlaccēri festival, 1986.

features of the tapas pole correspond to Arjuna's purpose in climbing it and also complement and reinforce features mentioned earlier in connection with the symbolism of the northeast. Where it is further a question of eighteen steps, this suggests a correlation with Arjuna's mastery of the restraint of destructive powers, always toward auspicious ends, for the eighteen-day war.

The raising of the tapas maram begins in late afternoon, between about 4:00 and 6:00 P.M. A hole about four feet deep is prepared for the pole. At Tindivanam, I was told that some silver or gold should be put in it. The pūcāri threw in three twenty-five-paise coins instead.[17] Next, a coconut and a lemon were opened with a knife and their juice was poured into the hole. The pūcāri then performed

seen as a kind of penance pole for the performance of tapas. Such asceticism is focused on storing up sexual energy for rechanneling into alternate uses."

17. Cf. Babb 1974, 13: at Singapore, a scramble for coins buried at the last year's festival when the hole was filled.

dīpārādhanā, waving a tray of turmeric with a camphor flame on it before dropping both turmeric and flame into the hole. The base of the tree should be set into the hole while the camphor can be seen still burning.

This ceremony combines elements similar to those found at post installation rites elsewhere. For instance, at the installation of the Khambheśvarī post among the Dumals in Orissa, separate pieces of the five metals (which include gold and silver) are placed in the hole, and then three golden nails are inserted in the post, one each at the top, middle, and bottom, before it is erected (Eschmann 1978c, 273). These acts were not performed at Mēlaccēri, but an additional preparation was made for the post as it lay on the ground. Just before it was raised, it was strewn from top to bottom with darbha grass, suggesting (like the strewing on the vedi in the Vedic sacrifice) the function of an altar—for Arjuna to offer himself upon to Śiva—and also reminiscent of the darbha tied to the flagpole.

Finally the pole is set in place, lifted and pushed into the hole and up from beneath its far end until it can be further raised with ropes attached to the top. It always seems to take three tries, the last accompanied by the sound of the pampai drum and, finally, triumphant shouts of "Govinda!" Coconuts and dīpārādhanā are offered again (in this case at both sites). The ropes are then removed from the top, and the crowd can take its first *darśan,* or "viewing," of the tapacu maram. The post remains in place until its next use at daybreak.

Before the drama "Arjuna's Tapas" moves from the stage to the tapas tree, virtually all the action dwells on Arjuna's march toward Mount Kailāsa. His advance is punctuated by as many as four seduction attempts, involving seven women (counting Viṣṇu disguised as Mohinī, the Enchantress). Arjuna's ascetic resolve does not waver (Hiltebeitel 1988a, 283–84). If we remind ourselves, again following Beck, that tapas is a heat "built up as a result of sexual abstinence," it can be no accident that when Arjuna finally reaches the tapas tree it has become, besides Mount Kailāsa, a symbol of sexual potency: in short, a ritually transparent phallic symbol.[18] Instead of the band of temptresses now left behind, Arjuna is joined at the base of the pole by a circle of local town or village women with fertility problems who have come there to perform a ritual to help them get pregnant.[19]

18. As my Sinologist colleague Jonathan Chaves put it, seeing Hiltebeitel 1988b, "for once a phallic symbol is a phallic symbol." I leave the matter unbelabored.

19. This was the sole explanation I met at both Tindivanam and Mēlaccēri. Frasca,

It is about 4:30 A.M., with a faint but growing hint of dawn in the sky.[20] At both Tindivanam and Mēlaccēri, there are about ten women. As the audience shifts to leave an open circle around them and the pole, the women smear a section above the base with turmeric and dot it with kuṅkum. Then each individually circumambulates the pole three times, keeping it to her right (*pradakṣiṇa*), holding a tray with a coconut and other offerings (variously bananas and cooked rice) that she places at the base of the pole after her last round. The women then sit in an arc at the edge of the circle (to the northeast at Mēlaccēri) while the upayatār (patron) for the drama sits across from them, at Mēlaccēri with his son. The women and members of the audience offer items of cloth, especially sarees at Tindivanam, which are folded and hung from the steps or tied around the pole. At Mēlaccēri a young man brings a baby in a cloth cradle and hangs it from the fourth rung. The baby's protests lead to its quick removal, but the cradle remains. The sarees hung from the tapas tree evoke the pan-Indian practice of tying bits of cloth to a tree (often a temple tree) to fulfill wishes (often for children). They also recall the sarees stolen from the Gopīs and pulled at Draupadī's disrobing in earlier dramas of the same festival cycle. Here what has been stolen in play and peeled in anger in the dramas is now offered to enhance similar auspicious ends in the ritual.[21] The same may be said of the baby in the cradle, but here we have an additional reminder, via the story and cult of Kāttavarāyaṉ, that the scene of Arjuna's tapas, and thus the pole that represents it, evokes the initiatory symbolism of death and rebirth (in epic and Vedic terms, Arjuna undergoes a dīkṣā), through which the sacrificer-hero is reborn.[22] On his impalement stake, after he has suffered and blessed everyone, Kāttavarāyaṉ dies (according to one text) "like a child in a crib": an apparent evocation of a traditional punishment of criminals, who would be placed into a basket or box and hung from a pole for several days (Masilamani-

---

however, mentions that the women come for relief from physical ailments "ranging from infertility to epilepsy and depression" (1984, 298). A close-up study of this ritual, with interviews of the women participants, would be rewarding.

20. Frasca, however, found that in Iruṅkal these events begin at 7:00 A.M.

21. For more on the symbolism of fabrics, particularly sarees, in Draupadī cult contexts, see Hiltebeitel 1988a, index, s.v. sarees, and 1989c.

22. See Biardeau 1976, 227, 241, 245; 1978, 149–59; Hiltebeitel 1980c, 149. Cf. Beck 1982, 166, referring to both Arjuna's penance and Tāmarai's (the main heroes' mother) in the *Elder Brothers Story*: "Penance itself is a kind of metonym for giving up life." Tāmarai's penance, seated on a pole prepared by Viṣṇu with seven needles and performed to overcome her barrenness, is compared to Arjuna's (Beck 1975, 130, 135).

Meyer 1989a, 87, 101–2). In another version, while he writhes on the stake's nails and hooks, his wives are said to stand around him in boxes, nests, or baskets that also hang from the stake (ibid., 87; see chap. 5, sec. C). In ritual enactments of his impalement, his impersonator may climb a sixty-foot pole or be hung from a hook-swinging beam holding (cradling) a succession of babies, whose parents believe this will bless the children with "a long and healthy life" (ibid., 95–98). Kāttavarāyaṉ's "mounting of the stake" brings out a violence in the symbolism of self-offering that is only latent in Arjuna's tapas.[23]

Arjuna, covered with ashes as a Śaivite ascetic, comes to the tapas tree with his bow and arrow (both beautifully made of sugarcane at Mēlaccēri). He places them at the base of the pole and also does a pradakṣiṇa circumambulation around it, first along with the women, then alone with a tray of turmeric and lit camphor. Finally, he prostrates himself before the pole and then begins his step-by-step ascent, singing songs to Śiva.[24] While he climbs, possessions may occur (as they did at Mēlaccēri, but not at Tindivanam) among women in the audience, but the women in the inner circle remain seated.[25] After about an hour of such step-by-step ascent, he reaches the top, symbolizing, as Frasca puts it, "the deepest points of his meditation on Śiva and his arrival at the Lord's abode" (1984, 298). There he remains for about a half an hour, the first part of which is spent in acts that display his fervent asceticism. At Tindivanam he sits cross-legged on the platform and holds his palms above his head like one of the portable wooden icons that occasionally portrays this scene (see chap. 3, sec. B). At Mēlaccēri he sits for a while and then makes offerings to Śiva: first he breaks coconuts on the metal rod that extends up from the pole and holds the platform in place; then he stands, holds the rod with his left hand, and leans out eastward offering Śiva a tray from which rises a quite large and long-burning flame. At Iruṅkal, he "causes the pole to sway back and forth sometimes as much as ten feet by rocking his body" (Frasca 1984, 299). According to V. S. Purushottama Chettiyar at

23. Kāttavarāyaṉ is brought to the stake as a punishment by Śiva, meted out for his violation of a Brahman woman, whereas Arjuna comes to the tapas maram chastely and with devotion, with no hint of punishment.

24. Some of the songs are from the *Tēvāram,* the classical Śaivite hymnal, as confirmed by both Frasca (1984, 298) and J. Rajasekaran (at Mēlaccēri).

25. Cf. Frasca 1984, 298, 300: however, the inner-circle women at Iruṅkal stand and may also get possessed (apparently only after Arjuna reaches the top). At Mēlaccēri one woman of the inner circle stood up abruptly, faced west, and joined her palms together when a woman in the crowd got possessed.

Tindivanam and various informants at Mēlaccēri, Garuḍa should appear in the sky. And though it was acknowledged that he failed to do so at Tindivanam, where at the time I seriously thought my chief trustee informant was pulling my leg, Garuḍa was indeed spotted at Mēlaccēri—with excitement and a palpable sense of blessing (implicitly Viṣṇu's or Kṛṣṇa's)—in the form of a circling Brahmany kite. Since this is our only actually experienced *Garuḍa-darśana* (the term for the ritual "sighting of Garuḍa"; Tamil *karuṭatarica<u>n</u>am* [Winslow (1862) 1979, 249]), let us just recall—as evident parallels—our earlier reference to the mythical appearances of Garuḍa at the salvific deaths of Aravā<u>n</u> and Karṇa (chap. 3, end).

For the next phase of Arjuna's stay on the tapas pole, Śiva is temporarily forgotten, and attention returns to the women. Arjuna suspends his austerities. A bag of items is brought up the pole for him to drop to the women below as a kind of prasādam. The women now stand at the base of the pole and make the shoulder-pieces of their sarees into aprons to catch the falling items in between their outstretched arms (see plate 9). They jockey for position, all in jovial good spirits. The items vary: at Tindivanam flowers (jasmine and marigolds); at Mēlaccēri limes and cut up bits of mango leaves; at Iruṅkal limes, ash, and flowers (Frasca 1984, 300). Whatever they are, these items carry the blessings of Arjuna and Śiva and are said to induce pregnancy. Limes are particularly appropriate in this connection. Heroes and heroines—in a list that includes Kāttavarāya<u>n</u> and the heroic twins (and sometimes their sister) in the *Elder Brothers Story* (Masilamani-Meyer 1989a, 73; Shulman 1989, 40, cf. 45; Beck 1982, 126, 184; cf. Roghair 1982, 243–44)—are often conceived in South Indian folklore after their mothers have swallowed a lime. At Mēlaccēri limes that bounced out of the saree ends on the ladies' first attempts to catch them were returned to them by well-meaning older men and boys. The limes, dropped first, were clearly of more potency than the mango leaf bits, but the latter are also interesting. They come from the leaves that Arjuna has torn off during his ascent of the pole. Similarly, the greenery on the extremity of the pole at the Bisket Jātrā New Year festival at Bhaktapur, Nepal, is assimilated "to fecundating semen eagerly sought by barren couples" (Chalier-Visuvalingam 1989, 1985). The ceremony is also very much like one that occurs in the Palnad hero cult. There too, women who seek a cure to infertility hold the shoulder-pieces of their sarees out in the same fashion, only in this cult the items that drop into them come from the heroes' weapons: elaborate, long, and essentially "trident"-like implements that the heroes' impersonators thrust back and forth above the women so that the flower petals and so forth fall into their "aprons."[26] If the tapas pole is not a weapon itself, it is, as I have stressed, the means to Arjuna's attainment of the ultimate weapon, pāśupata.

As Velcheru Narayana Rao has indicated, it is a recurring feature of Indian hero cults to avail women of the means to get children, indeed heroic children, since the means the heroes supply are extraordinary. Heroes are like special ancestors whose extraordinary feats and ultimate deaths have given fertility to the people and the land (Narayana Rao, personal communication, 1988). Recall that in the Dharma and Śiva gājans, fruit is placed on the spikes of the Bāṇeśvar and pāṭā and that either the fruit itself or water poured over the same spot is sought by women as a source of fertility. The Dharma gājan hero himself, Lausen, is conceived when his mother Rañjāvatī falls on such a spiked board, while in the *Elder Brothers Story* the twins and their sister can be born only after their barren mother does tapas on a needle-topped pole and then receives the limes from Śiva.[27] In the case of Arjuna's tapas, children are the indirect "fruits," as it were, of his asceticism: the direct fruit is his attainment of Śiva's grace and supreme weapon. We shall meet with other Draupadī cult examples of ways to get pregnant from heroes.

The women's ritual closes with a reverse circumambulation (*apradakṣiṇa*) of the tapas maram, keeping the post to their left, after which they retreat into the general crowd. Arjuna now remains atop the pole for only one more thing, his encounter with Śiva, who now makes a raucous approach with Pārvatī, the two of them disguised as hunter and huntress. Beyond what is described in volume 1 (285), I would stress only two things that were new to me in the 1986 Mēlaccēri performance, since each has its ritual implications. Before Śiva and Pārvatī's appearance, a circle of straw is strewn there around the tapas pole, essentially where the women had performed their ritual. The narrative explanation is that Duryodhana has sent incendiaries to burn Mount Kailāsa and destroy Arjuna and his penance. The only effect, however, is to intensify his tapas and to deepen its evocation of a fire sacrifice. One suspects, however, that it also serves to purify the ritual ground after the fertility rituals performed by the women.

26. I thank V. Narayana Rao for letting me see his videotape footage on this and other features of the festival of the heroes at Kārempūḍi.

27. See n. 22. Flowers are also strewn from the caṛak hook-swinging post in the Dharma and Śiva gājans (Robinson 1980, 364; Bhowmick 1964, 332).

Second, once Śiva and Pārvatī arrive, Śiva and Arjuna's encounter takes place over their simultaneous shooting of a boar, which, according to the dramas, was sent by Duryodhana to uproot the pole. Arjuna's tapas holds numerous evocations of initiatory death, but the killing of the boar as substitute victim is the one that is most revealing in the performance context, since it takes place while Arjuna is on the top of the pole.[28] As Beck has seen (1982, 166), the epic incident resonates with the boar-killing scene in the *Elder Brothers Story,* which in turn sheds light on the Draupadī cult's folk innovations.

Beck stresses the sacrificial nature of the boar killing. The heroic twins' sister foretells: "If you go to the boar, O brothers / there will be a sacrifice." Once the boar is killed, Viṣṇu demands its head for his share, leading the brothers to foresee their own deaths: "So we shall now give up our own heads" (1982, 166–67). But there is more to it than this. The twins will not actually die by being beheaded. They will die by impaling themselves on their own swords. Indeed, the site where they die in the Viramalai Hills is marked by a vaṉṉi-śamī tree from which Viṣṇu, hiding in a hollow, shoots at them with a plaintain stalk bow and jasmine arrow, cutting their sacred threads as a sign that their time has come. Not only do they fall on their swords, but their Untouchable companion follows their example by impaling himself on a branch from the same vaṉṉi tree (Beck 1975, 275–78). The whole sequence appears to be a mythic inversion, and thus evocation, of the Tamil Dasarā-Vijayādaśamī rite of shooting arrows (or an arrow) into a śamī that represents an "enemy" or "demon" (see chap. 5, sec. C). Here the tree, as it were, does the shooting and, in the companion's case, supplies the branch for the impaling as well. But for present purposes what is most important is that the symbolism of impalement is further evoked by the prior boar victim, whose death presages those of the heroes. The gigantic boar is named Kompaṉ, the "Tusked" or "Horned," and the prophecy is made several times that his two tusks are destined for the brothers: "With it their guts will be lifted out" (Beck 1975, 122; cf. 235, 244). Moreover, his tusks are sixty feet long (ibid., 270), a measurement also mentioned above in connection with Kāttavarāyaṉ's impalement stake and within the range of Draupadī cult tapas poles. Now when this boar is slain, it is at-

28. At the bottom of the pole an initiatory death is implied when Arjuna wrestles with Śiva, who hurls him to the sky, apparently replacing his reduction to a "ball of flesh" in the classical epic (Hiltebeitel 1988a, 285). On the boar as sacrificial substitute in the epic, see Biardeau 1978, 151–52.

tacked, as it were, from two ends. While one of the heroes (either the youngest brother, in the story, or the Untouchable ally riding a tiger, on a temple fresco) spears Kompaṉ in the back, a little female dog, performing an indispensable role, bites the boar's testicles from behind (Beck 1982, 150–51, 167 and photo, p. 98; 1975, plates 12 and 13).[29]

It is here that we have one small but telling point of contact with the joint killing of the boar by Arjuna and Śiva. As the chapbook version of "Arjuna's Tapas" puts it, Arjuna, shooting from above, splits the boar's face in two, while Śiva's arrow cuts up the boar's body (Hiltebeitel 1988a, 285). In the performed version recorded on videotape at Mēlaccēri, the dialogue is more revealing.

> Pārvatī (to Śiva, as they discover the tapas maram with Arjuna on top): What is this post [*kampam*]? Hey, give way.
> Śiva (to Arjuna): We sent an arrow [*pāṇam*] to kill a pig [*paṉṟi*].
> Arjuna (challengingly): Is it a back arrow [*piṉ-pāṇam*] or a front arrow [*muṉ-pāṇam*]?
> Pārvatī: We sent a back arrow. We shot it through the asshole [*cūttu*].[30]

The whole scene is done with lowbrow humor. In their hunter guise, Śiva and Pārvatī are outcastes. Similarly, among local audiences of bardic performances of the *Elder Brothers Story,* the scene of the little female dog biting the huge boar's testicles "is especially loved, . . . and they demand that it be performed regularly" (Beck 1982, 150). With all the explicit emphasis on impalement in the *Elder Brothers Story,* there is nothing about anal impalement. The little dog attacks from the rear, but only to bite the boar's testicles. In the Draupadī cult, however, Śiva's attack from the rear is anal, but has no explicit reference to impalement. What the goddess says in humor, however, is undoubtedly an allusion to impalement and is funny, at least in part, because it reveals the shadow side of Arjuna's tapas. As we have seen, arrows (*pāṇam,* Sanskrit *bāṇa:* recall Bāṇāsura and Bāṇeśvar) impale. And Arjuna has been sitting on a pole topped by a metal rod for a long time. Indeed, at this point the Kāttavarāyaṉ parallel is once again telling. In one version of his story, he journeys to his mother Kāmākṣī's place: "There, beyond many forests, in the middle of a flower garden, Kāttavarāyaṉ does tapas by *standing* [my italics] on a copper needle which is on top of

29. I will discuss these episodes further in volume 3.
30. My thanks to J. Rajasekaran for translating this dialogue. One should note that the Sanskrit *Mahābhārata* invites no such controversy over the entry point of the arrows: the boar is struck by "many arrows" from both archers (3.40.14–15).

a copper pot which is in turn on top of a sixty foot pole (kampam)" (Masilamani-Meyer 1989a, 88). Tāmarai's tapas pole is also topped with needles (cf. n. 22). It must be stressed, however, that this has indeed been a circuitous route to make another case for a Draupadī cult symbolism of impalement. As elsewhere, such themes are muted and deflected and, if one prefers, unconscious at least as regards informants. I would still argue that as part of a multi- and intercultic symbolism, the theme is pervasive.

The tapas maram rituals described till now—involving interplay with the Terukkūttu and rapports with the paṭukaḷam and the firepit—can be regarded as typical of the core area, and variations can best be understood as different kinds of departures: eliminations, substitutions, attenuations, fossilizations, conflations, and losses of meaning.[31] At certain festivals, for instance, Arjuna's tapas would remain only a subject of Pāratam narrative, with all ritual representation eliminated, as at the Sowcarpet temple in Madras. Most likely this is due to urban restrictions there, although nothing has prevented the erection of a tapas maram for the festival of the Teynampet temple in Madras.[32]

At Pondicherry, elaborate decoration of the processional icons has apparently displaced the Terukkūttu, reflecting what must at one time have been a determination to accentuate the temple rather than the dramas in the ritual cycle. Without dramas, the transition from Draupadī's disrobing to Arjuna's tapas is handled rather ingeniously. Three days before the firewalk (which occurs on the festival's nineteenth day), the processional chariot displays Draupadī and Arjuna's marriage. On the next day, it combines a portrayal of Arjuna's penance and Draupadī as Mahiṣāsuramardinī (Shideler 1987, 104, 118). Shideler does not indicate how Arjuna is portrayed in this latter tableau, nor in particular whether there is a pole or even his old or new weapons. Probably Arjuna is only in his conventional tapas pose, either standing or seated with his palms joined over his head. Nor does there seem to be any local version of the ritual involving the ascent of a tapas pole by a local resident rather than a visiting actor, such as is often done at temples outside the core area range of the kūttu troupes.[33] What is striking is that

31. For other brief discussions of rituals for Arjuna's tapas beyond those treated below, see Tanaka 1987, 374–75; Gros and Nagaswamy 1970, 121; Somander 1951, 612–13 (including a "cage" for Arjuna atop the pole); Richards 1910, 30.

32. In 1977. Personal communication from C. T. Rajan, who lived in the temple's neighborhood at that time.

33. I say this cautiously. Shideler is unlikely to have missed it, but he does skip from the sixteenth to the nineteenth day (1987, 151–52).

there is also no *ritual* representation of Draupadī's disrobing. From the joint appearance portraying their marriage, one moves directly to a joint appearance evoking their power to gain revenge: Arjuna obtaining the doomsday weapon of Śiva, and Draupadī with her trident (which, as we have seen, is ultimately the same weapon) impaling the Buffalo Demon.[34]

Across the Andhra border, troupes perform Draupadī cult dramas in Telugu. At Kārvēṭinagaram (Chittoor District), "Arjuna's Tapas" is one of four dramas out of ten performed in the afternoon rather than at night. On the eighth day, in correlation with recitation of the same story by a *Paurāṇika*—a reciter of purāṇic, or "old," stories—Arjuna climbs a tall palmyra singing Śiva's praises till he reaches an "arch-like seat" at the top. "Before he climbs down, he showers from his shoulder bag flowers, lemon fruits, holy ash balls etc., and the audience below almost create a stampede to collect them as they are considered to be very sacred" (Reddy 1985, 9–12). The delicacy of the women's ritual is lost to a general free-for-all.

Beyond the core area, such attenuations multiply. In the Thanjavur area, the main difference is that rather than being played by an actor from a Terukkūttu troupe, Arjuna is a local villager, normally in a role that has been in his family before him. At Cattiram Karuppūr, for instance, Arjuna is played by a Nāṭar coconut tree climber or toddy tapper, who dresses in the saffron-colored shirt and dhoti of a *saṃnyāsin* renunciant. From the top of the tapas maram, he throws down a variety of things: flowers, turmeric, bananas, limes, coconuts, kuṅkum. Everyone catches them, not just the ladies. Upon his descent, a fire is made around the pole, but now with a different explanation. Arjuna crosses the fire, enabled by his tapas. But since his tapas was constantly disturbed by Arakkis (female demons), the circle of fire is lit to prevent them from following him.

In Singapore, the Draupadī festival reported by Babb takes place over two and a half months, with the culminating events coinciding with a Navarātri festival performed for Māriyammaṉ, to whose main temple the Draupadī temple is annexed as a sort of side chapel. Babb says that the Navarātri is "completely unrelated" (1974, 12) to the Draupadī temple's firewalk, but the matter deserves further study. The ritual for Arjuna's tapas occurs at a cru-

34. As Mahiṣāsuramardinī, Draupadī is "twelve armed, . . . dressed in magenta with gold trim," holding a trident with her two extended hands over a "90 cm. long prostrate, blue painted plywood Mahiṣa/goat" (Shideler 1987, 118).

cial point where the two festivals seem to converge.[35] The firewalk of the Draupadī festival is set at least eighteen days after the ritual for Aravāṉ's sacrifice, which serves at Singapore to mark the ritual ground of Kurukṣetra (the term paṭukaḷam is not mentioned) with a trident (ibid., 10). In a narrative anachronism, Arjuna's tapas is performed after Aravāṉ's sacrifice, but this has the clear ritual result that Arjuna's tapas thus falls within the temporal and spatial frame of Kurukṣetra (this order is also reversed at Cattiram Karuppūr, where the proper sequence, though known, is changed to allow the tapas to be part of the culminating Sunday-through-Monday sequence of war-ending rituals).[36] At Singapore, its performance on the penultimate day of this eighteen-day battle cycle coincides with "one of the most important processions of the ceremonial year" of the Māriyammaṉ temple. On this evening, Māriyammaṉ is "drawn around the city on a chariot" (more recently a truck). When she is returned to her temple, her devotees undertake acts involving possession. Within the main hall of the Māriyammaṉ temple, women "swing their unbound hair about their heads in an ecstatic dance," while in the outer precincts mainly men undergo rites of flesh piercing, invoking Murukaṉ's *vēl*, or spear (ibid., 14–15). It is in this setting and at this time that Arjuna performs his tapas. A thirty-foot pole has been erected the same morning within the double temple compound. A local ritualist, his skin dyed a brilliant green, comes forth from the Draupadī temple, does homage to Śiva, circumambulates the pole, and then climbs it. "After remaining on the platform for a few minutes he shoots an arrow down and showers those below with flowers" (ibid., 16). Here we have but a fossil of the women's rite and the shooting of the boar, of which the ritual seems to bear no recollection. Once Arjuna descends, rites of possession continue through the night in the Māriyammaṉ temple (ibid., 15), but now various rites typical of the worship of Māriyammaṉ and Murukaṉ—preparation of flour lamps (māviḷakku), carrying *kāvaṭi*s (decorated poles, topped by arches and carried on the shoulders with offerings)—are also included in the nightlong observation of vows that is preliminary to the next day's firewalk for Draupadī. All this suggests a clear syncretism between the two cults. The connection with Māriyammaṉ deepens the background in which the Draupadī cult's prefirewalking vows resonate with

35. I cannot be more precise on this point, since Babb does not say whether the Māriyammaṉ rites in question are part of her Navarātri celebration.

36. As we shall see, the Singapore temple and festival have their roots in the Thanjavur area.

possession and impalement. And Arjuna's tapas is set at the boundary, or transition, between the rites for these two goddesses as the Draupadī cult exemplar of all ascetic acts.

At Cōḻavantāṉ, between Madurai and Dindigul, there is also a revealing conflation. According to one of the trustees at this Draupadī temple, when the tapas maram is erected, branches cut from vaṉṉi or śamī trees that grow wild in the region are tied to the pole. This is because Arjuna climbed a vaṉṉi maram in the original story. Of course he did do this, but not when he climbed Mount Kailāsa to perform his tapas. Rather, he climbed a śamī when the Pāṇḍavas hid their weapons, again when he retrieved his own weapons to defend the cattle of Matsya against the Kaurava raiding party, and, at least in folk accounts, when he and his brothers retrieved all their weapons at the end of their exile (see chap. 6, sec. B). It is easy to see how these stories could merge into one ritual. The mythical mountain has been lost to the combination of ritual trees. Indeed, unless it was concealed in his thigh, the pāśupata would have been among the weapons Arjuna retrieved from the śamī. As at Pondicherry, Singapore, and Cattiram Karuppūr, Arjuna's tapas is drawn closer to the war.

In this vein, one final, rather fascinating conflation must also be mentioned. At Draupadī festivals in Réunion there is a rite known as "the ceremony of the pole and the five dead cousins." It is not done in Mauritius, where it is considered—one might say correctly—to arise out of a confusion with other rites. At first cock crow, signaling the end of night, a pole with a platform on top, about thirty-five to forty feet high and with eight zigzag steps, is decorated with pennants and streamers. It is climbed by a young man made up with ashes, richly appareled, loaded with flowers, and carrying a bow and three arrows over his shoulder. At the summit, he waits until full daylight and then throws the flowers and his jewels on the ground to those below. Much as at Kārvēṭinagaram in Andhra, there is a rush for them—here by laughing women and children, suggesting that something remains of the women's rite. At about 6:00 A.M. he descends, having apparently done nothing with the bow and arrows. When he reaches the ground, five of the men who will walk over coals in the evening are lying under cloths. While the chief priest chants a prayer for them, the young man just down from the pole dances around the bodies as if molesting them. A cock is sacrificed, and drops of blood are sprinkled on the five "deceased," who then return to life, rise up, and join the others (Blaive, Penaud, and Nicoli 1974, 358–59).

This phase of the ritual is certainly an adaptation of the death and revival rites for the Young Pañcapāṇḍavas, which will be discussed in chapter 11. The children's young "molester" slayer is Aśvatthāman. But the pole is clearly what remains of Arjuna's tapas tree, now adopted into a war-*ending* scene. What then is Aśvatthāman doing climbing the pole instead of Arjuna? As noted earlier, he is Arjuna's chief Kaurava adversary to hold the pāśupata weapon. It seems that the pole survives as a reminder of this weapon and of Aśvatthāman's possession by Śiva before he kills Draupadī's sons. Therefore it is probably not an omission that the young man does nothing while atop the pole with his bow and arrows. He has no boar to shoot.[37] Were there any recollection of his use of the pāśupata, it would be in the sequel where Arjuna finally does release his pāśupata to neutralize Aśvatthāman's pāśupata, which was released in wrath.

The additional throwing of jewels from the top of the pole is also interesting. In the classical epic, when Draupadī demands revenge against Aśvatthāman for killing her children, she demands the jewel that was "natural born" in his head (*Mbh* 10.11.20; 16.21), which the Pāṇḍavas then obtain for her. In Draupadī cult dramas, instead of the head jewel, and also in lieu of Aśvatthāman's head itself, Draupadī receives the diadem that the dying Duryodhana gave to Aśvatthāman when he consecrated him as his fifth and last marshal.[38] In the Réunion rite, however, the women receive the jewels before Aśvatthāman descends to kill Draupadī's children. So if they receive the jewels as a memory of Draupadī's demand, it would have to be in a form that transfers the jewel bestowal to a moment before the killing, so as to retain the ritual emphasis on the women's auspiciousness.

Beyond the Draupadī cult, one could no doubt explore many Indian rituals for further light on Arjuna's tapas. Among the most revealing would be the climbing of a yūpa at the end of the Vājapeya sacrifice (Thite 1975, 82–83), the Indradhvaja (connected with Indra, Arjuna's father), and especially the Indra Jātrā and Bisket Jātrā festivals of Nepal.[39] One could also find analogues to the bow tree. In the Kerala festival for the hair (muṭi) of the goddess Bhadrakālī,

37. In a note to Blaive, Penaud, and Nicoli 1974, 364, Jean Filliozat correctly identifies the concluding phase of this ritual with the slaying of Draupadī's children but misinterprets the pole: "There is a pole but no one climbs it: it carries the flag of the Kauravas."

38. See Hiltebeitel 1988a, 419, 426–31; 1976a, 312–35; on the jewel theme, these remarks extend what is said in idem 1980–81, 194.

39. On the Indra pole festival, see chapter 5, n. 30 (one text stipulates it should be made of an Arjuna tree; Chalier-Visuvalingam 1989, 223 n. 94); on Indra Jātrā (with

under the "shelter of the muṭi," slightly off the central axis and apparently to the northeast, is set a lamp-bearing post called the "bow tree" (*dhanumaram*) that serves as the residence of either Vīrabhadra, as the chief of the goddess's army, or the redoubtable demon Ghaṇṭakarṇṇan.[40]

But an inquiry must have its limits. As a closing reminder of affinities between the pole and the bow, and also between the paṭukaḷam and folk variations on Dasarā, I mention only a ritual performed at a Dasarā festival for the god Mailāra in Karnataka.[41] As part of a sequence involving mock battles representing the god's contest with the demons Maṇi and Malla, on the evening of the penultimate ninth day of the festival, before the final fight with Malla, a member of a special group of quasi-ascetic ritualists, after lengthy fasting, climbs an eighteen-foot-high bow, becomes possessed by the god at the top, and utters prophesies for the coming year (Sontheimer 1989a, 314–18). The group of ritualists in question, called Gorappas or Vaggayyas, are in fact the counterparts in Karnataka of the dog-impersonating Vāghyās ("Tigers") of Maharashtra (Hiltebeitel 1988a, 123–24), worshipers of Khaṇḍobā, who is Mailāra by another name and the conqueror of the same two demons. In Karnataka, before sunrise on the day of the bowclimb, "thousands of devotees, many of them temporary or lifelong Gorappas dressed in their long, black woolen gowns," converge silently on a hillock where they are said to form the seven crores (*yeḷkoṭi*) of the god's army or, alternatively, the number that the demon slays, or demons who have become the god's devotees (Sontheimer 1989a, 317). Here we have a bow that is also a sort of tapas pole on the terrain of a battlefield ritual (cf. ibid., 329). In view of other connections between Dasarā and the Hindu epics, it is also worth wondering whether eighteen feet and seven crores (compare the seven *akṣauhiṇī*s of the Pāṇḍavas' army) are not ritual allusions to the *Mahābhārata*.

---

statues of Indra bound in cords and placed in prisonlike cages at the foot of the pole) and Bisket Jātrā (with assimilation of the pole to the *khāṭvaṅga* staff, topped by a Brahman skull and thus resonant with the pāśupata-head of Brahmā obtained atop the tapas pole), see Chalier-Visuvalingam 1989, 183–86; Visuvalingam 1989, 445.

40. See chapter 7, section B and Tarabout 1986, 119, 126. I only infer that the bow tree is to the northeast: it is slightly off the main axis (ibid., 119), and when the inferior divinities are fed at the northeast (ibid., 126), a torch is placed at the bow tree's foot for their leader (Vīrabhadra or Ghaṇṭākarṇṇan).

41. The same festival is also performed in February-March at a different site (Sontheimer 1989a, 314).

B. Arjuna's Driving of the Bulls

Remaining at the general level before moving back to the particular, *māṭu miraṭṭal*, "the driving [literally 'frightening'] of the bulls," is a rite that occurs widely in Tamilnadu and is by no means limited to the Draupadī cult. It is performed as part of the four-day Poṅkal festival that opens the month of Tai (January-February) and marks the beginning of the sun's ascent. Arunachalam describes its performance in Thanjavur and "adjoining districts." After receiving pūjās and having their horns (and other parts of their bodies) decorated earlier in the day, "all the cows, bulls and calves of the village are gathered together in a common large open space and driven around by the owners themselves, with loud noises and the sounding of the village drums."[42] All honor seems to go to the cows, not to any deity. At Mēlaccēri and Pakkiripāḷaiyam, however, the ceremony is done at this time using the Draupadī temple icons. At Mēlaccēri, on Kanu poṅkal, about 4:00 P.M. all the village's cattle and oxen are driven into the village "green" or *maitāṉam*, where the paṭukaḷam is during the festival. The pañcalōkam images of Arjuna, Draupadī, Subhadrā, and Pōttu Rāja are carried three times around the cattle, after which the cattle are driven away. Pāratam is then recited at the same maṇḍapa, beside the maitāṉam, where it is done during the festival. Pōttu Rāja is there to the right front of Draupadī, who is to Arjuna's right while Subhadrā is to his left. Then the icons are taken on procession through the village. At Pakkiripāḷaiyam, where temples to Draupadī and Aiyaṉār abut the open area, Arjuna is honored alone. At nightfall on māṭṭuppoṅkal, hundreds of cattle, many pulling bullock carts, are driven into the maitāṉam. As they mill about, lowing and lunging, Arjuna's icon, bow in hand, is carried out from the Draupadī temple on a palanquin for a torch-led circumambulation among them. Once he has blessed them and made their tour, all the cattle go home, and Arjuna's icon is returned to the temple.[43]

Arjuna's icon is also the principal one at a rite of the same, or a similar, name at Draupadī festivals. Another Draupadī cult name for the rite is *māṭu tirupputal*, "the turning back of the cattle," which is used not only at the Chinna Salem Draupadī festival but also at a festival in Kongunad where the goddess is not Draupadī

42. 1980, 222, and 212–27 on the full poṅkal cycle.

43. Observed January 15, 1982: a ceremony of magical quality that caught me by surprise, since I was in Pakkiripāḷaiyam to see dramas.

but Kālī (Vīrakāḷi), and the ritual a buffalo sacrifice. The myth evoked, however, still seems to be that of Arjuna's recovery of king Virāṭa's cattle from the Kauravas at the end the year the Pāṇḍavas spend incognito (Biardeau 1989a, 24–25). The *Virāṭaparvan* of the *Mahābhārata,* where this episode occurs, is widely recited in Tamilnadu, not to mention other parts of India, as a precaution against drought, or a stimulus to good rainfall. Indeed, Tamilnadu has its own local "City of Virāṭa" (Virāṭanakar), unconnected with the Draupadī cult, at proverbially prosperous Dharapuram (Coimbatore District), where surrounding villages are also identified with characters and scenes from the *Virāṭaparvan.*[44] The rite and the myth thus both have various settings and extensions. But where they converge at Draupadī festivals is in the ritual commemoration of the cattle-retrieving episode, which is also the subject of a Terukkūttu drama—*Māṭupiṭi Caṇṭai,* "The Fight over the Seizure of the Cattle" (Hiltebeitel 1988a, 299–300)—and Pāratam narration.[45]

At Draupadī festivals, māṭu miraṭṭal is often performed several days before paṭukaḷam and firewalking day, in connection with the corresponding narration and nighttime drama. It is sometimes held at a lake, and especially a dry lake bed, to reinforce the encouragement of rainfall.[46] In such circumstances, there would be no direct link between māṭu miraṭṭal and the paṭukaḷam, since the bull-driving ritual would occur before the paṭukaḷam was prepared, and in a different place.

Since I have not covered any of these pre-paṭukaḷam forms of māṭu miraṭṭal in my fieldwork, I will rely on accounts by Frasca, who describes the ritual at Iruṅkal, and Biardeau, who describes matters at Pondicherry.[47] In each case the ceremony is called *Māṭupiṭi Caṇṭai,* the usual name for the drama, perhaps chosen to cover both the drama and the ritual, which would be especially plausible at Pondicherry, since no dramas are performed there. At Iruṅkal the ceremony occurs three days before paṭukaḷam day, at Pondicherry two, in each case at a spot denoting a boundary location. At Iruṅkal this is a *veṭṭu-veḷi,* or "cleared field," "from which rice

44. On Dharapuram, on *Virāṭaparvan* recitation in Tamilnadu for good rainfall, and on localizations of Virāṭadeśa outside Tamilnadu, see Biardeau 1989b, 214–15 and plate 84; citations in Hiltebeitel 1988a, 299 n. 21; Zvelebil 1973, 215; Frasca 1984, 303 n. 18.

45. For alternate titles, see Hiltebeitel 1988a, 295 nn. 14–15.

46. Information so far supplied by V. M. Brameesa Mudaliyar.

47. Shideler (1987) does not mention this ritual as part of the cycle at this same temple. At Mēlaccēri, where the drama *Māṭupiṭi Caṇṭai* was performed three (1977) and four (1982) days before paṭukaḷam day, I did not hear of a corresponding ritual at that time but unfortunately did not inquire.

has been harvested and that is now dried and cleared." It is described as "outside the village." At Pondicherry, the ceremony takes place on a road toward the outskirts of town. Otherwise, however, it is difficult to generalize because these authors emphasize different things and because the ceremonies appear to be rather different.

At Iruṅkal, where the drama troupe is involved, "the entire village drives all its cattle" to the open field. There, actors in full makeup portray Arjuna "disguised as an hermaphrodite" and Uttara, the "ineffectual" son of Virāṭa, as they first repulse the Kauravas, and then run "up and down the veṭṭu-veḷi and eventually driv[e] the cattle back to the village to the overall rejoicing of the inhabitants." Frasca emphasizes Arjuna's role of driving the cows from outside the village back into it, "thereby safeguard[ing] its resources and main source of nourishment." There is no mention here of how or whether the enactment (or Pāratam recital) registers the epic detail that Arjuna must retrieve his weapons from a śamī tree (Frasca 1984, 302–3). The details, present and missing, remind one, however, of the gāmār tree at the edge of the open rice field outside of town in the Vishnupur Śiva gājan.

In any case, it is this matter of the śamī that Biardeau underscores. At Pondicherry, where no dramas or actors are involved, a small booth is constructed on the road heading out of town for Pōttu Rāja's wooden processional icon. As the pāratiyār describes the scene in which the Pāṇḍavas hide their weapons in the śamī tree, Arjuna arrives on his chariot, garlanded, with his bow and arrow. His progress is stopped facing Pōttu Rāja's booth, and Pōttu Rāja is offered a pūjā. Then the pāratiyār continues the story to the death of Kīcaka. At this point—without narrative prelude to the rescue of the cattle—an officiant (I assume the pūcāri) arrives attended by tambourines and trumpets and makes a second pūjā to Pōttu Rāja. Then the cattle are pushed into the streets to the sound of firecrackers and driven (no direction is given) by Arjuna on his chariot. The two pūjās to Pōttu Rāja—one in the name of Arjuna, the other by the officiant—both occur at points that logically correspond to epic incidents involving the śamī tree. The first corresponds to the Pāṇḍavas' concealment of their weapons in the śamī, and the second corresponds to Arjuna's retrieval of his weapons from the tree to win back the cattle from the Kaurava raiding party. In asking why Pōttu Rāja was worshiped in connection with this ceremony, however, Biardeau was told simply that he presides over every event of good augur. His connection with the śamī has become unconscious (Biardeau 1989b, 117).

The enactment of the recovery of the cattle several days before the performance of paṭukaḷam, in correlation with the unfolding of the epic through Pāratam and drama, is no doubt the most common timing for this ritual. In terms of a connection with the paṭukaḷam, all one would want to emphasize is that Arjuna's fight with the Kauravas over the cattle is a prefiguration of Kurukṣetra,[48] which the paṭukaḷam represents, and that his retrieval of weapons from the śamī, which all classical versions of the epic relate, is compounded by folk accounts (linked with Dasarā) of the incident (missing in classical accounts) in which all five Pāṇḍavas (must) return to the śamī to retrieve the weapons they will use at Kurukṣetra.[49] These, however, are both narrative connections, one classical and the other popular. The only hint of a ritual connection in either case is the honoring at Mēlaccēri and Pondicherry of Pōttu Rāja, who not only seems to retain a trace identity with the śamī, but who mythically, like the śamī, supplies the Pāṇḍavas—or better, supplies Draupadī—with weapons for the Kurukṣetra war. In any case, this connection still relies on myths for its linking threads. The rituals take place at two different sites. All this is different at Tindivanam, where the connections between the two terrains are made ritually. The myths, however, are certainly not irrelevant. I would argue that the mythic connections just cited are among the determinants of Tindivanam's ritual condensations.

On paṭukaḷam morning at Tindivanam, from about 10:00 to 11:00 A.M., the pāratiyār recites and lectures on the *Virāṭaparvan* at a clearing alongside the Tindivanam-Gingee road beside the base of the municipal water tank (see map 5). The site is thus both on the way out of town and near a modern, steel-girdered equivalent of a reservoir. The water tank is a secondary feature, however, since the temple pūcāri says that the ceremony was performed at this site before the tank was built, when the area was a maitāṉam, or open field. Beside the pāratiyār is Arjuna's portable wooden icon. It is the only icon present for the ceremony (there is no Pōttu Rāja), and it is there even before the pāratiyār. Arjuna is shown with his Gāṇḍīva bow to his left and a red-tipped arrow to his right. Below his bright green face hangs an unusual garland of vivid purple, orange, and yellow flowers. No white or red. Though I have no ex-

48. Arjuna's exchange of charioteer and driver roles with Uttara is a comic foreshadowing of his victory at Kurukṣetra with Kṛṣṇa as charioteer; Hiltebeitel 1988a, 299–300; Shulman 1985, 269–76. According to one Mēlaccēri informant, a Terukkūttu performer named Rajan, Uttara first vomits when he sees the eunuch whom Draupadī recommends as his driver.

49. See chapter 6, section B.

egesis to confirm it, this seems to be the only feature that might identify him as a eunuch. He is mounted on a "chariot" that is strapped to poles, making it something of a palanquin. Except for the painted platform, this is a simple structure with four corner poles and a plain flat roof. Each of the four poles has a freshly cut section of a plantain tree tied to it, so that the broad green leaves rise upward and surround Arjuna on all sides. To the front of the roof, on one side, is attached a cut-out, red and yellow painted, wooden pennant figuring a green Hanumān against a yellow background. Arjuna's icon remains stationary through the account of the *Virāṭaparvan* up to his retrieval of Gāṇḍīva from the śamī tree. At this point, the story comes au courant with his bow-and-arrow-bearing image.

The ritual now picks up where the recitation leaves off. Several cows and bulls are brought forward, carefully tended (mostly by Vaṉṉiyars, but also by a few Kōṉār herders). Though I had been led to expect fifty or sixty bulls *and buffaloes* by Purushottama Chettiyar, the temple's chief trustee, there were only three or four cattle in both 1977 and 1981. But given this informant's flair for precious details, we may be confident that water buffaloes have had their day in this stampede. As the Pāratam assemblage breaks up, firecrackers are lit, and the cattle break into a run. The palanquin bearing Arjuna's chariot is lifted on to eight men's shoulders and led by the most senior Vaṉṉiyar trustee, who looks as if he has perhaps assumed the role of Uttara, Arjuna's charioteer. In this fashion Arjuna drives the cattle back from town, having recovered them from Duryodhana, who is said to have treated them cruelly. He does not, however, simply drive them back toward town. He drives them to the paṭukaḷam area, where they quickly pass by the large supine effigy of the fallen Duryodhana, which is at this point still in need of some finishing artistic and ritual touches before it will be ready for further paṭukaḷam ceremonies. In being led through the paṭukaḷam, the bulls are said to represent Duryodhana's army as it is scattered in defeat: either a foreshadowing, or an actual representation, of the Kauravas' performance at Kurukṣetra. After the cattle are taken away, Arjuna's chariot, remaining in motion but slowed down by the thickening paṭukaḷam crowd, is carried once around the supine Duryodhana, whom Arjuna also stupefies and immobilizes in the *Virāṭaparvan*. Finally Arjuna and his chariot are set down at Duryodhana's feet, to his north, and thus facing south. Henceforth he remains throughout the morning paṭukaḷam ceremonies to "watch" the events that take place directly before his eyes, beginning with the sacrifice of his son Aravāṉ, which he will be able to see directly over Duryodhana's effigy and through the work going on to complete it.

One thing is certain. The local variations of this ritual all have at least one or two similarities with each other, but they lack the clear one-to-one resonances with the epic of such rituals as Arjuna's tapas and most of the other paṭukaḷam ceremonies yet to be discussed. The only constants are a spot on the edge of town and the driving of the bulls. Otherwise one has alternatives: the dry bed of a reservoir or an open field; ritual to Pōttu Rāja without any sense that he is related to the epic śamī tree, or no Pōttu Rāja; all the cattle of the village, or a token group of cattle with reports of larger numbers, including buffaloes; a pre-paṭukaḷam ceremony, or a ceremony that becomes part of the paṭukaḷam. Let me add that there are still further variations at Chinna Salem, which has the only other festival I have found besides Tindivanam's that combines māṭu miraṭṭal (there called *arccuṉaṉ māṭu tirupputal*) with other rituals, including firewalking, on the culminating day. There māṭu tirupputal comes after Aravāṉ's sacrifice rather than before it and thus seems to stand for part of the war itself (a tendency we have also noted for the tapas maram). But it is linked with and followed by not the usual paṭukaḷam rituals, but an alternate ceremony enacting the destruction of the Kauravas' fort (see chap. 13, sec. A).

Without epic constants for this ritual, it looks as if different epic themes have been freely evoked. And among these, it seems, are various evocations, separate or combined, of classical and folk versions of the retrieval of the weapons. Either Arjuna retrieves his alone, as in classdical versions of the epic, and the rest is left muted or is transfigured into the presence of Pōttu Rāja as the substitute for the śamī as source of weapons. Or Arjuna brings his weapons directly from the śamī (of the pāratiyār's narrative) to the paṭukaḷam, as at Tindivanam, leaving Pōttu Rāja out but also rendering him superfluous, since if Arjuna beings his weapons directly from the śamī to Kurukṣetra, this implies that the other Pāṇḍavas' weapons have also been brought from the śamī as well. Yet from the parallel angle of the Draupadī cult's popular mythology, Pōttu Rāja cannot be fully superfluous, since it is from Pōrmaṉṉaṉ, his alter ego, that Arjuna, in his alternate effeminate guise of Vijayāmpāḷ, brings the weapons for Draupadī. In one case Arjuna, disguised as a eunuch, obtains weapons from the śamī; in the other, disguised as the "Goddess of Victory," he obtains weapons from Pōrmaṉṉaṉ.

Given the fragmented and multivocal character of this ritual, the Tindivanam condensation presents its special problems, which I will take up from the angle of Arjuna's presence there on the paṭukaḷam. Two approaches suggest themselves. First is the possibility that, in some faint measure, in the Tindivanam version of māṭu mirattal Arjuna brings the symbolism of the śamī, and with it that of the buffalo sacrifice, to Kurukṣetra. As we have seen, the term māṭu can cover both cattle and buffaloes, and in Kongunad the "turning aside of the cattle" ritual can even involve a buffalo sacrifice. At Tindivanam, buffaloes are "supposed" to join the cattle in being driven through the paṭukaḷam, a place of sacrifice. As we noted in chapter 7 (sec. B), there is folklore in both Tamilnadu and Kerala that the Kaurava women are (metaphorically) female buffaloes. As we shall see, they too have a ritual presence on the paṭukaḷam. If the bulls are Duryodhana's army, what is Duryodhana?

These possibilities are enhanced by comparison with the analogous battlefield rituals in the Palnad and Elder Brothers hero cults. At Kārempūḍi, the battlefield site of the "horror [? *kalli*] and desolation/falling [*pāḍu*/*paḍu*]" (see chap. 7, sec. A) is marked by a representation of Pōta Rāju called "Kalli Potharaju" (Chandra Sekhar 1961, 184), to which a "procession goes . . . and the heroes fall on the armours to remind [i.e., recall] the heroic death of the departed heroes" (ibid.). Pōta Rāju's affinities with the śamī-jammi are clear in Andhra, and this cult is no exception. It should also be noted that the rituals at Kārempūḍi include—"at a designated spot on the battlefield"—an equivalent to māṭu mirattal called *Manda Pōru*, or "The Attack on the Herd" (Roghair 1982, 27). I will discuss it further in chapter 11, but note for now that according to V. Narayana Rao, the spot is near the marker for Pōta Rāju (personal communication, 1988). Meanwhile, the paṭukaḷam in the Viramalai Hills, glorified as Kurukṣetra itself, is marked by the trunk of a vaṉṉi tree enclosed in a small shrine to Viṣṇu (Beck 1982, 149, 212, map 8).[50] In each of these folk epics, the śamī also figures in the heroes' battlefield deaths, as we have just seen in the one case of the Elder Brothers and their Untouchable companion.[51] Moreover, Beck's map shows that the Viramalai vaṉṉi marks a spot at the north of the paṭukaḷam, just as Arjuna is placed to the north of the Tindivanam paṭukaḷam. These details satisfy a criterion of the *Mahābhārata*, but by ritually transposing it: the epic śamī tree is to the north of Virāṭa's capital (Hiltebeitel 1988a, 300), not Kurukṣetra.

There is thus a strong suggestion that a paṭukaḷam ritual requires the presence of a śamī or, if not a śamī, then a substitute for

50. Actually, as of 1990, a small vaṉṉi sapling *behind* the Mahāviṣṇu shrine is all that is left of what is said to have been the tree.

51. See section A. I reserve the subject as a whole for volume 3.

it. At Kārempūḍi, one has the stone pillar of Pōta Rāju. At Draupadī festivals, the usual substitute is, of course, the portable Pōttu Rāja that is brought to the paṭukaḷam in the lead of other icons, as if at the head of the Pāṇḍavas' army. This is the regular option, and Tindivanam incorporates it. Indeed, at both Tindivanam and Mēlaccēri, Pōttu Rāja arrives at (that is, his icon is carried to) the paṭukaḷam from the north.

Arjuna, then, seems to supply another substitute, a highly complex double of this symbolism: one of which I know of no other example than the one at Tindivanam. He comes directly from the śamī to Kurukṣetra, recalling both the retrieval of his own weapons (a classical episode) and the retrieval of all the Pāṇḍavas' weapons for the war (a folk episode, parallel to the provision of the weapons by Pōttu Rāja–Pōrmaṉṉaṉ, but involving only classical epic characters). Once Arjuna's "chariot" is stationed to supply the paṭukaḷam's northern marker, the weapon that seems to define his place there is the blood-tipped arrow that is set to stand point upward beside him. Let us recall Pōta Rāju's memorable form in Andhra as a post that "faintly resembles a spear and is called Sulam," and the Cūlam or Stūpi post outside the Forest Draupadī temple at Tiruvannamalai. From this perspective, the Tindivanam and Viramalai paṭukaḷams would each be equivalent to a north-facing goddess temple, with Pōttu Rāja (or the śamī, or Arjuna with the weapons from the śamī) facing in from the north rather than from the east. Let us recall that there is a variant of regional Gingee area mythology that Draupadī's original temple at Mēlaccēri faces north (Hiltebeitel 1988a, 68–70). Perhaps it is a *meaningful* coincidence that this temple marks the spot where Draupadī defeats the hundred-headed demon Acalammaṉ (a multiform of the hundred Kauravas) and secures the services of Pōttu Rāja as her temple guardian (ibid., 76–88). In other words, in the *mythic* original temple (the real Mēlaccēri temple faces east), which marks the site of Draupadī's battle alone (as distinct from the battle of Kurukṣetra, in which she is joined by the Pāṇḍavas), Pōttu Rāja guards the temple from the north. Further, if, as I argued in chapter 6, the temple recapitulates the structure of the uttaravedi, then the same would apply to the paṭukaḷam as an extension of the temple. More precisely, the paṭukaḷam would be equivalent to an uttaravedi with the yūpa at the north. This could further explain the presence of Arjuna, since he is the true sacrificer, and as such, equivalent to the yūpa. The blood-tipped arrow is in any case another reminder of the connection between arrows, the battlefield, and impalement. Now that we have seen that the tapas tree also has an impalement symbolism, one that even ties in with Arjuna shooting arrows, it also suggests a similar symbolism—additional to its representation of Mount Kailāsa—for the unusual placement of Arjuna's tapas tree as the northern marker of the Mēlaccēri paṭukaḷam. As at Cōḻavantāṉ, the tapas tree and the śamī tree have become interchangeable.

But is there evidence, other than his blood-tipped arrow and his northern position overseeing the paṭukaḷam, that Arjuna still represents the śamī itself, after coming from it? To this question I can only answer with a suspicion. As we saw in chapter 5 (sec. C), one way of performing a substitute for the śamīpūjā in Tamilnadu is to shoot an arrow at a vaṉṉi (śamī) tree, a plantain (or banana) tree, or some combination of vaṉṉi tree and plantain. The main vaṉṉi or plantain (*vāḻai*) tree target is identified as a demon foe: usually Vaṉṉiyacuraṉ (after the vaṉṉi tree), but sometimes Mahiṣāsura, for whom Vaṉṉiyacuraṉ seems to be a substitute. Masilamani-Meyer mentions two examples where it is a question of five plantain saplings set in a pantal *before a temple,* with the sapling in the middle recognized in one case as Mahiṣāsura. The central stalk represents him and receives the last arrow. The four corner stalks are given no demon identities and seem to represent only the four directions, into which additional arrows are shot (in press-a, 13–14).

Now Arjuna's "chariot" has a cut plantain sapling bound to each of the four corner posts. The Tindivanam pūcāri assured me that such a use of plantain saplings is no more than a very common indication of auspiciousness, as in the example of marriage pavilions.[52] But are they so innocent? To connect the four plantains on Arjuna's "chariot" with those surrounding a demon requires an inversion: rather than being the final target for an arrow within the four plantains, Arjuna stands with his red-tipped arrow as if he were shooting out from them. He is not the demon but the conqueror of demon foes. We know, however, that such an inversion is not simply a structuralist artifice, since we have already met a parallel in the *Elder Brothers Story,* where Viṣṇu shoots the jasmine arrow *from within the śamī* at the site of the original Viramalai paṭukaḷam. Even so, I would happily leave such complications aside, were it not that one Draupadī temple holds a ritual that seems to combine these very ingredients in a way that could supply a parallel and a complement to the kind of thinking that lies behind Arjuna's representation at the Tindivanam paṭukaḷam.

52. Recall that Arjuna's tapas tree platform has banana stalk cuttings on it at Iruṅkal (see n. 14): from here too he shoots arrows.

At Muthialpet—where Arjuna shoots his arrows at the śamī behind the temple at Vijayādaśamī to impress Draupadī before marrying her (chap. 5, sec. C)—there is no māṭu miraṭṭal ritual at the temple's regular Draupadī festival. Rather, the following rite, so far found at no other Draupadī temple, seems to replace it. On the day before the paṭukaḷam ceremonies and two days before firewalking, a plantain trunk called *vaṉṉi-vāḻai-maram* is planted before the entrance to the temple (that is, in the place of Pōttu Rāja). This name, the vaṉṉi [śamī]-plantain tree, combines the two trees, clearly identifying the plantain with the vaṉṉi and possibly with its additional meaning of "fire." The name might also hold an echo of the demon Vaṉṉiyacuraṉ, though the Kurukkaḷ rejected such a suggestion. Arjuna's icon, adorned as if he were hunting (*pārivēṭṭai*) and riding a horse vehicle (*kutirai vākaṉam*), comes to this plantain stalk and cuts it down "like a sacrifice." As was noted earlier, as part of Dasarā, the royal hunt can be an alternative pretext for the arrow-shooting visit to the demon tree.[53] The tree itself is not one demon but four. Each of its four leaves represents a different demon: Ikṣukaṇṭaṉ, Vāmaṉarāmaṉ, Karkoṭakaṉ, and Kuḷikaṉ.[54] Their defeat is said to pave the way for the Pāṇḍavas to win the Kurukṣetra war.

Instead of Arjuna's going to a śamī to obtain weapons that will enable the Pāṇḍavas to win the war, he now goes to a śamī substitute (the plantain) that conceals four demons and kills or sacrifices it, and them, to secure the victory. It thus seems that the usual śamī-plantain combination has been split at this temple, leaving the śamī where one might sooner expect the plantain (at Vijayādaśamī), and the plantain (named, however, the "śamī-plantain") where one would rather expect the śamī (in a ritual portraying a supposed prewar scene from the *Mahābhārata*). Along with holding a paṭukaḷam ceremony for Duryodhana on the ninth day, this temple also sends Draupadī in procession on the ninth night adorned as Mahiṣāsuramardinī (Makiṣācuramarttiṉi alaṅkāra), with eighteen weapon-holding arms to represent the eighteen-day war. It is thus not only the plantain sacrifice that is inserted from

53. See chapter 5, nn. 25–27. The hunt—a wild boar hunt—as a rite on Dasarā day is found in Goa (Silva 1955, 583).

54. The Kurukkaḷ was silent on these four demons. Kuḷikaṉ (Guḷikan), known in South Kanara (Prabhu 1977, 27) and Kerala, figures in exorcisms (Logan 1906, 176; cf. Ayrookuzhiel 1983, 14, 41–42, 47–48, 146, 152–53), is the "one of the seven invisible planets, said to be the son of Saturn" (Winslow [1862] 1979, s.v.), and is apparently equivalent to the Sanskrit "comet"-demon Ketu (see Merry 1982, 12; Clothey 1982, 160). Ikṣukantaṉ means Sugarcane Lord; Vāmaṉarāmaṉ means Dwarf-Rāma. Karkoṭakaṉ reminds one of Ghaṭotkaca, son of Bhīma and Hiḍimbā. An odd lot.

Vijayādaśamī, but the whole mythology of Durgā as slayer of the Buffalo Demon. More than this, the temporal placement of Arjuna's "sacrifice" of the plantain just before these representations of the war is an indication of a connection between the two rituals. It seems that Arjuna kills the demon in this fourfold plantain tree form so that Draupadī can manifest herself in the pose of victor over the same demon in his buffalo form, with the paṭukaḷam ceremony for Duryodhana's effigy set between these two ceremonies as if to link him in series with these other demons. This is similar to the combination we found among the chariot decorations at Pondicherry, where Draupadī as Mahiṣāsuramardinī is set beside Arjuna performing his tapas. Within such chains of associations as these, it is certainly possible that the four plantain stalks around Arjuna at Tindivanam are reminders—or perhaps remainders—of his connection with the śamī, akin to the four demons he kills at Muthialpet to pave the way to victory. Surrounded by the plantain stalks, Arjuna would thus not be the śamī as demon, but as the bearer of its connection with weapons, and ultimately a reminder that the śamī is a form of the goddess of Victory, Aparājitā, the Unvanquished, just as Arjuna-Vijaya is himself a form of this same goddess when he takes on the disguise of Vijayāmpāḷ, "Victory-Mother," to trick Pōrmaṉṉaṉ (alias the śamī) into handing over the ritual weapons that will allow Draupadī to win the war.

If this final example from Muthialpet is a substitute for māṭu mirattal, it has, of course, transformed its symbolism beyond immediate recognition. Much the same could be said of the "ceremony of the pole and the five dead cousins" as a transformation of Arjuna's tapas. In each case it is specific ritual forms that continue, while the myth changes. This brings us to the second approach to Arjuna's presence on the Tindivanam paṭukaḷam, which has none of the complications of the first. It may be observed that Arjuna's presence at the Tindivanam paṭukaḷam with his bow and blood-tipped arrow is, from a certain angle, a replication of his bow and tapas trees. In each case it is the same combination: the bow and the arrow, with hints at a symbolism of impalement. In their barest essentials, as when reduced to iconic tableaux, the two rituals can even be interchangeable. Other than such consistencies, however, the striking thing is that Arjuna's presences at the paṭukaḷam are so mute, distanced, and ritually nonessential. The greatest hero at Kurukṣetra is marginalized at the rituals that represent it. He is separated from his charioteer Kṛṣṇa, whose icon rides Garuḍa. So his many deeds at Kurukṣetra go ritually unreenacted. At the most, his icon's presence overlooking the Tindivanam paṭukaḷam can only signal his witness to the sacrifice of his son Aravāṉ and his scattering of the Kaurava army and possibly recall his collusion in the death of Duryodhana.[55] Elsewhere, the most we shall find in addition is that his icon is brought to the paṭukaḷam along with others. The main ritual actors at the paṭukaḷam, whether in the form of their icons or their human impersonators, are usually Pōttu Rāja, Aravāṉ, Bhīma, Duryodhana, the Young Pañcapāṇḍavas, and Draupadī. Yet this does not mean that Arjuna is irrelevant or forgotten. The Terukkūttu dramas highlight Arjuna and Kṛṣṇa in ways that more than sufficiently compensate for his ritual marginality. Yet the significance of this marginality itself must not be underestimated. Arjuna's ascent of the tapas maram shares another feature with his visit to the śamī tree. They are both indications that the greatest warrior of Kurukṣetra holds his profound and impeccable power in reserve and is present above all by his self-mastery and self-restraint.

55. He is supposed to pass on to Bhīma Kṛṣṇa's sign that Bhīma should club Duryodhana illegally on the thigh. But the paṭukaḷam reenactment usually omits this role; cf. Hiltebeitel 1988a, 417–18.

1. The pāratiyār S. Nagarajan reciting from the *Villipāratam* while dressed as Draupadī, beginning morning performance of "Eighteenth-Day War." Cattiram Karuppūr, 1990.

2. Mēlaccēri pañcalōkam icons: Pōttu Rāja bearing head and sword, Draupadī with parrot closed lotus bud, Arjuna with bow and half-moon arrow, Subhadrā with opening lotus.

3. Tindivanam Draupadī temple inner sanctum: Vināyakar, Dharma, Draupadī (central figure), and Kuntī, with standing Draupadī in back holding parrot.

4. Vīrāṇantal Dharmarāja temple inner sanctum: Draupadī (set to front), smaller Kuntī, Dharma (central figure), and Vināyakar, with Dharma in back seated in royal ease.

5. Tindivanam wooden processional icon of Dharma in disguise as Keṅkupaṭṭar, the "Kite-" or "Heron-Brahman," bearing staff and book called "Liking to Do Dharma."

6. Tindivanam wooden processional icon of four-armed Kṛṣṇa riding winged, beakless Garuḍa.

7. Four-armed Vīrapattiraṉ, head in hand, with two cukkumāttāṭi clubs.
Vaṭukku Poykaiyūr.

8. Pōttu Rāja with liṅgam and yoni on head. Ceṉpākkam Hamlet Draupadī temple, Vellore.

9. Women at base of tapas tree open ends of sarees to catch lemons dropped from above by Arjuna. Mēlaccēri 1986. Upper end of bow tree appears in upper right corner.

10. Head of standing Aravāṉ overlooking chest and head of Duryodhana's effigy at Tindivanam paṭukaḷam, 1977. Photo by Robert Mayes.

11. Runway cleared for pūcāri V. Govindaswami to approach Aravāṉ with blood rice; vīracāṭṭi whip is coiled in vīrakuntam to left. Tindivanam 1977. Photo by Robert Mayes.

12. Blood rice for Aravāṉ, later eaten to induce pregnancy, removed by devotees. Tindivanam 1977.

13. Permanent prone concrete effigy of Aravāṉ in its shed. Chinna Salem.

14. Kālī, her lap at ground level for Aravāṉ to lay his head on so he can look toward Kurukṣetra. Halved coconuts, rice pot, and rooster in readiness for Aravāṉ's sacrifice. Cattiram Karuppūr, 1990.

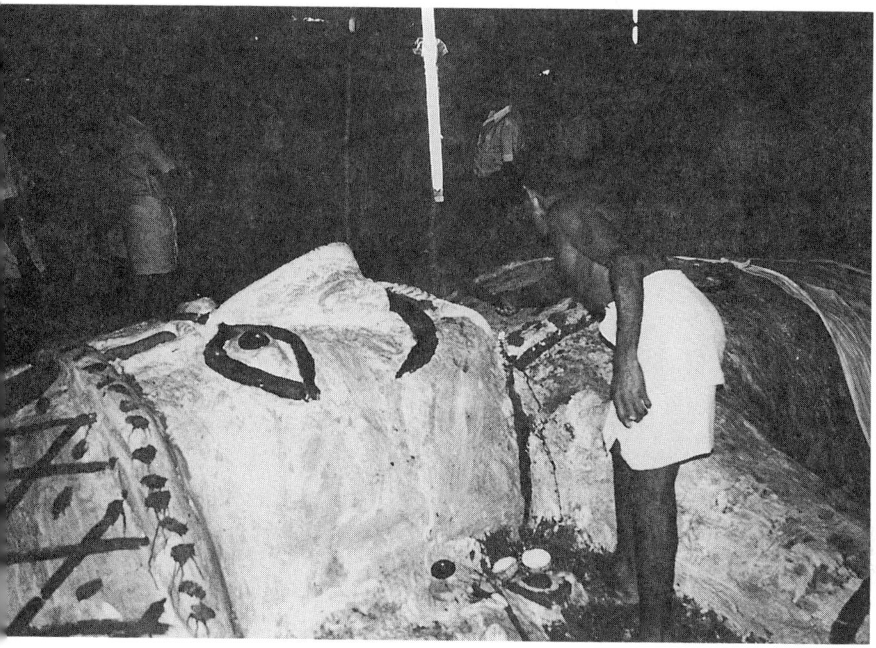

Tracing of arivāl sickle-knife over neck of prone Aravāṉ effigy after rooster sacrifice above neck. Cattiram Karuppūr, 1990.

16. Shrine for Nākakkaṉṉi, Kālī, and Aravāṉ facing north toward Muttāl Rāvuttaṉ. Aḻakār Tirupputtūr.

.7. Retying of Draupadī's wooden processional icon's hair as it is carried over Duryodhana's rampled effigy. Tindivanam 1977. Photo by Robert Mayes.

18. Postfestival remains of massive ninety-foot-long effigy of Duryodhana. Uttiramērūr, 1982.

. Bhīma actor clubs Duryodhana effigy's right thigh at point where blood has been placed in
t. Maṅkalam 1982.

20. Draupadī actor reties hair standing on chest of Duryodhana's effigy. Maṅkalam 1982.

21. Pāratiyār S. Nagarajan as Draupadī approaches bound Duryodhana before hair tying. Wheel-trident combination vīrakuntam is held beyond Duryodhana's head. Cattiram Karuppūr, 1990.

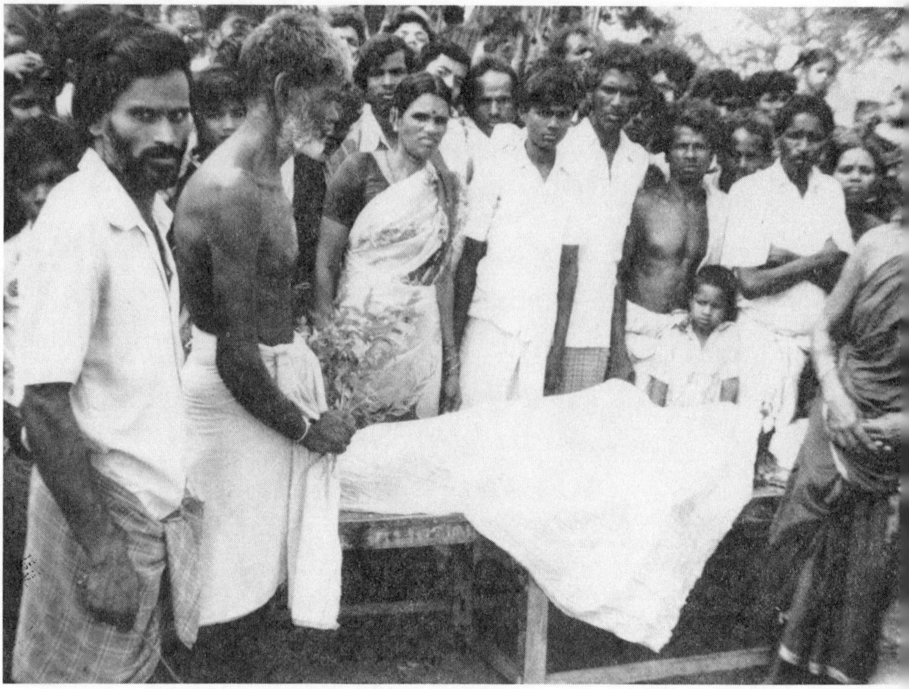

22. "Chief of Pūtams," "Chief of Guards," or "Bhīṣma" on elevated bench; holder of margosa sprigs and female family member in attendance. Maṅkalam 1982.

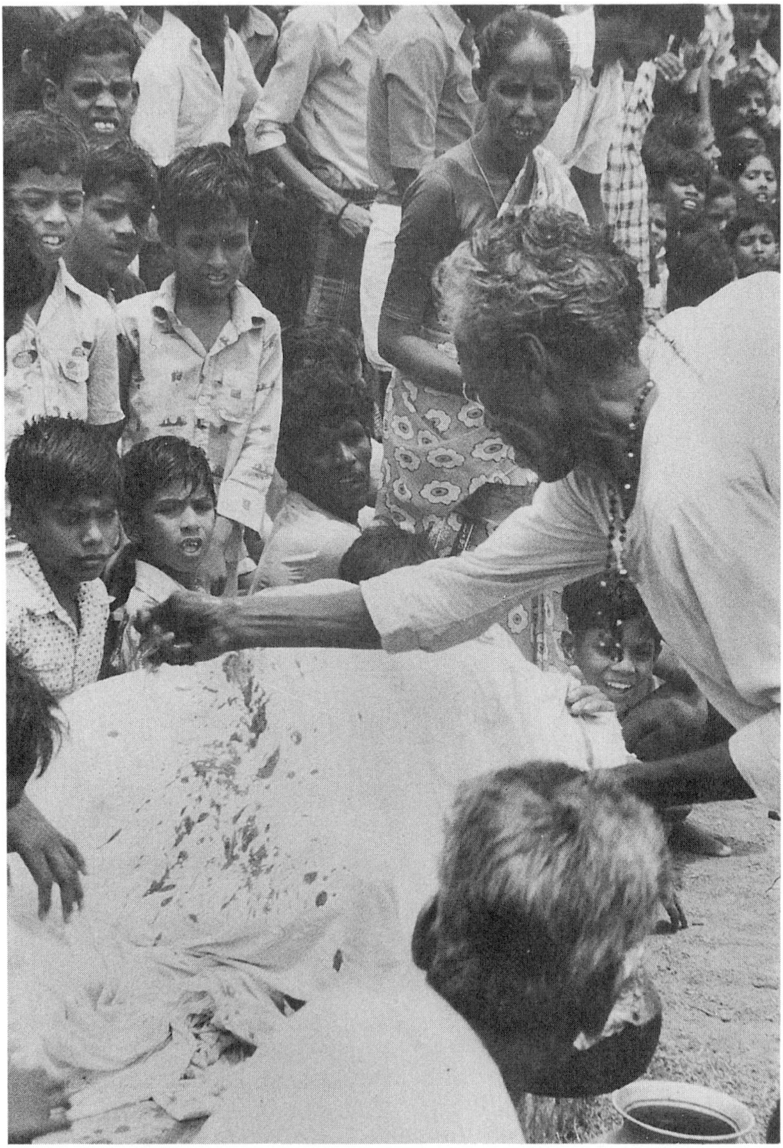

23. Kuṅkum-water "blood" sprinkled on one of Young Pañcapāṇḍavas. Tindivanam 1981.

24. Icons of Draupadī, Pōttu Rāja, and head of Aravāṉ regaled with whips and swords, approached by devotees for katti cēvai, or sword pressing. Sowcarpet, Madras, 1975.

25. Oleograph of Camuṇḍīśvarī slaying Mahiṣāsura, with her lion chomping the demon's human right thigh. Mysore Camuṇḍīśvarī temple in background, source of print.

26. Remains of circular "Aravāṉ Kaḷappali Fort" walls. Kīḻperumpākkam Hamlet. Villupuram, 1982.

27. Kōṭṭai Kāḷi, or "Kālī of the Fort," in black saree with cūlam, Kīḻperumpākkam Hamlet, Villupuram.

28. Fanged Kālī and Duryodhana (the pūcāri) arrive at Cakkaravartti Fort on chariot with pañcalōkam icons of Draupadī, Arjuna, and Kṛṣṇa. Cattiram Karuppūr, 1990.

29. Egg-eyed head of effigy of Vallāḷarājaṉ, victim of Aṅkāḷammaṉ, made from cremation ground ashes. Krishnampet, Madras, 1982.

30. Procession of two karakam pots from tank to temple before firewalk, led by rice mill owner and temple trustee M. Durai. Maṅkalam 1982.

31. Possessions during karakam procession to temple. Maṅkalam 1982. Weapons borne in procession include vīrakuntam (upper left), koṭicīlai pennant (center), and katti tipped with a lemon held front center.

32. Alaku-niṟuttal: standing of sword on karakam pot. Veḷḷimēṭupēṭṭai sanctum, 1977. Phot by Robert Mayes.

. Ramalinga Goundar, age 103 in 1986, grandfather of M. Durai (plate 30), goes first across e coals at Maṅkalam in 1982. Ball of jasmine and lemon gathered up by man to right. Tapas aram at northeast corner of firepit.

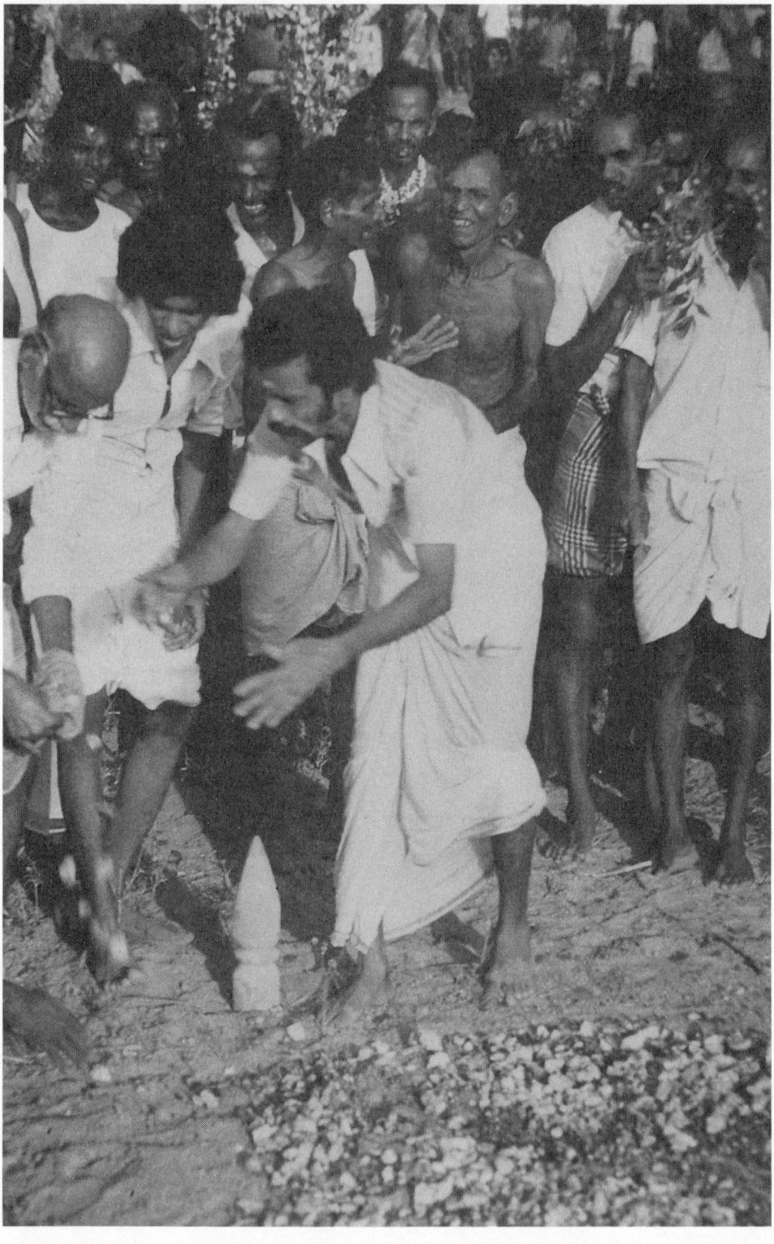

34. Yellow-painted akkiṉikampam set at northeast corner of firepit, just before firewalk. Mēlaccēri 1982.

35. Tindivanam pūcāri V. Govindaswamy first across the coals bearing flower karakam. Tindivanam 1977. Photo by Robert Mayes.

36. Lithograph from Pierre Sonnerat's 1782 *Voyage aux Indes orientales* showing a Draupadī cult firewalk. Uncustomarily in terms of currently known practices, it appears that a woman goes first, followed by the karakam bearer carrying a fruit-impaled alaku sword.

37. Pūcāri V. Govindaswamy performs karumāti funerary rites for remains of Duryodhana's effigy. Tindivanam 1981.

38. After tarumar paṭṭāpiṣēkam, or coronation of Dharma, in temple, Dharma's richly decorated image is lifted up and into chariot for procession through streets. Pondicherry 1977. Photo by Robert Mayes.

9 Aravāṉ's Battlefield Sacrifice to Kālī

We cannot begin to set forth the rituals of Aravāṉ's sacrifice without recalling his story. It is so packed with ritual allusions, however, that no summary could include them all. Moreover, such an effort would repeat material from volume 1. Since a principle of selection is called for, I offer a ritually scored account based on popular versions of the story known through the Terukkūttu.[1] There are now, however, two distinct published versions of "Aravāṉ's Sacrifice," each reflecting a different Draupadī cult milieu. I will continue, as in volume 1, to follow in the main the Irattiṉa Nāyakar version (*Aravāṉ Kaṭapali Nāṭakam* 1977) rather than the recently edited Sarasvati Mahal version (Cēturāmaṉ 1986), since the former is closest to the cultic themes of the core area.[2] But the Sarasvati Mahal version, edited and commented upon by Kō. Cēturāmaṉ, is invaluable for its differences, which reflect traditions of the Thanjavur area. I saw a variation on this second version performed as part of the festival at Cattiram Karuppūr (May 1990), with local actors all trained by the pāratiyār, who took the leading role of Draupadī (see chap. 2, n. 1).

The themes selected from our primary text will resonate not only with the Draupadī festival paṭukaḷam, but also with the Kūttāṇṭavar cult and its aḻukaḷam, or "weeping ground" (see chap. 7, sec. A), since Kūttāṇṭavar is identified with Aravāṉ. Only the Irattiṉa Nāyakar version touches base with both cults, reflecting the common mythology they share in the core area, and particularly in southern and coastal areas of South Arcot. As far as I have been able to determine, there are no Kūttāṇṭavar temples in Thanjavur

1. I omit discussion of echoes of Vedic ritual already treated in volume 1 (Aravāṉ=Irāvat in Sanskrit, possibly "possessor of the *iḍā*," the part of the oblation eaten in common as source of fecundity; the "head of the sacrifice" theme).
2. See Hiltebeitel 1988a, 160, 320–31.

District, which suggests an explanation for some of the differences that will be noted between the two versions of the story.

Kaḷappali, "sacrifice to the battlefield," is a prebattle ritual that secures victory. As far as I can tell, the term has no usage outside Tamil versions of the *Mahābhārata,* but there may well be ritual precedent in Caṅkam-period descriptions of human sacrifice before and after raiding expeditions.[3] In any case, just before the battle of Kurukṣetra, Duryodhana learns from the Pāṇḍava Sahadeva, renowned as an astrologer, that the optimal time for kaḷappali is the *amāvācai,* or new-moon night, which is one day hence, and gets Aravāṉ to agree to be the victim. Kṛṣṇa, seeing the danger, works things out so that Aravāṉ will perform this sacrifice for the Pāṇḍavas instead of the Kauravas. He explains to the Pāṇḍavas that it will be an offering to Kālī as part of the āyudhapūjā, or "worship of weapons." Though Kṛṣṇa does not mention it, the āyudhapūjā is a subrite of Dasarā, the royal festival that opens military campaigns at the end of the rainy season. Here one finds remarkable legendary parallels in Karnataka (North Kanara) traditions of human sacrifices on the day after Dasarā: the victim (or three victims) is beheaded at a stone altar outside a goddess temple, after which warriors can leave home for their military camps. The alleged practice is reenacted in various ritual forms—all with Draupadī cult parallels—that include simulated human decapitations, gourd offerings, and cock sacrifices.[4] An ordinary Dasarā would involve, of course, not a human sacrifice but a buffalo sacrifice. We may assume, however, that the play's allusion to Dasarā is self-conscious, since Yudhiṣṭhira asks whether a wild buffalo, elephant, boar, horse, or some other animal might not be more appropriate. It is worth recalling that Dasarā rites may also include a symbolic

3. The *Tamil Lexicon* gives no reference other than "*Pārata.*" The oldest partially surviving Tamil version of the epic, Peruntēvaṉār's ninth-century *Pārata Vēṇpa,* includes Aravāṉ's kaḷappali (Venketesa Acharya 1981, 137–44). Pre–raiding expedition human sacrifice is suggested in the *Cilappatikāram* (Dikshitar 1939, 187f.); post–raiding expedition human sacrifice in other Caṅkam texts (Kailasapathy 1968, 241–42; see Parpola in press, sec. 3.2.3. According to Nandi (1973, 40), a king desiring victory could perform *mahānavamī* or Dasarā rituals at any time. On head offerings more generally, see Nagaswamy 1982, 26–27, 33–34.

4. Silva 1955, 579–84; Parpola in press, sec. 3.2.3. I do not follow Silva (and Parpola, who follows him), who views the rituals as "circumstantial evidence" for actual human sacrifice (ibid., 577) and gourd and cock sacrifices as introduced only after the latter was "abolished" (ibid., 582–83). There is no evidence for a linear development of "substitutions." Silva shows only that a "conception" or "idea" of human sacrifice has "survived" (ibid., 580), not the actual practice. See Gonda 1987, 22 n. 105; Biardeau 1989b, 49–50 n. 22 and 78 n. 26, making in principle the same point.

slaying of an enemy or rival, with overtones of a relative, by the shooting of arrows.[5]

Kṛṣṇa reaffirms that kaḷappali requires a human victim and sets to working things out so that Aravāṉ—who is content either way—offers himself on behalf of the Pāṇḍavas. This requires moving the amāvācai ahead to the day before the real amāvācai. He convinces some Brahmans that their almanacs say it is already the amāvācai and gets them to perform the ancestral offerings (*tarppaṇam*) appropriate to the day. When Sūrya and Candra, the sun and moon gods, see this, they come together in the sky to question the Brahmans' irregularity. Kṛṣṇa seizes upon this moment to explain that an amāvācai is by definition the "coming together" of the sun and the moon (in Sanskrit, *sūryendu saṅgamam;* Venkatesa Acharya 1981, 141). This rather technical spoof is enough to supply Aravāṉ with an early amāvācai so that he can fulfill his promise to perform kaḷappali, but now for the Pāṇḍavas.[6]

Aravāṉ then secures three boons from Kṛṣṇa that reflect a fusion of ritual themes from his different portrayals in the two cults. First, that he will not die a bachelor, a problem that Kṛṣṇa solves by taking the form of Mohinī, the Enchantress, and marrying him in a last-minute wedding. This reflects the Kūttāṇṭavar cult rituals of South Arcot, in which devotees, including eunuchs and transvestites, take on Kṛṣṇa's role of Aravāṉ's bride and then widow. Second, that he will die in the war at the hands of a great hero, already his destiny in the classical epic, and also ritualized only in the Kūttāṇṭavar cult. Third, that he will see the entire war, a theme ritualized primarily in the Draupadī cult, where his head overlooks the paṭukaḷam. Significantly, the Sarasvati Mahal version from the Thanjavur area preserves only the one boon pertinent to the Draupadī cult: life (*uyir*) to his eyes and breath (*pirāṇaṉ*), so that he can watch the eighteen-day war (Cēturāmaṉ 1986, 68).[7] Indeed, in the

5. See chapter 5, section C and chapter 8, sections A and B. Aravāṉ is a relative of both sides and an enemy at least of the Kauravas, who plan to offer him first. Cf. also Hiltebeitel 1988a, 329, 331, and Cēturāmaṉ 1986, xiii, on the sense in which he endangers the Pāṇḍavas' vows by being able to destroy the Kauravas in a single day.
6. According to *Mahābhārata* 3.213.26–32, the time of the amāvasyā, when the moon enters into conjunction with the sun, is a fearful (*raudra*) time in which the Devas fight the Asuras; see Hopkins [1915] 1969, 93. The Aravāṉ myth seems to transpose that theme into the corresponding epic setting of the battle, about to take place, between the Pāṇḍavas and Kauravas.
7. Cf. Babb 1974, 9, with the same reduction to one boon at Singapore: "He agreed to the sacrifice on one condition, namely that he should be allowed to watch the coming war." On the Singapore festival's roots in the Thanjavur area, see chapter 8, n. 36.

Thanjavur area Aravāṉ's marriage to Mohinī seems to be unknown. According to the pāratiyār S. Nagarajan, whom I met in performance at Cattiram Karuppūr, Aravāṉ's last-minute marriage is to an entirely new woman: Paravanācciyāḷ, the daughter of Kṛṣṇa's "younger brother" (*tampi*) Sātyaki.[8]

At evening, Kṛṣṇa then declares it is time to go to Kurukṣetra. Yudhiṣṭhira worships Kālī in his "hall of weapons" (*āyutacālai*), and Kālī then appears before all on the battlefield. Aravāṉ's mother Ulūpī or Nākakkaṉṉi (serpent-maiden) weeps for him (as we shall see, it is Draupadī who does this in the Thanjavur versions). Aravāṉ does obeisance to Kālī, then removes his chestplate and epaulets and cuts flesh from his body in thirty-two places, putting the offerings in a copper pot (*kopparai*). While the rest of his body is draped from the neck down in a cloth, his head remains to watch the war. Kālī blesses the Pāṇḍavas for victory.

There is then a sequel that has its most evident ritual significance in the Kūttāṇṭavar cult, but is also significant, though less obviously, at the Draupadī cult paṭukaḷam. As Kṛṣṇa had promised, on the war's eighth day, despite his mutilated and skeletal body, Aravāṉ must be able to die heroically in battle: as in classical accounts, fighting the Rākṣasa Alambuṣa. Kṛṣṇa tells him to call on the "Primal Serpent-Remainder," Ādiśeṣa, who, as the father of Nākakkaṉṉi, is Aravāṉ's maternal grandfather. Ādiśeṣa comes from Nāgaloka, the world of serpents, and coils around Aravāṉ to reconstitute his body with flesh. Once Aravāṉ has distinguished himself in battle, Kṛṣṇa then either calls upon Garuḍa or inspires Alambuṣa to disguise himself as Garuḍa, and when the primal serpent sees his perennial "eagle" adversary, he fearfully uncoils himself from Aravāṉ's remains and leaves him for Alambuṣa to behead.

Since the Draupadī and Kūttāṇṭavar cults make selective ritual use of this one epic myth, we must not proceed as if the Draupadī cult ceremonies for Aravāṉ can be treated in isolation. Accordingly, after discussing the Draupadī cult rites, I will compare them with those done for Aravāṉ as Kūttāṇṭavar. Then I will attempt to show that the myth-ritual complex we find in these two cults has counterparts in other hero cults already met. Finally, I will discuss the significance of Kālī's arrival at Kurukṣetra.

8. Sātyaki, Kṛṣṇa's paternal uncle's grandson through the male line, is his tampi or younger brother in this extended classificatory sense only. S. Nagarajan was also familiar with the boon that Aravāṉ should die in battle, but neither this nor the variant on his marriage was enacted dramatically or ritually. In performing Pāratam, he had never traveled north of the Coleroon River, the traditional boundary between the Gingee and Thanjavur Nayakates (Hiltebeitel 1988a, 22).

A. Draupadī Cult Rites for Aravāṉ

As with māṭu miraṭṭal, the rituals for Aravāṉ's sacrifice can be performed before paṭukaḷam day. Where the play "Aravāṉ's Sacrifice" is included in the drama cycle, it could suggest an earlier coinciding slot for the rite, or even possible combinations of ritual and drama, as happens with māṭu miraṭṭal and the play *Māṭupiṭi Caṇṭai*. The play generally occurs anywhere between two and six days before paṭukaḷam (Hiltebeitel 1988a, 167). Surprisingly, however, there is little incidence of correlation between the drama and the ritual. The closest thing to a correspondence I know of is at Iruṅkal, where the ritual is performed two days before paṭukaḷam, on the sixteenth day, and involves collaboration between the dramatists (one of whom appears as Aravāṉ's Nāgī mother to lament over his effigy) and the villagers. But here there is no performance of the actual drama, and the ritual is slotted on the eve of the drama "Abhimanyu's Fight" instead.[9] At the early nineteenth-century Dindigul festival, the ritual occurred on day sixteen of an eighteen-day festival, one day before paṭukaḷam and two days before firewalking. But that festival had no independent drama cycle, only processions with "street drama" components (Hiltebeitel 1988a, 46–47, 152). At Singapore, again without separate dramas, it occurs in two linked parts, the second of which (the actual sacrifice) falls on the amāvācai of the Tamil month of Puraṭṭāci (September-October), and must be at least eighteen days before the culminating day of paṭukaḷam-type rites and firewalking. Here the timing retains the theme of the amāvācai and takes literally the eighteen-day vigil, but at the ex-

9. Frasca 1984, 305–9, 327a: at one point the seventeenth day (306), at three others the sixteenth. In Draupadī cult mythology, both sons of Arjuna are Rākṣasic, dismembered, associated with the number sixteen, and ultimately victims of Kṛṣṇa's design to keep them from upstaging their father (Hiltebeitel 1988a, 328, 401–4). According to the pāratiyār S. Nagarajan, Aravāṉ has also taken on Abhimanyu's trait of rolling over the Kaurava armies by turning into a grinding stone (*kuḻavi*) during his eighth-day fight (cf. Hiltebeitel 1988a, 402–3). It is tempting to think that the common numerical symbolism would be lunar: Abhimanyu incarnates the moon's "splendor"; Aravāṉ performs kaḷappali on the amāvācai. The *tithis*, "digits" or "segments of the sun's reflections on the moon" (Clothey 1982, 163), total fifteen in each of the waxing and waning halves of the month. The amāvācai is counted as the thirtieth tithi (Merrey 1982, 2). However, according to an epic passage (*Mbh.* 12.305.3 = Critical ed. 12.293.4) cited by Hopkins ([1915] 1969, 91), "the moon has sixteen parts, only one of which remains intact, the others increasing and decreasing." The Ganguli translation reads, with gloss: "Only fifteen of these are subject to increase and decrease. The sixteenth (i.e., that portion which remains invisible and which appears on the night of the New moon) remains constant" ([1884–96] 1970, 10:426). Cf. *Chandogya Upaniṣad* 6.7.1–5.

pense of other mythical continuities, such as placing the rituals for the death of Kīcaka and Arjuna's tapas after Aravāṉ's sacrifice (Babb 1974, 9–11, 15–16).

At certain shorter festivals, notably ten- or twelve-day cycles in and around Madras (Sowcarpet, Ālantūr, Pūṉamalli) and Bangalore (Richards 1910, 29–30), it is common for kaḷappali to be performed on the night (in most cases the ninth) before the culminating (usually tenth) day. At Sowcarpet, there is no paṭukaḷam, the big day building up solely to the late evening firewalk. In this instance the ninth night features the 4:00 A.M. braiding of the Draupadī icon's hair as an evident paṭukaḷam substitute or "part for the whole." This late-night adornment suggests itself further as an alternative to the ninth-night alaṅkāra at nearby Muthialpet, which explicitly evokes Navarātri, and Durgā's triumph over Mahiṣāsura, by dressing Draupadī as the eighteen-armed Mahiṣāsuramardinī in anticipation of her morning appearance on the paṭukaḷam (see chap. 8, sec. B). These all seem to be urban and diaspora modifications, as does the use of semipermanent wooden heads of Aravāṉ at temples in Madras and Pondicherry (Shideler 1987, 156, 201 fig. 13). In the core area, it is more common to find clay heads, with both the head and body destroyed at the end of the festival. Such usages call upon caste-specific roles that are typical of towns and villages.

Even where Aravāṉ's sacrifice is performed before paṭukaḷam day, it marks out the same ritual space as it does when the two rituals are continuous. At Singapore, immediately after Aravāṉ's sacrifice, a trident is implanted in the ground, occasioning "violent manifestations of trance" and marking "this spot as Kurukshetra" (Babb 1974, 10–11). At Dindigul, the Mackenzie manuscript's description informs us that "Kurukṣetra is named kaḷappali" (*kaṭapolli eṅkira kurukṣēttiram*), presumably indicating that the terrain becomes Kurukṣetra once kaḷappali is performed.[10] At Iruṅkal, the spatial rapport between the site of Aravāṉ's sacrifice and the paṭukaḷam is no different from what one finds at most other core area festivals, despite the ceremony's earlier performance. The most common core area pattern, however, is for Aravāṉ's sacrifice to be the ritual that opens the battlefield ceremonies on paṭukaḷam day. For our prime example of this we may return to Tindivanam, as well as to some instructive variations at Mēlaccēri. I will then look at the alternate kaḷappali rituals from south of the core area and

10. Mackenzie Collection, Mackenzie Manuscripts, no. 68, 135–46 (authorship uncertain [see Hiltebeitel 1988a, 43 n. 18]); this Tamil manuscript is briefly described by Mahalingam (1972, 104) as "Account of the various ceremonies of the Dharmaraja temple in Dindigul").

close this section with a discussion of some of the major kaḷappali subrites.

We left the Tindivanam paṭukaḷam with the placement of Arjuna's icon at the north, facing south over the preparations of Duryodhana's effigy toward Aravāṉ, his son. Upon his icon's arrival, Arjuna can see only Aravāṉ's headless body, roughly modeled of fresh mud and straw around a thick bamboo trunk, in a "heroic" pose: the left leg back so the knee almost touches the ground, the right leg and foot planted forward, and arms and hands extended on stick supports to hold a taut bow and bowstring.[11] The kneeling position is also sometimes found on sanctum-facing images of Pōttu Rāja (e.g., at Mēlkarippūr).[12] The modeling is the work of members of the potter (*Maṇ uṭaiyār, Kuyavar*) community. Following mātu miraṭṭal, the crowd continues to swell, packing the rooftops around the open area and the ridge down from the temple, and pressing in on the ritual scenes. A temporarily fenced-off area protects the sculptor and others who are applying finishing touches to Duryodhana's effigy. But around Aravāṉ's there is no enclosure, and the temple personnel must continually push and prod to keep an open space around it and to make passageways for arrivals and departures.

First to arrive is the chief potter, whose hereditary and caste role it is to make Aravāṉ's head out of clay. A group of drummers is sent for him. They return leading a procession up the road that curves around the paṭukaḷam area toward the temple. Behind the drummers, the potmaker and his family tend to Aravāṉ's head, which is covered by a cloth, as it is brought up the slope on the seat of a cycle rickshaw. Arriving above the ceremonial grounds, the potter and his party, to the sound of drums, carry the covered head down the passageway to the effigy. The thick bamboo pole that supports the trunk of the sculpture emerges to supply a neck between the shoulders and the head, and the potter and assistants fix the head on this pole. With its head, Aravāṉ's kneeling effigy will be about

11. Shideler 1987, 156, has the Pondicherry Aravāṉ kneeling on the left knee, but in 1977 it was the right, as also at Veḷḷimēṭupēṭṭai. It seems to be a position from which he can shoot his bow, but is also that of the actor as he performs kaḷappali in the drama (Hiltebeitel 1988a, 326). The standing position, ankles joined at the base of the pole, is found at Mēlaccēri and Maṅkalam.

12. A detail of interest, since Eveline Masilamani-Meyer has found the posture typical of "front-runner" (muṉṉoṭiyaṉ) deities like Pōttu Rāja, most particularly that of Aiyaṉār's Untouchable guardian Noṇṭi, "the Lame," whose backward leg betokens his lameness (personal communication, 1990). The theme of a lame "frontrunner" is intriguing: cf. Sontheimer 1989b, 219–21: "the lame temple servant" who dances in processions, and the one-legged dancing Duryodhana (chap. 7, sec. B).

seven feet tall (including the crown).[13] The potter then offers certain items at Aravāṉ's feet: a coconut, betel leaf and areca nut, bananas, and a rupee note, all on a banana leaf, and a green pumpkin (*pūcaṇikāy*) beside the banana leaf. All these articles will go to the potter's family upon the completion of the rites. Then the potter and his group go to the temple to invite the pūcāri and his assistants to continue the ceremonies.

The pūcāri, kaṇāccāri, and sword bearer, followed by drummers, now approach, entering the paṭukaḷam from the east rather than from the southern passageway directly behind and above Aravāṉ. They circumambulate Duryodhana before their arrival. Aravāṉ's sacrifice marks what appears to be the first time in the festival that lemons, each one coated with a dot of red kuṅkum paste, are impaled on the weapons: on the central prong of the three-pronged vīrakuntam, or heroic multi-tined lance, carried by the kaṇāccāri; and on the tip of the sword (*katti*), carried by the sword bearer (cf. Babb 1974, 9). A vīracāṭṭi, or heroic whip, yellowed with turmeric (vīrakantakam), is coiled in the vīrakuntam. And both weapons are garlanded, the vīrakuntam by a string of jasmine and varicolored flowers, also hung from its prongs, and the sword by a circlet of pink flowers (blood?) just below the lemon. Before this, as far as I was able to observe, when the vīrakuntam and katti were carried in festival processions, they were not adorned in these ways. Thus, although Aravāṉ's sacrifice will require his self-dismemberment, there is a second register on which it coincides with a symbolism of impalement. Indeed, at Singapore, his sacrifice coincides with the marking of Kurukṣetra by a trident. We have met this combination before in the myths and rituals of Śiva and Dharma gājans.

The pūcāri, meanwhile, carries a small clay pot, surmounted by a scaffolding of three sticks that meet at a point, to which brightly colored pennants are attached (yellow in 1977; purple, pink, and aquamarine in 1981). Inside the pot is cooked rice. One of his assistants also brings a clay cup containing either kuṅkum-reddened water (as I was told in 1977) or goat's blood (in 1981). All three officiants wear yellow, turmeric-dyed vēṣṭis, and their bodies are

13. Frasca mentions an elaborately constructed and painted twenty-five-foot effigy at Iruṅkal that the pūcāri must climb with a ladder (1984, 305–6; see now idem 1990, 17th plate). At certain festivals there is no clay and straw molding of the effigy, just straw (Pondicherry: Shideler 1987, 156), or the minimal body of a post ("a pole surmounted with a hideous red mask" at Ellappādi, Shankari Taluk, Salem District [Richards 1918, 115]).

streaked with sandalwood paste. In addition, the pūcāri's forehead is entirely covered with turmeric, except for kuṅkum above the eyebrows, and he also wears a yellow sacred thread over his shoulder. He looks dazed and has to be guided and restrained throughout these ceremonies by assistants, who are dressed in ordinary street clothes.

On this first arrival of the pūcāri and his train, he offers the coconut at Aravāṉ's feet and removes the cloth covering his head. In doing so, he completes the ceremony of "opening the eyes" (*kaṇ tiṟappu*) of the icon (normally this would include painting the pupils, but this has been done earlier). The "eye opening" imparts "life" (*uyir*) to the image and enables Aravāṉ to see the paṭukaḷam-battlefield as it is represented directly before him by the prone Duryodhana and his father Arjuna (see plate 10). It also allows the crowd to see Aravāṉ, whose red face, bulging eyes, huge lips, and other grotesque features (elsewhere including protruding canines) are ready for his gruesome task. One of the pūcāri's assistants then cuts a square piece from the shell of the pumpkin at Aravāṉ's feet and mixes some of the red liquid from the cup into the hole. After this cut is made, the pūcāri becomes possessed. He stiffens, twists and leaps, arches his back, and flings a handful of cooked rice into the air. All this is done in one sudden movement, and just as quickly he is restrained by his attendants and rushed back to the temple. The pot of rice with the pennants, however, is left behind at Aravāṉ's feet, beside the pumpkin and banana leaf with the other articles on it. Some of the rice is taken from the pot and placed on the banana leaf with the other offerings.

All this is preliminary to the pūcāri's second and final appearance before Aravāṉ.[14] Again leaving the temple, he and his entourage arrive, first circumambulating Duryodhana again, this time bringing a platter called the *ney kopparai,* or "ghee cauldron."[15] Upon arrival, the pūcāri completes the pūja to Aravāṉ by offering dīpārādhanā, holding the lighted camphor on the ney kopparai while the vīrakuntam and sword are also raised aloft nearby. Then the pāratiyār steps into this group to recite a few verses from the *Villipāratam* and offer some brief expository words, leading up to

14. I was told in 1981 that he should come three times, but this was not done in either of the years I attended. Photographing the same ceremony, see Frasca 1990, 20th and 21st plates, as cited below; the "ritual functionary" in his captions is the pūcāri V. Govindaswamy.

15. *Ney* also has the meanings of grease or fat and blood, but ghee is said to be what is meant.

the point where Aravāṉ begins to cut his flesh. With vigorous efforts by temple personnel, including some of the trustees, the area immediately around Aravāṉ is then cleared.

The pūcāri now receives the sword (katti) from the sword bearer and approaches the effigy. First, he slices bits from the head at what I take to represent the facial component of the thirty-two places of Aravāṉ's self-mutilation (see Frasca 1990, 20th plate). This leaves chipped white marks on the red- or black-painted eyeballs, tip of the tongue, tip of the nose, earlobes, and cheeks. Then, with one stroke, he cuts up the pumpkin at Aravāṉ's feet and puts the pieces in the ney kopparai. The pieces represent the full thirty-two cuts of Aravāṉ's flesh. He then takes up the pennant-topped pot of cooked rice and the clay cup full of reddened water (or goat's blood). This is meant to be taken as the blood from the pumpkin, but it seems to be what is left in the pot of the "blood" that went into the pumpkin. The pūcāri now holds the cup and pot aloft and mixes the blood with the rice. Then he takes the pot of rice mixed with blood. A path is cleared for him from Aravāṉ into the crowd, while the lemon-tipped vīrakuntam and katti (back in the hands of its bearer) are held aloft before Aravāṉ at his sides. Attended by his assistants, the pūcāri is led to the far end of this runway (see plate 11). From there, facing south, with the pot under his left arm, he races toward Aravāṉ. When he reaches him, he flings a handful of the bloody rice into Aravāṉ's face. He repeats this a second time, and then on his third approach he crashes the pot to the ground at Aravāṉ's feet, again gets wildly possessed, and is carried off to the temple (see Frasca 1990, 21st plate). This rite is supposed to feed Aravāṉ, who, it can be seen, is thus fed with pumpkin "blood" that is supposed to be his own. It is also said that women who take the blood rice from Aravāṉ's face and eat it will be able to get pregnant. But most of the people who sampled it were men and boys, one of whom looked quite revolted at the taste (see plate 12). From this point on through the rest of the paṭukaḷam ceremonies, Aravāṉ bears a ghoulish look, and the white cloth that covers his neck like a huge napkin is marked with red stains and covered with flower petals and bits of red rice: the "remains" of his heroic self-offering.

The rite of Mēlaccēri is in some regards less complex and less charged in its culmination. On the paṭukaḷam morning, there are similar elements in a somewhat different order: modeling the effigy, placing the head (here made of wood and kept from one festival to the next) on the post, removing the cloth and opening the eyes by the pūcāri, reciting by the pāratiyār, quartering a pumpkin, chipping the face, and placing the pieces in a pot. But there are also some noteworthy differences. For one thing, the pūcāri, a far quieter and also older man (if that has anything to do with it), yields a number of the more dynamic roles to assistants.[16] The sword bearer (one of Mēlaccēri's "Tigers of the Lion Throne") cuts the pumpkin into quarters, and instead of placing the pieces into the pot or mixing their "blood" with rice, he throws the quarters into the four directions to ward off noxious spirits from the ritual terrain. Rather than feeding Aravāṉ as he begins his "living death," Pēy or Bhūtas (ghosts, demons) like him are fed before his kaḷappali proper (the face chipping) to keep them away from him. Or if the pumpkin still represents Aravāṉ, the Bhūtas are fed with his flesh. In cutting the pumpkin and throwing its pieces, the sword bearer and an assistant are energetic, but there is no possession. Rather, the prime moment of possession occurs before this series of rites even begins.

At about 7:00 A.M., the thirteen-night drama cycle (one that omits "Aravāṉ's Sacrifice") comes to a close with the conclusion of "Eighteenth-Day War" and the tying of Draupadī's hair. For this scene, the actor portraying Draupadī—who appears only at the end of this play—is the "buffoon," or kaṭṭiyaṅkāraṉ. After the hair tying, this often rather incongruous Draupadī has an additional role that normally is not part of the drama but a ritual extension called for by the coordinators of the Mēlaccēri festival, one of whom told me that "it creates a feeling among the audience." I have not found it elsewhere. The kaṭṭiyaṅkāraṉ, still dressed as Draupadī but once again disheveled, gets possessed. In both 1982 and 1986, he carried a fire pot in his arms out from the area of the chariot on which Draupadī's icon had watched the drama. Supported by assistants, he lurched toward the paṭukaḷam area, where he was helped to deposit the pot on the ground. In 1982, he swallowed flame from a camphor light pūjā at this point and collapsed until relieved by a plate of turmeric set on his head (Hiltebeitel 1988a, 433 and plate 34). In 1986 there was no fire-swallowing, just sprinkling turmeric powder on the head. The common denominator seems to be the actor's possessed movement, bearing a fire pot, to a spot in the area that will become the paṭukaḷam, and his swallowing, or at least depositing, the fire there. The spot where the pot is left then becomes the site of Aravāṉ's sacrifice. It is supposed to be the same spot each year and to have been so for generations. The post for the molding of Aravāṉ's effigy was then placed right be-

16. Adikeshava Pillai, the pūcāri, is a Kōṉār, and a knowledgeable authority on the temple's traditions (Hiltebeitel 1988a, 90–95, 327), though he lives in another village.

hind the pot, and the pot remained in place, at Aravāṉ's feet, during the entire kaḷappali ritual. It appears that the Draupadī actor makes the transition from the drama stage to the paṭukaḷam—moving, let us note, from north to south—by portraying Draupadī in a sudden transformation into the fire-devouring or fire-bearing, and disheveled, Kālī. It is, of course, Kālī who must be present at the site of Aravāṉ's sacrifice, to receive his flesh in a ghee cauldron. The fire pot seems to be equivalent to the ghee cauldron, though unfortunately I did not confirm this.

I will return to the interplay between Draupadī and Kālī at the end of this chapter. But for the moment, the aforementioned southern variant of Aravāṉ's kaḷappali must be noted, since it sets the two goddesses in a suggestive rapport and also connects Kālī with fire handling. At Draupadī festivals to the immediate south and southwest of the core area, in southwestern South Arcot and Thanjavur Districts, kaḷappali has a strikingly different look. Instead of a standing or kneeling effigy, designed to support an elevated head that can "watch" over the paṭukaḷam and the eighteen-day war, Aravāṉ's effigies are prone, showing him lying on his back. Especially remarkable are the concrete effigies of Aravāṉ at Muṭiyaṉūr and Chinna Salem (see plate 13), both in Kallakuruchi Taluk, South Arcot. I describe the ritual, however, as it was observed at Cattiram Karuppūr, near Kumbhakonam.

From morning to evening, a group of Ācāris (artisans, masons; it was formerly done by potters) shapes a mound of dirt into Aravāṉ's body, about twenty-five feet long, head to the south. The effigy lies within the temple grounds, to the temple's northeast.[17] Before the drama starts in the evening, it is painted white, with a few blue and red touches on the crown, face, and chest. Aravāṉ bears a sickle sword (*arivāl*) raised in his right hand. In addition, a small figure of Kālī, about two feet high, is sculpted just beyond Aravāṉ's crown, to his south. This Kālī is without legs and rises from the ground as if to lean with heavy white arms, pendant blue breasts (actually, the color of her *choli,* or bodice), and lolling red tongue over her earthen lap. Though Aravāṉ appears to be looking skyward, in a position that would make it difficult to watch the war, he is said to have his head in Kālī's lap so that he can face north, the direction of Kurukṣetra.

At about 2:00 A.M., the drama reaches a point where Draupadī,

17. This is also the position at Chinna Salem, while at Muṭiyaṉūr the effigy is directly before the temple: in all cases east-facing temples with the effigy's head to the south.

played by the pāratiyār, performs a lengthy and energetic lament for Aravāṉ, among other things, rocking back and forth on her knees while twirling jasmine garlands above her head so that the buds spin off like popcorn. Significantly, Draupadī plays the role of the grieved mother rather than Nākakkaṉṉi. Thanjavur area temples seem to highlight Draupadī's rapport with Kālī at the expense of other epic female figures. At temples in the transitional area between the core and Thanjavur regions (Muṭiyaṉūr, Vriddhachalam), the lament is done by Nākakkaṉṉi.

After Draupadī's histrionics, the drama pauses for a ritual break. A rooster has been placed next to Kālī, and two halves of a broken coconut have been set in front of her breasts (plate 14). Nearby, on a bank of the Kaveri River, beneath a margosa tree, preparations are made by the group that will enact Aravāṉ's sacrifice. Various articles are prepared for procession: a karakam pot, to be carried by the pūcāri, a fire pot, and the weapons of Kālī (her cūlam) and Draupadī (her vīrakuntam and whip, which earlier in the evening had been placed to her left on her chariot as she watched the play). At the riverside, *aruḷ*, "grace," comes upon the person dressed as Kālī (in *Kāḷi vēṣam*), possessing him. As he makes his way toward Aravāṉ's effigy, leading this procession, it is said that his possession makes the task of guiding him there very difficult. When Kālī arrives—in green saree, red face makeup, and with protruding white canines—she holds a sword between her teeth with burning torches (*tī-p-pantams*) at the ends. In three clusters—one centered on Kālī, the others centered on the bearers of the two goddesses' weapons—the group circumambulates Aravāṉ three times. Then, while the possessed Kālī is restrained behind the clay image of Kālī near Aravāṉ's head, a rooster is beheaded with an arivāl, Aravāṉ's (and Kālī's) weapon, just over the Aravāṉ effigy's neck so that it stains the neck with blood. The rooster's body is then bled into a clay pot with rice in it that has been set beside Kālī (or the two Kālīs, earthen and human). The man carrying Kālī's cūlam then rushes out with the pot of blood rice to throw it up in the air. The arivāl is left momentarily at the effigy's neck, until one man takes it and cuts a line through the blood remaining there on the neck itself, as if marking the line of a severed throat or neck (plate 15). Then, after another break, the drama rejoins the ritual. The pāratiyār, still playing Draupadī, comes before Aravāṉ's effigy and laments like a mother who has lost her son. Another rooster is then sacrificed to Kālī, and bled to make more blood rice. The drama concludes with Duryodhana offering a countersacrifice of a white elephant, getting Bhīma—the only person, according to Śakuni,

Duryodhana's counselor, who can fulfill the task—to sever its head in one blow. Then a dīpārādhanā is offered over the prostrate Aravāṉ; blood-soaked rice is distributed to men and women, but especially to childless women; a lime is cut into four pieces and thrown in the four directions; and finally the ritualists and dramatists circumambulate the temple.

Cēturāmaṉ describes a similar ritual from the same Thanjavur area. A hole is made in the sand effigy's neck, and a small mud vessel filled with red liquid (made by mixing turmeric and lime) is placed in the hole. The neck is then covered with a white or yellow (*mañcaḷ*) cloth. About 7:00 P.M., after Aravāṉ's story is narrated, a man costumed as Draupadī in a yellow (*mañcaḷ*) colored dress comes to weep over Aravāṉ. Then, near the temple, another man dressed in red as Kālī, with red color on the face, comes holding seven or eight wiry sticks in his hand as torches (*kaiyil kampikaḷil amaikkap peṟṟa ēḷeṭṭu tīppantaṅkaḷuṭaṉ*), and with a horrific expression cuts Aravāṉ's neck with a sword (*vāḷ*). The cutting removes the cloth and releases the "blood" in the neck, which people then take and place on their foreheads. The Kālī actor then retreats from the scene while the Draupadī actor returns to continue a convulsive lament for her "dear son Aravāṉ" (Cēturāmaṉ 1986, 149–50). Other examples could be cited with further variations, but only two points need detain us. The fire pot and torches at these rites seem to confirm that the fire pot and fire swallowing at Mēlaccēri are signs that the possessed Draupadī has taken on the character of Kālī. Second, it seems to be a generalizable rule that where Aravāṉ has a prone effigy, Duryodhana does not, and vice versa (see chap. 2, n. 4). That there is a continuity between these effigy rites is clear from a transitional case at C. Kīraṉūr, near Vriddhachalam, where the blood for Aravāṉ is placed not in his neck but, as with Duryodhana, in his thigh (see chap. 10). These southern variants include a number of elements—pot of "blood," neckcloth, rooster or goat sacrifice (at C. Kīraṉūr; Junction Road temple, Vriddhachalam)—that have counterparts in core-area rites. But they are clearly part of a distinctive complex—one that will reward further discussion in this and later chapters.

With these southern variations in mind, it is worth reviewing two of the subrites of kaḷappali in the core area: the cutting of the pumpkin and the throwing of the rice.

The pumpkin, as one might guess, is not always a pumpkin. At Ālantūr and Pūṉamalli, a goat is sacrificed before Aravāṉ; at Cuddalore, Pātirikkuppam, and Villupuram it is a cock, at the latter temple sacrificed by the potmaker; and in rites described by Richards toward the beginning of this century, in one case the goat sacrificed before Aravāṉ provided the entrails that garlanded the pole below Aravāṉ's head (in Salem District), and in the other a sheep supplied entrails for a garland over a turmeric-dyed cloth around Aravāṉ's neck (in Bangalore) (1918, 115; 1910, 30). At Tindivanam, where goat's blood was said to have replaced reddened water from 1977 to 1981, the information is uncertain. In neither case did it come from the pūcāri, and I did not check it with him. If a goat was offered, it was not sacrificed before Aravāṉ. Perhaps it is common for the animal to be offered by the potmaker, as in the one case above. But the pūcāri did join others at Tindivanam in agreeing that a goat used to be sacrificed before Aravāṉ, and that the pumpkin (supplied by the potmaker) is a replacement for it. At Singapore, there is a doubling of pumpkins ("gourds"). The first, an offering to Aravāṉ (*aravāṉ pūcai*), is supposed to represent a bull, while the second, as part of his kaḷappali, is cut into thirty-two pieces that are placed on his neckcloth, representing Aravāṉ's own flesh (Babb 1974, 10–11), an effect achieved at Tindivanam by red rice and flower petals. The pumpkin as a substitute for animal sacrifice is a commonplace of Indian ritual,[18] though as we have seen, the substitution can work both ways. What is striking is that the pumpkin, the animal (cock, goat, sheep, "bull"), and the hero are in various ways interchangeable.

As to the throwing of the rice, let us note that the first pumpkin at Singapore, the one that represents the bull, is filled with red powder and quartered, and that the four pieces, which are said to have the odor of blood, are thrown onto the corners of the temple roof to feed the "evil supernaturals who lurk near the corners of the temple" and "clear the air of evil influences in preparation for his coming sacrifice" (Babb 1974, 9). At Sowcarpet, after red kuṅkum powder is placed in a square hole made in the pumpkin, five dabs of reddened pumpkin "meat" are then applied to the pumpkin itself (four around the hole and one over the piece that had been removed and replaced) to ward off the "evil eye" from Aravāṉ. Here the four corners of the square seem to correspond to the four directions around Aravāṉ, where, with their evil eye, the supernaturals must be kept at bay (though in this case not fed). We have seen that at Mēlaccēri the quarters of the pumpkin, cut before the kaḷappali proper, are thrown in the four directions to ward off lurking spirits from the kaḷappali area, which extends into the paṭukaḷam. In early

18. See Tanaka 1987, 213 with citations, including Östör 1980, 56; Clothey 1983, 114 123 n. 11.

nineteenth-century Dindigul, the processional enactment of Aravāṉ's sacrifice included the practice of mixing rice with the blood of a sheep and throwing it into the sky at midnight. Here it is not only a question of clearing the air. The blood rice should not fall back down to the ground; were it to do so, it would bring ill upon the pūcāri and the temple.[19] Again, it is no doubt kept from falling by the hungry supernaturals, as also at Cattiram Karuppūr. At Tindivanam, where there is no hurling of the quartered pumpkin, the apotropaic function finds its equivalent when the pūcāri, on his first appearance before Aravāṉ, throws the cooked rice into the air after the pumpkin has been filled with "blood." Yet there it is not only a matter there of throwing rice into the air but of throwing blood rice into Aravāṉ's face. According to the Tindivanam temple's chief trustee, the latter is done to sustain Aravāṉ through his vigil of the eighteen-day war. Basically the same rite and rationale are said to apply at Ālantūr, Pūṉamalli, and Villupuram. This feeding of Aravāṉ at the ritual battlefield and the rice thrown onto the corners of the temples at Singapore may remind us that at numerous Draupadī temples Aravāṉ's head (or sometimes several heads) is placed on corners and edges of the temple roof or the top of the temple compound wall (see chap. 3, n. 12). As a Pēy or Bhūta himself, Aravāṉ guards both the paṭukaḷam and the temple from those of his own kind.

Yet this feature of Aravāṉ kaḷappali is also a condensate of other ritual elements. It evokes, for one thing, the ritual feeding of water and balls of rice in Brahmanical ancestral rites, such as one is reminded of by the Brahmans' offering of *tarppaṇam*—"satiation," the name of the rite of giving them water—on the "false" amāvācai in the Aravāṉ myth, a day before they would otherwise do it correctly. Yet the amāvācai that Kṛṣṇa moves up by a day does not lose its ancestor-feeding symbolism. It becomes inverted into a sort of witches' sabbath or all souls' day amāvācai, since Aravāṉ (and perhaps even the other supernaturals) is an ancestor of sorts as well. On the one hand, although Aravāṉ is granted the boon of marriage just before his death, he probably does not consummate the marriage (see chap. 4, n. 11), and dies without issue. On the other hand, the blood rice that feeds him induces pregnancy. The equivalence of rice and semen is a commonplace of long standing in India.[20]

19. Mackenzie Collection, Mackenzie Manuscripts, no. 68, 104; Mahalingam 1972, 104; Hiltebeitel 1988a, 408.

20. On rice and semen, cf. Hiltebeitel 1988a, 192; O'Flaherty 1980, 48–53, 106, 155–56, 175–76. On rice in funerary rites, see Knipe 1977, 115; Hart 1975, 82: offerings of rice and wine to memorial stones in early Tamil Caṅkam literature; Knipe

It thus staggers the imagination to think how many people may have Aravāṉ, like Arjuna, as one of their "fathers." As with Arjuna on the tapas pole, the semen substitute comes from a hero who has undergone a heroic act of sexual self-denial.

One last feature of the throwing of the blood rice must also be mentioned: its connection with boundary symbolism. Many village and temple ceremonies could be cited, but none to greater advantage than the "boundary stone" rites from Tiruchirappalli District described by Whitehead.[21] They are remarkably like the Tindivanam rites for Aravāṉ. In one instance, at Irunganallur Village (fourteen miles from Trichy), the culminating day of the festival, featuring a karakam procession and numerous animal sacrifices, begins as follows: At 7:00 A.M. a lamb is killed. Blood drawn from its neck is collected in a clay pot filled with boiled rice and taken by the pūcāri to a four-foot-high boundary stone (*ellaikkal*) that represents the deity Kaṟuppu as "the Black God of the Boundary Stone." As the pūcāri runs to the stone "in a frantic state," he is "supposed to be possessed" by the goddess Karumbai. Upon arrival, "he runs around it thrice, and the third time throws the pot over his shoulder behind him on to another smaller stone . . . which stands at the foot of the ellaikkal. The earthen pot is dashed to pieces and the rice and blood scatter over the two stones." The pūcāri then rushes back to the goddess's pantal without looking back (1921, 101). There is no need to belabor the parallels and minor differences in the rites at Tindivanam. At another village (Pullambadi) in the same district, a sheep is offered to Kaṟuppu at the beginning of the festival, and rites to the boundary stone—not identified with Kaṟuppu here, but otherwise like those just described—are offered at the end of the festival, in this case with the head of the lamb being "placed on top of the stone" (ibid., 102–3).

B. From Paṭukaḷam to Aḻukaḷam

The Draupadī and Kūttāṇṭavar cults both draw ritually on the same myth, accenting it differently. Kūttāṇṭavar rituals vary remarkably

1989, 132–34: in a Vīrabhadra cult at Rajahmundry, coastal Andhra, children who have died prematurely are commemorated by liṅga-shaped "ash-fruit" icons, said to grow through the attentions they receive in their cult, that are made by potters from cow-dung ash mixed with acacia gum and given names by size after measures of rice.

21. See also Beck 1969, 558, 563; Hiltebeitel 1980a, 193–96; Tanaka 1987, 249. On boundary symbolism in Aravāṉ's sacrifice, cf. Cēturāmaṉ (1986, 6).

from region to region, so I will discuss only those that are closest to the Draupadī cult in the core area: in fact, the most renowned of them all, those of the Kūvākkam festival near Villupuram.[22]

I will not highlight the role of eunuchs at Kūttāṇṭavar festivals, other than to say that it is more prominent at Kūvākkam than anywhere else. Beyond this, suffice it to say that they are among those who don a tāli (marriage badge) around their necks to impersonate Kṛṣṇa-Mohinī in his/her last-minute marriage to Kūttāṇṭavar, and that they perform ritual laments during Kūttāṇṭavar's death march toward the "weeping ground" (aḻukaḷam) and at the weeping ground itself. These roles are included within the main ceremonies at Kūvākkam, which occur from the fourteenth through the sixteenth (again) day of an eighteen-day festival.[23] It is during this span that the rituals for Kūttāṇṭavar have their closest Draupadī cult analogues. An outline will suffice (see table 4).

It is clear that these two *Mahābhārata* hero cults are carried along by a similar ritual momentum. The Kūttāṇṭavar cult focuses all its rites on Aravāṉ. The Draupadī cult, on the other hand, thins out the rituals for Aravāṉ, and at some of the parallel points—the lamentations and revivals of items 6 and 8—Aravāṉ is not the focus at all. One might say, in terms of their hero cult contexts, that these two rituals are more basic than their particular mythologies.

In the Kūttāṇṭavar cult all the rituals refer to the mythology of one hero, whereas in the Draupadī cult they extend to embrace a number of heroes. The Kūttāṇṭavar cult thus condenses in the area of its epic mythology. In contrast, the Draupadī cult condenses in its rituals. The analogues to what takes place in three Kūttāṇṭavar cult locations—the site of turning to the north for kaḷappali, the aḻukaḷam, and the Kālī temple—all take place on one terrain—the paṭukaḷam—in the Draupadī cult.

One last contrast: In the Draupadī cult, once Aravāṉ's head reaches his post, except for his famous eyes, he never moves again. At the end of the festival, as we shall see, he may attain mokṣa, but from the very spot of his kaḷappali. In contrast, in the Kūttāṇṭavar cult everything hinges on Kūttāṇṭavar's movements. These are made possible first by the portable platform (kēṭayam) that takes his head around the village, and then by the chariot (tēr) that takes his head and body through the scenes of his kaḷappali, defeat at Kurukṣetra, and lamentation on the aḻukaḷam, to the Kāḷi shrine

22. I intend a separate study of the Kūttāṇṭavar cult.

23. The seventeenth day is for "leave-taking" and the eighteenth for the coronation of Dharma; cf. chapter 2, section A and chapter 14.

Table 4. Kūttāṇṭavar and Draupadī Cult Ritual Parallels

1. Fourteenth day evening: the "standing of the post" (*kampam niṟuttutal*). The post, about twenty feet high to support the body and head of Kūttāṇṭavar, is raised on his processional chariot. There is an analogy here with the use of a post to support Aravāṉ's head and body on the paṭukaḷam.
2. Fifteenth day, after midnight (actually early sixteenth day):
   A. 2:00 A.M. Completion of repainting of Kūttāṇṭavar's head, from which previous paint had been removed as one equivalent of the god's death.
   B. *Cuvāmi tirukkaṇ tiṟattal*, "opening of the god's holy eyes": renewing his "life" (uyir) with the painting of the pupils so that he can go on procession. Parallel with opening of Aravāṉ's eyes at paṭukaḷam.
   C. About 3:00 A.M., Kūttāṇṭavar's head brought out from the painting shed and placed on a portable platform (*kēṭayam*); the god's are eyes (re-)opened when cloth is removed and dīpārādhanā performed. Head on kēṭayam taken around village.
3. Sixteenth day, dawn. After being carried through the village, Kūttāṇṭavar's head is fixed to the post on the chariot, and his large epaulets (*pujaṅkaḷ*) and chest plate (*mārkkaṇṭam*) are attached to his body, which is filled out with straw and covered with garlands. Head then placed on top of chariot pole. At paṭukaḷam, no processions for Aravāṉ, except the bringing of his head; reference to epaulets and chest plate only in dramas.[24]
4. Sixteenth day, about noon. The chariot, having toured the village, turns north, facing toward the aḻukaḷam (and Kurukṣetra). The point of turning north is Kūttāṇṭavar's kaḷappali, marked by the beginning of the removal of his garlands. Aravāṉ also faces north on the paṭukaḷam, sometimes with a Kālī shrine or figure beside him.
5. Kūttāṇṭavar marches north, entering Kurukṣetra, and loses his eighth-day fight, which is indicated by the removal of all the rest his garlands (his flesh). In the Draupadī cult Aravāṉ never enters the paṭukaḷam to fight, but only watches over it.
6. The procession continues to the *aḻukaḷam*. When the giant figure arrives all his garlands are gone, leaving him dead, with only straw on his "skeleton." Aravāṉ may also be lamented on the paṭukaḷam, but not centrally.
7. Late afternoon: "Distribution of sacrificial rice" (*pali cātam paṭaittal*). A huge basket of clean cooked rice is brought from the village, offered in name to the deceased Kūttāṇṭavar, and distributed to the public. Compare the various blood-rice offerings to and around Aravāṉ.
8. 6:00 to 9:00 P.M.: Kūttāṇṭavar's chariot is taken to the embankment near the Kālī shrine. The head is removed, brought near Kālī, and revived. Draupadī cult revival rites do not include Aravāṉ.[25]

for his revival. The chariot serves as Kūttāṇṭavar's portable sacrificial altar. Once his head is removed from it, the tēr must be left by the reservoir bund for several months since it has been a "death house" and is polluted. This chariot movement makes it clear that

24. On the epaulets and chest plate in the dramas, see Hiltebeitel 1988a, 326.
25. See chapter 11.

in his own cult, Kūttāṇṭavar is the exemplary warrior-deity. There are no chariots for anyone else. In the Draupadī cult, nearly every hero and heroine can move on a chariot, though more often than not with Draupadī. The main chariot, unless in a postwar ritual for Dharma, is always hers.

C. Other Hero Cult Parallels

In volume 1, I began my discussion of the mythology of Aravāṉ's sacrifice by citing three rather fragmentary parallel stories of heroes who, through boons or acts of Kṛṣṇa, find themselves able to watch the *Mahābhārata* war with their severed heads. One legend is from Nepal; one from the Kurukṣetra area in Haryana state, North India; and the third—and closest to Aravāṉ's—is from Andhra, introducing a "new" epic hero called Barbareeka, a son of Ghaṭotkaca, himself the son of Bhīma and the Rākṣasī Hiḍimbā (1988a, 317). There is virtually no information on whether there are rituals tied in with any of these figures, and it seems that the theme is part of a free-floating *Mahābhārata* folklore. There do not, in any case, appear to be hero cult traditions linking any of these other seeing heads with battlefield rituals, whether commemorating the *Mahābhārata* or some other folk epic.[26] That distinction appears to remain Aravāṉ's.

We have, however, already seen that there are other ritual implications packed into Aravāṉ's myth besides those concerning severed heads watching wars. Some of these are best appreciated by looking at partially parallel episodes in the folk epics of other hero cults. Again, these are narrative episodes, not all of them necessarily ritualized. But whether ritualized or not in their own cults, they illuminate features of Draupadī cult ritual.

The most striking and complex parallel is found in the Dharma cult of West Bengal. As was stressed in chapter 7, the Dharma gājan has a hero-cult dimension, its rituals being tied in with the martial folk epic about Lausen. I have already mentioned the manner of Lausen's birth and death. We must now look at his story more closely. Behind Lausen's battlefield sacrifice is, of course, a whole complex folk epic that we can give no more than a capsule treatment, itself relying on others' summaries.

Lausen comes into the world with two enemies. One is Icchāi Ghōṣ, whose rebellion against the emperor of Gauṛ results in the

26. The Nepalese example of King Yalambar is linked with the royal Indra Jātrā festival; see Anderson 1971, 128.

killing of the six sons of the aged rāja Karṇa Sen, prompting the emperor to show gratitude for Karṇa Sen's loss by giving him his beautiful sister-in-law Rañjāvatī in marriage. The other is Lausen's maternal uncle Mahāmada, the emperor's minister (a Brahman?) and Rañjāvatī's brother, who, absent from the arrangement of her marriage, resents its outcome.[27] Mahāmada curses Rañjāvatī to be barren, and she is so until she lies down on iron spikes in devotion to Dharma. The god brings her back from death and gives her the boon of a son, Lausen. In coming of age, Lausen must overcome trials set for him by the goddess (see n. 29) as well as attempts by Mahāmada to have him killed. But he proves himself before the emperor and obtains an army of Ḍom Untouchables as his followers, led by thirteen Ḍom retainers. Finally, Mahāmada schemes to have him collect long-overdue taxes from Icchāi Ghōṣ. Lausen must thus champion the emperor's cause against his father's former conqueror. Dharma protects Lausen, while the goddess favors Icchāi. Every time Lausen cuts off Icchāi's head, the head utters the goddess's name, and she rejoins it to his body. Finally Lausen (or Nārada) succeeds in distracting the goddess so that Icchāi can be killed. Lausen and his army of Ḍoms thus triumph, but now Mahāmada prevails upon the emperor to divert Lausen with an elaborate Dharma pūjā. Lausen undertakes harsh austerities in his worship of Dharma, invoking the god to make the sun rise in the west so that "those who challenge Dharma's power will acquiesce to his supremacy" (Robinson 1980, 28; cf. 22–24). "The legend further says that the consummation of Dharma worship is to make the sun rise in the west in a new-moon night" (A. Bhattacharyya 1952, 146). Indeed, it is Mahāmada who concocts the idea as a means to provoke Lausen to kill himself, saying that "the divinely decreed evil of the whole country could be remedied only if Lāusen could make the sun rise in the west at the dead of night on the new moon" (Dasgupta [1946] 1962, 410–11). Dharma remains unresponsive until Lausen offers *nabakhaṇḍa*, the "nine-part sacrifice":

> Lausen unhesitatingly took the billhook in his hands and chopped off the flesh of his right thigh. When he placed it forward as an offering, the fire quickened. As he presented the remaining eight portions of his body, each offering was transformed by the fire into flowers of different kinds. The final

27. Mahāmada is an interesting figure: a minister, taking neither side in the final battle, not killing anyone himself, "yet . . . ultimately responsible for all the violent developments in the narrative. He facilitates death, somewhat inefficaciously" (Robinson 1980, 41–42).

> offering was his severed head, from which there came a cry praying for the sun to rise in the west. (Robinson 1980, 28)

While Lausen is performing this ritual, Mahāmada kills Lausen's Ḍom soldiers and razes his kingdom. "Death reigned everywhere" at the site of Lausen's sacrifice, with everyone dying in sympathy except the dog, mentioned earlier, who senses that Dharma will come.[28] At last Dharma appears, brings Lausen back to life and fulfills his two requests: that his Ḍom followers be revived, and that the sun rise in the west. There is a tradition at Baruipur, the folk epic site of Lausen's sacrifice, that Dharma takes on the aspect of Nārāyaṇa when he brings Lausen back to life (Robinson 1980, 72). It is not indicated whether this also applies to Dharma's revival of the Ḍom army and his raising the sun in the west. But it seems, at least in the latter case, that there are strong reasons to suspect so. The dog who waits for Dharma "obstinately obstructs" Dharma's path while the god is on his way to make the sun rise in the west and will not let him pass until he assumes the blue, four-armed form of Viṣṇu (Dasgupta [1946] 1962, 295).[29]

Ritual evocations of Lausen's nabakhaṇḍa appear to be diffuse. The vegetarian *homa* offerings into a fire, performed by a Brahman, may stand for his sacrifice, especially at Baruipur, where the homa is said to mark the original epic site (Robinson 1980, 245–46). It may also be commemorated in rites of stacking flowers (Lausen's flesh) on the fermented rice wine jug and the Bāṇeśvar (ibid., 123–24); in the side-piercing rite known as "nine-jewel arrow" (*nabaratna bāṇ),* recalling the nine pieces of flesh—pierced rather than cut off—as "jewels" (ibid., 289); and especially in goat sacrifices.[30] As Chattopadhyay (1942, 117) and Robinson (1980, 243) insist, there are strong reasons, including etymological ones, to underscore an identity between Lausen and the Dharma gājan ritual of the *loue bali,* or sacrifice of the loue goat. At Baruipur, the loue goat's blood is mixed with the ashes from the homa fire over Lausen's original sacrifice, renewing Lausen's own ashes beneath the earthen altar (Robinson, 1980, 231, 245). At some villages, one black loue goat is beheaded for Dharma while a second, smaller one, a kid called the kol loue, is beheaded for Kālī as Dharma's *kāminyā,* or consort

28. See chapter 7, n. 27.

29. The summary is drawn mainly from Robinson 1980, 22–24, 28. Certain details differ in R. M. Sarkar's recounting: nine Ḍoms; the names Durgā and Bhavanī for the goddess rather than Pārvatī (1986, 74–79). Cf. also Dasgupta [1946] 1962, 408–12.

30. "Nine at a time *balidān,*" the cutting of nine goats with a single stroke, apparently before a single sacrificial post (Robinson 1980, 238), also suggests a connection with Lausen.

(Chattopadhyay 1942, 116–17, 125; Robinson 1980, 241–45). But it is actually Kālī who gives ritual approval for both sacrifices (Chattopadhyay 1942, 124). I will return to the loue goat in chapter 11, but for the present it must be mentioned that the rites of its sacrifice and "revival" at the Birsinha Dharma gājan frame the ritual for Lausen's nabakhaṇḍa: the only instance I have found involving an enactment of the full folk epic scene.

From the first day of this Birsinha gājan, the two loue goats are tied at the southern extremity of the maṇḍapa that serves as the main center of ritual activity. On the culminating full-moon night, the devotees don turmeric-dyed cotton wristlets in the evening. After they visit the gāmār tree to bring back a branch to place beside Dharma and swing over coals brought from the cremation ground, the chief flesh-piercing rite—an elaborate form of tongue piercing—is performed about 4:30 A.M. Just before this comes Lausen's nabakhaṇḍa:

> A human figure was drawn with *ātap* rice, measuring nine poās (a poā = half a pound), to represent Lāusen who had offered his nine limbs to Dharma. Nine areca nuts were placed on the figure, two on feet, two on hands, two on the sides, two more on body and one on tongue (head). Near the upper extremity of the figure was a tripod of bamboo sticks . . . [to hold] a white round lump and a wick of cotton impregnated with clarified butter. It was said to represent the head of Lāusen. The earthen pot for the head of the goat was now made ready. It was a big earthen cooking vessel known as *hā̃ḍi*. . . . The singer of Dharmāyaṇa now sang of Lāusen's offer of his own body in nine parts, to Dharma. As he mentioned the offering of a limb, the singer gave a demonstration by cutting off that limb of the rice figure. (Chattopadhyay 1942, 121)

When this is completed, the body is covered with a red cloth and the lamp is lit on the head held by the tripod. It is not clear from the description where Lausen's sacrifice occurs in (or possibly outside) the maṇḍapa. But at this point, to the south of the maṇḍapa yet still within it—that is, near the goats—a rectangular pit is dug, east to west, with three compartments—one for each of the three bhaktas who hereditarily perform the complex tongue-piercing rite with a trident-shaped bāṇa, or "spear," that has earlier received the blessing of Kālī. The three perform this ceremony "to emulate Lausen," once again demonstrating the symbolic cross-referencing of dismemberment and impalement. Finally, as "the first streaks of dawn" appear, the priest lights a bundle of straw to the west of the pit. The bhaktas turn west to face it, thus seeing the "sunrise in the west" caused by Lausen. After vigorous dancing by the bhaktas, the tongue bāṇas are removed. Then the goats are sacrificed, the head of the loue goat going into the big earthen cooking vessel and that of the kol loue being set before Kālī, topped by a ghee lamp (Chattopadhyay 1942, 117–24).

The rite of *navakaṇṭam* (the Tamil term equivalent to nabakhaṇḍa)—offering the goddess flesh from nine parts of the body, the last offering being the head—is known in South India and is most likely a prototype for Aravāṉ's sacrifice. It is thus hard to resist the impression that a single ritual tradition lies behind the myths of Aravāṉ and Lausen.[31] Above all, it is like the rites for the prone effigies of Aravāṉ south of the core area. Indeed, though the motivations differ, the myths themselves are suspiciously similar. The most intriguing affinity is the coincidence of each sacrifice with a displacement of the sun on a new-moon night.[32] In one case Kṛṣṇa tricks the sun into appearing one day (or better, night) early in its "meeting" with the moon; in the other Lausen gets Dharma, with allusions to his "reviving" aspect as Viṣṇu-Nārāyaṇa, to make the sun rise in the west. In one case it is nine cuts; in the other it is thirty-two cuts with nine as precedent.[33] The dismemberment theme no doubt harks back to the world-creative dismemberment of Puruṣa in *Ṛg Veda* 10.90, from which, among other things, comes the sun. Indeed, it is possible, though I say this with hestiation, to discern a total of thirty-two for Puruṣa's divisions, or number of parts.[34] In any case, in the *Śatapatha Brāhmaṇa*, the primal dismemberment becomes the prototype for an "Asuric" performance of a

31. On the South Indian navakaṇṭam, mentioned in a tenth-century inscription from Nellore District, Andhra, see K. R. Srinivasan 1960, 29–30; Harle 1963, 243; Hiltebeitel 1988a, 319; Nandi 1973, 146, citing *Kālikā Purāṇa* (67.50 and 52) and *Tantrasāra* passages involving the "offering of flesh from different parts of the body" (their number not mentioned).

32. Note that here it is the two myths that share this feature. The Dharma cult ritual occurs on a full-moon night. That the Lausen story retains this feature despite the ritual contradiction suggests it is a tenacious piece of the myth.

33. The Tindivanam ritual suggests that there may be a retention of the ninefold numerology for Aravāṉ in the chipping of the face: two eyeballs, earlobes, and cheeks, plus one tip of the nose and tip of the tongue, making eight cuts, with the ninth being that of the neck, as represented by the bloodied "napkin." The thirty-two cuts are most regularly enacted with the pumpkin. Aravāṉ is also said to have thirty-two bodily perfections.

34. The divisions of Puruṣa are made in verses 8–14. The number thirty-two is reached by counting twice for the arms, thighs, feet, and ears, and twice for the emergence of Indra and Agni from the mouth. I know of no exegetic confirmation of this enumeration, which is made problematic by the fact that Puruṣa has a thousand

"first sacrifice," possibly of a human being, though the context suggests an animal victim:

> Then as to why he does not make cuttings of the head, nor the shoulders, nor the neck, nor the hind-thighs. Now the Asuras, in the beginning, seized a victim. The gods, from fear, did not go near it. The earth then said unto them, "Heed ye not this: I will myself be an eye-witness thereof, in whatever manner they will perform this (offering). . . . The Asuras then made portions of the head, the shoulders, the neck, and the hind-thighs: therefore let him not make portions of these (*ŚB* 3.8.3.27–29; Eggeling [1882] 1966, 2:206–7)

It would be purely hypothetical to read a real ritual, much less one involving human sacrifice, into this "in the beginning" rite.[35] One is reminded of the impalement in the "original paṭayaṇi." The Asuras are the mythic exemplars of how to do the ritual in the wrong way. But this Brāhmaṇic mythical rethinking of the primal sacrifice is most intriguing. With the Earth as witness (Is this because she receives the blood?), one has a prototype for the role of Kālī in the mythic and ritual complexes surrounding the figures of Aravāṉ and Lausen. And it is, of course, the demonic Kauravas who get the idea to perform kaḷappali in the first place.

Beyond this, there are also partial similarities between the Aravāṉ and Lausen myths that suggest further investigation. In one case it is a prewar sacrifice, performed so that Dharma (Yudhiṣṭhira) can win the war; in the other it is a postwar sacrifice, offered so that Dharma can win adherents. In one case Kṛṣṇa and Kālī collaborate, in the other Dharma and the goddess (Pārvatī or Durgā) champion opposite head-offering heroes.

When one brings the myths together with the two ritual traditions, however, it is clear that the affinities are even deeper. Lausen is not sacrificed at the beginning of the war, but the two goats are tied up at the beginning of the gājan. Dharma and the goddess are not opposed; rather, Dharma and Kālī receive the two goats' heads

heads and feet. The number of portions into which the animal is cut in the Vedic sacrifice is given as thirty-three or thirty-five (Malamoud 1989, 214–15): close but probably irrelevant. S. Bayly (1989, 201) offers similar reflections on the dismemberment of the Tamil Muslim warrior-saint Yusuf Khan, on whom see chapter 11, section B.

35. To the contrary, see Parpola in press, sec. 3.2.3, citing this passage and humanizing or euhemerizing the Asuras as reflectors of practices of the Dāsa enemies of the Vedic Aryans. His documentation, however, is rich and provocative; see further Parpola 1988.

together: Dharma's in a cooking pot (recall Aravāṉ's ghee vessel for his thirty-two bits of flesh), Kālī's facing her with a lamp on it. Lausen's double form allows him to be a rice body that can be dismembered as well as a severed head on a tripod platform, with a lamp on it, like the head of the kol loue. Given Lausen's ritual and even verbal equivalence with the two goats, which may recall Aravāṉ's interchangeability with goats and pumpkins, it is likely that the myth of Lausen's nabakhaṇḍa to Dharma also has behind it a ritual originally dedicated to Kālī, or to Kālī in collaboration with Dharma. For let us not forget that in these hero cults, Dharma always seems to retain a fundamental identity of Yama. In this vein, the two goats are tied up at the south of the maṇḍapa where Lausen's sacrifice is performed. The south is Yama's direction, and also, as we have seen and as I shall stress further in a moment, has its significance for Kālī.

Closer to Draupadī cult traditions geographically, and offering stronger possibilities of cross-pollination, are the *Elder Brothers* and *Palnāḍu* folk epics. Each has an important episode with striking similarities to Aravāṉ's sacrifice, though apparently without ritual reenactment. In each case, it is a question of a war-beginning episode.

Briefly, since I will discuss it more fully in volume 3, the parallel in the *Elder Brothers Story* concerns the boar Kompaṉ—like Aravāṉ, a prewar sacrifice to Kālī whose head is demanded by Viṣṇu, and whose body is cut in thirty-two places.[36] Recall that in the drama "Aravāṉ's Sacrifice" Yudhiṣṭhira asks whether, rather than sacrificing Aravāṉ, it might not be more appropriate to sacrifice a buffalo, a boar, or some other animal.

For present purposes, however, the *Epic of Palnāḍu* brings out a more instructive set of Aravāṉesque themes. The actual beginning of the battle of Kārempūḍi occurs after war is made unavoidable by a fateful intercaste meal that breaks into a furor, with everyone lusting for battle. At this point, Brahma Nāyuḍu—Viṣṇu incarnate—insists on a curious rite. For three and a half months he has kept all the battle-proud heroes of Palnāḍu from obtaining what each coveted: the right to start the war and thus connect it with his name. This is because "he had a son named Bālacandruḍu. The war belonged to him." But since Bālacandruḍu (or Bāluḍu) has come to the battlefield for only one day, Brahma Nāyuḍu has to devise a means for him to obtain what is rightfully his that will be within the bounds of *dharma:*

36. On Kompaṉ, see also above, chapter 8, section A.

> He had ripe sorghum brought. He had an Ādiśēṣa fashioned from the sorghum. He gave Ādiśēṣa an eye. . . . Near the mouth of the Guttikoṇḍa cave is a great anthill. He put Ādiśēṣa in the anthill. Round Ādiśēṣa's eye he put sacred ash, heroic sandal, and *tāmbūlam* [betel nut, wrapped in a leaf]. (Roghair 1982, 348)

Brahma Nāyuḍu then says that whoever retrieves these items will have the war in his name.

> As Brahma Nāyuḍu spoke, Ādiśēṣa flicked his tongue and hissed. The grass on all sides was burnt. . . . All the Heroes, who spread from Kāryamapūḍi [Kārempūḍi] to Guttikoṇḍa cave, went running. No one could approach. (Ibid.)

Bāluḍu leaps up, but he realizes that even with all his weapons he cannot approach the Ādiśeṣa. Then he recalls instructions his wife gave him before battle. Knowing that Brahma Nāyuḍu would construct this Ādiśeṣa, she advised Bāluḍu to call on Garutmantuḍu (Garuḍa).

> "Garutmantuḍu and Ādiśēṣa are enemies. He is in league with Viṣṇu. Therefore when you go pray to Garutmantuḍu, he will come on his great wings that are acres in extent. Being afraid that Garutmantuḍu will strike his head, Ādiśēṣa will draw his head into the hole in the anthill. You must watch for the chance." (Ibid., 349)

Following this advice, Bāluḍu secures the three items and is honored as the "bridegroom of war" (ibid.).

The "rite" of this sorghum Ādiśeṣa is known only in this narrative form. I know of no indications that it is performed or ritually recalled during the festival of the heroes at Kārempūḍi. But the thematic affinities with Draupadī cult rituals, and myths, are worth exploring. Like Aravāṉ's head, it is strangely alive, though in its tongue and its capacity to duck rather than in its eyes. Aravāṉ is not only, by some accounts, Ādiśeṣa's grandson. He also has nāga traits: a name locally derived from *aravu*, "snake," and frequently a cobra hood over his crown, with such variations as sprouting cobra heads throughout the crown (Veḷḷimēṭupēṭṭai), or a snake's body mounting the crown from behind (Tindivanam). When Ādiśeṣa, or a combination of Aravāṉ's snake-relatives, supplies the flesh that allows Aravāṉ to fight Alambuṣa in his eighth-day battle, he loses only when Garuḍa, with Kṛṣṇa's collaboration, makes Ādiśeṣa, or the various snakes, abandon him. Thus in one case it is Kṛṣṇa, and in the other Viṣṇu, who motivates Ādiśeṣa's removals through Garuḍa's "appearances" (in the "illusory" or "magical" sense of *māyā*): in each case a sort of Garuḍadarśana, but without ritual sighting as such. We may also assume that the sorghum Ādiśeṣa is placed at a boundary: not only between Kārempūḍi and the Guttikoṇḍa cave, to which Brahma Nāyuḍu will lead the heroes after their deaths, but between this world and the underworld, the realm of nāgas, since it is set in an anthill. Indeed, the heavenly world is indicated as well by the appearance of Garuḍa. The convergence of these themes points us toward an enriched understanding of the strains that link Aravāṉ with Ādiśeṣa in Draupadī cult ritual.

Ādiśeṣa is, of course, precisely the serpent who encircles, the serpent who marks boundaries. He encircles the universe of time: when he appears on the waters for Viṣṇu to lie on, it is the end of a *kalpa* and the beginning of a night of Brahmā after a *naimittika*, or "occasional" pralaya; when Viṣṇu awakens from Ādiśeṣa's serpent couch, it is the beginning of a re-creation and a new kalpa, or day of Brahmā. Ādiśeṣa's appearances thus mark the outer boundaries of the rhythm of time, since a *prākṛta* pralaya, or "dissolution of matter," is also the end of time (*kālānta*). He also "repeatedly" (that is, with temporal implications) encircles the universe of space. Without his head touching his tail, he moves around the zodiac from east to south to west to north in the course of a year (Kramrisch [1947] 1976, 1:62 n. 105). In some South Indian accounts he encircles Mount Meru (Shulman 1980a, 123). At Madurai, he retraces the boundaries of the city after a pralaya-like flood (ibid., 123–24; Dessigane, Pattabiramin, and Filliozat 1960, 76). He also encircles the building site of the classical Hindu temple, as well as other ritual sites and constructions (Kramrisch [1947] 1976, 1:60 n. 105, 90 n. 89). We already know that when he encloses the body of Aravāṉ, he encircles the hero whose eighteen-day vigil oversees the temporal limits of the battle of Kurukṣetra. Let us then see whether his connection with Aravāṉ has anything to do with defining the spatial boundaries of the paṭukaḷam.

Toward the ends of chapters 6 and 8, I called attention to a thread that must be traced further into the paṭukaḷam's ritual fabric. The paṭukaḷam looks to be a transposition of a north-facing temple. It is thus worth looking further into the manner in which Ādiśeṣa circumscribes a temple. Now it is well known that the foundation of a Hindu temple is laid out according to a square geometric diagram known as the *vāstu-puruṣa-maṇḍala*, the "circle [even though the design is square] of the Puruṣa of the site." Mythically, the Vāstupuruṣa is sacrificed to create the diagram he becomes, through his division into parts. This sacrifice evokes that of the primal Puruṣa of *Ṛg Veda* 10.90, whose hymn has sixteen verses, whose body may have thirty-two subdivisions, and whose dismemberment produces the universe. But the Vāstupuruṣa is also identified as a demon: a goat-headed demon (Kramrisch [1947] 1976, 1:75–78). Indeed, Tanaka has found at a Kālī temple in Udappu, Sri Lanka, that the recurrent Brahman-performed ritual of *vāstu śānti*, which "appeases the site" and "gives peace" to its Puruṣa (Kramrisch 1:74), is commemorated by a fire sacrifice of the demon Vāsturājupuruṣaṉ, a "demon-king" Vāstupuruṣa: A pumpkin is cut and smeared with red vermilion powder; pieces of its "flesh" are offered in the fire; then a six-foot-long straw figure—Tamil *Vāstu pommai*, the "site doll"—is half thrown in the fire as well; finally, what remains of the pumpkin and straw figure is thrown away at the edge of a lagoon or crossroad (Tanaka 1987, 213–15). The pumpkin, straw figure, and boundary symbolism clearly find their counterparts at Aravāṉ's kaḷappali. But most important, for present purposes, the vāstupuruṣamaṇḍala also has "the shape of a nāga" and can be referred to as the vāstunāga, a technical term for Ananta or Śeṣa himself (Kramrisch 1:85 n. 75, 287 n. 95).

The two most common vāstupuruṣamaṇḍala designs are those having sides of eight by eight squares, with sixty-four small squares (or *pāda*s), like a chessboard, and those with nine by nine sides, with eighty-one pādas. "In both kinds of mandala," writes Volwashen, "32 'outer gods' cover the pādas around the border." In the eighty-one pāda maṇḍala, there are precisely thirty-two pādas for these deities, while in the sixty-four pāda maṇḍala, the thirty-two gods must fit into twenty-eight pādas by doubling at the corners. The two schemes are described in the *Mayamata*, a South Indian (probably Śaiva Siddhānta) *Vastuśāstra* text, and nicely diagramed by Dagens (1985, 20–22, figs. 5 and 6). The exterior ring of pādas is thus in either case "divided into 32 units," which, according to Volwashen, "represent the 'lunar mansions'" of the zodiac, a numerology that plays "an important part in all astrological predictions about circumstances in which the building should be begun and continued" (1969, 45; cf. Kramrisch 1:85–86).[37] We have already seen that the serpent Śeṣa moves through the zodiac. He thus moves through the outer squares of the temple diagram, marking a division of his body into thirty-two parts.[38] Here we have the most

37. The apparent relation of this numerology to lunar symbolism has been mentioned in n. 9.

38. I have not found textual evidence of such a division of Śeṣa, but the idea is clearly found for the parallel division into nine parts to represent the "peripheral

decisive model for this feature of Aravāṉ's sacrifice, and the change from nine cuts to thirty-two. The correct performance of his rite, which ensures victory in battle, thus involves astrological predictions about when the war, as the equivalent of a building, "should be begun and continued." More than this, just as the founding of a temple requires a metaphoric "cutting" of Śeṣa's body into thirty-two parts, so the paṭukaḷam-founding rite of his grandson Aravāṉ's sacrifice calls for cutting Aravāṉ's flesh into thirty-two pieces (which Ādiśeṣa temporarily replaces). To be sure, the thirty-two pieces are not set around the paṭukaḷam's borders. They are offered to the goddess Kālī in a vessel of ghee. The symbolism is condensed to this one point, the point at which the sacrifice takes place—which is, of course, on the paṭukaḷam's boundaries. But there is reason to be confident that this is the right track. At the vanayāgas, or "forest sacrifices," before the margosa trees that supply the wood for the four icons of the Jagannātha festival at Puri, there is not only a pitcher for Durgā at the western end, corresponding to the garbhagṛha of this transposed Durgā temple (see chap. 6 and map 4). "Another 32 pitchers are placed on the different spots of [the] Yajñaśālā to worship various Hinduistic deities (e.g., the ten Dikpālas, Gaṇeśa, Kālī, Sarasvātī [sic], Bhairava, Kṣetrapāla, the eight Vasus, Nāgas, Nāginīs)" (Tripathi 1978, 243). One should not miss the inclusion of the serpents, or the symmetry between these forest and battlefield terrains as transposed temples. We must now take our discussion of the paṭukaḷam as a temple one step further and demonstrate that the temple transposed upon it is one to Kālī.

D. Kālī at Kurukṣetra

The simplest pieces of the puzzle, decisive in themselves, are three. First, Kālī temples in Tamilnadu generally face to the north.[39] Sec-

---

sense" in which the "serpent of the site" moves around it: the Orissan *Bhubanapradīpa* enjoins that "the body of the snake be divided into 8 (or 9) equal parts, head, heart, stomach, navel, knee, chin, ankle, and tail" (Kramrisch [1947] 1976, 1:90 n. 89). Shulman 1980a shows further the connection between the Vāstupuruṣa and Ādiśeṣa as the "remainder" of the sacrifice: "The temple is erected upon the foundation of this symbolic sacrifice: just as Ādiśeṣa supports the universe, the Vāstupuruṣa sustains the shrine." Cf. Biardeau 1989b, 84 and n. 6.

39. See Hiltebeitel 1988a, 72–73; van den Hoek 1978, 119; Pate 1917, 110–11; Beck 1981a, 84, 99; Reiniche 1987, 90. There has been a recent spurt of adding north-facing images of Kālī at Draupadī temples: on the vimāna at Tindivanam during a recent 1989 *kumbhabhiṣeka* (temple reconsecration); a new maṇḍapa "desired by the young people" being built at Cattiram Karuppūr, where Kālī's present shrine faces east, adjacent and to the south of Draupadī's sanctum.

ond, there is sometimes a north-facing shrine to Kālī beside Aravāṉ's effigy, on the southern boundary of the paṭukaḷam. Third, since at least the time of the Tamil *Paraṇi* poems of the tenth or eleventh to twelfth centuries, Kālī is regarded as the goddess of the battlefield.[40] Not incidentally, the Paraṇi poems derive their name "from the calendrical asterism Bharaṇi, sacred to the god of death, Yama, but in South India also to his female counterpart, the 'black' goddess Kālī,"[41] and describe phantasmagoric temples to Kālī made, among other things, of the remains of human sacrificial victims and war elephants (Nagaswamy 1982, 25–26). These three pieces together are sufficient to tell us that the ritual battleground is an equivalent of a north-facing Kālī temple or maṇḍapa. Let us then look at the evidence and some of its ramifications.

There is a good core area example of a north-facing shrine to Kālī beside Aravāṉ at Iruṅkal, where, to the south of the paṭukaḷam rectangle, the twenty-five-foot effigy of Aravāṉ stands beside a "small Kali shrine," just to Aravāṉ's left (west).[42] At the Sowcarpet temple in Madras, where the braiding of Draupadī's hair at 4:00 A.M. on the ninth night stands for the paṭukaḷam pars pro toto, the temple is opened at 10:00 P.M. Shortly thereafter (marking the beginning of the night's reduced paṭukaḷam ceremonies), a small group of devotees races about a hundred yards from the temple with the wooden head of Aravāṉ to a north-facing, temporarily constructed bamboo and palm leaf pantal for Kālī on the south side of the street. There a pumpkin is cut, and goat's blood is said to be poured on Aravāṉ's head. Where there is no actual shrine for Kālī at the paṭukaḷam, one may find an alternate representation, as with the variety of pots, including fire pots and ghee cauldrons. One may also be reminded of the kol loue goat that Kālī receives at the south end of the Dharma gājan maṇḍapa in conjunction with the sacrifice of Lausen.

40. In the earlier Caṅkam-period poems, it is Koṟṟavai or Koṟṟi who receives post-victory battlefield sacrifice, which the medieval commentator Nacciṉārkkiṉiyar summarizes from the earlier works as involving the cooking of the blood and fat from the "'minced' corpses" in a "huge pot" as "libation to the gods" (Parpola in press, sec. 3.2.3; Kailasapathy 1968, 241–42; Nagaswamy 1982, 22–28).
41. Parpola in press, sec. 3.2.3. The name and timing recur in the *Bharaṇi* (= Paraṇi) festival for Bhadrakālī of Kodungallur, celebrating her war against the demon Dārikan in ceremonies that take place before the temple, considered the goddess's "principal sanctuary for all of Kerala" and linked by some with the former Cēra capital. Bhadrakālī is "represented in her terrible form, facing north" (Tarabout 1986, 369–73).
42. Frasca 1984, 329, figure 34; see chapter 8 n. 3 for the adjustments one must make to read Frasca's map correctly.

But it is especially in Thanjavur District, where one finds prone earthen effigies of Aravāṉ, that the pattern is reinforced. Not only can Kālī provide her lap for Aravāṉ's head on the paṭukaḷam, their rapport is frequently registered as a permanent feature of the temples themselves. Especially at temples in Thanjavur, Kumbhakonam, and Pattukkottai taluks, it is common to find a permanent large head of Aravāṉ, sometimes in a maṇḍapa, sometimes within a niche of the south wall of the temple itself, facing north directly opposite a figure of Muttāl Rāvuttaṉ, who will be similarly ensconced facing Aravāṉ to the south. In other words, Aravāṉ is to the southeast of the sanctum, Muttāl Rāvuttaṉ as usual to the northeast, and they face each other. Often beside Aravāṉ, again sometimes in a separate maṇḍapa of her own, is Kālī, facing north like Aravāṉ. One finds such an arrangement, for instance, at the Hajiyar Teru temple in Kumbhakonam, which has the largest known head of Aravāṉ (Shastri [1916] 1974, 127–28 and fig. 139; Hiltebeitel 1988a, 327); at the East Gate temple in Thanjavur; at Tirumaṅkalakkuṭi; and at Pattukkottai. At Aḻakār Tirupputtūr, Muttāl Rāvuttaṉ faces not only Aravāṉ and Kālī, but also Nākakkaṉṉi, all three on one platform in a maṇḍapa outside the temple proper (plate 16). What is striking is that the temples thus have double axes. On the east-west axis, Draupadī is faced by Vīrapattiraṉ, her stand-in for Pōttu Rāja. And on the south-north axis, Aravāṉ and Kālī are faced by Muttāl Rāvuttaṉ. While Aravāṉ's clay effigy defines the ritual ground before the temple as the paṭukaḷam, the head of Aravāṉ incorporates the orientation of the paṭukaḷam into a feature of the temple itself. Most striking, it is Muttāl Rāvuttaṉ whom we now find in the pain-absorbing, "temple"-facing position of this interior axis. He must be there to absorb the sacrificial suffering of Aravāṉ and to neutralize the dangerous power of Kālī.[43]

In any case, Kālī must be present with Aravāṉ, as required by the myth. As we have seen, in the Irattiṉa Nāyakar version of *Aravāṉ Kaṭapali*, Kālī appears at Kurukṣetra to receive Aravāṉ's sacrifice after Dharma performs her worship in his hall of weapons. Here the Sarasvati Mahal version pares down the story as usual, but for once it introduces an interesting twist through its reduction. In this version there is nothing about Duryodhana's wanting to perform kaḷap-

43. Curiously, while Muttāl Rāvuttaṉ holds securely to his place, the figures facing him change once one moves out of these central Thanjavur area taluks. At Vaṭukku Poykaiyūr, he is faced by Kamalakkaṉṉi-Hiḍimbā (see Hiltebeitel 1988a, 213–15); at Chinna Salem by Duḥśālā (ibid., map 5); at Cōḻavantāṉ by Kamalakkaṉṉi, Nākakkaṉṉi, and Iṭumpavaṉṉi (who seems to be a double for Kamalakkaṉṉi, identified as a wife of Bhīma).

pali first, of his receiving advice from Sahadeva, and of Kṛṣṇa's, as a result, having to move up the amāvācai. The sole and stark motivation for Aravāṉ's kaḷappali is that Kṛṣṇa advises it as a means for each of the Pāṇḍavas to secure victory through their weapons: Dharma with his sword (*katti*), Bhīma with his mace (*katāyutam*), Arjuna and Nakula with the tips of their arrows (*pāṇamuṉai*), and Sahadeva with his dagger (*camutāṭu*; Cēturāmaṉ 1986, 19, 28, 35, 43, 48). The play ends, after a long lament by Draupadī rather than by Nākakkaṉṉi, with Aravāṉ empowered to see the eighteen-day war, but still preparing to perform kaḷappali. One will recall that at Cattiram Karuppūr, Kālī appears at this point only as part of a ritual break from the drama. Nevertheless, the Sarasvati Mahal drama does have a sort of appendix (*iṇaippu*, "join"), in manuscript by a different hand (ibid., 129), in which Kālī does makes an appearance (*kāṭci*) for a song (*viruttam, pāṭal*) and speech (*vacaṉam*). Holding a skull and trident, she describes how, when the Pāṇḍavas set out on their forest exile (*vaṉam celakālam, vaṉattukkup pōy*), they left their weapons under her protection in the hole of a *vākai* tree, thus "placing the weapons in me" (or "in my place": *āyutaṅkaḷai enniṭattil vaittuviṭṭu*). Having waited thirteen years, it is now a "good time" for them to retrieve them, she says. This time turns out to be Aravāṉ's sacrifice. From her tree, Kālī addresses some people nearby: "Hey humans, tell them to take the weapons having given the sacrifice which was worthy of gold as they gave me their word" (ibid., 129–30).

The story is clearly garbled. As Cēturāmaṉ (131) points out, it is normally a vaṉṉi (śamī) tree, not a vākai tree (*Mimosa flexuosa*). Kālī also seems to forget that the Pāṇḍavas deposit their weapons not at the beginning of their exile, but at the beginning of its thirteenth year, when they go into hiding. As Cēturāmaṉ says, the author has "shown his talent and imagination" (*kaṟpaṉait tiṟattaik kāṭṭukiṟatu*; 131). But it is a fascinating condensation, since it provides another indication that the folk tradition is bothered and fertile in posing answers to the question of how the Pāṇḍavas got their weapons back from the vaṉṉi-śamī tree. Aravāṉ's kaḷappali has become a means to retrieve the weapons from the vākai tree, alias the vaṉṉi tree, via Kālī. Moreover, in the *Villipāratam*, the vaṉṉi tree in which the Pāṇḍavas conceal their weapons is near a Kālī temple, where they offer her worship (*kāḷikōyil*; *Villipāratam* 4.1.9; Cēturāmaṉ 132). The Pāṇḍavas also worship Kālī at the vaṉṉi tree before leaving their weapons there in other Draupadī cult dramas that cover the *Virāṭaparvan* (Hiltebeitel 1988a, 296). She is thus consistently the protector of their weapons.

This makes Arjuna's presence at the Tindivanam paṭukaḷam all the more interesting. He comes from māṭu miraṭṭal, the "driving of the bulls," after his own one-man visit to the vaṉṉi tree, precisely with the red-tipped arrow (*pāṇam*) that Kālī has protected. Indeed, in the Sarasvati Mahal drama, it is the tip of Arjuna's arrow that Kṛṣṇa says will be rendered victorious by Aravāṉ's sacrifice. The blood-tipped arrow thus comes straight from one Kālī "temple" to another. From the vaṉṉi-śamī tree, which, according to the Sanskrit epic, is also near a cremation ground and north of Virāṭa's capital, it is brought to the paṭukaḷam. There it marks the entrance point from the north and faces the Kālī shrine (at Tindivanam, by implication only) to the south. Significantly, then, each edition of "Aravāṉ's Sacrifice" connects his kaḷappali with ritual features of Dasarā. The Irattiṉa Nāyakar version associates it with the "worship of the weapons," which brings forth Kālī's appearance at Kurukṣetra in time for Aravāṉ's sacrifice to secure the Pāṇḍavas' victory. The Sarasvati Mahal *appendix* links it with a dim echo of a "worship of the śamī tree," with Kālī inviting the Pāṇḍavas to visit her in the vākai tree, instead of the śamī, to retrieve their weapons, which, as Kṛṣṇa has planned, are now assured of victory as a result of Aravāṉ's sacrifice. This latter story is unusual and seems to involve a further forgetting of stories in which Pōrmaṉṉaṉ provides an answer to how the Pāṇḍavas get the weapons from the śamī. As we have seen, Pōrmaṉṉaṉ-Pōttu Rāja is replaced in the Thanjavur region by Vīrapattiraṉ. And on the north-south axis of the Thanjavur area temples, these various markers of the northern entrance of the paṭukaḷam are replaced by Muttāl Rāvuttaṉ.

The argument that the Draupadī cult paṭukaḷam is a transposed Kālī temple finds further corroboration when it is compared with the grounds of other South Indian battlefield rituals. In Tiruchirappalli District, certain Kālī temples linked especially with weavers hold paṭukaḷam ceremonies (using this specific term) that reenact the defeat of a demonic king Vallāṉ and the death (there are both pre- and post-battle beheadings to Kālī) and revival of his conquerors. The temple faces north, the paṭukaḷam is an open space north of the temple, and the ritualists who impersonate the dead warriors sit or lie in holes (*kuḻi*), facing south (Reiniche 1987, 90, 94–96). Here it would be more correct to say that the paṭukaḷam is the extension of a Kālī temple, since the main temple is a north-facing temple of Kālī herself.

More revealingly, the Viramalai Hills paṭukaḷam of the Elder Brothers cult shows an interplay between the east-facing temple of the goddess Periyakkāṇṭi (which stands on the west side of the paṭukaḷam) and the north-facing icons of the twin Elder Brothers (in two aspects), their sister Taṅkāḷ, the Seven Virgins, and Viṣṇu-Māyavar (in the south) (Beck 1982, 51, 212 map 8). As mentioned in chapter 8, the northern marker that the heroes and their sister face is the trunk of a vaṉṉi tree that plays an important role in connection with the brothers' deaths. Now as Beck says, Periyakkāṇṭi has "the place of honor," while the others "and even Vishnu himself face in a subordinate (northerly) direction" (ibid., 51). Periyakkāṇṭi is the "major goddess of the complex," and her own temple five miles away from the paṭukaḷam faces east like the one on the paṭukaḷam itself (ibid., 51, 208 map 1a). There is no shrine for Kālī at this paṭukaḷam. But the brothers launch the series of events that lead to their deaths there by killing the boar Kompaṉ, who *is* a sacrifice to Kālī. Moreover, there is a transformation of Taṅkāḷ, the younger sister, as she makes her way to the paṭukaḷam. First, having let loose her hair (Beck 1975, 284), she has an exchange with Periyakkāṇṭi (or Arukkaṇṭi) that suggests to Beck "the merger of these two women as one" (Beck 1982, 51). The goddess then has her bird vehicle carry Taṅkāḷ to the site of the boar's sacrifice, which is near enough to the paṭukaḷam for Taṅkāḷ to search from there for her brothers (Beck 1975, 290). At the paṭukaḷam, as she laments over them and revives them, she faces north (ibid., 293), like her icon. If it is too much to say that she is transformed into Kālī (she is called Pārvatī in this portion of the story), it is not too much to say she takes on some of Kālī's ritual features. Most temples to the Elder Brothers and their sister seem to have them facing north from their position in the sanctum, as they do from their position on the paṭukaḷam (Beck 1982, 208 map 1b, 210 map 3, 211 maps 5 and 6). There is thus a double orientational interplay and transformation of the heroine at the Viramalai paṭukaḷam. This should remind us of the interplay between the temple and the paṭukaḷam in the Draupadī cult, and the transformation of the Draupadī actor at Mēlaccēri into an image of Kālī as he moves from the east-facing chariot (the portable temple) to place the pot that defines the north-facing orientation of the paṭukaḷam.[44] Let us also recall that at Tindivanam, Draupadī goes on procession with Kālī on the night that

44. The essentials of Draupadī's transfigured movement toward Kālī and the latter's collaboration, through Draupadī, with Dharma both seem to underlie the grim enactment of Aravāṉ's sacrifice at Pāṇṭirappu, Sri Lanka: local temple actors representing Dharma and Draupadī "together under one cloth go and kill her son, Arāpān, represented in the form of a soft wet clay figure kept under a triangular cloth covered framework (tripod-like). They take a knife and slice off the head, exposing 'blood' filling made with turmeric and lime mixture, whereupon Tarumar and Drau-

"Aravāṉ's Sacrifice" is performed as a drama,[45] and that she takes on Kālīrūpa, the "form of Kālī," in Draupadī cult folklore, both in the forest and on the battlefield (Hiltebeitel 1988a, 289–94).[46]

There will be more to unfold from this recognition of the paṭukaḷam as a transposed or extended Kālī temple, but for the moment it will suffice to conclude by addressing two remaining anomalies concerning Aravāṉ. One is that Aravāṉ's effigy is sometimes placed to the southwest of the paṭukaḷam (and of Duryodhana's head) rather than due south. This is what one finds, for instance, at Mēlaccēri, Maṅkalam, Tūci, and Uttiramērūr.[47] In Tamil eight-directional rituals, southwest is the region of Nirṛti, adjacent to the southern position of Yama and opposite the northeast position of Īśāna (see, e.g., Beck 1981a, 99). Nirṛti—"Decomposition, Decay," "the earth's evil aspect," although in processes linked with ritual rebirth (Heesterman 1957, 15–17; Malamound 1989, 74–75)—is a Vedic deity, like all the gods of the eight directions, and the only female among them. Clearly Aravāṉ is placed in this position because Nirṛti is resonant with Kālī. Let us recall that at Iruṅkaḷ, Kālī's "small shrine" is to Aravāṉ's left (that is, southwest with respect to Duryodhana). Moreover, confirmation comes from another kaḷam-type ritual. In the kaḷaris of Kerala, the southwest is the "virgin's corner" for the altar of Bhagavati-Bhadrakālī as goddess of war.[48]

This brings me to one final point. In the core area, Aravāṉ's head is normally, though not always, placed on a post: usually a bamboo post, which may be left with no more adornment than garlands of entrails or may supply the support for a body molded of mud and straw. In volume 1 I hinted, I think now somewhat prematurely, that this post is a multiform of a sacrificial stake (331 and n. 24). I would not entirely abandon that idea, since the analogue in the Kūttāṇṭavar cult is to place the head on a post that rises from the center of a chariot. As we have seen, chariots are widely equipped

padī return to the temple and sing a wailing lament over the loss of their son. The sacrifice was necessary as an offering to goddess Kali" (McGilvray 1975). The tripod, found at Aravāṉ's and Lausen's sacrifices, may replicate the trident.

45. See chapter 3, section A.

46. Cf. Choondal 1980, 43: in *Mavarattham Pattu*, a Malayalam "ballad" on the *Mahābhārata*, "Kali who has no place in the epic is invoked which is rather unusual." One might also think of the shift in focus from Kāmākṣī to Kālī in the narrative scenes concerning Kāttavarāyaṉ's impalement (Masilamani-Meyer 1989 and in press-b; Shulman 1989; see above, chap. 5, sec. C).

47. On the latter, see Gros and Nagaswamy 1970, plate 16a, showing a seated Aravāṉ, his arms upheld by sticks, beside a massive effigy of Duryodhana.

48. See chapter 7, section B. Cēturāmaṉ refers to Kālī as "Bhadrakālī of the Battlefield," Raṇapattirakāḷi, in his recounting of earlier versions of the story (1986, ix).

with multiforms of the sacrificial stake. But if, as I have argued, the paṭukaḷam is configured as a north-facing Kālī temple with the underlying plan of a Vedic mahāvedi, the place for such posts would be at the northern boundary, where we do indeed find Pōttu Rāja making his entrances, reminders of the śamī tree, transpositions involving Muttāl Rāvuttaṉ, and, at Tindivanam, Arjuna's blood-tipped arrow. Meanwhile, the post for Aravāṉ is not essential. His head may simply be set in a Kālī shrine, with no post, as at Sowcarpet. Or in the Thanjavur region, he may be lying down, with his head in Kālī's lap, or in his own separate shrine. This leads me to the conclusion that the post with Aravāṉ's head on it is above all, and rather simply, his body or its support. If it is more than that, whether it is to the south or southwest of the paṭukaḷam, it is part of Kālī's altar, like the post on the chariot in the Kūttāṇṭavar cult. In any case, it is part of the paṭukaḷam equivalent of Kālī's sanctum.

10 Paṭukaḷam Sequences

Core area paṭukaḷam rites can be reduced to two main components: an effigy of Duryodhana for Draupadī's hair tying, and what I will call rites of revival, usually for her children, the Young Pañcapāṇḍavas. Where the effigy is of Duryodhana, rites without revivals are few and far between. The only instances I have found are at Kalahasti, on the Telugu fringe of the core area to the north, and at temples within (Sowcarpet) and just beyond (Pūṉamalli) Madras. Revivals without a Duryodhana effigy are even rarer, having surfaced only at the "ceremony of the pole and the five dead cousins" in Réunion, and the unique joint Draupadī-Kūttāṇṭavar festival at Tailāpuram. These appear to be exceptions that prove the rule.

At the urban temples without revivals, the revivals have probably been replaced by other rites, as we shall see in chapter 11. The other instances of absent revival rites could result from peripheralization, though one could plausibly argue that the cases of Kalahasti and Pūṉamalli, both within the core area, present evidence for an older, pre- or subcore area tradition of effigies without revivals. As we shall see, these two temples have an interesting variant on the effigy rites. In any case, revivals without effigies are clearly exceptional. The peripherality and peculiarities of the Réunion ceremony have already been discussed (chap. 8, sec. A). At Tailāpuram, there are no paṭukaḷam rites for Duryodhana on the festival calendar. Duryodhana's death is covered only in the Pāratam recitation. The rites for the Young Pañcapāṇḍavas are part of the following sequence that closes out the Draupadī temple phase of the festival: Aravāṉ kaḷappali, Arjuna's tapas (ninth day and night), Young Pañcapāṇḍavas, and firewalk (tenth day, morning and evening). The final three days are then dedicated to Kūttāṇṭavar rituals, culminating in his eighth-day fight and "weeping ground rites." These supply the ritualized war scenes that the festival accentuates rather than those involving the death of Duryodhana. At the Draupadī festival in Kiḷiyaṉūr, only two miles from Tailāpuram, the effigy and revival rites occur together as usual.

Within the core area, then, the normal situation is to find the two fundamental rites of the paṭukaḷam inextricably interlinked. The first order of business is thus to describe them together. Our primary example will once again be Tindivanam, rounded out by additional observations mainly at Mēlaccēri and Maṅkalam. We will then discuss the intriguing exceptions at Pūṉamalli and Kalahasti and glance at the diffused light that is shed back on Thanjavur area rites by those of the Draupadī festival at Singapore. Subsequent chapters will then take up the revival and effigy rites separately.

A. The Paṭukaḷam Rites at Tindivanam

On the night that the Terukkūttu troupe performs its climactic play, "Eighteenth-Day War," preparations for the construction of Duryodhana's effigy begin at about 8:00 P.M. with the dumping of about five tons of earth on the paṭukaḷam grounds. Not far in back of the drama audience, the chief mason (Kottaṉār) and one assistant, who do the sculpting as a hereditary right, work well into the night to give the image its basic contours by morning. Then, with the area fenced off to separate them from the swelling crowds, they continue to work as the performances of māṭu mirattal and Aravāṉ kaḷappali occur around them. While Arjuna is set at Duryodhana's feet, the mason is fixing Duryodhana's protruding tongue in place; during the crowded rites for Aravāṉ, he and his assistant are applying red, white, and blue-gray washes to Duryodhana's crown. Ultimately the whole body is painted from crown to heel, the full figure measuring about thirty-five to forty feet. The final form at Tindivanam is a quite handsome and regal Duryodhana, well sculpted in a rounded style. He lies on his back with bulging eyes, protruding tongue, right arm raised, left arm lowered, legs separated, feet splayed to the outside, a mace in his raised right hand and a shield in his lowered left.[1]

1. Cf. Frasca 1990, 22d plate; Gros and Nagaswamy 1970, 120; Richards 1910, 30. The possibility of Duryodhana's revival, as well as an explanation for his position on his back with his head to the south, can be inferred from Thurston and Rangachari's account of Untouchable Māla funeral rites: "the head of the dying is always placed to the south [the realm of Yama]. . . . Consequently, if the dead arose, if facing south he would go to an evil place. By lying on the back with the head to the south, they rise facing north, and so escape an evil fate" ([1904] 1965, 4:372–73). Positionally, this would also apply to Aravāṉ effigies with the head in Kālī's lap.

While kaḷappali is occurring, certain other paṭukaḷam preparations are also made. Six rectangular concrete blocks, about five feet long and nearly two feet wide, surround the Duryodhana effigy. These are washed with turmeric water and covered with margosa leaves. According to local understanding, five of these slabs are to serve as beds (*paṭukkai:* the etymological affinity with paṭukaḷam was noted) for the Young Pañcapāṇḍavas. The sixth, nearest Arjuna and Duryodhana's left leg, was said in 1975 to be for Droṇa, in 1977 for Bhīṣma, and in 1981 for Aśvatthāman, each identification being supplied by a different informant (see below). While these beds are being prepared, the individuals who will lie on them sit cross-legged beside them and are doused with water to cool them. Meanwhile, a pumpkin filled with kuṅkum-reddened water is placed between Duryodhana's thighs, and a hole is made in his right thigh and filled with some of the same mixture (1977), or with goat's blood (1981), and covered over again.[2]

After Aravāṉ kaḷappali, and before the pūcāri and his entourage return to the scene, a brief ceremony is performed for the "opening of Duryodhana's eyes." While a pūjā is offered, a white cloth is held as a screen over Duryodhana's chest. Behind the screen, the mason-sculptor paints the pupils on Duryodhana's bulging round eyeballs. This invests Duryodhana with life—really the last moments of his life—so that he can "see" the deaths of the Young Pañcapāṇḍavas, as the story requires, before dying.[3]

Soon after Duryodhana's eyes are opened, the ceremony gathers momentum. As a dramatic and stately procession begins to descend from the temple, the men who represent the five Young Pañcapāṇḍavas, and the sixth who (following my most recent and best-documented information) impersonates Aśvatthāman, lie down on the concrete blocks and are covered with sheets. First comes a pair of drummers, then the kaṇāccāri holding aloft the garlanded vīrakuntam with the whip coiled through its prongs and the red-dotted lemon on its central tine, the holder of the lemon-impaled katti, the pūcāri holding a tray with articles for pūjā, including powdered turmeric (vīrakantakam), and the wooden processional icons of Bhīma and Draupadī, Pōttu Rāja, Kṛṣṇa on Garuḍa, Dharma, Nakula, and Sahadeva. They enter the paṭukaḷam from the north, make two turns around Duryodhana (in both 1977 and 1981 they

2. These variations correspond to those for Aravāṉ kaḷappali in these same years; see chapter 9, section A. At Mēlaccēri and Maṅkalam a small earthenware pot of reddened water is lodged in a hole in the thigh.

3. For Draupadī cult treatments of this episode, see Hiltebeitel 1988a, 421–24; 1988b, part 2; 1989d.

were supposed to do three, as with Aravāṉ, but shortened the ritual because of the pressure of the crowd). It is on their two tours around Duryodhana that the pūcāri and his entourage administer the rites of dying and revival, which we shall discuss in chapter 11.

Here, however, we must recognize a discordance between epic and ritual. In the epic, and in the dramas that reenact it, Duryodhana lies dying because he has been felled by Bhīma with a mace blow to the thigh. It is after this that Aśvatthāman goes to avenge him by killing the Pāṇḍavas and kills their children instead. On the Tindivanam paṭukaḷam, however, the blow to Duryodhana's thigh is enacted *after* the massacre of the Young Pañcapāṇḍavas. Moreover, this is not all that is compacted into this ritual scene. The death of Duryodhana overlaps with the Young Pañcapāṇḍavas' revival.[4] While the revivals continue, the pūcāri and his entourage make their way to Duryodhana's right thigh. The pūcāri takes the sword from the sword bearer, and with two swift strokes quarters the pumpkin lying between the thighs (in 1977 the lemon, which flew off the tip of the sword, left an imprint in the left thigh). The pumpkin-cutting is said to remove the evil eye from the subsequent cutting of the right thigh (this is one of the explanations for the same rite at Aravāṉ kaḷappali, though at Sowcarpet in Madras rather than at Tindivanam). Then, with the same sword, the pūcāri slashes into the right thigh of Duryodhana at the spot where the "blood" has been placed in a hole and then covered. For the effigy, this appears to be the moment of death.

At this point things happen very quickly. The wooden image of Draupadī is brought before the thigh, and the oozing mixture of mud and "blood" is caressed into the long, disheveled hair that hangs down her back. Then her icon is lifted onto its bearer's head, and Draupadī joins Bhīma's icon—also separately held—in a triumphant procession over the prostrate form of her victim. Leading the crossing, moving from the thighs over the chest, head, and crown, is the pūcāri's entourage: first the kaṇāccāri with the lofted vīrakuntam, its whip removed but its lemon and garland still intact; then the sword bearer with the lofted katti; then the pūcāri; then the icons. Reaching up behind Draupadī as she crosses the corpse are many anonymous hands, which place more mud and blood in her hair while tying it into a knot (kūntal, koṇṭai) interlaced with red and orange flowers (plate 17). A thick, exuberant

4. I use the term "overlap" to cover such variations as sequential and simultaneous, both of which one finds at different festivals. At Mēlaccēri they follow the same sequence; at Maṅkalam they are simultaneous.

crush of people join the wake of this crossing, as Draupadī's victory over Duryodhana becomes participatory. When the march is complete, nothing remains of Duryodhana but a long heap of mud. The procession returns to the temple, where a pūjā is conducted for the icons by the pūcāri. Meanwhile, the crowd left on the paṭukaḷam is entertained by a trio of actors from the Terukkūttu troupe, who rush onto the scene to perform a raucous mock lament, impersonating three Kaurava women: Duryodhana's wife Peruntiruvaḷ, mother Gāndhārī, and sister Duḥśālā. The three mourners wear their hair disheveled, thus reversing their position with Draupadī and fulfilling her vow—made even in the classical *Mahābhārata*—that she would live to see the Kaurava women with the unkempt hair of widows (Hiltebeitel 1981, 188; cf. 1988a, 306). Peruntiruvaḷ in particular arrives borne on a ladder (a mock palanquin-chariot?) and carrying a winnow. This appearance of Duryodhana's widow amid the other Kaurava women has a parallel in one of the paṭayaṇi ("battle formation") sequences of Kerala, where the widow of Dārikan, the goddess Bhadrakālī's victim, leads a dance procession of "other mothers" who rush among the audience symbolizing the dissemination of smallpox (Tarabout 1986, 233–34; cf. Raghavan 1947, 25).[5] The winnow, which separates chaff from grain and is thus expressive of the metaphoric significance of the paṭukaḷam as a threshing ground, is also a funerary symbol that is often linked with destructive goddesses of the crematorium such as Kālī and Aṅkāḷammaṉ.[6] Note that this is the only appearance of the actors on the paṭukaḷam at Tindivanam. With these activities the paṭukaḷam ceremony there comes to an end.

B. Core Area Variations

These rites are anything but uniform from place to place. Let us first get a sense of the basic core area paradigm, and its main regional variations, by looking at the corresponding rites at other sites, especially Mēlaccēri and Maṅkalam. Then we can look farther afield. The first thing to appreciate is that the Tindivanam rites

5. Cf. the mock possession of the dissolute "prostitute" in one of the Dharma gājans (Robinson 1980, 137–38).

6. On Aṅkāḷammaṉ's winnow, see Meyer 1986, 110, 115, 129 (carried by a person dressed as Kālī), 139–40 (similarly by one dressed as Pecciyammaṉ), 142–43, 173–75, 213–14 ("considered to be 'unclean'"). On a funerary usage by widows among Oddēs in both Andhra and Tamilnadu, see Thurston and Ragachari [1904] 1965, 5:433 (the rite also involves an effigy for the deceased; cf. ibid., 2:211; Meyer 1986, 230 n. 1). On usages in Śiva and Dharma gājans, see above, chapter 7, section C. Cf. Tarabout 1986, 565: a symbol of the decapitation of grain.

are typical of the core area in their overall structure. The only features I have not observed elsewhere are the following: the concrete blocks (see chap. 8, n. 4); the cutting of a pumpkin between Duryodhana's thighs; a sixth-man role for Aśvatthāman; problems of crowd control that are not met in villages; and a reduction of roles for the Terukkūttu actors. To this may be added some details that V. M. Brameesa Mudaliyar spotted as Tindivanam irregularities. At most places, he said, a potter sculpts the effigy (as at Maṅkalam) rather than a mason. Perhaps the elaborate painting of the effigy with colored washes is the mason's touch.[7] And the bedsheets for the Young Pañcapāṇḍavas should, he said, be stained with turmeric: something I did find at other festivals. These, however, are but incidental variations of the fundamental paṭukaḷam components—effigy, revivals, and hair tying—that could be found at any core area Draupadī festival.

Core area temples, then, have their variations on each of these three components, which we may take up one at a time. First, Duryodhana's effigies at Mēlaccēri and Maṅkalam are about the same size as the one at Tindivanam. One must, however, mention the grandiose effigy at Uttiramērūr, which is about ninety feet from crown to heel. I did not see it at festival time, but even after months of weathering it was still at least seven feet high at the head and chest (plate 18).[8] Kaḷampūr also claims a ninety-one-foot Duryodhana,[9] while those at Tūci and Māṉāmpāṭi are about seventy and nearly sixty feet, respectively. From these examples, it seems that such gigantic Duryodhanas are a North Arcot tradition. The intended impact is nicely phrased in the 1980 festival poster from Māṉāmpāṭi: "Seeing the astounding shape (*piramikkattakka uruvam kāṇal*) of Duryodhana is a very great sight that holds the eyes."

The head of the Maṅkalam effigy is painted a ghostly white, with black eyeballs, mustache, and goatee. But the rest of the figure (crown, body) is coated with red (kuṅkum) and yellow (turmeric) powders. The Mēlaccēri effigy (in both 1982 and 1986) was

7. The effigy is whitewashed and partially painted, but less "professionally," at Pondicherry, Maṅkalam, and Avalūrpēṭṭai. Recall that masons have replaced potters at Cattiram Karuppūr in the construction of Aravāṉ's effigy. Probably concrete effigies for either figure have such a background of social change as well.

8. Cf. Gros and Nagaswamy 1970, plates 16 a and b (with facial and other details intact), 119–20: "gigantic"; "not less than twelve to fifteen meters long and rising to the height of a man" (as shown in plate 18; my translation). The remains of the effigy I saw in 1982 were surely longer than that estimate.

9. Information from written answer to questionnaire (1982). I visited this temple in 1986, but it had been too long since the most recent festival to estimate the size of the figure from its remains.

unpainted and coated entirely with turmeric powder. Rather than the idealized rounded and regal features of the Tindivanam effigy, these Duryodhanas are more angular and grotesque,[10] especially the one at Mēlaccēri, with its broad, flat nose and two full rows of protruding teeth made of coconut shells (cf. Babb 1974, 18). They are also more demonic, corpselike, and ghoulish, the effect enhanced by the glint of red or yellow powder, such as one uses to cover a corpse, on the body of dirt. Finally there is also variation in the way the effigy is treated at the end of the rite. It is not uncommon for Duryodhana to be trampled back into mud, as he is at Tindivanam. This was also done at Veḷḷimēṭupēṭṭai in 1977 and at Mēlaccēri in 1986 (see Hiltebeitel 1988b, part 2). But at the 1982 Mēlaccēri festival, and also at Maṅkalam (1982), there was no such mass crossing of the effigy. In these cases the effigy may remain largely intact for additional rites.[11] At Maṅkalam, a young man passes out handfuls of muddy "blood" from the thigh to people in the crowd—both men and women—to put into their own hair, an alternative means of communal involvement and identification with Draupadī. At both Maṅkalam and Mēlaccēri, women and boys take up pinches of turmeric-sprinkled mud from the crown. At Maṅkalam this was identified as another enhancement for women who want to get pregnant. At Pondicherry, after Draupadī's processional icon has watched the death and revival rites from her chariot, the chariot is driven over Duryodhana's thighs (both of them), leaving tracks on the otherwise intact effigy (see Gros and Nagaswamy 1970, 122; Shideler 1987, 121, 157, fig. 16). Pondicherry women and some men rush to obtain the "sand loam" from the broken thighs, and one man later sells small pots of it at the temple (Shideler 1987, 157, 159, unexplained). In these cases, after the ceremony the effigy is left to face the elements: first—to judge from those I have seen in varied states of decomposition—to dry in the sun until cracks show, and then, with the rains, to lose its human features and be breached by rivulets.

As to the revivals, the sole difference to note at this point is that instead of lying on concrete blocks, most of the men who undergo this ritual at Mēlaccēri and Maṅkalam lie in pits (*kuḻi*) in the ground, but in each case one lies on a bench. As with the concrete slabs, the

10. The same contrast is also found in the processional wooden icons as one moves from South Arcot to North Arcot; see chapter 3, section B (Maṅkalam is in North Arcot; Mēlaccēri is in the direction of North Arcot from Tindivanam).

11. Effigies for Aravāṉ have similar variations in coloring (at Muṭiyaṉūr his body is yellow, his face red; at Chinna Salem his body and face are both red), but Aravāṉ effigies do not ever seem to be trampled.

pits and benches are lined with margosa leaves. I leave further discussion of these matters for chapter 11.

Finally, significant variation is also found in the hair tying. The pāratiyār, for one, may take a far more active role than he does at Tindivanam. At Mēlaccēri in 1986, for instance, N. Kannapiran not only recited a few verses of Pāratam but was the evident master of ceremonies and choreographer, beckoning and halting the flow of ritual actions and ultimately tying the knot in the Draupadī icon's hair himself as it was carried over the effigy. Variation in the tying of the hair depends above all, however, on the handling of the icons and the roles assumed by the Terukkūttu actors.

Both the icons and the actors can provide means of representing Draupadī's kūntal muṭittal that are independent of the paṭukaḷam. If a festival includes a drama cycle, it will almost invariably end on the climactic morning, a few hours before the paṭukaḷam rites, with Draupadī's hair tying by Kṛṣṇa in the play "Eighteenth-Day War" (Hiltebeitel 1988a, 432; 1988b, part 2). Draupadī's processional icon may watch the drama on her chariot, but it will not be braided until later. On the other hand, at festivals where there is no Terukkūttu, the decoration (alaṅkāra) of Draupadī's processional icon can be the chief ritual means to represent the hair tying. Such is the case at Pondicherry. Indeed, we have noted certain urban temples in Madras where the adornment of Draupadī's icon on the ninth night stands for the paṭukaḷam pars pro toto. Thus in being braided, her icon may be adorned as the disheveled Kālī (at Cintadripet [Gopalakrishnan 1953, 107] and at Sowcarpet, at 4:00 A.M.) or as Durgā-Mahiṣāsuramardinī (at Muthialpet; see chap. 9, secs. A and D). On the paṭukaḷam, however, these two means—the iconic and the dramatic—can be variously combined and are more than just ritual replication of the hair tying at the end of the drama. In the typical core area rites, one may speak of the hair tying on the paṭukaḷam as the point where each festival shows its originality in bringing the three "scripts" of recitation (Pārata Piracaṅkam), drama (Terukkūttu), and iconic ritual (involving both temple personnel and crowd participation) together.[12] It is on the paṭukaḷam that these scripts converge with the greatest intensity and finality. They are rebraided like Draupadī's hair, which is in turn a metaphor for the binding together of these social, ritual, and narrative processes.[13]

12. See Hiltebeitel 1988a, 139, showing the convergence of these three scripts (denoted by a row of asterisks) in diagram.

13. At the firewalk that follows, the actors are normally absent or at least have no scripted role.

Table 5. Paṭukaḷam Alternatives at Maṅkalam and Mēlaccēri

Maṅkalam 1982	Mēlaccēri 1982, 1986
1. Wooden icons of Draupadī and Bhīma, held aloft on their platforms, face Duryodhana's head from the southwest corner of the paṭukaḷam, between his head and the standing effigy of Aravāṉ.	
2. Revival rites begin, men under sheets.	
3. Draupadī actor enters paṭukaḷam from temple (which opens onto the paṭukaḷam's northwest corner).	A. Actors representing Draupadī, Nākakkaṉṉi (Ulūpī, Aravāṉ's mother), and a third woman, variously said to be Kuntī or Gāndhārī, enter the paṭukaḷam from the dramatists' green room (1982).
4. Next from the temple come the temple officiants, weapon bearers, musicians, and a file of disheveled women, who join in procession behind the Bhīma and Draupadī icons in a circumambulation of Duryodhana, with frantic displays of possession by the weapon bearers and women.	
5. Draupadī actor laments before Aravāṉ, beats breasts.	B. Draupadī, Nākakkaṉṉi, and the third woman lament before Aravāṉ, beat breasts, sit on ground in a circle with arms locked over shoulders (1982).[14]
	C. Revival rites begin.
6. Draupadī's wooden icon and platform are set facing east on Duryodhana's chest; icon's hair is braided by pūcāri. Bhīma icon watches. Revivals from under sheets begin.	
7. Pūcāri cuts effigy's thigh.	
8. Beside the effigy (not on it) Draupadī actor ties his (Draupadī's) hair into knot with string of marigolds, then unties it.	
9. Revival rites conclude.	D. Revival rites conclude (1986).

14. The same ritualized gestures of lamentation are performed for Aravāṉ-Kūttāṇṭavar at Kūvākkam.

Table 5 (*continued*)

Maṅkalam 1982	Mēlaccēri 1982, 1986
10. Bhīma and Duryodhana actors enter paṭukaḷam from temple, begin duel, chase, pas de deux.	E. Bhīma and Duryodhana actors enter paṭukaḷam from green room, begin duel, chase, pas de deux (1982, 1986). Revival rites continue to conclusion (1982).
11. Bhīma actor clubs effigy's right thigh with mace, falls back possessed, and is carried off (plate 19).	F. Duryodhana actor ends chase lying on effigy's right thigh, then gets up. Bhīma actor cuts effigy's thigh with sword, gets possessed, and is carried off (1986). Cimmācaṉapuli cuts thigh, Bhīma actor falls back in possession, and Draupadī actor falls forward in possession onto wound.[15] Both must be carried off (1982).
	G. Chariot bearing crowned pañcalōkam (five metal) icons of Arjuna, Draupadī to his right, and Subhadrā to his left is carried onto effigy from north. Pōttu Rāja icon is carried alongside (1982), along with Kṛṣṇa (1986). Chariot bearers hold icons aloft for hair tying, done during pause for dīpārādhanā offering on Duryodhana's chest (1982), or cross effigy without interruption while hair dressing occurs in motion (1986).
12. Draupadī actor takes up blood mixed with mud from thigh, smoothes it into hair, then mounts Duryodhana effigy's chest.	H. Draupadī actor returns to take up blood, dress it in hair, knot the hair, and enter brief possession. Effigy still intact (1982); demolished (1986).
13. Dīpārādhanā tray with lit camphor offered on effigy's chest before Draupadī actor.	
14. Standing on effigy's chest, Draupadī actor reties hair into a bun with string of marigolds (see plate 20).	
	I. Duryodhana's widow appears with a winnow for mock lament: screeching, grimacing (1982); beating oversized breasts (1986). Played by the kattiyaṅkāraṉ.

15. On the cimmācaṉapuli, a local ritual title at Mēlaccēri, see chapter 2, section B.

Against this background, the interplay of icons and actors at Mēlaccēri and Maṅkalam is more complex than at Tindivanam, where the only Terukkūttu presence comes at the end in the person of the lamenting Kaurava women. For simplicity's sake, I outline these sequences in parallel in table 5, to show the contrasts.

There are two major ways, which might be called tone and design, in which these paṭukaḷam scenarios differ. The key tonal indicator is whether, in what ways, and for whom the ceremonies include and enhance possession. Of the three temples under discussion, possession was least in evidence at Tindivanam and most in evidence at Maṅkalam, with Mēlaccēri in the middle but closer to Maṅkalam. For Mēlaccēri and Tindivanam, this reverses the emphasis in the prior rites for Aravāṉ on the same morning.[16] Thus at Tindivanam, the pūcāri's deep and wild possession at Aravāṉ's sacrifice has no counterpart during his pumpkin cutting and thigh cutting on the paṭukaḷam. Nor is there any emphasis on possession during the rites of dying and revival. At Mēlaccēri and Maṅkalam, the actors introduce notes of possession at the scene of killing Duryodhana: the Bhīma actor becomes possessed in all cases (11, F). At Mēlaccēri, the Draupadī actor is also possessed at this point (F), while at other festivals both Bhīma and Duryodhana become possessed.[17] At Mēlaccēri, there is also a further possession of the Draupadī actor when he enacts the dressing of her hair on the effigy (H). Only at Maṅkalam, however, is the paṭukaḷam an arena for possessions by local villagers: above all in the procession of the weapons (4), but also in the dying and reviving rites. I will return to both of these matters in chapter 11, since they appear to be connected. In sum, at Tindivanam possession is the province of the pūcāri, and only at the preliminary rite of Aravāṉ's sacrifice. At Mēlaccēri and Maṅkalam, it is primarily the province of the actors. Only at Maṅkalam does it also include the villagers.

As one can see, a common overall design appears at six points (3 = A, 5 = B, 9 = D, 10 = E, 11 = F, 12 = H), while a number of common elements occur at different points (2 and C, 6 and G, 13 and G, 14 and H). The only elements that occur at one festival and not at the other are the procession with the weapon bearers at Maṅkalam (4) and the arrival of Duryodhana's widow at Mēlaccēri

16. See chapter 9, section A. I did not see the Aravāṉ kaḷappali ritual at Maṅkalam.
17. C. Jagannathachariar (personal communication), recalling festivals from his native village of Tūci (Cheyyar Taluk, North Arcot), says that both actors may remain possessed for as long as half an hour after these scenes. Cf. Gros and Nagaswamy 1970, 121: Bhīma is supposed to be in such a state of trance that the effigy must be placed before him lest he kill the actor instead (at Uttiramērūr).

(I), but these both have their equivalents at Tindivanam. Meanwhile, the preliminary lamentation before Aravāṉ (5, B), in which the mourning is not for his kaḷappali or his fight with Alambuṣa (as on the Kūttāṇṭavar cult aḻukaḷam) but for the end of the eighteen-day grace period during which his head remained alive to watch the war, is performed at Mēlaccēri and Maṅkalam, but not at Tindivanam. Of these three subrites, each temple thus performs two out of three.

In these circumstances, differences are striking only in terms of accentuations. Since the hair tying is the central rite, and the one with the greatest replication, the most prominent point of distinction between festivals is which hair tying receives the greatest accent. At Tindivanam, the only hair tying on the paṭukaḷam is that of Draupadī's icon. At Maṅkalam, the hair tying of the icon is first (6). This is linked to temple and local rites: the cutting of the thigh by the pūcāri (7), and the simultaneity with the emergence of the local temple elders from under the sheets in the revival rites (6–9). But the greatest accentuation is placed on the Terukkūttu performance that follows this. During the first hair tying on the effigy's chest—that of the icon—the Draupadī actor is already in evidence, performing a complementary preliminary hair tying of his (Draupadī's) own on the sidelines, beside the effigy (8). Even at this point, the actor's hair tying, not the icon's, is the one that follows the thigh cutting, as befits the narrative sequence. The accentuated hair tying, which follows a second thigh cutting by the Bhīma and Duryodhana actors (11), is then the one where the Draupadī actor steps on Duryodhana's chest to do it again (12). This is the climax, and a quite stunning young Draupadī, in a blue saree, was there to perform it (plate 20). Both the icon and the actor represent the victorious goddess. At Mēlaccēri, on the other hand, the high point of hair tying is focused on the temple's valuable pañcalōkam icons and the finely decorated palanquin-chariot that carries them. The Terukkūttu duel between Bhīma and Duryodhana builds up to the crossing of these icons over the effigy, not to the triumphant stance of the actor. When the Draupadī actor finally does appear on Duryodhana's chest, it is only an aftermath, linked with no separate thigh cutting of its own, and part of a confused scene that comes quickly to focus on the macabre humor of Draupadī's counterpart, the widow of Duryodhana. In this case there is a contrast: the purer icon represents the goddess in her victorious aspect, atop her fallen foe; the possessed actor represents the suffering goddess, the heated goddess, who has lost her children.

C. Rites with Double Effigies

Moving away from these typical core area variations, these rituals do not give expression to any of the lurid details that form part of the scene's mythology, particularly in the Terukkūttu. For Draupadī's icon and actor, there is neither a comb made from Duryodhana's ribs nor a garland made of his intestines: only the hair oil (*eṇṇai*) from the blood of his thigh (Hiltebeitel 1988a, 236–37, 306–7, 432–33; cf. 260, plates 30, 32–33). But the rib comb and garland of guts have been ritualized in some places. At Pūṉamalli a goat "used to be"[18] sacrificed before Aravāṉ early on the culminating ninth night to mark the beginning of the war, and during the night two effigies were prepared, one of Duryodhana and the other of Duḥśāsana, both (as elsewhere with Duryodhana alone) with their heads to the south. Not only was the goat's blood placed in Duryodhana's thigh, but its intestines were implanted in the effigy of Duḥśāsana. At about 5:00 A.M. of the tenth day, in a ceremony called "the Destruction of Duryodhana and Duḥśāsana" (*Turiyōtaṉaṉ-Tuṟcātaṉaṉ-Cammāram*), a Terukkūttu actor personifying Bhīma led the local celebrants in the demolition of both effigies. The concomitant hair tying (kūntal muṭittal) of Draupadī, however, still made use only of the blood from Duryodhana's thigh, and not Duḥśāsana's intestines, which were only submitted to the general "destruction."

It is, then, Duḥśāsana's intestines rather than Duryodhana's that feature in the ritual, and only in this secondary place. After all, in the Draupadī cult, Draupadī's vow concerns only Duryodhana, not Duḥśāsana, whose blood and guts are solely the concern of Bhīma. Indeed, there is a Terukkūttu explanation of how it comes about that Duḥśāsana has left no corpse on the paṭukaḷam. In one performance of "Eighteenth-Day War" by the Pakkiripāḷaiyam troupe, Kṛṣṇa tells Draupadī, as he shows her the paṭukaḷam while circling the drama stage, that Duḥśāsana has left no dead body (*pretam*) there, since Bhīma was so angry that he squeezed all Duḥśāsana's muscles to bits and offered them up to Vāyu, the Wind.[19] It is likely

18. According to an elderly Vaṉṉiyar senior trustee, who had been ousted from his position. As of late 1981, the festival had not been performed since 1977, since the paṭukaḷam grounds of the temple had been occupied by squatters and were the subject of pending litigation.

19. Hiltebeitel 1988b, part 2. For other variations of Bhīma's vows concerning Duḥśāsana's blood and intestines, see Hiltebeitel 1988a, 237 (the blood compared to spray from water pounded with Bhīma's mace) and 407–9 (represented by ashes offered to the wind).

that this explanation reflects the core area norm by providing a "theological" justification, from the mouth of Kṛṣṇa, for the one-effigy rite, as distinct from the no doubt familiar but irregular two-effigy rite.

The only other place I have found such a two-effigy rite in my fieldwork is at Kalahasti. There again, as I indicated at the beginning of this chapter, the effigy rites are performed without revival rites. As was noted, this might reflect a distinctive early ritual tradition. In any case, there is no reason to think that the Duḥśāsana effigy is in any way a replacement for the revival rites, or vice versa for that matter. What, then, might be the character of such a distinctive strand? Some clues can be found in K. Venkatesa Acharya's description of Tamil double effigy rites in connection with the *Vikramārjuna Vijaya,* the tenth-century Kannada version of the *Mahābhārata* by Pampa:

> In Tamilnadu there is a tradition which is slowly dying. After the Bharata *Pravachana* [or piracaṅkam] is over, in the country yards, the killing of Dussasana and Duryodhana will be displayed. In a large piece of plain land the figures of Duryodhana and Dussasana are constructed. A person who plays the role of Bhimasena undergoes many rituals like fasting. On that particular day the person will be led to the field in a procession. Drums and many other instruments will be played to rouse the martial spirit for the ensuing show. Old people who have seen the show say that it presents the picture of the gruesome killings of Bhimasena. The person who takes off [impersonates] Bhimasena, it is said, would lose all sense except the ghastly martial instinct. After destroying the figures, the man, like a devil dances and finally falls exhausted to regain senses after long. Such country-yard-shows must have been fresh in Pampa's mind while he conceived the Bhima-Dussasana duel. (1981, 360–61)

Venkatesa Acharya does not locate these Tamil ceremonies for us, but they are certainly akin to the one just described at Pūṉamalli, with the exception that the impersonator of Bhīma is a local ritualist rather than a Terukkūttu actor. This would not discourage one from pursuing the possibility that this ritual strand has early elements.

It is Pampa who seems to provide the earliest known literary version of the tradition that it is not Duryodhana's blood but Duḥśāsana's, released when Bhīma opens Duḥśāsana's chest to drink it, that Draupadī dresses into her hair. "Pampa's Bhimasena does the job in an extremely gruesome manner. Drenching her hair with the blood and combing it with his teeth and garlanding her with the intestines, . . . Bhimasena repeatedly drinks the blood . . . [and] on and off eats the flesh of Dussasana" (Venkatesa Acharya 1981, 360). It seems to be this "inhuman and cannibalistic" (ibid.) strand, with its earliest roots in Karnataka, that the Draupadī cult *normally* rejects in its de-emphasis of the Duḥśāsana tradition in favor of the Duryodhana tradition. In doing so, the Draupadī cult upholds what seems to be not only the older tradition,[20] but also the tradition with the most evident royal implications.[21] I thus suggest that the double effigy tradition within the Draupadī cult, which from the available evidence seems to occur most often in northern parts of the core area,[22] shows the results of fusion with a Kannada tradition that in its origins probably had nothing to do with the Tamil Draupadī cult. If, as Venkatesa Acharya says, Pampa had such "country-yard-shows" fresh in his mind, and not just a mythic phantasmagoria, he would be more likely to have seen an early and distinct Kannada tradition that a Tamil one.[23]

D. Showing Draupadī the Battlefield

The double effigy tradition may also contribute to a further paṭukaḷam variation found in the Thanjavur area. We will retrace this variant back to Thanjavur after looking at Babb's description of one of its transplants in Singapore. After daybreak on the culminating morning of firewalking day, "five large humanoid figures are fash-

20. The earliest variant, found in Bhaṭṭa Nārāyaṇa's Sanskrit drama *Veṇīsaṃhāra* (ca. 675–725 C.E.), has it as Duryodhana's blood, but aside from the Draupadī cult, other South Indian versions from Kerala (including Kathakali drama) and Karnataka (including Hoysala sculptures) favor the Duḥśāsana variant (see Hiltebeitel 1981, 180; 1988a, 21, 241 plate 4; Sitaramiah 1967, 26, 146). Subrahmanya Bharati's *Pāñcāli Capatam* ("The Vow of Pāñcāli") has Draupadī put up her hair with the combined blood of both (Valam [1957] 1972, 124).

21. Unlike Duḥśāsana, Duryodhana is the king. On further royal dimensions of the Draupadī cult hair tying, see chapter 12.

22. I have been told, however, of instances of double effigy rites in Tirunelveli District (by V. Vijaya Venugopal), and Eveline Masilamani-Meyer observed and photographed such rites at the Pūmal Rāvuttar Kōyil Street temple in Thanjavur (1985 or 1986). The pāratiyār S. Nagarajan, in a recorded narrative, indicated that Draupadī gets the blood, bone (for her comb), and veins (for her ribbon) from Duḥśāsana, but in the ritual he orchestrated at Cattiram Karuppūr, these things were taken from beneath Duryodhana's bench, and in any case from a man impersonating Duryodhana rather than an effigy.

23. Blackburn 1989, 30 n. 23, calls attention to "the *Mahābhārata* Yajnam festivals of southern Andhra Pradesh and Karnataka," which, till now unknown to me, might bear looking into in this connection (and many others related).

ioned out of sand on the ground near the south wall of the temple," each lying on its back face upward. These "dying warriors" are each visited in turn by a procession consisting of the images of Vīrapattiraṉ, Kṛṣṇa, Arjuna, and Draupadī. While the icons then watch from a position on the ground, the local actors also approach each figure in turn. Each time, Draupadī asks Kṛṣṇa who the dying warrior is. The first three are Abhimanyu, Droṇa, and Karṇa. Kṛṣṇa says each will go to heaven, and Draupadī "sprinkles powdered turmeric on the figure and then obliterates it gently with her hand."[24] When Draupadī hears that the fourth figure is Duḥśāsana, she flies into a rage and "instead of obliterating the image with her hand she kicks it to bits." This seems to be another variant of the pulverization of Duḥśāsana that reduces him to thin air. Finally, when she learns that the last effigy is Duryodhana, she "flies into a fit of anger." Very quickly, "a cloth is laid over the image and the washerman lies down on top and is completely wrapped up. At about the same moment Draupadi digs into the side of the image and withdraws a mirror, a comb, and a box of kunkumam. The washerman is pinched sharply on his legs. Then he is picked up and rushed to Draupadi's shrine. Once in the shrine he is held in the posture appropriate for whipping and is lashed on the wrists" (Babb 1974, 18–20).

The catalog of ritual transformations, already begun, is easy to extend. The box of kuṅkum substitutes for the blood from the thigh. At last the comb enters the ritual from the dramas (Hiltebeitel 1988a, 306, 432), plus the useful mirror for her long-awaited cosmetics. Recall that the muṭi-coiffure of the goddess in Kerala is formed around a mirror.[25] The washerman, who earlier exhibits "behaviour suggestive of trance" and carries a five-pointed spear (equivalent to the vīrakuntam) in processions (Babb 1974, 6), performs ritual roles that recall such core area activities as the kaṇāccāri carrying the vīrakuntam, the Duryodhana actor lying on the effigy, and the elders who undergo the rites of death and revival while being covered with sheets.

Babb tells us it was "claimed by some" of his Singapore informants "that the shrine of Draupadi was originally established by a community of boat repairmen from the village of Vadukku Poigaiyoor near Nagapattinam," on the Thanjavur District coast of the Kaveri delta. Other informants disagreed (1974, 3). The Draupadī

24. I take it that this happens over all three, as elsewhere. Babb describes the full rite only for Abhimanyu.
25. See chapter 7, section B.

festival at Singapore is highly complex and draws on a diverse Tamil population, so one would not expect all of its elements to be traceable to one region. But the memory of a connection with Vaṭukku Poykaiyūr proves to have been worth investigating for the ceremony in question. At this temple near the shore, five paṭukaḷam effigies are made of mud: Duryodhana and Duḥśāsana side by side with their heads to the south; Abhimanyu, Karṇa, and Bhīṣma side by side with their heads to the north: each row heads outward, feet toward the middle. The only difference from the group at Singapore is Bhīṣma instead of Droṇa. Kṛṣṇa leads Draupadī on a tour of this battlefield, shows her the dead, and, in the case of Bhīṣma, the dying (his bed of arrows is remembered but not represented), and she sings laments (*oppāri*) over them, considering them her children. When it comes to Duryodhana, Kṛṣṇa tells Draupadī that she can now fulfill her vow. Played by the pāratiyār, Draupadī stands on top of a bench above the Duryodhana effigy and ties up her hair, using a comb (the mirror and kuṅkum were not mentioned). There is no sprinkling of turmeric or promise of heaven or mokṣa here: the latter is only for Aravāṉ.

This rite has at least three variations. One, to which it is probably traceable, is its presence in core area Terukkūttu dramas. Kṛṣṇa circling the battlefield with Draupadī to show her the slain warriors before she comes to Duryodhana for her hair tying can form a vivid scene in "Eighteenth-Day War" (Hiltebeitel 1988a, 419; 1988b, part 2). Second, as just indicated, it may be performed with effigies. The only other place I have found the five or more figures made into earthen effigies is at Pattukkottai. There it is a question of Droṇa, Karṇa, Cayintavaṉ (= Jayadratha), Duḥśāsana, and Duryodhana. Each has his own "paṭukaḷam" on a separate street. The pūcāri, rather than Kṛṣṇa (who is said not to be represented by the pūcāri), leads Draupadī to the five paṭukaḷams one after the other. At each of the first four, the pūcāri announces the name of the figure, Draupadī laments, they each sprinkle water on it, and then they destroy the figure. Each hero obtains mokṣa. Last, at Duryodhana's effigy, when they rub out the figure, a mirror, comb, ribbon, and some oil are found in the effigy's chest for Draupadī to put up her hair. There is no cutting of the leg.

More common, however, is the third variation. Instead of using effigies, the heroes lying on the battlefield are represented by men. The effigies have been found in eastern and southern parts of Thanjavur District, the human figures in more central and northern parts (Tiruppālatturai; Aḻakār Tirupputtūr, Cattiram Karuppūr), as well as in southern South Arcot (Junction Road, Vriddhachalam; C. Kīraṉūr). At C. Kīraṉūr, one man lies as Duryodhana, head to the south, to the west of a circle made up of six additional men representing Duḥśāsana, Bhīṣma, Abhimanyu, Aravāṉ, Droṇa, and Karṇa; all seven are covered with shawls (*cālvai*). First the pūcāri uses the comb, mirror, and kuṅkum to tie up the hair of Draupadī's icon. After that a local actor dressed as Kṛṣṇa and the pāratiyār dressed as Draupadī tour the circle. Pausing at each "kaḷam," Kṛṣṇa tells Draupadī who lies there. She weeps (*pulampal*) and tells Kṛṣṇa to grant the hero mokṣa, to which he agrees. They then sprinkle water, make the figure sit up, hold the vīrakuntam in place, and whip him with the vīracāṭṭi. At last Draupadī comes to Duryodhana's "paṭukaḷam." Kṛṣṇa tells her who he is. She becomes furious. They hold a board a little in front of Duryodhana. Draupadī puts her foot on the board and ties up her hair.

At Aḻakār Tirupputtūr, this rite is magnified. There 150 people lie down in rows, forming a square. They are "all the soldiers on both sides." Kṛṣṇa shows them to Draupadī. She weeps and sprinkles turmeric water on them, and Kṛṣṇa bestows mokṣa. About an hour after that, Draupadī stands on a plank and puts up her hair before Duryodhana.

Finally, at Cattiram Karuppūr, a local man impersonating Kṛṣṇa simply reads Draupadī (the pāratiyār S. Nagarajan) a list of the major heroes in the order in which they died, before he finally shows her Duryodhana, who is actually the pūcāri lying on a bench, covered with a cloth, periodically writhing in possession, restrained by three men with the vīracāṭṭi, and occasionally pausing to drink soda. The vīrakuntam, a cakra with three branch tridents spiking nine lemons, is held upright at Duryodhana's head, a second whip coiled through it (plate 21). Draupadī steps with one foot on a board, as above, and puts up her hair with a mirror, wooden comb, and, instead of powdered kuṅkum, a large forehead smear of red liquid "Eyetex Poornima Kunkum" from a bottle. She then falls back in possession and is carried toward the sanctum tying a garland of flowers in her own hair.

It seems that the core area Terukkūttu theme has been doubly elaborated as one moves farther and farther south: first with the slain represented by local people, and then, as also in Singapore, with effigies. Let us also note the evident fusion of effigy rites with revival rites. At Singapore, the washerman identifies with the Duryodhana effigy by having his legs (thighs?) pinched. But he also undergoes the sheet-covering and arm-whipping rites that are found in the revival ceremonies. More than this, the five effigies look like a fusion of the double effigy rite for Duryodhana and

Duḥśāsana with the typical five-person revival rite. With regard to the former, there is an interesting if baffling solution: Draupadī vows to do up her hair with Duḥśāsana's blood (Babb 1974, 8) but gets the articles for doing so, as we have just seen, from Duryodhana. One finds the same contradiction between the pāratiyār S. Nagarajan's narrative and the ritual he participates in at Cattiram Karuppūr (see n. 22). In other cases, the ultimate focus on Duryodhana helps explain how Draupadī can urge Kṛṣṇa to grant mokṣa to Duḥśāsana: he has receded back into the general circle of heroes. Meanwhile, the revival rites are recalled not only in the sheet coverings and arm whippings, but also in the various sprinklings and promises of mokṣa. Ritual fragments survive without their myths, taking on alternative epic myths to explain them. Nowhere is such a process more in evidence than in the further transmigrations of the Draupadī cult revival rites.

11 Death and Revival

The ritually enacted deaths and revivals that take place on the Draupadī cult paṭukaḷam are based upon two fundamentally distinct understandings of one epic scene. Since each requires radical reinterpretation of the classical (both Sanskrit and Tamil) epic story, it is reasonable to seek their sources outside the epic proper. In this chapter, after detailing the Draupadī cult revival rituals and myths, I will turn first to analogous rituals in similar cults of the larger area in which the Draupadī cult is found. They are akin to a number of well-documented "folk" rituals of popular Hinduism and, as Obeyesekere (1984) has shown, of popular Sinhalese Buddhism. With Obeyesekere, but in a different direction, we may then look beyond these south Indian–Sri Lankan horizons to the comparative question of "dying and rising gods" and to the larger South Asian context.

A. Five Children, Four Guardians

In the Draupadī cult's core area, the two basic understandings of the revival rituals have distinct subregional distributions and seem to be further differentiated according to the main sponsoring castes of the festivals in these two areas. Generally, in most of South Arcot and on up the coast through eastern portions of Chingleput District toward Madras, Draupadī temples and festivals are controlled mainly by Vaṉṉiyars, the numerically dominant agricultural caste in these areas. In these circumstances, the revival rituals focus on the "Young Pañcapāṇḍavas" (iḷam pañcapāṇṭavarkaḷ), also called the Upapāṇḍavas, the "lesser" or "younger" Pāṇḍavas: that is, Draupadī's five sons by her five Pāṇḍava husbands. The alternative form of the revival rite has been found widely in North Arcot, and also in northwestern portions of South Arcot (at Nallāṉpiḷḷaiperṟāḷ, Gingee Taluk) and Chingleput districts that border on

North Arcot. Some of the festivals where it has been found are sponsored by temples in the hands not of Vaṉṉiyars, but of Vēḷāḷar Mutaliyārs, increasingly the dominant agricultural caste as one moves north and westward into those areas. Here the ceremony focuses on the "Four Survivors" of the Kaurava army, or better, the "Four Guardians" of Duryodhana.

In either variant, the deaths and revivals are related to the additional—and indeed central—death of Duryodhana, which, as we have seen, occurs conjointly with them. But we have noted that there is a persistent narrative incongruity. In classical accounts, the blow to Duryodhana's thigh comes before the killing of Draupadī's children, whereas in the rituals it usually comes after. Most centrally, however, the *Mahābhārata* knows nothing of the revival of the Young Pañcapāṇḍavas. Such a notion is evoked only by the ritual-related versions of the story that exist within the cult. What is surprising, however, is that despite the prominence of this ritual, its version coexists in the cult with denials that any such revival takes place. The icon sculptor N. Dandapani says Draupadī's children are simply dead and gone; they do not come back to life. Most pāratiyārs say the same thing. Similarly, Terukkūttu actors may concur. My two main dramatist informants claimed it is just for ritual effect that the Upapāṇḍavas rise up. When their troupe performs its nightlong versions of "Eighteenth-Day War," Draupadī sees her dead sons and sings: "Could the dried nel [paddy] sprout? Could the five dead come again? Could the black milk become white . . . ?" (song handwritten by R. S. Mayakrishnan). There is nothing in the drama to indicate that the five revive. In fact, Draupadī often shows little concern for her children's fate in these dramas and, if anything, is more outraged that Aśvatthāman has slain her brother Dhṛṣṭadyumna along with them.[1] She thus breaks into lamentation and anger and vows she will again keep her hair disheveled until she is avenged against the slayer of her brother, not her sons (Hiltebeitel 1988a, 420–31).

The five children and four guardian variants must be described separately, but it is important to note that the rituals *look* fundamentally the same. Moreover, either rite may be done with five officiants. This is because an additional officiant, beyond the four or five, may in either case represent an additional epic hero, usually one singled out for an accented ritual treatment. At Tindivanam, such treatment befalls Aśvatthāman (or in earlier years Droṇa or

1. The dramatists were not familiar with any of Draupadī's other brothers, also slain at this time in the classical versions of the epic.

Bhīṣma). Furthermore, one can hear both explanations for the rites at the same temple or in neighboring villages. This is not to say that there are no irregular variants. At Pondicherry, for instance, Shideler found the five "sleeping warriors" identified not only as "Pāñcāli's sons," but also as "the Pāṇḍavas" as well as a group including Draupadī's brother Śikhaṇḍin and the Matsya king Virāṭa.[2]

Of the three main core area paṭukaḷam ceremonies discussed in chapter 10, two (Tindivanam and Mēlaccēri) unequivocally involve the Upapāṇḍavas. But Maṅkalam presents a seeming third possibility that is probably only an intermediate solution, with traces of both main variants. At this temple, some informants identified the revived heroes as the Young Pañcapāṇḍavas; but others, including members of the family of the chief trustee, identified them as five *Pūtams* (Sanskrit Bhūtas), literally "ghosts" or "elements." Both meanings are suggestive. The Sāṃkhya theory of the five elements (*pañcabhūtam*, Tamil *pañcapūtam*) pervades Hinduism and supplies a recurrent metaphor for the process of dying: one "returns to the five elements" (earth, water, fire, wind, space).[3] One might imagine that the five pūtams are the elements to which Duryodhana returns while dying. On the other hand, let us recall that Duryodhana's former concrete effigy at Tindivanam was destroyed because it attracted (other) Bhūtams, "ghosts."[4] Also, in the chapbook version of "Eighteenth-Day War," Kṛṣṇa calls upon a *host* of Pūtams to guard the Pāṇḍavas' army camp on the night that Aśvatthāman kills their children (Hiltebeitel 1988a, 420). N. Dandapani, the icon sculptor, says that *four* such Pūtams guard the Young Pañcapāṇḍavas. Alternatively, according to the pāratiyār M.C. Venkatesha Bhagavatar, Kṛṣṇa leaves *two* Pūtams to guard them, one of whom swallows Aśvatthāman's arrows "like biscuits" before Aśvatthāman dispatches him. These are elaborations of a classical theme, for it is a *single* Pūtam or Bhūtam who delays Aśvatthāman's progress, until Aśvatthāman worships Śiva, in both the *Villipāratam* (*Patiṉeṭṭāmpōr Carukam* 2.2–8) and the Sanskrit epic (10.6.10–29). If the Pāṇḍavas and their children have Pūtam guardians, why not Duryodhana?

Of the two possibilities, however, only the second had local, if

2. See Frasca 1984, 313; Shideler 1987, 180–81, discussed below. In what looks to be a drastic simplification, at Udappu, Sri Lanka, it is Duryodhana who "is revived by Draupadī's compassion" (Tanaka 1987, 383).
3. On the five elements in Tamil symbolism, particularly in connection with the five shrines housing the different elemental liṅgams of Śiva, see Shulman 1980a, 82 and n. 12; Das 1964, 196; in the *Mahābhārata*, see esp. 14.17.2–23.
4. See chapter 2, n. 4.

lukewarm, endorsement at Maṅkalam. According to the 103-year-old Ramalinga Goundar, a firewalker since childhood and the chief trustee's grandfather (Hiltebeitel 1988a, 68; 1988b, part 1), the five Pūtams are to be understood not as "ghosts," but as Duryodhana's guards (*kāval*). But according to the temple's pūcāri, they were indeed pēy, or "ghosts," as well, to which Ramalinga Goundar replied that "the pūcāri may not be knowing everything." Indeed, neither knew whether the five had any names. Only Ramalinga Goundar had anything to offer on this account: the four in the pits around Duryodhana are the four guards; the fifth, on a bench beyond his head, is the "chief of the guards" (plate 22). But to get their names, he said, one would have to go to the *Mahābhārata*. This we will do shortly. The mixed situation at Maṅkalam may reflect the combination of Vaṉṉiyar control in a North Arcot setting near the South Arcot border of Gingee Taluk. Four or five miles north of Maṅkalam at the Avalūrpēṭṭai Draupadī temple, rather than Pūtams or guardians of any kind, the rite is once again concerned with the Young Pañcapāṇḍavas. The South Arcot–North Arcot border seems to be transitional for these rites. The four-guardian rite has also been found just over the South Arcot side, at Nallāṉpiḷḷaiperṟāḷ.

Let us then look more closely at these two versions. We can take up the Upapāṇḍava rite as it was observed and explained at Tindivanam and Mēlaccēri, and the Four Guardians rite, which was observed, but poorly explained, at Maṅkalam, as it was better described elsewhere. Bear in mind that my main informants at Tindivanam were the temple pūcāri and the chief trustee, in that order, while at Mēlaccēri interviews were carried out with the Young Pañcapāṇḍavas themselves: with Gopala Goundar, chief trustee, in 1982, and with the other four in 1986.[5]

Recall that in the paṭukaḷam sequence at Tindivanam, the pūcāri and his entourage enter the ritual grounds and twice circumambulate Duryodhana's effigy. It is on the first round that they attend to the killing of the Upapāṇḍavas. The five men who personify the latter, plus the sixth who impersonates Aśvatthāman, are all senior members of Vaṉṉiyar families loyal to the temple, but without particular temple titles. Their bodies are covered with sheets from the head to above the ankles, leaving the ankles and feet bare. According to Tindivanam informants, it is Kṛṣṇa who placed the bedsheets over the heads of Draupadī's sons as one of his ways of

5. The latter interviews were carried out by J. Rajasekaran for Hiltebeitel 1988b; portions of them can be seen in part 2 (longer version only).

tricking Aśvatthāman into killing them rather than their fathers.[6] Aśvatthāman thus fails to recognize that the sleeping children are not the Pāṇḍavas, whose heads he has promised to bring to the dying Duryodhana.

Each of the Young Pañcapāṇḍavas has a small retinue of male attendants (sons or younger brothers) to minister to him. One of them continues to douse each sheet-covered figure with water, while another taps his ankles with a cluster of leafy margosa twigs. The tapping with margosa leaves is said to prevent sleeping. If one falls asleep, it is said he will die, and Purushottama Chettiar, the chief trustee, recalled that this had once actually happened. Let us note that this is not just a case of a trance state bordering upon death, but a living out of the implications of the myth: the Young Pañcapāṇḍavas die *while they are sleeping*.

The pūcāri and his assistants then splash reddened kuṅkum water from a small earthen pot onto the sheets covering each of the Upapāṇḍavas (plate 23). This signifies that they are slain in their sleep. The pūcāri also sprinkles turmeric powder on the sheets, while the kaṇāccāri and sword bearer stand by at each station with their weapons aloft. The sixth figure, Aśvatthāman, lies beneath his cloth and is tapped with margosa and sprinkled with water, but no "blood" or turmeric is sprinkled on him.[7]

When the ritual slaying of the sleeping figures is complete, the vīracāṭṭi (heroic whip) is removed from the prongs of the upraised vīrakuntam. Then, on the second circumambulation, the pūcāri and company administer the rites of revival. While a hereditary whip bearer holds the vīracāṭṭi, the pūcāri takes the vīrakuntam. As they make their rounds, he touches it to the side of each of the dormant Upapāṇḍavas. It is, he says, this touch—the touch of the weapon of Ammaṉ (Mother, the goddess)—that brings each of the Young Pañcapāṇḍavas back to life. He also throws more turmeric powder on them.[8] And while he applies this touch of the goddess's weapon, he sings a song for the "calling" or "invitation" of the goddess (*ampāḷai aḻaittal*). The song is one he normally sings while invoking Draupadī in her temple. Though it glorifies the goddess's exploits, beauty, and power, it makes no reference to the theme of revival. But it does indicate a conception of the goddess appropriate to this ritual moment and will be referred to later.

6. For another trick by Kṛṣṇa in the same situation, see Hiltebeitel 1988b, part 2.
7. This distinction might be erased if the figure under the sixth sheet is Droṇa or Bhīṣma. Mythically, neither should be "sleeping."
8. On the revival power of turmeric alone, see Sontheimer 1989a, 323.

Once the Young Pañcapāṇḍavas are touched with the vīrakuntam and revived, the pāratiyār recites a few verses. The sheets are then lifted from the five figures, and their attendants help them recover. Some are in a limp swoon, or look dazed, and must be helped to their feet. When they are able to do so, they extend their arms upward so that they are joined together, and the whipbearer lashes them three times each on the wrists with the vīracāṭṭi. This is said to bring them out from their sleeplike trance and to end their deathlike condition. In the case of Aśvatthāman, however, there is no whipping. After his victims have been revived, he is given some water to drink, and then the narrowed tip of the whip is tied around his left arm and he is led away from the scene lest he escape and become possessed and do more harm. Even though he too has been under a sheet, it is understood that Aśvatthāman has been possessed while slaying the Upapāṇḍavas and might now continue this possession with the same murderous results upon other victims. To describe his possession, the pūcāri used the term *maruḷu,* literally "delusion, bewilderment" (cf. Meyer 1986, 110 and n. 2), rather than *āvēcam,* the term normally used to describe (and sometimes debate about) incidents of possession. The Upapāṇḍavas' revivals then run their course as they depart from the paṭukaḷam while the pūcāri and his assistants turn their attention to the ritual killing of Duryodhana. The overlap of these rites can be significant in relation to the supporting version of the epic story, since, as Draupadī prepares to tie up her hair on Duryodhana's effigy, she can lament the deaths of her children. At Mutikai Nallāṉkuppam, the only place where I have found the revivals to occur *after* the enactment of Duryodhana's death and Draupadī's rebraiding, it is fittingly the Upapāṇḍavas, not the Four Guardians, who are revived.

At Mēlaccēri, the most evident differences in the Upapāṇḍava rite have already been signaled: no Aśvatthāman or any other sixth figure; the conventional bench and pits lined with margosa leaves rather than the concrete blocks. There are, however, a number of more subtle differences, some immediately observable, others detectable from clues gathered from the interviews with the Mēlaccēri contingent of Upapāṇḍavas. A major difference is that at Mēlaccēri the impersonators of the Young Pañcapāṇḍavas are nearly all important senior office bearers of the temple. The one to lie on the bench is Gopala Goundar, chief trustee. In 1982 he claimed that it was his honor to choose the other four, but this must be a pro forma honor, since, according to interviews with the other four in 1986, their participation derives from long-held family traditions.

One is the kaṇāccāri, who recalls that his elder brother, father, and grandfather performed the same role with the same title, which he thinks has been in his family for at least five generations. Another is the camayam, who likewise claimed that his charge as a son of Draupadī is a hereditary one (*paramparai*) in his family and will pass on to his son. A third is one of the holders of the office of cimmācaṉapuli, or Tiger of the Lion Throne, who claims the latter title came to an ancestor in the Nayak period, while the role of Upapāṇḍava goes back four generations. The last had no specific temple office but claimed the role of Young Pañcapāṇḍava passed to him from his grandfather through his elder brother. Clearly, these offices and ritual prerogatives are passed on among *paṅkāḷis*, the "co-sharers" in a lineage of males who can trace their descent from a common male ancestor.

It may be noted that the epic identities of this group are usually undifferentiated, like the four Pūtams. Beyond being the Pāṇḍavas' and Draupadī's children, they have no patronyms. When asked which of the Upapāṇdavas they were, none of them knew, and only one of them—the kaṇāccāri—had anything to offer on the subject, which was the confused thought that he might be Sahadeva: not, that is, the son of Sahadeva. I could thus find no hints that the use of the bench for Gopala Goundar might have reference to any differentiation among the brothers.[9] It was only said to register his preeminence among the ritualists.

The Upapāṇḍava role requires all five to undergo a preparatory penance (*viratam*), which all but one (the camayam) said goes back to his donning of kāppu at flag hoisting. Each defined the penance differently, however. Strictest was the kaṇāccāri, who maintains not only a no-food (only milk) diet, but sleeps on a mat without bedsheets (which implies sexual abstinence) rather than on a mattress. Most relaxed was the camayam, who claims he does nothing else than have no food other than milk on the morning of the rite. The association between bedsheets and sexual impurity invites one to ponder the use of sheets to cover the presumably pure and chaste Upapāṇḍavas. Indeed, at Mēlaccēri in 1982, two sheets were used: one covering the bed of margosa leaves, the other over the ritualist. In 1986, only the latter was used. In earlier times the sheets could not have been the store-bought variety one sees now, and in fact one of these informants, the camayam, used the term *pōrvai*—an upper

9. At Maṅkalam, one informant who identified the five figures as the Young Pañcapāṇḍavas, rather than Pūtam-guardians, said the bench was for the son of Bhīma, presumably as the biggest. The pāratiyār K. Muttuswami Pillai says the figure on the bench should be the son of Dharma, in the center of the other four.

garment, cloak, or mantle—for the sheet covering. This may recall both earlier ritual conditions and the narrative setting of the battlefield. In any case, the covering, of whatever sort, may be part of an obstetric symbolism of ritual rebirth.

As at Tindivanam, each Upapāṇḍava's retinue of attendants (in most cases composed of paṅkāḷis) keeps the sheets doused with water and taps his body with wands of margosa leaves: one on the ankles, another on the shoulders. Again, while the Upapāṇḍavas' heads are covered, their feet are uncovered. Here we learn that the attendants must be able to observe the Young Pañcapāṇḍavas' big toes. As each Upapāṇḍava confirmed, for the approximately ten minutes that they are under the sheets, their main preoccupation is to keep shaking one of their big toes (*kālperuviral*). The tapping with margosa and the shaking of the toe combine to keep them conscious. Indeed, as the cimmācaṉapuli explained, to keep his mind (*ñāṉam*) on the tapping of the neem leaves is to keep it on the deity (cāmi), presumably Draupadī, since the margosa leaves have her śakti.

While members of the public who attended the performance are under the impression that possession (āvēcam) comes upon the Young Pañcapāṇḍavas during this rite, several of the latter said that this was not the case in their own experience. The important thing is to remain conscious. One even keeps his eyes open. Rather than possession, they described the state as one in which one remembers nothing; in which one drifts back and forth from feeling unconscious to regaining consciousness. Another repeatedly feels dizzy. As at Tindivanam, they must not fall asleep. But at Tindivanam, nothing was mentioned about the big toe. The death and revival of the Young Pañcapāṇḍavas is also handled differently. At Mēlaccēri, the pūcāri and his entourage, which of course does not include the kaṇāccāri or camayam (who are under the sheets), make only one round of the effigy. The pūcāri sprinkles more water and turmeric powder over the sheet-covered bodies, but no red liquid for blood. Nor does anyone apply the goddess's vīrakuntam. Here turmeric is also sprinkled earlier over the margosa pits and the surrounding ground. As to the accounts of the Young Pañcapāṇḍavas, according to Gopala Goundar, while they are in their deathlike condition, the Draupadī actor weeps over them and vows that she will not put up her hair until they—her sons—revive. This lament involves no special songs, prayers, or mantras. But her five sons are now enabled to rise up: in part through the lament, and in part through the śakti of the goddess that is present in the cooling neem leaves and the turmeric. I did not, however, observe the Draupadī actor weeping over the Upapāṇḍavas in 1982, and in fact Gopala Goundar was describing the ritual from memory—which does not make his account less interesting. Another Upapāṇḍava spoke of the Draupadī icon watching over them during their rite, before her hair tying, which clearly did happen in both 1982 and 1986. One also spoke of the pāratiyār singing of the goddess's power as he passed among them. This will remind us of the invocatory song of the Tindivanam pūcāri.

Finally, as the Young Pañcapāṇḍavas rise up, two whip bearers—at least one of them is another of the five cimmācaṉapulis at Mēlaccēri—administer the customary lashing of their wrists. Only Gopala Goundar rises unflailed, showing his submission to the whip by the alternative act of wearing an identical tapered, turmeric-dyed whip around his neck during his full stint under the sheets. Let us recall here the affinities between this heroic whip and the cord that binds the victim to the Vedic yūpa, signifying its submission to the sacrifice.[10] Similarly, at Tindivanam, the unwhipped Aśvatthāman is led away from the paṭukaḷam with the whip's tapered end around his wrist. It seems that in each of these cases involving a distinctive ritual treatment with the whip, it is one that brings out a symbolism latent for all the Young Pañcapāṇḍavas: they are being treated like paśu, sacrificial animals. In fact, the identification of Aśvatthāman's victims as paśu is underscored by the portrayal of their "brutal deaths" in the Sanskrit *Mahābhārata* (Hiltebeitel 1976a [1990], 320–24).

Turning now to the story told in connection with the otherwise similar rites of the Four Kaurava Survivors or Four Guardians of Duryodhana, we can now satisfy ourselves as to how Duryodhana comes to have a fourth survivor of the war to guard him. The traditional epic knows of only three: Aśvatthāman, Kṛpa, and Kṛtavarman. Two Mutaliyār informants, in both cases pāratiyārs, did identify this fourth. Venkatesha Bhagavatar claimed that the fourth survivor was Cutāṉikkaṉ, "a member of Śalya's army" (a figure I cannot trace further). For him, however, the four survivors were not to be confused with the four Pūtams, who he said shared the paṭukaḷam rites beneath the sheets with Bhīṣma. In fact, his reason for the four lying in the pits around Duryodhana is that they are hiding and secretly overhear the conversation in which Duryodhana tells Aśvatthāman, the chief survivor, to go kill the Pāṇḍavas. Should they sleep, Duryodhana will be unprotected. Brameesa Mudaliyar, on the other hand, dispensing with the notion of Pū-

10. See chapter 6, section A, 8.

tams, identified the four guards as the four survivors and the fourth among them as the Rākṣasa Cañcakattakaṉ. This intriguing figure turns out to be none other than the collectivity of the Saṃśaptakas (those "sworn together" in a suicide pact to detain Arjuna away from the central action of the war) hypostatized into one individual. According to former members of the Pakkiripāḷaiyam Terukkūttu troupe I interviewed in 1977, this same Cañcakattakaṉ has a body made out of bell metal! The leaders of the same troupe, interviewed in 1981, also gave his name as Cañcīvi-karttā, "the One Who Makes Rejuvenation." I suspect that the Saṃśaptakas' habit in the Sanskrit epic of never quite allowing Arjuna to definitively eliminate them stands behind their hypostatization into a single survivor, who in turn stands for the revivability of the Saṃśaptaka army. In any case, the supporting version of the epic story, as told by Brameesa Mudaliyar, is the following.

When Duryodhana was hiding in the water doing tapas and reciting mantras to revive his army, the four survivors came searching for him: first on the battlefield and then, seeing his backward steps into a pond or tank, in the water.[11] Aśvatthāman urged Duryodhana to come out and change his hiding place, since the Pāṇḍavas would surely find him there. But Duryodhana told the four of his plans to revive the army and ordered them to hide nearby and be his guardians while he completed the mantras. They went to a nearby banyan tree. But instead of guarding Duryodhana they fell asleep in its shade. They were not supposed to sleep, but they did, right through the entire period when Duryodhana was found and defeated by Bhīma.[12] During the rituals that enact this scene, precautions identical with those described in the Young Pañcapāṇḍava rite (neem, whipping, turmeric: I did not hear about shaking the big toe) are taken to see to it that no one actually sleeps under the sheets. If they do, they may die: something Brameesa Mudaliyar assured me has happened more than once.

As noted earlier, the two paṭukaḷam variants look essentially the same, and one must suspect that they are in origin one ritual. One of the few differences evident at the Four Guardians rite as I saw it performed at Maṅkalam is that some of the attendants of the men under the sheets were women (see plate 22). They were said to be the ritualists' wives and daughters-in-law. I do not know whether

11. For the Terukkūttu version of this background story, see Hiltebeitel 1988a, 415. Note that Duryodhana's *cañjīvi mantiram* is a long hymn to the goddess, calling on her as the one to revive his army.

12. One Maṅkalam informant claimed the Pūtams must not sleep lest Duryodhana's life be taken away by Yama.

this occurs elsewhere or bears any relation to the alternative myth. The Young Pañcapāṇḍavas, being unmarried, would not have wives or daughters-in-law. Another difference was the greater incidence of possession, which affected not only the frantic weapon-bearing procession that entered the paṭukaḷam toward the beginning of the death and revival rites, but also, later, some of the reviving Pūtams themselves. Local informants explained the opening rush as a group heightening of the pūcāri's possession, but this was given no epic explanation. In any case, the figures under the sheets are not Draupadī's children, so no one is killing or weeping over them.

One hint of a common prototype for the two rites is their numerology. According to Brameesa Mudaliyar, the Four Guardians rite should involve a fifth figure, that of Bhīṣma, lying elevated on a bench, as he sometimes does as a *sixth* figure among the Upapāṇḍavas (recall the 1982 paṭukaḷam ceremonies at Tindivanam; see n. 7). The number five thus keeps recurring, as it still does, despite modifications, at festivals in the Thanjavur area and at the "immigrant" Draupadī temple in Singapore (see chap. 10, sec. D). Of our two main variants, it seems that the Young Pañcapāṇḍava rite holds here to what is most essential. In the Four Guardians rite, the themes of death and revival are severely attenuated. As with the Upapāṇḍavas, the four bodyguards are kept from sleeping, which would incur either their deaths or Duryodhana's. But unlike the Upapāṇḍavas, their deaths have no epic reference unless one is incorporated in the notion that they are Pūtams, ghosts. Nor is there anything in the accounts to suggest that their rising up at the end of the ritual has to do with a revival. It is only in an inverse sense that the story refers to a revival: had his guards remained awake, Duryodhana would have been able to call upon the goddess to revive his entire army—a theme drawn from epic and ultimately Indo-European sources that tell of the power of the demons, and in particular of their chief priest Śukra, to revive their armies (see n. 11). In this light, with the Four Guardians only sleeping when they should not be, the paṭukaḷam scene requires no additional rites of killing besides the slaying of Duryodhana. This may reflect the more Brahmanically defined leanings of the Vēḷāḷar Mutaliyārs who have the main hand in some of the temples where this variant occurs (Māṉāmpāṭi, Perunakar). For Brameesa Mudaliyar and Venkatesha Bhagavatar, the two pāratiyārs from this community who supplied versions of this story, it seems to reflect a knowledge, and a determination to emphasize, that the Young Pañcapāṇḍavas should stay dead. In this regard it may also be noted that Draupadī should have nothing to lament when she mounts the body of Duryodhana, since she certainly cannot lament the sleeping Kaurava survivors *who have not yet awakened to kill her children and brother(s).* From the angle of the Four Guardians rite, Draupadī's lament can only be a sidelight, or mythical postscript, to the ceremony. Accordingly, at Maṅkalam, the only place where I have seen a variant of the Four Guardians rite performed, the Terukkūttu actor impersonating Draupadī never laments or shows signs of possession during either of the moments that he enacts the goddess's rebraiding.[13] In short, the Four Guardians rite requires no enactment or acknowledgment of the death, much less revival, of the goddess's children.

As we saw in chapter 2, according to Brameesa Mudaliyar, the four survivor-guardians should be impersonated by four temple officiants: Cañcakattakaṉ by the kaṇāccāri, bearing a water pot; Aśvatthāman by the kuntam, holding the vīrakuntam; Kṛpa by the camayam, in charge of the offering tray with turmeric powder; and Kṛtavarman by the kumāravarkkam, holding the sword (katti, alaku). It was found, however, that even when I was led on a search by Brameesa Mudaliyar himself, these correlations were never quite met. Uttiramērūr, the only temple with a full variation on them, had all four paired differently: the kaṇāccāri was Kṛpa, the camayam Aśvatthāman, the kuntam Kṛtavarman, and the kumāravarkkam Cañcakattakaṉ. All four, plus a fifth to represent Bhīṣma, were in fact Vaṉṉiyars. Yet even in these circumstances, it seemed that Brameesa Mudaliyar was teasing out this partial confirmation from the local informants. The notion of a set of four epic-ritual correlations, and possibly the office of kuntam, were in his head far more clearly than in theirs. For him, it was an ideal case—which is not to deny its significance. Brameesa Mudaliyar had performed Pāratam at most of the temples on this tour. He could well have given instruction on these epic-rite correspondences that such local authorities had not assimilated. In the fluid interplay between Pāratam and local ritual, there will not often be an exact match between the pāratiyār's knowledge of the epic and the local understanding of the ritual.

A deeper problem, however, was also evident in our findings that two of the offices, kuntam and kumāravarkkam, were uncommon at the visited temples and call for explanations outside the Four Guardians rite. If the office of kuntam is to be found anywhere beside the uncertain instance at Uttiramērūr, it appears to have splintered off from that of the kaṇāccāri, whose usual charge

13. See chapter 10, section B, items 8 and 12 of outline of Maṅkalam paṭukaḷam ceremony.

is to hold the vīrakuntam or kuntam. More important, the kumāra-varkkam as (ideally) the sword-bearing Kṛtavarman is but a pale shadow of this resonant title as it is known at certain other Draupadī festivals, principally among Vaṉṉiyars, in connection with variations on what may be called the "youth" or "kumāra function." On the one hand, we have seen that at Nallāṉpettāḷ the term kumāravarkkam can be used to refer to the five officiants who represent the Young Pañcapāṇḍavas themselves.[14] On the other hand, the term kumāravarkkam and variants can be used to refer to the group of youths, often called kumāras or vīrakumāras, who perform the sword-pressing feat known as *katti* or *alaku cēvai*, "sword service." In fact, the identifications of the kumāravarkkam as the sword bearer and the rejuvenating Cañcakattakaṉ may be a parallel to this set of associations. As was suggested in chapter 2, katti cēvai, prominent at Draupadī temples in Bangalore and Madras, appears to be an urban alternative for the Young Pañcapāṇḍava rites of the core area. The katti cēvai at the Sowcarpet temple in Madras, which I observed in 1975, offers much to confirm this.

On the afternoon of the penultimate ninth day of the Sowcarpet festival, the kumāras, all boys and young men, having completed nine of ten days of fasting, come to the temple dressed only in yellow vēṣṭis. They assemble as a group under the pantal that extends out from the temple, between the balipīṭha-flagstaff complex and the wooden processional icons of Draupadī (facing east), Pōttu Rāja (before and below her to her left: to her northeast), and Aravāṉ's head (set back into a niche in the temple wall). Pōttu Rāja has three vīracāṭṭi whips around his neck, while Draupadī and Aravāṉ each have one around theirs. Pōttu Rāja and Draupadī each also have a long curved sword leaning on their right arms and set to lie across their chests, points upward, with lemons impaled on the tips. Pōttu Rāja then has two additional lemons on the end of his icon's raised knife, while Draupadī has behind her palanquin a multi-tined vīrakuntam, also spiked with numerous lemons (see plate 24). The goddess and Pōttu Rāja thus both hold the swords to their chests as the kumāras do, while registering as well, with the lemons on the tips of the swords and other weapons, that sword pressing is a form of impalement. Meanwhile, as elsewhere, the whips around the necks suggest a submission to sacrifice for all the icons, including Aravāṉ, a "youth" like the kumāras, and present as he would be on the paṭukaḷam with the Young Pañcapāṇḍavas.

One at a time, the kumāras then come to stand before the three

14. Cf. further chapter 10, section B.

icons, offer reverence, and do a series of maneuvers with the sword (katti, alaku), passing it in a downward motion in a crisscross pattern using both hands, and pressing it against the bare chest at different positions and angles. Thanks to Draupadī and Pōttu Rāja's protection, there is no bloodshed. Then in the evening, at about 8:00 P.M., the kumāras gather again at the temple, form a line for worship in the garbhagṛha, and break for a circuit of local Śiva and Viṣṇu temples to bathe in their tanks. At about 9:15, they join a grand procession of the goddess's karakam (decorated pot) and pañcalōkam icon, the latter housed on an elaborately decorated portable platform backed with an arched frame.[15] This procession has also made a tour of surrounding streets and is heading back to the Draupadī temple. As in the culminating karakam procession that includes the vīrakumāras in Bangalore,[16] the weapons of Pōttu Rāja—here vīrakuntam, vīrakantakam, vīracāṭṭi, sword—are all carried as part of this approach. Just before reaching the temple area, still on the street, the kumāras are met by men bearing vīracāṭṭi whips. The youths crouch or kneel, protecting their heads with one arm while raising the other straight up to be whipped three times around the wrist. Sometimes two boys join arms together to share the whipping. The lashes leave no traces, again thanks to the goddess's protection. Meanwhile, some return to the wooden icons of Draupadī and Pōttu Rāja for further sword pressing. At midnight, Draupadī's wooden icon is adorned as Kālī, and at 4:00 A.M. the icon's hair is finally tied, supplying the substitute for this feature of the paṭukaḷam complex without a Duryodhana effigy. In terms of the epic story, this of course marks the end of the war. Now on this night, the kumāras are supposed to sleep in the temple. Their sleep must be minimal in these conditions and must amount to a combination sleep and vigil. In other words, it bears a resemblance to the sleep of the Young Pañcapāṇḍavas, the other chief element of the core area paṭukaḷam complex that is missing at Sowcarpet. It was, however, the chief whip bearer, Madurai Muttu, who supplied the clinching information.[17] The youths who withstand the sword feats and whipping after nine days of fasting "prove that they are the sons of Draupadī" and are ready to carry out the battle on the Pāṇḍavas' side.

Katti or alaku cēvai is a rite performed elsewhere, especially in

15. The conveyance was called a *toṭṭil*, "a cradle, crib, or swinging cot, for a child" (Winslow [1862] 1979, s.v.), rather than a "chariot."

16. Described in chapter 2, section C; cf. also Babb 1974, 22.

17. On this exuberant informant, often a virtual bodyguard for me and C. T. Rajan during the tumult at this festival, see chapter 2, n. 27.

other hero cults.[18] But in Draupadī cult contexts, its predominantly urban provenance suggests that of the two alternatives, it is the modification, not the modified. In urban conditions, Draupadī temples must find the core area paṭukaḷam rites, which require a large open space for the construction of effigies and the digging of pits, increasingly difficult to perform. So it appears that while some urban festivals (Muthialpet, Ālantūr, and Teynampet in Madras, Kalassipalaiyam in Bangalore [Richards 1910, 30], even Singapore) continued to construct features of a paṭukaḷam, others have adapted by drawing upon this alternative hero cult option, which requires no more than a place before the icons. I have, in any case, found no instance where alaku cēvai and the rites of dying and revival for the Young Pañcapāṇḍavas are *both* performed.

In the one case, then, we have actual Vaṉṉiyar youths performing a feat of submission to the goddess through a symbolism of martial bravado that evokes the facing of death and calls for the goddess's power (śakti) to bless and protect them as her sons. In the other we have Vaṉṉiyar men of middle and late years who impersonate youths—Draupadī's sons, precisely—who undergo rites of symbolic death that similarly call upon the goddess's power not only to bless and protect, but—most poignantly for the age group—to revive. In either case, this "youth function" has clear pertinence to Vaṉṉiyars, as was demonstrated in connection with that community's experience in Karnataka, in chapter 2. On the contrary, the Four Guardians rite has eliminated this "youth function" and truncated, along with it, the themes of death and revival. I hypothesize that this happened as the ceremonies lost the meaning they had to Vaṉṉiyars, and took on new meanings under the influence of others, especially of Vēḷāḷar Mutaliyārs. Thus, however risky the conclusion may be, given the limited nature of my information, I would urge that the Four Guardians rite is an erudite and toned-down Vēḷāḷar modification of the more coherent, dramatic, and profound Vaṉṉiyar rite of the death and revival of the Young Pañcapāṇḍavas.

Finally, in addition to the four guardians or the five Pāṇḍava children, we have seen that there is often a fifth or sixth figure singled out for special treatment. Aśvatthāman (alias Bhīṣma, alias Droṇa) at Tindivanam goes unwhipped. Elsewhere, one of the five or six lies on a bench, and may also go unwhipped. Shideler found at Pondicherry that the sixth figure was Dhṛṣṭadyumna, Draupadī's

18. More generally, see Thurston and Rangachari [1904] 1965, 2:158–59 (note the related *jammi* or śamī tree rituals); 5:406; 7:320, 360, 410; Blackburn 1988, 95.

brother (1987, 180), born before her from the same sacrificial fire. At Mēlaccēri, however, the bench is there for the chief trustee Gopala Goundar, but he is still only one of the Young Pañcapāṇḍavas.

The hero most frequently mentioned, however, is Bhīṣma. On my tour with Brameesa Mudaliyar, his insistence that the Four Guardians should be joined by Bhīṣma as a fifth was confirmed at Māṉāmpāṭi, Tūci, and Perunakar. Venkatesha Bhagavatar, the other Vēḷāḷar Mutaliyār pāratiyār who provided a version of the Four Guardians rite, also said that the fifth figure should be Bhīṣma. And at Maṅkalam, some informants also said the elevated figure—corresponding to Ramalinga Goundar's "chief of Duryodhana's guards"—was Bhīṣma. At Mutikai Nallāṉkuppam, on the other hand, it is again the five Young Pañcapāṇḍavas who are joined by Bhīṣma on the elevated bench. Why Bhīṣma? And why the elevated bench? About the latter, most informants had no idea, unless it was suitable for someone senior: either the chief trustee among the ritualists, as at both Maṅkalam and Mēlaccēri, or a major epic dignitary. But at Mutikai Nallāṉkuppam a more satisfying answer was offered by the visiting pāratiyār K. Radhakrishnan. The bench is Bhīṣma's bed of arrows, which in the epic keeps his body from touching the ground. I suspect that this is the best explanation of this ritual feature. As Brameesa Mudaliyar indicated, at festivals where the Four Guardians rite predominates there can also be a later ceremony, quite lengthy in some instances, in which the pāratiyār recites and discourses upon sections of the epic's *Śāntiparvan*, commemorating Bhīṣma's postwar speeches to the Pāṇḍavas as he lies dying, filled with arrows, before obtaining mokṣa (Hiltebeitel 1988a, 140–41 n. 9). We have seen Bhīṣma's bed of arrows before as a symbol of impalement (chap. 7, sec. C). That also seems to be one significance of his elevated bed on the paṭukaḷam. Though he and his bench may be positioned at Duryodhana's head, as at Maṅkalam, he is usually at Duryodhana's feet, in the position that marks the northern entrance to the paṭukaḷam that is also, at Tindivanam, the site of Arjuna's blood-tipped arrow, the entrance point of Pōttu Rāja (with evocations of the śamī), and, on the south-north axis of Thanjavur area temples, the position of Muttāl Rāvuttaṉ facing Aravāṉ and Kālī (chap. 9, sec. D). The entrance point to the paṭukaḷam thus bristles with a variety of raised weapons, or their humanized "post" equivalents, like the entrances to many goddess temples (see Biardeau 1989b, photos 53, 59, 81, 85). Let us also recall that one of the ways the Young Pañcapāṇḍavas may be revived is with the touch of the Mother's trident.

B. Words, Water, Wands, and Weapons

These rites are part of a widely diffused South Indian mythic and ritual complex. In terms of the actual lamentation and revival rituals, the closest known parallels are to be found in the battlefield rites that reenact key episodes in the *Elder Brothers Story* and the *Epic of Palnāḍu*.

In the Elder Brothers cult, both at the "graveyard" paṭukaḷam sanctified by the story in the Viramalai Hills and in annual rites at lineage temples where the paṭukaḷam is represented locally, the following rites occur. When the death of the heroes is recited, certain males in the audience are possessed by the heroes' spirits, particularly those of the two principal twin heroes Caṅkar and Poṉṉar. Under this influence, they seize weapons or sticks, or make violent arm movements, and "begin a period of wild swirling and swaying . . . 'dancing' or 'fighting.'" Then they begin to fall to the ground, and though some are helped up, eventually all fall, leaving the ground "covered with bodies." Assistants then "move them to a 'graveyard' along one side of the larger area" and arrange the "corpses" into a north-south queue, their feet facing east. "The men are then covered with white cloth. . . . Any untouchables who have participated (there should be at least one according to custom) are also laid out, as above, but slightly separated from the other bodies." Thus the twins' Untouchable ally Cāmpukā is represented. Then the bard, taking on the role of Taṅkāḷ, the twins' sister, sings the precise lament that the heroine sang to revive her brothers and Cāmpukā in the epic. Indeed, an important point: Taṅkāḷ's words have the power to revive not only her brothers, but if they wake up, "all the dead warriors"—that is, the entire army (Beck 1982, 39, 41). While the bard, playing Taṅkāḷ, recites, "a ritual assistant sprinkles a little water from a hand-held pot over each supine body," and "each participant then returns magically to life, rising slowly to a sitting position" (Beck 1982, 37–46).

Beck has translated Taṅkāḷ's ritual lament both from a recorded performance text and from a temple manuscript (1982, 38–46). It is clearly a precious bardic tradition, one for which I could find no precise parallel in the diffuse world of Draupadī cult revivals, where the pāratiyārs in particular often deny that any such revivals occur. The most typical form of mock battle on the Draupadī cult paṭukaḷam is the duel between Duryodhana and Bhīma. When staged by Terukkūttu actors, it is more a carefully choreographed duel than a battlefield mêlée. But where local people take on the combat roles, the results can be closer to those in the Elder Brothers cult. At Cuṇṇāmpukuḷam, on the northern fringes of the core area, the ninth day "depicts the battle between the Panchapandavas and Kauravas headed by Duriyodhana. Two batches of persons appear in the costume of the Kauravas and Pandavas respectively and a pole fight takes place between them" (Moses 1961, 85). Unfortunately this report does not tell how deaths are handled (if at all), and whether or not there are revivals. One does, however, find something of a mock battle mêlée at Maṅkalam in the possessed procession with ritual weapons that coincides with the beginning of the death and revival rites.[19]

Similar elements, in different combinations, are also reported in the cult of the Heroes of Palnāḍu and are worth setting forth in their festival context. Every year on the full moon of Kārttika (October-November), Brahma Nāyuḍu, Viṣṇu incarnate, is said to descend to the Temple of the Heroes from the Guttikoṇḍa cave, to which he led the heroes who had been slain on the battlefield of Kārempūḍi after bringing them back to life. The sixteenth day, that of the new moon, then begins the main festival sequence with the honoring of the heroes themselves in the form of their reliquary weapons (daivālu), some of which (or better, of whom) are brought from distant districts and joined with those kept in the local temples of the cult's battlefield site. The seventeenth day is then for ceremonies known as *rācagāvu*, involving "the sacrifice of a ram to Pōtarāju": a Māla Untouchable bites its jugular and pulls off its skin with his teeth; a buffalo is offered at the same time; and the story of Pōta Rāju and his Śivanandi Fort is told in the evening. Draupadī festival parallels involving Pōttu Rāja–Pōrmaṉṉaṉ—in particular, Pōrmaṉṉaṉ's "Fight," his fort-city of Śivānandapuri, and the indispensability of his weapons for the battle of Kurukṣetra—are now evident.[20]

After the eighteenth day's recitation of the episode that makes the battle of Kārempūḍi inevitable (see chap. 9, sec. C), the nineteenth day is the occasion for an account of a cattle raid, known as *Manda Pōru*, "The Attack on the Herd," or alternatively as "The Death of Lankanna." As at Draupadī festivals, elements of the forthcoming battle are prefigured by the ritual commemoration of an epic cattle raid, here including the theme of death and resurrection.[21] From about 3:00 A.M. till morning, a ritual "said to be en-

19. See chapter 10, section B, table 5, items 2–4.
20. Roghair 1982, 26–27; Hiltebeitel 1988a, 336–93; 1988b, part 1.
21. See chapter 8, section B. Both accounts reflect the interplay between cowherd

dowed with great power" recreates the scene. A man who assumes the role hereditarily impersonates the herdsman (Golla or Bōya) Lankanna, chief keeper of Brahma Nāyuḍu's cattle. As the story tells, he is trampled, beheaded, and dismembered as the cattle stampede past the gate he is supposed to guard. The ritualist lies on the ground covered with cloth, his face invisible and his body totally still, with weapons set around him as if he were slain. Another man then comes as Brahma Nāyuḍu, sits by him, and sprinkles turmeric water (tīrtham) on him for several hours, before finally removing the cloth to reveal his revival. The story, as Roghair summarizes it, is as follows: Brahma Nāyuḍu gathers up the parts of Lankanna's body, "puts each limb and organ in its proper place, . . . whispers a spell in Lankanna's ear, and soon he comes back to life." But when Lankanna wants to go to Vaikuṇṭha (Viṣṇu's heaven) rather than rejoin the living, Brahma Nāyuḍu removes the *tulasi* (basil seed) necklace from Lankanna's neck and releases him heavenward.[22]

Following the twentieth day, which includes sword feats (*katti sēva* = katti cēvai), the twenty-first day brings on the rites of kalli paḍu, "falling down" (or kalli pāḍu, "the horror and the desolation"), in which the participants touch the weapons—the divine heroes—to thorny greens on the ground, signifying their deaths, and then fall on them at the Temple of the Heroes in the presence of the limestone slab of Pōta Rāju.[23] As far as I can tell, unlike his revival of Lankanna, Brahma Nāyuḍu's revival of all the heroes on the battlefield, and their return to the Guttikoṇḍa Cave, takes place only in the story and not in the ritual. It is in any case a revival of the entire army, as in the Elder Brothers cult. Let us recall the Draupadī cult's paṭukaḷam-generated elaborations on this increasingly important theme: the fourth Kaurava survivor, who personifies the revival of the Saṃśaptaka army; the prevention, mainly by Kṛṣṇa, of the revival of Duryodhana's entire army; and Draupadī's weeping, sprinkling of turmeric water, and Kṛṣṇa's bestowal of mokṣa for the hundred and fifty soldiers representing *both* armies at Aḻakār Tirupputtūr (chap. 10, sec. D).

These revival scenarios are not reducible to generalized cults of the deified dead (contrary to Blackburn 1988, 215–16). Comparable

---

and Kṣatriya traditions, on which see especially Narayana Rao 1989, 105–8, 110–21; also Hiltebeitel 1988a, 185, 220; 1989b, 5–7, 11–13.

22. All details on the late night ritual are from Velcheru Narayana Rao (personal communication, November 1988, for which I am grateful). See also Roghair 1982, 27, 253–58, including all quoted material.

23. Details again from Narayana Rao; cf. Roghair 1982, 29 and above, chapter 7, section A.

revival rites could be cited at the paṭukaḷams for Māriyammaṉ (see chap. 7, n. 2) and Kāḷiyammaṉ (Reiniche 1987, 90) in Tiruchirappalli District, the aḻukaḷam-cremation ground for Kūttāṇṭavar, and in the Pattini cult in Sri Lanka. We shall note some of their features shortly. But the "kaḷam" rituals of the Kongunad and Palnad hero cults, whose affinities with the Draupadī cult continue to deserve our closest attention, are sufficient to show that the revival rites in question form part of a common complex and share specific ritual features: lying under sheets, lamentation, sprinkling, secret songs in Kongunad; covering with cloth, sprinkling with turmeric water, and thorny greens for the daivālu-heroes in Palnad. Indeed, the touching of the daivālu to the thorny greens, followed by the ritualists' falling on the weapons themselves in the presence of Pōta Rāju, is reminiscent of the margosa-leaf beds for the dying and rising heroes in the Draupadī cult, which are also surrounded by symbols of impalement that include the sword-bearing Pōttu Rāja and may even be equated with them, since the margosa leaves combine with the raised bench to represent Bhīṣma's bed of arrows.[24]

Beyond these parallels, however, are deeper issues that can be approached only by looking at the narratives that tie in with these rites and at other folk epic and ritual variations on the same themes. Let us first address the issue of *how* the revivals are accomplished. In the *Elder Brothers Story,* Viṣṇu tells Taṅkāḷ to think of Śiva and a golden wand will descend from heaven that she can use, along with a water pot, to revive her brothers. These devices have close counterparts in the "Khan Sahib Caṇṭai," a Tamil ballad on the historical figure of Muhummad Yusuf or Yusuf Khan, whom the British promoted to Subadhar of Madurai and then hanged for treason in 1764. According to this story, three nights after he was hanged, Yusuf Khan appeared to the sepoys in a dream and told them to go to his sweetheart for a magical golden cane and a ruby cup of water; by sprinkling him with water from the cup and tapping him gently with the cane, his body could be revived. When the British heard of this, however, they tested his corpse's vitality, then cut the body in pieces and buried them far and wide to prevent his resuscitation (Arunachalam 1976, 143–44; cf. Bayly 1989, 193–215, 236–37).

In the *Epic of Palnāḍu,* Brahma Nāyuḍu reassembles the pieces of Lankanna and then revives him, not only by whispering in his ear, but apparently with a tulasi necklace. The tulasi necklace is part of

24. Margosa twigs and leaves, however, are not thorny. But see n. 27.

the apparatus of revival at an earlier war when Brahma Nāyuḍu uses it along with a five-colored, lotus-shaped diagram to revive the slain (1982, 187). It is no doubt with some similar combination that he revives the dead at the end of the battle of Kārempūḍi.[25]

Distilling what is most recurrent in these legendary accounts, we find that revivals require the combination of powerful words, cooling fluids, and the touch of some kind of empowered staff or other object (golden wand, golden cane, golden necklace). When we turn back to the actual revival rituals, there is good reason to think that these paraphernalia can be identified with the articles mentioned in the myths. Taṅkāḷ's lament and the words Brahma Nāyuḍu whispers in Lankanna's ear remind one of the Draupadī actor's lament (at Mēlaccēri), her pūcāri's song (at Tindivanam), her pāratiyār's recitation (at Mutikai Nallāṉkuppam), or the mantras of an aged Brahman, brought in specially for the rite (at Aṉmarutai).

Water is sprinkled on the sheets at the Elder Brothers paṭukaḷam. At the Māriyammaṉ paṭukaḷams in Trichy District, the Paṟaiyar priest, after descending from his impalement stake, also sprinkles water on the sheets of the four other Harijans who lie at the base of the stake. In the Pattini cult revival rituals among Sinhalese Buddhists in Sri Lanka, Pattini revives Kōvalaṉ by making use of the water from "an ambrosia pond" created for her by Indra, and then also with her shawl, which she wets with this water (Obeyesekere 1984, 269–70).[26] Draupadī cult ritualists are also doused with water, often turmeric water.

Various articles meet the criteria of the wand. One is the bundles of margosa sprigs used to tap the bodies. This practice in fact has a general application known as *kuḻaiyaṭikka*, literally "to beat (*aṭi*) with young leaves or twigs (*kuḻai*)," which is nicely summarized by Winslow: "To recite incantations while shaking or drawing a handful of margosa twigs over a sick or possessed person or animal, or one bitten by a snake" (Winslow [1862] 1979, s.v. kuḻai, p. 337). But according to informants, while the neem wands help to empower the revival, they do not actually effect it. This is usually said—as it was by informants at Mēlaccēri, Mutikai Nallāṉkuppam, and Teynampet (in Madras)—to be accomplished by the vīracāṭṭi, the tapered, turmeric-colored "hero whip." Indeed, not only does this

25. Roghair leaves out this part of the epic, but Sewell's summary (1882, xi) indicates that Brahma Nāyuḍu "sent two women to procure all kinds of herbs and drugs" for him to use to bring about the revivals.

26. Cf. Obeyesekere 1984, 244: Kaṇṇaki revives the slain with her shawl, which also has the power to dispel pestilences (ibid., 133–34).

"golden" whip bring the Young Pañcapāṇḍavas back to life when it is flailed across their wrists, but it can also be worn as a "golden" necklace, as at Mēlaccēri.

One other implement can revive the Young Pañcapāṇḍavas. At Tindivanam, although the whip is applied as elsewhere, the true revival—according to the pūcāri—is caused by the touch of the vīrakuntam, "Ammaṉ's weapon." Obeyesekere has found a similar account at the Madurai Cellattammaṉ temple: when Kaṇṇaki revives Kōvalaṉ, "she touches him with a spear, and he comes back to life" (1984, 541, n. 4). The vīrakuntam and spear are special cases, because they are different forms of the goddess's main weapon of combat. Behind these accounts, it seems, there is thus a likely allusion to the goddess's combat with her demon foes. In Kōvalaṉ's case this seems odd, since I know of nothing to suggest that he is in any way a demon. But the Madurai Cellattammaṉ temple features a myth of the goddess's triumph over the Buffalo Demon (van den Hoek 1978, 120; Hiltebeitel 1988a, 74). Possibly the use of the sword to revive Kōvalaṉ there is a reflex of that myth. In such accounts, however, the touch of the goddess's weapon brings not revival from death, but salvation in extremis. The touch of Draupadī's vīrakuntam seems to be a ready evocation of this theme, since the Young Pañcapāṇḍavas are Arakkaṉs, that is, demons or Rākṣasas (Hiltebeitel 1988a, 429). It is thus probably no coincidence that the "song of invitation" the Tindivanam pūcāri sings as he goes about reviving them with this "weapon of Ammaṉ" begins by invoking Draupadī under the following names of the goddess: "Cuntari Cakuntari Tikampari Parampari Cumaṅkaḷila Vāli Makiṣācūra Caṅkāri [Destroyer of Mahiṣāsura]." Here we see that revival can shade over into mokṣa or liberation, as it does also with Lankanna; with the Elder Brothers, who likewise see and talk with their sister after she has revived them before they "quickly ascend to heaven" (Beck 1982, 57; cf. 39; 1975, 292–95); and in the transformation of Draupadī cult revival rites into bestowals of mokṣa in the Thanjavur area.

In this vein, one other figure must be mentioned in connection with the total paraphernalia of revival. This is Pōttu Rāja, whose identity as the Buffalo King conceals a prior identity as the Buffalo Demon and thus an unstated myth of his own death and revival, or at least death and reincarnation. Whether this tacit myth could have any bearing on our rites must remain a moot point, but Pōttu Rāja certainly has multiple presences on the paṭukaḷam where the rites are carried out. His weapons of death and revival are virtually omnipresent. Even the margosa tree is connected with Pōttu Rāja, for it is the most common substitute for the śamī or vaṉṉi tree that is his trademark. A striking convergence in nearly all the death and revival rituals and related myths is the presence of the śamī or the margosa.[27] In the *Elder Brothers Story* and the *Epic of Palnāḍu* the heroes die beside the śamī. Margosa leaves line the pits on the Draupadī cult paṭukaḷam, and also on the paṭukaḷam in the weavers' cult to Kālī in Trichinopoly district (Reiniche 1987, 90). In the Sri Lankan Pattini cult, Kōvalaṉ dies beneath a margosa tree (Obeyesekere 1984, 245–46, 265, 267, 282). A rich Draupadī cult parallel is to be found at Pondicherry.

There does not appear to be any use of margosa leaves at Pondicherry to line the pits or bench, or tap the bodies, of the six "sleeping warriors" (generally understood as the Young Pañcapāṇḍavas and their maternal uncle Dhṛṣṭadyumna). Instead, bedsheets are laid out on the bench and sandy soil. Six ritualists lie on these, each covered by an additional sheet. Nor do the six surround the effigy of Duryodhana, which is nearby; rather, the five on the ground surround the sixth on the bench. The ceremony takes place in a square area marked at the corners "by five-meter high posts decorated with palm branches" and margosa leaves. In the center, by the figure on the bench, rises a still taller post that is also wrapped in margosa leaves, but not topped with palm, and connected to the other posts on the corners by cords bearing varicolored pennants. This post is topped by a red flag showing a five-headed cobra that is said to represent Aravāṉ, whose "blood" (kuṅkum water) is mixed with rice and flung over each warrior's heart region, after which they are revived with the turmeric whips (Shideler 1987, 99, 156–57 and 201, fig. 14). Here, as at Tindivanam, the blood of Aravāṉ reappears to mark the ritualists' deaths, but the addition of the rice suggests that the six are also being fed, like demons. The flagpost in the center displaces the effigy of Duryodhana: a distant reminder of the Réunion rite of the "ceremony of the pole and the five dead cousins" (chap. 8, sec. A). More specifically, the central pole transposes the symbolism of the flagstaff, linked at the temple with Pōttu Rāja and the balipīṭha as pluriforms of the yūpa, to the very middle of the ritual battlefield. And the corner posts—wrapped in margosa leaves up to a fan of spiky palm fronds, beyond which the post is unadorned—strikingly effect the image of green, arboreal versions of the vīrakuntam, the multi-tined imple-

27. Margosa is used to decorate Pōta Rāju's portable pole in the procession before an Andhra village buffalo sacrifice; Biardeau 1989b, 13. Recall also that in the Dharma gājans, the margosa, identified as Bāṇ Gosāin, is a multiform of the śamī-like gāmar tree and the Bāṇeśvar: "playing with flowers" (coals) is done before the Bāṇ Gosāin-margosa at Baruipur (Robinson 1980, 265).

ment of impalement, with an extended central prong. On the one hand, the uses of margosa and palm suggest a combination of these trees as a sacrificial grove. On the other hand, one has the more specific evocation of margosa-wrapped "tridents" surrounding a margosa-wrapped flagstaff–sacrificial post. The function of the margosa would presumably be to represent the goddess's power to mitigate the pain of the six ritualists' sacrificial deaths.[28]

C. The Revivers and the Revived

It is best to begin with the female-male combinations. Clearly, the kin relations differ: wife-husband (Kaṇṇaki and Kōvalaṉ); younger sister–elder brother (Taṅkāḷ and her brothers, Draupadī and Dhṛṣṭadyumna); mother-sons (Draupadī and the Young Pañcapāṇḍavas, Kālī and Kūttāṇṭavar); lover-sweetheart (story of Khan Sahib). But in most cases, the relationship is more than one-dimensional. The weeping Draupadī is in fact not only a mother and sister, but also a widow (her husbands are symbolically dead to her until they accomplish the destruction of Duryodhana, her defiler). Similarly, Taṅkāḷ laments her brothers as their stand-in widow. And Kaṇṇaki, at least at Pattini in Sri Lanka, not only is a wife but speaks of herself as Kōvalaṉ's mother precisely at the point when she revives him (Obeyesekere 1984, 266 and passim). In the revival of Kūttāṇṭavar, the roles that converge in these other situations are separated but are still both present: eunuchs and transvestites impersonate ViṣṇuMohinī to marry and widow him, while Kālī, who revives him, is announced as his true mother (Hiltebeitel 1988a, 326).

Thus no one of these kinship relationships exhausts the depth of the female-male rapport that is found in these various rituals and related myths. But two powerful themes are recurrent, no matter what the main kinship link. First, the lamentation by the disheveled goddess or heroine evokes the theme of widowhood. Second, despite the fact that all the female figures are real or symbolic wives, all are in some manner *virgin wives*, a symbolism that the myths and rites themselves constantly return to and reinforce at crucial moments. The classical *Cilappatikāram* is, of course, an exception. But in all other cases, including both the Tamil and Sinhalese folk versions, one finds repeated reinforcement of the virginity theme, usually in the most highly charged and paradoxical circumstances. In South Indian oral versions, "it is made clear that Kaṇṇaki never

28. This interpretation relies entirely on Shideler's description and photograph (1987, fig. 14).

knew her husband's body and perhaps never even touched him. Instead Kōvalaṉ leaves her on the very day of their wedding. . . . It is implied that she remains in this state of a pristine newlywed forever and that her special power stems from this condition" (Beck 1972b, 25). Such notions are also found in Sinhala versions of the same story; alternatively, Pattini's purity is guaranteed by Pālanga-Kōvalaṉ's impotence (Obeyesekere 1984, 230, 293, 456–470). The eunuchs and transvestites who impersonate Mohinī marry Kūttāṇṭavar only so that he will not die an unmarried bachelor; the consummation of the marriage is questionable.[29] Correspondingly complex situations safeguard the regenerative virginity of Taṅkāḷ (Beck 1982, 45) and the reviving heroines of the *Epic of Palnāḍu*.[30] Finally, mother Draupadī is unequivocally a virgin (*kaṉṉi*) in the mythology of her cult (Hiltebeitel 1988a, 8–9, 222–23, 291–95, and passim).

Although the goddess who revives may be sister, wife, or mother, in her most highly charged images, she thus combines aspects of the *virgin widow.* These two roles fuse together two of the primary identities of the goddess: the virgin Durgā and the deranged and disheveled widow Kālī. Let us recall that in Madras temples, a substitute for the paṭukaḷam rites is to adorn Draupadī as *either* Durgā or Kālī. Moreover, though these two roles may be fused, as they certainly are in the figure of Draupadī, they should not be confused.[31] Let us thus appreciate some of the ways that the goddess, in varying identities, is implicated in scenarios of revival.

First, she is featured in the intermediate role of wife and source of prosperity in the well-known iconic scene in which Viṣṇu revives the cosmos as Nārāyaṇa or Anantaśāyin ("He who reclines on the serpent Ananta"). As Viṣṇu awakens from his yogic sleep and Brahmā rises on the lotus that surges from his navel, it is Lakṣmī whom one sees pressing Viṣṇu's feet. Her position suggests itself as a variation on some of the ritual revival scenes described above: in particular, those where the attendant is, or impersonates, a woman.[32] With her mysterious gesture, one that seems to have received little comment, Lakṣmī has apparently been massaging Viṣṇu's feet, or even more commonly his ankles, as he lies on his

29. See chapter 4, n. 11.
30. See below on the roles of Māncāla and Akka Pinakka in the Palnad epic.
31. See Obeyesekere 1984, 440, 540, n. 4: a point he obscures.
32. See especially the photos of the bard as Taṅkāḷ (Beck 1982, 97); the drawing of the same scene (Beck 1975, 293a); the photo of the *kapurāla* as Pattini (Obeyesekere 1984, plate 21); and recall that at Maṅkalam the attendants include female members of the family.

serpent couch for a whole night of Brahmā or kalpa. Is she seeing to it that he only sleeps? With Viṣṇu's awakening comes the revival of the triple world. Not only is Lakṣmī the source of the triple world's prosperity, the lotus that rises from Viṣṇu's navel, with the demiurge upon it, is her earth-symbolizing flower.

The main iconic complement to this tableau is Śakti-Kālī's revival of the corpse (*śava*) of Śiva. The one is concerned with the rhythm of the kalpa and the revival of the triple world, the other with the mahākalpa and the revival of the entire universe. Here we have Kālī the widow, whose disheveled hair, as she dances over the funeral of the cosmos, is an image of the unraveling of the three strands of *prakṛti,* or matter (Hiltebeitel 1981, 210). Kālī revives Śiva by her "power" of erotic fascination, which transforms his corpse into her reanimated and sometimes sexually aroused consort. This tantric tableau, however, also has purāṇic variations in which the widow-husband rapport is transformed into that of the mother-child. Here Śiva stops Kālī's mad dance of destruction, and thus the untimely dissolution of the universe, by appearing before her in the form of a baby, whom she picks up and suckles (Shulman 1980a, 95; Dimmitt and van Buitenen 1978, 201). Draupadī cult folklore has its own variation on this theme. During her nights in exile, Draupadī assumes the "form of Kālī" and roams the forests devouring flesh, until one night, returning unsatiated, she is barred by Bhīma, and produces her children when five drops of Bhīma's blood touch the ground after her fingernails have dug into his arm. She is then pacified by her newborn children's cries of "Mother" (Hiltebeitel 1988a, 293–94). One is, of course, struck by the fact that these Young Pañcapāṇḍavas rise from the ground to recognize their mother at birth in Kālīrūpa. Similarly, it is normally the disheveled Draupadī, in the image of Kālī, whom the Young Pañcapāṇḍavas rise to see on the paṭukaḷam, just before the rebraiding of her hair.[33] Through all this, she is a virgin.

We have seen the regenerative force of the goddess's virginity, and transformation to marriageability, in the seedling ceremonies, linked with Durgā through their performance at Dasarā. In the Draupadī cult, they are clearly a temple counterpart to the rites of dying and revival on the paṭukaḷam. In this regard it is also worth recalling the alternative meaning of the five pūtams as elements. In his Tamil version of the epic, Villipputtūr compares the birth of the

33. In the Sanskrit epic, as the doomed warriors awaken to their deaths, they see a vision of the goddess Kālarātri, the destructive "Night of Time," described adjectivally as *kālī,* "black" (*Mbh.* 10.8.64–65: probably one of the earliest allusions to Kālī herself).

sons of Draupadī to the emergence of the five elements (*pūtaṅkaḷ-aintum; Villipāratam* 1.7.87) from prakṛti. The *Villipāratam* is, of course, a primary source for the pāratiyārs who recite at Draupadī festivals. One might thus suspect that the dying and rising of the five Pūtams on the paṭukaḷam has another variant, linked not with Duryodhana's guardians, but with the Young Pañcapāṇḍavas.[34] As a widow, the disheveled goddess dances through the prākṛta pralaya; as a virgin, she renews the cosmos by the asexual production of the five elements from her body (prakṛti).

Finally, let us turn to the question of *who* effects the revivals. For despite the centrality of the goddess, it is obvious that it is not a simple question. A recurrent pattern is that the revivals result from the goddess's collaboration with Kṛṣṇa or Viṣṇu. In the *Elder Brothers Story,* Taṅkāḷ revives her brothers and Cāmpukā with the help of Viṣṇu, though in this case Śiva is also involved (Beck 1975, 286–95; 1982, 39–41). In the *Epic of Palnāḍu,* Brahma Nāyuḍu, Viṣṇu incarnate, collaborates in the revivals with two virgin heroines, Māncāla (who keeps the tulasi-pearl necklace used to revive the dead in earlier episodes) and Akka Pinakka, the virginal "elder" (*akka*) sister of the previously revived Lankanna.[35] In the Kūttāṇṭavar cult, the collaboration involves a precise division of roles: it is the impersonators of Kṛṣṇa-Mohinī who lament and Kālī who revives. It is even possible that Pattini's collaboration with Indra in Buddhist Sri Lanka is a reflex of such a pattern, since Indra tends to figure in Buddhist mythology as a concentration figure for mythemes connected in Hinduism with both Viṣṇu and Śiva.[36]

The same pattern pertains to the revivals of the Young Pañcapāṇḍavas, but much more diffusely, since the mythology that supports the ceremony is so underdeveloped. It is in the Thanjavur area and its Singapore transplant that Draupadī and Kṛṣṇa collaborate most consistently on the ritual battlefield, but there it is not so much a revival as a liberation, and of different sets of heroes (chap. 10, sec. D). But core area Draupadī cult informants do sometimes have views on these matters. Of those who think revivals do take place, most said it was Draupadī who effects them, while one—the pāratiyār K. Radhakrishnan, met at Mutikai Nallāṉkuppam—said it was Kṛṣṇa. But the most reflective answer came from the Tindivanam pūcāri, who remarked with a smile that, though the song

34. Villi alters a Sanskrit epic theme in which the five elements are identified with the Pāṇḍavas (*Mbh.* 5.63.2; 12.38.37; 12.53.18).
35. I will discuss these matters further in volume 3.
36. On Śiva, see Obeyesekere 1984, 334.

he sings during the revivals is an invitation to Draupadī, it closes with an invocation of her relationship with Kṛṣṇa: "Āti-nārāyaṇaṉ taṅkaiyai tiraupatā aruṅkiḷi pāñcāliyē"—"Younger Sister of the Primal Nārāyaṇa, O Draupadī, Graceful Parrot Pāñcāli." In fact, this response presupposes a wider set of associations, drawn both from the *Mahābhārata* and from other parts of the Draupadī festival cycle, that reinforce Kṛṣṇa and Draupadī's regenerative collaboration many times over: most notably, as we have seen, in the nine grains ceremonies.[37]

There is a temptation to argue that this collaboration results from projections of a generally "epic" or "purāṇic" typology upon a prior situation in which it is the goddess who revives alone. Clearly it is in some of our older scenarios that she does so, lending some weight to the argument that her collaboration with Viṣṇu might be modeled on the Anantaśāyin myth, or on the generalized avatāra myth of the unburdening of the earth. In our oldest South Indian "revival" document, the *Cilappatikāram,* Kaṇṇaki revives Kōvalaṉ without help from any male. As Obeyesekere observes, Indra's collaboration with Pattini in the Sinhalese Buddhist revival rituals is inconsistent, leaving it "possible that Pattini directly awakening her husband is an older version of the myth" (1984, 270). Śakti is also unaccompanied in her revival of Śiva.

But as a matter of method, we must be wary of isolating one figure in Hindu mythology from the rest, and treating that one as if he or she was once the "original" center of an autonomous mythology, onto which the complexities of classical Hindu mythology and cosmology have only been superimposed. These sources do not allow us to reconstruct an "original" reviving mythology of the Indian goddess.

D. Dying and Rising Gods and the Sacrificer's Wife

Such a construct is not, however, unimaginable. Here we have one of the classic problems for a theory of diffusion, since it would be a mistake not to recognize that the revived heroes, in their cults, are "dying and rising gods." Obeyesekere has taken one route in addressing these issues in connection with the Pattini cult, the oldest version of whose story, the *Cilappatikāram,* perhaps from about A.D. 400–600,[38] he regards as our oldest source on this pattern in South Asia. In a now familiar sequence, Kaṇṇaki's lamentation mo-

37. See chapter 4. Kṛṣṇa's replenishing of Draupadī's sarees is also an image of the earth's regeneration; see Hiltebeitel 1988a, 264–65; 1980b.

38. Arguing for a later dating, see Hikosaka 1989, 83–94 (eighth century).

mentarily revives her unjustly slain husband Kōvalaṉ so that he can see and speak to her before he goes to heaven, where she will soon join him after carrying out the vengeful rectifying acts that establish her as a goddess (Dikshitar 1939, 245–70). Obeyesekere opts for an argument of diffusion from West Asia, not ruling out ancient contacts via the Indus Valley Civilization, but choosing rather to "limit the argument to continuous and intensive contact between West Asia and Kerala, so as to render plausible the hypothesis of the West Asian origin of the Pattini cult" (1984, 530–31). He further argues that Pattini is originally a Jaina-Buddhist deity, fitting his hypothesis that the diffusion from West Asia was carried out through coastal trade routes that penetrated into the "*popular* [Obeyesekere's italics] religion of the new local entrepreneurs" to be grafted onto "the worship of the goddess (if not the dying god)" that was, according to him, "a preexisting feature of Dravidian folk religion" (ibid., 531–33; quotes 533). The Jaina-Buddhist argument is buttressed by the comment that "the drama of 'death and resurrection' is alien to Hinduism," a claim supported by the admission that "as far as I know the dramatic enactment of the death and resurrection theme is not found anywhere in Hindu ritual, though the theme of the wife resurrecting her husband is found in myth" (ibid., 530).

We have now reviewed enough death and resurrection enactments to know that they are not alien to Hindu ritual. The rest of this argument is also very shaky. I leave aside the issue of whether the category of dying and rising gods is a "misnomer" for the ancient Near Eastern and Mediterranean pattern argued for by Frazer. Though Obeyesekere calls upon Frazer for background support, his argument allows for a Christian interpretation of the dying and rising theme by the time it would have allegedly influenced the Pattini cult.[39] It is still not clear what the evidence is for a preexisting Dravidian folk "mother goddess" cult, not to mention the evidence that it did *not* have dying and rising gods. As far as I know, all evidence on popular Dravidian goddess cults comes from recent centuries. Nor am I convinced that Pattini, even in the *Cilappatikāram,* can be claimed as originally Jaina-Buddhist but not Hindu: a reservation that is even more acute for the features of her cult (cf. Tarabout 1986, 612). But more to the point, we have seen that the "drama of death and resurrection" is hardly alien to Hinduism or undocumentable in Hindu ritual.[40]

39. Obeyesekere 1984, 532; J. Z. Smith argues that the category "dying and rising gods" is a "misnomer" before the *interpretatio Christiana* (1987, 521–27; 1978, 72).
40. Blackburn 1989, 22 n. 13, also finds Obeyesekere's argument "difficult to accept."

Evidence for kaḷam and paṭukaḷam rituals is, of course, relatively recent, as the cults in question have been traced back no further than the twelfth to the fifteenth century. There is also no guarantee that they included these dying and rising rituals from the beginning. One could thus argue that the Pattini cult has diffused this theme into such later cults, something that for South India cannot be disregarded as a contributing factor.[41] There is, however, an important difference between the Kaṇṇaki-Pattini tradition as we find it in the *Cilappatikāram* and the kaḷam and paṭukaḷam traditions. Whereas the *Cilappatikāram* centers its story on a hero and heroine from merchant families and is written by a Jain (all of which feeds into Obeyesekere's Jaina-Buddhist hypothesis), most kaḷam and paṭukaḷam rituals, and the epic and folk epic traditions connected with them, are centered on, and can indeed be said to belong to, landed dominant castes. Moreover, I suspect that the same could be said for the ritual reenactments of the Pattini myth in Sri Lanka, which are *village* rituals (*gammaḍuva*) with a royal prototype (Obeyesekere 1984, 34–45, 119 and passim) that contain an ideology like that in South India, where dominant-caste rituals on the village and regional level stress the rapport between kingship and the prosperity of the land. In other words, most paṭukaḷam rituals of death and revival, like the Sri Lankan gammaḍuva for Pattini, express a rapport that is difficult to explain by, or trace back to, the interests of merchants. And indeed, the *Cilappatikāram* itself is also about kings who seem to be no less Hindu than Jaina or Buddhist, and who proclaim Pattini a goddess. Here we can simply turn the tables and point out that this text is not evidence, or at least direct evidence, of a ritual.

In fact, the type of revival rituals I have been describing do seem to be linked primarily with the values of landed dominant castes rater than merchant communities. Or more accurately, to use the terminology developed by Beck (1972a, xiv–xvi, 34–35, and passim) and Narayana Rao (1986, 134–43; 1989, 113–14) in connection with the *Elder Brothers* and *Palnāḍu* folk epics, they reflect a right-handed caste ideology rather than a left-handed one.[42] This means

41. At the death of Palakan-Kōvalaṉ in Kerala, the "shelter of the muṭi" (Bhadrakālī's hair chignon) closes, and it is reopened several hours later with a song for Palakan's "resurrection" (*tōṟṟam pāṭṭu;* Tarabout 1986, 135). As in the Draupadī cult, one finds the hair tying and revival themes together. I would still stress, however, that a one-to-one Kaṇṇaki-Draupadī link is strained; see Hiltebeitel 1988a, 17 n. 11, 149, 201 n. 25. One suspects a motivation to find Dravidian epic roots for the *cult* of the allegedly "northern Aryan" Draupadī.

42. The Tiruchirappali District paṭukaḷam cult for Kālī among Kaikkōḷar or Ceṅkunta Mutaliyār weavers (Reiniche 1987, 90; chap. 7, sec. A) is no real exception. As

that it is not just a question of the dominant landed castes themselves, but of the landed ideology that relates them to various service castes, especially Untouchable laborers, and Brahmans. Left-hand communities of the merchant-artisan cluster may have folk epics and rituals of revival, but I am not aware of them.[43] Their known folk epics, however, are not linked with the land; with the revival of the young who fight and die for the land—indeed, with the revivals of whole armies who fight and die for the land;[44] or with the goddess *of* the land as the source of their regeneration. It is thus not surprising that we find the closest parallels to Draupadī cult paṭukaḷam rites in other variations on royal and dominant caste ideology: a popular Dasarā in Karnataka, and a village buffalo sacrifice in Andhra.

On Dasarā day at Devaragudda (or alternatively, in February-March at another site in the same cult), the god Mailāra's conquest of the demon Malla involves the performance of heroic feats of self-mutilation by a group from among the army of the god's "seven crores" of devotees (or alternatively, the demon's army, presumably revived). They are recruited among Kuruba Vaggayyas (the shepherd caste "tiger-dog" worshipers of Mailāra) and Māḍiga Untouchables and are called Kañcavīras, "said to be a corrupt form of pañcavīras, that is, 'five heroes,' who voluntarily cut off their heads

---

Beck shows for Kongunad, Mutaliyārs (Ceṅkunta Mutaliyārs included) have "split loyalties": though officially left, "many members of this group fought loyally for right-division kings, and were granted land in Koṅku for their heroism," leading to "right-division . . . attitudes, mannerisms, and traditions" (1972a, 101; cf. 37–39, 233, 266). Reiniche, discussing a weaver-warrior sacrificial symbolism, shows that this paṭukaḷam cult belongs to weavers in an area that was formerly a military camp (1987, 96–99). Piḷḷai Vēḷāḷars are the dominants at the paṭukaḷam ceremonies mentioned in chapter 7, n. 2.

43. One could follow up Beck 1972a, 35–40, to argue that left-hand communities are disposed toward miraculous survival, rather than revival, myths. Other revival myths familiar to me, though not centered on landed dominant-caste heroes, are still arguably expressive of "right-hand" ideology: for instance, the "Ciṉṉattampi Story," about an Untouchable cobbler hero (Nirmala Devi and Murugan 1987, 49), the thwarted revival of the demon Dārikan (Tarabout 1986, 153), or even the Paraśurāma-Rēṇukā myth (e.g., Thurston and Rangachari [1904] 1965, 7:302). For revival rituals, see ibid., 4:383, 6:38.

44. As not only with the Elder Brothers' resident army, the Heroes of Palnāḍu, and Duryodhana's army (see above, sec. B), but the army of Lausen in the Dharma cult (see chapter 7, section C and below in this section). Recall Draupadī's identity as Yākacēṉi, "she whose army is the sacrifice"; the vēlakaḷi danced combat at Trivandrum as a sacrifice of the "revived" Kaurava army before Padmanabhaswamy-Nārāyaṇa; the "parades of edifices" as offerings of the army (chap. 7, sec. B), and hints at Duryodhana's own revival (chap. 10, n. 1; above n. 2). Cf. Tarabout 1986, 31, on the "sacrifice of a multitude."

in front of the god" (Sontheimer 1989a, 318). The most important among them must be twelve years old and unmarried. According to Sontheimer, the explanation of the name recalls "the tradition of Mhaskobā in Maharashtra where the god demanded as proof of faith the five immature children of the founder of the cult," whom the deity saved by turning them into lambs.[45]

Again, at a village buffalo sacrifice in Cuddapah District, Andhra, after two buffaloes have been sacrificed to the village goddesses Peddamma and Chinnamma,

> One is cut open, and some of the flesh is cooked near the shrine. Part of it, with some cholam [boiled millet, soaked with the buffalo's blood] offered before the images, is given to five Māla [i.e., Untouchable] children called Siddhulu, i.e., holy or sinless, who, in some cases, are covered with a cloth during the meal. (Thurston and Rangachari [1904] 1965, 4:334)

It is especially the Draupadī cult affinities that are striking in these two cases: rituals, or at least myths, of death and revival by groups of five pure youths around a fallen demon or buffalo; ritualists from either the landed dominant caste itself (the Draupadī cult Vaṉṉiyars) or the Untouchable groups who serve them and would have traditionally fought beside them in their armies. The Elder Brothers and Palnad Heroes' cults include roles for members of both groups, as do the Tiruchirappalli area paṭukaḷam rites for Māriyammaṉ.

With such considerations as these, we can pose an explanation of why Draupadī cult paṭukaḷam ceremonies include dying and rising rituals for the Young Pañcapāṇḍavas mainly in parts of the core area where Vaṉṉiyars are more dominant, modify them west of that area, where the Vaṉṉiyar population thins out, and replace them in urban and extracore areas with transformations into sword-pressing and bestowals of mokṣa. It is because those who transplanted the Draupadī cult away from its Vaṉṉiyar matrix either were not Vaṉṉiyars, and modified the rite, or were Vaṉṉiyars but were in areas where they could not retain their status as dominant landed castes. It is where Vaṉṉiyars *could* retain that position that the rites had the most profound meaning because of their ties to the land. Away from the core area, the paṭukaḷam rites are thus re-

45. Sontheimer 1989a, 317–18 (and above, chap. 8, sec. A, end). A version of the beheading of the five Pāṇḍava children much like the Draupadī cult version is found in the related Khaṇḍobā cult (ibid., 337 n. 70).

placed by others—some that we have met already, and others that I will describe in chapter 13. Paṭukaḷam rituals of dying and rising can thus be said to have diffused from one kaḷam cult to another, but not within such cults (at least in the case of the Draupadī cult) beyond their core areas.

In revisiting Indian "dying and rising gods," we thus reach the same conclusions we did in revisiting Indian "gardens of Adonis." Ancient Near Eastern, Dravidian, and tribal continuities are possible, but are yet to be made compelling. However, it is possible to identify significant continuities within Hinduism. Moreover, in each case it is not just a matter of classical and folk forms, but of Vedic ones. In the case of the sprouting rituals, the main Vedic prototype was found in the *devasū* offerings, the quickly sprouting plants that form part of the preliminaries to the royal consecration within the Rājasūya. Let us now take a look at death and revival within the Vedic sacrifice.

Within the prototypical Vedic animal sacrifice, there is a sequence known as the *paripaśavya* oblation ("those surrounding, related to the victim" [Vogel 1910–11, 47]) that, as far as I have found, has received remarkably little scholarly attention.[46] Let us follow the description in the *Śatapatha Brāhmaṇa* and then note some instructive variations in the later *Śrautasūtra* literature.

After the śamitar has announced that the animal, the exemplary goat, has been "quieted" by strangulation or suffocation at the śamitar's shed (śāmitra), the adhvaryu says to one of his assistants, "'Neṣṭṛ, lead the lady!' The Neṣṭṛ leads up the (sacrificer's) wife bearing a vessel of water for washing the feet" (*ŚB* 3.8.2.1).[47] Having brought her to the śāmitra, the neṣṭṛ instructs her to address a series of *yajus* formulas: first to the victim, identifying him as the "wide-stretched" sacrifice, to propitiate him; then urging him to "advance unresisted" and "free from injury" on heavenly paths to the "rivers of ghee"; and then purifying the water in her vessel by invoking the waters to prepare the victim's way to the gods (*ŚB* 3.8.2.2–3):

> 4. Thereupon the wife cleanses with the water the (openings of the) vital airs of the victim. The reason why she thus cleanses

46. See the brief discussions in Schwab 1886, 110–11; Vogel 1910–11, 47 ("optional"); Keith [1925] 1971, 2:325; Chaudhuri 1940, 77–78; Thite 1975, 150, 197; Malamoud 1989, 217.

47. Eggeling [1882] 1966, 2:190, quoted but with the Sanskrit transliterated as elsewhere in this volume.

> with water the (openings of the) vital airs is this: the food of the gods is living, is immortal (ambrosia) for the immortals; but in quieting and cutting up the victim they kill it. Now the vital airs are water; hence she now puts into it those vital airs, and thus that food of the gods becomes truly living, becomes immortal for the immortals. (Eggeling [1882] 1966, 2:191)

It is explained that the sacrificer's wife does the cleansing because, since women bring forth progeny, the neṣṭṛ can cause the victim to be born from her (5), a process that then takes place:

> 6. With (*Vājasaneyi Saṃhitā* 6.14) "Thy speech I cleanse" she wipes the mouth; with "Thy breath I cleanse," the nostrils . . . [so on with the eye, ear, navel, penis, and hind part]. Thus she puts vital airs into it, revives it. Thereupon, holding the legs together, (she wipes them) with "Thy feet I cleanse"; for it is on its feet that it stands firmly; she thus makes it stand (on its feet) for the sake of a firm position. (Eggeling [1882] 1966, 2:191–92)

As the opening stanza indicates, it is above all the washing of the feet that is important. Reborn from the sacrificer's wife, the "stretched out" victim is imagined to stand up: "His resurrection is a new birth" (Malamoud 1989, 217: "Sa résurrection est une nouvelle naissance"). The adhvaryu and yajamāna (or in some readings the wife and yajamāna) then continue "to put the vital airs into it and revive it" (*ŚB* 3.8.2.9; Eggeling [1882] 1966, 2:192) by using some of the remaining water to sprinkle the victim "from the head" with yajus for his mind, speech, breath, eye, and ear, and then they finally pour out the last of the water behind him. The sprinkling renders the victim pure and soothes and heals the cuts that the śamitar can now begin to make in his role as butcher (7–11). It is presumably the goat's resurrected form that does not suffer the pain.

The *Śrautasūtra*s show the different authorities quite divided on the extent of the wife's role. *Baudhāyana* has the wife pour out the remaining water as well as make the earlier sprinklings, and it also indicates that after the last of the water is poured the adhvaryu's assistant (the pratiprasthātṛ now instead of the neṣṭṛ) leads her back to her seat (Kashikar and Dandekar 1962, 818; Kashikar 1958, 996). *Bhāradvāja* registers a controversy: "The sacrificer's wife should make the breaths (that is, the various limbs) of the animal swell, and the adhvaryu should pour down water (upon them). According to some teachers [however], the adhvaryu should make the breaths swell and the sacrificer's wife should pour down water" (Kashikar and Dandekar 1962, 821). *Mānava,* for instance, speaks for the second option (ibid., 825). *Āpastamba* has the adhvaryu's assistant (pratiprasthātṛ) say the early yajus formulas rather than the wife (ibid., 823). And several authorities, in what seems to be the basic drift of the changing times that these texts reflect, mention no role for the wife at all (ibid., 826–28). One can hardly doubt that the wife's role is diminished by the controversies and equivocations over who makes the breaths and the limbs, one after another, "swell" (*ā-pyai*). Not only is the goat supposed to stand up, but so is its penis. As *Āpastamba* makes clear, each of the goat's limbs, including the penis, should be made to swell (*āpyāyatām*) by the recitation of the appropriate formula—said now by the pratiprasthātṛ (ibid., 823). But *Kātyāyana,* following *Śatapatha Brāhmaṇa,* recalls that the wife speaks the formula while washing the penis (ibid., 827). The simmering scandal here should remind us of the famous moment in the Aśvamedha sacrifice when the king's chief wife cohabits with the slain horse. That scene is but a rich and royal elaboration of this one, as will be clear shortly. But before we turn to the horse sacrifice to close this chapter, let us examine a case that might make the path between the Vedic goat sacrifice and hero cult revival rituals shorter and clearer.

The Dharma gājans of Bengal have inspired a literature, the *Dharma Mangals*, that is so rich in themes of "death and 'revivification'" as to have inspired two studies on the subject by Robinson (1976; 1980, 20–48, 227–28). Among the revived, we have already noted Lausen himself, his mother Rañjāvatī, his foe Icchāi Ghōṣ, and his army of Ḍom soldiers. It is once again the revival of Lausen and his army that interests us, now for their connection with the ritual of the loue bali, or sacrifice of the loue goat.

Recall that when Lausen cuts off his head as the final gesture of his nine-part sacrifice, the severed head cries out for the sun to rise in the west. Dharma responds (in one local account in the form of Nārāyaṇa) first by reviving Lausen, and then by granting him two boons: the miraculous sunrise, and the revival of his army. Now, at the Birsinha Dharma gājan, Lausen's sacrifice, reenacted with a prone effigy of rice that is first cut in nine places and then covered with a red cloth, is co-orchestrated with the sacrifice of the black loue goat to Dharma and the smaller black kol loue goat to Kālī, with Kālī giving ritual permission for both (see chap. 9, sec. C):

> A woman devotee has to perform those rites and bear the expenses. They are carried out for the birth of a son. In view of

> the expenses and the poverty of the villagers, there was some difficulty in getting a woman to act as "mother" of the Loue as this devotee is termed. In the old days women would beg for this honor and many were disappointed. A son was said to be born if the rites were correctly performed (leaving an ample loophole in case of disappointment). The name given to the son was Luidhar, Lāusen or the like. . . . The people who join the rite say that the name is given as the son has been obtained by taking the Loue on the lap. (Chattopadhyay 1942, 117–18)

Here Chattopadhyay makes the point, cited earlier (chap. 9, sec. C.; cf. Robinson 1980, 243), that Lausen's name is etymologically linked with that of the loue goat.

In 1939 the "'mother' of the Loue" came to Birsinha from a distant village, joined by her husband, who was initiated like other bhaktas. They each fasted, eating vegetarian food only, on the penultimate day, and joined in processions. At sunset the bhaktas surrounded her by making an enclosure with their canes and led her to a body of water for a purifying bath (Chattopadhyay 1942, 119). This sunset immersion is tied in with the theme of revival, which will be ritually played out with the next two sunrises. In this regard, the bhaktas' enclosure of canes deserves special notice. In the Bhaktapur Śiva gājan, canes (*beṭ*)—made from saplings of gāmār, bel, or margosa, rubbed with oil and turmeric and passed down through the generations—are struck together over the spiked pāṭā board, with the pāṭbhakta lying on it, to make a sound that breaks Śiva's meditation and induces a "joyful" trance among the dancing bhaktas surrounding the pāṭā on its procession (Östör 1980, 138). At Dharma gājans, "the *beṭ* is the weapon of the bhaktas of Lausen's army; it is the magical stick that resuscitates" (Robinson 1980, 361). A ritual called *Bhakta marā*, "Dead Bhaktas"—now defunct at two villages where it was recalled—was said to reenact this revival of Lausen's army: the devotees would lie down "forming a human chain along the path between the two villages," and the priest would "walk over and among them, touching their heads with a cane (*beṭ*) whereupon they would rise up" (ibid., 367). The similarities to Draupadī cult rites and the row of dead warriors on the Elder Brothers paṭukaḷam are evident. Indeed, at Birsinha, there is another variant of this rite that looks closer in still other ways to Draupadī cult ceremonies. Come morning, just before Lausen's sacrifice is enacted and recited, three men will lie in rectangular pits, six feet long by three feet wide and one foot deep, undergoing rites of tongue piercing "to emulate Lausen." It was also said at Birsinha in 1939 that a gāmār branch used to be cut and fixed by the blacksmith with iron nails, to be "pressed against the chest" at this time (Chattopadhyay 1942, 120–23), another variant of katti cēvai.

After the tongue-piercing ceremony for the men in the pits and the reenactment of Lausen's nabakhaṇḍa, the sacrifice of the loue and the kol loue is offered to Dharma and Kālī. Most of the details of the slayings are conventional for "village" goat sacrifices. While an oil lamp is lit, the head of the loue goat is placed in an earthen pot with five fruits and five precious items in its mouth. The pot is covered with a lid, and the lamp, representing the loue's life, is set on top of it. Then it placed on the lap of the loue's mother. After the kol loue is offered to Kālī, a Śrotriya Brahman performs a homa "on behalf of the 'mother of Loue' at her expense." At evening, hearing songs of the loue's resuscitation, she is then taken to the Dharma temple to sit—still bearing the pot—facing a floor design representing Dharma's "house." "The husband and the Paṇḍits remained outside the door. As the night ended and the day began to dawn, the woman asked, 'Bābā Loue, have you awakened?' The form of address was that used towards a son in endearment. The head responds, it is said, by waving its ears so that they may strike the head, and the sides of the pot with a tapping sound." The ceremony closes when the woman carries the pot on her head, with the lamp closed inside it while still burning, to a tank and immerses it. "On return, the he-goat for the next ceremony"—that is, the next loue goat—is set free to "graze at will, unmolested for the next few years" (Chattopadhyay 1942, 124–26).

To be sure, the mode of goat sacrifice and revival is decidedly un-Vedic. I propose, however, that beheading, which in general may be said to mark the main distinction between the Vedic sacrifice and sacrifices to the goddess, is also the point around which continuities between these two sacrificial systems would be rearranged. The revival, instead of taking place after the animal's suffocation and before it is cut, must occur after it is beheaded, as with Lausen himself. In the case of the loue goat, it must be the head that is revived rather than the whole goat. And instead of the fertilizing rite's being focused on the male organ, it is focused on the woman's lap (like Kālī's lap for Aravāṉ's head at Cattiram Karuppūr) and the pot, which is presumably a symbol of her womb and the awakening of the child within it. Beyond this, however, there are a few features of the loue bali that do have a Vedic look: the requirement that a woman perform the rites of revival, and the goat's freedom to wander at will before its sacrifice. To explore these parallels further, we must look beyond the Vedic goat sacrifice to the Aśvamedha.[48]

Let us start off by noting that when the Aśvamedha horse is directed toward the northeast and set free to wander for the year before its sacrifice, it has a protective escort of four hundred young men: a hundred princes or sons of the king (*rājaputrāḥ*), a hundred Kṣatriyas (*rājanyāḥ*), a hundred sons of bards and village headmen (*sūtagrāmaṇyām putrāḥ*), and a hundred sons of attendants (*kṣattar*) and charioteers (*saṃgrahītar*) (P.-E. Dumont 1927, 37). Their main charges are to see to it that the horse does not couple with a mare and that it is not taken by enemies (ibid., iii). The escort, in other words, is a miniature army. This escort finds its exact complement during the Aśvamedha's elaborations of the wife's foot-washing and limb-swelling "revival" of the sacrificial animal. When the neṣṭṛ leads the sacrificer-king's four richly appareled queens, plus a young girl (*kumārī*) as the fifth, toward the suffocated horse, the queens are accompanied by four hundred maids: the chief wife (*mahiṣī*) by a hundred princesses or daughters of the king; the favorite wife (*vāvatā*) by a hundred Kṣatriya girls (*rājanyās*), the discarded wife (*parivṛktā*) by a hundred daughters of bards and village headmen, and the least respected or lower-caste wife (*pālāgalī*) by a hundred daughters of attendants and charioteers (ibid., 16–17, 180–81; for variants see Chaudhuri 1940, 84).

The four women and the girl carry pitchers containing "foot-washing" (*pannejanī*) waters. The neṣṭṛ first makes the wives recite the customary formulas for the animal sacrifice, summarized above, and then the formula special for the Aśvamedha: "Mother! Little mother! Dear little mother. No one leads me!—The little horse sleeps—(No one leads me), the fair one attired in Kāmpīla" (*ambe ambike 'mbālike na mā nayati kaścana sasaty aśvakaḥ subhadrīkām kāmpīlavāsinīm*). The four wives then circumambulate the horse nine times, alternating directions twice and fanning it: according to Dumont, either with fans, or with the ends of their garments (according to *Baudhāyana Śrautasūtra* 15.29, with a golden fan held by the mahiṣī [P.-E. Dumont 1927, 337]). Then, back in the manner of the typical animal sacrifice, they purify the horse's vital breaths, sprinkling water on the limbs to swell them, then do the same to the numerous other suffocated victims. It is only after this that the most

48. Positing a "tribal" loue bali before Brahmanization, see Robinson 1980, 243–45. At a South Kanara hog sacrifice, at the place prepared for cutting up the animals, "at first ladies rubbed the body [of each hog] all over with turmeric" (Parpola 1989, 22).

famous part of the rite occurs: unique to the Aśvamedha, but with its obvious counterpart in the "scandal" of the normal animal sacrifice. The chief queen lies near the horse, invoking its power to produce an embryo. She and the horse are then covered with a cloth by the adhvaryu, and beneath the cloth she spreads her thighs, takes the horse's member, and places it in her vagina, calling for the "vigorous male" to emit semen. Then, after the sacrificer-king enjoins the horse to do the same, the priests, wives, and young girl exchange a series of crude insults. Only the young girl, however, speaks for herself, in answer to the first insult, which comes from the adhvaryu.[49] According to most schools, the insults addressed to the four wives are responded to, as if in chorus, by their maids. After the women return to their place, or after the mahiṣī rises, the male participants, or alternatively all the participants, then "utter a purifying stanza" (cf. P.-E. Dumont 1948, 484). Finally, each of the three primary wives takes 101 needles—the mahiṣī golden ones, the favorite silver ones, and the discarded wife copper or lead ones—to mark off the "paths of the knife" (*asipathān*). That is, they pierce the horse's skin with them, tracing the lines by which the śamitar will then cut the victim. The 303 needles, quite a striking image on the horse's body, are said to represent the union of the people (*viś*) with the royal power, the multiformity of the regions of space, the sacrificer's bridge to heaven, and a means "to know (the way) to the heavenly world" (P.-E. Dumont 1948, 483).[50]

At this point, let me formulate a working hypothesis. It seems that with the discontinuation of Vedic animal sacrifices, the prestige of the Aśvamedha as the royal animal sacrifice par excellence—the one that most clearly ties together the rapport between the king, his army, and the prosperity and fertility of royal line, land,

49. Parpola (in press, sec. 3.2.8) observes that only the "archaic *Vādhūlasūtra*" informs us of the full role of this "virgin." After the mahiṣī wipes a blade of grass that is cut at both ends on the part of her body "where the member of the stallion is placed," she throws it on the virgin (a Kṣatriyā or Vaiśyā) saying, "I pierce you with the burning of sexual union." "From the sequel, which is somewhat corrupt, it appears that she now enters the playing-hall (*sabhā*), i.e., becomes a prostitite." The same sūtra also mentions a male youth (*kumāra*), also a virgin, who "in ancient times" slaughtered the horse: "He was led to the place adorned and with lamentation (*rudantaḥ*), for he was to die: his head fell severed" (Parpola in press, sec. 3.2.4; P.-E. Dumont 1927, 371–72). I would not go so far as Parpola, however, to identify this lamented youth with Ishtar's Dumuzi.

50. Unless otherwise cited, summarizing P.-E. Dumont 1927, 175–83, mainly from *Vājasaneyi Saṃhitā* and *Śatapatha Brāhmaṇa;* see also O'Flaherty 1988, 15–18, translating the insults into something besides Latin and Greek; Malamoud 1989, 216 on the "paths of the knife."

and people—enabled its fractured fragments to survive, transformed and recontextualized, in rituals that translate the same rapport into other terms, royal (Dasarā), as well as regional (hero cults) and local (village buffalo and goat sacrifices).[51] I will discuss what I feel is the best Draupadī cult evidence for such continuities in the next chapter. In connection with rites of revival, it is not so much the Draupadī cult rites themselves that hold distinctive analogies, but the class of revival rites to which they belong.

There is every reason to suspect that there is indeed a continuity from the mysterious revival of the Vedic sacrificial animal, and its symbolism, to the ideology of resuscitation that one finds expressed in so many later Hindu rituals, myths, and icons. The role of the sacrificer's wife, and especially the king's four wives in the Aśvamedha, abounds in resonances that recur in these contexts. Not only is she the wife, she is the mother, or the "three mothers." In the Aśvamedha, the horse, identified with both the royal yajamāna and the god Prajāpati, imparts through the wives, and the mahiṣī in particular, a mysterious embryo that takes the form of "progeny and cattle" for the king and his kingdom (P.-E. Dumont 1927, 178; *ŚB* 13.2.8.5). Dumont even refers to the mahiṣī as "the 'sakti' of the god [Prajāpati], that is, the feminine form of the divine power, and the 'sakti' of the king, that is, the feminine form of the royal power" (1927, xii; my translation).

Moreover, the Vedic goat and horse, and the kol loue of the Dharma gājan, are revived only momentarily. Similarly, one repeatedly hears that folk epic heroes are revived only briefly, vouchsafed their return from death for only a few words, or eye contact, with the reviver. What is important is that the victim is made whole before his ascent to heaven: a far cry, by the way, from the dying and rising gods of the ancient world, whose revival is supposedly "seasonal" and without such a heavenly aftermath. The making whole, however, differs, as does the role of the reviver, or revivers. Whereas the suffocated Vedic goat can stand on its feet before it is butchered (there is no mention of the horse's doing this in the Aśvamedha), the folk epic hero, like the loue goat, must some-

51. Cf. Biardeau 1989a, 23–28; 1989b, 184–95; Tarabout 1986, 470. The equivalent rite, the "calling of the mother" or "mothers" (*ammai aḻaittal*), takes place at the endpoint of a procession of the buffalo and the mare, symbolically married, to the northeast (Biardeau 1989a, 24; 1989b, 185). This, the initial direction for the wanderings of the sacrificial horse (P.-E. Dumont 1927, iii), is the "unconquerable" (*aparājitā*) direction according to *Aitareya Brāhmaṇa* 1.14, and later a frequent direction from the capital for the śamīpūja of Dasarā, which is connected with the worship of the goddess as Aparājitā (Biardeau 1981a, 226; Parpola in press, sec. 3.1.3).

how be reassembled, as in the case mentioned earlier of Brahma Nāyuḍu and the dismembered Lankanna.

Most intriguing in this regard are the instances where the heroine, along with using other means mentioned earlier, revives the hero by sewing his body back together, severed head and all. This occurs in Tamil folk versions of the *Cilappatikāram* (Arunachalam 1976, 30–31, 119) and the *Elder Brothers Story.* In a chapbook version of the latter, Taṅkāḷ stitches up both of her twin brothers (ibid., 175), while in the oral version translated by Beck, though she intends to sew up both of them, only the younger's revival is described (1975, 293–95). In asking Śiva for the boon to revive them, she says, "I must have the boon to use the golden thread with the golden needle." It may not be enough to say that the "needle seems to be a metaphor for the body and the thread for his life" (ibid., n. 2), or that the "trick" of restoring life in this fashion and then withdrawing it by removing the sutures reflects a "primitive popular belief" (Arunachalam 1976, 31). With her golden needle, Taṅkāḷ, who takes on aspects of mother (the name Pārvatī) and widow in this episode, may remind us of the golden needles of the mahiṣī, who, with the two other queens, marks out the "paths of the knife." Some texts, in fact, say that the mahiṣī's golden needles are for the forepart of the horse, including the head (Chaudhuri 1940, 87). One need only posit an inversion of a type often found in survivals of rituals in myths: the needles, which trace the lines of cutting before the horse's dismemberment, would be recollected by the needle and thread that sew the body together after it has been dismembered: the closing act of a revival ritual transformed into a revival myth.

Such possibilities are only tantalizing, but they are cumulative. In the Sri Lankan ritual drama of "Killing and Resurrection," when Kaṇṇaki revies Pālanga, "She created a pond of ambrosia that day / She wetted the end of her shawl with it / Brought blessing on all by *fanning*" (Obeyesekere 1984, 272; my italics). In the Aśvamedha, "the little horse sleeps," under a blanket. The recurrent collaborations of the goddess and Viṣṇu are also reminiscent of the alternating collaborations between the sacrificer's wife (or wives) and the adhvaryu (either himself or through his assistants). Kṛṣṇa is identified as the adhvaryu priest in the *Mahābhārata*'s "sacrifice of weapons" (*Mbh.* 5.139.29; Hiltebeitel 1976, 15), and it is above all the tradition of the adhvaryu's Veda, the *Yajur Veda,* and especially the *Śatapatha Brāhmaṇa,* the adhvaryu's manual, that exalts Viṣṇu as the sacrifice (see, e.g., Biardeau, in Biardeau and Malamoud 1976, 89–90).

Finally, it is worth thinking about the Aśvamedha as a ritualized war, and about the destiny of the miniature army that constitutes the horse's escort. Though the ritual texts underplay this aspect, it is clear that the escort was frequently expected to use force, and that by reputation the Aśvamedha was "much like a war during its important phases" (Biardeau 1989a, 25). In particular, the Aśvamedha that the Pāṇḍavas perform, so soon after the *Mahābhārata* war, is replete with violent encounters between the escort, led by Arjuna, and the heirs of the kings whom the Pāṇḍavas had defeated at Kurukṣetra. In fact, it is amid these encounters, rather than in the horse sacrifice proper, that the *Mahābhārata*'s Aśvamedha gives us a revival scenario, a matter I will return to in volume 3. For the present, however, the *Mahābhārata* shows us that the combats fought while protecting the horse are not perfunctory. The escort would have suffered casualties; there would not be four hundred returnees. But there are four hundred maids from the same precise classes and occupation groups who form the chorus of the four queens in the exchange of insults over the revived horse. I propose that it is not reading too much into this ritual to suggest that they too share in the revivification of this rite. They contribute the reviving feminine element to the "kumāra or youth function" of an early ritual of battle. In complementing the number of young warriors who had left with the horse, which must surely have been higher than the number that returned, their symbolic function is to represent the restoration, the potential revival, of this miniature army of young men.

12 Thighs and Hair

Core area paṭukaḷam rites involving Duryodhana's effigy have now been sufficiently detailed. We can thus turn to the problems of interpretation that they raise. Certain things are striking. For one, while the death and revival rites that coincide with them are illuminated by parallels from local goddess cults, regional folk epics, and hero cults, it is far less common to find effigy rites in such sources.[1] Duryodhana's effigy calls for different comparative strategies. Second, the rites over Duryodhana's effigy are distinctive for their combination of activities concerning his thigh and Draupadī's hair. We must look further into other uses of these symbols, particularly in rituals. Finally, we have noted festivals, particularly in urban settings, in which the tying of Draupadī's hair involves only her icon, and no effigy, and for that matter, no paṭukaḷam. We must also discuss one more effigyless variant in which the hair tying follows rituals in a fort: a setting that in turn will being us back to our discussion of the paṭukaḷam as a transposed Kālī temple.

A. Duryodhana's Thighs

The general hypothesis that I will pursue here is that effigy rites involving thighs and hair have a royal character. It appears to be a symbolism that goes back to Ṛg Vedic portrayals of the king of the gods:

> Thou, O Indra, lovest our rites; thou tramplest down those that revile thee; thou, vigorous hero, guard thyself in thy vital parts [literally thighs (*ūrvoḥ*)]; thou hast smitten the Dāsa with thy blows. (*ṚV* 8.70.10, cited and translated in Parpola 1984, 226)

1. The only instance I know of is Lausen's effigy (chap. 9, sec. C).

Ritually speaking, however, we can return to where we left off in chapter 11, with the Aśvamedha, noting that in this case we are dealing not with an elaboration on a more general sacrificial theme (as with the revival of the animal), but with a feature of Vedic ritual that is especially important to this royal rite. Outside the White Yajur Veda school, whose texts supplied our main guide through the Aśvamedha's revival rites, we find that Black Yajur Veda texts mention something additional going on in the very midst of these same activities.

In *Āpastamba Śrautasūtra* 20.17.12–18.7, as the mahiṣī recites the Aśvamedha formula about the three mothers, the pratiprasthātṛ leads the sacrificer's wives around the horse. First the queens take up and tie the hair on the right side of their heads, untie the hair on the left side, strike their right thighs, and fan the horse with the end of their garments, circumambulating it from left to right (in the direction of the path of the sun, or a pradakṣiṇa). Then, going three times in the opposite direction, they reverse all this: hair loosened on the right, tied on the left, striking the left thigh, and not fanning. Finally, they reverse direction again and do as they did on the first three circuits. Then follows the mahiṣī's cohabitation with the horse, the exchange of obscenities, and the needles to mark the "paths of the knife" (P.-E. Dumont 1927, 275–77). *Vādhūla Śrautasūtra* (fragment 90) keeps the three-times-three circuits of the horse but has them undertaken in turn by the three main queens independently, with variations on the treatment of the thighs and hair. On the first-round pradakṣiṇas, the mahiṣī, followed by her maids, keeps to the same order with the thighs, slapping her right one, but reverses the treatment of the hair, loosening it on her right. Then the favorite wife, maids in train, does the opposite. And finally the discarded wife, maids behind her, loosens her hair on both sides and strikes both thighs (ibid., 370–71). Finally, *Baudhāyana Śrautasūtra* 15.29 mentions that the mahiṣī, maids in tow, unties her hair, presumably all of it, but says nothing about her thighs. The favorite and discarded wives then are said simply to do the same. Here, however, we learn that after each has made her three circuits, they stop at the horse's north, after which an enclosure is made around the horse with an opening from the northern side, through which the mahiṣī is then led to the north side of the horse for their cohabitation. Significantly, in this text it is emphasized that she should express her spite or chagrin (*nihnuvānām*) (ibid., 337–38).

Already we see some remarkable convergences. The alternating of the different sides of the queens' hair reminds us that Draupadī often ties, unties, and then reties her hair on the paṭukaḷam. More than this, her final hair tying is often complemented by the appearance of the disheveled Kaurava mothers and widows, whose hair is thus untied at the close of the rite like the discarded wife in the *Vādhūla Śrautasūtra.* The alternating of the thighs is also instructive. While there is no thigh slapping on the paṭukaḷam, there is in the drama that sets its ritual stage. In performed versions of "Eighteenth-Day War," Kṛṣṇa, who is after all only reminding Bhīma of how he must fulfill his own and Draupadī's vows, slaps his *right* thigh to show how Bhīma should end his duel with Duryodhana.[2] And of course Duryodhana's effigy is struck on the right thigh either by Bhīma (an actor) with his mace or by a temple officiant with what is ultimately the goddess's sword. One can also infer that the striking of the *left* thigh in the middle three circuits of the horse is associated, at least in *Āpastamba,* with themes of inauspiciousness (reverse circumambulation; probably hair loosened on the right, tied on the left) and death (no fanning). This accords with a double tradition in the Sanskrit epic. Bhīma breaks both of Duryodhana's thighs, recalling the queens' slapping of both thighs. But Duryodhana's death results from his having bared his left thigh to Draupadī at the dice match (Hiltebeitel 1988a, 418 n. 34; Biardeau 1989b, 98). We shall return to the problem of the right and left thighs shortly. Finally, in *Baudhāyana,* the chagrined and disheveled mahiṣī enters the sacrificial enclosure from the north just as Draupadī does the paṭukaḷam. Indeed, at Mēlaccēri, where the royal Gingee connections can be said to be strongest, Draupadī is carried on her chariot with Arjuna and Subhadrā: the mahiṣī, the true king, and the "favorite."

Were these convergences limited to only these two settings, they could be dismissed as coincidental. We have already caught glimpses, however, of similar elements in Kerala: in Southern Travancore, blood offerings with the elevation of the goddess's disheveled muṭi, held *facing south,* like Draupadī entering the paṭukaḷam and the disheveled mahiṣī entering the horse's enclosure from the north; in Central Travancore, the parades of horse "edifices" (which Tarabout treats as substitute horse sacrifices, representing the offering of the warrior class) combined with the impersonation of Duryodhana, chief of the goddess's army, dancing on one leg.[3] It would be enough to see these as fragments of the same Aśvamedha scenario,

2. In classical epic sources (Sanskrit and Tamil), and even in the chapbook version of the play, the gesture is Arjuna's (Hiltebeitel 1988a, 417–18).

3. See chapter 7, section B: also on the horse sacrifice and parades of horse edifices linked with the *Mahābhārata,* Tarabout 1986, 483, 488–91, 503, 521–22.

dispersed into a variety of "royal" Nāyar rites. But there is also an instance where the horses, hair, and thigh rites are connected.

In the southeastern part of the ancient province of Valluvanad in central Travancore, a type of festival occurs in which the grounds are laid out as a sort of war stage to reenact a historic regional battle in which the local rāja was defeated by the Zamorin of Calicut.[4] The two armies are represented by rows of horse and bull "edifices" and elephants. In the example observed by Tarabout, adjacent temples of Kālī-Bhagavati and Śiva face this terrain from the north, looking south, the goddess's temple being the one that is most active for the festival (Tarabout 1986, 498–501). After various preliminaries, a zone is cleared out in the middle of the grounds, and a man, garlanded around the neck, tours this space striking his right thigh while running and making a plaintive cry of "ayayoo," referring to a local myth in which this cry is made by the goddess (ibid., 501–2, 509). Then, after the goddess's long-haired, disheveled male oracles (*veḷiccappāṭu*) touch their swords to the stretchers that bear the horses, a "game of the horses" (*kutira kali*) begins, in which each faction agitates the horses one at a time, beginning with the one on each side identified as the "king," offering them before the goddess and the flagpost outside the Śiva temple (ibid., 509–10). This is then followed by a series of cortèges. In one, the women in a procession of Ceṟuman agriculturalist Untouchables perform a dance resembling a movement called *muṭiyāṭṭam*, "the dance of the head-dress (*coiffe*)," in which they whirl about with loosened hair, betokening feminine possession, and make the goddess's cry of "ayayoo" (ibid., 514–15). In another, the two central elephants each carry a mobile image of a goddess made of a metallic mirror surrounded by a fan of folded fabric, which Tarabout compares to the muṭi I described earlier (ibid., 515). After the succession of ritual dishevelments,[5] this seems to introduce the note of bound-up hair. Finally, at dawn, the horse offerings and thigh-slapping routines are done one more time, closing the festival (ibid., 520).

Tarabout sees the treatment of the horses as an echo of the Aś-

4. See Tarabout 1986, 427–38, stressing a "convergence profonde" between the role of Valluvanad in the Māmānkaṃ festival and the *uccāral* festival there for the earth's menstruation. Whereas the duodecennial Māmānkam renewed the kingdom and its royal allegiances and tenures, the uccāral, occurring in the same period, involves more local alliances and echoes the royal festival with mock battles involving parades of edifices.

5. As part of the sequence of parades of edifices, a small cortège of Parayan Untouchables carries a sort of "*coiffe*" or muṭi (Tarabout 1986, 509).

vamedha. As he says, "The edifices are offerings: the sacrificial logic is maintained, in the devotional frame" (ibid., 496; my translation). But he oddly makes no such connection for the thigh slapping and the alternate treatments—disheveled and tied—of the hair. More than likely, they are part of this same transposition. In particular, the gestures with the hair and thighs, whether enacted by men or women, are those of the goddess, uttered with her plaintive cry, and seem to devolve upon her from the king's wives, especially the mahiṣī, in the Aśvamedha. Repeatedly we find these affinities between the mahiṣī and the goddess, particularly in her inauspicious and sacrificially destructive forms (cf. Biardeau, in Biardeau and Malamoud 1976, 149; Parpola in press, sections 3.1.3, 3.2.6). Moreover, the Aśvamedha itself is an invitation to combat between armies, with the possibility that two kings could offer rival Aśvamedhas at the same time, as the double parades of edifices, with two horse "kings," seem to recall.[6] The main things that separate these Kerala rites from those of the Draupadī cult are thus that they commemorate a local war rather than the *Mahābhārata* and that two kings are offered in the form of horses rather than one king in the form of an effigy.

For such fragments of Vedic royal ritual to have survived as an ensemble in the festivals of regionally dominant castes is plausible in itself. But the rapport is strengthened by similar echoes in the intermediary, and prototypically royal, rituals of Navarātri-Dasarā and their variants of Durgā pūjā and Rām Līlā. In fact, it has become almost fashionable lately to invoke connections between the Aśvamedha and Dasarā, at least with the buffalo sacrifice.[7] One recent perspective on this subject bears special notice.

Parpola has attempted to show that the Dāsas or Dasyus, mentioned frequently in the *Ṛg Veda* as the enemies of the Vedic Aryans, were an earlier wave of Aryans that entered northwest India carrying the Bronze Age culture of greater Iran (known archaeologically as Namazga V) and speaking a pre-Vedic Aryan language. What most distinguished them in the eyes of the Vedic Aryans was their forts, which the invading Aryans did without, and their lack of a

6. The double Aśvamedha is Biardeau's key to the *Mahābhārata*'s sacrifice of battle; see Biardeau and Péterfalvi 1986, 329; Biardeau 1989b, 236–37; Hiltebeitel 1988a, 396, with prior citations of Biardeau.

7. See Stein 1980, 386–87; Sontheimer 1989a, 320; cf. Biardeau 1989a, 23–28; 1989b, 184–95, 233–41, 325; on the Aśvamedha and buffalo sacrifice, see chapter 11, section D and n. 51. Krishnamurthy Hanur also argues for such continuities (see chap. 2, n. 30).

soma cult. Though they were not the original people of the Indus Valley Civilization, who, Parpola still feels, probably spoke a proto-Dravidian language, they were "quickly" absorbed into it "culturally and linguistically" (1988, 211–12, 226–27, 238 [quote]). This argument allows Parpola to claim a lineage, mainly via an Indus Valley cylinder seal from Kalibangan "showing a Durgā-like goddess of war, who is associated with the tiger" (238 and 294, fig. 24a), in two directions: not only back to the West Asian and Mediterranean cults of goddesses of city walls (or forts) who were connected with felines, but forward, through the Dāsas' influence on the later cult of the goddess. He is particularly interested in Durgā and Tripurasundarī, the "Beautiful Lady of the Triple Fort" (in press, sections 1–1.2.5).

The discussion of Durgā's link to more ancient fort goddesses with felines (lions, tigers, leopards) is tempting, as is the identification of the Dāsas as an early wave of non-soma-offering Aryans. But the relation between these arguments is still uncertain. Parpola's reconstruction of Dāsa religion is hypothetical, and also problematic as it bears on several issues in this chapter and the next. A successful argument is made that the Dāsas' forts were real rather than figments of nature myth, as others have argued, and further, drawing on both archaeological and Ṛg Vedic descriptive evidence, that they were circular, typically with three concentric rings (1988, 216–17, 237; in press, secs. 3.1.7–8; cf. Rau 1973, 24). One may also accept that the Brāhmaṇa myths of the gods' conquest by ritual means of the triple forts of the Asuras are transpositions of these down-to-earth conditions.[8] That the name Durgā should derive from the Vedic word *durga,* an "inaccessible place" or "fort" (ibid., 1988, 259; in press, sec. 1), is also more than likely. But Parpola's "proposed association of Dāsa forts with the worship of Durgā" (1988, 257) is highly conjectural.

It is important that "sacrifices of hundreds of buffaloes are mentioned as conducive to victory in a few early hymns of the Veda (6, 17, 11; 5, 29, 7–8; 8, 12, 8), but not in later Vedic literature" (ibid., 1988, 256 n. 472; cf. in press, sec. 3.2.6). But can one say that the earlier Ṛg Vedic Aryans adopted the buffalo sacrifice "from their enemies and rivals, . . . who lived in forts with concentric ramparts along with hundreds of buffaloes"? It is a big leap to argue

8. With no fort, the gods usually conquer the Asuras with *upasad* ceremonies and drive them from the triple world that is represented by their three altars. The demons have both seven-walled and three-walled forts (Rau 1973, 19–23 with citations). Cf. Narayana Rao 1989, 116: The Andhra cattle herder hero Kāṭamarāju agrees to eschew forts—"your forts are your cattle"—in true "Aryan" fashion.

that the early Dāsas "were worshiping Durgā as the goddess of the stronghold."[9]

I will return to the matter of forts in the next chapter, but for the moment Parpola's argument also bears on the relation between the Aśvamedha and Dasarā. He argues that the violent, agonistic, and orgiastic elements in the Vedic śrauta rituals are fossils of the earlier religion of the Dāsas (1988, 251, 254). In particular, he regards the obscenities, thigh slapping, and related rites of the Aśvamedha as having been imported into the śrauta ritual under the influence of originally Dāsa rites, which he sees evidence for in the *vrātya* rites of the Mahāvrata and Vrātyastomas. In the Mahāvrata, one finds thigh slapping and obscenities (1988, 253 n. 455; cf. Rolland 1973, 65–67). He sees continuations of these rites in the sexualized ritual abuse (though with no thigh slapping) that is said to delight the goddess in the Śābarotsava, a feature of Durgā pūjā that is traditionally explained as "tribal" from its presumed link with the tribal Śabaras or Saoras (1984, 219–20, n. 194, citing Kane [1930–62] 1975, 5,1:177; cf. Parpola in press, secs. 3.2.2, 3.2.4). The Śābarotsava, however, is only found in the Durgā pūjā of Śākta Bengal, not in other variants of Dasarā, though it certainly has counterparts in abuse rituals found in other goddess cults, including Draupadī's (see Hiltebeitel 1988a, 263–71; Tarabout 1986, 359–411).

In brief, Parpola reads Śākta and Tantric cult and imagery back into the hypothetical religion of the Dāsas and keys on it to draw a continuum, through this Dāsa religion, from West Asia and the Indus Valley to later Hinduism. In any case, as regards the rites of the hair and the thigh, I see no reason not to think that the Aśvamedha, rather than the Mahāvrata and the religion of the Dāsas, is still our primary source and, because of its royal character, the most important one connecting these gestures with Dasarā and Draupadī's paṭukaḷam.

Curiously, I know of no rites or other evocations of the hair and the thigh together in any one Dasarā-type festival. But they do occur separately. In the Navarātri festival at Madurai, on the eighth night the goddess Mīnākṣī is depicted in the pose of beheading Mahiṣāsura. On the ninth night she worships Śiva, atoning for her sin in killing Mahiṣa, Śiva's devotee. And on the following "tenth

9. Parpola in press, sec. 3.2.6. The Asuras live in their forts and harbor the boar Emuṣa in an "inaccessible place" (*durga*); Indra must obtain Emuṣa to win Viṣṇu, identified as "the sacrifice" (ibid.). The wild boar is concealed "behind twenty-one stone *puraḥ*," or forts (ibid.; Rau 1973, 18–21 for texts): not necessarily the same as buffaloes kept in a stronghold, as above. Nor do the Asuras sacrifice either Emuṣa or the buffaloes.

day" of Dasarā, she undergoes a "hair-washing" ritual before her procession with Śiva around the temple (Fuller 1980, 339–40; Fuller and Logan 1985, 79–83). It is understood to be a washing with water, which is cooling, though no actual water is used.[10] Furthermore, since her atonement for killing Mahiṣa is "insufficient," the hair washing removes the additional sin or taint (*doṣa*) that remains in her hair.[11] Fuller and Logan have nicely followed up my article (1981) on textual treatments of Draupadī's hair to bring out the pertinent parallels, which are equally valid for Draupadī festivals:

> Although the Mīnākṣī Temple ritual is said to be a hair-washing, rather than a hair-binding, the two actions do in fact go together and it therefore seems legitimate to regard Mīnākṣī's state during Navarātri as similar to Draupadī's during the *Mahābhārata* war. . . . Mīnākṣī is said to have taken a vow at the start of Navarātri, which is explicitly symbolized by the cord she wears, and all the cords are removed at the hair-washing ritual. Consequently, the hair-washing can be interpreted as marking the termination of the goddess's vow, just as Draupadī's hair-binding does at the end of her "sacrifice of battle." (1985, 94)

Furthermore, at her next major festival, Mīnākṣī has her hair combed and actually anointed with oil, which is heating, after which she looks in a mirror (Fuller 1980, 341; Fuller and Logan 1985, 95): elements that recurs at Thanjavur area (and Singapore) paṭukaḷam rites for Draupadī.[12] Also reminding us of the Thanjavur area rites, preparations for Durgā pūjā include offering "materials such as sandal-wood paste, myrolaban for purifying the hair and also a comb . . . a silken ribbon for keeping the hair in position, . . . vermilion for putting it on the head, a mirror for observing the face" (Kane [1930–62] 1975, 5,1:159).

As to the thigh, matters are more complicated. It does not seem to be a question of rites prescribed for these festivals in Brahmanical texts or temples, but in folk or popular variations on Dasarā themes. In oleographs sold at the Cāmuṇḍīśvarī temple on the Cāmuṇḍī Hill that rises above Mysore, the goddess's lion is shown with his teeth sunk into the bloody right thigh of Mahiṣāsura. Or, more precisely, while the buffalo carcass of Mahiṣāsura lies on the ground

10. Fuller and Logan 1985, 95. Fuller mentions that Māriyammaṉ's hair is actually washed at her Samayapuram festival (1980, 340 n. 40).

11. Fuller and Logan 1985, 93–94.

12. See chapter 10, section D.

beheaded by Cāmuṇḍī's blood-tipped sword, the lion attacks the right thigh of Mahiṣāsura's *human* form, which has escaped from his buffalo body at the moment of death. At the same time, the goddess holds this human Mahiṣa's head by the hair in readiness to behead him, in his human form as well, and pierces him with her trident in the chest (see plate 25).

Now the Cāmuṇḍīśvarī temple is one of the two temples, the other being another Cāmuṇḍī temple in the royal palace, to celebrate conjointly the famous Navarātri-Dasarā festival at Mysore, the city named after Mahiṣāsura himself. The print is not, of course, an iconographic representation of a Dasarā buffalo sacrifice, which would not include the lion or an emergent human as the demon's final form. In fact the buffalo sacrifice at Mysore, in which the king and Brahmans of the Cāmuṇḍī temple are involved, but at a distance and at another time, has been displaced from Cāmuṇḍī to her "younger sister" Tripurasundarī, the Beautiful Lady of the Triple Fort, whose temple is on a neighboring hill.[13] The print thus represents an interpretation of the myth that continues despite these ritual displacements, retaining a popular iconography.

It might seem a minor detail or coincidence that the goddess's lion should bite the right thigh of the human form of the Buffalo Demon. But a search of other sculptures, paintings, and poster art representations of the killing of the Mahiṣāsura shows the Mysore picture to be unique in this feature and invites an inquiry as to what might lie behind it.[14] I have found two parallels.

A second case of thigh-biting animals representing possession in the conquest of demons comes from an unexpected quarter: paintings of the *Rāmāyaṇa* found in a late sixteenth-century translation of that epic commissioned by the emperor Akbar from the hands of his own mainly Muslim artists, so as to familiarize himself and his courtiers with Hindu traditions. One of these paintings, by the Muslim artist Fazl, shows several monkeys biting the legs of the fallen Rāvaṇa: one attacking his upper right thigh, another his right calf, and a third his left leg just above the knee (Beach 1981, 131, 134; 1983, 56). It is likely that we meet again a depiction that relies on folk elaborations of the monkeys as embodiments of the

13. Biardeau shows "the ties that weave themselves to form a continuous chain from Cāmuṇḍī to the buffalo, by way of the Brahmans and the king but also Cāmuṇḍī's younger sister"—and also Mādiga Untouchables (1989b, 314–17; my translation).

14. Closest is the colored print facing Pāṇḍeya Pam n.d., 59: Durgā's lion claws the human Mahiṣa's left thigh as he emerges full-bodied from the severed buffalo neck. Elsewhere the goddess's lion or tiger usually goes after the buffalo's animal head or his human right arm (in Bengal, connected with Durgā Pūjā).

possessed frenzy of battle, a role they play even in the *Rāmāyaṇa*.[15] But here there is also the possibility, which will find some supporting evidence in the next chapter, that the painting is an imaginative interpretation of contemporary North Indian rites of Rām Līlā, themselves a transformation of Dasarā, at which the scenes of Rāvaṇa's defeat are reenacted.

The most significant parallel, however, is to be found in Maharashtra, in popular oleographs that show the god Khaṇḍobā and his consort Mhālsā defeating the demons Maṇi and Malla. While Khaṇḍobā rides his horse and is attacked by one of the demons, who stands with a raised mace, Mhālsā spears the other demon in the side while Khaṇḍobā's dog draws droplets of blood from the falling demon's right thigh. It is not certain which of these demon brothers is attacked in this fashion, but it is probably Maṇi, since in the myths he is the first to fall, leaving the dog to concern itself with his blood in another way: it must try to prevent it from touching the ground lest it regenerate more demons (another variation on the revival of the demon army).[16] Again, this is certainly not a Dasarā ritual, but the defeat of Maṇi and Malla is enacted at Dasarā in Karnataka, where Mailāra (Khaṇḍobā's Kannada name) has a Dasarā festival at Devaragudda.[17] Moreover, the dog represents the Khaṇḍobā cult's male ecstatics, the Vāghyās, or "tigers," who impersonate dogs at ceremonial occasions, while at Mailar they form the god's army. The tiger is, of course, the alternate mount of the goddess when she defeats Mahiṣāsura. It is likely that in its attack on the demon's thigh, the possessed frenzy of Khaṇḍobā's tiger-dog is modeled on the ferocity of Durgā's tiger. Let us recall that Duryodhana's right thigh is cut by a possessed actor impersonating Bhīma, who in the *Mahābhārata* is linked with both lions and tigers. Indeed, at Mēlaccēri in 1986, not only did the Bhīma actor cut Duryodhana's right thigh, but so did a "tiger of the lion throne" (cimmācaṉapuli) act out the same cutting in mime. If not possessed, the cimmācaṉapuli was at least very highly and sympathetically excited.[18]

The connections with Dasarā, no more than tangential in any of

15. Hiltebeitel 1980a, 204; cf. *Rām.* 5.59–61: *madhuvana* episode.

16. See Stanley 1989, 280–84, including plates 23 and 24; Sontheimer 1984, 164–65 and plate 2: neither suggests which demon is which.

17. See chapter 8, section A.

18. See chapter 10, section B, item F. Cf. Hiltebeitel 1988a, 123–24 (vāghyās and other tiger-dog and lion-dog combinations); 125 (Bhīma-"Wolfbelly"); 335–36, 365–66 (lion and tiger traits of Pōttu Rāja). The cimmācaṉapuli's miming of the thigh cutting can be seen in Hiltebeitel 1988b, part 2.

these instances, are not ritual ones on the precise point in question: that is, the thigh. Indeed, only in the case of Duryodhana's effigy is there a thigh-cutting ritual at all. But the similarities between these possessed assaults on the right thighs of demon kings cannot be illusory. Setting Akbar's *Rāmāyaṇa* illustrations momentarily aside, the other three instances mark out a most plausible cultural continuum from Maharashtra through Karnataka to northern Tamilnadu, allowing us to perceive the milieu in which Draupadī cult ritualists would have sensed that Duryodhana's right thigh, rather than the classically favored left, would be the appropriate one for smashing. If such connections are real, however, they must draw on a shared symbolism. It seems there are two orders of facts to consider.

First, there are other rituals involving bloodletting from the thigh, and in some cases the right thigh. Lausen's nabakhaṇḍa begins as follows: "After preparations were made, Lausen unhesitatingly took the billhook in his hands and chopped off the flesh of his right thigh" (Robinson 1980, 28). His other eight self-dismemberments, culminating with the head, then follow. Presumably this would be reflected in effigy rites for Lausen. At the Chola-period Puḷḷamaṅkai Śiva temple near Thanjavur, a kneeling suppliant before Durgā is shown performing a phase of the same navakhaṇḍa ritual, South India style, cutting a piece of flesh from his right thigh (Vogel 1930–32, 541; Hiltebeitel 1988a, 318). Similarly, although Aravāṉ's thighs are omitted from the thirty-two cuts that were enumerated by the Mēlaccēri pūcāri (Hiltebeitel 1988a, 327), one of them becomes ritually important at Pondicherry, where Shideler found that the blood sprinkled over the six "sleeping warriors" was taken from a bowl set beneath Aravāṉ's left thigh (1987, 156). At C. Kīraṉūr, blood is taken from one of the thighs of Aravāṉ's *effigy* (chap. 9, sec. A). According to N. Dandapani, Arjuna is reminded by Kṛṣṇa to retrieve the pāśupata weapon from his right thigh (chap. 8, sec. A). Let us also recall that Kāttavarāyaṉ ornaments his impalement stake with huge hooks as big as a thigh.[19]

Most interesting, however, are the thigh-piercing rites of Maharashtra, which appear to be part of the Khaṇḍobā cult. My introduction to them comes from Meera Kosambi (1984; parentheses hers):

> A village about forty miles from Poona had an annual festival (April 1978 was the date that I recall) at which the ceremony

19. See chapter 5, section C; chapter 7, section C.

> was held late in the evening. The persons (originally sacrificial subjects?) chosen were a young Mahar couple; only Mahars were considered suitable, an honour jealously guarded by the community. The man underwent the ceremony of *māṇḍi foḍaṇe,* literally "breaking the thigh," in which a long iron pin was pierced into the thigh to the accompaniment of music, drums, and shouts. I personally was able to witness not this ceremony but its counterpart where the woman had her forearm similarly pierced (to all appearances only superficially); however, the actual ritual was known as *danḍa foḍaṇe,* "breaking the upper arm." The wound was rubbed over with holy powder (I forget whether it was the usual vermilion and turmeric or a special powder) which was supposed to heal it immediately and prevent any sensation of pain; the woman's face did, however, register pain and shock. The man and woman were then taken in separate processions to the main temple and around the village.

It seems that Sontheimer describes a variant of this ritual, called *pavāḍā,* "a 'heroic, magical feat,'" performed at Devaragudda on Dasarā day, and at Mailar after the slaying of the demon. It is a function of the Kañcavīras, or "five heroes" (see chap. 11, sec. D), who are "recruited especially from Kuruba Vaggayyas and (in Devaragudda) also by Mādigas" (Sontheimer 1989a, 318; 1981, 13). The Vaggayyas are the Kannada equivalent to the Marathi Vāghyās, or "tigers":

> They wield weapons like iron prongs, swords, or tridents, and pierce their calves with painted iron rods, or with an instrument resembling a pointed tent peg made of wood of the palm tree. The most important incident of the ritual is carried out by a young unmarried Vaggayya preferably twelve years old. He is the one who has to first perform the ritual of piercing the leg in front of the god. He then simultaneously passes two thorny twigs of the *babbuli* tree through the wound. After that he passes a long rope through the wound. (ibid., 1989a, 318)

Behind the temple where the pavāḍā is performed are "some exquisitely carved medieval stone heads," said to be those of Kañcavīras "who died in self-sacrifice" (ibid.). There is thus a hint that the exemplary Kañcavīra carries the pavāḍā to the same conclusion as Lausen and Aravāṉ: self-decapitation.

Though it is risky to generalize on these practices, there appear to be some common denominators. Those who undergo these rites of thigh piercing seem to be substitutionary victims of low status. This is especially clear in the last two cases. The Untouchable Mahar performs the rite on behalf of the village and appears to be the substitute for the patron of the annual village festival, probably the village headman, or even the community itself. In Karnataka, the low-caste Kuruba Vaggayyas and Untouchable Māḍigas perform a rite like the Maharashtrian one to the god Mailāra, offering their heroic feat as a substitutionary sacrifice for the god's army, of which the god himself is king. It can hardly be accidental that Maharashtrian oleographs show Khaṇḍobā's "tiger"-dog as the agent in the thigh biting of the demon. The coincidence of the rite with Dasarā in one place and the death of the demon in the other is itself evidence for such a parallelism. The thigh biting seems to be a symbolic representation of the rite, showing a correspondence between the heroic bhakti feats of the Vaggayyas and Māḍigas—and the thigh-piercing Mahar—with the fate of Maṇi, Mailāra-Khaṇḍobā's demon devotee.[20] One may be reminded of the washerman whose legs are pinched as he lies on the effigy of Duryodhana at Singapore: himself a low-caste ritual substitute for King Duryodhana.[21] The thigh-sized hooks for Kāttavarāyaṉ do not seem to have ritual use. But they are still part of the symbolic sacrificial apparatus of this Untouchable god of multicaste traits, who equates himself with a king as he announces his death by impalement, then dons a royal guise for the ordeal, with the king and Brahmans in attendance, and the king in particular as organizer and patron of the ceremonies (Masilamani-Meyer in press-b, 164–79; Shulman 1989, 52–53). Finally, Lausen, king of an Untouchable army, offers himself on behalf of that army's revival, while Aravāṉ, of mixed Kṣatriya-Nāga parentage, offers himself for the Pāṇḍavas' victory at Kurukṣetra: explicitly, in one of the Terukkūttu plays, as a substitute for Arjuna or Kṛṣṇa (Hiltebeitel 1988a, 322).

In other words, these rites of thigh cutting and thigh piercing seem to play upon themes of substitutionary sacrifice by a low-status figure for a king, or someone who represents the royal sacrificial function locally. The same appears to apply to the various demons, whose sacrificial deaths are substitutionary offerings for sacrificers, who are themselves royal heroes and gods. This interpretation seems to find some confirmation in the purificatory rite for the patron or chief trustee (upayakkāraṉ) at the Udappu, Sri Lanka Draupadī festival (cf. chap. 2, sec. B; chap. 5, sec. A). When

20. On Maṇi in this guise, see Stanley 1989.
21. See chapter 10, section C.

the priest puts a darbha-grass ring on the patron's finger, the patron, seated, "places a sprig of darbha grass under his right leg . . . [and] places his left hand, palm upwards, on his right thigh with his right hand, palm downwards over it and closes it for a while" (Tanaka 1987, 199). Darbha or kuśa grass, proverbially sharp (Indra uses it to pierce the Asuras' seven hills; *TS* 6.2.4.2–3; Rau 1973, 21), is the sacrificial grass par excellence. Here it seems to imply a thigh offering by the patron himself. Rather than having it performed through a low-status substitute, he performs it bloodlessly through a symbolic ritual substitution.

If rituals of thigh cutting seem to call for substitutes or symbolic equivalents and seem to be found only in popular religious contexts, myths—notably classical myths—are less reluctant to accord the gesture to kings. A vivid example is the story of King Śibi, whose great generosity is exemplified by his offering his own body, piece by piece, to ransom a pigeon chased by a hawk that has come to him for refuge. The birds are really the gods Viśvakarma (pigeon) and Indra (hawk), who put Śibi's generosity to the test by agreeing to ransom the piegon only if Śibi matches its weight with his own flesh. Ultimately, Śibi must offer pieces of flesh from all the parts of his body, since the divine pigeon overweighs the scales. He begins, as the hawk demands, by cutting the flesh from his right thigh (*ūrordakṣiṇād-utkṛtya; Mbh.* 3, appendix 1, no. 21, colophon 5, 84–85). Here the king offers the substitutionary sacrifice for the god.

Another example is India's most prominent myth of the origin of kingship and, with it, the milking of the earth for prosperity. The adharmic rule of King Vena is followed, after his death, by the good rule of his son Pṛthu, "the broad," after whom the "broad earth" (*pṛthivī*) is named because she yields her milk to him like a cow. Since Vena dies sonless, a special form of generation is required: the Ṛṣis "churn" parts of his body, usually two, to produce two sons: a mytheme that evokes the churning of the firesticks and the churning of the ocean, out of which comes the goddess of Prosperity, Śrī-Lakṣmī. Different texts locate the double churnings in different parts of the body (O'Flaherty 1976, 331–32), but it is again a *Mahābhārata* version that is most relevant to our theme. The sages, having killed Vena because of his adharmic rule, first churn his right thigh to produce a dark, deformed ancestor of the "barbaric" mixed-caste Niṣādas, and then churn his right hand to produce Pṛthu. (ibid., 333; *Mbh.* 12.59.99–103). In Andhra Pradesh, a version of this myth is told by Bōyas (traditionally hunters), who claim to be "descendants of Nishadu": their ancestor was born from Vena's right thigh and his brother from the right shoulder. While the latter became king, Nishadu became "ruler over the forests" (Thurston and Rangachari [1904] 1965, 1:187–88). The good king and his low- and mixed-caste counterpart, the outlet for Vena's evil and impurity and the outcome of his adharmic mixing of castes, are thus born together, both of them being necessary to milk the earth of prosperity (O'Flaherty 1976, 321–31). The rapport between the arm-born Pṛthu and the thigh-born Niṣāda suggests a prototype for the rapport between the royal function and the low-caste ritual service functions that we have seen in the various thigh-piercing rituals just described.

Biardeau (1989b, 55) calls attention to *Āśvalāyana Gṛhyasūtra* 4.3.1ff., which specifies that when one prepares the corpse of a regular sacrificer (*āhitāgni*) for cremation, the two firesticks should be placed on the thighs, suggesting that the thighs themselves are the parts of the body suitable for churning. Duryodhana's thighs are not exactly churned, however, but are crushed or pounded like the soma plant.[22] A widely found "interpolated" *Rāmāyaṇa* verse has it that at Rāvaṇa's funeral rites, "a cart (*śakaṭam*) was placed between his feet and a wooden mortar (*ulūkhalam*) between his thighs" (*Rām.* 6. app. 1, no. 69, l. 26, following 6.99.41). The mortar's connotation of "pounding" is evident. In either case, whether pounding or churning, we have an image of the release of a sacrificial essence. Duryodhana's right thigh, in terms of the Terukkūttu drama on his death, is his "life spot," his "vital place" (*uyir nilai;* Hiltebeitel 1988a, 417), and there is certainly something similar in the iconography of royal thighs being bitten by animals representing states of possession. In fact the male thigh, and particularly the right thigh, seems to be a seat of fertility. This brings us to the most obvious instance of thigh symbolism in the Hindu lexicon. In the cosmogonic sacrifice of Puruṣa, it is from the thighs of the primal male that the Vaiśyas are born, those who see to the welfare of plants and herds and form the economic base of the popular mass (*viś*) of Vedic society. Here the symbolism is that of dismemberment, not churning or pounding. But the means of sacrificial violence are, as we have seen, interchangeable often enough. It may be pertinent to note here that the armed human figure that emerges from the Buffalo Demon is, according to *Vāmana Purāṇa* 20.47, his puruṣa, or "soul" (Biardeau, in Biardeau and Malamoud 1976, 148).

22. On Duryodhana's death as part of a double Aśvamedha (see n. 6), in the role of the Pāṇḍavas' primary soma victim, but one whose somic death is left incomplete because Dharma prevents Bhīma from crushing his head, see Biardeau CR 91, 166–67; Biardeau and Péterfalvi 1986, 246–47; Hiltebeitel 1988a, 418). The crushing of the thighs, however, seems to be part of the same symbolism.

It is certainly also the royal persona of the Buffalo Demon as victim of the goddess's sacrifice. Here we have a tempting convergence. The human form of the demon who offers blood from his thigh is an image of the royal sacrificer as victim, and also an evocation of the regenerative cosmogonic sacrifice of Puruṣa. Where the thigh offering concerns the goddess, whether it is the result of dismemberment, pounding, or churning, the vital sacrificial essence released from the thigh is obviously, in all cases, the demon-victim's blood.

B. Blood and Hair

This discussion of thigh symbolism has been only selective. Let it suffice to mention that the thigh offering to the goddess is an ancient Near Eastern motif[23] and that Viṣṇu, the supreme Puruṣa who incarnates the sacrifice, uses his own thighs virtually as an altar in the sacrifice of demons.[24] The point to bear in mind as we move back to Draupadī's hair is the last one. With all its implications of regenerative fertility and sexual potency, it is thigh blood that the goddess demands. In Draupadī's case, taking it from Duryodhana's thigh has in addition a dimension of sexual revenge. When Duḥśāsana drags her by the hair into the dicing hall and Duryodhana bares his thigh to her, Draupadī is menstruating. Her hair is loose for that reason. Her vow to keep it that way until she can oil it with Duryodhana's thigh blood is tantamount to an extended condition of interrupted menstrual purification, since normally a hair washing with cooling water rather than freshly warm blood—in the *Villipāratam,* Draupadī's vow calls for the "hot blood" of her victims, Duryodhana included (2.2.25; Hiltebeitel 1988a, 237)—would mark the end of her period (1981, 189–90, 203–11). Duryodhana's thigh thus becomes an altar of offering to her. It is an image of sexual revenge that finds its inversion in Tantric circles, in which the thighs may be considered the altar one prepares for the act of sexual union. Among the cakras that the Tantric *sādhaka* (adept) places and worships on the *śakti*'s body before ritual intercourse, one is placed on "the sloping ground," a term referring to the thighs and "also used to describe the sides of the Vedic sacrificial

23. In the *Gilgamesh Epic,* Enkidu tears loose the Bull of Heaven's right thigh and hurls it at Ishtar; see discussion in Hiltebeitel 1980a, 216–27.

24. Viṣṇu slays Madhu and Kaiṭabha on his thighs or "loins" (*jaghana*) when he awakens from his yogic sleep to recreate the universe (*Devī Māhātmyam* 1.103; Jagadīśvarananda 1972, 21), and also Hiraṇyakaśipu in his Man-Lion avatar. See further Hiltebeitel 1982a, 111 n. 93.

altar" (Finn 1986, 110 and nn. 160, 165; *Kulacūḍāmaṇi Tantra* 4.56–58). It should also not be missed that when Draupadī's icon or chariot is carried onto Duryodhana's effigy from the north, she mounts him *between* his thighs. She ascends his body by climbing over his groin: an inverse sexual position reminiscent of Kālī standing on the prone corpse of Śiva (cf. Hiltebeitel 1988a, 294).[25] Having had the "form of Kālī" to this point, she deactivates that form with the tying of her hair.[26]

In this vein, the logic of the thigh and hair rites on the Draupadī cult paṭukaḷam finally becomes rather evident. If Draupadī's menstruation has been interrupted and she cannot wash her hair with cooling water at its end, she demands to oil it with hot, menstrual-like blood from the right thigh, the male fertility seat, the "life point," of her chief violator.[27] Indeed, it is usually blood from a small earthen pot—an inevitable womb symbol—set at this vital spot in Duryodhana's earthen effigy. There is thus an affinity between Draupadī and the menstruating goddess who is worshiped in India in many forms.[28]

In Tamilnadu, for instance, Mīnākṣī's menses are celebrated not at Navarātri, when her hair is washed, but at her Āṭi Pūram festival (Fuller 1980, 334–37; Fuller and Logan 1985, 94). According to Fuller (1980, 333), the latter is a temple equivalent to the festival of Āṭipperukku that, especially in the Kaveri delta, celebrates the river's flooding or overflow (*perukku*) on the eighteenth of Āṭi (July-August). "It is commonly believed" that the Kaveri's menstruation is indicated by her waters turning "red for the three days preceding Āṭipperukku" (ibid., 333). It is a time when newlyweds perform a rite in which the husband reties the tāli around the wife's neck, replacing the cotton thread from the wedding with a golden chain, and then offering the cotton thread, soaked in turmeric, along with flowers, in the river (Arunachalam 1980, 91–93). One could draw an analogy here with the rebinding of Draupadī's hair as a restoration

25. At Sri Lankan festivals, Draupadī takes Duryodhana's chest blood (Tanaka 1987, 382) or puts up her hair standing on his head (Macready 1888–89, 191)!

26. Recall that Bhagavati-Bhadrakālī's muṭi is deactivated in an opposite sense when it is untied, leaving only a remainder of its dangerous power to face south for a blood sacrifice (chap. 7, sec. B).

27. The thigh symbolism in the Aśvamedha is explicitly sexual: the mahiṣī opens her thighs to the seed of the horse; the horse, like the king, remains continent for the year, its departure marking the point at which the king last lay between the thighs of his favorite wife, but without uniting with her, beginning for both king and horse a year of chastity (P.-E. Dumont 1927, 18).

28. In North India, for Gaṅgā, see Agrawala 1966, 37; Fuller 1980, 336 n. 34. For Kerala, see n. 4 above; Vaidyanathan 1982, 45–49.

of her marital status. In Kongunad, this same date is recalled as the time Pārvatī first menstruated, and the first eighteen days of this dangerous and inauspicious month are further identified as the eighteen days it took the Pāṇḍavas to defeat the Kauravas in the *Mahābhārata* war (Beck 1972a, 53). One could say that the symbolism of Draupadī's hair hangs here pending. Indeed, as we saw in chapter 2, Āṭipperukku coincided at the 1981 Tindivanam Draupadī festival with the day of paṭukaḷam, on which Draupadī does tie up her hair.

Most interesting, however, are the Orissan rites of the earth's menses (*raja parba*), celebrated over three days at the onset of the rainy season in Āṣāḍha (June-July), followed by a purifying bath on the fourth day. One of the five temples that hold this festival with a fair is a hill temple to the goddess Haracaṇḍī. While the women stay in the village for the three days in a seclusion that corresponds to that of the goddess's period, the men—who cannot stay in the village because of the symbolism it thus takes on—go to Haracaṇḍī's temple to offer her goats and rams. "According to popular tradition (*lokācāra*), Haracaṇḍī is Draupadī" (Marglin 1988). Marglin's interviews show how the connection is formulated. I choose one of several, an interview with a man, that could make the point:

> A. She was disturbed during her *ritu* [period]; she was taken by the hair and she was angry and the result was very bad. . . . Everything was destroyed, blood was shed.
> Q. Your observation of *raja parba* does it mean to give rest to mother earth?
> A. Yes. If we do not allow her to rest during her menses, the results will not be good. Our works will not be fruitful. So that's why our women are given lots of rest as the representatives of mother earth. (Marglin, 1988)

Draupadī cult paṭukaḷam rites look like a variation on such themes, with the difference that Draupadī, in her cult, is the menstruating goddess in a vengeful mode, with the full *Mahābhārata* myth behind her. The postmenstrual tying of her hair is thus not so much a symbol of fertility, as with the various earth and river goddesses, as one of victory over a demonic foe, as with Mīnākṣī and Mahiṣāsura. Indeed, in classical epic terms, the release of Aśvatthāman's weapon into the wombs of the Pāṇḍava women has rendered Draupadī barren. Yet it cannot be insignificant, and it is also rather beautiful, that the heated, bloody, and impure rites that mark the end of her extended menstrual condition often coincide with the rites for the revival of her children.

13 Effigies and Forts

We now come to one of the most surprising incongruities between popular Draupadī cult understandings of the *Mahābhārata* war and the classical epic texts. Though it is, I suspect, universally known in Draupadī cult circles that the war takes place at Kurukṣetra, the "Field of the Kurus," it is not uniformly thought that Kurukṣetra is a battle-*field*. Instead, it is sometimes conceived of as a fort (*kōṭṭai*); or, in variants, a fort or palace (*araṉmaṉai*) plays a crucial part in the war.[1]

Through most of the core area, however, the fort tradition is limited only to myths. My two main Terukkūttu informants—R. S. Mayakrishnan speaking, as usual, for both himself and his brother R. S. Natarajan—provided a typical example:

> The entire eighteen-day war took place in a fort. Each night Draupadī would assume the form of Kālī (*kāḷi uruvam*), enter the fort, and devour the bodies of the slain. It was just as she began to do after her disrobing, when she went out each night to devour the creatures of the forest. She never stopped it, and continued it through the war until the binding of her hair.

At the Sowcarpet temple in Madras, where Draupadī's hair tying is done not upon a paṭukaḷam effigy but to her icon, adorned as Kālī, on the night before the firewalk, a similar story is told by the temple's Brahman pūcāri. Here the "palace"-fort is not the battlefield but the Draupadī temple:

> On the eighteenth day of battle, Kṛṣṇa reveals to Bhīma and Arjuna how Draupadī had assumed Kālīrūpa at nights during

1. Actually, Kurukṣetra has four gateways guarded by four Yakṣas (*Mbh.* 3.81.7–42). In Kurukṣetra area folklore, the four are "said to have sung and danced with joy during the battle, while they drank the blood of the slain" (Cunningham 1970, 89). But the epic never identifies Kurukṣetra as a fort.

> the war, and tells Bhīma to watch for her that morning. When she returns at 4:00 A.M., she will be in a fierce mood from sucking up the blood on the battlefield, and might even kill the Pāṇḍavas. He instructs Bhīma, the strongest, to close the front gate of the palace and watch from a side window. At 4:00 A.M. Draupadī returns, sees the gate, and calls out in her real voice, as Draupadī, even though she is still in Kālīrūpa. Bhīma sustains an hour's argument with her until he extracts her promise that she won't kill them, and will help them win the war. Since she assumes Kālīrūpa only from midnight to 4:00 A.M., she is in danger of losing this power if she doesn't get in before dawn. Thus she agrees and comes in as Draupadī.

The hair tying of Draupadī's icon is done at this point, representing the end of the war, whose eighteenth-day battle is understood here to have been fought on this night. Draupadī returns to her palace-temple after negotiating a termination of her battlefield Kālīrūpa that is clearly only provisional.[2]

Two other fort myths, both well represented in the core area through dramas, are familiar from earlier discussion: "Pōrmaṉṉaṉ's Fight," involving the destruction of his own fort, and "Draupadī the Gypsy," in which Draupadī enters the Kaurava fort to predict the outcome of the war. We shall return to these later.

A. From the Core Area to Thanjavur

What one does not find in the core area are paṭukaḷam fort rituals. Or, more precisely, one does not find them until one reaches a transitional zone between the Gingee core region and the Thanjavur–northeastern Trichy region. For the present, it is possible to trace this transitional area along a southward curve through southern South Arcot, east to west, from Cuddalore, Villupuram, Ulundurpet, and Vriddhachalam to Chinna Salem, and on into Salem in Salem District.[3] At these sites, the fort rituals tend to combine core

2. Similar myths are told about Draupadī's time in the forest; see Hiltebeitel 1988a, 290–95.

3. From Salem, a line might be further traced to Bangalore's Hulsoor Gate temple festival. A karakam pot is carried, with the Vīrakumāras in attendance performing alaku cēvai, to the location of an unnamed and now extinct seven-ringed fort, at the site of what is now an anthill. Everyone rushes the site, at the northern part of the municipal Corporation Office building, and then circumambulates it seven or nine times before returning to the temple (Munivenkatappa, 1965). A round fort is made there of small stones, this being the last ritual before the goat biting by Pōttu Rāja (Krishnamurthy Hanur, personal communication, 1990; see chap. 5, n. 37).

area elements with Thanjavur area elements. As we have now seen, it is also, roughly speaking, along this same line that Aravāṉ effigies begin to replace Duryodhana effigies,[4] Vīrapattiraṉ to replace Pōttu Rāja, and Draupadī viewing the battlefield to replace rites for the Young Pañcapāṇḍavas or Duryodhana's four guardians. The southern fort traditions thus have their place within a distinctive set of transformations (see map 1).

I will initially follow this line from east to west, and then move from north to south. In doing so, we will be looking at two different versions of what the ritual represents in the *Mahābhārata*. There appear to be two main complexes involving both myths and rituals: one that links the attack of a fort to the end of the war, and one that is more free floating but usually linked to a prewar episode. The end-of-the-war setting is most prevalent along the transitional line, while the earlier settings predominate farther to the south. But as we shall see, the narration and sometimes the ritual enactment of fort myths portraying a prewar episode can be ritually slotted to coincide with the end of the war as well. No matter what the setting, all the following versions of the story and ritual can be evoked by asking how a particular temple, or festival, narrates or performs (or both) its *kōṭṭai iṭittal*—its "destruction" or "demolition of the fort." The verb *iṭi* also means "to grind grain," "to pulverize,"evoking the same agricultural metaphors as the terms *kaḷam* and *paṭukaḷam*. Since the ritual end of the war seems to draw fort myths to itself whether the episodes are early or late, let us begin with the complex that straightforwardly connects the destruction of the fort with the war's end.

Examples of actual fusion between fort and core area paṭukaḷam rites are found in similar ceremonies at Tēvaṉampaṭṭaṉam on the coast near Cuddalore, Matukkarai (Pondicherry State), and Villupuram (Kīḻperumpākkam Hamlet). At the latter site, a fort called Aravāṉ Kaḷappali Kōṭṭai, the Fort of Aravāṉ's Battlefield Sacrifice, is constructed of circular mud walls about four feet high, with four entrances (*vaḻi*) between them (plate 26). A standing effigy (*pommai*) of Aravāṉ faces the southern gate, looking north. Within this fort, a circle of about twenty feet in diameter, Duryodhana is represented in the center either by a person lying on a raised mound of earth (*mēṭu*) or by an earthen effigy (*pommai*). Informants simply

4. The only place I have found prone effigies of both Duryodhana and Aravāṉ is at Lalgudi. They are made on successive days, and uniquely, within my findings, their bodies are both formed of straw (rather than earth or concrete) and provided with papier-mâché masks for their heads.

did not agree, nor did they agree on whether Duryodhana was surrounded by four guards, or "relatives," or by the Young Pañcapāṇḍavas. In 1982 informants, including the pūcāri, said it was a Duryodhana effigy in the middle of the fort surrounded by the Young Pañcapāṇḍavas, but a more random gathering in 1990 introduced notes of uncertainty. Perhaps there have been changes. At Tēvaṉampaṭṭaṇam there is a similar circular walled fort made of sand with four gates, and inside is a Duryodhana effigy around which rites are performed for the Young Pañcapāṇḍavas.

In any case, at Villupuram, before noon on firewalking day, the pūcāri in Kāḷi vēṣam (dressed as Kālī) comes to feed Aravāṉ with blood-soaked rice, while a second man with a whip flails the figures lying on the ground inside the fort. The Kālī priest bites off the neck of a chicken to provide the blood for the rice, goes around throwing the blood rice in the different directions, then swoons and is carried away to a body of water to cool his possession. Pāratam is then recited in the fort area, not by a pāratiyār but by a learned man from a nearby town. Then, at noon, a palanquin bearing a processional image of Kōṭṭai Kāḷi, "Kālī of the Fort," is brought by four men from the Draupadī temple (where the icon is kept against the south wall, like Kālī and Aravāṉ shrines in the Thanjavur area to the south). Kōṭṭai Kāḷi is red-faced with protruding canines, bears a trident, is dressed in a black garment, and given disheveled hair for the occasion (plate 27). She is taken around the fort several times, with the icons of the Pāṇḍavas behind her, until all of a sudden she enters the fort. At this point the fort is demolished, principally by Kālī, but also by Arjuna and the other Pāṇḍavas, and more generally by the participating public. Kōṭṭai Kāḷi is none other than the "angry" Draupadī in Kālīrūpa, so the tying of Draupadī's hair is now done to the Kōṭṭai Kāḷī icon. The temple also has a wooden icon of Draupadī that is not brought out for the destruction of the fort but appears only later that day for the firewalk.

At Tēvaṉampaṭṭaṇam there is no Kōṭṭai Kāḷi image, only a man dressed as Draupadī in black to look like Kālī, who enters the fort through the northern gate (as also at Matukkarai), offers a chicken, throws blood rice in the four directions, and then attacks Duryodhana by striking him first on the thigh, then in the chest. There is no hair tying at this point. It is done earlier that morning in the Terukkūttu, and then, to the hair of Draupadī's icon, on the next day before the firewalk.

Just a bit to the southwest, an informed overview of end-of-the-war fort rituals was available from the pāratiyār K. Muttuswami Pillai. Interviewed during his performance at the 1990 Kūttāṇṭavar festival at Kūvākkam (see chap. 3, n. 15), he claims to do all his other Pāratam at Draupadī temples around the same Villupuram-Ulundurpet area. First of all, he says, Kūttāṇṭavar's weeping ground (aḻukaḷam) is nothing but the name for the paṭukaḷam at Kūttāṇṭavar festivals. On the sixteenth day of the Kūvākkam festival, Kūttāṇṭavar's huge chariot is brought to the outdoor "temple" at the aḻukaḷam grove (chap. 9, sec. B). There, instead of reciting Kūttāṇṭavar's eighth-day fight and death in battle, which is what the ritual commemorates, he recites the eighteenth-day war's events of the deaths of Śakuni, Śalya, and Duryodhana. His job is to bring the festival's war-closing rituals (concerning Kūttāṇṭavar) together with the war-closing myth (concerning Duryodhana). The latter, here, is without any ritual enactment. He thus makes the equation between the aḻukaḷam and the paṭukaḷam himself and conveys it to the small circle close and interested enough to hear him recite amid a vast hubbub. Local Kūvākkam informants make no such equation. Meanwhile, Muttuswami Pillai also extends his equation to Draupadī cult rituals. At Draupadī festivals, he says, the paṭukaḷam is called Cakkaravartti Kōṭṭai, the "Wheel-Turner Fort." The Cakkaravartti Fort is the place where Śakuni, Śalya, and Duryodhana die in the eighteenth-day war. All of these (aḻukaḷam included) are names for Kurukṣetra. At the Draupadī festivals, he says, a fort is made. In different places they do it different ways: for example, making the fort walls of earth or strings. Dharma's son Pirativintiyaṉ should lie on a bench in the center, while the other four Young Pañcapāṇḍavas lie in pits on the ground.[5] Sometimes there will also be a cement Duryodhana effigy in the fort. The pāratiyār goes around as if he were Aśvatthāman, cutting the five youths, who should be guarded not only by four Pūtams, but also by Kālī, since Kṛṣṇa had promised her a *kapālam,* or skull bowl, to gather up the blood of Kurukṣetra. First the Pūtams and Kālī resist Aśvatthāman, but when he shows that he has Śiva's pāśupata weapon, they just withdraw, since "Kālī cannot disobey the orders of Śiva."

Here, amid a number of variations on the familiar, we now meet a new term. The fort is not Aravāṉ Kaḷappali Fort (a name I have heard nowhere besides Villupuram). It is the Cakkaravartti Fort, identified not only as Kurukṣetra but also as the place where the war ends. We must keep it in mind, but first let us look at the war-ending fort rituals at the western end of our transitional line.

Two temples where I have found it, at Chinna Salem and Salem

5. See chapter 11, n. 9.

Table 6. The Destruction of the Fort at Chinna Salem and Salem

Chinna Salem	Salem
Sunday	**All on one day**
1. Aravāṉ's sacrifice[6]	1. Aravāṉ's sacrifice
2. Arjuna's turning back of the bulls	
3. Demolition of the fort and tying of Kālī	2. Demolition of the fort
4. Firewalk	3. Firewalk
Monday	4. Hair tying
5. Turmeric water bath, morning	5. Turmeric water bath
6. Hair-tying and coronation of Dharma	

(on the northwest side of the city), perform the ceremony similarly, calling the ritual by its simplest name, kōṭṭai iṭittal, "the destruction of the fort." My 1984 fieldwork there was done before I became aware that "paṭukaḷam"-forts often had the term "wheel" (*cakkara*, Skt. *cakra*) in their names, but nothing of this sort was mentioned. The Chinna Salem poster announcing the festival says that the "demolition of the fort" is performed on the same "fort ground" (*kōṭṭai maitāṉattil*) as Aravāṉ's sacrifice, and includes not only the destruction of the fort but the "tying of Kālī" (*kāḷi kaṭṭutal*). Keeping in mind that there is no Duryodhana effigy nor any rites of dying and rising at these festivals, the essentially common sequence of the Chinna Salem and Salem rituals shows that the fort ceremony not only replaces the paṭukaḷam, but also displaces Draupadī's hair tying (see table 6).

Both temples are administered by Vaṉṉiyars and are proud to involve many other castes in their festivals. Although the Salem temple is a small private one, the Chinna Salem temple is much more ample and is famous for its festival throughout southwestern South Arcot (Francis 1906, 328; Hiltebeitel 1988a, 110). Since its rites are ampler too, I take them as the primary example.

When visited several months after the last festival, in 1984, the "fort ground" was no more than an open area filled with debris to the south of the temple and west of the shed housing the prone concrete effigy of Aravāṉ (plate 13). There the ramparts of a square fort, said to rise to about three feet, are constructed on the morning of firewalking day. The fort is Duryodhana's, and it is guarded by Kālī, who is understood at Chinna Salem to have taken on the identity of Duḥśālā (Tuṟcāttai), the hundred Kauravas' only sister and wife of Jayadratha Saindhava. (At Salem this fort-guardian is identified only as Kālī.) An old Vaṉṉiyar impersonates Kālī-

6. Using the concrete effigy shown in plate 13.

Duḥśālā as a hereditary role. Unfortunately I did not learn at either place whether Kālī[-Duḥśālā] enters the fort from a particular side. Within the Chinna Salem temple, however, Duḥśālā-Kālī is posted as one of Draupadī's and the Pāṇḍavas' guardians. While Pōrmaṉṉaṉ (next to Caṅkuvati) is said to guard the main eastern gate and Muttāl Rāvuttaṉ the northern gate, she occupies a maṇḍapa on the south wall, guarding the southern gate (see Hiltebeitel 1988a, 111, map 5). But from that position she faces north, as Kālī would from one of her typical north-facing temples. As suggested earlier, her position also seems to be a variant of the Kālī shrines that face Muttāl Rāvuttaṉ on the south-north axis of Draupadī temples in the Thanjavur region.[7] Kālī and her surrogates (including the fire-pot-bearing Draupadī at Mēlaccēri [chap. 9, sec. A]) thus ordinarily enter the battlefield from the north but may also protect the battlefield (or temple) by facing north, the direction from which dangers (like herself) are said to come (Hiltebeitel 1988a, 70, 127). In any case, Duḥśālā guards the temple as a result of her "failure" to prevent the demolition of her brothers' fort.

The five Pāṇḍavas come, having won the war (!). They are represented by a group of about forty men, all in hereditary roles, and led by a Vaṉṉiyar who acts as Arjuna. They circumambulate the fort three times, then "arrest" Duḥśālā-Kālī and her two oldest brothers, Duryodhana and Duḥśāsana (also Vaṉṉiyars). No one is killed. The "arrest" is accomplished by tying them with the end of a vīracāṭṭi whip, referred to as the "tying of Kālī." Once "tied," Duḥśālā-Kālī disposes herself favorably toward the Pāṇḍavas. She circumambulates the fort once, and that is the signal for the fort's demolition. The forty attendants of Arjuna then carry out this operation for about an hour. The ceremony ends when Arjuna pulls the three under arrest by a rope (possibly the vīracāṭṭi whip again) through the village in a scene that is said to be an occasion for fun.

At Salem, icons of Arjuna, Bhīma, Nakula, and Sahadeva are placed on the four corners of the fort. It is they who are said to destroy it, along with Pōrmaṉṉaṉ, while Dharma abstains, although the demolition itself is done by the local celebrants.

A number of elements here seem to be the equivalents of features of the absent paṭukaḷam rituals. The "tying" of Kālī-Duḥśālā and her transformation from the Pāṇḍavas' adversary to their protector looks like an allomorph of Draupadī's hair tying, which elsewhere marks the deactivation of her Kālīrūpa. The demolition of

7. See chapter 9, section D and n. 43.

the fort is like the demolition of Duryodhana's effigy. Both rituals mark the true end of the war. Pōrmaṉṉaṉ and Caṅkuvati carry over from the core area into the iconography of the two temples, and, at least at Salem, Pōrmaṉṉaṉ has a role in the ritual. But the differences from the typical core area paṭukaḷam rites are staggering. Duryodhana and Duḥśāsana are not killed. The former provides no blood for Draupadī to oil into her hair. And when she does put up her hair, it is after the firewalk rather than before it, as part of Dharma's coronation. This seems to take the sexual revenge out of the hair tying and to make the firewalk a preliminary purification before a final hair tying can be accomplished in conjunction with Dharma's paṭṭāpiṣēkam. As I demonstrated in volume 1, that is not the sense of the main core area myth of Draupadī's firewalk, which explains that she did it to make the Kaurava widows into suttees (1988a, 441–42). Rather, it is like a variant known in the Thanjavur area in which Draupadī prepares, after the war, to put up her hair with a heavenly flower, only to find that one petal has wilted. Seeing this, Bhīma tells her she should walk on fire to prove her chastity.[8] The Thanjavur area story of the wilted petal implies the deferment of Draupadī's hair tying, at least in its final unblemished form, to after the firewalk. The Chinna Salem and Salem variants thus seem to fuse elements from both regions.

B. The Wheel Fort

Moving back to the center of this transitional corridor and beginning to head south, one hears more about a cakra-named fort at Draupadī temples around Vriddhachalam. Here, however, at two temples no more than ten miles apart, the fort is linked in one case with the end of the war and in the other with its beginning. In turning again to the wheel-named fort and to such shifts of setting in the epic narrative, we begin, in this location, to trace the extensions of further Thanjavur area elements up into southern South Arcot. One last example of an end-of-war setting will exemplify this influence from the south.

8. See Hiltebeitel 1988a, 439–40. The Thanjavur-Trichy provenance of this story was further confirmed by two Thanjavur area pāratiyārs: S. Nagarajan (who was unfamiliar with the core area suttee story) and G. Ramachandra Bharati, from near Kumbhakonam (Cēturāmaṉ, personal interview, March 1990). In Nagarajan's version, Draupadī keeps the *pārijāta* flower in her *maṭi* (the lap fold of her saree) from the time Bhīma gets it for her in the forest until she takes it out for her hair tying. Seeing the one wilted petal, Bhīma tells her to walk on fire to remove any doubts about her tryst with Kīcaka and other rumors: "If you make it through you will be worshiped as a goddess. If not, perish in the fire that you were born in."

The Junction Road temple in Vriddhachalam has the following sequence of rituals: Aravāṉ kaḷappali, tying of Kālī, paṭukaḷam, and firewalking. For Aravāṉ's sacrifice, a Cempaṭavar (inland fisherman) in Kāḷi vēṣam sacrifices a goat over the neck of Aravāṉ's prone effigy. Now Kālī must be appeased. A fort is built, about four or five inches high and with four unguarded gateways at the cardinal points. Śiva sent this fort down from Kailāsa to earth so that Kālī would have a place to get her *balis*, her sacrificial offerings, including "chickens, goats, everything, even warriors." The appeasing of Kālī takes two forms, one in myth, the other in ritual. The story is as follows. Abhimanyu has a very small boy (*ciṉṉa kuḻantai*) named Ciruttoṅku. This boy asks Kālī how he can appease her, and because he is a small child, she tells him. Her fort is called the Cakkara Āyutam Kōṭṭai, the "Wheel Weapon Fort," because a wheel whirls around above it. She will be appeased only if he can stop its turning. For that, she says, he needs the inner stalk, or spadix, of a plantain tree: that is, a *vāḻaittaṇṭu*. If he touches the cakra with the vāḻaittaṇṭu, it will stop revolving. Then, when the cakra stops, they can tie Kālī's hands.

The ritual, however, includes none of the specifics of this myth. The Cempaṭavar, who remains possessed after sacrificing the goat over Aravāṉ's neck, and still of course in Kāḷi vēṣam, enacts Kālī's appeasement with the help of the temple pūcāri, a Vaṉṉiyar. Kālī, we now learn, is not content with the Aravāṉ's thirty-two pieces of flesh; she wants his head. This she should not have, for the obvious reason that without it, Aravāṉ could not watch the eighteen-day war, or for that matter fight on its eighth day. So instead of giving her Aravāṉ's head, the pūcāri offers her a pūjā with the breaking of a coconut and the beheading of a chicken, and he appeases her by putting the chicken's blood on her forehead. Then, on the very grounds of the demolished fort, five men, impersonating the slain heroes Śakuni, Duḥśāsana, Bhīṣma, Droṇa, and Abhimanyu, lie down in a circle with a sixth representing Duryodhana on a bench in the middle. All are covered with vēṣṭis. Another local actor in Draupadī's vēṣam then goes around the outer five and revives them by lamenting, sprinkling water, whipping their wrists, and placing poṭṭu on their foreheads, whereupon they go to Vaikuṇṭam, the highest heaven of Viṣṇu. No one represents Kṛṣṇa, so presumably it is Draupadī who bestows the ultimate reward herself. Then Draupadī goes to Duryodhana, stands with her leg on his chest, takes up blood from his thigh, and puts up her hair. In this case, then, the destruction of the fort is fused not with the paṭukaḷam rituals of the core area but with those of the Thanjavur area, involving Draupadī's viewing of the battlefield. The Wheel Weapon Fort simply becomes Kurukṣetra.

Before we turn to the Thanjavur traditions themselves, however, it is worth introducing them, as we did for the rituals of Kṛṣṇa showing Draupadī the battlefield, with questions raised by the transplanted Draupadī festival at Singapore.

The Singapore fort ceremonies occur not on the festival's culminating day (with the five-effigy rites and firewalk; chap. 10, sec. D), but earlier, after Aravāṉ's sacrifice and Arjuna's climbing of the tapas tree. Near Aravāṉ's shrine, preparations are made for "the ritual storming of an enemy's castle." As was noted in chapter 9 (sec. A), as a sequel to Aravāṉ's sacrifice, a trident was planted in the ground near the same shrine, marking the spot as Kurukṣetra (Babb 1974, 10–11):

> A rectangle, about ten feet by six, has been formed by sand ridges on the ground. Each wall of this rectangle has been broken in the middle by forming four "doors." A long table is set up nearby. When the procession arrives the image of Virapatra [Vīrapattiraṉ] is deposited on the ground facing the rectangle. A sword-bearer is stationed at each of the doors and another swordsman, having made one circuit of the rectangle without gaining entrance, rushes in with a great shout from the crowd.

From this point on, the washerman—who will later, as we have seen, undergo similar rites representing Duryodhana—is the main ritual actor. Having so far "been standing by in a trance, [he] is lifted up and deposited on the table" and covered with a white cloth. Then he is "immediately rushed into the shrine of Draupadi," where "he is whipped three times across the wrists." Many other people then go into trance and are treated similarly, the whipping continuing for about ten minutes, after which Vīrapattiraṉ's processional image is "taken into the main hall of the temple and deposited on the floor facing the apron in front of Draupadi's shrine."

Babb's informants "were unable to explicate these events with any degree of precision":

> The drama at the rectangle is said to be the Pandavas' "first victory" in the war. None of my informants was able to identify the owner of the "castle" that the sand rectangle represents. Some say the central figure who storms the fortress is

Krishna; others are not so sure. Deities guard each of the doors, and the invader must obtain permission from each to enter the fortress; permission obtained, he enters. (Babb 1974, 13–14)

Most of the mysteries of this account can be resolved by tracing the ceremony and its minimal narrative content back to fuller versions of the Thanjavur region.[9] In brief, however, we will find that Vīrapattiran̲ is first placed outside the fort because it has to be conquered for him. And once it is conquered, he is placed before Draupadī in the sanctum because, as the guardian of her fort, he is also the guardian of her temple.

Some preliminary clarification can be found in Cēturāman̲'s description of a story and related ritual called *Cakkara Ārakkōṭṭai Piṭikkum Vil̲ā*, the "Festival of the Seizing of the Cakkara Āram Fort." His informant on the story was the pāratiyār G. Ramachandra Bharati, for whom, according to Cēturāman̲, the meaning of the fort's name is the "Wheel Spoke Fort" (personal communication; see n. 8). While the ceremony is happening, the following "imaginative story (*kar̲pan̲aik katai*), one that is not in the *Bhārata* text" and for which he says there is no text at all, is recounted by someone from a "lineage (*paramparai*) of gurus" familiar with it (1986, 150, 152):

> Having given Dharma's sister Caṅkāmirtam in marriage to Vīrapattiran̲, the Pāṇḍavas gave them a Vibhūti Fort [*oru vipūti kōṭṭai*] in which to live. A battle then occurred between a horse [-riding] hero [*kutirai vīran̲*] who was standing guard at the fort and a horse[-riding] hero of Duryodhana's army. In the battle, Vīrapattiran̲'s horse hero, who was the head-man [*talaivan̲*] of the Cakkara Ārakkōṭṭai, obtained victory, disgracing Duryodhana's horse hero and sending him running, and he also sent [running?] and cut the leg and tail of the horse. Learning of this, Duryodhana came with the army and began to do battle with Vīrapattiran̲. In the course of this war, needing to seize this fort, Duryodhana opposed the fort guards in the four directions. . . . Then Vīrapattiran̲'s wife Caṅkāmirtam said that to make war with Duryodhana without the permission of her elder brothers [the Pāṇḍavas] was not wanted [*vēṇṭām*], and as a result of her preventing her husband [from defeating him], Duryodhana took possession of the fort. The Pāṇḍavas who

9. There is, however, no wheel-fort rite at Vaṭukku Poykaiyūr, linked with the Singapore temple's origins; see chapter 10, section D.

heard the news, with the help of Kṛṣṇa, again took possession of the Vibhūti Fort, and they entrusted it to Vīrapattiraṉ. (Cēturāmaṉ 1986, 150–52)[10]

In this account, there are thus three battles connected with the fort: the first between the two "horse heroes," the second matching Duryodhana against Vīrapattiraṉ and Kālī, and the third pitting the Pāṇḍavas and Kṛṣṇa against Duryodhana. Clearly, only the third could correspond to the Singapore ritual of the Pāṇḍavas' "first victory." This might also square with the uncertain recollection there (the only one offered) that the central figure to storm the fort is Kṛṣṇa. But as we shall see, Kṛṣṇa usually offers "help" of other kinds. As to the further uncertainty at Singapore over whose fort it is, the washerman there seems to have his counterpart either in Duryodhana's "horse hero" or, as he does later in the Singapore festival—when the washerman gets his legs pinched—with Duryodhana himself (chap. 10, sec. D). As we shall see, Thanjavur area myths and rituals will allow for both possibilities.

Cēturāmaṉ's discussion of the actual ritual is minimal, but he says it is done in numerous towns, and with "a unique excellence" at the Thanjavur East Gate (*kīḻavācal*) Tiraupatiyammaṉ Temple. There, he says, "the story is arranged as if Kāḷi Tēvi had assumed the responsibility for guarding the northern gate, and an excellent scene is arranged in which Duryodhana's armies do battle with Kāḷi" (ibid., 151). Curiously, however, the festival at the Thanjavur East Gate Draupadī temple is quite different from this brief description, and also from the story above. According to the temple's pūcāri, the paṭukaḷam they make is called Cayintavaṉ Kōṭṭai, the "Fort of Cayintavaṉ," or Jayadratha, though it is also known as the Vibhūti Fort, as above, or *Tirunīṟu* Fort (in spoken Tamil, *Tuṇṇūṟu* Kōṭṭai): in either case, the "Sacred Ash Fort." A four-sided fort is made of festoons (tōraṇams). In the center they make a platform from a mound of earth. One man impersonating Cayintavaṉ lies on the platform. After Cayintavaṉ is offered dīpārādhanā and a coconut, a man in Kāḷi vēṣam comes around the fort, and enters it from the north. At the sign that Kālī should kill Cayintavaṉ, a cock is killed. Its intestines are taken out and tied around Kālī's left hand. Kālī is really Draupadī in Kālīrūpa, and this is done because Draupadī is said to have made a vow that she would wear Cayintavaṉ's intestines as her garland. The fort is now hers, and she and the Pāṇḍavas give it to Vīrapattiraṉ. As above, he is

10. Cēturāmaṉ's source for this story was Ramachandra Bharati; see n. 8. I thank Abbie Ziffren for her help in translating this passage.

their brother-in-law, married to their only sister Caṅkāmirtam. Henceforth the fort is theirs, and he becomes Draupadī's kāval, or guardian.

Fortunately, two much fuller, and also quite similar, accounts of the story were obtained from the pāratiyārs S. Jegadisan at C. Kīraṉūr (near Vriddhachalam) and S. Nagarajan at Cattiram Karuppūr (near Kumbhakonam).[11] Once again we will follow our north-to-south route, beginning with a brief retelling of the prewar account that comes from the same Vriddhachalam area as the end-of-the-war story from the Junction Road temple. S. Nagarajan's account will then deserve our fullest attention, not only because it is the richest, but also because I was able to see him perform it as part of a Cakkaravartti Fort ritual.

According to S. Jegadisan, the Cakkaravartti Fort is none other than Upaplavya, the town of epic fame given to the Pāṇḍavas by Virāṭa after their thirteenth year of exile spent incognito in his kingdom.[12] In a "folkloric" twist, it had originally been given to Draupadī as dowry (*strī-taṉam*), but Duryodhana went and captured it for Ceyittarācaṉ [= Jayadratha-Cayintavaṉ] just before the war, to keep the Pāṇḍavas from occupying it. As long as the fort's cakra turned, Cayintavaṉ would rule it. In fact, the fort itself rotated and was identical with the cakra. Kṛṣṇa then interceded, saying only he or Sahadeva had the power to stop it. Sahadeva agreed to go. With his heroic sword (*vīra-vāl*) he cut down all the guards. Then he stopped the rotating wheel with the vāḻaittaṇṭu, or plantain stalk, entered by the northern gate, and severed the head of Ceyittarācaṉ. Then all the Pāṇḍavas went to rule in this place, prepared their armies for the eighteen-day war, performed Aravāṉ kaḷappali, got their weapons ready, killed everybody at Kurukṣetra, and fulfilled Pāñcāli's vow.

Here Vīrapattiraṉ is one of the original guardians of the fort and does not seem to become Draupadī's guardian as a result of the fort's conquest. The fort that the Pāṇḍavas (re)capture before the war is originally part of Draupadī's dowry, not the residence they give to Vīrapattiraṉ and Caṅkāmirtam, their sister. Vīrapattiraṉ seems to take over this fort most explicitly in the Thanjavur area.

11. I thank Eveline Masilamani-Meyer for her help in conducting and translating these two interviews.

12. The link with Upaplavya finds a variant in the early nineteenth-century Dindigul festival, where the Pāṇḍavas' "buying" of the Cēkkirāyaṉ Kōṭṭai (perhaps a distortion of Cakkara-Rājaṉ, the "Wheel King Fort"?) is the result of an alliance between the "the cities of Indraprastha and Upaplavya" (Mackenzie Collection, no. 68; Hiltebeitel 1988a, 152).

Let us then turn to the account of S. Nagarajan, recorded toward the beginning of his participation in the festival at Cattiram Karuppūr, near Kumbhakonam.

> Śiva and Pārvatī came down to earth. They went to have a bath. While they were bathing, Śiva took off his earring (*kuṇṭalam*). He put it down, but it started to whirl around and around and became a big fort (kōṭṭai). When Pārvatī came out from her bath, she said, "What is this?" Śiva said, "Let it be." So where is this fort located? It stays on earth in a place belonging to Hāstinapura and belongs to the king who rules there. At that time, Duryodhana was the oldest of a hundred brothers, and had a sister called Duḥśālā. He gave her to Cayintavaṉ in marriage. He wanted to settle the two of them in this fort. At that time the Pāṇḍavas were in the forest for twelve years. During that time they married their younger sister Caṅkāmirtam to Vīrapattiraṉ, and had settled them in that fort. So while the Pāṇḍavas were in the forest, Duryodhana fought with Vīrapattiraṉ, threw the two of them out of the fort, and replaced them, settling Duḥśālā and Cayintavaṉ there. Now Vīrapattiraṉ was not an ordinary human being, and could have defeated anyone. But Caṅkāmirtam told him, "He fights us while my brothers are away in the forest. Let us be patient and not fight back. I will go and tell my brothers." When the Pāṇḍavas heard, they said, "Now we have to recapture the fort." But Dharma said, "Before we do this, I will have to find out some secrets. Let us wait awhile." So they could not do anything. The only one who could do anything was Kṛṣṇa. So they called on Kṛṣṇa. Dharma said, "My sister's husband (*maittuṉaṉ*) and my sister have been thrown out of the fort, and Duryodhana has settled his own maittuṉaṉ there. How can I capture this fort?" Kṛṣṇa replied, "This is not an ordinary fort. It whirls around. At the bottom is the *vāl āyutam* (sword weapon), going round with the sound *kaṭakaṭakaṭakaṭa*. Whatever you place there, it will cut. Not only that, if any enemy comes, the conch will be blown. Whenever this conch blows, the enemy will stop in his tracks. Not only that, you have four guardians in the fort's four directions: at the east Vikkiṉēcuraṉ [Gaṇeśa], at the south Taṭcaṇāmūrtti [Śiva], at the west Cuppiramaṇiyaṉ [Murukaṉ], and at the north Kālī. It is very difficult to get inside. We must stop the sword, fight all these guards, and, to enter, get Kālī on our side. Only Kālī knows the secret, and we must somehow get it from her. So we'll make Arjuna's son Ab-

himanyu into a child and bring him to Kālī." Kṛṣṇa gave a means (*tantiram*) and changed Abhimanyu into a child, and Sahadeva dressed like a lady. So Sahadeva came to the fort and said she wanted to sell the child. When Kālī saw this, she said "Why, mother, are you selling your own child, the one that you bore?" "My husband died. I have difficulty feeding myself; how can I raise this child?" So Kālī said, "Okay, give the child to me."

Once adopted, Abhimanyu asked Kālī, "When you go outside and enemies come, what do I do?" Kālī told him about the four guardians. The other three no one can pass. "One can enter only by the northern side, where I am, by deceiving (*ēmāṟṟu*) me, and I'm not easily deceived. Even if they deceive me, they cannot get by me because the cakra is whirling around, and they'll be cut by the sword. And on top of that, the conch is blowing. You cannot very quickly take possession of me by charms." As soon as Abhimanyu learned all this, he wrote a palm leaf (*ōlai*) to his father and sent it through the wind. When they received the letters, the Pāṇḍavas said, "It sounds easy," and set off for the fort. They approached Gaṇeśa with steamed rice cakes (*koḻukkaṭṭai*) and rice flakes (*aviḻ*), Śiva with worship (*pajaṉai*), and Murukaṉ with beautiful girls, but all three refused to yield. At last they came to Kālī. Abhimanyu asked her further. She said, "When it's amāvācai, at midnight, I get thoroughly drunk with alcohol and intoxicating things (*pōtaivastu*). At that time I fall down drunk. You have to loosen my hair and tie it. And while I am unconscious, you have to break and take out my two teeth [her protruding canines]. When my teeth are taken out, all my śakti goes, and I don't know what anyone is doing. Only then, when I have no power, can you go past me. Otherwise it is impossible." Abhimanyu sent this secret to the Pāṇḍavas, and awaited the proper time. While she was lying drunk, he tied her hair and broke out her teeth. While she was there like that, they went inside.[13] They stopped the cakra from going round with the vāḻaittaṇṭu. The wheel got stuck in its milk. They stopped the conch by filling it with cotton. [Nothing was said about the neutralization of the sword.] Then they went inside and tied up Cayintavaṉ. After that the real war started, the eighteen-day war.

13. In the version sung by S. Nagarajan in the Cakkaravartti Kōṭṭai ritual (see below), it is clear that it is the Pāṇḍavas who get Kālī drunk by offering her toddy, marijuana, and whiskey.

Asked if this happened before or after Aravāṉ's sacrifice, the pāratiyār said the two have no relation to each other, and he launched into a description of the latter. I take this as a recognition that Aravāṉ's sacrifice is fixed textually in the *Mahābhārata*, and thus in the ritual sequence of a festival, whereas the fort story is not. But the evasion only masks an obvious congruity. Both stories, at least with the fort story told in this form, occur on an amāvācai, with Kālī drunk on either liquor or blood, at the very beginning of the eighteen-day war. As we just saw, the story does occur before Aravāṉ's sacrifice, according to S. Jegadisan, as part of the end of the Pāṇḍavas' sojourn with Virāṭa. But that will hardly fix this free-floating story for us.

As to wheel-fort rituals in the Thanjavur area, much of what goes on has, at least on the surface, surprisingly little to do with this story. It seems that there are two primary elements, which can either be performed separately or combined. One, which can relate to the story and which we have already noted at the East Gate temple in Thanjavur, is to have an enactment of Cayintavaṉ's defeat, with either his killing or his arrest and expulsion from the fort. But one also finds ostensibly the same ritual performed for Duryodhana rather than Cayintavaṉ. One example is at Lalgudi, where Cakkarapuṟakkōṭṭai (Wheel Exterior Fort) is simply the name for the site where Draupadī puts up her hair, taking the necessary articles from an unusual prone straw effigy of Duryodhana with a papier-mâché mask (see n. 4). On the festival announcement, the ritual is thus called *Cakkarapuṟakkōṭṭai kūntal muṭi*, the "Cakkarapuṟa Fort hair tying," and occurs on the day between Aravāṉ's sacrifice and firewalking.

The other is to have local people dress up in a variety of vēṣams or costumes, varying from place to place, and be taken about in cycle rickshaws and bullock carts in a display that seems to span two possibilities: recreating the appropriate epic scene, or a variant, with Pāratam recitation; or exhibiting a generous portion of the Hindu pantheon. According to S. Nagarajan, it is done with proper epic panache at the Periya Katai Teru Draupadī temple in Kumbhakonam.[14] A square or rectangle is drawn on the ground with four entrances. At each gate, one person stands with a stick, impersonating one of the four divine guards. People dress up in costumes of the Pāṇḍavas, enter the fort through the northern gate, capture Cayintavaṉ, "arrest" him like a prisoner, and lead

14. Eveline Masilamani-Meyer observed this ritual performed by the Thanjavur Pūmal Rāvuttaṉ Kōyil Street temple in 1985 or 1986 (personal communication, 1990).

him away with ropes. One is reminded of the ritual at Chinna Salem, except there the arrests are made of Duryodhana, Duḥśāsana, and their sister Duḥśālā, Cayintavan-Jayadratha's wife (who at Chinna Salem is identified with Kālī). Nothing is done for her at Kumbhakonam, just as nothing is done for him at Chinna Salem. But the Chinna Salem rite now seems to retain a trace of this southern tradition about the Cayintavaṉ family. At Kumbhakonam, however, the tying of Kālī is part of the story but not the ritual, whereas at Chinna Salem the tying of Duḥśāla-Kālī has a place in both the myth and ritual. Certain features of the Thanjavur area story—the stopping of the cakra with the plantain stalk, the extraction of Kālī's canines—do not seem to be ritualized anywhere.[15]

In contrast, the Cakkaravartti Kōṭṭai ritual at Cattiram Karuppūr had a little bit of everything else. Soon after nightfall, the chariot bearing Draupadī, Arjuna, and Kṛṣṇa's pañcalōkam icons is decorated to leave the temple and join six other chariots on the street, all lined up facing east for the procession to the Cakkaravartti Kōṭṭai. People of every age come dressed up as all variety of Hindu gods and sages, with epic heroes almost lost among the throng. After much posing for pictures and other amusements, once they all get in their chariots, the order is as follows. The first chariot, a cycle rickshaw, bears Karṇa on a peacock throne. He leads this procession because the total Pāratam covered by this ceremony includes his seventeenth-day fight and death. But there was nothing else to indicate it, either in the Pāratam or in the ritual. All the following chariots are double bullock carts, each provided with two vertical tube lights with an arc of little red lights above them, all run by a generator. The second chariot bears Rāma, Lakṣmaṇa, Sītā, and Hanumān; the third, Kṛṣṇa, the Pāṇḍavas, and Draupadī; the fourth, five children as the Young Pañcapāṇḍavas; the fifth, Murukaṉ, his wives Vaḷḷi and Tēvāṉai, Nārada, and other child-Ṛṣis; the sixth, Śiva, Pārvatī, Gaṇeśa, Murukaṉ, and Vaḷḷi (again), and more little Ṛṣis; and on the seventh and last (see plate 28), along with the pañcalōkam icons and vīrakuntam (front left of Draupadī: that is, facing northeast), sit Duryodhana (the temple's Kōttaṉar pūcāri, bearing a lemon-tipped sword) and Kālī (in a green saree, bearing her trident, wearing a golden crown, and red faced with white canines).[16] The procession makes its way for over an hour to the Cak-

15. The plantain is probably a śamī equivalent again, as when either represents demons at Dasara (chapter 8, section B); like other "milky śamī substitutes (chapter 6, section B), it now appeases weapons!
16. Dressed again as at Aravāṉ's sacrifice; see chapter 9, section A.

karavartti Fort, which is situated at a hamlet called Manañcēri. This site is chosen because it is the boundary of the Draupadī temple's power and said to be the boundary of Cattiram Karuppūr. However, no significance was attached to its boundary location, since it was pointed out that at some festivals the ceremony is performed on the temple grounds.

At no point in my efforts to get advance information about a ritual have I found greater confusion. The pāratiyār S. Nagarajan was at pains to explain that the ceremony was not done properly here, as it was in downtown Kumbhakonam. Nothing special would be done to represent the fort, he said. One was built there long ago, but no more. No one would lie down there either. He would sing his story of Cayintavaṉ, but there would be too much noise. Just then, an old man came walking by and said that the whole idea of the ritual is to go to capture the fort of Duryodhana. The pāratiyār smiled knowingly and said, "Some people say so." Indeed, that was the public understanding of the rite, and after observing the rite, it was evident that the pāratiyār was wrong about two things. Someone did lie down, but as Duryodhana, not Cayintavaṉ. And something special was done to represent the fort. The pāratiyār seemed to recall the ritual only to the degree that it corresponded to his Pāratam.

At it turned out, the Cakkaravartti Fort was a large square kōlam, close to twenty feet on each side, under a pantal that extended out from a house owned and rented out by the temple. After the chariots arrived and turned around, two sets of benches were laid out. In a perfect execution of simultaneous ritual doubling, while the pāratiyār sang his account of the Pāṇḍavas' capture of the Cakkaravartti fort from Cayintavaṉ before the war begins, the ritual enacted the capture of the Cakkaravartti fort (= Hāstinapura) from Duryodhana as the war ends. The Kōttaṉar pūcāri, impersonating Duryodhana, after being shown a dīpārādhanā, gets possessed (by Duryodhana, according to one informant). It was he who had borne the lemon-topped sword beside Kālī on Draupadī's chariot, presumably as a sign that he was to be the sacrificial victim to Draupadī in Kālīrūpa.[17] He lies on a bench held down by three or four attendants, is fanned, and is restrained by the vīracāṭṭi whip from getting too thoroughly possessed. Periodically he struggles, and supposedly gives oracles about people's grievances (*kuṟaikaḷ*),

17. Recall Draupadī's icon on procession with Kālī's at Tindivanam for the Terukkūttu performance of Aravāṉ's sacrifice (chap. 3, sec. A).

though I saw nothing to confirm this.[18] Mostly he just grunted and writhed. The local idea is that Duryodhana is captured in the fort. I was told the next morning, when the same Duryodhana did much the same thing at the paṭukaḷam, but this time with the pāratiyār as Draupadī putting up her hair (plate 21), that Duryodhana's two parts used to be continuous. The problem was that it would last too late into the night, so the practice was stopped. So the hair-tying sequel to his capture was moved to the separate but highly similar morning ritual that was described in chapter 10 (sec. D). The only noticeable distinctions are that in the morning ritual, Duryodhana writhes but does not grunt and is covered with a brown cloth: both changes no doubt reflect that he is now dead.

Finally, at Dharmarāja temples in Coimbatore District, kōṭṭai iṭittal evokes an entirely different story. In oral versions, the fort in question—the Cakkarapuram or Cakkarapuri Kōṭṭai (Wheel City Fort)—belongs to two demonic (Arakki) magician sisters named Āravalli and Cūravalli. The Pāṇḍavas determine to conquer it during their period of forest exile. In the version of the pāratiyār Val Bhiman of Aṉṉūr, Abhimanyu is sent as a child to get the fort's secrets from Kālī. This is not, however, Arjuna's son Abhimanyu but another Abhimanyu, the son of Sahadeva, known as Vālāl Apimaṉṉaṉ, Abhimanyu with the sword! Clearly we have here a distorted trace of the story that Sahadeva disguises himself as a woman to take the "real" Abhimanyu, transformed by Kṛṣṇa to appear as Sahadeva's child, on her hip. First this new Abhimanyu uses his sword to stop the river that protects the fort. Once inside, Kālī tells him how to stop the cakra above her fort by throwing a magic stone (*mantirakkal*) at it. Then Sahadeva, a great *jñāni* (man of knowledge), enters the fort, defeats Āravalli and Cūravalli, and is able to control Kālī because he is a "portion of Śiva" (Śivāṃśa), whom Kālī is unable to fight.[19] Bhīma then uses his mace to destroy the fort.

18. Recall that the leader of the Kaurava-Kuravans gives oracles in Kerala, while Duryodhana dances at another Kerala temple on one leg (see chap. 7, n. 22).

19. Here there is no "tying of Kālī" as a multiform of Draupadī's hair tying such as we have seen in various forms at Muthialpet (Draupadī's icon decorated as Kālī), Villupuram (Kōṭṭai Kāḷi), Chinna Salem (tying of Duḥśālā), Junction Road, Vriddhachalam, and East Gate temple, Thanjavur (tying Kālī's hands); and in S. Nagarajan's account (her hair tied when she is drunk). These tyings seem to bind the goddess to her various victims, who may also be tied or "arrested" (e.g., Duryodhana at Cattiram Karuppūr; Cayintavaṉ at Periya Katai Teru, Kumbhakonam; and Duryodhana and Duḥśāsana at Chinna Salem; recall also the arrest of Aśvatthāman at Tindivanam, linked with the symbolism of binding a sacrificial victim; chap. 11, sec. A).

Āravalli and Cūravalli then go to Kerala, where, linked with Bhagavati, they continue to exercise their magic powers. The Coimbatore area festivals studied include no ritual enactment of the destruction of this fort. At Aṉṉūr, however, despite its prewar epic setting, the story is recited on the festival's eighteenth day, as if it retained a ritual correspondence with the end of the war.

This oral version, similar to one heard at nearby Veḷḷalūr, differs significantly from the chapbook ballad of the story called *Āravalli Cūravalli Katai* (Pukaḻēntip Pulavar, n.d.). Here events occur before the gambling match, when the Pāṇḍavas and Kauravas ruled their separate kingdoms (ibid., 4), the Pāṇḍavas' known as Tarumapuram (ibid., 89).[20]

> Āravalli and Cūravalli are two of seven Reṭṭi women, fearsome magicians, who rule a fort in Nellūrupaṭṭaṇam (Nellur) in Southern Andhra. Bhīma fails in an initial attempt to defeat them, is imprisoned, and has to be rescued by Kṛṣṇa. Āravalli sends a message to the Pāṇḍavas belittling their manhood and dynasty. The Pāṇḍavas decide to avenge themselves and learn through Sahadeva's astrology that only Allimuttu (also called Allirājaṉ) can do so. While his father Pōrmaṉṉaṉ is out hunting, his mother Caṅkuvati, the Pāṇḍavas' sister, refuses. But Dharma convinces her. The Pāṇḍavas adopt Allimuttu and Caṅkuvati adopts Abhimanyu for the duration of Allimuttu's mission. Bhadrakālī gives him sacred ash and a sword. He uses the ash to burn away all the magical forces that Āravalli sends against him, camps before the fort and confronts them. They challenge him to a series of wagers (*pantayam*s), and he wins each time, calling on Draupadī, Kṛṣṇa, Bhadrakālī, and the Pāṇḍavas and applying the ash to his forehead. Āravalli then offers him her daughter Pal Varicai. He suspects she will be a magician too, but Āravalli promises him she is an innocent girl who grew up in an underground cell (*nilavaṟai;* 63) and has never seen the sun nor any king. Pal Varicai is indeed innocent, but Āravalli tricks her into carrying a clump of jasmine and a lemon that she says will relieve Allimuttu when there is no water on their journey to get the Pāṇḍavas' permission. On the way, overcome by thirst, he smells the jasmine and faints, and when she squeezes the lemon for him to drink he shivers and dies. Pal Varicai sees she has been tricked by Āravalli, weeps, and prays to Viṣṇu and Śiva to revive Allimuttu so

20. I thank Pon Kothandaraman for going over this text with me.

that he can conquer her mother's city and marry her. Back at Nellur, Āravalli and Cūravalli put her back into her cell.

The Pāṇḍavas learn what has happened and set out toward Nellur. Caṅkuvati weeps. Pōrmaṉṉaṉ arrives and blames her for letting Allimuttu go. Abhimanyu overhears and vows that he will retrieve Allimuttu's soul (*uyir*) even if he is in some afterworld. He sets out with Pōrmaṉṉaṉ. When they find the body, Abhimanyu tells Pōrmaṉṉaṉ to guard it while he searches the heavens. Now Ātinārāyaṇaṉ [Kṛṣṇa] decides to test Pōrmaṉṉaṉ. He takes the form of a poor almanac-bearing Brahman from Kāśī (75–76, 93) and pretends to be hungry, unable to eat before he performs a pūjā, and unable to perform the pūjā because he has seen a corpse. He can eat only if the corpse is cremated. He chides Pōrmaṉṉaṉ for thinking that a soul can be retrieved and says Pōrmaṉṉaṉ will be responsible for killing him, and thus guilty of Brahmanicide, if he does not cremate his son. Pōrmaṉṉaṉ agrees. The Brahman sends him off for special firewood, and while he is away, he orders the goddess Earth to open, take in the body, and guard it. Then he piles up wood as if the corpse were beneath it, adds the wood Pōrmaṉṉaṉ soon brings, and sets the false pyre alight. The Brahman then leaves and orders a great rain from Varuṇa, which washes everything away, leaving the spot without traces.

Abhimanyu finds Allimuttu's soul in Indraloka and brings it back in a precious casket (*cimil;* 79). He finds Pōrmaṉṉaṉ weeping and hears what has happened. They look in vain for the remains of the pyre. But Allimuttu's protective *rājāḷi* bird (a falcon or hawk) has seen everything and leads them to the spot. Not understanding, Abhimanyu—repeatedly called Vālāl-Apimaṉṉaṉ, "Abhimanyu with the sword"—plants his sword there, point upward, and prepares to impale himself, thinking he will die like his "brother." When he jumps on the sword it goes into the earth, and Allimuttu's soul reenters his body through it. Allimuttu comes out from the ground, asking, "Where is Pal Varicai?" He determines to conquer Nellur, and all three set out on their horses. Meanwhile, the Pāṇḍavas (minus Dharma) also set out on their chariots. Āravalli sees seven men approaching her fort: Bhīma from the south; Arjuna, Nakula, and Sahadeva from the east; Pōrmaṉṉaṉ from the west, and Abhimanyu and Allimuttu from the north (82). Allimuttu praises Bhadrakālī and asks her to come from her temple to the battlefield (*raṇakaḷam*) to fill it with blood and

> flesh so that he should be able to make a Pāratam war here (83). While the others fight outside the fort, Allimuttu and Abhimanyu enter it from the northern side and cut off many heads. They capture all but one of the seven women. The one escapes to Kerala, where she takes the name Pakavatiyammaṉ (Bhagavati; 84). Trying to learn about the escapee, Allimuttu beats the other six with a thorn-tipped whip. Bhīma then comes and says that, rather than beating them, they should cut off their noses, upper lips, and ears. With this they feed Bhadrakālī's army of demons. They then destroy the fort, sow it over with castor seed (86, 88), and visit Bhadrakālī's temple to praise her for the victory. Kālī asks for the six noses to be strung on a tōraṇam before her temple. The party then leaves for Tarumapuram, where Dharma and Draupadī greet them for the wedding. Draupadī blesses Allimuttu, saying, "Till the end of the Kaliyuga, your story will be remembered. People will consider it as Pāratam" (91). Kṛṣṇa then reappears as the Kāśī Brahman to perform the wedding. But before he does so, he says everyone should forget the name Pal Varicai; he will rename her Vālammāḷ, and she will live long (*vāḻ;* 93).

Vālammāḷ means the "Youthful Lady" or "Young Mother" and is clearly meant to be an improvement over Pal Varicai, "Row of Teeth," whatever unpleasantness that may mean (see Hiltebeitel 1988a, 109). She is also no doubt the same person as Vālāmpāḷ, whose wooden processional icon we found a singular example of at Chinna Salem (chap. 3, sec. B): a suggestion of a folkloric continuum between this latter temple at the southwest of the core area (in which Pōrmaṉṉaṉ and Caṅkuvati are represented together facing the sanctum [1988a, map 5]) and the further southwestern traditions of Coimbatore.

For immediate purposes, however, what is most significant is that the oral versions of *Āravalli Cūravalli* are thematically and narratively close to oral versions from the Thanjavur area (the wheel theme; Abhimanyu sent as a child in a variation on his collaboration with his "parent" [now father] Sahadeva). At no point in the chapbook is there any suggestion that the fort bears a wheel-related name or has any cakra to protect it. The chapbook version, on the other hand, links up with core area traditions by centering much of the story of Pōrmaṉṉaṉ, his son Allimuttu, and the latter's marriage to Pal Varicai–Vālāmpāḷ. In *central* core area mythology, however, Pal Varicai is the pregnant sister of Muttāl Rāvuttaṉ, whom he almost sacrifices to Draupadī, while Allimuttu marries not her, but Mallikā, Muttāl Rāvuttaṉ's magically created daughter (Hiltebeitel 1988a, 105–16).

This cluster of characters seems to have flourished in Coimbatore area traditions, where Pōttu Rāja is again known as Draupadī's temple guardian rather than Vīrapattiraṉ, who replaces Pōttu Rāja as the central figures in the Thanjavur area. At Aṉṉūr, for instance, Pōttu Rāja is represented by three conical stones facing Dharma and Draupadī's sanctum on a platform next to Nandi. At Veḷḷalūr, he is said to be Draupadī's army marshal (*cēnātipati*), the husband of Caṅkuvati, Dharma's sister, and brother of Muttālakkaṉṉi, Dharma's wife. Muttālakkaṉṉi is also Dharma's wife in an oral account from Chinna Salem, again pointing to the same continuum. But there, instead of being linked with the Pāṇḍavas as Pōttu Rāja's sister, she is the daughter of Muttāla Mahārāja, the Hindu king whom Muttāl Rāvuttaṉ first served as marshal until he accompanied Muttālakkaṉṉi to serve Dharma and Draupadī in the same capacity (Hiltebeitel 1988a, 110–15).

Coimbatore area temples thus provide a likely background for the chapbook ballad no less than for the oral accounts (note the common interest in explaining how one or more of the sisters escapes to nearby Kerala to become, or join magical forces with, Bhagavati). But it replaces certain Thanjavur area themes with core area ones not only by focusing on the family of Pōttu Rāja–Pōrmaṉṉaṉ, but by incorporating into his family two women—Pal Varicai and Muttālakkaṉṉi—who in the core area are connected instead with Muttāl Rāvuttaṉ. Indeed, one may suspect that the losses to Muttāl Rāvuttaṉ's family are really transfers of the magician themes in the story from him to Āravalli and Cūravalli. Moreover, one can detect further core area multiforms in the chapbook's spoof on Pōrmaṉṉaṉ's near Brahmanicide (cf. ibid., 377–78, 424–48) and in his son Allimuttu's handling of the thorn-tipped whip. On the other hand, the four-sided attack on the fort, with Allimuttu and Abhimanyu entering with Kālī's blessings from the north, plus all the riding around the fort on chariots, remind one of the wheel-fort myths and rituals of the Thanjavur area. Allimuttu's prayer that Bhadrakālī make the battle within the fort a Pāratam and Draupadī's assurance that the story will be recognized as Pāratam also help to explain how *Āravalli Cūravalli* can be recited on a festival's eighteenth day as an equivalent to the Kurukṣetra paṭukaḷam rites, like the wheel-fort myths of Thanjavur.

So much, then, for variations on kōṭṭai iṭittal. We must now look into some of the themes that hold this complex together. We need go no further in discussing *Āravalli Cūravalli Katai* and the Coimbatore area's coalescence of core area and Thanjavur area themes. The real problem lies in the relation between core area fort myths and Thanjavur area fort myths *and rituals*. Clearly, the place to start is with Caṅkuvati-Caṅkāmirtam, the Pāṇḍavas' younger sister. She is unquestionably one and the same person. In the core area she is the wife of Pōrmaṉṉaṉ–Pōttu Rāja. In the Thanjavur area she is the wife of Vīrapattiraṉ.[21] It is at this point that I will try to justify my continued reference to Vīrapattiraṉ as Pōttu Rāja's substitute and, in making that point, to further buttress my argument that the Gingee region is the core area and source of the Draupadī cult's diffusion.

The core area myth in which Caṅkuvati marries Pōrmaṉṉaṉ is "Pōrmaṉṉaṉ's Fight," in which Pōrmaṉṉaṉ is tricked into destroying his own, or his father's, fort, and sowing it over with castor and cotton. After this, he brings his ritual weapons to serve Draupadī so that she can successfully begin the *Mahābhārata* war with him as her marshal, and he gets Caṅkuvati in the bargain. According to the Tindivanam pūcāri, in fact, Pōrmaṉṉaṉ stands guarding the fort in which the war takes place, holding the head of his father "Pōttu Rāja" (Hiltebeitel 1988, 344). Moreover, as we have seen, Pōttu Rāja is associated with the śamī tree and particularly, in Draupadī cult rituals, with the vaṉṉimaram (śamī) that conceals the Pāṇḍavas' weapons during their period of disguise in the kingdom of Virāṭa. The Pāṇḍavas cannot wage war without these weapons any more than they can do so without the ritual weapons brought by Pōrmaṉṉaṉ. In core area circles, the two stories are each others' classical-popular multiforms.[22]

In the Thanjavur area, however, while Vīrapattiraṉ retains a connection with the liṅgam and the yūpa-like post (see chap. 5, sec. D), he retains no evident connection with the śamī. The śamī is replaced by Upaplavya. In each case, what is required is that the Pāṇḍavas secure something necessary for their victory at the end of their year of concealment. In the one case it is the weapons from the śamī outside Virāṭa's capital, with their multiform in the weapons of Pōrmaṉṉaṉ. In the other it is the wheel-fort of Upaplavya, also outside Virāṭa's capital, as their base of operations to begin the eighteen-day war by readying their armies and weapons. As we saw in chapter 2, there is an affinity between Virāṭa's Matsya king-

21. Outside Thanjavur District proper, one may still find Vīrapattiraṉ a bachelor (that is, unmarried to Caṅkāmirtam): e.g., at Lalgudi, and at Junction Road, Vriddhachalam. At the latter temple, he is single even though he is said to be the Pāṇḍavas' maittuṉuṉ or "sister's husband."

22. See chapter 6, section B; chapter 8, section B; and chapter 9, section D.

dom, with its chaotic shadings, and the festival-holding temple and village, from which (no less than in which), in one manner or another, the Pāṇḍavas go to war. The boundaries of the temple and village are thus especially significant in relation to these *Virāṭaparvan* themes. Despite the warning that it is not significant, let us remind ourselves of the boundary location of the Cakkaravartti fort at Cattiram Karuppūr. As regards Vīrapattiraṉ, he thus guards the fort and the temple in the same manner as Pōttu Rāja. It is the boundary fort *from* which the Pāṇḍavas wage war at Kurukṣetra. But it is also the fort *in* which they wage war, since the wheel-fort can also *be* Kurukṣetra.

Other continuities between the two fort myths are also evident. In one account, Pōrmaṉṉaṉ's Śivānandapuri was created when Pārvatī drew a kōlam design on the ground, placing a fort inside it. When Śiva awoke he brought the city to life and gave it its name (Hiltebeitel 1988a, 340; Biardeau 1989b, 114). The wheel-fort in one account comes from Śiva's fallen earring; in another it is sent from Mount Kailāsa. At Cattiram Karuppūr it is represented by a kōlam. Moreover, it also bears the name Vibhūti Fort, the fort of Śiva's sacred ash. To be sure, Śivānandapuri is never possessed by Duryodhana. But Pōrmaṉṉaṉ's father had to be killed because he was a partisan of the Kauravas, thus marking in each case a change in the fort's allegiance from the one side to the other. In each case the Pāṇḍavas gain entry to the fort with the help of tricks by Kṛṣṇa. The winning of Pōrmaṉṉaṉ's allegiance and weapons is also an initial victory for the Pāṇḍavas, though won without a fight (Hiltebeitel 1988a, 370). Vīrapattiraṉ's Ash Fort stays standing for him to guard, while Pōrmaṉṉaṉ's Fort is demolished. But what it means for an "ash fort" to stand is a good question, especially since it is destroyed in the rituals.[23] In any case, the result is that both Pōrmaṉṉaṉ and Vīrapattiraṉ guard not only the fort of Kurukṣetra, but also the Draupadī temple, itself a fort (as well as a chariot).

More than this, the wheel-fort myths take a somewhat tacit theme from the core area treatment of Pōrmaṉṉaṉ and extend it into a central episode involving Vīrapattiraṉ. Being married to Caṅkuvati–Caṅkāmirtam, each is the Pāṇḍavas' only sister's husband (maittuṉaṉ). For each, the parallel figure in the Kaurava camp is thus Jayadratha-Saindhava, the husband of the Kauravas' only sister, Duḥśālā. In the core area, the rapport is thematically enriched in the Terukkūttu renditions of *Cayintavaṉ Caṇṭai*, "Sain-

23. I am not tempted by Cēturāmaṉ's explanation that it refers to cement (personal interview; see n. 8).

dhava's Fight," through a set of extended folkloric parallels and inversions that were detailed in volume 1. But in brief, in the Pōrmaṉṉaṉ myth, the son holds the father's head and keeps it from falling, whereas in the Jayadratha story the father holds the son's head and drops it.[24] In the Thanjavur cycle, the structural opposition turns into a narrative one. In one account, the fort was originally the Pāṇḍavas' wedding gift to their sister and Vīrapattiraṉ. Then, as Dharma tells Kṛṣṇa (according to S. Nagarajan): "My sister's husband (maittuṉaṉ) and sister have been thrown out of the fort, and Duryodhana has settled his own maittuṉaṉ there." Though Vīrapattiraṉ could have prevented Duryodhana's takeover of the fort, he refrains from doing so at the bidding of Caṅkāmirtam so that the Pāṇḍavas can recapture it for him.

As regards the setting of these stories in the *Mahābhārata*, it clearly makes a difference in terms of fidelity to the classical story whether Cayintavaṉ is killed in the fort or just expelled from it. If he is only expelled, his death can be preserved for the fourteenth day of the war, when Arjuna should behead him for his part in killing Abhimanyu. As one would expect, the expulsion stories come primarily from pāratiyārs, who know the classical epic. Where he is killed, one can infer that the wheel-fort story has been conflated with the killing of Cayintavaṉ on the fourteenth day, a story that itself involves the Kauravas' formation of a circular array around Jayadratha in an attempt to protect him against Arjuna's assault. In contrast, the understanding that Cayintavaṉ is killed emerges primarily from local temple informants, as at the East Gate temple in Thanjavur and at Cōḻavantāṉ. The only exception I have found was the pāratiyār's account from C. Kīraṉūr, where, quite logically, it is Sahadeva rather than Abhimanyu (who has died the day before) who must stop the cakra with the vāḻaittaṇṭu. In these cases, the killing of Cayintavaṉ represents his fourteenth-day fight.

At Cōḻavantāṉ, beyond Thanjavur District in Madurai District to the south, a fort for Cayintavaṉ is prepared in the sands of the nearby Vaikai River. Seven ridged squares of sand are built, one within another and each about a foot high. In the middle, a small stage is built for Cayintavaṉ. A local ritualist impersonating him comes with another representing Droṇa, leading the processional image of Draupadī, who is borne on a horse vāhana. While Draupadī stays outside the seventh wall on her horse, Cayintavaṉ goes to the innermost fort and lies down on the platform. There Droṇa

24. See further Hiltebeitel 1988a, 405–6.

and other guards are supposed to protect him, as they do in the *Mahābhārata*, by forming a circular array around him. While one party (the Kauravas) guards the seven entrances bearing swords and flags, another (the Pāṇḍavas), led by the pūcāri, fights past them in mock combat. On both sides, the participants wear protective kāppu. When the Pāṇḍavas party finally reaches Cayintavaṉ, the pūcāri cuts a lime, throws its quarters in the four directions for Pūtams, and then cuts Cayintavaṉ's tongue, making it bleed. He then puts turmeric on it, but it leaves a scar. In the epic story, Jayadratha is beheaded.

More interesting is Draupadī's horse vehicle. Biardeau has argued that Jayadratha symbolizes the horse that Duryodhana fails to protect in his battlefield equivalent of a flawed Aśvamedha. The alternation of victories and defeats in the wheel-fort myths may contain an echo of the type of double horse sacrifice that Biardeau posits as the symbolism behind the last days of the war (see chap. 12, nn. 6, 22). Let us recall that in one account, the first fight at the wheel-fort is between two "horse heroes": Duryodhana's and Vīrapattiraṉ's. "In the battle, Vīrapattiraṉ's horse hero, who was the head-man [*talaivaṉ*] of the Cakkara Ārakkōṭṭai, obtained victory, disgracing Duryodhana's horse hero and sending him running, and he also sent [running?] and cut the leg and tail of the horse." The battle between Kaurava and Pāṇḍava horse heroes thus has the result that Duryodhana's horse hero suffers the humiliation of the maiming of his horse's leg and tail. One suspects an evocation here of some kind of horse sacrifice. And one may further suspect that Duryodhana's horse hero is none other than Jayadratha himself, or a double for him, just as Vīrapattiraṉ's horse hero is probably a double for his cavalier colleague, Muttāl Rāvuttaṉ. Alternatively, Draupadī comes on her horse vāhana to witness the sacrificial maiming of Jayadratha himself.[25]

In terms of its epic context, it also makes a difference whether the story or ritual features Abhimanyu (or one of his doubles: his son, or Sahadeva's son Abhimanyu). As noted, if the ritual portrays the death of Jayadratha on the fourteenth day, it can have no part for Abhimanyu, whom Jayadratha helped to kill on the thirteenth day. Not surprisingly, then, the rituals that reenact the story as one of Cayintavaṉ's death have no part for Abhimanyu. On the contrary,

25. Recall the game of horses (kutira kali) outside goddess temples in Central Travancore, each side agitating horse figures in mock combat; also the chagrined and disheveled mahiṣī approaching the Aśvamedha horse from the northern side of the enclosure.

the accounts that feature Abhimanyu in the conquest of the fort are all prewar episodes. Indeed, insofar as the wheel-fort myths usually involve an opposition between Abhimanyu and Jayadratha in which Abhimanyu comes out victorious, they are an inverse playback and conflation of the epic's thirteenth- and fourteenth-day battles: first, the thirteenth-day war in which Abhimanyu penetrates the Kauravas' *cakravyūha,* the "wheel" or "circular array," only to be caught and slain within it; and then the fourteenth-day war in which Arjuna must penetrate the circular array that protects Jayadratha. The wheel-fort narratives are in effect initiatory episodes for Abhimanyu, trials in which he becomes a child of Kālī to play out a victory that is denied him in the classical epic. Rather than dying in the cakravyūha, he is "reborn" as Kālī's child in the cakra-fort. In the classical epic, Abhimanyu marries Virāṭa's daughter Uttarā at the end of the *Virāṭaparvan* and sires the child Parikṣit who will be the miraculous sole survivor of the Pāṇḍava-Kaurava line. In these stories he is transformed into a child himself or replaced by his otherwise unknown "additional" child Ciruttoṅku. Just as the Pāṇḍavas undergo a sort of initiatory dīkṣā in the "womb" of Virāṭa's kingdom of Matsya, the "Fish" (Hiltebeitel 1988a, 301), so does Abhimanyu, at "Upaplavya," as the child of Kālī. The initiatory theme is especially clear at Aḻakār Tirupputtūr. Here the fort is a "maṇḍala" called Cakkarāparaṇam Kōṭṭai, the "Wheel Ornament Fort." Draupadī (not Sahadeva) brings Abhimanyu as a little baby (*kuḻantai, cinna pāyaṉ*) and gives him to Kālī so she can raise him to learn the arts of war (*pōrvittai, pōrvidyā*). This time he is told nothing about getting her drunk. Rather, she tells him the fort is protected by bees. He must put flowers over the well where the bees are kept so they will not sting the fort's attackers.

Indeed, the baby theme in the Thanjavur accounts is also a multiform of another core area fort myth, already summarized at the end of chapter 4. In "Draupadī the Gypsy," Draupadī, in the guise of a gypsy fortune-teller, enters Duryodhana's palace or fort (Hāstinapura) carrying Sahadeva disguised as a baby on her hip, to tell the Kauravas' fortunes to the Kaurava women. In Duryodhana's absence (he is out trying to kill the Pāṇḍavas in the forest), she predicts in vivid terms how she will put up her kūntal on the paṭukaḷam "standing on the king of the earth," "on your husband" (to Duryodhana's wife), and how she "will come to rule the earth" herself (Hiltebeitel 1988a, 306). Here we have a fusion of fort and paṭukaḷam images. Having entered the fort of her enemy, she announces the paṭukaḷam rites. Similarly, when Abhimanyu is brought to Kālī on the feminine hip of Sahadeva or Draupadī, he enters the fort that doubles for the paṭukaḷam itself.[26]

Finally, what about the name of this fort? Clearly its middle element is rampant. *Cakkara* has been noted as the modifier for six different terms: *-vartti* (turner), *-āyutam* (weapon), *-āram* (spoke), *-āparaṇam* (ornament), *puṟam* (exterior), and *-puram* or *-puri* (city). Its presumed circular character is in any case one feature that does not match the square or rectangular forts that sometimes represent it ritually; but it sometimes is a circular fort, and possibly has a long prehistory, as we have seen from Parpola. The variations in the name might suggest that an original middle term has been forgotten and replaced. If this is so, an answer may lie in a Tamil classic. I follow Parpola's summary of the "description of a temple to the dread goddess of war, death and [the] forest (*kāṭu*), called *Kāṭamar Celvi*" (Parpola in press, sec. 3.1.7), in chapter 6 of the *Maṇimēkalai*, the Old Tamil epic of the sixth century (Richman 1988, 7) or ninth to tenth century A.D. (Hikosaka 1989, 75–94):

> The temple was situated outside the city of Pukār that had come into being along with it, in a nearby grove that functioned as a cemetery. The temple, surrounded by an enclosure wall with a gate in each of the cardinal directions, was called *cakkara-vāḷa-kōṭṭam:* it represented Mt. Meru (6.193) in the center of the earth, surrounded by circular continents topped by high mountain ridges and separated from each other by oceans. . . . Emaciated ascetics doing penance in the cremation ground made garlands of broken skulls. Other ascetics offered cooked food under *vanni* trees. (Parpola in press, sec. 3.1.7; cf. Krishnaswami Aiyangar 1928, 126–29; Nandakumar 1989, 33–41; Nagaswamy 1982, 16–18)

The *Maṇimēkalai* also refers to this Cakkaravāḷakōṭṭam as Cuṭukāṭṭu Kōṭṭam, "the temple of the burning ghat," and as containing a

26. Two variants: In Tamilnadu, Aṅkāḷammaṉ, disguised as a gypsy fortune-teller and with her child Vīrabhadra on her hip, enters the fort of king Vallāḷarājaṉ, disembowels his pregnant queen, and leaves Vīrabhadra to kill king Vallāḷarājaṉ, hold his head, and turn his fort into a cremation ground (Meyer 1986, 14; Hiltebeitel 1988a, 355–63). In Kerala, Bhagavati-Kālī goes to Dārikan's fort as a beggarwoman clad in rags, with disheveled hair and a broom and winnow in her hand, and accompanied by her attendant Vetalam, chief of Bhūtas. She learns the mantras that protect Dārikan's life, defeats him in battle, drags him from his fort by the hair, and kills him on the doorstep of his castle's northern room by "applying her left big toe to his right ear." Ritual reenactment involves the fort's destruction from within by a possessed *veḷiccapāṭu* dancer (Raghavan 1947, 25–27).

"temple dedicated to Kāli" (Krishnaswami Aiyangar 1928, 125). Moreover, as Richman observes, the author, Cāttaṉār, "describes the cremation ground as 'surrounded by a guarded fortress wall divided by these four clearly marked, towering gates.' . . . These terms are part of an architectural context, particularly one that emphasizes the fortified and 'battle-ready' nature of a city" (1988, 98). Normally, as Richman says, a cremation ground is neither walled nor fortified. But this one is described "as *ār*, 'rare,' 'unusual,' 'unique'" (ibid.). In fact, it is an image of the classical Buddhist cosmogram, the *cakravāla*, as a fortified cremation ground Kālī "temple" (*kōṭṭam*). It is an evocation of the Buddhist teaching of impermanence, a place where the heroine Kōtamai learns from Campāpati, patron goddess of Pukār, that neither she nor any of the gods in the entire cakravāla-universe has the power to revive her dead son.[27] This is in marked contrast to the revival scenario in the *Maṇimēkalai*'s companion epic, the *Cilappatikāram* (Hikosaka 1989, 114), in which the heroine Kaṇṇaki revives her husband (see chap. 11). And it is also contrary to the revival scenarios of Draupadī cult paṭukaḷam and fort rituals, in which the fort is sometimes the very place that heroes are revived or, alternatively, ritually rise up, blessed with mokṣa. Remarkably, the Buddhist Cakkaravāḷakōṭṭam, no doubt sustained by its early association with Kālī, whose Hindu temple was similarly conceived in medieval poems,[28] seems to have survived in Hindu Draupadī cult folklore, from much the same Thanjavur Delta region as the ancient city of Pukār itself. Of all the variants of the name, it is of course Cakkara Ārakkōṭṭai that looks most like a possible transformation.[29] It has at least the merit of deriving from an esteemed pāratiyār (see n. 8). In the center of the Buddhist cakravāla, Mount Meru is surrounded by seven ring mountains.[30] Let us note that Vīrapattiraṉ also guards the temple of

27. Hikosaka (1989, 115) and Richman (1988, 79–82, 92–94) are probably right that Kōtamai's story is an elaboration of that of Kisāgotamī, who learns from the Buddha that she cannot revive her son by being told to seek out a house that has not known death (building on the Buddhist house-universe homology).

28. See Nagaswamy 1982, 31–33: In the twelfth-century *Takkayākapparaṇi* by Oṭṭakūttar, Kālī's temple consists of all fourteen worlds; Mount Meru forms its balipīṭhas; it outlasts the pralaya; and it has the desert as its landscape.

29. *Āra* as spoke, derived from Sanskrit *ara* or *āra*, may also recall the Jaina usage of the term as a unit of time, a "spoke" in the "wheel of time" (Randolph Kloetzli, personal communication, 1990; Monier-Williams [1899] 1964, s.v. *ara*): another cosmogram, but one emphasizing time rather than space.

30. On the cakravāla as cosmogram, see Kloetzli 1983, 23–50; Richman 1988, 79–100, with further discussion of the *Maṇimēkalai* passage, noting that it is the first usage of the term *cakravāla* in Tamil (ibid., 95).

Aṅkāḷammaṉ, whose cremation ground and "hunt" rituals can result in the destruction of her demon foe's seven-ringed fort (Meyer 1986, 146, 172). Both Aṅkāḷammaṉ and Draupadī have their affinities with Kālī and links with the cremation ground. The presence of the vaṉṉi (śamī) tree must also remind us of the śamī tree beside the cremation ground where the Pāṇḍavas hide their weapons, outside the city of Virāṭa. That the "original" Cakkravāḷa "temple" should have vaṉṉi trees beside it also reinforces the possibility that Pōttu Rāja's connection with this tree lingers in his substitute Vīrapattiraṉ's associations with the wheel-fort and the vāḻaittaṇṭu (see n. 15). Its characterization as a Vibhūti Fort, however, now looks like another evocation of a correlation between the battlefield and the cremation ground.

With Vīrapattiraṉ and Kālī playing such prominent parts in this wheel-fort complex, we are now able to see the roots of some of the Thanjavur area's transformations of the Draupadī cult. In part, the wheel-fort complex looks like a folk variation on an ancient, classical Tamil theme. Beyond that, however, Vīrapattiraṉ looks like a Brahmanical and Śaivite substitute for Pōttu Rāja in an area dominated by Brahmanical and Śaivite culture. And the heightened accentuation of Draupadī's identity with Kālī in the Thanjavur area—in connection with Aravāṉ, Muttāl Rāvuttaṉ, and the wheel-fort—probably has the same background.

C. Forts and Temples

The Draupadī cult fort mythology is thus ultimately about two forts. One is the fort of the enemy (Jayadratha, Duryodhana). The other is the Pāṇḍavas' palace and the Draupadī temple. The prototype for the relation between the two is the rapport between the Vedic altars of the gods, which serve the gods instead of forts and provide the analogue (and model) for the temple, and the triple and seven-ringed forts of the demons, which the "enemy" forts keep replicating (see chap. 12, n. 8). In Draupadī cult ritual, it seems that either may be identified as the battlefield of Kurukṣetra. Though I know of no instance where the war is explicitly said to take place in the Draupadī temple, the image of the temple under siege has a rich development at the Madurai Mīnākṣī temple, where, on the eighth night of Navarātri, Mahiṣāsura succeeds in penetrating not only the temple but the sanctum. There Mīnākṣī must carry out the combat in her own contained space lest it spread to the world (Fuller and Logan 1985, 86–88, 104). If Draupadī does not fight the Kauravas within her temple, her mūlavar, or temple icon, is nonetheless theologically one with her processional icon, which does go out to battle.[31] Moreover, the temple is a fort and the fort is a temple. As I urged earlier, the paṭukaḷam is a Kālī temple transposed, while its fort variant is guarded by Kālī or is even—where she is called Kōṭṭai Kāḷi—her own fort. More precisely, it is a temple of Draupadī in Kālīrūpa.

It is now time to turn to a pair of questions I have left unformulated to this point. So far, the rites of Duryodhana's effigy have been interpreted in relation to the horse of the Aśvamedha and the buffalo sacrifice of Dasarā. While these comparisons have illuminated some ritual details, they have told us little about the effigy itself. Duryodhana's effigy is neither a horse nor a buffalo. And on the one point—the cutting of the right thigh—where the effigy is treated in a fashion that recalls these animal sacrifices, it is not the horse or buffalo whose thigh it cut, but queens who slap their thighs, or the Buffalo Demon's ultimate human form that has his right thigh bitten.[32] It is thus the royal human thigh, not the thigh of the animal victim, that seems always to be in question, at least in the Indian tradition.[33] Effigy rites are distinctive in themselves and must be so interpreted. This task remains before us and may be framed by the questions just mentioned: What is Duryodhana's effigy doing in a fort? And by the same token, what is it doing in a temple? And for the Thanjavur area, how do the same questions apply to prone effigies of Aravāṉ?

As to forts, or rather forts by themselves, only one example need be mentioned for its obvious parallels: the effigies of Rāvaṇa at North Indian Rām Līlās. Rām Līlā is explicitly a variation on Dasarā: one that is usually performed without a king or, more exactly, with Rāma as the king. The Rām Līlā seems to exercise and build upon the Dasarā option, mentioned in chapter 5 (sec. C), that the king—that is, the festival-performing town or village's local version of Rāma—may make an effigy of his enemy or bring him before

31. Unlike Dharma, who by various accounts does not leave the temple in a processional warrior form; see chapter 3, section B; chapter 5, section D; his abstention from the fort destruction at Salem; and *Āravalli Cūravalli Katai,* in which only his chariot does not join the attack of the fort.

32. We are not told enough about the cutting of the horse's leg of Duryodhana's horse hero to insist on what might be an interesting exception.

33. I no longer maintain a significant affinity between the treatment of Duryodhana's right thigh and that of the right foreleg of the sacrificial buffalo (and sometimes goat), placed crosswise in the severed head's mouth. Both rites evoke themes of sexual revenge, but a foreleg is not a thigh (cf. Hiltebeitel 1982b, 88–97 and 110 n. 90; 1988a, 305 and n. 31).

his mind. Rām Līlā is mainly popular in villages and towns, and within wards of cities, much as is the case with Draupadī festivals. The best-documented Rām Līlā, however, the one at Ramnagar across the Ganges from Banaras, is an exception, the festival there having apparently been royally appropriated (though the royal family is Brahman) and reformed at the end of the eighteenth century or beginning of the nineteenth (Hess 1988, 4; Schechner 1983, 226, 256, 258).

Three days before Vijayādaśamī[34] or Dasarā, the death of Rāvaṇa's gigantic and gluttonous brother Kumbhakarṇa is enacted at the staged environment of Laṅkā, where a walled fort has been constructed with Kumbhakarṇa's effigy, the largest in the līlā at a height of four stories (Hess 1988, 50), outside the fort's walls (Schechner 1983, plate 37). First, the impersonators of Rāma's monkey army attack the effigy. Sugrīva, the monkey king, mounts the effigy's shoulder and "bites off the monster's nose and ears" until "'blood' rushes out." Sugrīva's biting of Kumbhakarṇa's nose is indeed shown in one of the *Rāmāyaṇa* paintings commissioned by Akbar (Beach 1981, 149; 1983, 46): a reminder, though this incident is from the classical *Rāmāyaṇa*, that earlier Rām Līlās may have influenced the portrayal of leg-biting monkeys in the same manuscript. Then the boy impersonating Rāma, firing a volley of arrows at the effigy, "shoots off the giant's right arm, then the left, then the head, and finally the torso. These parts of the effigy fall to the ground one by one," the effigy itself having been specially constructed to enable this (Hess 1988, 38, 51). Kumbhakarṇa's preliminary sacrifice by dismemberment (through arrows!) thus has an affinity with the prewar sacrifice of Aravāṉ: both are at a gate or boundary of a battlefield-fort.[35] Then, on Dasarā day, the Mahāraja of Vārāṇasī performs the āyudhapūjā, or worship of the weapons, in the courtyard of *his* fort, which is also the staged environment for Rāma's fort-capital of Ayodhyā, and "in an extraordinary and magnificently theatrical procession of elephants," sets off the more than five kilometers to Laṅkā, to the southeast, where Rāvaṇa is represented within his fort by his large standing effigy. Before he reaches the fort of Rāvaṇa, at what appears to be a boundary point between the

34. Vijaya-, masculine, for Rāma, rather than Vijayā-, for Durgā.

35. The points in common are all traceable to, and even clearer in, the Vālmīki *Rāmāyaṇa:* to fight, Kumbhakarṇa crosses the wall (*prākāram*) of Laṅkā (6.53.46) or its fort gate (*puradvāra;* 54.1153*); Sugrīva bites off his nose and ears (55.67); Rāma dismembers and beheads him (55.111–23), leaving his body to block Laṅkā's gate (*ruddhvā dvāram;* 56.1222*, line 6).

two forts, the king comes to a śamī tree, which he circumambulates and worships.[36] As we have seen, the origin of the śamīpūjā is often credited to Rāma, though it does not appear in the *Rāmāyaṇa* (Biardeau 1984, 6; 1989b, 302–3), just as it is often given a source in popular versions of the *Mahābhārata*. The king then rides up, over, and past the battleground outside Rāvaṇa's fort, whereupon, after a brief ten minutes, he turns around to make his way back to his own fort. Schechner senses the mystery—"it is the only time in the Ramlila that the Maharaja literally invades the performing space"—and rightly calls attention to the combination of āyudhapūjā and sīmollaṅghana, though not mentioning the related śamīpūjā: that it was the royal practice of kings "to march their armies to the borders of their domain, proclaim the territory as theirs, confront their opposing number across the border, and go home" (1983, 249–50, 270–71). Significantly, the Mahāraja also explains the brevity of his stay in Laṅkā by his reluctance to see "the killing of a king" (ibid., 269; cf. Hess 1988, 40). Hein describes what is surely a more typical enactment (one that is reminiscent of the well-choreographed dance-duels between Bhīma and Duryodhana around Duryodhana's effigy): "Two carriages bearing impersonators of Rāma and Rāvaṇa circled round and round in lively imitation of the tactical gyration of the chariots of the two champions in combat. A great shout went up as Rāvaṇa was struck down," after which Laṅkā is stormed and the effigies are burned (1972, 76–77). Here we have both the storming of the fort and the destruction of the effigy. At Banaras, the Rāma actor shoots thirty-one arrows at the effigy: one to dry up Rāvaṇa's navel (his vital point), the rest for his twenty arms and ten heads. The Rāvaṇa actor then shows these effects by removing his twenty arms and ten heads and bowing before Rāma, "symbolizing his union with the lord in death." After nightfall, the effigy is then burned to represent Rāvaṇa's cremation (Hess 1988, 41).

Unlike the prone earthen effigy of Duryodhana, Rāvaṇa's effigy stands in his fort for his last battle and is demolished by burning. But it is clear that the Rām Līlā and the Draupadī cult paṭukaḷam have similar elements: a preliminary battlefield sacrifice by dismemberment (Kumbhakarṇa's name means "Pot ear"; Aravāṉ's head is made by potters); a battle between royal forts (or between Rāma's temple and a fort); representation or evocation of the śamīpūja; and demolition of the effigies. The founding of these līlās seems to go back to the sixteenth to seventeenth century (Hein

36. I thank Philip Lutgendorf and Linda Hess for their information on this point, which is not mentioned in the sources I have consulted.

1972, 108–9, 224–27, 274), a time that also could well be that of the consolidation of Draupadī cult paṭukaḷam rites in the Gingee core area. Not only are both epics tied into the popular mythology of Dasarā, but they have supplied the myths for similar battlefield rituals that in each case involve popular transpositions of Dasarā rites into idioms of ritualized epic conflict.

Finally, regarding the presence of Duryodhana's effigy in a temple, let us recall the many instances already cited in this chapter of the interchangeability of forts, palaces and temples. This fluidity is reflected in the range of the Tamil word *kōyil/kōvil* ("king's house," "palace," "temple"; Hart 1975, 13), and in the possible semantic continuity in the transformation of Cakkaravāḷakōṭṭam (*kōṭṭam:* "place," "temple") to Cakkara Ārakkōṭṭai (*kōṭṭai:* "fort, castle"). Indeed, the Hindu temple itself shows traces through the years of increasing "fortification." Meister observes that by the seventh century, in Central India "fort"-like brick temples to Śiva begin to suggest "an attempt to reinforce and fortify the interior deity," with increasing emphasis on guardian deities at the corners, especially when the corner deities are doubled to fit an eight-by-eight square temple plan (1981, 82; 1984, 119; see also chap. 9, sec. D). The impression of a fort then becomes evident in many of the great multiple-walled temples of South India: "The *prākāra* walls surrounding south Indian temples seem extensions, to a degree, of the citadel, with the innermost wall, called *āvaraṇa,* forming a protective 'sheath' around the sanctum" (1984, 138). Drawing on the work of Kramrisch, Meister notes the vulnerability of the corners as the "point of attack" upon the square vedi altar within, which represents the "earth in its sacral aspect [as] the site of the sacrifice" (ibid., 139). This is the terrain that Madurai Mīnākṣī must defend within her temple-fortress against the assault of Mahiṣāsura. As we have seen, goddess temples in particular have an association with forts through the identity of Durgā as goddess of the "inaccessible fort," or *durga,* and of Tripurasundarī as Beautiful Lady of the Triple Fort.

There is, however, no more fruitful way to bring out the rapport between Draupadī's fort-temple and the Kālī temple- and fortlike character of her paṭukaḷam, along with the place of Duryodhana's or Aravāṉ's effigy upon it, than to look at the corresponding components in the festivals of Draupadī's sister goddess Aṅkāḷammaṉ. As at a Draupadī festival, there is of course a rapport between the temple, where the goddess is pure, and an area of ritual action that involves varieties of impurity. In the Aṅkāḷammaṉ cult, the latter is the cremation ground, which can also be known as the "northern ground" (*uttirapūmi;* Meyer 1986, 148), perhaps reminiscent of the uttaravedi, and apparently also as a paṭukaḷam.[37] There an effigy is customarily constructed from earth and the ashes of the deceased.

There are many local and regional variations on the identity of the effigy. Usually it is of the goddess, though under different names and "avatars" (Meyer 1986, 198). Rather rarely, in what is the closest parallel to Duryodhana's effigy, it is of the goddess's demon foe, Vallāḷarājaṉ (plate 29; cf. Meyer 1986, 132 and n. 2, 140, 171).[38] And quite often it is Vallāḷarājaṉ's pregnant queen, who is a multiform of the goddess herself as a sacrificial victim (ibid., 216).[39] A ritual called "pillaging the crematorium" involves the demolition of the effigies, whichever one or more may be involved, and a wild scramble for the contents. If there is an effigy of Vallāḷarājaṉ's wife but none of Vallāḷarājaṉ, it is still understood that he is killed, as in the myth cited above where he is beheaded by Vīrapattiraṉ. Generally, if the effigy is of the goddess, her stomach is filled with food. And if it is of the pregnant queen, her womb and embryo, represented by the viscera (liver, intestines) of a goat or sheep, are ripped open by the goddess as the fortune-teller–midwife of the Vallāḷarājaṉ myth that parallels "Draupadī the Gypsy" (see n. 26). Where it is the goddess, the primary myths evoked are not the story of Vallāḷarājaṉ, but Śiva's Brahmanicide and (or) the destruction of Dakṣa's sacrifice. In the latter case, "the destruction of the sacrifice by Śiva, or by Kālī aided by Vīrabhadra, is equivalent to the sacrifice of the sacrifice" (Biardeau 1989b, 298; my translation). Here the ash-and-earthen goddess as victim is ultimately Satī, with the sacrificial fire altar as her crematorium (ibid., 299; cf. Meyer 1986, 169) and her corpse as the womb of life (Meyer 1986, 217). The role of Vīrapattiraṉ thus differs in these myths. In the Vallāḷarājaṉ myth, he is the goddess's child-guardian in her assault on the king's fort, whereas in the Dakṣa myth he guards the sacrifice of the goddess herself, the sacrifice turned in upon itself (Hiltebeitel 1989b, 8; cf. 1988a, 356–59, 372–73). In either case, however, the cremation

37. See chapter 7, n. 3. According to Tailāpuram informants, any sacrifice to Kālī should be done facing north.

38. Of the two festivals I studied, both in Madras City, the Ice House area temple in Krishnampet (T'Nagar) constructed effigies of both Vallāḷarājaṉ and his wife, while the Mylapore temple at Mundakanniyamman Koil Street had four effigies, all of the wife.

39. Other possibilities: it may be a male god, Mācāṉakkaruppucuvāmi ("the black god of the cremation ground"; Meyer 1986, 170–71), or even Vīrabhadra (76, 167); and it may be a corpse (168–69).

ground is both a temple and a fort. Likewise, in the Thanjavur area Draupadī cult, he guards both the Draupadī temple and the wheel-fort of ashes that is either the base of the Pāṇḍavas' operations at Kurukṣetra or equivalent to the battlefield itself.

For our purposes, it is best to emphasize Masilamani-Meyer's descriptions of rituals from Coimbatore and Salem Districts, where the effigy is named Mācāṇiyammaṉ or Mācāṇiyāttā, "Mother of the cremation ground." A distinction between the pure (*cutta*) goddess Aṅkāḷammaṉ in the temple and the impure (*acutta*) form she takes on the cremation ground is registered in the understanding that Mācāṇiyammaṉ is one of Aṅkāḷammaṉ's avatāras (Meyer 1986, 76). The association of the cremation ground with a temple is vividly illustrated by the permanent construction in some villages of cement effigies of Mācāṇiyammaṉ—"an imposing female, measuring 6 to 8 metres, stretched out on her back and looking skywards" (ibid., 84)—that then have temples built around them close to the cremation ground (ibid., 76 and n. 2, 84, plates 8–10). One will recall the concrete effigies of Duryodhana and Aravāṉ. In cases where the effigy is still made annually for the festival out of ashes and earth, the combined fort-temple symbolism becomes evident. Like Duryodhana and Aravāṉ, who also always lie on their backs, Mācāṇiyammaṉ's head is to the south (ibid., 109, 117). A number of conical shapes, called guards (kāvals) or Piḷḷaiyārs (Gaṇeśas), often said to be the goddess's children (*kuḻantai*), are placed around the effigy, with a string connecting them. These figures "are also called *kōṭṭai* . . . or Vallāḷa *kōṭṭai* (forts), the reason being that the guards and the string tied around them represent the ramparts of a fort in the middle of which the goddess lies." On the other hand, "They are the *dvārapālaka,* the door-keepers of the shrine," their positioning being "similar to the function of the walls of a shrine" (ibid., 171–72; cf. 109, 118, 134).[40] Let us recall the two varieties of "sleeping warriors" around Duryodhana: either his guardians, or the goddess's children.

For the pūcāri and others to enter such a fort-temple of Mācāṇiyammaṉ, the string is removed to leave an opening at the feet or at the head and feet (ibid., 118, 134). In other words, the entrance is made from the north, as in Draupadī cult paṭukaḷam and fort rituals. The myths speak of her arrival at Vallāḷarājaṉ's fort in a palanquin (ibid., 187, 197), presumably reflecting the movements of the goddess's processional icon to the same point: the north of Vallāḷarājaṉ's

40. Similar items may be used around the Draupadī cult firepit (see chap. 14, sec. F).

fort, where Aṅkāḷammaṉ disembowels the queen (ibid., 14). The pūcāri, or whoever else becomes possessed by the goddess, often takes on the character or dress of Kālī (ibid., 111–12, 129–30, 173, 175), who is Aṅkāḷammaṉ in her horrific (*akōra*) form (ibid., 37, 77, 80). Here, however, in contrast to the Draupadī cult, the rapport between the temple and the ritual ground is not one between an eastern and a northern orientation. Aṅkāḷammaṉ temples, like Kālī temples, "should be facing north" themselves (ibid., 72). The difference here is between the northern, protective orientation of the goddess in her temple and her southern, destructive orientation, facing the realm of death, as she enters the cremation ground: a pattern we have noticed at Thanjavur area Draupadī temples, where Kālī has her north-facing shrines but enters the paṭukaḷam from the north for Aravāṉ's sacrifice. As to the demolition and "pillaging" of the effigies in the Aṅkāḷammaṉ cult, we need only note that in one instance, when the effigy is of Aṅkāḷammaṉ herself, a comb, a mirror, turmeric, kuṅkum, and eye black are among the articles placed on the yellow cloth over her body (ibid., 134; cf. 133).

Finally, it must also be noted that there is a variant ritual called *pārivēṭṭai*, a "hunt," performed at Trichinopoly District Aṅkāḷammaṉ temples, that can involve the destruction of Vallāḷarājaṉ's fort (made of stones and strings) *without* an effigy. Here the goddess is the hunter (ibid., 146, 244–47). Both cults thus have fort and effigy variants.

But back to our closing question: What are Duryodhana's and Aravāṉ's effigies doing in a transposed Kālī temple? In their variety, the Aṅkāḷammaṉ cult effigies are of two main types, with a third as intermediary. In one, the effigy is of the goddess. In the other it is of the demon. And in the intermediary, it is of the wife of the demon who is also a multiform of the goddess. Looked at in this way, matters become rather straightforward. It is conventional for South Indian temples to show a correspondence between the body of the deity and the ground plan of the temple. Śiva temples in particular are represented in this fashion, with the deity on his back facing upward, his head in the area of the sanctum, and his prone body extending outward to outline the ground plan.[41] Masilamani-Meyer shows a similar scheme as the ground plan of an Aiyaṉār temple: one that is particularly interesting for its representation of Aiyaṉār as a king and the various zones of his body as

41. See Beck 1976, 239; Vanmikanathan 1971, 118–19; Curtis 1973, 32–34; see also above, chapter 6, section A, 5 and n. 21.

linked with different guardian deities, animals, and his army (in press-b). Correspondingly, a goddess temple would show the body of the goddess as the ground plan, and this is what one finds where Aṅkāḷammaṉ and her avatāras such as Mācāṇiyammaṉ lie in this fashion on the cremation ground: in Mācāṇiyammaṉ's case sometimes in an actual temple.

The other main alternative is for the ground plan to represent the body of a sacrificial victim. In the Aṅkāḷammaṉ cult, we have seen that the goddess, the demon's wife, and the demon all meet this criterion. But it is, of course, the demon, Vallāḷarājaṉ, who is most like Duryodhana or Aravāṉ. Ultimately, where the ground plan of a temple schematizes the body of a sacrificial victim, the prototype is the Vāstupuruṣa, or "Puruṣa of the Site." The Vāstupuruṣa is commonly identified as a demon (Kramrisch [1947] 1976, 1:75–84) and, as Beck puts it, as "some sort of corpse that 'fell' to earth as what was 'left-over' after the great, original sacrifice" (1976, 227). The Vāstupuruṣa, however, is not represented as a prone effigy with his head in the sanctum and body and legs extended. Rather, as was noted in chapter 9, he is made to fit a square, in particular the nine-by-nine square that has thirty-two outer pādas, or squares, on its border (Kramrisch [1947] 1976, 1:49, 79), with his head to the northeast, feet to the southeast, and knees and elbows touching at the other two corners (ibid., 56; Beck 1976, diagram 4). Graphically, this cannot be the model for such demon effigies as Vallāḷarājaṉ, Duryodhana, and Aravāṉ. Indeed, as we saw in chapter 9, the typical outer division of the Vāstupuruṣa's body into thirty-two parts is a prototype for Aravāṉ's boundary sacrifice to Kālī. In effect, his sacrifice is equivalent to that of the Vāstupuruṣa or Vāstunāga. Where the demon victim has his prone body extended, as it is in these cases, it has an affinity with the deities who are represented this way. The most immediate correlation is for the demon to be a king, like Aiyaṉār and Vallāḷarājaṉ. In the Draupadī cult, however, this applies only to core area rites where the effigy is of Duryodhana. Aravāṉ is not a king, though he could be construed as a substitute sacrifice for his royal father Arjuna. This is one more indication that it is the Thanjavur area rites that have modified a core area norm, in clear consonance with the increasing emphasis placed on Kālī in that area's paṭukaḷam rituals. Though in either case the goddess is Draupadī in Kalīrūpa, Duryodhana is ultimately Draupadī's victim, whereas Aravāṉ is Kālī's. Where Duryodhana is the victim, Draupadī enters the paṭukaḷam from the north in her Kālīrūpa, faces south in a destructive capacity, mounts the groin and chest of her victim's corpse, and ties her hair with the thigh blood of the demon "king of the earth." On the other hand, where the effigy is of Aravāṉ, it is no more than the materialization of something only implicit in the core area: that he is the true Vāstunāga of Kurukṣetra.

14 Tīmiti, the Firewalk

Since it is high spectacle and usually the culmination of the festival, it is not surprising that firewalking has been the main, and often sole, focus of the briefer notices of the Draupadī cult that have appeared sporadically over the past two hundred years in travelers' accounts, journals, district gazetteers and manuals, and scholarly notices.[1] Until recently, this literature was descriptive rather than interpretative and, with the exception of Richards (1910; 1918, 115–16), said nothing about the relation between the firewalk and other ceremonies. Among recent authors, Brown (1976, 1984) has retained this emphasis, perhaps because the Fiji festival she describes seems to have raised the firewalk to such importance as to have preempted other rites.

Even since 1970, when the first studies appeared that were attentive to the integration of Draupadī's firewalk in the larger temple and festival cycles, the greatest interpretative flair has remained focused on the firewalk.[2] Meanwhile, recent accounts of firewalking rituals in other cults, not only for other South Indian goddesses (Beck 1969, 564; Meyer 1986, 242–44; Biardeau 1989b, 143–56, 286–95; Tarabout 1986, 351) but for Pattini (Obeyesekere 1984, 41–43, 139–56, 220–22) and Kataragama (a form of the god Murukaṉ) in Sri Lanka (Obeyesekere 1978) and for Saints Constantine and Helen in Greece (Danforth 1989), make it possible to interpret the Draupadī cult firewalk in a comparative light as well.[3] Our task is to

1. Sonnerat 1782, 247–48 provides the first description, with a plate of the firewalk (plate 36). Reports . . . 1854 is an early government-sponsored study of the prevalence of firewalking and hook swinging in different South Indian districts.
2. See especially Babb (1974, 23–44), Biardeau (1989b, 113–22), Tanaka (1987, 152–53, 333–412), and Brown (1976, 1984), and also Hiltebeitel 1982b, 74–84, 93–95; Gros and Nagaswamy 1970, 119–23; Blaive, Penaud, and Nicoli 1974; Frasca 1984, 316–21; Shideler 1987, 158–66.
3. Firewalking in South India (for Andhra, see, e.g., Tapper 1979, 13–17; 1987, 176–78: a festival involving Pōta Rāju; for Karnataka, Prabhu 1977, 59, 86, 101), and

appreciate the bounty offered by these sources without losing sight of our primary purpose: to set the Draupadī cult ceremonies in their larger festival context while recognizing that the firewalk is indeed what the paṭukaḷam rites, or their equivalents, build up to as the festival's climax.

A. Vows

Ordinarily, a firewalker makes a vow to walk on fire for Draupadī in a situation of distress, hoping to receive a favor or blessing from her: a change in some undesired condition (cf. Reiniche 1979, 162). Should the favor be granted before the firewalk is carried out, the firewalk fulfills a debt, offers thanks, and completes a process in which the individual and the goddess share a victory over inimical or destructive forces. But the firewalk can also be done while still hoping for the favorable outcome. A person may also vow to cross the coals any number of times, frequently over three successive festivals, but sometimes many more. So early crossings could involve supplication and later ones not only discharge of the obligation, but thanksgiving or a hoped-for continuation of good health or other blessings. The most frequent impulse behind a firewalking vow is illness or disablement. The vow may be taken not only on one's own behalf, but for the sake of another, especially an ill family member (usually a child). Draupadī's favor knows no restrictions, however, and people ask her to overcome infertility, end unemployment, or bring success in business, school examinations, building a house, or even the lottery.[4]

---

on into Orissa (Freeman 1974), seems to be performed mainly for goddesses—too many to mention. But it is also done for male deities, especially ones linked with Śiva: Vīrabhadra in Andhra (Reports . . . 1854, 33–34); Śiva in Bengal (see chap. 7, sec. C); Kataragama (Skanda-Murukaṉ) in Sri Lanka, and the Bhūtas Vishnumurthy, Pañjorli, and Kundodara, a form of Mahiṣāsura, in South Kanara (Prabhu 1977, 49, 94–96, 110), where firewalking often combines with worship of a *nāgamaṇḍala* (snake maṇḍala) reminiscent of Aravāṉ's connection with Ādiśeṣa (ibid., 63, 75, 91, 94). As a cross-cultural phenomenon, firewalking has attracted some of the great names: see Lang 1900–1901; Frazer [1913] 1936, 1–20; Hopkins 1913; Leroy 1931; Eliade 1964, 54, 112, 206, 372–73, 442–43; [1958] 1965, 85–86. It is done during Muharram in India, often with Hindus among the firewalkers; see Derrett 1979, 287; Hjortshoj 1987, 296; Jaffri 1979, 225; Nambiar, Karup, et al. 1968, 58; Bayly 1989, 142; Reports . . . 1854, 20, 31, 34, 36–37. My colleague Seyyed Hossein Nasr (personal communication, January 1991) confirms my inference from sources on Muharram in Iran and West Asia, that the festival includes firewalking only in South Asia.

4. The last four examples provided by V. S. Purushottama Chettiyar, chief trustee, Tindivanam. Cf. Babb 1974, 35; Tanaka 1987, 157–68, 369–71.

Come festival time, the preliminaries of the vow consist of individual variations on renunciations that mainly concern food and sex. Length and intensity depend on one's means, one's dedication, and the structure of a particular festival. At Tindivanam, where both men and women do the firewalk, both practice sexual abstinence. They may in addition sleep on a mat to avoid contact with the sexually polluted mattress (cf. Babb 1982, 32). The Tindivanam pūcāri lives entirely in the temple, sleeping and taking his food there, for the twenty days between the beginning of the dramas and the firewalk. The firewalkers, however, do not sleep there, as they do at the Sowcarpet temple in Madras (see chap. 10, sec. A).[5] As regards food restrictions, all meat eating ceases. In addition, the number of meals each day can be reduced to two or one. Some subsist on fruit and milk, and some only drink water between morning and evening. Smoking is discontinued. The period of one's vows will normally begin with the donning of the kāppu wristlet. As we saw in chapter 4, this can take place at different points at different festivals and, within the same festival, earlier for temple officiants than for the larger mass of firewalkers (as at Tindivanam).

As mentioned in chapter 5, the wearing of kāppu symbolizes the goddess's protection and also a sort of chaste marriage to her. This sheds some light on the nature of infractions. Most of the restrictions just mentioned seem to be regularly followed and are not thought of as major sources of danger if broken. On the contrary, two self-evident prohibitions—drinking and contact with menstruating women—were mentioned not among the vows themselves, but as the violations that inevitably explained mishaps in the firewalk (cf. Babb 1974). These are both highly charged restrictions, since both are broken. At some festivals, at least, drinking can be documented, even as part of the ritual (Shideler 1987, 158–59; cf. chap. 2, n. 27). Moreover, Draupadī is a menstruating woman with whom contact is not only necessary but desired throughout her festival. If the firewalk represents the point, after her hair tying, when her extended menstrual period is ended, it would be all the more a violation to pollute one's worship of her by crossing the coals after contact with an ordinary menstruating woman.

On tīmiti day, beginning early in the morning, after the completion of the drama "Eighteenth-Day War," there is a further proliferation of individual and family-related vows. These are carried

5. Firewalkers sleep in the temple at Iruṅkal (Frasca 1984, 274); at Muthialpet (Madras), only the Kurukkaḷ does so. Cf. Babb 1974, 32; Tanaka 1987, 350–51.

out within the grounds of the Draupadī temple, which thus becomes the scene of daylong activities. A time of high intensity in the morning before the paṭukaḷam ceremonies is followed by a midday slackening, then by periods of peak intensity before and after the firewalk in the late afternoon or evening. The vows carried out within the temple grounds may be independent of any intent to participate in the firewalk. Two occur most regularly in the core area, one by women and one by men.[6]

Most typical of the early morning period (ca. 8:00–11:00 A.M.), though at some temples it may be done throughout the day, is the preparation by women of sweet rice poṅkal. Bringing dried cowdung cakes, metal pots, and cooking ingredients, they set up their small fires around the sides and back of the temple while the thick smoke fills the air around and above them. Once it is cooked, the poṅkal is offered to Draupadī and then taken home to be eaten by the woman's family. Because it is cooked in the temple, it is considered especially salubrious. Generally, poṅkal is a symbol of overflowing abundance.[7]

Meanwhile, other vows are undertaken principally by men. Most dramatic is the *aṅkap-piratatṭciṇam,* or "circumambulation by the limbs," in which the individual rolls his body in the auspicious clockwise direction around the temple with his arms outstretched over his head. Attendants douse him and his path with water, thus not only soaking him but leaving him covered with mud. At Tindivanam, the circuit is completed with prostration before an elevated brass pot lodged in a brace atop a post at the outer southwest corner of the temple. Men wear turmeric-dyed vēṣṭis while performing this vow, just as they do for the firewalk.[8]

B. Fire Lighting

At about 2:00 P.M., the firewalkers first gather together as a group for the "fire-kindling" (*tī mūṭṭal*) ceremony. At Tindivanam, a Brahman Aiyar priest or kurukkaḷ is brought in for this rite, as he is for the fire at Draupadī's birth. His mantras are said to purify the firepit. He offers a dīpārādhanā to the site, then kindles a fire with the

6. The Tindivanam pūcāri says that some also bring cocks and other items to offer to Muttāl Rāvuttaṉ on this day.

7. Recall Draupadī's *akṣayapātra,* the "inexhaustible vessel" she uses to feed the Pāṇḍavas in the forest (Hiltebeitel 1988a, 154–55, 288). On victorious connotations of poṅkal, see Biardeau 1989b, 211–12.

8. As performed for other Tamil deities (*Tamil Lexicon,* s.v.), it seems to represent an offering of all one's limbs to the deity.

camphor flame from the offering tray and feeds it with coconut fiber, ghee, and finally some wood. A large mound of split wood, reportedly two tons, stands by, and each of the firewalkers takes a piece and places it on the fire before departing. This group participation in the building of the fire is also done at Sowcarpet in Madras, but not at Mēlaccēri. At Tindivanam the main wood used is casuarina, but several other trees also contribute to the fire. Frequently mentioned at other festivals is *aracu* wood: that is, pipal or aśvattha.[9] There is too little consistency, however, to support any inferences. The presence of a Brahman at the firelighting will, however, no longer surprise us (cf. Tanaka 1987, 380, 395).

From this point, it is possible to recognize four phases in the firewalking rites at most Draupadī festivals: a ceremony at the bank of a tank or reservoir (or alternatively a riverbank or seacoast), a procession from the water to the temple, rites within the temple, and the firewalk itself. We will now follow this progression.

C. The Ceremony by the Water

At Tindivanam, the firewalkers assemble at the Tīrthaṅkuḷam tank, a kilometer north of the paṭukaḷam and firepit, between 3:00 and 4:30 P.M. Certain preparations are made by all the firewalkers, while others are idiosyncratic. Everyone bathes in the tank, and many of those who do so apply turmeric water to the face and body. All devotees intending to cross the coals must also purchase a firewalking ticket for fifty paise (half a rupee) from a temple officiant and a kāppu wristlet of turmeric-dyed string, to which a piece of turmeric is tied. About 650 tickets with kāppu were sold in 1977, and more than 800 in 1981. Most firewalkers also pick up a handful of margosa sprigs from the front of the Murukaṉ temple at the southeast corner of the tank. Generally it is men who carry the clutches of margosa; women only rarely do. Both turmeric and margosa are said to contain the goddess's śakti, or power of cooling and healing (cf. Beck 1972a, 205–6; Brubaker 1978, 323–31; Tanaka 1987, 278). Perhaps the men have the greater need. Most of the men and women wear yellow garments: the men usually wear turmeric-dyed vēṣṭis and the women brilliant yellow and orange sarees and

9. E.g., at Muthialpet (where vaṉṉi wood is also used); Chintadripet (Gopalakrishnan 1953, 108); Singapore (Babb 1974, 22); cf. also Mitra 1936, 177, citing a newspaper article by "an European gentlemen" stating that "Medieval law laid down that innocence was proved by the suspect walking on the embers of pipal-wood." Dharmaśāstra ordeal literature also stipulates use of aśvattha leaves in carrying a red hot iron ball; see Lariviere 1981, 33–37; Khan 1787, 388, 403.

cholis. Women firewalkers let their hair loose by the tank and then bind it with flowers into a kūntal. They will thus cross the coals like Draupadī.

At villages like Mēlaccēri, Maṅkalam, and Veḷḷimēṭupēṭṭai, where only thirty or forty people cross the coals, there is less uniformity in dress and less accent on yellow and orange garments. There is also no selling of tickets. At urban festivals, on the other hand, the yellow dress becomes even more conspicuous. The application of striped and patched turmeric powder designs on the face and body may also be more extensive, as at Pondicherry (cf. Robinson 1980, 191–92). Young male firewalkers—at some temples those who have earlier performed sword-pressing feats—will wear garlands or, at Pondicherry, bands of red and white flowers crossed at the chest. According to Biardeau, the latter is a sign of the victorious warrior (1989b, 121; cf. Hart 1975, 135). At Pondicherry and Sowcarpet, men of all ages also carry yellow cloth sacks across the stomach packed with lemons. The lemons are said to have a cooling śakti like the margosa, and are distributed after the firewalk as prasādam to friends and family. It seems that such contrasts must result in part from the greater financial resources of town and urban firewalkers, and in part from a need to forge the firewalkers there into a collectivity. In the villages, where everyone knows everyone else and usually even the nature of each devotee's vow, the firewalkers are a distinctive group without such trappings. But the yellow garments, tied in with the various uses of turmeric, are still in evidence and are favored throughout all areas of the Draupadī cult's diffusion.

The applications of turmeric and the wearing of yellow are actually synonymous, since the ordinary Tamil word for turmeric (*mañcaḷ*) is also the word for yellow. Turmeric powder and yellow garments also adorn firewalkers for other goddesses,[10] and they figure both together and separately in countless Indian myths and rituals.[11] In chapter 6 (sec. A, 8) I introduced the notion that, as one of the five ritual weapons brought to Draupadī by Pōrmaṉṉaṉ, turmeric powder has an anointing function in Draupadī cult ritual comparable to its use in animal sacrifices to the goddess, in which

10. Yellow is worn by firewalkers for other South Indian goddesses as well; see Biardeau 1989b, 146 (for Māriyammaṉ); 293 (for Paccaivāḻiyammaṉ); Whitehead 1921, 96 (for Piṭāriyammaṉ). Yellow garments and thick turmeric paste on the body are worn for Pattirakāḷi's firewalk at a village in Tamil Sri Lanka (McGilvray 1986).

11. Beyond the following discussion, see Sontheimer 1989, 307, 323 (turmeric powder used to revive sheep), 326 (= gold); Courtright 1985, 102; Tanaka 1987, 203 (Gaṇeśa born from turmeric and represented by it ritually); Jagadisa Ayyar 1982, 74–75 (yellow garments may be worn by saṃnyāsins).

the buffalo in particular is not only sprinkled with turmeric but also garlanded before his beheading.[12] I also urged that both such uses are reminiscent of the anointing functions of ghee in the Vedic sacrifice. A sacrificial model applies to many uses of turmeric that resonate with Draupadī cult firewalking rituals. Among many South Indian communities, including Vaṉṉiyars, women (and sometimes men) color their face and limbs with turmeric for their weddings, which, as we saw in chapter 3, are offerings of young men and women to each other.[13] As if for a marriage, suttees also ascend the funeral pyre "in a robe dyed with turmeric" (Dymock 1890, 466; cf. Roghair 1982, 355). And in an episode in the *Epic of Palnāḍu*, the virgin Māncāla arranges a seven-pot turmeric bath that douses the clothes of the young heroes who will soon die in battle, including her estranged husband, Bāluḍu, in his "virginal battle" as the "bridegroom of war" (Roghair 1982, 315, 319, 349).[14] It seems that the various applications of turmeric have a general sense of anointing one for a ritual transformation, one that may involve the cooling or healing of sacrificial pain and symbolic death, whether from fire (turmeric is rubbed over burns from the firewalk) or weapons (it is applied medicinally to cuts and wounds).

The Draupadī cult, however, also deepens these resonances. The term *vīrakantakam*, used for turmeric as one of Draupadī's ritual weapons, has in fact an alchemical background. *Gandhaka* (Tamil *kantakam*) is the alchemical word for sulfur, which is thought to have the property of being able to calcinate, or "fix," mercury. Whereas mercury is the essence of Śiva, deriving from his semen, gandhaka, or sulfur, is the essence of Śakti, originating from her "fragrant" (*gandha*) menstrual blood that mingled in the Milk Ocean when she once left her bloodstained garments on the shore while bathing.[15] The alchemist purifies and stabilizes mercury through the use of sulfur, "killing" and "resurrecting" it into "younger" and "subtler"

12. See, e.g., Artal 1907, 642; Whitehead 1921, 48, 56–57, 72, 83; Elliot 1860, 1:402, 416–17; Hiltebeitel 1980a, 161; recall the hog sacrifice in Parpola 1989, 22 (see chap. 11, n. 48).

13. Nanjundayya and Iyer 1928–35, 4:613; Sontheimer 1989, 308–9, 326; recall Flueckiger 1983, 30, 40 (see chap. 4, sec. B). See Hiltebeitel 1982b, 51, with further references. Many South Indian women also take a daily turmeric bath (Jagadisa Ayyar 1982, 74–77); cf. Shulman 1989, 41: Kāttavarāyaṉ's Āriyamālai bathes in rivers of turmeric. The oblong basin called "Draupadī's Bath" at Mahabalipuram is perhaps, like other *Mahābhārata* monuments there, given its name through Draupadī cult associations.

14. Rajput warriors wore yellow "when about to sacrifice themselves in a desperate conflict, a sacrifice to their supposed ancestor Sūrya" (Dymock 1890, 447).

15. See White 1984, 46–47, including the pertinent myths.

forms through a series of alchemical processes that involve the mercury's penetrating the sulfur and "absorbing" or "sucking into itself the subtleness that lays embedded in the female elements, in order to make itself all the more subtle" (White 1984, 49–52).

As *vīra-kantakam,* or "heroic sulfur," turmeric powder seems to be a popular or "poor man's" ritual equivalent of sulfur, having similar transmutative or rejuvenating properties. According to the pāratiyār V. Venugopala Aiyar, vīrakantakam is born with Draupadī, from the fire of her birth; it is a "śakti of Amman̲, and men put it on to get that śakti."[16] Note that turmeric, in its ritual uses, is called the same thing (*vīragandhaka*) in the cult of the heroes of Palnāḍu.[17] The origin of turmeric and kuṅkum from the goddess is also found in a Telugu Māḍiga myth: the two substances come from the brains and blood of the original Mātaṅgi, an Untouchable woman who impersonates the goddess (Clough 1899, 71–72). Even in its everyday preparation, kuṅkum is made from the "transmutative" process of mixing turmeric with lime. The red "blood" of kuṅkum is ready to be released from within turmeric.

For Draupadī, the mañcaḷ saree that her icon wears can represent her both as a chaste virgin and as a mother. When Duḥśāsana attempts to tear off her sarees, the last one, the unremovable one that Kṛṣṇa passes down over her shoulder, should be mañcaḷ, symbolizing her chastity and, in terms of her cult's mythology, her status as a kan̲n̲i, or virgin.[18] On the other hand, Brown cites a pamphlet prepared by a former Madras "pandit" for the Fiji firewalk that claims the turmeric-dyed yellow robes worn by the men "represent the robes of the Mother" (1984, 228). Though only men are supposed to cross the coals at some Draupadī festivals, the view at Tindivanam, according to V. S. Purushottama Chettiyar, the temple's chief trustee, is that firewalking is really a women's rite.[19] In the chief core area firewalking myth of Draupadī luring the

16. According to the icon sculptor N. Dandapani, the lotus that opens at Draupadī's feet on her processional icons is supposed to be mañcaḷ, or yellow, to symbolize the fire of her birth.

17. Velcheru Narayana Rao, personal communication, 1988; also *vīragandham* for "hero-sandal paste" (idem, 1983).

18. Cf. Egnor 1986, 307: "A young girl's garment (*cittāṭai*) is the top piece draped over the shoulder, worn by girls come of age but not married. The same garment is tied on statues of female deities, because a deity is always young and always a virgin." Cf. Hiltebeitel 1989c; 1988a, 236, 247 plate 13. A Sanskrit term for turmeric is *yuvatī,* "young girl" or "virgin." At Udappu, Sri Lanka, "Draupadī is said to wear a yellow sari, which is the color of a virgin" (Tanaka 1987, 409).

19. Of the three men-only firewalks I saw, only at Pondicherry was the rule kept. At both Sowcarpet and Veḷḷimēṭupēṭṭai, one woman crossed, at the former site with an

Kaurava widows into becoming suttees, it is only women who join Draupadī in her original crossing (Hiltebeitel 1988a, 440–42). For women firewalkers, then, Draupadī herself is one model, the suttee another. As to male firewalkers, the wearing of turmeric and turmeric-dyed garments has a number of connotations. It is an absorbing of the goddess's virginal and rejuvenating śakti, a means of being reborn through her as her "sons," and the taking on of a feminine aspect. In some cases, as at the Bangalore Hulsoor Gate Dharmarāja Temple festival, one of the devotees undergoes a complete transformation:

> The priest adorns himself and his hair with white jasmine garlands. He is made to wear a turmeric colored saree and blouse. Strings of jasmine buds of special variety decorate the hands. The strings of flowers flow from the hair all over his back. On the chest he wears necklaces, strings of beads, etc. The priest looking like a lady, shines like a bride.[20]

But Draupadī's male firewalkers can also take on the aspect of warriors ready for battle, as with the turmeric-bathed young heroes of Palnāḍu. Like the paṭukaḷam, the firepit can be an image of Kurukṣetra or even, as in the suttee myth, the battlefield's cremation ground.

Eight hundred men and women bathing at the edge of the Tīrthaṅkuḷam tank, dressing themselves in yellow on its east bank and steps, picking up their green sprigs of margosa, putting on their red and white garlands, is a vivid sight.[21] At the center of it all, almost inconspicuous, is the nuclear group that will fuse this gathering into a unity. It consists of the pūcāri, the kaṇāccāri, the camayam's replacement, the whip bearer, their various assistants,

---

astonishing twirling dance. Cf. Brown 1984, 229 (both men and women, "but ordinarily only men do"); Richards 1910, 31; Tanaka 1987, 383 (apparently men only); Babb 1974, 24–25 and Blaive, Penaud, and Nicoli 1974, 360–61 (men cross coals, women circumambulate firepit); Nevill 1887a, 58–59 (men and prepubescent girls only); Richards 1918, 115; Gopalakrishnan 1953, 108; Moses 1961, 85; Nambiar et al. 1965, 73, 88–89 (both men and women); Lewis 1931, 513 (both men and women, apparently at the same temple described fifty years later by Babb as for men). Cf. Biardeau 1989b, 146 for similar variation at Māriyammaṉ firewalks.

20. Munivenkatappa 1965. Cf. Nanjundayya and Iyer 1928–35, 4:618–19, emphasizing the feminine apparel of the karakam carrier, who is perhaps also the pūcāri.

21. See Frasca's photos from the 1981 Tindivanam festival (1990, 18th and 19th plates). The scene varies from festival to festival. At Mēlaccēri, bathers go individually or in small groups to the pentagonal Pañcapāṇṭava Tank (*kuḷam*) near the temple; at Maṅkalam in 1982, the tank being dry, women and then men merrily doused each other with water from a tap near the tank.

and the musicians of the *kōyil mēḷam* (the temple's processional band, composed of a *mattaḷam* drum player and one or two *nākacuram* [a clarinetlike instrument] players). The main officiants sit at the very edge of the water, at the center of all the bathing and other activities, while the assistants and musicians stand a sort of guard around them. Placed in their midst are a number of items that the pūcāri prepares for the rites that follow. Foremost is the *alaku karakam,* a large-bowled earthenware pot (*karakam*) that will have a sword (alaku) stood upon its outer curved surface. The preparations at the tank are said to transform it from an ordinary pot (*kalacam*) into a karakam (cf. Biardeau 1989b, 144). First the pot is washed. Then sandal and turmeric powder are applied in a band around the upper part of the outer bowl. Some raw rice and a lemon are put inside. Mango leaves are set around the mouth and a coconut is placed on them to close off the opening. A scaffolding is then built up from the top and decorated with flowers (mainly orange and yellow marigolds with a sprinkling of jasmine), so that the flowers form a crownlike cone atop the pot.[22] Finally a lemon is set at the peak of the cone, and four other lemons are placed at the cardinal points, near the top. Other implements assembled around the *alaku karakam* include the alaku sword itself and the vīrakuntam, held upright with a lemon on its central prong and a vīracāṭṭi coiled within it. There is also a kuṭṭi piḷḷaiyār, or "little Gaṇeśa," elsewhere known as akkiṉikampam, or "fire-post," about which more will be said shortly.[23]

D. Procession to the Temple

After a lull in activity between 4:30 and 6:00 P.M., which corresponds to the inauspicious *irākukālam* on the firewalk Sunday,[24] the karakam procession to the temple begins about 6:00 P.M. In both 1977 and 1981, I was warned that the press of the crowd and the commotion of the firewalkers would make it impossible to get near the firepit if I arrived with their procession, and I was urged to secure a place near the coals early, before the procession arrived. This meant that at Tindivanam I did not see the rites performed in the second and third phases of the firewalk sequence: the procession itself and the rites at the temple. The Tindivanam temple trustees

22. Cf. Brown 1976, 23: "Some say the *kargam* is the crown of the Mother" (omitted from Brown 1984).

23. On the akkiṉikampam and alternative names, see chapter 6, section B.

24. The irākukālam, dominated by the eclipse demon Rāhu, occurs at different times on different days of the week.

also took this option, not participating in the procession (as their counterparts did at Maṅkalam and Mēlaccēri) but remaining at the firepit in the double capacity of dignitaries and overseers of order in the crowd. For Tindivanam, I thus rely mainly on the pūcāri's description and draw comparatively on observation of the corresponding rites at Maṅkalam, Mēlaccēri, and Veḷḷimēṭupēṭṭai.

According to the Tindivanam pūcāri, the procession from the tank to the temple takes the following order: kōyil mēḷam (musicians); pampaikkāraṉ (pampai drum player); alaku karakam bearer; pūcāri carrying the alaku (sword) and kuṭṭi piḷḷaiyār; kaṇāccāri carrying the vīrakuntam; and the mass of firewalkers, referred to as bhaktas, "devotees." The whip bearer, who uses a new whip freshly made for each festival rather than the one in the vīrakuntam, is not counted separately, as he roves among the firewalkers lashing their raised wrists in groups of ten or fifteen. It was emphasized that the alaku karakam is carried in the center of the procession. It is borne atop the head, by a Vaṉṉiyar in a hereditary role (see chap. 2, sec. B.). According to the temple's chief trustee, there should be another Garuḍadarśana during this procession, but no Garuḍa was sighted in either year.[25]

The comparative study of processions in India is in its infancy, but Herrenschmidt's cautious beginnings suggest that three functions may be repeatedly encountered, in the following order: musicians, carriers of symbols, and bringing up the rear, the "place of honor" (1982, 45–49). One could construe this to imply that the firewalkers have the place of honor at Tindivanam, which is possible, perhaps as the collectivity that offers itself in sacrifice. But it seems more likely that the honored place is indicated by the "central" position of the alaku karakam, which represents the goddess.[26] At Maṅkalam, in fact, two karakams are brought from the tank to the temple precisely in the rear position (plate 30). There the order is vīrakuntam bearer, lemon-tipped sword bearer, pampaikkāraṉ, koṭicīlai flag bearer (a red flag on a long pole), holder of a tray with a camphor flame, musicians and firewalkers together, and, in the rear, the two karakam bearers, each holding his pot on his head atop the rolled end of a yellow cloth that trails in a long drape be-

25. The only actual sighting I was present for was thus the one at Mēlaccēri during Arjuna's tapas; see chapter 8, section A. Cf. Biardeau 1989b, 156: a garuḍadarśana connected with firewalk and impalement in the Māriyammaṉ cult.

26. As Draupadī says in her *Māṉmiyam,* "I will appear in a karakam and I will walk across the fire with the devotees" (see Appendix). The position of the pāṭbhakta and *sāddhu,* last in the culminating procession at the Bhaktapur Śiva gājan (Östör 1980, 129), is, however, a parallel to that of that bhaktas.

hind it, the ends held by a third man so that they come in contact with the point of a sword. This sword, called the *pūkkatti* ("flower sword"), is strung with circlets of jasmine, its handle held aloft toward the space between the two pots. The chief karakam, the one on the right, and the flowered sword are carried by male members of the family of the chief trustee.[27]

The differences between these two processions, however, already warn us against generalizations. The mēḷam at Tindivanam does not include the ankle-bracelet rattle (*cilampu*) or hourglass-shaped drum (*uṭukkai*) that one finds at Maṅkalam, and at Maṅkalam no one wields the vīracāṭṭi whip (it is carried on a tray). Meanwhile, the single karakam pot carried from the tank at Mēlaccēri is positioned at neither the center nor the rear of the procession, but directly behind the pampaikkāraṉ toward the front. In 1986 it was carried atop the head of the elderly chief trustee Gopala Goundar, who also carried a raised lemon-tipped sword in his right hand. At Mēlaccēri, this procession is without any musical instruments other than the pampai drum, and no whipping is done during it.

No matter what musical instruments and ritual implements are involved, however, they contribute, along with the goddess's presence in the karakam, to the heightening of possession among some of the firewalker-bhaktas. At Maṅkalam in particular, the various weapon bearers and flag bearers toward the lead all acted out gestures of martial possession (plate 31); the women near the cilampu and uṭukkai players in the center performed possessed dance movements, flailing their loosened hair, beckoning the flow of the goddess's śakti from the karakams. The local rice mill owner, leading the two karakams, kept biting his left forearm, with popping eyes.[28] Whatever the items carried at a particular festival, virtually all the paraphernalia of possession—cilampu, uṭukkai, vīracāṭṭi, vīrakuntam, koṭicīlai, akkiṉikampam, lemon-tipped sword, even the karakam—find their place, at different temples, among the ritual

27. For other Draupadī cult karakam processions, see Brown 1976, 26, 29; Richards 1910, 32 (karakam first in firewalk procession); Babb 1974, 24 (again, karakam first); for Māriyammaṉ, see Moffatt 1979, 258–59 (karakam carriers last).

28. He explained that he had gotten possessed (āvēcam) at the time because some of the women in the procession were menstruating. His body got irritated. Other men felt it too. They could not identify the women but took the countermeasures of putting turmeric water on their bodies and cutting a lemon. At the Udappu, Sri Lanka, Kālī festival, a "medium possessed by the goddess tried to bite his own arm"; villagers and Kālī, speaking through the medium, said this was a form of "*narapali* or human sacrifice" (Tanaka 1987, 149).

weapons that Pōrmaṉṉaṉ-Pōttu Rāja brings to the service of Draupadī (Hiltebeitel 1988a, 387–88 and table 10). Yet surprisingly, Pōttu Rāja's icon is not part of these processions, as it is in so many others. It is possible that the karakam brought up from the water represents an emergence or "birth" of the goddess.[29] If this is so, it would parallel Draupadī's birth from fire, and thus the myth in which the ritual implements are born with her rather than brought to her by her guardian (Hiltebeitel 1988a, 386–93), thereby accounting for Pōttu Rāja's absence. Alternatively, however, it should be pointed out that there are no portable icons in this procession—other, that is, than the karakam. The portable icons will often join the next procession from the temple to the firepit.[30]

E. Return to the Temple

At this point, with the arrival of the karakam procession at the temple, we face a confusing situation, one that has already revealed itself in the presence of two karakams at Maṅkalam. There can be as many as four types of karakams at a Draupadī festival,[31] and those having the same functions can have different names. Moreover, not all festivals divide the functions in the same way. At Tindivanam there are three types of karakams, one of which we met in chapter 4: the cāl karakam, two of which are used in the nine grains sprouting rites. These cāl karakams are not brought into the firewalk sequence directly, but the other two karakams are. When the alaku karakam reaches the temple from the tank, it is brought into the sanctum and placed before Draupadī's permanent stone icon beside another karakam called either the *pū* ("flower") karakam or *cakti* ("power," Sanskrit *śakti*) karakam. A dīpārādhanā is done to both of them. This second karakam, on which a cone

29. At Udappu, Sri Lanka, there are daily karakam processions from the seacoast to the temple, which Tanaka views as invitations to Draupadī to come from the sea, where she is seen in visions walking on the waters (1987, 352, 357, 379). Cf. the pots bought from the water in the Dharma and Śiva gājans (chap. 7, sec. C), especially the *pūr kalasī,* representing either the androgynous Dharma or the goddess as his consort and connected with ecstatic dancing (Robinson 1980, 307–19).

30. Cf. Biardeau 1989b, 144–45: karakam processions from Kaveri river to Māriyammaṉ temple with ritual weapons of her guardians Kāttavarāyaṉ and Kaṟuppucāmi, but not their icons.

31. At Veḷḷimēṭupēṭṭai, an *apiṣēka* ("consecration") *cakti karakam* used in navadhānya rites, an *alaku* ("sword") *cakti karakam* for the standing of the sword, an *alaṅkāra* ("decoration") *cakti karakam* of copper decorated with pennants and flowers, and an *akkiṉi* ("fire") *cakti karakam* or *pū* ("flower") *karakam* (= *pūṅkarakam*), the last two both carried across the fire (N. M. Adikeshava Bharatiyar, informant).

of paper flowers is kept throughout the year, is decorated for the firewalk with real flowers at the temple itself and with water from the nearby Rājaṅkuḷam tank rather than the more distant Tīrthaṅkuḷam. Unlike the alaku karakam, it is half filled with water. Otherwise it is similarly scaffolded with sticks of margosa, covered with flowers, and topped with a lemon dotted with a red poṭṭu mark of kuṅkum. According to the pūcāri, it should be decorated on the day of Arjuna's tapas, but since hands were short in 1981, the task was done only on the morning of firewalking day. It is this second pū or cakti karakam that will be carried over the coals.

These names and functions are anything but uniform from festival to festival. At Maṅkalam, the names alaku karakam and pūṅkarakam are used for both of the two pots decorated at the tank and carried in the procession from the tank to the temple. Though the sword is stood on the one carried by the tarumakarttā's nephew, two pots are carried because odd numbers are said to be inauspicious. Meanwhile, the pot to be carried across the fire is again decorated in the sanctum but is called *ammaṉ cakti karakam.* So far, the differences lie only in numbers and names. But at Vēḷḷimēṭupēṭṭai, the functions are compounded. There, the sword-standing pot, called *alaku cakti karakam,* does not come from the tank but is decorated and stays put in the sanctum. And the *two* pots that cross the fire—the copper *alaṅkāra cakti karakam* and the *akkiṉi cakti karakam* or pūṅkarakam—go together on both processions: the first from the tank to the temple, the second from the temple across the coals. These variations, which could be extended not only with other Draupadī cult examples but from other firewalking cults as well, will suffice to outline the difficulties.[32] For simplicity's sake, however, it is still possible to observe a few consistencies. The sword-standing pot, which can be called the alaku karakam, is never confused with the pot carried across the coals, which can most profitably be called the pū ("flower") karakam, or the akkiṉi or tī ("fire") karakam.

32. Cf. Babb 1974, 22–23; Richards 1910, 32 (karakam at firepit guarded by Pōttu Rāja); Hasan 1970, 149–50 ("Karaga festival"); and especially Brown 1984, 233–39 (Śakti karagam in Māriyammaṉ temple, Agni and Gaṅgā karagams at Draupadī's firepit facing the Māri temple; no sword standing; each decorated at seashore, and supposed to contain the five elements [Brown 1984, 234]). For other goddesses, see Whitehead 1921, 37–38 and plate 3; Diehl 1956, 176–77; Moffatt 1979, 255, 267 (a "lower form" of the goddess); Reiniche 1979, 166–71; Hiltebeitel 1985a, 183–85 (at Gingee buffalo sacrifice); Meyer 1986, 234–42; Tanaka 1987, 271–88 (Kālī festival); and especially Biardeau 1989b, 292–93 (for Paccaivāḷiyammaṉ's firewalk, a *pūṅkarakam* first across the coals, followed by an *agnikarakam* with actual fire in it, and a *gaṅgaikarakam* [= Gaṅgā karakam] that appeases the fire, with water in it).

These two pots clearly figure in an opposition. One pot emerges from the bank or shore of a body of water; the other crosses the coals. The former is an almost birthlike emergence of the goddess (see n. 29); the latter fulfills her destination. Biardeau clarifies a similar opposition at Thanjavur District firewalks for Māriyamman̠. The pot that remains in the temple represents "the creative face of the divinity who presides over the conservation of the world and oversees its regeneration," while the fire-crossing pot represents "her martial and destructive aspect, necessary to renew the world, which would otherwise sink into an irremediable chaos," "the warrior goddess traversing the fires of war" (1989b, 154, 148; my translation). The parallel with Draupadī's fire-crossing pot is tempting. Her firepit is frequently linked with Kurukṣetra. According to a pamphlet on the Karagam festival of the Dharmaraya Temple, Hulsoor Gate, Bangalore, "Some people believed that Draupadī appeared in an awesome and fearful form when she entered the battlefield and the karakam is supposed to represent that" (Munivenkatappa 1965). This description refers only to Draupadī's processional movements, but it could easily extend to the firepit.

In any case, when the two (main) karakams join each other in the sanctum, the temple is, for the moment, the center of all activity and divine power. It has not had this centrality since flag-hoisting day, and has never had so much concentrated power (śakti) at any prior point in the festival. The goddess, who has suffered and triumphed her *Mahābhārata* at various degrees of distance from her temple (at the Pāratam pantal, drama stage, and paṭukaḷam), and through various forms of embodiment (verbal, dramatic, ritual, iconic), has re-presented herself in her temple, before her mūlavar, in what appears to be her most elemental and basic form of all, the earthen karakams.[33] At Tindivanam, according to the pūcāri, after he offers dīpārādhanā to the two pots, while a few assistants stand in attendance and two thousand devotees wait outside, he stands the alaku sword on the outer curve of the alaku karakam. The rite is called *alaku niṟuttal*, "'to place a pointed weapon' or 'to cause a pointed weapon to stand upright'" (Meyer 1986, 238). He uses no tricks, in particular no smear of turmeric paste to hold the point in place, such as I saw on my first visit to Tindivanam in 1975, when the trustees, in the festival off-season, invited a local pāratiyār to show me how it was done.[34] At Tindivanam, as at many other

33. See nn. 26, 32 and Appendix.
34. According to several pāratiyārs, alaku standing is frequently done by the pāratiyār, though I was not at any festival where this was the case.

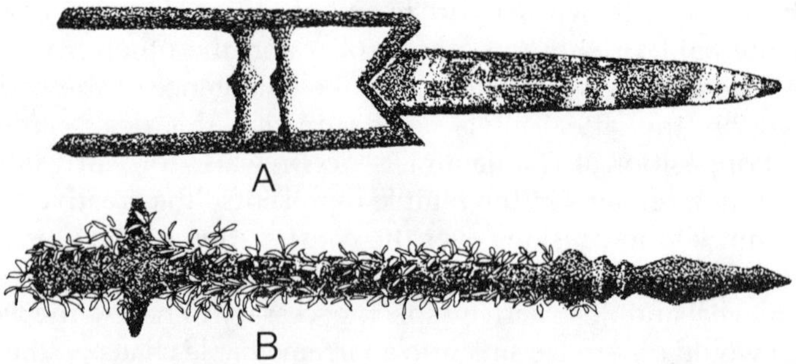

Figure 15. Different types of alaku swords for standing on karakam pots: (A) Tindivanam; (B) Maṅkalam.

Draupadī temples, the alaku is a peculiar type of sword, having a straight double-edged blade that tapers to its point, and an open-bar, double-grip hilt that is perpendicular to the blade and enclosed in a protective frame (see fig. 15A).[35] On my first visit to Tindivanam, I was told by the trustees that the alaku automatically falls after the firewalk is over. But the pūcāri said this is just the trustees' "gas": "How would they know? They never come to the temple." He insists that the alaku stands until the next day, when he takes it down from the pot himself (see plate 32).

Before I attempt to add to what is already a shrewd scholarly discussion of alaku niṟuttal, let me give the rite an air of immediacy by describing its 1982 performance at Maṅkalam, which I attended and attempted to record by hand in my notebook. Recall that at this temple, two alaku or "flower" karakams have arrived from the tank on the heads of their bearers, while a third, the ammaṉ cakti karakam, is in place after having been decorated earlier at the temple. I was with about thirty other people in a sanctum about ten by ten feet in size.

> Inside. The pots are taken down, set on sand. Dīpārādhanā to pots. Chanting to Draupadī, "Ammā!" Calling "Kōvintā!" Drumming very loud, with cilampu, cymbals, etc. Prostrations of two women in front and to sides of pots. Women rocking, bowing. Crush of bodies. Woman next to me helps me clear my elbows for writing. Same woman was possessed in procession,

35. Another term for this implement, mentioned at several villages, is *kaṭṭāri,* for which the *Tamil Lexicon* gives "1. Cross-hilted dagger. . . . 2. Trident of Śiva." The Tindivanam pūcāri said the kaṭṭāri is an ancient weapon of Tamil kings, and can be used for cutting trees! As a fighting weapon, it seems most suitable for close-in jabbing.

> dancing with gestures of beckoning to the karakams. Now same gesture imploring the śakti to flow from the image to the karakam. Water poured over man doing prostrations. Hundred-year-old man [Ramalinga Goundar] kneels down, touches head to steps leading up to images. Pause. Prayers. Cries to Kōvintā. Man holding small pot sprinkles water about, cooling. Man holding flower-sword (pūkkatti) goes into possession, leaps, shouts "Kōvintā" for half a minute. Falls to floor. Pūkkatti rested near [main] pūṅkarakam. Old man beside karakams kneels and dances, knees to the floor, women follow in circle. Floor all soaked. A hothouse. The pūkkatti man gets up, takes up the pūkkatti, pumps it up and down to the music like a drill, dances with legs in squat toward the karakams, sword held upright between his thighs. Places sword tip on pot. Sword shivers, shakes, falls. Another man grasps the alaku karakam, works it into sand, stabilizing it. Turmeric powder sprinkled on sword. It almost stands. Noise fierce. Dīpārādhanā to sword. It almost stands again, totters after three seconds. It stands for five seconds. Shouts of "Kōvintā!" It falls. Frenzy. More Kōvintās. Everyone shakes right forefingers at the sword. Scolding it? Songs of coming of Draupadī-ammaṉ. Another try. Falls again. Another dance, same squatting fashion, around the pots. Sidling zigzag approach to pot. It stands.

I do not know how long this sword stood. But I doubt it could have been for very long, since, unlike the more balanced and sturdy alaku at Tindivanam, this *katti* was a long, thin, regularly hilted sword with a pliancy that made it shiver, not to mention the circlets of jasmine on it that would vibrate with it (see fig. 15).[36]

Needless to say, I was struck by an erotic component in this Maṅkalam performance, one that makes almost (if not actually) overt the sword's phallic connotation in relation to the womblike pot. Of course I was observing it through the filter of Beck's classic two paragraphs on a similar ceremony for Aṅkāḷammaṉ: the sword "laid across the neck of the pot" is a token of his [Śiva's] visit and sexual union" with Aṅkāḷammaṉ; when "her sexual desire is satis-

36. The terms katti and alaku are not consistently differentiated. The alaku-sword can also be called a katti. And katti cēvai, involving the regular sword, can also be called alaku cēvai (see chapter 2, section B; chapter 11, section A). However, the Tindivanam pūcāri maintained that alaku should refer only to the sword stood on the pot, while katti is what is carried by the sword bearer. I have not met the term *katti niṟuttal*. The term *alaku* is also used for flesh-piercing needles (Biardeau 1989b, 146, 153). *Katti* may derive from Sanskrit *khaḍga* (ibid., 150).

fied by intercourse with Śiva," she can then demonstrate "her new, cooled state by absorbing the heat that burns her devotees, as they walk the burning coals" (1969, 564). It is doubtful, however, that one can easily transfer this interpretation to the Draupadī cult.[37] For one thing, I know of nothing to indicate that the alaku karakam (or Draupadī's mūlavar beside it) absorbs the heat. We shall see that heat control is accounted for differently. More important, what kind of sexual union can the sword and pot represent? Are we to understand that the goddess and her male consort (Śiva? Arjuna? Dharma, with whom Draupadī often shares the sanctum? Bhīma?[38]) are simply satisfying themselves while their devotees are engaged in rites that rely upon their own absolute purity and sexual self-denial?[39] One can argue for such a displacement by a selective interpretation of the symbols. Could it not be that when the sword is said to fall "on its own" just before or after the firewalk[40] it indicates the sexual fulfillment and abatement of desire of both the god and goddess? Do not the devotees as "sacrificers" offer up to the goddess what they themselves renounce—meat, blood, and sex, in symbolic forms, on the paṭukaḷum—in order that they may walk the coals? I must admit that these propositions are my own (1982b, 82–83, 93). But I think now that it is better not to push for such a projection on the theological plane. Draupadī is a virgin. Her devotees simply would not countenance such an interpretation. The sexual themes are there, but, at least at Maṅkalam, their force is in their being acted out, thinly (if at all) sublimated, by the devotees themselves. As with the women's rites at the base of Arjuna's tapas

37. As does Brown 1984, 235: "During their union, the Goddess's passion absorbs the heat of the fire so the firewalkers can cross over the coals safely." Śiva, however, is said to absorb the firewalkers' heat in his gājan from within his sanctum (see chap. 7, sec. C). Presumably this refers to his liṅgam. Here again, however, a sexual component is not made explicit.

38. Tanaka's view of this rite at Udappu, citing Beck 1969 and Hiltebeitel 1982b, should be read cautiously: "The sword is the weapon of Bhimasena, . . . and represents him, whilst the *karakam*-pot represents Draupadī. More generally speaking, the sword is a phallus and the pot a womb. Thus this ritual act symbolically implies a union between Draupadī and Bhimasena during the festival" (1987, 352). Note that this sword standing occurs at flag hoisting, not in connection with the firewalk.

39. If the sword wavers, it is a sign that someone impure is about to participate in the ceremony, which must be immediately interrupted until the cause of pollution is removed (Gros and Nagaswamy 1970, 121).

40. Said not only by the Tindivanam trustees but at Muthialpet and Chintadripet (Gopalakrishnan 1953, 108), while at Sowcarpet—vive la différence—the sword is said to fall miraculously when the first firewalker *enters* the firepit. Cf. Hemingway 1907, 294: the goddess gives her consent after a sword remains standing when stuck in the ground.

tree, people's gestures have sexual implications that go unacknowledged in the symbolic object itself. The symbols may be sexual but sexually pure, and they free symbolic actions that, while having a sexual referent and atmosphere, are themselves also renunciatory. Thus even when a sword is placed on the pot in the sanctum, the pure and renunciatory dimension of the karakam, insisted on by Biardeau, seems to retain prominence.[41] Moreover, as Meyer has argued, there are too many instances of swords' being "the weapon *par excellence* of the goddess" and even "identified" with her (1986, 240), rather than with a god or hero for one to insist, without informant support, that the sword is a male symbol. Where the sword standing is taken as the first and foremost sign of the goddess's permission to undertake the firewalk, there is nothing to indicate that the miracle—as it is understood—is not entirely her own. Indeed, according to N. M. Adikeshava Bharatiyar, at Draupadī festivals the karakam is śakti and the alaku is śakti.

Moreover, though alaku niṟuttal is widely understood at core area Draupadī temples to be the first test to see whether the goddess gives her "green signal" for the firewalk, this is not a uniform feature of the rite, as Beck's full interpretation requires. Usually, when it is performed for Aṅkāḷammaṉ it has no connection with firewalking (Meyer 1986, 238–42), as is also the case where it is done by Dēvāṅga weavers for their goddess Chaudhēśvari (Thurston and Rangachari [1904] 1965, 2:158–59). At Draupadī temples themselves, it may also be done at times other than firewalking. Winslow associates the rite specifically with Draupadī but says that it is performed in her "pagoda" "before the festival in her honour is commenced" ([1862] 1979, 41): presumably, that is, in connection with flag-hoisting ceremonies. At the Udappu, Sri Lanka Draupadī festival, it is done on the first day, along with flag hoisting, and involves a squatting dance called *ānanta naṭanam* ("walking of joy") that is reminiscent of the one at Maṅkalam, except that here it is done by Draupadī's medium as he brings the pot into the temple on his head, balancing it with a cane in one hand and a knife in the other (Tanaka 1987, 351–52). According to Adikeshava Bharatiyar,

41. Contrary to Hiltebeitel 1982b, stressing a rapport between "orectic" and "normative" dimensions of the symbol. That Turnerian approach is oversusceptible to arguments from the unconscious and to superinscribing seeming parallels on the symbol, even ones from the same culture, that may lie in the interpreter's eyes only. Hiltebeitel 1982b, 82–83, and Brown 1984, 225, 235 (arguing, I believe unconvincingly, that the central stick of mango wood "carefully shoved into the pot" is the equivalent of the missing "sword of Śiva" from Beck's article) should be rejected in this light.

alaku niṟuttal is done at some festivals three times: at flag hoisting (further confirmation of Winslow from the core area), at Draupadī's marriage, and for the firewalk by the pāratiyār. The pāratiyār Brameesa Mudaliyar adds that it is done at some festivals three days before the firewalk. Meanwhile, at urban Madras temples, a pattern seems to have evolved in which it is performed on the night before tīmiti, prior to the dressing of Draupadī's icon as Kālī or Mahiṣāsuramardinī.[42] It seems that in these temples, though it remains connected with the firewalk, alaku niṟuttal has also been drawn into the penumbra of paṭukaḷam substitutions because of the sword's connotation as the *goddess's* weapon. In fact, at Chintadripet it is connected directly with alaku cēvai: the sword pressers continue this ordeal until the sword stands, indicating a connection between Draupadī's favor and her satisfaction with the purity of her votaries (Gopalakrishnan 1953, 106; similarly Thurston and Rangachari [1904] 1965, 2:159 among the Dēvāṅgas).

F. Crossing the Coals

As soon as the Tindivanam pūcāri completes his standing of the sword, he does a dīpārādhanā to Draupadī's pañcalōkam processional icon, which has been richly decorated with garlands and a silver crown and now rests in the temple's front maṇḍapa with the other processional icons. The *cāmi* (that is, the "deity" Draupadī in this form) is then taken outside the temple along with Arjuna's pañcalōkam icon, and the pair are tied to a large and colorfully painted four-poster, roofed palanquin that takes eight men to carry it, four on each side. With shouts and drumming, the pūṅkarakam is also taken from the sanctum and lifted onto the pūcāri's head. Now a new procession forms for the approach to the firepit. This time the order is kōyil mēḷam, pampaikkāraṉ, pūṅkarakam, palanquin, kaṇāccāri, firewalkers. One of the pūcāri's assistants also brings the kuṭṭi piḷḷaiyār on a tray with a coconut and other pūjā items (betel nut, camphor, *mullai* flowers [a kind of jasmine], and a lemon).

Meanwhile, final preparations are undertaken at the firewalking area. At larger towns (Tindivanam, Pondicherry) and in Madras City (Sowcarpet), the area is set off by an enclosure of rope or bamboo fencing. Those admitted inside (trustees, other dignitaries, visiting researchers) have to remove their sandals so as not to pollute this ground. More important, in these urban and town settings the enclosure serves to mark a barrier against the swelling crowd

42. At Chintadripet (Gopalakrishnan 1953, 107), Muthialpet, and Sowcarpet.

that pushes in dangerously from all sides, despite not only the fence but also the vigorous and repeated *lathi* (truncheon) charges of the police (cf. Shideler 1987, 163). The firepit is an object not only of seeing, or darśan, but also, I would have to say, of longing: and not only for the firewalkers but also for the crowd, which swells toward it and then recedes in a kind of tidal rhythm.[43] At village festivals (Mēlaccēri, Maṅkalam, Veḷḷimēṭupēṭṭai), neither barriers nor police were necessary, the crowds being smaller and far more orderly on their own, and the firepit forming its own natural boundaries. But everywhere the crowd that gathers for the firewalk is impressive, drawing on family and residential networks that extend beyond the immediate location. People fill every available vantage point (rooftops, trees, electricity towers, the wonderful boulders of Mēlaccēri) to take it all in. The allure of the firepit is sometimes linked with a vision of Draupadī (Tanaka 1987, 152–153) or with a concentration that must not be distracted by "a pretty girl" in the crowd as one draws toward it (Brown 1976, 33; cf. Lal and Seruvakula 1974, 49). There is also a notion that Draupadī will protect the firewalkers by spreading her hair or sarees over the coals (Babb 1974, 1, 40–41; Macready 1888–89, 192; Somander 1951, 614; cf. McGilvray 1986) or that the coals will feel like cool flowers (Babb 1974, 41).[44]

As the time for the firewalkers' approach draws near, all remaining stumps are removed and the coals are raked out into a rectangular bed to form the firepit (*tīkkuḻi; akkiṉikuṇṭam*). Usually, in what seems to be the norm, a shallow trench has been dug out at the far side so that the firewalkers will cross it immediately after the coals. This is called the "milk pit" (*pāl kuḻi*) or "milk river" (*pāl āru*). Ordinarily it is filled with water, but at some diaspora sites real milk is supplied by donors (Babb 1974, 22; Lewis 1931, 513: both for Singapore) or coconut milk is used (Blaive, Penaud, and Nicoli 1974, 160: Réunion). The crossing length of the milk pits I have seen is between four and seven feet.[45] The firepits vary in depth and

43. Brown 1976, 32, describes a similar "impel-restrain" pattern, and the firepit as "a longed for object"; cf. Lal and Seruvakula 1974, 49.

44. Cf. Babb 1974, 32–33. At a Māriyammaṉ firewalk, while the men cross the coals, the pūcāri pours red-hot embers over the women's hair (Oppert 1893, 480). The "flower-coals" equation is widespread: see Eichinger Ferro-Luzzi 1983, 214–15; Lal and Seruvakula 1974, 48; Tanaka 1987, 374: Draupadī's firepit is called the *pū niṭam* or "flower place"; for other goddess cults, cf. McGilvray 1986; Mackenzie 1874, 8: the firepit filled after the last crossing with flowers; Thurston 1906, 485: flowers instead of fire. Recall the "flower play" with hot coals in the Dharma gājans (chap. 7, sec. C).

45. Conditions vary. Of the six firewalks I have seen, three did without a milk pit: Sowcarpet, Maṅkalam, and Pondicherry. For the milk pit at other Draupadī fes-

length. The deeper the coals, the more intense the heat and the greater the danger. Those at Tindivanam and Sowcarpet, when freshly raked, were the deepest and freshest, and the most dangerous I saw: in each case about three inches deep. At Pondicherry and Veḷḷimēṭupēṭṭai the coals were about half as deep, but still beds, whereas those at Maṅkalam and Mēlaccēri were so thinned out that at many points there were only patches of cinder rather than living coals. As to length, the temples with the deeper coals also had the longer crossings: roughly twenty-five feet for the first two pairs, twenty feet for the last.[46] Here there is another factor: number of crossings. The longer and deeper crossings were in most cases made only once, while the shorter and shallower ones are often made three times.[47] The town and urban festivals accentuate the goddess's power to protect by increasing the risks that test that power, whereas in the villages, there seems to be more concern for caution. Most of the injuries and the single death that resulted from the firewalks I witnessed occurred where the coals were deepest. The death occurred at Tindivanam in 1981. The mattaḷam drum player fell on the coals and was then trampled by onrushing firewalkers for several seconds before he could be retrieved by a man whose charge it was to meet such emergencies. He died four days later at Jipmer Hospital in Pondicherry. Curiously, a few months after it had happened, several of the first local informants to speak of it gave me the stock explanation: he was drunk, or he had been in contact with a menstruating woman. But the pūcāri said three years later that the drummer had forgotten to do some *cāntikam* (propitiation).[48]

---

tivals, see Richards 1910, 32; 1918, 115; Stokes 1873, 190; Beauchamp 1901, 57; Frasca 1984, 317. Sayce (1933, 3) diagrams a three-pit site for a Natal Māriyammaṉ firewalk: a small turmeric water pit to "purify" the feet before the firepit and a real-milk milk pit.

46. This range of depth and length is common at Draupadī festivals (Babb 1974, 22; Brown 1976, 10; Richards 1910, 32; 1918, 115; Stokes 1873, 190). At Veḷḷalūr (Coimbatore District), however, the pit is one meter deep, one meter wide, and sixty feet long (with a "milk pit" beyond it): a type met at festivals for other goddesses (see Oppert 1893, 480, 492–94; McGilvray 1986).

47. On triple crossings, see Firewalking . . . 1900, 320; Richards 1910, 32; 1918, 115–16; Blaive, Penaud, and Nicoli 1974, 361–62; Frasca 1984, 317; and below in this section.

48. At the 1977 Tindivanam festival, the goddess's palanquin was almost dropped when, of the eight men carrying it, those at the forward right corner lost control. This was said to be because they were drinking. Cf. chapter 2, n. 27. Stokes 1873, 190–91, reports a death at a village ceremony; similarly Reports . . . 1854, 28, 30–32; Lewis 1931, 516, a bad injury; Thurston 1906, 485, a firewalking death at Muharram attributed to "the influence of liquor."

In approaching the firepit, the procession may be quite orderly. At Maṅkalam, following an exuberant rush from the temple after the standing of the sword, the firewalkers gathered for a long time at the eastern edge of the firepit and formed themselves several rows deep, with the prominent ritualists all in front. Here there were no possessions at this point.[49] Elsewhere, however, some of the firewalkers were possessed and, fervent to cross the coals before they should, had to be restrained. At this highly intense point, there are usually three rites of thermostatic regulation: an offering to the kuṭṭi piḷḷaiyār or akkiṉikampam; the testing of coals in a turmeric-dyed cloth; and a freshness test on a bouquet of flowers tied around a lemon that is tossed on the coals and retrieved. Though variants of the last two rites may be spoken of as "tests" like alaku niṟuttal (Beauchamp 1901, 57), they differ from it in being directly concerned with the heat of the fire.

At Tindivanam, amid the tumult that attends the arrival of the firewalkers at the firepit, the pūcāri does two of these rites but not the third. Once he reaches the firepit, he removes the flower karakam from his head at the firepit's caṉi mūlai, or northeast corner. There he takes the kūṭṭi piḷḷaiyār, sets it down at the same corner, offers the coconut and other pūjā items to it, and does a dīpārādhanā before it. Then he takes a specially prepared turmeric-dyed cloth (*mañcaḷ tuṇi*) from around his waist, opens it on the ground, places some coals from the fire in it, and closes the cloth around them. He rapidly circumambulates the firepit with the coals in the cloth, and puts the coals back in place on the firepit. He then repeats this with a second circumambulation. Each time, he must determine that the coals have not burned the cloth. If there are such burns, it indicates that the goddess will not protect the firewalkers; the coals are too hot, and the firewalk should be either delayed or canceled. Finally, one lemon and flower are thrown on the fire but not picked up to test their freshness. The crowd, however, has done its own form of this rite while waiting for the procession to arrive. Men and women repeatedly toss limes and flowers (especially from women's hair) onto the coals. The fire tenders rake or scoop off many of these while they are still fresh and hand them back into the crowd as prasādam.[50]

49. The firewalk is not a scene of possessions at Maṅkalam, whereas the paṭukaḷam ceremony there includes more possessions than usual.

50. Cf. Shideler 1987, 163–64; Tanaka 1987, 385. These rites have other variations. At Sowcarpet, the wrapped-up coals are taken into the sanctum and tied around the mūlavār's lap before the cloth is opened; cf. Gros and Nagaswamy 1970, 121; Frasca 1984, 317. The coals may also be tested in the firewalkers own waistsashes or on

According to the pāratiyār Brameesa Mudaliyar, the manner in which these rites are performed at Tindivanam is filled with censurable shortcuts. His description not only presents a cogent and well-synthesized "ideal" village case (very close to what I observed at Maṅkalam and Mēlaccēri in 1982) but integrates the precautionary tests with our best information about the akkiṉikampam (including its source in wood from the "milky" atti tree).[51]

First the akkiṉikampam or *neruppu stampam* (in either case, "fire-post"), brought from the tank and worshiped with the goddess, should be set near the firepit and offered a pūjā consisting of curd, rice, plantains, and ghee. The heat of the fire, the *neruppu śakti* ("fire power"), is absorbed into the akkiṉikampam by the pūjā and the accompanying recitation of mantras. Let me add that it may also be sprinkled (as at Maṅkalam) or coated (as at Mēlaccēri in 1986) with cooling turmeric (Hiltebeitel 1988b, part 2) or painted yellow (as at Mēlaccēri in 1982).[52] Then the coals held in the turmeric-dyed cloth should be taken and tied in the tummy fold (*maṭi*) of the Ammaṉ's mūlavar in the sanctum of the temple.[53] If the cloth does not burn, it is proof that the akkiṉikampam holds the heat. Finally, a lemon covered with a ball of jasmine and red flowers should be placed on the fire. The man who has the honor of walking first on the coals should pick it up (plate 33). Brameesa Mudaliyar frequently did this himself in his role as pāratiyār, often picking up more than one ball of flower-covered lemons. These he would carry across the fire and then into the sanctum, after which, having placed them before the goddess, he would give them to barren women who had requested them from him beforehand. The women would then have to swallow the entire lemon, even the seeds, in order to conceive: a procedure for which the pāratiyār claimed a 100 percent success rate and the births of hundreds of children given by the goddess. The firepit seems to be an image here of a barren womb turned fertile.[54]

---

their bodies (Richards 1918, 116; Moses 1961, 85; Sonnerat 1782, 248). On the flower and lime tests, cf. Babb 1974, 23, 33; Blaive, Penaud, and Nicoli 1974, 361. Cf. Beauchamp 1901: "A few flowers and limes, thrown into the lap of the idol a few days before, should keep fresh till the last day."

51. For earlier discussion, see chapter 5, section D; chapter 6, section B.

52. Cf. chapter 6, section A, 2: ghee applied to the cutting point of the Vedic yūpa.

53. Cf. Frasca 1984, 317: carrying the coals to the lap of the icon is done by the pāratiyār.

54. Other instances of fruits eaten or swallowed to induce pregnancy associate asceticism with practices or themes of impalement (chap. 7, sec. C; chap. 8, sec. A). The lemons are sacrificially offered on the fire as they are on the nails or posts.

As to the akkiṉikampam, the pūcāri's specification that it is placed at the caṉi mūlai, or northeast corner, of the firepit is not without interest. Indeed, in the two cases—at Mēlaccēri and Tindivanam—where I observed firewalks with a single akkiṉikampam (or kuṭṭi piḷḷaiyār), it was set for its pūjā at the firepit's northeast (plate 34). Caṉi mūlai means "Saturn's corner," Saturn (Sanskrit Śani) being the most baneful of the seven planets. There may be a sense here that the appeasement of the fire through the akkiṉikampam is linked with the propitiation of Caṉi. Recall that the nine planets protect the firewalkers at Muthialpet (see chap. 4, sec. A). But our primary interest in these fire-posts is that they are miniature portable replicas of the yūpa and multiforms of Pōttu Rāja.[55] We now see that their northeast position at the firepit is equivalent to that of other "pacifying" functionaries of the northeast (see chap. 6, sec. A, 8). Though formally the akkiṉikampam can be thought of as a miniature Pōttu Rāja post and named a "Dwarf Gaṇeśa," it can also—like other posts and swords we have met—be regarded as feminine. At Cantavācal, it is said to be "Ammaṉ." What is striking, however, is that the tapas maram and the akkiṉikampam now have this position in rapport with the firepit, itself a multiform of the sacrificial fire. The firepit receives the self-offerings of the firewalking devotees. As a miniature yūpa, the "milky" akkiṉikampam is thus first placed at this appeasing position, where it contains the heat of the fire to remove the pain and danger of this devotional form of self-sacrifice. As a "Dwarf Gaṇeśa," it is also—like Gaṇeśa himself—a "remover of obstacles."

Unlike the tapas maram, the akkiṉikampam does not normally remain at this northeast point. But before we follow its progress, we should note some variations on its deployment. At Maṅkalam, there are four akkiṉikampams, one at each corner of the firepit. Each one is offered a pūjā of the type described by Brameesa Mudaliyar. Here the akkiṉikampams begin to look, in these positions, like the "guardian" cones that represent the corners of the "fort" at Aṅkāḷammaṉ's cremation ground. And indeed, one finds a development of this type at the Draupadī festival in Udappu, Sri Lanka: "Four small mounds (*matai*), representing the shrines of Kali (north), Virapattiran (east), Vairavar (south) and Aiyanar (west), are placed around the pit. These deities are all *akkiṉikuṇṭakkāvals* (guards of the fire pit). They are impersonated by four *karikampus* (sticks of joy), and are installed on the mounds by four villagers," who are possessed by the four deities while implanting

55. See chapter 6, section B.

them (Tanaka 1987, 375–76). Vīrapattiraṉ probably again "replaces" Pōttu Rāja at the east.[56] Later, when the fire is lit, they are moved from the cardinal points to the corners (ibid., 411, n. 21; cf. 379). At C. Kīraṉūr, a stick is set at each corner, one of margosa in the northeast. Alternatively, at Sowcarpet, where there is no akkiṉikampam, there is a molded earthen curb around the firepit with turret-like cones built up at both the corners and the intermediate points, each of which receives a sprinkling of turmeric and an offering of flowers before the firewalk. And at Muthialpet, nine dishes of navadhānya are placed around the firepit at its points of "fortification" (see chap. 4, sec. A). These guards, turrets, and fortification points all seem to extend the heat-"containing" function of the akkiṉikampam and to define the firepit, like the paṭukaḷam, as another Kurukṣetra "fort."[57]

We now come to the firewalk itself. At Tindivanam, after the pūcāri makes his two circumambulations with the turmeric-coated sack of coals, each time starting from and returning to the kuṭṭi piḷḷaiyār at the northeast corner, he then takes up the pūṅkarakam, which had been deposited there before the first circuit, raises it onto his head, and circles the pit once more. He completes this round not at the northeast corner where he started it, but by passing that point and coming to the theoretical head of the line of firewalkers at the midpoint of the east end of the firepit. Meanwhile, the assistant who has carried the kuṭṭi piḷḷaiyār puts it back on its tray and brings it to join those behind the pūcāri near the head of the line. From there, immediately after the last lime and flowers are tossed on the coals (and left there), the pūcāri, pūṅkarakam on head, goes straight across the firepit as the first to cross it (plate 35). Or, to put the

56. Actually, Pōttu Rāja is not absent at Udappu. He and Vīrapattiraṉ are the north and south gatekeepers, respectively, at the entrance to the sanctum. Vīrapattiraṉ, however, is at the flagpole-balipīṭham complex at the temple's eastern entrance (Tanaka 1987, 128–30), corresponding to his apparent position at the firepit. A fragment of Caṅkuvati's marriage is also known as Udappu: a goat is symbolically sacrificed "as part of the dowry of Arjuna's younger sister's marriage" (Tanaka 1987, 381). But it is not indicated which guardian is her husband.

57. No other authors have mentioned the portable akkiṉikampam in Draupadī cult ritual, only likely alternatives or substitutes: Richards 1918, 116 ("a small 'milk-post' planted near the fire-pit"); Nevill 1887a, 59–60 (branches of the *pū-aracu* tree at ends and side); Shideler 1987, 164 (Draupadī's tēr and processional icon "rushed in near the northeast corner"). Cf. Biardeau 1989b, 153: a young banana plant as an *akkiṉikkāl* or *akkiṉikampam* set in the ground at the northeast corner of a firepit for Māriyammaṉ by a possessed man impersonating Kāttavarāyaṉ; similarly, Thurston and Rangachari [1904] 1965, 3:317. Pattini shares her fire-cooling power with her Pōttu Rāja–like, fire-born brother(s) known as Devol Deviyo or Gini ("Fire") Kurumbara (Obeyesekere 1984, 144–45, 150–54, 221).

emphasis where it belongs, he is the means by which Draupadī's flower karakam leads the firewalkers. He claims not to be possessed at this point, but the goddess gives him the śakti to bear the heavy pot and cross the coals unharmed.[58]

The new order behind the flower karakam should be: vīrakuntam, carried by the kaṇāccāri; palanquin for the two cāmis, Draupadī and Arjuna; kuṭṭi piḷḷaiyār; vīracāṭṭi; kōyil mēḷam; and the mass of firewalkers. At Tindivanam in 1977, however, an advance group of firewalkers proved unrestrainable and broke free over the coals in a wild rush before the crossing of the karakam. In any case, the kuṭṭi piḷḷaiyār or akkiṉikampam, our portable post, thus crosses the coals—as Brameesa Mudaliyar also says it should—from the midpoint of the east end of the firepit: the position of the yūpa and also that of Pōttu Rāja outside the Draupadī temple. I will return to these matters shortly.

After he crosses the firepit and the "milk river" (the term of choice here), the pūcāri carries the pūṅkarakam back to the temple. There he deposits it back beside the alaku karakam in the sanctum. The kuṭṭi piḷḷaiyār is also returned to its place against the rear wall of the sanctum. Meanwhile, the mass of firewalkers must not only make the same crossing of the firepit and milk river but must pass the whip bearer, who lashes many around their raised wrists with the turmeric-coated vīracāṭṭi. Some cross at a walk. Many run. Men often shout "Kōvintā," raising their right fists. For those who have crossed the fire possessed (in *āvēcam*) or who might faint, the whipping is supposed to help relieve their condition,[59] much as it does for the Young Pañcapāṇḍavas on the paṭukaḷam. The firewalkers then proceed to the temple, where they remove their kāppu wristlets and their handfuls of margosa leaves and garlands. Most leave

58. Frasca 1990, 23d plate, showing a wide-angle view of the same karakam-bearing pūcāri, and mēḷam and icon bearers in train, crossing the coals at Tindivanam in 1981, four years after my plate 35. According to Frasca 1984, 319, "all are in agreement that the individual carrying the karakam is possessed." Similarly Tanaka 1987, 152–53; he has had a vision of Draupadī before his first firewalk. On the other hand, at Bangalore Karagam festivals, possession is avoided; the karagam carrier practices in secret so he will not drop it, since tradition says he would be killed if he did so. In former times, it is said, he was killed after he completed his task and replaced by a new youth (kumāra) who would undergo an oath and dīkṣā to carry it the next year (Krishnamurthy Hanur, personal communication, 1990). We have seen that possession can be denied by an individual while attributed to him by others; see chapter 11, section A. Tindivanam firewalkers interviewed in 1981 gave estimates of those who get possessed ranging from "50 to 75 percent" to "very few."

59. Cf. Brown 1976, 33; Nevill 1887a, 59; Babb 1974, 23, 39: whipping apparently only before the firewalk, including a function of bringing on "quietude."

them at the Pōrmaṉṉaṉ maṇḍapa, creating a large pile, although some deposit them at the pantal outside the temple or beside the nearby tank. Later that evening the processional icons of Draupadī and Arjuna will be taken on the palanquin through the streets. The flower karakam remains beside the alaku karakam for the night and is removed the next morning by the kaṇāccāri, who gets to keep the pot as well as the paddy on which it has been placed, and the coconut set in its top. As we have seen, the pūcāri then takes down the alaku from the alaku karakam later that day.

Though such large single-crossing firewalks can be described as mass crossings, they have a different atmosphere from the smaller ones in the villages. At Mēlaccēri, Maṅkalam, and Vēḷḷimēṭupēṭṭai, the firewalkers line up two or three deep at the edge of the firepit and prepare to cross in unison. When the first firewalker steps into the coals to pick up the dropped ball of lime and flowers, others immediately join in, filling the firepit with moving people. The karakam does not so much lead the procession as form a nucleus, with other implements and processional images of the deities in train, through the center of the firepit. At Maṅkalam and Veḷḷimēṭupēṭṭai, where there are three such crossings (see n. 47)—over, back, and over again—movement must be carefully choreographed lest people bump into each other. Possessions were not in evidence. Indeed, the logistics would be unimaginable and terribly dangerous if the eight hundred firewalkers, many possessed, went back and forth across the deep firepit at Tindivanam.[60] The Tindivanam firewalk goes on as long as fifteen minutes. The village ones are over in seconds. At the village rites, the collectivity is formed by the individual firewalkers' going across, or back and forth, together. Individuals may make vows for their children, but they seldom carry them across the coals. At Tindivanam, Sowcarpet, and Pondicherry, there is a much higher frequency of children being carried or led across the coals, and of whole family units (father, mother, child) crossing together. There is also a higher frequency of young men among the firewalkers at the larger festivals—a pattern also noticed by Babb, who interprets their attraction to the ordeal as one of young men "blocked" economically who seek an alternative mode of empowerment (1974, 42–43; cf. Obeyesekere 1978, 465–66, 472–74; Danforth 1989, 103).

One consistent point, however: the firewalkers almost always

60. Similarly at Sowcarpet. Cf. also Babb 1974, 23–24; Nevill 1887a, 59; Brown 1976, 29–33.

line up on the east of the firepit to make their crossing (or first and last crossings where there are three) westward. This means that they face the goddess in her temple and cross the firepit moving toward her.[61] In many cases, as at Mēlaccēri (see Hiltebeitel 1988b, part 2), Sowcarpet, and Veḷḷalūr, the firepit is directly in front of the temple. In others, as at Tindivanam (see map 5), the firepit is at an angle to, or beside the temple. But the east-to-west movement of the firewalkers, ultimately toward the temple, still pertains.

Sometimes the processional image of the goddess is also placed, along with other icons, facing eastward across the firepit toward the approaching firewalkers. At Mēlaccēri, for instance, the icons of Draupadī, Arjuna, Subhadrā, and Pōttu Rāja are set or held aloft beyond the firepit and milk pit on the same east-west axis that extends toward the temple. One will recognize two alternatives here. In one, Draupadī's processional icon follows her flower karakam over the coals. In the other, only the flower karakam crosses the coals, while the icon is placed at an intermediary point between the firepit and the temple. At Mēlaccēri, her icon's intermediary position marks a sort of way station, where the whipping is done and pinches of turmeric are handed out, especially to apply to burns (see Hiltebeitel 1988b, part 2). There are other examples of both options, but it is more common to find the icons in their intermediary receiving position at the far end of the firepit and milk pit. There is also, in either case, considerable variety in the icons present.

In cases where the icons cross the coals, Draupadī is always present. She crosses alone at Maṅkalam and Kūttampākkam (Biardeau 1989b, 120), and also in Sonnerat's lithograph from 1782 (plate 36). Led by Pōttu Rāja, she is with Arjuna on their palanquin at Tindivanam; with Pōttu Rāja, the Pāṇḍavas, and Kṛṣṇa on Garuḍa at Vēḷḷimēṭupēṭṭai; and with Pōttu Rāja (who "guards" her karakam), a "*chakram*" on a pole and Dharmarāja at the Kalassipalaiyam temple in Bangalore (Richards 1910, 32). At Veḷḷimētupēṭṭai, Pōttu Rāja's icon, facing backward, leads Draupadī's icon toward the firepit and then follows her icon onto it, along with those of the Pāṇḍavas, each on a bearer's head. This variety may reflect the variety of

61. Cf. Biardeau 1989b, 146, 293: the same at firewalks for Māriyammaṉ and Paccaivāḻiyammaṉ. For Draupadī, cf. Stokes 1873, 190; Nevill 1887a, 58–59; Firewalking . . . 1900, 320; Richards 1910, 32; Frasca 1984, 316; Hiltebeitel 1988b, part 2. For exceptions, see Richards 1910, 32, and Beauchamp 1901, 57 (both north to south). Either the latter is wrong, however, or the Ālantūr "platform" (a raised, walled pit with approach and descent ramps) has since been reoriented east to west. A raised pit is also found at Kalahasti.

Draupadī cult firewalking myths. Where Draupadī's is the only icon, it could be to lead the Kaurava widows to become suttees (Hiltebeitel 1988a, 440–42). Where she shares her palanquin with Arjuna, it seems to thematize their victory, and Draupadī's cycle-ending reunion with her most Śiva-like husband (ibid., 448).[62] Where she leads the Pāṇḍavas, it could be to purify them of the sins accrued on the battlefield (ibid., 442–46; Tanaka 1987, 345, 385). The presence of the head-holding Pōttu Rāja may evoke the Pāṇḍavas' particular sin of Brahmanicide, from the killing of Droṇa (Hiltebeitel 1988a, 444–48). Pōttu Rāja also leads Draupadī's army at Kurukṣetra. Kṛṣṇa's presence on Garuḍa will remind us that a Garuḍadarśana is hoped for on the way to the Tindivanam firepit. People also shout "Kōvintā" as they cross the coals (cf. Richards 1910, 32; Brown 1976, 28–29, 32). According to one Tindivanam firewalker, the fire belongs to Draupadī, but calling upon Kṛṣṇa gives them courage to cross it. The cry is also said to bring Kṛṣṇa's grace even to Draupadī and to induce a "peaceful" state of *cāntam* (Hiltebeitel 1988a, 277).

In cases where the firewalkers cross toward the icons, Draupadī's is again always there. Sometimes, if one can trust all the reports, she is alone (Stokes 1873, 190; Blaive, Penaud and Nicoli 1974, 359–61; Brown 1976, 34). At Pondicherry she is joined by Arjuna; at Alantūr by Arjuna and Kṛṣṇa;[63] at Mēlaccēri by the pañcalōkam images of Arjuna, Subhadrā, Pōttu Rāja, and Kṛṣṇa; and at Singapore by Arjuna, Kṛṣṇa, Vīrabhadra, and Aravāṉ's head, the latter still looking at Kurukṣetra, now in its firepit form, one must assume. Indeed, at Pattukkottai, a head of Aravāṉ is left in an observant's position beneath the tapas tree until the firewalk is over.

G. Interpretations

Of all Draupadī festival rituals, the firewalk clearly has the greatest homogeneity from place to place. In contrast to paṭukaḷam rites, it remains basically the same ceremony, and not only as one moves out from the core area into surrounding districts, but also in the Draupadī cult diaspora as well. As I have tried to show, the varieties one finds in far-flung places are mostly traceable to variations within the core area itself. Indeed, the similarities between Drau-

62. At Udappu, Sri Lanka, Draupadī and Arjuna cross the fire impersonated by ritualists rather than icons (Tanaka 1987, 351, 383–84).
63. Not only in 1901 (Beauchamp 1901, 57), but also in 1981.

padī's firewalk and those for other deities—mainly but not solely goddesses (see n. 3)—allow us to speak of the firewalk as a cross-cult ritual unit.[64] This no doubt has something to do with its tenacity at diaspora Draupadī festivals: émigré Indians of different backgrounds can be drawn to the firewalk because it has a cross-cult intelligibility.[65] Thus, for example, the Fiji (Brown 1984, 231), Singapore (Babb 1974, 1), and Udappu, Sri Lanka (Tanaka 1987, 83) firewalks for Draupadī are connected with temples or priests of Māriyamman̲, a goddess who, as we have seen, has Tamil firewalking rituals of her own.[66]

This integrity of the firewalk by itself raises the possibility of viewing it as detachable from the rest of the Draupadī festival. The myths of Draupadī's firewalk are themselves independent of the *Mahābhārata*. Whereas paṭukaḷam rituals are rooted in the classical text, the stories of Draupadī's firewalk are rooted in the ritual, which has no textual basis (cf. Babb 1974, 29). They are a popular appendix. Similarly, the ritual itself can be looked at as an addendum to the more textually based ceremonies of the paṭukaḷam. Indeed, the Fiji festival provides the instructive case of a firewalk without any paṭukaḷam ceremonies or discernible equivalents. Is this just a result of diaspora dilution—the submergence of a Draupadī festival into a Māriyamman̲ festival?[67] Or is it also another form of paṭukaḷam substitution: a part for the whole? As we have seen, there is a certain interchangeability between the paṭukaḷam and the firepit. Both can be Kurukṣetra. In one form or another, and often in several forms, Draupadī crosses both ritual terrains, and those who follow her can be her festival army, sharing her triumph.[68] Apparently the appendix can replace or reject the body.

64. Different types of firewalking rituals include a single possessed priest crossing the coals alone, on behalf of others (Obeyesekere 1984, 41) or a fakir standing aside to retain the heat himself while enabling others to cross (Leroy 1931, 40–46), as Draupadī's possessed medium does at Udappu (Tanaka 1987, 384).

65. The relation between goddess festivals with firewalking, ten-day Muharram festivals with firewalking in India (see nn. 3, 48), and ten-day Dasarā festivals, normally without firewalking, deserves consideration. Cf. chapter 7, section C on convergences between Muharram and gājan festivals in West Bengal.

66. As also at Tindivanam and Mēlaccēri; see chapter 3, n. 8.

67. Describing observation of the 1970 and 1972 festivals, three years before Brown's fieldwork at the same site, Lal and Seruvakula (1974, 41–58) make no mention of Draupadī and treat the festival as if it were entirely Māriyamman̲'s.

68. Certain myths of the origins of the Anastenaria identify the firewalkers with Saint Constantine's army, which entered fire behind him, in one case to escape a walled city circled by fire (Danforth 1989, 86–87, 127).

Interpretation of the Draupadī cult firewalk has more or less presumed such a detachable character for it and has left us little to distinguish it from the firewalks of other cults.[69] For Babb, it is a form of reality testing. Through the construction of an alternate reality or "atmosphere of verisimilitude," "walking on fire constitutes an incontestable demonstration of the fundamental reality" and "validity of a particular view of the world"; one that enables a divine empowerment of the bhakta participants, who in recent years have been predominantly young men "blocked" economically and educationally from gaining full access to "the material possibilities of life in a metropolitan center like Singapore" (1974, 37–43). For Brown, it is scored with sexual symbols, and driven by motivations of union with the divine mother (1984, 226–38). For Frasca, "it appears that the fire-walk is conceived as a mass possession ritual not only involving the initiated ones who are crossing the coals but also the spectators themselves. . . . In a sense, the village as a whole is possessed and pervaded by the power of the goddess" (1984, 318–19).[70] For Tanaka, the firewalk and the votive rites and possessions preceding it are pervaded by idioms of sacrifice, which he interprets in ideological and "political" dimensions bearing on power and patronage.[71] For Biardeau, Draupadī's firewalk reorients themes found more generally in other firewalks: the victory march of Māriyamman̲ (1989b, 148), a "signification 'eschatologique'" in the cult of Paccaivāḻiyamman̲ (ibid., 284). In the latter cult, the firewalkers "traverse a 'devouring fire'; the firewalking area is a cosmos in flames, Śiva unleashed, a periodic renewal of the world. The devotees who aid in this renovation—no doubt hardly conscious of it, since their vows are personal—participate in the tapas of the Earth in the midst of fire," their penance reproducing the earth's fiery ordeal and renewal (ibid.). Biardeau sees this pralayic dimension retained in Draupadī's firewalk, but reenvisioned, in epic terms, as a fire of war that burns the goddess Earth, who suf-

69. I leave aside the question of how firewalking is done, other than to observe that skepticism about "tricks," discussion of "evidence," demonstrations that it can be done just as well with a scientific or Marxist "faith" (as at Tindivanam in 1981), and advocacy of what seem to be simplistic scientific explanations are wearisome to firewalking bhaktas I have questioned. Cf. Danforth 1989, 191 (a mock firewalk), 207–13. For discussion, see Gaddis 1967, 133–55; Brewster 1977, 43–47; Leikind and McCarthy 1985. The question dominated turn-of-the-century writings: e.g., Firewalking . . . 1900, 316; Leroy 1931, 50–51 (in summation).

70. Cf. Babb 1974, 38: "It might be said that trance becomes one of the dominant themes of the cycle as the hour of firewalking approaches."

71. Tanaka 1987, 48–49, 55–56, 179–85, 323, 339–40, especially 370–80 on the firewalk itself, 414–15.

fers for the loss of her protective warriors but must be periodically cleansed of their violations of the dharma (ibid.).[72]

As I indicated in volume 1, fire is the most overdetermined symbol in the Draupadī cult (1988a, 446). The firewalk is what gives it its force. There is thus no reason to wholly reject any of these interpretations, though Brown's and Frasca's must be qualified (see nn. 37, 41, 58) and Babb's confined to a specific type of festival. Indeed, Danforth's emphasis on the therapeutic dimension of the firewalk is just as pertinent to the Draupadī cult as it is to the Greek cult of Saints Constantine and Helen (1989, 84–131).

We must not, however, content ourselves with the idea that the firewalk is only an appendix. First, there is more to say about its place within the cult's sacrificial ensemble. And in closing, we must address its place amid the Draupadī festival's processual movements.

According to V. S. Purushottama Chettiyar, the Tindivanam chief trustee with an eye for the odd detail, there have been firewalks at Tindivanam in which not only humans crossed the coals, but as many as ten or fifteen cows and she-buffalo as well, driven across by their owners, who wished to cure them of some illness or to improve their milk. Warned by him to be on the watch in both 1977 and 1981, and skeptical as usual, I was finally rewarded when one lone cow was led across by its owner in 1981. Rites in which cattle are driven over fires are widely known, not only in South India, where they may be very ancient,[73] but in other parts of the world, including ancient Rome and eighteenth-century Ireland (Walhouse 1878, 129; Allchin 1963, 129–37). One might be hesitant to go beyond Purushottama Chettiyar's explanation to a sacrificial

72. Cf. the combination of images in the mythology of Pattini's firewalk in Sri Lanka: "seven mountains of fire," approached "as if ready for battle" (Obeyesekere 1984, 149–50). The seven mountains of fire are a pralayic image of the dissolution of the cakravāla by fire, akin to the pralaya-surviving Cakkaravāḷa-kōṭṭam-cremation ground and Kālī temples discussed in chapter 13, section B. Cf. the pralayic themes in the crematorium dances of the Dharma gājans and the Aṅkāḷammaṉ cult (chap. 7, n. 30). Fire ordeals may also have a similar cosmological structure; see *Chāndogya Upaniṣad* 6; Hiltebeitel 1983a. In dharmaśāstra literature, the accused must demonstrate innocence by carrying a red-hot iron ball through seven circles arranged serially (Lariviere 1981, 33–38; Khan 1787, 403–4). Saṃsāra, Nāropa sings, is "an unbearable fire-bowl" (Guenther 1963, 25).

73. See Allchin 1963, 1–99, on neolithic cow dung/ash mounds in the Deccan; 135 fire crossing by cattle at Māṭṭu Poṅkal (Bulls' Poṅkal) led by Golla herdsmen and "dedicated to the god Kātama-rāya" (that is, Kāṭamarāju, on whom see Narayana Rao 1989). Cf. Thurston 1906, 477; Thurston and Rangachari [1904] 1965, 1:101: a young bull precedes the firewalkers "partly across the fire-pit," after which milk from young cows is sprinkled over the coals.

one. After all, at Tindivanam, the animals driven across the coals are cows and female buffaloes, for whom the healing and milk-enhancing properties of the rite might well be taken as sufficient. Indeed, such an explanation might also suffice for the neolithic rites imagined by Allchin. But there is no escaping the sacrificial implications of South Indian firepits. As in the Draupadī cult, the firepit (akkiṉikuṇṭam) is a *kuṇṭam* (Sanskrit *kuṇḍa*): that is, a dug-out sacrificial "altar," as distinct from a raised fire altar, or vedi (Khan 1787, 398–400). Moreover, as Purushottama Chettiyar has insisted, the firewalk is a woman's rite. If cows and she-buffaloes cross the fire, their bulls may not be far behind. As we saw in chapter 8 (sec. B), bulls and (theoretically) buffaloes are driven earlier on the same day past Duryodhana on the paṭukaḷam, symbolizing the scattering of what is left of the defeated Kaurava army. Though no informant made a connection with these bulls and buffaloes explicit, a remnant of the Kaurava army does cross the firepit wherever the kaṇāccāri and the other weapon-bearing officiants are said to represent the Kaurava survivors. Let us also recall that the same Kaurava widows whom Draupadī leads across the coals to ensure that they become suttees are imagined in one of the dramas by Gāndhārī, their mother-in-law, as a herd of she-buffaloes.[74]

In fact, the bulls are not far behind, as can be seen at a "village goddess" festival for "Mariyama" held near Bangalore in the 1870s. What is striking about this ceremony is that it combines the firewalk not only with a sacrificial post and real male animal victims, but with a Potail—the local name for a Potrāj, the Untouchable ritualist who in parts of Andhra, Karnataka, and Maharashtra is none other than Pōta Rāju in human form. I confine attention to the rites involving a small firepit, about four feet long, two feet wide, and nine inches deep. First the pūjārī goes back and forth across the pit three times with a flowered basket on his head. Then the Potail brings a black ram to the edge of the firepit where it can face the goddess, over the coals, in her temple. When the ram grows still and looks straight ahead, it is decapitated. Then the women from the village, at least one from each household (widows excluded), cross the fire, egged on by the men. After this, those of ranking caste who have participated go home, and the Potail invites the Untouchable Holeyas into the village, from which at other times they are excluded. They bring their women, and also four buffaloes: three that they have dedicated, and one that is dedicated by the village as a whole. The buffaloes are led around the temple and

74. See chapter 7, section B; chapter 8, section B; and Hiltebeitel 1988a, 232, 434.

made to jump over the firepit. Then they are taken to a "stone pillar about twenty yards in front of the temple." A beam of wood is tied to this pillar. The Potail consecrates the four animals, and they are tied to the beam and beheaded. Their heads are then placed on flowers in front of the firepit. The one dedicated by the village is the first slain and is the only one to have its right foreleg placed in its mouth. Probably it faces the goddess beyond it like the black ram that was sacrificed before it (summarizing Mackenzie 1874, 6–9). Unlike the ram, whose sacrifice opens the firepit for everyone (women and buffaloes) except the pūjāri but does not get to cross it himself, the buffaloes cross the pit before their sacrifice. This is another variation on the preliminary ram or goat sacrifice that we have seen echoed in Aravāṉ's kaḷappali. Indeed, one cannot miss the similar structures of these firewalking rites. The sacrificial "victims"—firewalkers and animals alike—face the goddess in her temple. In one case their self-offerings are mediated by the Potail and the stone pillar, in the other by Pōttu Rāja and his multiform, the akkiṉikampam. The fire itself is not the recipient of the offering, but the means of a crossing that makes the offering acceptable to the goddess. It is, like Agni, the "bearer of oblations."

With these analogies in mind, let us retrace the processual movement of the Tindivanam Draupadī festival, our representative core area example, from the paṭukaḷam through the firewalk. For if we are to catch the spirit of this thing, it is best, finally, to move with one festival and to recognize that, short of fully participating, our imaginations must be our guides. Led by Pōttu Rāja, Draupadī enters the paṭukaḷam from the north. Having mounted Duryodhana's effigy, retied her hair, and deactivated her "form of Kālī" in the battlefield or fort equivalent of a Kālī temple, she is then newly represented in the form of two karakams. They will now be the active intermediaries between her relinquished "form of Kālī" and her mūlavar, which will ultimately be her true form once the festival is over. One karakam, decorated at and carried from a body of water, seems to represent her in an elemental, regenerated form and is usually taken to the temple sanctum to support a sword on its bowl during the firewalk. The other, decorated in the temple, which seems to represent her in a conquering, victorious aspect, is taken from the sanctum to the firepit. There this second flower or fire karakam is joined by the heat-containing akkiṉikampam, at the east end of the firepit, from which point, approaching the sanctum either directly or indirectly, they are among the paraphernalia that lead the firewalkers over the coals and milk river, and back to the temple. There the devotees may leave their clutches of margosa and turmeric-dyed kāppu wristlets at the Pōrmaṉṉaṉ maṇḍapa before entering the sanctum itself.

At the paṭukaḷam, Pōttu Rāja leads the way, as the marshal of Draupadī's army, to her triumph at Kurukṣetra. At the firepit, his post-multiform, the akkiṉikampam, defines the firepit as a sacrificial terrain, one where the firewalkers are like cattle, *paśu:* that is, sacrificial victims.[75] They may still be Draupadī's festival army, or they may be the Kaurava widows, both of whom were represented at the paṭukaḷam and have ritually moved on from it. Their march is oblatory, but it is also salvific. Not only does each person fulfill an individual vow, there is also a collective dimension to the firewalk that reminds one of the collective salvation at the pralaya (Biardeau 1981c, 122–23; 1981d, 110–19, 152, 155–57), supporting Biardeau's interpretation of the firepit as an image of the end and renewal of the universe (see also n. 72). In a certain sense, if the paṭukaḷam is the Kurukṣetra of the war, the firepit is the Kurukṣetra of the pralaya: the Draupadī cult's ritual equivalent of Arjuna's fiery pralayic vision of the world-devouring Kṛṣṇa in the eleventh chapter of the *Bhagavad Gītā* or of Śiva dancing in his circle of flames.[76] At Draupadī festivals, the *Gītā* generally is given attention only by the pāratiyārs, and even then not regularly (see Hiltebeitel 1988a, 140). Draupadī cult narrative, ritual, drama, and songs, such as in the verses below, are more interested in the goddess's destructive cosmic forms than Kṛṣṇa's or Śiva's:

> "Not touchable, my mother, you are indeed fire, mother [*nēruppēyammā*][77]
> Who cannot be controlled by anyone else, my mother Draupadī.
> You are the great fire, my mother, not touchable.
> You are the lady who burned the Triple City.
> (Hiltebeitel 1988a, 11)

Indeed, it is tempting to think that the crossing of the "milk river" is an allusion to the Ākāśa Gaṅgā, the Heavenly Ganges or Milky Way. The firewalkers would thus cross not only the fires of the pralaya but the salvific river in its cosmic form. Their victorious

75. Draupadī's firewalk is "one of numerous substitutes for human sacrifice associated with temples" (Biardeau 1981c, 152; my translation): a collective sacrifice or, in Tarabout's terms, the "sacrifice of a multitude" (see chap. 7, n. 18).

76. See Brown 1976, 37; Hiltebeitel 1982b, 84 and n. 66 (my father, George Hiltebeitel, first suggested to me the analogy with Śiva). Cf. Blaive, Penaud, and Nicoli 1974, 360–61 (firewalkers "dance"); Östör 1980, 147; Shulman 1980a, 213–23.

77. Retranslated from Hiltebeitel 1988a, 11, following Zvelebil 1989, 359.

march behind the flower or fire karakam is then one that leads them back to Draupadī's temple.[78] At Pōttu Rāja's maṇḍapa, where they leave behind their margosa and kāppu—the amulets of personal protection and the restraining symbols of their vows—they reach the point beyond which one may stand before Draupadī with a devotion like his: that of the saved victim and demon devotee. Her sanctum-"home" is open to them, with the alaku karakam inside it, which now appears to represent the elemental potentiality of the goddess and the source of physical, spiritual, and cosmic renewal toward which the firewalkers' movements aspire.

78. Though read too late for it to be discussed in this chapter, Gombrich and Obeyesekere's treatment of the "Sinhala Buddhicization" (1988, 414) of the Kataragama firewalk deserves appreciation. Sinhala Buddhists have recently provided a new charter myth for this originally Hindu rite, deriving it from the ancient king Duṭugämuṇu's conquest of the Tamil king Alāra, with Kataragama-Skanda inspiring him "for the glory of Buddhism" (ibid., 425–31). Destroying Alāra's fort and city (ibid., 427, 430; cf. 180: an alternate fort theme), Duṭugämuṇu in one account returns as the first firewalker (ibid., 434). A Muslim shrine for self-infliction of wounds stands nearby (ibid., 164). These interreligious dimensions of the cult's dramatic growth suggest looking further into the relation between Hindu and Muslim firewalking in India (see above nn. 3, 65). The new breed of middle-class "Protestant Buddhist" firewalk leaders prefer California firewalking to Indian (Gombrich and Obeyesekere 1988, 413) and discourage bhakti, possession, and purity (all with Hindu overtones) in favor of Buddhist morality and meditation as the means to cross the coals (ibid., 188–89, 414–15, 432). Firewalking healers "acquire the mental power (*cittabalaya*) to walk on fire by attaining the first *jhāna*" or meditation realm (ibid., 327), suggesting a pralayic image: when the cakravāla world system is destroyed by fire (as is most regular), so are the first and second meditation realms (Kloetzli 1983, 75). An alternative firewalking myth involves the testing of Kataragama's mistress Vallī's purity (Gombrich and Obeyesekere 1988, 423). Firewalking priests now claim a double descent from the army of Duṭugämuṇu and tribal Vädda hunters (ibid., 431–34).

15 Closures

In its aftermath, it is all the more evident that the firewalk is the climax of a Draupadī festival. Subsequent rituals draw no large public. They mainly either wind things down or tie up loose ends. They also tend to bring the local community into focus as one that can now return to normality by an evocation and implementation of images of peace or pacification, order, cooperation, celebration, and prosperity. As we saw in chapter 2, there are a number of such rites. They may include funerary ceremonies, offerings to guardian deities, the coronation of Dharma, a leave-taking with the festive throwing of turmeric water, flag lowering, dispersal of seedlings, and the removal of kāppu by the main officiants. Flag lowering and removal of kāppu are a must, as is the coronation of Dharma. Incidence of the other rites varies. For most of these rites, discussion has already been sufficient.[1] The exceptions are the funerary rites and the coronation of Dharma.

A. Funerary Rites, Karumāti

Before Dharma can rule, karumāti (a general term for purifying funeral rites) should be performed, as it is at most Draupadī festivals. According to Adikeshava Bharatiyar, Dharma remains reluctant to rule even after Draupadī has conducted the Kaurava widows across

1. On the offerings to guardian deities (kāval pūjā), see chapter 5, section D and n. 37; and further, Hiltebeitel 1988a, 118; 1989a, 363–64; Eichinger Ferro-Luzzi 1977, 548; Shideler 1987, 173. The food prepared may also be distributed to the poor, as at Maṇakuṭaiyaṉ (cf. Richards 1910, 30). On dispersal of seedlings, see chapter 4. On flag lowering and the removal of kāppu (basically symmetrical with flag raising and the donning of kāppu), see chapter 5, sections A and B. Leave-taking and turmeric water sprinkling are common to many goddess festivals and are not unusual at Draupadī's. But a number of Draupadī temples, like Tindivanam's, have discontinued this supposedly joyful and cooling rite because it got too rowdy; cf. Meyer

the firepit to heaven,[2] because the bodies of some of "the V.I.P.s" who died at Kurukṣetra have been preserved with herbal juices. Dharma's coronation is impossible while the corpses remain in place. So Bhīṣma, still lying on his bed of arrows, advises Dharma to cremate the dead and complete the postmortem purifying rites. Asked who the V.I.P.s were, the pāratiyār mentioned only "Karṇa, Abhimanyu, and others." He had certainly not run out of epic names. The list's brevity may reflect the fact that the ceremony is concerned not so much with epic heroes as with ritual artifacts.

At Tindivanam, the only place I have observed it, karumāti is performed only one day after the paṭukaḷam and tīmiti ceremonies it commemorates, at about 10:00 A.M. Normally, as a family rite, karumāti would conclude a much longer period of impurity and mourning for the deceased. There is variation from village to village and caste to caste, but among Vaṉṉiyars and others involved in the Draupadī cult, the norm (a conventional one) is said to be sixteen days. But because Dharma's rule is not to be postponed and, one sometimes hears, because the ritual remains of the "deceased" are themselves polluting to the village, it is rare to find karumāti so long after tīmiti. Of sites visited, only at Marutāṭu is it performed on the sixteenth day, still just before the coronation of Dharma. According to Brameesa Mudaliyar, it is usually performed on the tenth day after tīmiti. At Tindivanam and Veḷḷimēṭupēṭṭai, however, one day was thought sufficient, for the reasons just mentioned.

In these ceremonies, it is considered essential that the kaṇāccāri and camayam participate along with the pūcāri. At Tindivanam, where the camayam office has been discontinued, an assistant to the pūcāri took his part, carrying the sword used at Aravāṉ's kaḷappali and in cutting the pumpkin at Duryodhana's thighs the previous day. The kaṇāccāri, however, did not carry the vīrakuntam, as he had done the day before. In addition, the pūcāri was assisted by his relative and colleague, the pūcāri of the Tindivanam Māriyammaṉ temple.

Two reasons were given for the required participation of the kaṇāccāri and camayam. According to Brameesa Mudaliyar, since

---

1986, 247. Ceremonies reported at only one temple (Pondicherry) include a "swing festival" before Dharma's coronation, in which Arjuna's icon reclines with his head on the Draupadī icon's left thigh! (Shideler 1987, 174); and a *Śāntiparvan* ceremony for Bhīṣma's mokṣa begun right after Dharma's coronation and continued for thirty days at Perunakar (Hiltebeitel 1988a, 140–41, n. 9).

2. See Hiltebeitel 1988a, 440–41: Adikeshava Bharatiyar told the suttee and karumāti myths as one narrative sequence.

they are two of the "four" Kaurava survivors of the war—for him, let us recall, the kaṇāccāri is Cañcakattakaṉ, the camayam is Kṛpa—they must represent the Kauravas at Duryodhana's karumāti. By his reckoning, the kuntam (Aśvatthāman) and kumāravarkam (Kṛtavarman) should also be there, but were, as we have seen, missing at Tindivanam (as indeed at most other festivals). But according to Purushottama Chettiyar, the Tindivanam temple's chief trustee, it was when Aśvatthāman, Kṛpa, and Kṛtavarman had killed the Young Pañcapāṇḍavas that Duryodhana's heart softened, and he insisted they should perform the karumāti not for him, but for them, his nephews. Each of these variants is a continuation of one of the alternative identifications of the "sleeping warriors" around Duryodhana, with the surprising agreement that in either case, certain of the temple officiants represent the Kaurava survivors, whether three or four of them, who must be present for the karumāti rites.[3] The Pāṇḍavas, meanwhile, will be present in their icons. There is, however, nothing in the actual ceremonies at Tindivanam directed toward a commemoration of the deaths of the Young Pañcapāṇḍavas, or anything that ostensibly connects the kaṇāccāri or the camayam's replacement with the Kaurava survivors.

At Tindivanam, there are six "deceased" for whom the same basic karumāti is performed: Aravāṉ, Duryodhana, the tapas pole (tapas maram), the firepit, Arjuna's bow tree (vil maram), and the Terukkūttu musicians' platform. The aforementioned priestly contingent, including the only men still wearing kāppu and turmeric-dyed vēṣṭis, leads a small procession from the temple to these "remains," then back to the temple. In the procession, the wooden icons of the five Pāṇḍavas and Pōttu Rāja are each carried separately, while a bullock cart that is pushed and pulled manually holds the wooden icons of Draupadī and Kṛṣṇa. Draupadī's hair is bound up into a richly flowered bun, or koṇṭai. Kṛṣṇa, quite appropriately for this funerary round, is riding Garuḍa.

The sequence begins with the karumāti for the two heroes, who seem to stand as well for such other heroes as one may imagine. But it is clear that what ties these rites together is not that the deceased are slain warriors, but the physical remains of rituals. At each of the six stopping points, the same basic sequence is performed. I will describe it in full only for Aravāṉ, whose rites open the closing of the paṭukaḷam as they opened its opening.

First, Aravāṉ's large pottery head is pushed backward from his body and broken on the ground. Its large pieces are further hacked

3. See chapter 2, section B; chapter 11, section A.

to bits and pulverized. Then his body, built around a bamboo pole with straw covered by mud, is pried apart and dismantled with the sword (katti), and the straw is used to light a small fire.[4] This is allowed to burn for a few seconds and is then extinguished with water. On top of these ashes and remains, the pūcāri then sprinkles milk from a pot. This is a featured subrite and can provide an alternative name for the entire ceremony: "milk releasing" (*pāl viṭutal*) or "milk sprinkling" (*pāl teḷittal*). Traditionally this offering of milk, and what follows, is a means of feeding the individual's soul (*ātmā*) as he or she becomes an ancestor.[5] Accordingly, the rite is described as an *ātmā cānti*, a "pacification of the soul."[6] After the milk sprinkling, dīpārādhanā is offered to the remains. Then a coconut is broken, and a piece of it is left along with a handful of cooked rice, a banana, betel leaf, and a piece of betel nut, all on a plate of stitched dried banyan leaves (a poor man's setting, as distinct from a banana leaf). Much of this same ceremony is then performed, though without the dramatic destruction of the effigy, for the remains of each of the other ritual objects, beginning with the long mud pile that was just the day before the body of Duryodhana. At all but the last two points, straw from Aravāṉ's body supplies the fuel for the fire. According to Brameesa Mudaliyar, if Duryodhana's effigy remains untrampled, as it does at many festivals, the milk should be poured into his mouth. At Tindivanam, some of the milk for Duryodhana is sprinkled over the entire remains of his effigy, the rest over the ashes of his straw fire (see plate 37). After this, the same straw fires, food offerings, and dīpārādhanā are conducted at the base of the tapas pole and the middle of the firepit, in the latter case beside a small mound of gathered ashes. Here also, some coins that were buried beneath the firepit site before its lighting are now dug up and made off with by children. The bow tree and musicians' platform receive no fires, only the food offerings and dīpārādhanā. All the while, the pampai and mattaḷam drums are

4. A similar rite, solely for Aravāṉ, involving breaking his head and dismantling his straw body, but apparently no fire, is performed at Pondicherry and is concerned with Aravāṉ's mokṣa (Shideler 1987, 170–71).

5. Recall Aravāṉ's connections with ancestral rites, and the last-minute marriage to Mohinī that makes him fit for them as a nonbachelor (chap. 9, beginning and sec. A).

6. According to Brameesa Mudaliyar, who added that a family sixteen-day karumāti would involve addressing mantras to three stones, representing the deceased, his father, and his grandfather: a variation on a pan-Indian pattern involving three rice balls (*piṇḍis*; see Knipe 1977, 115); cf. Thurston 1906, 143–220, with numerous examples of corresponding rites in different communities; Beck 1975, 175, 189 (karumāti ceremonies in the *Elder Brothers Story*).

played. Finally, the icons are returned to the temple and placed under the pantal that extends from its entrance.

This is an entirely peaceful ceremony, with real touches of sadness. One suspects that the sword is present only to aid in the dismantling of Aravāṉ, while the vīrakuntam and whip are absent because the war is over. The ritualists and the icons have the whole scene to themselves. There is no public aside from the few curious children. Indeed, one senses that karumāti is taken as a private family matter. As we have seen, except for the two pūcāris, whom we can regard in this context as family priests, those who are present—people and icons—are, in mythic terms, primarily the Kaurava and Pāṇḍava survivors.[7] It is after this ceremony that V. Govindaswamy, the Tindivanam pūcāri, breaking his twenty days of sleeping at the temple, goes home to take water with his wife and children for the first time since then and to do a pūjā before two pictures he keeps, one of his father and the other "of Ammaṉ."

Since karumāti is an ancestral rite (see nn. 5 and 6), a strong family bond is maintained between the epic heroes and the villagers. Indeed, this is just the other face of the various rites that link the heroes and villagers through ritual means of overcoming infertility. Moreover, it is not just the heroes who are ancestors. As we have seen, substances dropped from the tapas pole or picked up from the effigies of Duryodhana or Aravāṉ, or from the firepit, can induce pregnancy. Now these same ritual objects are treated like ancestors as well.

Karumāti finally and fully closes off the martial phase of the festival. It is a purifying adieu to the deceased and the festival's spectacular ritual artifacts. But it is also a closing off of all the major arenas, away from the temple, at which the different phases of the *Mahābhārata*—in particular, the buildup to the war (Arjuna's tapas tree and bow tree), the war itself (the paṭukaḷam effigies of Aravāṉ and Duryodhana), and the war's aftermath (the firepit)—have been dramatically and ritually enacted. It is the ritual that best exem-

7. According to Adikeshava Bharaityar, *all* the male survivors of the war are present. His way of supporting this was to inform me that Sātyaki, who survives the war in the Sanskrit epic, was killed by Aśvatthāman, and that Kṛṣṇa does not count as a survivor. Kṛṣṇa, in any case, is present for the karumāti at Tindivanam. The classical list would be seven Pāṇḍavas (the five brothers plus Kṛṣṇa and Sātyaki) and three Kauravas. The 1981 Tindivanam procession also had a single woman in it, dressed in a bright red saree. I wondered whether she had a ritual or epic identity, but the pūcāri assured me she did not—that she was no one in particular and just there because she wanted to be. In any case, if Draupadī has conducted the Kaurava widows to heaven, this woman should not be one of them.

plifies the coherence of what I introduced at the beginning of chapter 8 as the larger or extended unity of paṭukaḷam rites.

B. Coronation of Dharma

With karumāti complete, Dharma can be enthroned in the ceremony known as *tarumar paṭṭāpiṣēkam,* literally the "consecration (*apiṣēkam*) of Dharma with a gold forehead band or ornament (*paṭṭam*)." At Marutāṭu it is done later on the same day as karumāti, but usually it is done one to three days afterward. I will describe the rite as it is most familiar to me from observation at Pondicherry (in 1977), drawing also on the description of the Tindivanam pūcāri.

During the afternoon, the processional icons of Dharma and Draupadī are elaborately bathed and richly decorated with silk cloths, flowers, and garlands. If there is a choice, these are pañcalōkam rather than wooden icons. At Tindivanam and Pondicherry, Dharma has his own pañcalōkam icon. In the evening, once his image is decorated, he is shown seated at ease on a flower-backed throne.

The temple phase of the ceremony begins with an elaborate dīpārādhanā, using a variety of lamps with different odd numbers of wicks. Each lamp is waved singly before the icon, after which the celebrants hold their hands joined over the flames and touch hands to their foreheads. Then a processional icon of Kṛṣṇa is brought beside Dharma's icon for the coronation. Here the pāratiyār should recite the closing verse of the *Villipāratam,* in which Kṛṣṇa, before leaving for Dvārakā, crowns Dharma himself and calls upon the Pāṇḍavas to rule virtuously, according to aṟam or dharma (10.46). The paṭṭam is first offered to Kṛṣṇa and then placed on Dharma's head (Shideler 1987, 177). At Pondicherry and Tindivanam, the paṭṭam is actually a cupped silver crown—at Tindivanam, donated by the town's Laxmi Vilas Bank. At Veḷḷimēṭupēṭṭai, it is a gold-leaf band that is tied around Dharma's head, as also at Iruṅkal (Frasca 1984, 320). At Marutāṭu the crowning is done by a Brahman, brought in specially for this rite, but usually, it seems, it is done by the pūcāri, as at Tindivanam. At Pondicherry, Dharma's rapport with Draupadī is nicely symbolized by the staff of sovereignty (daṇḍa) he bears at this point. On its top is a parrot, one of Draupadī's symbols (see plate 38).

Dharma's icon is then taken out and placed on a tēr that will take him on procession through the town. The symbolism is transparent. Now that Draupadī has won the war, dharma rules incarnate in her husband Dharmarāja and extends their joint sovereignty over the town or village. This is no longer the disguised Dharma of earlier processions: Keṅkupaṭṭar, the "Kite-" or "Heron-Brahman," whose staff concealed his identity with Dharmarāja Yama as the lord of Death.[8] According to the Tindivanam pūcāri, the title of the book that Dharma carries in his Keṅkupaṭṭar disguise is *Aṟam Ceyya Virumpu*, "Liking to Do Dharma." This has been the thread through his identity all along, but it has meant that the Kauravas had to be defeated before he could justly rule. I once asked the pāratiyār V. Venugopala Aiyar what he considered to be the underlying purpose of a Draupadī festival. He responded simply and unexpectedly: "dharma." We do not need a long exegesis to make our own closure on this point. A Draupadī festival, through the *Mahābhārata* myth it reenacts, is all about dharma: its decline, crisis, and renovation. From flag hoisting through karumāti, the festival reenacts dharma's decline and crisis, and the terrible but still dharmic resolutions they require. With Dharma's postcoronation emergence from the temple and his procession through the village or town, the festival announces dharma's renovation, which now radiates from the sanctum, where Draupadī, no longer violent and dangerous, is henceforth regulated by dharma. This regulation of the goddess by dharma brings prosperity (*śrī*) in the various forms of good fortune, both individual and collective, that have been sought from her through the festival. More than this, dharma, in Tamil aṟam, is one of the four goals of human life (*puruṣārtha*s) and implies them all. At the 1986 Mēlaccēri festival (see Hiltebeitel 1988b, part 1), the pāratiyār N. Kannapiran opened his first day of pāratam recitation, at flag hoisting, with a reminder that the *Mahābhārata* teaches these four goals: aṟam, *poruḷ* (meaning, substance, wealth), *iṉpam* (delight, pleasure), and *vīṭu* (liberation, [the eternal] "home"). In his discourse, aṟam is at the foundation of the first three and prepares one for the fourth.[9] Indeed, let us recall the highly sexualized interplay between Dharma and Mukti in the Dharma gājans.[10] There is thus no contradiction between these two pāratiyārs' insistence on the primacy of dharma, on which they discourse, and the prominence of tapas and bhakti that is so evident in the cult's dramas and spectacular rituals, or the vows the bhaktas fulfill for the sake of wealth and pleasure.

8. See chapter 3, section B.

9. These terms carry some connotations different from the corresponding ones in Sanskrit: in the pāratiyār's unusual order, the equivalents are dharma, artha, kāma, and mokṣa (usually ordered kāma, artha, dharma, mokṣa). As David Shulman pointed out (a remark while watching Hiltebeitel 1988b), the pāratiyār's order suggests a higher value for iṉpam than is usually accorded to kāma.

10. See chapter 7, section C.

Appendix *Śrī Tiraupatātēvi Māṉmiyam*, "The Glorification of Draupadī"

King Cunītaṉ's Lunar Dynasty ancestry is traced back six generations to Arjuna.[1] His father Niccakkiramu moved the dynasty from Hāstinapura to Ānarttatēcam when the goddess Gaṅgā flooded Hāstinapura to prevent people in the Kali yuga from touching the holy ornaments (*tiruvāparaṇa*) and other things that the gods had given the Pāṇḍavas (18). Ruling Ānarttatēcam, Cunītaṉ subjugated the whole world according to dharma (aṟam).[2] The demon Acilōmaṉ's ancestry also goes back six generations to the whirlwind demon Tiruṇavarttaṉ (Tṛṇāvarta), who carried the baby Kṛṣṇa up to heaven, and to Tiruṇavarttaṉ's son Caṭācuraṉ (Jaṭāsura), who was slain by Bhīma.[3] With a hundred heads, two hundred arms, and the strength of a hundred thousand elephants, Acilōmaṉ considered Cunītaṉ his hereditary enemy. To kill him, he did penance to Brahmā and received boons. After a year's battle, Cunītaṉ, realiz-

1. I was referred to this text several times, under varying titles, during research for volume 1 but could not find it (1988a, 78 n. 13). I came across it by chance in April 1990 when P. Krishnaraju, hereditary administrator of the Pondicherry temple, divulged that he had an old copy, torn in places and frayed at many corners. He agreed to make two photocopies, one for me and one for himself, to best preserve the text as it now stands. *Tiraupatātēvi Māṉmiyam* (Ilaṭcumaṇappiḷḷai 1902) is the title of the whole work, but a section by that title is the second of five parts (pp. 11–42, with a misnumbering so that there are actually no pages 27–32). That is the section summarized here. The first part, *Śrī Pāṇṭava Tiṉacari*, gives information on the Pāṇḍavas' birthdays. The third, *Śrī Tiraupatātēvi Piratiṣṭai*, gives instruction on how to install the icons on a yantra, apparently for a kumbhābhiṣeka. The fourth is a recitation of Draupadī's 108 names. And the fifth is a song of praise to her (*Śrī Tiraupatātēvi Patikam*). I thank Lee Weissman for his help with the translation.
2. Ānarttatēcam (Ānartta is an epic-purāṇic site in Gujarat; Schwartzberg 1978, 14, 27) was not mentioned in any of the oral versions gathered for volume 1. Presumably it is a variant of the northern realm of Cunītaṉ, variously given as Kauśambī and "northern Gingee."
3. The name Acilōmaṉ was used by only one of the nine pāratiyārs (N. Kannapiran) interviewed about this story for volume 1. It represents a Sanskritic end of the spec-

ing he was losing, went to the ashram of the Pāṇḍava family guru, Dhaumya (Taumiyamuṉivar).[4] Acilōmaṉ then ruled Ānarttatēcam with a crooked scepter.

Dhaumya took Cunītaṉ to the shining world of Satyaloka and asked Brahmā if there was a way to defeat Acilōmaṉ. Brahmā told of the severity of Acilōmaṉ's penance: "The first year he ate dried leaves; the second he drank water; the third he ate wind; the fourth he went without food; the fifth he ate filings (*arappoṭi*); the sixth he ate fire; the seventh he lay in water; the eighth he lay on thorns; the ninth he stood on the edge of a sword (*kattimuṉai*); the tenth he stayed in fire (*neruppil iruntum*)."[5] Surprised at his cruel tapas (*koṭuntavam*), Brahmā granted his wishes. But since Acilōmaṉ was the "crown jewel of fools" (*mūṭacirōmaṇi*), thinking women of little strength, he did not ask for a boon to protect himself from them.

Brahmā then told Cunītaṉ and Dhaumya to go to the ashram of Upayāca Muṉivar.[6] They approached it, but it had been ravaged by Acilōmaṉ. They learned that Upayācar was across the Varākanati (The Varāha River) on the Varākaparuvatam (Varāha Mountain).[7] Seeing that they were coming, Upayācar came to greet them and heard what had happened. Upayācar told Cunītaṉ a secret teaching. Draupadī, in her previous life as Nāḷāyaṇi, married the Muṉi Mavutkalliyar (Maudgalya), who had the form of five lights. They made love for a thousand years. When Mavutkalliyar went to Brahmā for his religious duties, Nāḷāyaṇi, desiring his five forms, asked Śiva to give her a husband five times. As she stood in the

---

trum of this demon's names, since it probably derives from the *Devī Māhātmyam* (Hiltebeitel 1988a, 86–87). Oral versions usually traced the demon's enmity back to Bhīma's killing of Baka (ibid., 79, 81, 86–87). As further notes will suggest, the author seems to represent or at least draw from a learned, somewhat Sanskritized, pāratiyār tradition. Tṛṇāvarta, not mentioned by any of my earlier informants, is a purāṇic figure unknown to the Sanskrit *Mahābhārata*.

4. Dhaumya is indeed the Pāṇḍavas' family priest in the Sanskrit *Mahābhārata*.

5. These penances recall those of Baṇāsura and his followers in the gājans of West Bengal (see chap. 7, sec. C), but they also suggest an arrogant misuse and exaggeration of some of the rituals done for Draupadī: in particular, the last, staying in fire.

6. Only Brameesa Mudaliyar mentioned Upayācar's role in the sacrifice and added also his brother Yācaṉ's (Hiltebeitel 1988a, 81). At Draupadī's birth in the Sanskrit *Mahābhārata*, both brothers officiate. His is also the only account that brings Cunītaṉ to Gingee in his search for them.

7. Varākanati is the alternative name for the Caṅkarāparaṇi River that goes around Gingee; see Hiltebeitel 1988a, 52–56, with map and legends linking the river with Viṣṇu as Varāha, the Boar. Varākaparuvatam must be one of the Gingee mountains. From the *Māṉmiyam*, it appears to be the Rāja Giri, site of the King's Fort. But other accounts suggest it would be the mountain near Singavaram village, east of Mēlaccēri (ibid., 54).

heavenly Gaṅgā, the tears from each entreaty fell in the water and became a stalk with a golden lotus. Indra, going to Kailāsa to serve Śiva, saw the golden lotuses, followed them to Nāḷāyaṉi, realized what had happened, and then went on to Śiva. Turning prideful at seeing Śiva and Pārvatī, who were ignoring him while playing dice, Indra prepared to strike them with his thunderbolt. Śiva, with an affectionate sidelong look, made him stand for a thousand years like a column (*tūṇ*). He then put Indra in a cave with four other former Indras and determined that the five should become the husbands of Nāḷāyaṉi. Amid the celestials' rejoicing, however, the goddess Earth, unable to bear the weight of evildoers, took refuge with Viṣṇu. Viṣṇu distributed seven hairs. Śiva took five of them, joined each with his five-syllable mantra and with the *aṃśas* ("portions") of the five gods Yama, Vāyu, Indra, and the Aśvins. Viṣṇu then gave the five hairs to the five Indras in the cave, who were then born as the Pāṇḍavas.[8] The aṃśas of the remaining two hairs became Kṛṣṇa and Balarāma. Nāḷāyaṉi herself descended, with the youth of a fourteen-year-old girl, as Draupadī, in the middle of the yāka fire performed by Pāñcālarājaṉ through Upayācar's mantra power. She married the Pāṇḍavas, and because of the will of Śrīman Nārāyaṇa, destroyed Duryodhana and other Daityāṃśas, Kīcaka and other Rākṣasāṃśas, and Jayadratha and other Asurāṃśas.[9] All agreed that Acilōmaṉ should now be killed by that great goddess. He was ruling at Ceñci (Gingee), a city built on the peak of the Varāha Mountain, on the west side of the Varāha River (14), where Upayācar's leafy hut had formerly been. Ceñci was named after him, because he "overcame suffering" (*cemji*, with *cem* taken as *tuṉpam*, "suffering"; 24). There Ceñci-Acilōmaṉ built a sixteen-cornered [fort] on the Varāha Mountain, giving it the name Ceñcimalai and the city the name Ceñcinakaram.[10] From there he oppressed the three worlds.

8. The account is notable for combining variants on the background for Draupadī's polyandry into a sequential narrative (see Hiltebeitel 1976, 80–81, 170–75, on the five entreaties, golden lotuses, and former Indras; Scheuer 1982, 99–105 and Subramanian 1967, 47, on Nāḷāyaṉi and Maudgalya in the Southern Recension of the *Mahābhārata* and *Villipāratam*). Hairs for the Pāṇḍavas are new to me, and Śiva's role in investing them with his five-syllable (*pañcākṣara*) mantra is another reminder that the Pāṇḍavas embody him in different ways (see 1988a, 132, 196, 198–99, 213, 444). The five lights are also new to me (cf. Scheuer 1982, 101). Note also that it is Yama who provides the portion for Dharma (cf. chap. 3, sec. B; chap. 6, n. 13).
9. *Aṃśas*, or incarnate "portions," of these various types of demons.
10. We now see that this version incorporates the variant (Hiltebeitel 1988a, 83) that Acilōmaṉ is the demon of the Gingee Fort. Indeed, not only that, he gives the fort, mountain, and town his name (as Mahiṣāsura does for Mysore). I have not found

Upayācar then took Cunītan̲ and Dhaumya to another leafy hut on the Cintu (Indus) River and invited the best of Mun̲is and Brahmans to perform a yākam there. At this great sacrifice, among other presences, Uruttiramūrtti (Rudramūrti) was the cāmittaran̲ (śamitar) (25–26).[11] For forty-six days the sacrifice continued. Cunītan̲'s body withered, and his mind became submerged in bliss. He joined his hands. Gods, sages, and Apsarases rejoiced. Drums rolled. While this was happening, on a jeweled, golden chariot (*vimāna*) called Puṇṇiyakōṭi, the blue-jewel creeperlike body of Kiriyācatti (Kriyāśakti, the power of action) appeared in the middle of the yākakuṇṭam (firepit) only to those who had great merit.[12] She had shoulders like a lion's, hair that made you wonder whether it was black thread,[13] and a body the color of the dark *neytal* flower (*karuneytal*), good fragrance, the look of a fourteen-year-old, shining like lightning, bearing in her right hand a flower bud with a female green parrot on top, her left hand hanging.[14] Her eyes poured out a flood of mercy (*kirupāveḷḷam*) while giving fearlessness to her devotees. Happy in mind, Mahātēvi [i.e., Draupadī], appearing on the Puṇṇiyakōṭi chariot in the middle of the sacrificial fire, blessed Upayācar, and said, "Come close and listen with affection. I am Kiriyācatti who appeared from Kāriyacatti.[15] My body has the true form of Fire (*akkin̲icōrūpam*). Between me and Agni there is no difference (*akkin̲ikkum en̲akkum pētamēyillai*). In a former age, for the sake of the five Pāṇḍavas, for the sake of Pāñcālarājan̲, in order to rid the earth of its burden, you made me descend in the sacrifice. For what reason have you invited me to come now?" The gods told her how Acilōman̲, mighty in the arts of magic war (*māy-*

---

this etymology for Gingee mentioned elsewhere; cf. Srinivasachari 1943, 5, 21–25 (several different etymologies).

11. Another hint at a connection between Rudra-Śiva and the Vedic śamitar; cf. chapter 6, section A, 8, and Hiltebeitel 1988a, 126–27.

12. Unlike her prior (epic) birth, Draupadī is born with her war chariot. Presumably she is also born with her various (ritual) weapons, since in this account she does not get them from Pōttu Rāja (cf. Hiltebeitel 1988a, 81, 386–92). Only her bow and arrows will be mentioned, however. Nothing is said about the site of the sacrifice being near the river or on the spot of her Mēlaccēri-Gingee temple.

13. Like an icon's (cf. Hiltebeitel 1988a, plate 7)?

14. Later, when Draupadī tells how the temple icons should look, the flower in her right hand is said to be a blue lotus (*nilōṟpala malar*), and she should be standing as if adorned for a wedding. Presumably this refers to being in a *tribhaṅga* (three-bend) pose, since, with that addition, the same is said for Arjuna's icon (39).

15. The "power of action" that derives from the "causal power." The text relates this earlier to the Mavutkalliyar-Nāḷāyan̲i story: Mavutkalliyar's father Mutkalamun̲ivar (Mudgala) is born from the primal cause, the *karaṇapuruṣa* (22).

āyuttam), had taken over the three worlds and had defeated Cunītaṉ, who was standing before her with palms joined, a member of the Kuru clan. "O Tiraupatātēvi, you should destroy that villain." Before the Muṉis and Tēvars, Mahātēvi said to Cunītaṉ, "O child, you should not fear. I will send your enemy to the abode of Yama." Saying that, she sent the Puṇṇiyakōṭi chariot, made of extreme radiance (*atitējōmayam*), to Gingee (Ceñcippati), and the gods and Cunītaṉ with the chariot. Learning of her approach, Acilōmaṉ put his golden crowns on his hundred heads, mounted his chariot drawn by a thousand asses (*kaḻutaikaḷ*), and readied his vast army to fight, undeterred by bad omens.

"Just as in former times, Turkkātēvi (Durgā) fought with Makiṭācūraṉ (Mahiṣāsura), the Sattamātarkaḷ (Seven Mothers, Saptamātrikās) fought with Vakkirācūraṉ, and Cītā (Sītā) with the hundred-necked (*catakaṇṭa*) Rāvaṇa,[16] just so Tiraupatātēvi fought hotly with Acilōmaṉ." Each fought with a bow, releasing countless divine and magical arrows. "Getting very angry, thinking that Acilōmaṉ should be destroyed, preparing to use the Nārāyaṇa weapon (*astiram*), Draupadī pulled the bow all the way back to her ear, so that the entire world trembled. Then, even though she cut off and flung away ninety-nine of his heads, a holy voice spoke from the sky, saying: 'Because he has received a boon from Brahmā, if his hundredth head alone falls to the ground, it will explode (*veṭi*). You should fight without letting it fall to the ground.'" While Draupadī was considering this, the great Bhāgavata Nārada came and stood in the Ammaṉ's presence (*canniti*) and made a petition (*viṇṇipam*). He told her that Tarumaputtiraṉ's (Yudhiṣṭhira's) [former] minister (*mantiri*), the best of Brahmans, named Cuvētaṉ,[17] had a line of descendants through six generations, each one of whom served as minister to Dharma's descendants, down to Cunītaṉ. Cunītaṉ's minister was Pōtarājaṉ. "This Pōtarājaṉ is an extremely subtle person (*atinuṭpacāli*).[18] He knows the Vedas without any doubt or variation. He knows the science of mantras (*mantiracāstira*) to its limits. He will bear Acilōmaṉ's hundredth head by his mantra power (*mantirapalam*) without its falling to the ground." Draupadī then told Pōttu Rāja to hold the head by the power of his mantras. She

16. The text thus links Draupadī more with a folk Sītā than the classical one. On the hundred-necked Rāvaṇa, see Shulman 1986.
17. Unlike Dhaumya and Upayācar, Cuvētaṉ ("Good at Veda"), ancestor of Pōttu Rāja, is without a classical epic pedigree.
18. Cf. Hiltebeitel 1988a, 82, for the subtlety Arjuna must use to divert him. His lack of subtlety can also be something of a joke in the Pōrmaṉṉaṉ cycle (ibid., 339, 343, 358, 369).

prayed to Jaṉārttaṉaṉ (Janārdana-Viṣṇu), released the Nārāyaṇa weapon, and severed Acilōmaṉ's head. Before it touched the ground, Pōttu Rāja snatched it with his left hand.[19]

Draupadī then told Cunītaṉ he should return to his city and rule according to dharma. She would be going to the presence of Śrīman Nārāyaṇa, lying on the Milk Ocean. Cunītaṉ prostrated himself before her, his heart melting (*maṉaṅkaṉintu*), sang a song of praise, and requested her to always make him serve her at Gingee (Ceñcinakaram).[20] Draupadī said, "O child, in the Kali age humans all deviate from the way of dharma. Women transgress their bounds. Brahmans defame the dharma of their families. Śūdras oppress Brahmans. Therefore I will not live in Gingee alone. . . . You should hear the history of my chief marshal (*cēṉatipati*). At the confluence of the Tāmparaparaṇi River there is a small country named Muttuviḷaiyum.[21] A small king (*ciṟṟarācaṉ*) ruled there named Mavuttikēcaṉ. . . . [His fifth descendant] is Muttālaṉ, my chief marshal. Because he is fifteen years old, everybody calls him Muttālarājaputtiraṉ. Standing there with folded hands is [also] Pōtarājaṉ, the leader of my ministers (*mantirikaḷukkuḷ talaivar*)."[22] Cunītaṉ promised, "These two should always be with you, and you should stay in Gingee and grant us all wishes." Draupadī told Cunītaṉ that he should build her a temple where she would reside with Pōtarājaṉ and Muttālarājaputtiraṉ in the form of worshipful icons (*arccā rūpam*), and that he should also install images of Kṛṣṇa and the five Pāṇḍavas.[23] Then she blessed them individually. "O Pōtarājaṉ, you should stand on my ground across from my sanctum (*canniti*), holding Acilōmaṉ's head with your left hand by your mantra power, a sword in your right hand. O Muttālarājaputtiraṉ, you should be to my left side, with all weapons, on a white horse.[24] O my child Cunītaṉ, you should build a temple for me in Gingee, and according to my commandments you should install images of vari-

19. Note here and later the collaboration between Draupadī and Viṣṇu.

20. Either Cunītaṉ has forgotten about Āṉarttatēcam, or it has somehow turned into Gingee.

21. The Tambraparni is in Tirunelveli District, Tamilnadu. I have found no traces of the "small country" (*ciṟu tēcam*) of Muttuviḷaiyum there.

22. Once again Muttāl Rāvuttaṉ has become a Hindu, but linked with the adharma of the Kali age as, no doubt, he would be, in these circles, as a Muslim. Note also that he has taken over Pōttu Rāja's marshal role (or, more exactly, Pōrmaṉṉaṉ's marshal role, since, for the pāratiyārs, Pōttu Rāja is consistently a Brahman minister; Hiltebeitel 1988a, 79).

23. See chapter 3, n. 27.

24. On the implications of the deity's left side in the temple plan, see chapter 6, n. 21.

ous metals [named], and conduct a festival (*utcavam*). The first year you should have a great marriage festival, marrying me to Dharma; the second year with Bhīma, the third with Arjuna, the fourth with Nakula, the fifth with Sahadeva. Once that cycle is over, just begin it again.[25] Every year, the eighteenth day should be the first day of the month of Cittirai. On that day you should do a big fire festival (*akkiṉi makōtcavam*). On that day I will appear in a karakam and I will walk across the fire with the devotees. The next day they should do the *avapiratam* (*avabhṛtha*), and the day after that the paṭṭāpiṣēkam.[26] If you perform the festival in this manner, besides the miraculous great pleasure (*pēriṉpam*) that is mokṣa, I will give to my devotees everything else according to their desire, without a doubt. Who is fit to give mokṣa besides Śrīman Nārāyaṇa? No one. He is the ultimate giver. He is the ultimate *ātmā* [in verse].[27] In this Kali yuga I will be manifest for six thousand years in arccā rūpam. After that my śakti will no longer be on earth." Having said that, while Cunītaṉ stood praising Śrī Draupadī, the Kriyāśakti, she disappeared.

25. Nowhere is this a practice I know of, but it probably shows the author's familiarity with the *Villipāratam;* see Hiltebeitel 1988a, 438. The Mēlaccēri festival is, however, supposed to be held once every five years.
26. An avabhṛtham or purifying bath (for the icons? the participants?) is unfamiliar to me in this context and has the look of a "Vedic" addition.
27. Recall, however, that matters are not always so clear in the rites of revival and of Draupadī viewing the battlefield. In any case, it is again a matter of collaboration (see n. 19).

Abbreviations

Indian Texts

AB	*Aitareya Brāhmaṇa*
DM	*Devī Māhātmyam*
HV	*Harivaṃśa*
Mbh.	*Mahābhārata*
MS	*Maitrāyaṇī Saṃhitā*
Rām.	*Rāmāyaṇa*
ṚV	*Ṛg Veda*
ṢaḍB	*Ṣaḍviṃśa Brāhmaṇa*
ŚB	*Śatapatha Brāhmaṇa*
TB	*Taittirīya Brāhmaṇa*
TS	*Taittirīya Saṃhitā*
VS	*Vājasaneyi Saṃhitā*

Bibliographical Entries

AA	*Arts Asiatiques*
BEFEO	*Bulletin de l'Ecole Française d'Extrême Orient*
BSOAS	*Bulletin of the School of Oriental and African Studies*
CIS	*Contributions to Indian Sociology*
CR	comptes rendus (see Biardeau)
ERE	*Hastings' Encyclopaedia of Religion and Ethics*
HR	*History of Religions*
IA	*Indian Antiquary*
IESHR	*Indian Economic and Social History Review*
IIJ	*Indo-Iranian Journal*
JAOS	*Journal of the American Oriental Society*
JAS	*Journal of Asian Studies*
JASB	*Journal of the Anthropological Society of Bombay*
JTS	*Journal of Tamil Studies*
QJMS	*Quarterly Journal of the Mythic Society*

Bibliography

Works in Indian Languages

Aravāṉ Kaṭapali Nāṭakam. 1977. Madras: Irattiṉa Nāyakar and Sons.

Bhatt, G. H., et al., eds. 1960–75. *The Rāmāyaṇa, for the first time critically edited*. Baroda: University of Baroda.

Cēturāmaṉ, Kō., ed. 1986. *Aravāṉ Kaḷappali*. Tañcāvūr: Caracuvati Makāl Nūl Nilaiya Caṅkam.

Ilaṭcumaṇappiḷḷai, P. 1902. *Śrī Tiraupatātēvi Māṉmiyam*. Madras: Cuppiramaṇiya Aiyar (as reconstructed from title page, on which all that remains is "——ṉṉai: ——maṇiya Aiyar").

Irākavamūrtti, Pāṉāmpaṭṭi. [1907] 1979. *Śrī Virāṭaparva Nāṭakameṉṉum Māṭupiṭi Caṇṭai*. Madras: Irattiṉa Nāyakar and Sons.

Kashikar, C. G., ed. 1958. *Śrautakośa*. Vol. 1. *Sanskrit section*. Poona: Vaidika Saṃśodhana Maṇḍala.

Kīcaka Cammāra Nāṭakam. 1962. Madras: Irattiṉa Nāyakar and Sons.

Kinjawadekar, Ramachandrashāstri, ed. 1936. *Shriman-Mahābhāratam*. Part 7, 19. *Harivanshaparvan with Bhārata Bhāwadeepa by Neelakantha*. Pune: Chitrashala Press.

Kōpālakiruṣṇamācāriyār, Vai. Mu. 1976–78. *Villiputtūrār Iyaṟṟiya Makāpāratam*, with commentary. 9 vols. Madras: Kuvaippalikēṣaṉs.

Muller, F. Max. 1965. *The hymns of the Rig-Veda in the Samhita and Pada texts, reprinted from the editio princeps*. 3d ed. 2 vols. Kashi Sanskrit Series, no. 167. Varanasi: Chowkhamba Sanskrit Series Office.

Munivenkatappa, S. M. 1965. *Karaga Mahotsava* (a pamphlet in Kannada on the Karaga festival at Bangalore). Trans. for me privately by K. T. Pandurangi.

Pāṇḍeya Pam, Śrīrāmanārāyaṇadattaji Śāstri "Rāma." n.d. *Sacitra Śrīdurgāsaptaśatī: Hindi Anuvāda tathā Pāṭhavidhi sahita*. Gorakhpur: Gita Press.

Perumal, A. N., ed. 1983. *Veḷḷaikkāraṉ Katai*. Madras: International Institute of Tamil Studies.

Pukaḻēṇṭippulavar. 1909. *Turōpataikuṟam*. Ed. P. Etirāculu Nāyuṭu. Madras: Śrīkōpāvilāca Press.

——— [Pukaḻēntip Pulavar]. n.d. *Āravalli Cūravalli Katai*. Irattiṉa Nāyakar and Sons.

Sukthankar, Vishnu S., et al., eds. 1933–59. *The Mahābhārata, for the first time critically edited.* 37 fascs. Pune: Bhandarkar Oriental Research Institute.

Taṇikācala Mutaliyār, Tiṇṭivaṉam. 1979. *Turōpatai Kuṟavañci Nāṭakam.* Madras: Irattiṉa Nāyakar and Sons.

Vaidya, Parashuram Lakshman. 1969, 1971. *The Harivaṃśa, being the Khila or supplement to the Mahābhāratam for the first time critically edited.* 2 vols. Poona: Bhandarkar Oriental Research Institute.

Weber, Albrecht, ed. 1964. *The Çatapatha-Brāhmaṇa in the Mādhyandina-Çākhā with extracts from the commentaries of Sāyaṇa, Harisvāmin and Dvivedaganga.* Chowkhamba Sanskrit Series, no. 96. Varanasi: Chowkhamba Sanskrit Series.

Other References

Agrawala, V. S. 1966. *Śiva Mahādeva: The great god.* Varanasi: Veda Academy.

Allchin, F. R. 1963. *Neolithic cattle-keepers of the Deccan: A study of the Deccan ashmounds.* Cambridge: Cambridge University Press.

Ananthakrishna Iyer, L. K. 1909–12. *The Cochin tribes and castes.* 2 vols. Madras: Higginbotham/Government of Cochin.

Anderson, Mary M. 1971. *The festivals of Nepal.* London: Allen and Unwin.

Andric, Ivo. [1945] 1977. *The bridge on the Drina.* Trans. Lovett F. Edwards. Chicago: University of Chicago Press.

Appadurai, Arjun. 1981. *Worship and conflict under colonial rule: A South Indian case.* Cambridge: Cambridge University Press.

Archer, W. G. 1947. *The vertical man: A study in primitive Indian sculpture.* London: George Allen and Unwin.

———. 1974. *The hill of flutes.* Pittsburgh: University of Pittsburgh Press.

Artal, Rao Bahadur R. C. 1907. The village goddess Dyâmavva. *JASB* 7:632–47.

Arunachalam, M. 1976. *Peeps into Tamil literature: Ballad poetry.* Tiruchitrambalam: Gandhi Vidyalayam.

———. 1980. *Festivals of Tamilnadu: Peeps into Tamil culture* 3. Tiruchitrambalam: Gandhi Vidyalayam.

Ayrookuzhiel, A. M. Abraham. 1983. *The sacred in popular Hinduism.* Madras: Christian Literature Society.

Babb, Lawrence. 1974. *Walking on flowers: A Hindu festival cycle.* Singapore: Department of Sociology, University of Singapore, Working Papers no. 27.

———. 1975. *The divine hierarchy: Popular Hinduism in Central India.* New York: Columbia University Press.

Bang, B. C. 1973. Current concepts of the smallpox goddess in parts of West Bengal. *Man in India* 53:79–104.

Basham, A. L. [1951] 1981. *History and doctrine of the Ājīvakas.* Delhi: Motilal Banarsidass.

Bayly, Susan. 1989. *Saints, goddesses and kings: Muslims and Christians in South Indian society 1700–1900.* Cambridge: Cambridge University Press.

Beach, Milo Cleveland. 1981. *The imperial image: Paintings for the Mughal court.* Washington, D.C.: Freer Gallery of Art, Smithsonian Institution.

———. 1983. *The adventures of Rama, with illustrations from a sixteenth century Mughal manuscript.* Washington, D.C.: Freer Gallery of Art, Smithsonian Institution.

Beauchamp, H. 1901. Reproducing a letter to Mr. H. Beauchamp, editor of the "Madras Mail." *Madras Government Museum, Bulletin,* 4, 1. Madras: Government Press.

Beck, Brenda E. F. 1969. Colour and heat in South Indian ritual. *Man* 4:553–72.

———. 1972a. *Peasant society in Konku: A study of right and left subcastes in South India.* Vancouver: University of British Columbia Press.

———. 1972b. The study of a Tamil epic: Several versions of *Silappadikāram* compared. *JTS* 1:23–38.

———. 1975. The story of the brothers: An oral epic from the Coimbatore District of Tamilnadu. Collected in 1965. Mimeographed and privately circulated by the author.

———. 1976. The symbolic merger of body, space, and cosmos in Hindu Tamil Nadu. *CIS* 10, 2:213–43.

———. 1981a. The goddess and the demon: A local South Indian festival and its wider context. In *Autour de la déesse hindoue,* ed. Madeleine Biardeau. *Puruṣārtha* 5:83–136.

———. 1981b. Letter to author, 30 November.

———. 1982. *The three twins: The telling of a South Indian folk epic.* Bloomington: Indiana University Press.

Bell, Catherine. 1989. Religion and Chinese culture: Toward an assessment of popular religion. *HR* 29:58–64.

Bhattacharya, Bholanath. 1971. A note on Vausakhi Dharma Gajan of Bengal. *Folklore* (Calcutta) 12, 7:240–48.

Bhattacharyya, Asutosh. 1952. The Dharma-cult. *Bulletin of the Department of Anthropology* (Government of India). 1, 1:117–53.

Bhattacharyya, Narendra Nath. 1975. *Ancient Indian rituals and their social contents.* Delhi: Manohar, 1975.

Bhowmick, P. K. 1964. Gajan—a regional festival. *Folklore* (Calcutta) 5, 9: 321–33.

Biardeau, Madeleine. 1967–68. Brâhmaṇes combattantes dans un mythe du sud de l'Inde. *Adyar Library Bulletin, Dr. V. Raghavan Felicitation Volume* 31–32:519–530.

———. 1976. Etudes de mythologie hindoue: 4. *Bhakti* et *avatāra. BEFEO* 63:87–237.

———. 1978. Etudes de mythologie hindoue: 5. *Bhakti* et *avatāra. BEFEO* 65:111–263.

———. 1981a. L'arbre *śamī* et le buffle sacrificiel. In *Autour de la déesse hindoue,* ed. Biardeau. *Puruṣārtha* 5:215–244.

———. 1981b. Sacrifice: Le yūpa, poteau sacrificiel dans l'Hindouisme. In *Dictionnaire des mythologies,* 109–13 (offprints of Biardeau articles). Paris: Flammarion.

———. 1981c. *L'Hindouisme: Anthropologie d'une civilisation.* Paris: Flammarion.

———. 1981d. *Etudes de mythologie hindoue.* Vol. 1, *Cosmogonies purāṇiques.* Paris: Ecole Française d'Extrême Orient.

———. 1984. The Śamī tree and the sacrificial buffalo. *CIS,* n.s., 18, 1:1–23.

———. 1988. Semis de graines dans des pots: Reflexions sur une forme. In *Essais sur le rituel,* vol. 1, ed. Anne-Marie Blondeau and Kristofer Schipper, 93–117. Colloque du Centenaire de la Section de l'Ecole Pratique des Hautes Etudes, Bibliothèque de l'EPHE Sciences Religieuses, vol. 42. Louvain and Paris: Peeters.

———. 1989a. Brahmans and meat-eating gods. In Hiltebeitel 1989b, 19–33.

———. 1989b. *Histoires de poteaux: Variations védiques autour de la déesse hindoue.* Paris: Ecole Française d'Extrême Orient.

———. CR 77–91 (1969–1983). Comptes rendus of seminars on the *Mahābhārata. Annuaire de l'Ecole Pratique des Hautes Etudes,* V^e section, 77 (1969–70): 168–73; 78 (1970–71): 151–61; 79 (1971–72): 139–47; 80–81 (1973–74): 120–41; 82 (1973–74): 89–101; 83 (1975): 103–11; 84 (1975–76): 165–85; 85 (1976–77): 135–67; 86 (1977–78): 143–53; 87 (1978–79): 145–71; 88 (1979–80): 167–82; 89 (1980–81): 221–50; 90 (1981–82): 145–55; 91 (1982–83): 153–73.

Biardeau, Madeleine, and Charles Malamoud. 1976. *Le sacrifice dans l'Inde ancienne.* Paris: Presses Universitaires de France.

Biardeau, Madeleine, and Jean-Michel Péterfalvi. 1985. *Le Mahābhārata: Livres I à V.* Paris: Flammarion.

———. 1986. *Le Mahābhārata: Livres VI à XVIII.* Paris: Flammarion.

Blackburn, Stuart H. 1988. *Singing of birth and death: Texts in performance.* Philadelphia: University of Pennsylvania Press.

———. 1989. Patterns of development for Indian oral epics. In *Oral epics in India,* ed. Stuart H. Blackburn, Peter J. Claus, Joyce B. Flueckiger, and Susan S. Wadley. Berkeley and Los Angeles: University of California Press.

Blaive, Br., A. Penaud, and R. M. Nicoli. 1974. La marche sur le feu à l'Ile de la Réunion. *BEFEO* 61:355–364.

Bolle, Kees. 1983. A world of sacrifice. *HR* 23, 1:37–63.

Bollée, W. B. 1956. *Ṣaḍviṃśa-Brāhmaṇa: Introduction, translation, extracts from the commentary and notes.* Utrecht: Drukkerij A. Storm.

Breckenridge, Carol Appadurai. 1977. From protector to litigant—changing relations between Hindu temples and the Rāja of Ramnad. *IESHR* 14, 1:75–106.

Brewster, Paul G. 1977. The strange practice of firewalking. *Expedition* 19, 3:43–47.

Brown, Carolyn Henning. 1976. Ritual power and danger: Hindu firewalking in Fiji. Paper presented to American Anthropological Association, Washington, D.C.

———. 1984. Tourism and ethnic competition in a ritual form: The firewalkers of Fiji. *Oceania* 14:223–44 (revision of Brown 1976).

Brubaker, Richard Lee. 1978. The ambivalent mistress: A study of South Indian village goddesses and their religious meaning. Ph.D. diss., University of Chicago.

Burrow, Thomas, and Murray B. Emeneau. 1961. *Dravidian etymological dictionary.* London: Oxford University Press.

Caland, W. 1924. The sacrificial stake of Īsāpur. *Acta Orientalia* 3:92–93.

Chalier-Visuvalingam, Elizabeth. 1986. Bhairava: Kotwal of Vārāṇasī. In *Varanasi through the ages,* ed. T. P. Verma, D. P. Singh, and J. S. Mishra. Varanasi: Bharatiya Itihas Sankalan Samiti.

———. 1989. Bhairava's royal brahmanicide: The problem of the Mahābrāhmaṇa. In Hiltebeitel 1989b, 157–230.

Chandra Sekhar, A. 1961. *Fairs and festivals: 6. Guntur District.* Part 7B of *Census of India* 1961, vol. 2: *Andhra Pradesh.* Delhi: Manager of Publications.

Chattopadhyay, K. P. 1942. Dharma worship. *Journal of the Royal Asiatic Society of Bengal* 8:99–137.

Chaudhuri, J. B. 1940. The wife in the Vedic ritual. *Indian Historical Quarterly* 16:70–98.

Chellappan, K. 1990. Tamil culture in Mauritius: Past and present. *Indian Express,* Weekend section. Feb. 10, pp. 1 and 4.

Chhabra, B. Ch. 1947. Yūpa inscriptions. *India Antiqua* 6:77–82.

Chidanandamurti, M. 1982. Two Māsti temples in Karnataka. In Settar and Sontheimer 1982, 117–31.

Chokalingam, K., director. 1973–74. *Temples of Tamilnadu: 7. Thanjavur* (i–iii). In *Census of India 1961,* vol. 9: *Tamilnadu,* part 11D. Delhi: Manager of Publications.

Choondal, Chummar. 1978. *Studies in folklore of Kerala.* Trivandrum: College Book House.

———. 1980. Ballads of Kerala. *Sangeet Natak* 55:41–58.

Clothey, Fred W. 1982. Chronometry, cosmology and the festival calendar in the Murukaṉ cult. In *Religious festivals in South India and Sri Lanka,* ed. Guy R. Welbon and Glenn E. Yocum, 157–88. New Delhi: Manohar.

———. 1983. *Rhythm and intent: Ritual studies from South India.* Madras: Blackie.

Clough, Emma Rauschenbusch. 1899. *While sewing sandals.* London: Hodder and Stoughton.

Courtright, Paul B. 1985. *Gaṇeśa: Lord of obstacles, lord of beginnings.* New York: Oxford University Press.

Cousins, J. H. 1970. Dance-drama and shadow play. In *The arts and crafts of Kerala,* ed. Stella Kramrisch, J. H. Cousins, and R. Vasudeva Poduval. Cochin: Paico.

Cox, J. F. 1881. *A manual of the North Arcot District.* Madras: Government Press.

Crooke, William. 1914. Gurkhā, Gorkhā. *ERE* 6:456–57.

———. 1915. The Dasahra: An autumn festival of the Hindus. *Folklore* (London) 75:28–59.

Curtis. J. W. V. 1973. *Motivations of temple architecture in Śaiva Siddhānta.* Madras: Premier Press.

Dagens, Bruno. 1985. *Mayamata: An Indian treatise on housing architecture and iconography.* New Delhi: Sitaram Bhartia Institute of Scientific Research.

Danforth, Loring M. 1989. *Firewalking and religious healing.* Princeton: Princeton University Press.

Das, R. K. 1964. *Temples of Tamilnad.* Bombay: Bharatiya Vidya Bhavan.

Dasgupta, Sashibhusan. [1946] 1962. *Obscure religious cults.* Calcutta: K. L. Mukhopadhyay.

Derrett, J. D. M. 1979. Spirit possession and the Gerasene demoniac. *Man,* n.s., 14:286–93.

Dessigane, R., P. Z. Pattabiramin, and J. Filliozat. 1960. *La légende des jeux de Çiva à Madurai d'après les textes et peintures.* Publications de l'Institute Français d'Indologie, no. 19. Fasc. 1: text; fasc. 2: plates. Pondicherry: Institut Français d'Indologie.

Detienne, Marcel. 1977 [original French ed. 1972]. *The Gardens of Adonis: Spices in Greek mythology.* Trans. Janet Lloyd. Brighton: Harvester Press.

Devi, E. H. 1976. The military system as reflected in the ballads of North Malabar. *Journal of Kerala Studies* 3, 364:413–19.

Dharmadhikari, T. N., ed. 1989. *Yajñāyudhāni (an album of sacrificial utensils with descriptive notes).* Pune: Vaidika Saṃśodhana Maṇḍala.

Diehl, Carl Gustav. 1956. *Instrument and purpose: Studies on rites and rituals in South India.* Lund: C. W. K. Gleerup.

Dikshitar, V. R. Ramachandra, trans. 1939. *The Silappadikaram.* Madras: Oxford University Press.

Dimmitt, Cornelia, and J. A. B. van Buitenen, trans. 1978. *Classical Hindu mythology: A reader in the Sanskrit Purāṇas.* Philadelphia: Temple University Press.

Dimock, Edward C., Jr. 1982. A mythology of the repulsive: The myth of the goddess Sītalā. In *The divine consort: Rādhā and the goddesses of India,* ed. John Stratton Hawley and Donna Marie Wulff. Berkeley: Berkeley Religious Studies Series.

Dirks, Nicholas B. 1982. The pasts of a Pāḷaiyakarar: The ethnohistory of South Indian little king. *JAS* 3:655–83.

———. 1987. *The hollow crown: Ethnohistory of an Indian kingdom.* Cambridge: Cambridge University Press.

Dumézil, Georges. 1973. *The destiny of a king.* Trans. Alf Hiltebeitel. Chicago: University of Chicago Press.

Dumont, Louis. 1957. *Une sous-caste de l'Inde du Sud: Organisation sociale et religion des Pramalai Kallar.* Paris and the Hague: Mouton.

Dumont, P.-E. 1927. *L'Aśvamedha: Description du sacrifice solonnel du cheval dans le culte védique d'après les textes du Yajurveda blanc.* Paris: Paul Geuthner.

———. 1948. The horse-sacrifice in the *Taittirīya-Brāhmaṇa. Proceedings of the American Philosophical Society* 92, 6:447–503.

———. 1962. The animal sacrifice in the *Taittirīya-Brāhmana:* The part of the

Hotar and the part of the Maitrāvaruṇa in the animal sacrifice. *Proceedings of the American Philosophical Society* 106, 3:246–63.

Dutt, M. N. 1897. *A prose English translation of the Harivaṃśa.* Calcutta: Elusium Press.

Dymock, W. 1890. On the use of turmeric in Hindoo ceremonial. *JASB* 2:441–48.

Eggeling, Julius, trans. [1882] 1966. *The Śatapatha Brâhmaṇa* (in 5 parts). Sacred Books of the East, vols. 12, 26, 41, 43, 44. Delhi: Motilal Banarsidass.

Egnor, Margaret T. 1986. Internal iconicity in Paṟaiyar "crying songs." In *Another harmony: New essays on the folklore of India,* ed. Stuart H. Blackburn and A. K. Ramanujan. Berkeley and Los Angeles: University of California Press.

Eichinger Ferro-Luzzi, Gabriella. 1977. The logic of South Indian food offerings. *Anthropos* 72:529–56.

———. 1983. *Cool fire: Culture-specific themes in Tamil short stories.* Monographica 3. Gottingen: Edition Herodot.

Eliade, Mircea. 1964. *Shamanism: Archaic techniques of ecstasy.* Bollingen Series 76. New York: Pantheon Books.

———. [1958] 1965. *Rites and symbols of initiation.* New York: Harper Torchbooks.

Elliot, Sir Walter. 1860. Aboriginal caste book. 3 vols. London: India Office Library, manuscript.

Elmore, Wilbur Theodore. 1915. *Dravidian gods in modern Hinduism: A study of the local and village deities of Southern India.* Lincoln: University of Nebraska.

Eschmann, Anncharlott. 1978a. Hinduization and tribal deities in Orissa: The Śākta and Śaiva typology. In Eschmann, Kulke, and Tripathi 1978a, 79–97.

———. 1978b. The Vaiṣṇava typology of Hinduization and the origin of Jagannātha. In Eschmann, Kulke, and Tripathi 1978a, 99–117.

———. 1978c. Prototypes of the Navakalevara ritual and their relation to the Jagannātha cult. In Eschmann, Kulke, and Tripathi 1978a, 265–83.

Eschmann, Anncharlott, Hermann Kulke, and Gaya Charan Tripathi, eds. 1978a. *The cult of Jagannath and the regional tradition of Orissa.* South Asia Institute, New Delhi Branch, Heidelberg University. New Delhi: Manohar.

———. 1978b. The formation of the Jagannātha triad. In Eschmann, Kulke, and Tripathi 1978a, 169–96.

Fabricius, Johann Philip. 1972. *Tamil and English dictionary.* 4th ed. Tranquebar: Evangelical Lutheran Mission Publishing House.

Finn, Louise M. 1986. *The Kulacūḍamaṇi Tantra and the Vāmakeśvara Tantra with the Hayaratha commentary.* Wiesbaden: Otto Harrassowitz.

Firewalking ceremonies in India. 1900. *Journal of Society for Psychical Research* 9:312–21.

Fisher, Richard. 1974. Pain—warning signal for survival. *Observer Magazine,* December, 31–43.

Florescu, Radu, and Raymond T. McNally. 1973. *Dracula: A biography of Vlad the impaler.* New York: Hawthorn Books.

Flueckiger, Joyce Burkhalter. 1983. *Bhojalī:* Song, goddess, friend—a Chhastisgarhi women's oral tradition. *Asian Folklore Studies* 42:27–43.

Francis, W. 1906. *Madras District gazetteers: South Arcot.* Madras: Government Press.

Frasca, Richard. 1984. The Terukkūttu: Ritual theatre of Tamilnadu. Ph.D. diss., University of California, Berkeley.

———. 1990. *The theatre of the* Mahābhārata: *Terukkūttu Performances in South India.* Honolulu: University of Hawaii Press.

Frazer, James George. 1907. *The golden bough.* Part 4: Adonis Attis Osiris. London: Macmillan.

———. [1913] 1936. *Balder the beautiful: The fire-festivals of Europe and the doctrine of the external soul.* London: Macmillan.

Freeman, James M. 1974. Trial by fire. *Natural History* 83:55–62.

Fuller, C. J. 1980. The divine couple's relationship in a South Indian temple: Mīnākṣī and Sundareśvara at Madurai. *HR* 19:321–48.

———. 1987. Sacrifice (*bali*) in the South Indian temple. In *Religion and society in South India: A volume in honour of Prof. N. Subba Reddy,* ed. V. Sudarsen, G. Prakash Reddy, and M. Suryanarayana. Delhi: B. R. Publications.

Fuller, C. J., and Penny Logan. 1985. The Navarātri festival at Madurai. *BSOAS* 48:79–105.

Gaddis, Vincent H. 1967. *Mysterious fires and lights.* New York: David McKay.

Ganguli, Kisari Mohan, trans., and Pratap Chandra Roy, publisher. [1884–96] 1970. *The Mahabharata.* New Delhi: Munshiram Manoharlal.

Garstin, J. H. 1878. *Manual of the South Arcot District.* Madras: Lawrence Asylum Press.

Gehrts, Heino. 1975. *Mahābhārata: Das Geschehen und seine Bedeutung.* Bonn: Bouvier Verlag Herbert Grundmann.

Gold, Ann Grodzins. 1987. *Fruitful journeys: The ways of Rajasthani pilgrims.* Berkeley and Los Angeles: University of California Press.

Gombrich, Richard, and Gananath Obeyesekere. 1988. *Buddhism transformed: Religious change in Sri Lanka.* Princeton: Princeton University Press.

Gonda, Jan. 1967. The Indra festival according to the Atharvavedin. *JAOS* 87:413–29.

———. [1954] 1969. *Aspects of early Visnuism.* Delhi: Motilal Banarsidass.

———. [1966] 1969. *Ancient Indian kingship from the religious point of view.* Leiden: E. J. Brill.

———. 1980. *Vedic ritual: The non-solemn rites.* Handbuch der Orientalistik 2. Leiden: E. J. Brill.

———. 1987. *Rice and barley offerings in the Veda.* Leiden: E. J. Brill.

Gopalakrishnan, M. S. 1953. Mother goddess: A regional study (Madras and Malabar). M. Litt. thesis, University of Madras.

Gros, François, and R. Nagaswamy. 1970. *Uttaramērur: Légendes, histoire, monuments*. Publications de l'Institut Français d'Indologie, no. 39. Pondicherry: Institut Français d'Indologie.

Guenther, Herbert V. 1963. *The life and teaching of Nāropa: Translated from the original Tibetan with a philosophical commentary based on the oral transmission*. Oxford: Clarendon Press.

Gupta, Sanjukta. 1976. Viṣvaksena the divine protector. *Wiener Zeitschrift für die Kunde Südasiens und Archiv für Indische Philologie* 20:75–89.

Haekel, Josef. 1972. "Adonis-gärtchen" im Zeremonialwesen der Rathwa in Gujarat (Zentralindien): Vergleich und Problematik. *Ethnologische Zeitschrift Zürich* 1:167–75.

Harle, James C. 1963. Durgā, goddess of victory. *AA* 26:237–46.

———. 1986. *The art and architecture of the Indian subcontinent*. Harmondsworth: Penguin.

Harman, William P. 1989. *The sacred marriage of a Hindu goddess*. Bloomington: Indiana University Press.

Hart, George L. III. 1975. *The poems of ancient Tamil: Their milieu and their Sanskrit counterparts*. Berkeley and Los Angeles: University of California Press.

Hasan, M. Fazlul. 1971. *Bangalore through the centuries*. Bangalore: Historical Publications.

Haug, Martin. 1922. [reprint]. *The Aitareya Brahmanam of the Rigveda*. Allahabad: Sudhindra Nath Vasu, M. B., at the Panini Office.

Hawley, John Stratton. 1981. *At play with Krishna: Pilgrimage dramas from Brindavan*. Princeton: Princeton University Press.

Heesterman, Jan. 1957. *The ancient Indian royal consecration: The Rājasūya described according to the Yajus texts and annotated*. The Hague: Mouton.

———. 1985. *The inner conflict of tradition: Essays in Indian ritual, kingship, and society*. Chicago: University of Chicago Press.

Hein, Norvin. 1972. *The miracle plays of Mathurā*. New Haven: Yale University Press.

———. 1986. A revolution in Kṛṣṇaism: The cult of Gopāla. *HR* 25: 296–317.

Held, Garrett Jan. 1935. *The Mahābhārata: An ethnological study*. London: Kegan Paul, Trench, Trubner; Amsterdam: Uitgeversmaatschappij Holland.

Hemingway, F. R. 1907. *Trichinopoly District gazetteer*. Madras: Government Press.

Herrenschmidt, Olivier. 1982. Quelles fêtes pour quelles castes? *L'Homme* 22:31–56.

———. 1989. *Les meilleurs dieux sont Hindous*. Lausanne: L'Age d'Homme.

Hess, Linda. 1988. *The Ramlila of Ramnagar: An introduction and day-by-day description*. Berkeley and Varanasi: Anjaneya Publications.

Hikosaka, Shu. 1989. *Buddhism in Tamilnadu: A new perspective*. Madras: Institute of Asian Studies.

Hiltebeitel, Alf. 1976 [1990]. *The ritual of battle: Krishna in the Mahābhārata*.

Ithaca: Cornell University Press. Reprinted Albany: State University of New York Press.

———. 1977. Review of Gehrts 1975, in *Erasmus* 29:86–92.

———. 1978. The Indus Valley "Proto-Śiva," reexamined through reflections on the goddess, the buffalo, and the symbolism of *vāhanas*. *Anthropos* 73:767–97.

———. 1980a. Rāma and Gilgamesh: The sacrifices of the water buffalo and the bull of heaven. *HR* 19:187–223.

———. 1980b. Draupadī's garments. *IIJ* 22:97–112.

———. 1980c. Śiva, the goddess, and the disguises of the Pāṇḍavas and Draupadī. *HR* 20:147–74.

———. 1980–81. *Sītā vibhūṣitā:* The jewels for her journey. Ludwik Sternbach commemoration volume, *Indologica Taurinensia* 8–9:193–200.

———. 1981. Draupadī's hair. In *Autour de la déesse hindoue,* ed. Madeleine Biardeau. *Puruṣārtha* 5:179–214.

———. 1982a. Firewalking through the *Mahabharata:* The cult of Draupadi and the great Indian epic. *India Magazine* 2, 4:18–27.

———. 1982b. Sexuality and sacrifice: Convergent subcurrents in the firewalking cult of Draupadī. In *Images of man: Religion and historical process in South Asia,* ed. Fred W. Clothey. Madras: New Era Publications.

———. 1982c. Brothers, friends, and charioteers: Parallel episodes in the Irish and Indian epics. In *Homage to Georges Dumézil,* ed. Edgar C. Polomé. *Journal of Indo-European Studies* Monograph, no. 3, 85–112.

———. 1983. Die Gluhende Axt: Symbolik, Struktur und Dynamik in *Chāndogya Upaniṣad* 6. In *Sehnsucht nach dem Ursprung: Zu Mircea Eliade,* ed. Hanns Peter Duerr, 394–405. Frankfurt am Main: Syndikat.

———. 1984a. The two Kṛṣṇas on one chariot: Upaniṣadic imagery and epic mythology. *HR* 24:1–26.

———. 1984b. Two South Indian oral epics. *HR* 24:164–73.

———. 1985a. Purity and auspiciousness in the Sanskrit epics. In *Essays on purity and auspiciousness,* ed. Frédérique Appfel Marglin and John Carman. *Journal of Developing Societies* 1:41–54.

———. 1985b. On the handling of the meat, and related matters, in two South Indian buffalo sacrifices. In *Divisione della carni: Dinamica sociale e organizzazione del cosmo,* ed. Christiano Grottanelli. *L'Uomo* 9:171–99.

———. 1985c. Two Kṛṣṇas, three Kṛṣṇas, four Kṛṣṇas, more Kṛṣṇas: Dark interactions in the *Mahābhārata.* In Essays on the *Mahābhārata,* ed. Arvind Sharma. *Journal of South Asian Literature* 20:71–77.

———. 1987a,b. Gambling *and* Kurukṣetra. In *The encyclopedia of religion,* ed. Mircea Eliade. 5:468–74; 8:406–7. New York: Free Press.

———. 1988a. *The cult of Draupadī.* Vol. 1, *Mythologies: From Gingee to Kurukṣetra.* Chicago: University of Chicago Press.

———. 1988b. Director, *Lady of Gingee: South Indian Draupadi festivals,* parts 1 and 2. Videotape. Washington, D.C.: George Washington University. Distributed through University of Wisconsin South Asia Center.

———. 1988c. South Indian gardens of Adonis revisited. In *Essais sur le rituel,* vol. 1, ed. Anne-Marie Blondeau and Kristofer Schipper. Colloque du Centenaire de la Section des Sciences Religieuses de l'Ecole Pratique des Hautes Etudes. Bibliothèque de l'EPHE Sciences Religieuses, vol. 92. Louvain and Paris: Peeters.

———. 1988d. Orders of diffusion in a South Indian goddess cult. Paper delivered at the American Academy of Religion Annual Conference, Chicago.

———. 1988e. The Tamil Draupadī cult and the *Mahābhārata. Journal of the Institute of Asian Studies* (Madras) 6:31–37.

———. 1989a. Draupadī's two guardians: The buffalo king and the Muslim devotee. In Hiltebeitel 1989b, 339–71.

———, ed. 1989b. Introduction. In *Criminal gods and demon devotees: Essays on the guardians of popular Hinduism*, 3–18. Albany: State University of New York Press.

———. 1989c. The folklore of Draupadī: Sarees and hair. To appear in *Power, gender, and transmission: Essays on South Asian folklore*, ed. Arjun Appadurai, Frank Corom, and Margaret Mills. Philadelphia: University of Pennsylvania Press.

———. 1989d. Draupadī cult līlās. Paper presented at the Conference on the concept of Līlā in South Asia, Harvard University. To appear in a publication of the Conference Proceedings, ed. William S. Sax.

Hiltebeitel, Alf, and Thomas J. Hopkins. 1987. Indus Valley religion. In *The Macmillan encyclopedia of religion*, ed. Mircea Eliade. 7:215–23. New York: Free Press.

Hjortshoj, Keith. 1987. Shi'i identity and the significance of Muharram in Lucknow, India. In *Shi'ism, resistance, and revolution*, ed. Martin Kramer. Boulder, Colo.: Westview Press; London: Mansell.

Hopkins, Edward Washburn. 1913. Firewalk. *ERE* 6:30–31.

———. [1915] 1969. *Epic mythology*. New York: Biblo and Tannen.

Hudson, D. Dennis. 1971. Two Citrā festivals in Madurai. In *Asian Religions: 1971*, ed. Bardwell L. Smith. American Academy of Religion Annual Meeting 1971. Chambersburg, Pa.: Wilson College.

———. 1982. Two Citrā festivals in Madurai. In *Religious festivals in South India and Sri Lanka*, ed. Guy R. Welbon and Glenn E. Yocum. New Delhi: Manohar.

———. 1989. Violent and fanatical devotion among the Nāyaṉārs: A study in the *Periya Purāṇam* of Cēkkiḻār. In Hiltebeitel 1989b, 373–404.

Hudson, D. Dennis, Mira Rehm Binford, and Michael Camerini. 1976. *Wedding of the goddess*, parts 1 and 2. Film. Madison: University of Wisconsin South Asia Center.

Jaffri, Syed Husain Ali. 1979. Muharram ceremonies in India. In *Ta'ziyeh: Ritual and drama in Iran*, ed. Peter J. Chelkowski. New York: New York University Press and Soroush Press.

Jagadisa Ayyar, P. V. 1982. [1st ed. n.d.] *South Indian customs*. New Delhi: Asian Educational Services.

Jagadiśvarananda, Swami. 1972. *The Devī-Māhātmyam or Śrī Durgā Saptaśati*. Madras: Śrī Ramakrishna Math.

Jamison, Stephanie. In press. *Myth and ritual in ancient India.* Ithaca: Cornell University Press.

Janaki, S. S. 1988. Dhvaja-stambha (critical account of its structural and ritualistic details). In *Śiva temples and temple rituals,* ed. S. S. Janaki. Madras: Kuppuswami Sastri Research Institute.

Jones, Clifford R. 1982. Kaḷam Eḻuttu: Art and ritual in Kerala. In *Religious festivals in South India and Sri Lanka,* ed. Guy R. Welbon and Glenn E. Yocum. New Delhi: Manohar.

Kailasapathy, K. 1968. *Tamil heroic poetry.* Oxford: Clarendon Press.

Kalidos, Raju. 1989. *Temple cars of medieval Tamiḻaham.* Madurai: Vijay.

Kane, Pandurang Vaman. [1930–62] 1975. *History of Dharmaśāstra.* 5 vols. Poona: Bhandarkar Oriental Research Institute.

Kashikar, C. G., ed., and Dandekar, R. N. 1958, 1962. *Śrautakośa.* Vol. 1, English section, parts 1 and 2. Poona: Vaidika Saṃśodhana Maṇḍala.

Keith, Arthur Berriedale. 1914. *The Veda of the Black Yajus school entitled Taittiriya Saṃhitā,* part 1: Kāṇḍas I–III. Harvard Oriental Series, vol. 18. Cambridge: Harvard University Press.

———. [1925] 1971. *The religion and philosophy of the Veda and Upanishads.* 2 vols. Westport, Conn.: Greenwood Press.

Khan, Ali Ibrahim. 1787. On the trial by ordeal, among the Hindus. *Asiatick Researches,* 1:389–404.

Kinsley, David. 1986. *Hindu goddesses: Visions of the divine feminine in the Hindu religious tradition.* Berkeley and Los Angeles: University of California Press.

Kloetzli, W. Randolph. 1983. *Buddhist cosmology (from single world system to pure land: Science and theology in the images of motion and light).* Delhi: Motilal Banarsidass.

Knipe, David M. 1977. *Sapiṇḍīkaraṇa.* The Hindu rite of entry into heaven. In *Religious encounters with death,* ed. Frank E. Reynolds and Earle H. Waugh, 111–24. University Park: Pennsylvania State University Press.

———. 1989. Night of the growing dead: A cult of Vīrabhadra in coastal Andhra. In Hiltebeitel 1989b, 123–56.

Kosambi, Meera. 1984. Letter to author, 30 March.

Kramrisch, Stella. [1947] 1976. *The Hindu temple.* 2 vols. Delhi: Motilal Banarsidass.

Krishnaswami Aiyangar, Rao Bahadur S. 1928. *Manimekhalai in its historical setting.* London: Luzac.

Kulke, H. 1978. Royal temple policy and the structure of medieval Hindu kingdoms. In Eschmann, Kulke, and Tripathi 1978a, 125–37.

Lal, Bhairo, and Semi Seruvakula. 1974. Walking through fire. In *Holy torture in Fiji,* by Muneshwar Sahadeo, Sister Mary Stella, Bhairo Lal, Semi Seruvakula, Ron Crocombe, and Stan Ritowa. Sidney: Pacific.

Lang, Andrew. 1900–1. The firewalk. *Society for Psychical Research, Proceedings* 15:2–15.

Lariviere, Richard W. 1981. *The Divyatattva of Raghunanda Bhaṭṭācārya: Ordeals in classical Hindu law.* New Delhi: Manohar.

Leikind, Bernard J., and William J. McCarthy. 1985. An investigation of firewalking. *Skeptical Inquirer* 10, 1:23–40.

Leroy, Olivier. 1931. *Les hommes salamandres: Recherches et réflexions sur l'incombustibilité du corps humain.* "Questions disputées." Paris: Desclée, de Brouwer.

Lévi, Sylvain. 1966. *La doctrine du sacrifice dans les Brāhmaṇa.* 2d ed. Paris: Presses Universitaires de France.

Lévi-Strauss, Claude. 1971. *The naked man.* Vol. 4. *Introduction to a science of mythology.* Trans. John and Doreen Weightman. New York: Harper.

Lewis, L. Elizabeth. 1931. Fire walking Hindus in Singapore. *National Geographic* 59:513–22.

Logan, William. 1906. *Manual of the Malabar District.* Madras: Government Press.

Loud, John A. n.d. Translation of *Māriyammaṉ Tālāṭṭu* (Lullaby to Māriyammaṉ). Personal communication.

Macdonell, Arthur A., and A. B. Keith. [1912] 1967. *Vedic index of names and subjects.* 2 vols. Delhi: Motilal Banarsidass.

McGilvray, Dennis. 1970, 1975. Notes on the Pāṇṭirappu Tiraupatai Amman Kovil festival. Personal correspondence.

———. 1986. *Symbolic heat.* Video slide-tape, ten minutes. Boulder: University of Colorado Museum.

Mackenzie, J. S. F. 1874. The village feast. *IA* 3:6–9.

Macready, W. C. 1888–89. The jungles of Rājavanni Pattu and the ceremony of passing through fire. *Orientalist* 3:188–93.

Mahalingam, T. V., 1972. *Mackenzie manuscripts: Summaries of historical manuscripts in the Mackenzie Collection.* Madras University Historical Series, no. 25. Madras: University of Madras.

———. [1940] 1975. *Administrative and social life under Vijayanagar.* 2 vols. Madras: University of Madras.

Majumdar, B. C. 1911. The Stambhesvari, communicated with a note by R. D. Bannerji. *JASB* 7:443–47.

Makrakis, Basil, 1982. *Fire dances in Greece.* Heraclion: privately printed.

Malamoud, Charles. 1989. *Cuire le monde: Rite et pensée dans l'Inde ancienne.* Paris: Editions la Découverte.

Marglin, Frédérique Appfel. 1985. *Wives of the god-king: The rituals of the Devadasis of Puri.* Delhi: Oxford University Press.

———. 1988. Draft of untitled paper on modern western and traditional Indian attitudes toward menstrual taboos. Delivered at American Academy of Religion Annual Meeting, Chicago.

Masilamani-Meyer, Eveline [see also Meyer, Eveline]. 1989a. The changing face of Kāttavarāyaṉ. In Hiltebeitel 1989b, 69–103.

———. 1989b. Wächtergottheiten in Tamilnadu. Paper presented to the Völkskundemuseum, Zurich.

———. In press-a. Durgā in Tamilnadu. In *Durgā and the buffalo,* ed. Gunther D. Sontheimer and M. L. K. Murty. Heidelberg: South Asia Institute.

———, trans. and ed. In press-b. *The story of Kāttavarāyaṉ.*

Mathew, K. S. 1979. *Society in medieval Malabar: A study based on Vadakkan Pāṭṭukaḷ.* Kurichy: Jaffe Books.

Meister, Michael W. 1981. Muṇḍeśvarī: Ambiguity and certainty in the analysis of a temple plan. In *Kalādarśana: American studies in the art of India,* ed. Joanna G. Williams, 77–89. Studies in South Asian Culture, vol. 9. Leiden: E. J. Brill.

———. 1984. Śiva's forts in Central India: Temples in Dakṣiṇa Kosala and their "daemonic" plans. In *Discourses on Śiva,* ed. M. Meister. Philadelphia: University of Pennsylvania Press.

Merrey, Karen L. 1982. The Hindu festival calendar. In *Religious festivals in South India and Sri Lanka,* ed. Guy R. Welbon and Glenn E. Yocum, 1–26. New Delhi: Manohar.

Meyer, Eveline [see also Masilamani-Meyer, Eveline]. 1986. *Aṅkāḷaparamēcuvari: A goddess of Tamilnadu, her myths and cult.* Weisbaden: Franz Steiner.

Meyer, Johann Jakob. 1937. *Trilogie altindischer Mächte und Feste der Vegetation.* Vol. 3, *Indra: Der altindische Gott der Frühlingssonne und der Fruchtbarkeit und sein Fest.* Zurich and Leipzig: Max Niehaus.

Mialaret, Jean-Pierre. 1969. *Hinduism in Singapore: A guide to the Hindu temples of Singapore.* Singapore: Asia Pacific Press.

Miller, Jeanine. 1974. *The Vedas: Harmony, meditation, fulfillment.* Bombay: B. I. Publications.

Mitra, Sarat Chandra. 1936. On the fire-walking ceremony of the Dusādhs of Bihar. *QJMS* 27, 1:172–81.

Mitterwallner, Gritli von. 1984. Evolution of the liṅga. In *Discourses on Śiva,* ed. Michael W. Meister. Philadelphia: University of Pennsylvania Press.

Moffatt, Michael. 1979. *An Untouchable community in South India: Structure and consensus.* Princeton: Princeton University Press.

Monier-Williams, Sir Monier. [1899] 1964. *A Sanskrit-English dictionary.* Oxford: Clarendon Press.

Moses, F. A., et al., researchers. 1961. *Census of India 1961.* Vol. 9, *Madras.* Part 6. Village Survey Monographs, no. 28: *Sunnambukulam.* Ed. P. K. Nambiar. Delhi: Manager of Publications.

Nagaswamy, R. 1982. *Tantric cult of South India.* Delhi: Agam Kala Prakashan.

Nambiar, P. K., superintendent, et al. 1965. *Census of India 1961.* Vol. 9, *Madras.* Part 11D, *Temples of Madras State,* 1: *Chingleput District and Madras City.* Delhi: Manager of Publications.

———. 1966. *Census of India 1961 . . . Temples of Madras State,* 2: *Tiruchirapalli and South Arcot.* Delhi: Manager of Publications.

———. 1968a. *Census of India 1961 . . . Temples of Madras State,* 3: *Coimbatore and Salem.* Delhi: Manager of Publications.

———. 1968b. *Census of India 1961 . . . Temples of Madras State,* 4: *North Arcot and Nilgiris.* Delhi: Manager of Publications.

———. 1968c. *Census of India 1961 . . . Temples of Madras State,* 5: *Kanyakumari and Tirunelveli.* Delhi: Manager of Publications.

———. 1969. *Census of India 1961 . . . Temples of Madras State, 6: Madurai and Ramanathapuram.* Delhi: Manager of Publications.

Nambiar, P. K., K. C. Narayana Karup, et al. 1968. *Census of India 1961.* Vol. 9, *Madras.* Part 7B. *Fairs and festivals.* Delhi: Manager of Publications.

Nandakumar, Prema, trans. 1989. *Manimekalai.* Thanjavur: Tamil University.

Nandi, Ramendra Nath. 1973. *Religious institutions and cults of the Deccan.* Delhi: Motilal Banarsidass.

Nanjundayya, H. V., and L. Krishna Ananthakrishna Iyer. 1928–35. *The Mysore tribes and castes.* 4 vols. Mysore: Mysore University.

Narayana Rao, Velcheru. 1983. Letter to author, 16 August.

———. 1986. Epics and ideologies: Six Telugu folk epics. In *Another harmony: New essays on the folklore of India,* ed. Stuart H. Blackburn and A. K. Ramanujan, 131–66. Berkeley and Los Angeles: University of California Press.

———. 1989. Tricking the goddess: Cowherd Kāṭamarāju and goddess Gaṅga in the Telugu folk epic. In Hiltebeitel 1989b, 105–22.

Nayakar, T. Aiyakannu. 1891. *Vannikula Vilakkam: A treatise on the Vanniya caste.* Madras: Albion Press.

Nevill, Hugh. 1887a. Passing over fire, to Draupadi and the five Pândavas. *Taprobanian* 2, 2:58–60.

———. 1887b. Hymn to the five, or *Âyvar kâviyam. Taprobanian* 2, 6: 177–78.

Nicholas, Ralph. 1978. Sītalā and the art of printing: The transmission and propogation of the myth of the goddess of smallpox in rural West Bengal. In *Mass culture, language and arts in India,* ed. Mahadev L. Apte, 152–80. Bombay: Popular Prakashan.

Nirmala Devi, R., ed., and V. Murugan, trans. 1987. *The wandering voice: Three ballads from palm leaf manuscripts.* Folklore of Tamilnadu Series, no. 1. Thiruvanmiyur: Institute of Asian Studies.

Nishimura, Yuko. 1987. *A study on Māriyammaṉ worship in South India: A preliminary study on modern South Indian village Hinduism.* Tokyo: Institute for the Study of Languages and Cultures of Asia and Africa.

Obeyesekere, Gananath. 1978. The firewalkers of Kataragama: The rise of *bhakti* religiosity in Buddhist Sri Lanka. *JAS* 36:457–76.

———. 1984. *The cult of the goddess Pattini.* Chicago: University of Chicago Press.

O'Flaherty, Wendy Doniger. 1976. *The origins of evil in Hindu mythology.* Berkeley and Los Angeles: University of California Press.

———. 1980. *Women, androgynes, and other mythical beasts.* Chicago: University of Chicago Press.

———. 1984. *Dreams, illusion, and other realities.* Chicago: University of Chicago Press.

———. 1988, ed. and trans. *Textual sources for the study of Hinduism.* Totowa, N.J.: Barnes and Noble.

Oppert, Gustav. 1893. *The original inhabitants of Bharatavarṣa or India.* Westminster: Archibald Constable; Leipzig: Otto Harrassowitz.

Östör, Ákos. 1980. *The play of the gods: Locality, ideology, structure, and time in the festivals of a Bengali town.* Chicago: University of Chicago Press.

Parpola, Asko. 1983. The pre-Vedic Indian background of śrauta rituals. In Staal 1983, 2:41–75.

———. 1988. The coming of the Aryans to Iran and India and the cultural and ethnic identity of the Dāsas. *Studia Orientalia* 64:195–302.

———. 1989. Witnessing a hog sacrifice in South Kanara. *Nordic Institute of Folklore Newsletter* 4:20–24.

———. In press. From Ištar to Durgā: Sketch of a prehistory of India's feline-riding and buffalo-slaying goddess of victory. In *Durgā and the buffalo,* ed. Günther D. Sontheimer and M. L. K. Murty. Heidelberg: South Asia Institute.

Pate, H. R. 1917. *Madras District gazetteers: Tinnevelly.* 2 vols. Madras: Government Press.

Peterson, Indira. 1989. Śramaṇas against the Tamil way: Jainas and Buddhists in the hymns of the Tamil Śaiva saints. Paper presented at the Association of Asian Studies Annual Meeting.

Powell, J. H. 1914. "Hook-swinging" in India: A description of the ceremony, and an inquiry into its origin and significance. *Folklore: Transactions of the Folklore Society* 25:147–97.

Prabhu, K. Sanjiva. 1977. *Special study report on Bhuta cult in South Kanara District: Census of India 1971, Mysore,* series 14. Delhi: Controller of Publications.

Radhakrishna Aiyar, S. 1917. *A general history of Pudukkottai.* Pudukkottai: Sri Brihadambal State Press.

Raghavan, M. D. 1947. *Folk dances and plays of Kerala.* Trichur: Mangaladoyam Press.

———. 1961. *The Karāva of Ceylon: Society and culture.* Columbo: K. V. G. De Silva.

Ramachandra Rao, S. K. 1979. *The Indian temple: Its meaning.* Bangalore: I. B. H. Publications.

Ramakrishna Rao, Rajakaryaprasakta B. 1921. The Dasara celebrations in Mysore. *QJMS* 11:300–311.

Ramanayya, N. Venkata. [1930] 1983. *An essay on the origin of the South Indian temple.* New Delhi: Ramanand Vidya Bhavan.

Rangachari, K. 1930. The Śrī Vaiṣṇava Brahmans. *Bulletin of the Madras Government Museum,* n.s., general section, 2, 1:1–158.

Rao, C. Hayavardana. 1936a. *The Dasara in Mysore: Its origin and significance.* Bangalore: Bangalore Press (42 pp.).

———. 1936b. *The Dasara in Mysore: Its origin and significance.* Bangalore: Bangalore Printing and Publishing Company (200 pp.).

Rau, Wilhelm. 1973. *The meaning of "pur" in Vedic literature.* Abhandlungen der Marburger Gelehrten Gesellschaft, 1. Munich: Wilhelm Fink.

Reddy, G. N. 1985. Purāṇa performance: A case study from Telugu. Paper presented at Conference on the Purāṇas, University of Wisconsin, Madison.

Reiniche, Marie Louise. 1979. *Les dieux et les hommes: Etude des cultes d'un village du Tirunelveli Inde du Sud.* Cahiers de l'Homme Ethnologie-Géographie-Linguistique, n.s., 18. Paris: Mouton.

———. 1987. Worship of Kāḷiyammaṉ in some Tamil villages: The sacrifice of the warrior-weavers. In *Religion and society in South India (a volume in honour of Prof. N. Subba Reddy)*, by V. Sundarsen, G. Prakash Reddy, and M. Suryanarayana, 89–103. Delhi: B. R. Publishing.

Renou, Louis. 1954. *Vocabulaire du rituel védique.* Paris: C. Klinksieck.

Reports on the swinging festival, and the ceremony of walking through fire. 1854. *Selections from the records of the Madras government,* no. 7. Madras: Fort Saint George Gazette Press.

Richards, F. J. 1910. Fire-walking ceremony at the Dharmaraja festival, with note by S. Krishnaswami Aiyangar. *QJMS* 2, 1:29–32.

———. 1918. *Madras District gazetteers: Salem,* part 1. Madras: Government Press.

———. 1920. The village deities in Vellore Taluk, North Arcot District. *QJMS* 10, 2:109–20.

Richman, Paula. 1988. *Women, branch stories, and religious rhetoric in a Tamil Buddhist text.* Foreign and Comparative Studies/South Asian Series 12. Syracuse University: Maxwell School of Citizenship and Public Affairs.

Robinson, Sandra P. 1976. "Death" and "revivification" in the Dharmamangal. In *Bengal: Studies in literature, society and history,* ed. Marvin Davis. South Asia Series, Occasional Paper no. 27. East Lansing: Asian Studies Center, Michigan State University.

———. 1980. The Dharmapūjā: A study of rites and symbols associated with the Bengal deity Dharmarāj. Ph.D. diss., University of Chicago.

Roghair, Gene. H. 1982. *The epic of Palnāḍu: A study and translation of Palnāṭi Vīrula Katha, a Telugu oral tradition from Andhra Pradesh, India.* Oxford: Clarendon Press.

Rolland, Pierre. 1973. Le Mahāvrata: Contribution a l'étude d'un rituel solonnel védique. In *Nachrichten der Akademie der Wissenschaften in Göttingen,* 1:5–79. Philologisch-historische Klasse, no. 3. Göttingen: Vandenhoeck & Ruprecht.

Sarkar, Benoy Kumar. [1917] 1972. *The folk-element in Hindu culture: A contribution to socio-religious studies in Hindu folk-institutions.* Delhi: Munshiram Manoharlal.

Sarkar, H. 1978. *An architectural survey of temples of Kerala.* New Delhi: Archaeological Survey of India.

Sarkar, R. M. 1986. *Regional cults and rural traditions: An interacting pattern of divinity and humanity in rural Bengal.* New Delhi: Inter-India Publications.

Sarkar, R. M., and Arun Kumar Ghose. 1972. Socio-ritual impact of the Gajan festival on folk life. *Modern Review* 131:103–8.

Sarojini Devi, Konduri. 1990. *Religion in Vijayanagara empire.* New Delhi: Sterling.

Sayce, R. U. 1933. An Indian fire-walking ceremony in Natal. *Man* 33:2–7.

Schechner, Richard. 1983. *Performative circumstances from the avant garde to Ramlila.* Calcutta: Seagull Books.

Schechner, Richard, and Linda Hess. 1977. The Ramlila of Ramnagar. *Drama Review* 21, 3:51–82.
Scheuer, Jacques. 1982. *Śiva dans le Mahābhārata.* Bibliothèque de l'Ecole des Haute Etudes, Sciences Religieuses, vol. 56. Paris: Presses Universitaires de France.
Schomer, Karine. 1989. Paradigms for the Kali yuga: The heroes of the Ālhā epic and their fate. In *Oral epics of India,* ed. Stuart H. Blackburn, Peter J. Claus, Joyce B. Flueckiger, and Susan S. Wadley, 140–54. Berkeley and Los Angeles: University of California Press.
Schwab, Julius. 1886. *Das altindische Thieropfer.* Erlangen: Andreas Deichert.
Schwartzberg, Joseph E., ed. 1978. *A historical atlas of South Asia.* Chicago: University of Chicago Press.
Sen, Citrabhanu. 1978. *A dictionary of Vedic rituals.* Delhi: Concept.
Sen, Ram Comul. 1833. A short account of the Charak Púja ceremonies, and a description of the implements used. *Journal of the Asiatic Society of Bengal* 11:609–12.
Settar, G., and Günther D. Sontheimer, eds. 1982. *Memorial stones: A study of their origin, significance, and variety.* Dharwad: Karnatak University; Heidelberg: South Asia Institute, University of Heidelberg.
Sewell, Robert. 1882. *Lists of the antiquarian remains of the presidency of Madras.* Archaeological Survey of Southern India, vol. 1. Madras: Government Press.
Shah, Haku. 1985. *Votive terracottas of Gujarat.* Ed. Carmen Kagal. New York: Mapin International.
Shastri, H. Krishna. [1916] 1974. *South Indian images of gods and goddesses.* Varanasi: Bharatiya.
Shastri, J. L., ed. 1970. *The Śiva-Purāṇa.* Trans. A board of scholars. 4 vols. Delhi: Motilal Banarsidass.
Shideler, David William. 1987. Walking the path of Draupadī: Ritual vitalization of the *Mahābhārata* in a South Indian Draupadī Amman festival. M.A. diss., University of Hawaii.
Shulman, David Dean. 1980a. *Tamil temple myths: Sacrifice and divine marriage in South Indian Śaiva tradition.* Princeton: Princeton University Press.
———. 1980b. The green goddess of Tirumullaivāyil. *East and West* 30: 117–31.
———. 1985. *The king and the clown in South Indian myth and poetry.* Princeton: Princeton University Press.
———. 1986. Battle as metaphor in Tamil folk and classical traditions. In *Another harmony: New essays on the folklore of India,* ed. Stuart H. Blackburn and A. K. Ramanujan. Berkeley and Los Angeles: University of California Press.
———. 1989. Outcaste, guardian, and trickster: Notes on the myth of Kāttavarāyaṉ. In Hiltebeitel 1989b, 35–68.
Silva, Severine. 1955. Traces of human sacrifice in Kanara. *Anthropos* 50: 576–92.

Singh, Sarva Daman. 1965. *Ancient Indian warfare with special reference to the Vedic period*. Leiden: E. J. Brill.

Sircar, D. C. 1967. *The Śakti cult and Tārā*. Calcutta: University of Calcutta.

———. 1971. *Studies in the religious life of ancient and medieval India*. Delhi: Motilal Banarsidass.

Sitaramiah, V. 1967. *Mahakavi Pampa*. Bombay: Popular Prakashan.

Smith, H. Daniel. 1969. *Vaiṣṇava iconography*. Madras: Pāñcarātra Pariṣōdhana Pariṣad.

Smith, Jonathan Z. 1978. *Map is not territory: Studies in the history of religion*. Leiden: E. J. Brill.

———. 1987. Dying and rising gods. In *The encyclopedia of religion*, ed. M. Eliade, 4:521–27. New York: Macmillan.

Snodgrass, Adrian. 1985. *The symbolism of the stūpa*. Studies on Southeast Asia, Southeast Asia Program. Ithaca: Cornell University.

Somander, S. V. O. 1951. Fire-walking in Ceylon. *Chambers's Journal*, n.s., 611–14.

Sonnerat, Pierre. 1782. *Voyage aux Indes orientales*. Paris: privately printed.

Sontheimer, Günther-Dietz. 1981. Dasarā at Devaragudda: Ritual and play in the cult of Mailār/Khaṇḍobā. *South Asian Digest of Regional Writing* 10:1–28.

———. 1982. Hero and Satī-stones of Maharashtra. In Settar and Sontheimer 1982, 261–81.

———. 1984. The Mallāri/Khaṇḍobā myth as reflected in folk art and ritual. *Anthropos* 79:155–70.

———. 1989a. Between ghost and god: A folk deity of the Deccan. In Hiltebeitel 1989b, 299–338.

———. 1989b. *Pastoral deities in Western India*. Trans. Anne Feldhaus. New York: Oxford University Press.

Srinivas, M. N. 1942. *Marriage and family in Mysore*. Bombay: New Book Company.

———. 1965. *Religion and society among the Coorgs of South India*. Bombay: Asia Publishing House.

Srinivasachari, Rao Bahadur C. S. 1943. *A history of Gingee and its rulers*. Annamalai University Historical Series, no. 2. Annamalainagar: Annamalai University.

Srinivasan, Doris Meth. 1984. Significance of pre-Kuṣāna Śaivite iconography. In *Discourses on Śiva*, ed. Michael W. Meister, 32–46. Philadelphia: University of Pennsylvania Press.

Srinivasan, K. R. 1960. *Some aspects of religion as revealed by early monuments and literature of the South*. Madras: University of Madras.

———. 1964. *Cave-temples of the Pallavas*. Architectural Survey of Temples, no. 1. New Delhi: Archaeological Survey of India.

Staal, Frits. 1983. *Agni: The Vedic ritual of the fire altar*. 2 vols. Berkeley: Asian Humanities Press.

Stanley, John M. 1977. Special time, special power: The fluidity of power in a popular Hindu festival. *JAS* 37:27–43.

———. 1984. The Dassara divination ritual at Mangsuli. Paper presented at Association of Asian Studies annual meeting, Washington, D.C.

———. 1987. Niṣkāma and Sakāma, Bhakti: Pandharpur and Jejuri. In *Religion and society in Maharashtra,* ed. Milton Israel and N. K. Wagle. South Asian Studies Papers, no. 1. Toronto: University of Toronto Center for South Asian Studies.

———. 1989. The capitulation of Maṇi: A conversion myth in the cult of Khaṇḍobā. In Hiltebeitel 1989b, 271–98.

Stokes, H. J. 1873. Walking through fire. *IA* 2:190–91.

Subramanian, M. V. 1967. *Vyasa and variations: The Mahabharata story.* Madras: Higginbothams.

Tamil Lexicon. [1926–39] 1982. 6 vols. Madras: University of Madras.

Tanaka, Masakazu. 1987. *Sacrifice for power: Hindu temple rituals and village festivals in a fishing village, Sri Lanka.* Senri: National Museum of Ethnology.

Tapper, Bruce Elliot. 1979. Widows and goddesses: Female roles in deity symbolism in a South Indian village. *CIS,* n.s. 13, 1:1–31.

———. 1987. *Rivalry and tribute: Society and ritual in a Telugu village in South India.* Delhi: Hindustan.

Tarabout, Gilles. 1986. *Sacrifier et donner à voir en pays Malabar.* Paris: Ecole Française d'Extrême Orient.

Thite, Ganesh Umakant. 1975. *Sacrifice in the Brāhmaṇa-texts.* Poona: University of Poona.

Thurston, Edgar. 1906. *Ethnographic notes in Southern India.* Madras: Government Press.

Thurston, Edgar, and K. Rangachari. [1904] 1965. *Castes and tribes of Southern India.* 7 vols. Madras: Government Press.

Trautmann, Thomas R. 1988. Review of Heesterman 1985. *JAS* 47, 3:681–83.

Tripathi, G. C. 1978. Navakalevara: The unique ceremony of the "birth" and the death of the "Lord of the World." In Eschmann, Kulke, and Tripathi 1978a.

Underhill, M. M. 1921. *The Hindu religious year.* Calcutta: Association Press.

Vaidyanathan, K. R. 1982. *Temples and legends of Kerala.* Bombay: Bharatiya Vidya Bhavan.

Valam, H. K., trans. [1957] 1972. *Amarakavi Subrahmanya Bharati,* The vow of Panchali. Mylapore: Mohana Trust Pathippagam.

van Buitenen, J. A. B. 1973, 1975, 1978. *The Mahābhārata.* 1. *The book of beginnings;* 2. *The book of the assembly hall* and *The book of the forest;* 3. *The book of Virāṭa* and *The book of the effort.* Chicago: University of Chicago Press.

van den Hoek, A. W. 1978. The goddess of the northern gate: Cellattamman as the "Divine Warrior" of Madurai. In *Asie du Sud: Traditions et changements,* ed. Marc Gaborieau and Alice Thorner, 119–29. Colloques Internationaux du Centre National de la Recherche Scientifique, no. 582. Paris: Editions du CNRS.

Vanmikanathan, G. 1971. *Pathway to god through Tamil literature.* Delhi: Tamil Sangham.

Vanmikanathan, G., and N. Mahalingam. 1985. *Periya Puranam: Condensed English version.* Mylapore and Madras: Sri Ramakrishna Math.

Varadarajam Pillai, M. R. 1977. Folk songs of Kerala: A mirror of life in medieval Kerala. In *Conflict and culture: Sociological essays,* ed. K. Thullaseedharan. Trivandrum: College Book House.

Venkatesa Acharya, Kambaluru. 1981. *Mahabharata and variations: Perundevanar and Pampa (a comparative study).* Kurnool: Vyasaraja.

Vidyarthi, Govind. 1976. Mudiettu: Rare ritual theatre of Kerala. *Sangeet Natak* 42:51–59.

Visuvalingam, Sunthar. 1989. The transgressive sacrality of the Dīkṣita. In Hiltebeitel 1989b, 427–62.

Vogel, J. Ph. 1910–11. The sacrificial posts of Īsāpur. *Archaeological Survey of India Annual Report,* 39–48.

———. 1930–32. The head-offering to the goddess in Pallava sculpture. *BSOAS* 6, 2:539–43.

Volwashen, Andreas. 1969. *Living architecture: India.* New York: Grosset and Dunlap.

Waghorne, Joanne Punzo. 1989. From robber baron to royal servant of God? Gaining a divine body in South India. In Hiltebeitel 1989b, 405–26.

Walhouse, M. J. 1878. Passing through fire. *IA* 7:126–29.

White, David Gordon. 1984. Why gurus are heavy. *Numen* 31, 1:40–73.

Whitehead, Henry. 1921. *The village gods of South India.* Calcutta: Association Press.

Williams, R. 1963. *Jaina yoga: A survey of the mediaeval Śrāvakācāras.* London: Oxford University Press.

Winslow, M. [1862] 1979. *Winslow's comprehensive Tamil and English dictionary.* New Delhi: Asian Educational Services.

Zanen, M. 1978. Gardens of Adonis in the Mediterranean area and in South India: A comparison of their structure. In *Asie du Sud: Traditions et changements,* ed. Marc Gaborieau and Alice Thorner, 1–7. Colloques Internationaux du Centre National de la Recherche Scientifique No. 582. Paris: Editions du CNRS.

Zarrilli, Philip. 1979. Kalarippayatt, martial art of Kerala. *Drama Review* 23, 2:113–24.

———. 1984. From martial art to performance: Kaḷarippayaṯṯu and performance in Kerala, South India. Manuscript draft: from the author.

Zvelebil, Kamil Veith. 1973. *The smile of Murugan: On Tamil literature of South India.* Leiden: E. J. Brill.

———. 1989. Review of Hiltebeitel 1988a. *Journal of the Royal Asiatic Society of Great Britain and Ireland,* 357–60.

General Index

156, 158, 255 (plate 11), 275 (plate 31), 291–92, 295, 322–23, 335, 337, 343–44, 346, 350–52, 360–61, 449–50, 465; lemons impaled on, 62, 150, 151 (fig. 11), 265 (plate 21), 290, 448; other names of, 114, 152
Vīraṉs, heroes, 48, 107–8, 112–13
Vīrapampai, 149–50, 156. *See also* Drums
Vīrapattiraṉ, Vīrabhadra, 47, 103, 112–16 and fig. 4, 131 n. 18, 176, 215 (plate 7), 232, 299 n. 20, 314, 408–12, 421–25, 429, 440 n. 3, 463, 468; as Draupadī's guardian, 409, 411; as post, 114–15 and fig. 4, 152, 422. *See also* Pōttu Rāja
Virāṭa, *Virāṭaparvan*, 234, 237, 315, 341, 411, 414, 422, 426
Virginity, virgin goddess, 127, 171, 362–63, 377 n. 49. *See also* Draupadī, as virgin
Virgin Mary, 77 n. 21
Viṣṇu, 48, 91, 136, 145, 179–80, 206, 221 n. 22, 225, 239, 241, 308, 310, 317, 352, 358, 363–66, 379, 387 n. 9, 396, 484 n. 7, 485; as Nārāyaṇa, 179–80, 304, 306, 363, 366, 366 n. 44, 485, 487–89
Vows, 38, 229, 388, 440–42, 444, 466, 474, 482; Draupadī's, 340, 411
Vrātya rites, Mahāvrata, Vrātyastoma, 387

Waist curvature, female, 74, 121, 132
Washerman, 335, 337, 393, 408, 410
Whip, whipping, 28–30, 33, 34 n. 31, 145, 149, 156, 268 (plate 4), 295, 322–23, 335, 337–38, 348, 407–8, 420–21, 447, 449; whip worn around neck, 347, 351. See also *Vīracāṭṭi*
Widow, widows, 66, 75, 329–30, 362–65, 379, 474. *See also* Suttee
Winnow, 185, 192, 324, 329, 427 n. 26
Womb, 56, 60–62, 67, 69, 77, 157, 375, 397, 426, 434, 459, 462
Women's rituals and ritual roles, 192, 201, 205, 220–24, 228–31, 253 (plate 9), 256 (plate 12), 280 (plate 36), 292, 324 n. 5, 326, 363 n. 32, 373–75, 392, 442, 454–55, 459, 461, 472–73. *See also* Firewalkers, women; Pregnancy, rituals

Yajamāna, *yajman* (sacrificer), 17, 32–34, 56, 116, 124, 126, 377–78. *See also* Rival sacrificers; Sacrificer
Yākacālai, *yāgaśāla*, *yajñaśāla*, 59–61, 67, 69, 312
Yama, 50–51, 90 n. 20, 313, 318, 321 n. 1, 485, 487
Yellow-orange garments, 36, 43–44, 89, 217 n. 14, 290, 351, 442–43, 446–47, 478. *See also* Turmeric
Yoni, 60, 132–34, 137–38, 218 n. 15, 252 (plate 8)
Yoṉikuṇṭam, 60, 69
Young Pāñcapāṇḍavas, 67, 465; birth of, 364; differentiation among, 345, 403; dying and rising of, 38, 212, 231, 267 (plate 8), 320–23, 325, 339–47, 349, 352–54, 360–62, 364–65, 370, 398, 401–3, 435, 478. *See also* Five children, rites for
Youths, youth function, 25–26, 28–29, 33, 67, 351, 377 n. 49, 380
Yudhiṣṭhira. *See* Dharma, Dharmarāja
Yūpa, 98 n. 32, 105, 116, 117–24, 127, 129, 131–32, 135–40, 142–44, 146–50, 154–59, 164, 182, 231, 240, 347, 361; mobile, 143, 463; as phallic, 132; pointed, 138–39, 142, 144, 154, 164; sharp extensions of, 142–45, 156; tripartite form of, 121–23 and fig. 5; victim tied to, 121, 142–43, 150; *yūpa* tree as victim, 118, 120. See also *Akkiṉikampam*; *Liṅgam*; Post
Yusuf Khan, 307 n. 34, 358

Index of Temple and Festival Sites